SMALL-BUSINESS MANAGEMENT

Seventh Edition

Justin G. Longenecker, Ph.D.

Chavanne Professor Emeritus of Christian Ethics in Business
Baylor University

Carlos W. Moore, Ph.D.

Edwin Streetman Professor of Marketing
Baylor University

G26 **SOUTH-WESTERN PUBLISHING CO.**

CINCINNATI   WEST CHICAGO, IL   DALLAS   LIVERMORE, CA

COVER PHOTO: © Phillip A. Harrington

PREFACE

The Seventh Edition of *Small-Business Management* presents a thoroughly rewritten and updated treatment of the creation and management of small firms. We have included a strong emphasis on entrepreneurial opportunities and new-venture processes, as well as a coverage of managerial activities needed for successful operation of small firms. Revision highlights of this Seventh Edition include the following:

1. A new Chapter 2 on the family business.
2. Expanded coverage of the preparation of a new-business plan in Chapter 4.
3. Expanded treatment of financial management, including an extended discussion of cash flow analysis.
4. More material on personal computers and software in Chapter 21.
5. Expanded coverage of risk management and liability problems in Chapter 22.
6. A case following each chapter and a new Comprehensive Case at the end of the text.

Pedagogical Aids in the Textbook

In addition to its coverage of small-business concepts, *Small Business Management*, Seventh Edition, employs numerous features to facilitate student learning. Several of these aids are improved features continued from the previous edition. Others have been added to contribute to the attractiveness and usefulness of this Seventh Edition. The primary learning aids within the book are:

1. An "opener" for each chapter which features a specific small business firm in the context of that chapter.
2. *Action Reports*, many of them new, that dramatize text material with experiences of real-world entrepreneurs.
3. *Looking Ahead* and *Looking Back* sections for each chapter that give a preview and review of basic chapter topics.
4. Numerous new photographs, graphs, tables, and illustrations that communicate key concepts.
5. Annotated *References to Small Business in Action* at the end of

each chapter that identify articles describing actual applications of chapter topics.

6. A franchise investigation checklist (Appendix A) and a list of Small Business Administration Publications (Appendix B).

7. A glossary of terms used in the text.

Supplementary Publications

Several supplements are available to assist in the teaching and learning process of small-business management. These include:

1. *Small Business Management Using Lotus™ 1-2-3* (Stock No. G262). This workbook and its accompanying Small-Business Management System diskette (Stock No. G2681G)*, designed by Terry S. Maness, complements the textbook by allowing students to work with computerized versions of the quantitative concepts in the textbook. The workbook contains problems and a computerized, comprehensive model for developing a business plan for a new venture. It has a chapter that teaches students how to prepare their own worksheets using Lotus™ 1-2-3 and a formatted diskette.

2. An instructor's solution manual (Stock No. G262M)* for the problems in *Small Business Management Using Lotus™ 1-2-3* is available.

3. *MicroSWAT Testing Diskettes* (Stock No. G267-3T* for use with Apple computers and Stock No. G268-1T* for use with IBM computers). These are computerized test banks containing more than 1,000 questions, both objective and essay. An instructor can select questions from any chapter and also add his/her own questions.

4. *Student Learning Guide* (Stock No. G261). This supplement presents specific learning opportunities, key points and brief definitions to remember in understanding the chapter, comprehensive "programmed" self-reviews, and creative exercises for the application of learning. In addition, a series of "Pretests," based on each Part of the text, simulate actual testing situations and help students evaluate their learning prior to course examinations.

5. *Instructor's Manual* (Stock No. G26M*). The Instructor's Manual is an expanded supplement that contains suggested options for creative teaching, *new* lecture guides, answers to discussion questions in the textbook, discussion of text cases, more than 1,000 test questions, answers to test questions, and answers to exercises and questions in the *Student Learning Guide*. The Seventh Edition of the manual also includes over 80 new transparency masters, half of which are adapted from illustrations in the textbook.

*Items marked with an asterisk are provided free of charge to adopters of the textbook.

Acknowledgments

In preparing the Seventh Edition, the authors have been aided by colleagues, students, business owners, and others in providing case materials and in numerous other ways. In addition to those identified elsewhere, we especially acknowledge the contributions of Terry S. Maness, Daniel F. Jennings, John and Loretta Ambrose, and Dean M. Young. We are grateful for the special contribution of Kris K. Moore in supplying material for Chapter 21 and for the generous support of Mr. and Mrs. Edwin W. Streetman and our dean, Richard C. Scott. We are especially indebted to Dr. H. N. Broom for the material which was shaped by his co-authorship over the first six editions.

Justin G. Longenecker
Carlos W. Moore

Waco, Texas

CONTENTS

PART I—BENEFITS OF SMALL BUSINESS

1   Entrepreneurs: The Energizers of Small Business   2

Stories of Successful Entrepreneurial "Energizers" 3, Rewards of Entrepreneurship 9, Characteristics of Entrepreneurs 11, Readiness for Entrepreneurship 14, Entrepreneurial Roles, Ventures, and Styles 18, Case 1—Construction Equipment Dealership 26

2   The Family Business   29

The Family Business: A Unique Institution 30, Family Roles and Relationships 35, The Process of Succession 41, Case 2—The Woodward Well Company 51

3   Small Business: Vital Component of the Economy   54

Definition of Small Business 55, Small Business in the Major Industries 57, Small-Business Strength in Numbers 61, Special Contributions of Small Business 61, Case 3—Frost Jewelry Store 73

PART II—STARTING THE SMALL BUSINESS

4   Creating a New Venture and Preparing a Business Plan   78

Creating a New Venture, 79, Preparing a New-Venture Plan 85, Case 4—Asphera Lens Company 98

5   Analyzing the Market   103

Definitions of a Market 104, The Process of Market Analysis 105, Marketing Research 113, Sales Forecasting 120, Case 5—HOT Magazine 128

6   Franchising or Buying an Existing Business   134

Scope and Development of Franchising 135, Buying a Franchise 138, Evaluating Franchise Opportunities 145, Selling a Franchise 150, Buying an Existing Business 152, Case 6—Al's Car-Care 165

7   **Selecting a Location and Physical Facilities**   169

Importance of a Well-Chosen Location 170, Considerations in Selecting a Location 171, The Building and Its Layout 186, Equipment and Tooling 191, Case 7—The Fashion Attic 198

8   **Initial Financial Planning**   201

Nature of Financial Requirements 203, Estimating Financial Requirements 205, Locating Sources of Funds 210, Points to Consider in the Financing Proposal 223, Case 8—Walker Machine Works 230

9   **Legal Aspects of the Business**   233

Options for Legal Organization 234, Characteristics of the Proprietorship 235, Characteristics of the Partnership 236, Characteristics of the Corporation 239, Areas of Business Law Relevant to the Small Business 243, Choosing an Attorney 249, Case 9—"No Strain" Testers 254

PART III—SMALL-BUSINESS MARKETING

10   **Consumer Behavior and Product Strategies**   260

Scope of Marketing Activities for Small Businesses 261, Concepts of Consumer Behavior 263, Definitions of Product Terminology 272, Product Strategies for Small Business 273, Case 10—The Expectant Parent Center 285

11   **Distribution, Pricing, and Credit Policies**   288

Distribution Activities 289, Pricing Activities 299, Credit in Small Business 307, Case 11—The Jordan Construction Account 318

12   **Personal Selling, Advertising, and Sales Promotion**   321

Promotional Planning 322, Personal Selling 327, Advertising 333, Sales Promotion 336, Case 12—Mitchell Interiors 345

PART IV—MANAGING SMALL-BUSINESS OPERATIONS

13   **The Process of Management**   350

Management Functions in Small Business 351, Distinctive Features of Small-Firm Management 355, Time Management 363, Outside Management Assistance 364, Case 13—Central Engineering 377

14   **Objectives, Strategy, and Operational Planning**   380

Small-Business Objectives and Responsibilities 381, Small-Business Strategy 389, Operational Planning in Small Firms 394, Quantitative Tools to Aid Planning 400, Case 14—Emergency Filler Cap Case 408

15 Organizing the Small Firm   **411**

Types of Formal Organization Structure 412, Informal Organization 415,
Fundamentals of the Organizing Function 416, The Board of Directors in
Small Corporations 420, Case 15—Fourt Furniture Incorporated 427

16 Managing Human Resources in Small Firms   **431**

Recruiting and Selecting Personnel 432, Training and Development 439,
Compensation and Incentives for Small-Business Employees 442, Effective
Human Relationships in the Small Firm 445, Case 16—The Case of the
Dirty Washrooms 452

17 Operations Management   **454**

Production/Operations Control 455, Plant Maintenance 460, Quality Control 463, Work Improvement and Measurement 467, Industrial Research for
Small Plants 470, Case 17—Concessionaire Trailers 474

18 Purchasing and Managing Inventory   **477**

Purchasing 478, Inventory Control 487, Case 18—Mather's Heating and
Air Conditioning 498

PART V—FINANCIAL AND ADMINISTRATIVE CONTROLS

19 Accounting Systems, Financial Analysis, and Budgeting   **502**

Major Considerations Underlying an Accounting System 503, Selecting
Alternative Accounting Options 507, Typical Accounting Statements 510,
Analysis of Financial Statements 514, Budgeting in Small Firms 519, Case
19—Style Shop 529

20 Working-Capital Management and Capital Budgeting   **536**

Definitions of Key Financial Terms 537, Working-Capital Management 538,
Capital Budgeting in Small Business 548, Other Considerations in Evaluating
Expansion Opportunities 553, Case 20—Barton Sales and Service 560

21 Computerizing the Small Business   **565**

Computer Systems 566, Computer Applications for Small Business 571,
Deciding to Computerize the Small Business 578, The Future of Computers
584, Case 21—The Fair Store 588

22 Business Risks and Insurance   **590**

Common Small-Business Risks 591, Coping with Small-Business Risks 601,
Insurance for the Small Business 603, Case 22—Dale's Lawn Service 611

PART VI—STATUS AND FUTURE OF SMALL BUSINESS

23 Governmental Interaction with Small Business   616

Governmental Regulation 617, The Burdensome Nature of Regulation on Small Business 623, Taxation 626, Special Governmental Assistance 629, Case 23—The Terrell Company 636

24 Trends and Prospects for Small Business   638

Trends in Small-Business Activity 639, Competitive Strengths of Small Firms 640, Small-Business Problems and Failure Record 643, Prospects for the Future 650, Case 24—Classique Cabinets 658

COMPREHENSIVE CASE—The Mismatch   663

APPENDIX A—A FRANCHISE INVESTIGATION CHECKLIST   668

APPENDIX B—SBA PUBLICATIONS ON MANAGEMENT ASSISTANCE   671

GLOSSARY   675

INDEX   694

PART I
BENEFITS OF SMALL BUSINESS

1 – Entrepreneurs: The Energizers of Small Business

2 – The Family Business

3 – Small Business: Vital Component of the Economy

1

Entrepreneurs:
The Energizers of Small Business

Figure 1–1 Debbi Fields

In 1977, Debbi Fields, then 20, opened Mrs. Fields Cookies in Palo Alto, CA. By 1986, this business had grown to more than 300 cookie stores across the country (plus Australia, Tokyo, and Hong Kong), selling $60 million worth of cookies!

Debbi Fields is an entrepreneur—a person who created a profitable, new business. Seeing the potential for a specialized cookie shop, she dropped out of a community college to start baking cookies. As the business prospered, she surrounded herself with a professional management team, but she declined to enter a franchising pattern.

Debbi Fields is a "people person"—one who has concern for both employees and customers. Her personal philosophy, often expressed in such seemingly "corny" slogans as "Good is never good enough," continues to pervade the firm's operations.

Source: Various publications and phone conferences.

Watch for the following important topics:

1. Examples of highly successful entrepreneurs.
2. Rewards of entrepreneurship.
3. Personal characteristics of entrepreneurs.
4. Personal readiness for the various types of entrepreneurial roles and ventures.

Entrepreneurs provide the spark for our economic system by taking risks in producing goods and services. By choosing to own and manage their own firms, they become the *energizers* of small business. Each year, millions of individuals, from teenagers to retirees, respond to the call of entrepreneurship and the opportunity to pursue independent business careers. In ways that are competitive and innovative, they give dynamic leadership in our economic life.

Although some writers restrict the term *entrepreneur* to founders of business firms, in this text we use a broadened definition that includes all active owner–managers. Obviously this definition includes second-generation members of family-owned firms and owner–managers who buy out the founders of existing firms. Our definition, however, excludes salaried managers of large corporations, even those who are described as "entrepreneurial" because of their flair for innovation and their willingness to assume risk.[1]

Have you ever wondered what sorts of opportunities knock on the doors of would-be entrepreneurs? How attractive can the rewards of entrepreneurship be? Are there any special characteristics or personalities that entrepreneurs must possess in order to succeed? Is there a "right" time to plunge into entrepreneurship, or must some special events take place to trigger this plunge? In what types of roles, ventures, or styles can entrepreneurs be involved? This chapter will discuss each of these questions and thereby provide an introduction to the formation and management of small firms.

STORIES OF SUCCESSFUL ENTREPRENEURIAL "ENERGIZERS"

The reality of entrepreneurial opportunities can be communicated most vividly by giving examples of a few entrepreneurs who have succeeded. Reading these brief accounts of successful ventures should give you, the reader, a "feel" for the potential that you can achieve if you dream of having your own business. Even though these ventures are untypical in that each became a "smashing" success, they can be highly informative. They demonstrate the continued existence of opportunities and show the vast potential for at least some new ventures. And you should realize that less spectacular business ventures can still provide highly attractive career options!

Tom Fatjo's Business Ventures (Houston, TX)

Tom Fatjo is a highly successful entrepreneur who left a career in public accounting to go into the business of collecting garbage![2] After studying economics and accounting at Rice University, he went to work for Deloitte, Haskins and Sells, the Big-Eight accounting firm. In this profession he worked primarily with small to medium-sized firms, developed an acquaintance with small-business operations, and acquired an enthusiasm for entrepreneurship.

Fatjo's opportunity for business ownership emerged in the form of a community garbage-collection problem. When the private contractor who collected garbage in Fatjo's subdivision decided to concentrate on more lucrative routes, the community was left with a need for such service. Fatjo invested $500 in a garbage truck, hired a few employees, and began operation.

From that local base, Fatjo expanded by merging his business with Browning-Ferris and acquiring small waste disposal firms in various parts of the country. In only a short time, he became a multimillionaire. Browning-Ferris became the largest solid-waste disposal firm in the world and, in 1984, exceeded $1 billion in gross revenues.

In 1975, Fatjo stepped down as head of Browning-Ferris Industries and went on to other entrepreneurial ventures. One of these, the Houstonian, includes a 300-room hotel and conference complex, a health and fitness center, and a luxurious women's spa run by his wife, Judy Fatjo. This venture reflected Fatjo's concern for physical fitness and his desire to help people be more productive for a long period of time. "We thought," Fatjo said, "that by having an impact on the health and fitness of executives, we'd also have an impact on their employees."

In 1982, Fatjo turned in a new direction, teaming up with Charles and Beth Kuntzelman to market nationally a physical fitness program called "Living Well."[3] The Kuntzelmans had started their own firm, Fitness Finders, Inc., in Spring Arbor, MI, and offered a physical fitness package to corporations for their employees. This business had grown modestly to $500,000 in annual revenues, but its linkage with Fatjo's Houstonian permitted a dramatic expansion of the business. By 1984, it had become a $20-million-a-year operation, and Fatjo expressed his intention for this firm to

Figure 1-2   Tom Fatjo, Developer of Browning-Ferris, the Houstonian, and Living Well

become "the IBM of fitness," serving not only the corporate market but providing a number of athletic facilities in each of 50 to 75 major markets.

Fatjo's entrepreneurship is distinctive in a number of ways. First, he was well-prepared by virtue of a university business education and work experience with a major public accounting firm. Second, he saw opportunities where others saw only problems, particularly in the garbage disposal business. Third, he displayed a sense of mission in his desire to build a business and also to contribute to the physical fitness of Americans. A similar sense of mission also characterized the Kuntzelmans who had turned down an earlier offer to sell their firm, believing that the fitness program might not develop properly under that ownership.

Proctor and Gardner Advertising (Chicago, IL)

After earning an English degree at a small Alabama college, Barbara Gardner Proctor found a job as an advertising copywriter in Chicago.[4] As she gained experience in advertising, she also developed an appreciation for the quality of advertising. One particular concept suggested for a TV commercial struck her as tasteless and offensive, and this difference of opinion led to her being fired.

Following her dismissal, Proctor applied to the Small Business Administration for a loan. She obtained $80,000 in this way and promptly opened her own agency in 1970.

Proctor and Gardner Advertising is still relatively small among advertising agencies, but it is well-established and respected (having more than $12 million in billings in 1983). It specializes in advertising targeted to the black community and counts Kraft Foods and Sears among its clients. And Chicago's big Jewel Food Stores chain credits Proctor with helping make its generic foods campaign a success in 1978. In her business, Proctor refuses liquor or cigarette accounts, choosing to emphasize family products.

Figure 1–3   Barbara Gardner Moore, Founder of Proctor and Gardner Advertising

Barbara Gardner Proctor, as an entrepreneur in the area of business services, selected a strategic niche in which she could compete effectively. She also demonstrated the ability of women to function successfully in independent business careers, once considered to be largely the province of males.

Federal Express (Memphis, TN)

With annual revenue in excess of $1.4 billion, Federal Express is no longer a small business! But Federal Express is a relatively new business, having started operations only in 1971. Its business is that of delivering parcels overnight to all major cities in the United States. Using a hub-and-spokes pattern, its planes converge on Memphis nightly with incoming freight and then fly out with shipments to their respective home bases.

Federal Express originated in the mind of Frederick W. Smith, a student at Yale.[5] In 1965, he wrote a paper for an economics course proposing a new type of air freight service. According to his thesis, later proved successful by Federal Express, a company with its own planes dedicated to freight distribution should be superior to existing freight forwarders who were limited by the shifting schedules of passenger airlines.

Smith's professor (who surely made a name for himself in the annals of business history) pointed out the fallacy of Smith's reasoning and gave the paper a C! But entrepreneurs are not deterred by professors or others who lack their vision of the future. After his subsequent distinguished tours of military duty in Vietnam, Smith "dusted off" the idea and persuaded enough people of its potential value to obtain financial backing.

This venture has been unique in many ways. It was forced to start with a fleet of planes that could cover the entire country. The founder also came from a wealthy family and was able, as well as willing, to risk a substantial part of the family fortune by investing several millions of dollars. Nevertheless, the capital requirements were great, and Smith found it necessary to obtain the major portion of the financing from the venture capital industry. Ultimately, over a dozen equity groups participated in three major rounds of financing.

Although the startup is unusual in many ways, it is especially significant in showing the ability of one person, a potential entrepreneur, to conceptualize an entirely new type of business by studying business methods and new trends. The new concept was then implemented so successfully that it changed the very way in which business in America communicates and ships its freight.

Figure 1–4   Frederick W. Smith, Founder of Federal Express

Unlimited Entrepreneurial Opportunities

In a private enterprise system, any individual is free to enter business for himself or herself. In this chapter thus far, we have read of four different kinds of persons who took that step—a young mother in California, a businessman in Texas, an advertising copywriter in Chicago, and a wealthy heir in Memphis. In contrast to many others who tried and failed, these individuals achieved outstanding success.

At any time, such potentially profitable opportunities exist in the environment. But these opportunities must be recognized and grasped by individuals with the abilities and desire that are strong enough to assure success. The examples cited here can help you to visualize the broad spectrum of opportunities that await you. Of course, there are thousands of variations and alternatives for independent business careers. In fact, you may achieve great success in business endeavors that are far different from those described here. In these varied types of entrepreneurship, there are a number of potential rewards. We turn now to a consideration of these benefits.

REWARDS OF ENTREPRENEURSHIP

Individuals are *pulled* toward entrepreneurship by various powerful incentives, or rewards. These rewards may be grouped, for the sake of simplicity, into three basic categories: profit, independence, and a satisfying life-style.

Profit

The financial return of any business must compensate its owner for investing his or her personal time (a salary equivalent) and personal savings (an interest and/or dividend equivalent) in the business before any "true" profits are realized. All entrepreneurs expect a return that will not only compensate them for the time and money they invest, but also reward them *well* for the risks and initiative they take in operating their own businesses. Not surprisingly, however, the profit incentive is a more powerful motivator for some entrepreneurs than for others. For example, people like Billy J. (Red) McCombs of San Antonio, TX, have a rather simple objective of making as much money as they can. Even as a boy, Red McCombs possessed an obvious entrepreneurial instinct, as noted by one writer's account:

> This single-mindedness baffled and sometimes distressed his gentle, middle-class parents. "When I was 11, I'd wash dishes in a cafe downtown from 4 p.m. until midnight and deliver newspapers at 5 a.m.," he recalls. "My mother would get tears in her eyes. 'You don't need to do this,' she'd say, and of course she was right. My father was an auto mechanic and we never wanted for anything. But I wanted to make money."[6]

Red McCombs' desire to make money led him into many entrepreneurial ventures. He has ownership interests in a chain of 100 Mr. M convenience stores, 7 radio stations, oil exploration in 2 states, a contract drilling company, real estate, a Rolls-Royce dealership, and San Antonio's NBA (National Basketball Association) franchise—the Spurs.

The preceding example portrays an entrepreneur who possesses an extremely strong interest in financial rewards. However, there are also those for whom profits are primarily a way of "keeping score." Such entrepreneurs may spend their profit on themselves or give it away, although most of them are not satisfied unless they make a "reasonable" profit. Indeed, some profit is necessary for survival because a firm which continues to lose money eventually becomes insolvent.

Independence

Freedom to operate independently is another basic reward of entrepreneurship. We know that the United States has long been known as a nation of rugged individualists. Many of us have a strong, even fierce, desire to make our own decisions, take risks, and reap the rewards for ourselves. Being one's own boss seems an attractive ideal.

Professor Albert Shapero, who studied entrepreneurs in many countries, argued that their driving motivation is independence. Following are his comments on his research:

> In hundreds of interviews in many countries, my colleagues and I have asked entrepreneurs how much money they would take to work for someone else—to become a manager in a corporation. No matter how they've complained about the difficulty of dealing with the economy, government regulations, and the unions, the answer is always the same, "There is no way I will work for others!"[7]

An example of the quest for independence is found in the case of Philip Bredesen of Nashville, TN, who found the constraints of corporate life distasteful when his employer was acquired by a larger company.[8] Although he was named a vice-president, he found that the merger made his job bureaucratic and frustrating. In 1980, therefore, he founded his own firm (which manages health maintenance organizations). For Bredesen, running his own business has been exhilarating. He says, "Your mistakes are your own. Your successes are yours. There is a sense of controlling your own destiny."[9]

Of course, independence does not guarantee an easy life. Most entrepreneurs work very hard for long hours. But they do have the satisfaction of making their own decisions within the constraints imposed by economic and other environmental factors.

A Satisfying Way of Life

Entrepreneurs frequently speak of the personal satisfaction they experience in their own businesses. Some even refer to business as "fun." Part of this enjoyment may derive from the independence described above, but some of it also apparently comes from the peculiar nature of the business, the entrepreneur's role in the business, and the entrepreneur's opportunities to be of service.

One example is Dick Considine, founder of Lincoln Logs, Ltd., producer of logs for do-it-yourself log houses. In discussing his business, he emphasizes psychic as much as monetary rewards:

> I think my greatest satisfaction is knowing that hundreds of people are living in these houses today, people who in many cases didn't think they could afford their own homes. We've done surveys...and found that the typical log-home dweller is a romantic. I really feel that, by channeling my own romanticism into a practical direction, I've made it possible for a lot of people to lead better lives.[10]

Figure 1-5   Entrepreneurial Incentives

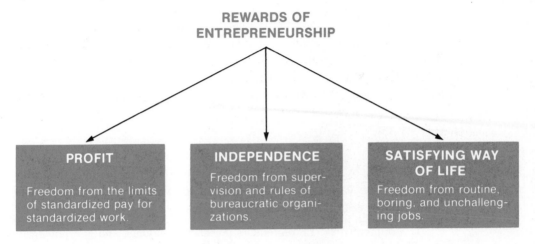

CHARACTERISTICS OF ENTREPRENEURS

Entrepreneurs have some qualities that distinguish them from the general population and even from professional managers. Researchers have emphasized such qualities as the need for achievement, willingness to take risks, self-confidence, and need to seek refuge from any of various environmental factors. However, research on this topic is far from definitive, and statements that identify entrepreneurial characteristics should be taken somewhat tentatively. Furthermore, since there are exceptions to every rule, some "unlikely" prospects may turn out to be highly successful entrepreneurs.

High Need for Achievement

Psychologists recognize that people differ in their need for achievement. Individuals with a low need for achievement are those who seem to be contented with their present status. On the other hand, individuals with a high need for achievement like to compete with some standard of excellence and prefer to be personally responsible for their own assigned tasks.

A leader in the study of achievement motivation is David C. McClelland, a Harvard psychologist.[11] He discovered a positive correlation between the need for achievement and entrepreneurial activity. In other words, those who become entrepreneurs have, on the average, a higher need for achievement than do members of the general population. Even among entrepreneurs, there are differences in achievement needs. Entrepreneurs heading faster-growing firms appear to have higher achievement needs than both nonentrepreneurs and entrepreneurs in slow-growth firms.[12]

This drive for achievement is reflected in the ambitious individuals who start new firms and then guide them in their growth. In some families, such entrepreneurial drive is evident at a very early stage. For example, sometimes a child takes a paper route, subcontracts it to a younger brother or sister, and then tries another venture. Also, some college students take over or start various types of student-related businesses or businesses that can be operated while pursuing an academic program.

Willingness to Take Risks

The risks that entrepreneurs take in starting and/or operating their own businesses are varied. Patrick R. Liles, a former Harvard professor, has identified four critical risk areas.[13] These are:

1. *Financial risk.* Entrepreneurs invest their savings and guarantee their bank loans.
2. *Career risk.* Entrepreneurs who fail may find it difficult to find employment afterward.
3. *Family risk.* The entrepreneur's spouse and children may suffer from inattention and emotional stress of coping with a business failure.
4. *Psychic risk.* The entrepreneur may be identified so closely with a venture that he or she takes business failure as a personal failure.

David C. McClelland discovered in his studies that individuals with a high need for achievement also have moderate risk-taking propensities.[14] This means that they prefer risky situations in which they can exert some control on the outcome, in contrast to gambling situations in which the outcome depends on pure luck. This preference for moderate risk reflects self-confidence, the next entrepreneurial characteristic that will be discussed.

Self-Confidence

Individuals who possess self-confidence feel that they can meet the challenges which confront them. They have a sense of mastery over the types of problems that they might encounter. Studies show that successful entrepreneurs tend to be self-reliant individuals who see the problems in launching a new venture but believe in their own ability to overcome these problems.

Some studies of entrepreneurs have measured the extent to which they are confident of their own abilities. According to J. B. Rotter, a psychologist, those who believe that their success depends upon their own efforts have an **internal locus of control**. In contrast, those who feel that their lives are controlled to a greater extent by luck or chance or fate have an **external locus of control**.[15] On the basis of research to date, it appears that entrepreneurs have a higher internal locus of control than is true of the population in general.

A Need to Seek Refuge

Although most people go into business to obtain the rewards of entrepreneurship discussed earlier, there are some who become entrepreneurs to escape from some environmental factor. Professor Russell M. Knight of the University of Western Ontario has identified a number of environmental factors that "push" people to found new firms and has labeled such entrepreneurs as "refugees."[16]

In thinking about these kinds of "refugees," we should recognize that many entrepreneurs are motivated as much or more by entrepreneurial rewards than by an "escapist" mind set. Indeed, there is often a mixture of positive and negative considerations in this regard. Nevertheless, this typology of "refugees" is suggestive, if not exhaustive, in clarifying some important considerations involved in much entrepreneurial activity.

The "Foreign Refugee"   There are many individuals who escape the political, religious, or economic constraints of their homelands by crossing national boundaries. Frequently such individuals face discrimination or handicaps in seeking salaried employment in the new country. As a result, many of them go into business for themselves. For example, Chris Nguyen came to the United States from South Vietnam at the age of 18 with no capital, no knowledge of business, and only a minimal proficiency in English.[17] After studying chemical engineering and business, he quit school in 1971 to start his own business. With a brother and sister, he founded a business to make Oriental eggrolls that he believed were far superior to those being sold in America. By 1984, the company was achieving sales of $4 million.

The "Corporate Refugee"   Individuals who flee the bureaucratic environment of big business (or even medium-size business) by going into business for themselves are identified by Professor Knight as **corporate refugees**. Some corporations spawn so many entrepreneurial offspring that they are described as "incubator organizations." For example, the Silicon Valley, a section south of San Francisco, CA, is populated by small electronic firms that have been "spun off" from large companies or otherwise started by corporate refugees.

Other "Refugees"   Other types of "refugees" mentioned by Professor Knight are the following:

Figure 1–6   The Entrepreneur as "Refugee"

B.C.   **BY JOHNNY HART**

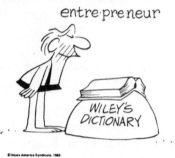

Source: By permission of Johnny Hart and News America Syndicate.

1. The *parental (paternal) refugee* who leaves a family business to show the parent that "I can do it alone."
2. The *feminist refugee* who experiences discrimination and elects to start a firm in which she can operate independently of male chauvinists.
3. The *housewife refugee* who starts her own business after her family is grown or at some other point when she can free herself from household responsibilities.
4. The *society refugee* who senses some alienation from the prevailing culture and expresses it by indulging in entrepreneurial activity—selling paintings to tourists, operating an energy-saving business, or starting some other type of firm.
5. The *educational refugee* who tires of an academic program and decides to enter the real world by going into business.

READINESS FOR ENTREPRENEURSHIP

Many people think about getting into business for themselves but are waiting for the right opportunity to come along. Others become so well-established in careers that they tend to get "locked into" salaried employment. They acquire interests in retirement programs and achieve promotion to positions of greater responsibility and higher salaries. And some look back over their careers as salaried personnel, thinking of "what might have been" if only they had gone into business for themselves, but recognize that it is now too late.

The Free-Choice Period

There is no question that education and experience are a part of the necessary preparation for most entrepreneurs. Although requirements vary with the nature and demands of a particular business, some type of "knowhow" is required. In addition, prospective entrepreneurs must build their financial resources in order to make initial investments. Nevertheless, there is a "right" time to get into business. As Figure 1–7 shows, the "free-choice period" occurs between a person's mid-twenties and mid-thirties. During this period, there tends to be a balance between preparatory experiences on the one hand and family obligations on the other.

Obviously, there are exceptions to this generalization. Some teenagers start their own firms. And other persons, even at 50 or 60 years of age, walk away from successful careers in big business when they become excited by the prospects of entrepreneurship.

Figure 1–7 The Free-Choice Period for Would-be Entrepreneurs

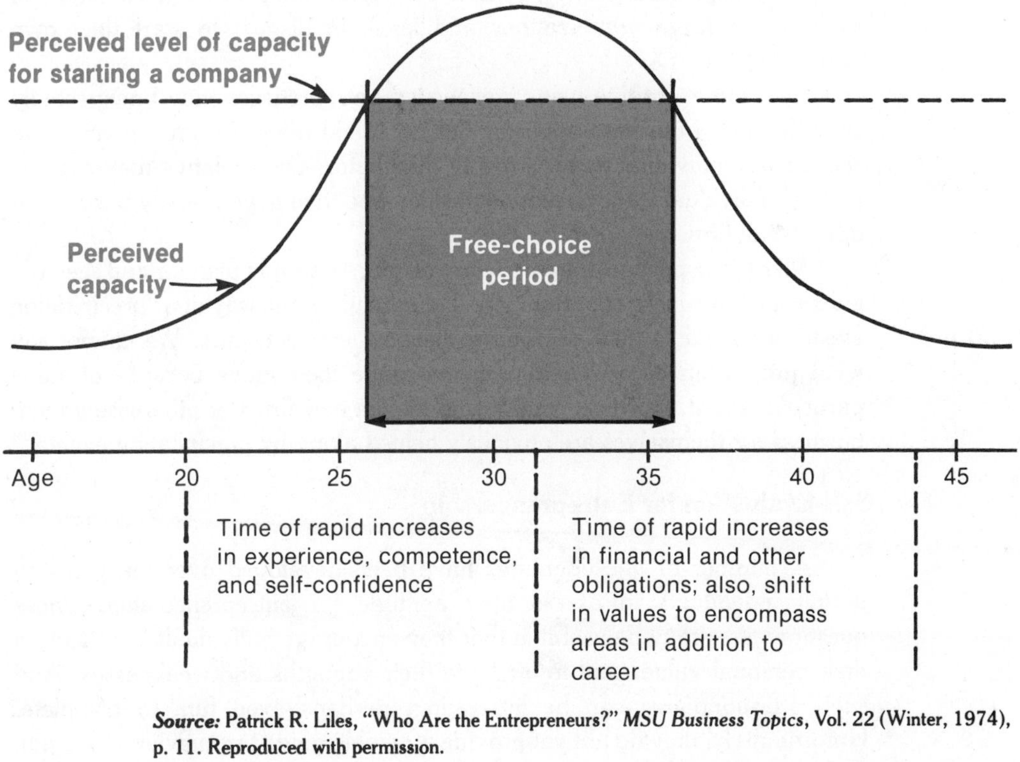

Source: **Patrick R. Liles, "Who Are the Entrepreneurs?"** ***MSU Business Topics*****, Vol. 22 (Winter, 1974), p. 11. Reproduced with permission.**

Precipitating Events

As suggested earlier, many potential entrepreneurs never take the fateful step of launching their own business ventures. Some of those who actually make the move are stimulated by **precipitating events** such as job termination, job dissatisfaction, or unexpected opportunities.

Charles E. Van Vorst has described how his dismissal from a large corporation caused him to start a small landscaping business.[18] After his executive job was abolished, he spent more than a year unsuccessfully seeking employment elsewhere and suffering the humiliation of standing in line for unemployment compensation. Finally, he started helping his two sons who had a weekend landscaping route. He enjoyed the work and began to build the route into a full-time business of his own, adding customer after customer as the weeks went by. His dismissal from corporate life had triggered his entry into a personally owned business.

Getting fired is only one of many types of experiences which may serve as a catalyst in "taking the plunge" as an entrepreneur. Some individuals become so disenchanted with formal academic programs that they simply walk away from the classroom and start new lives as entrepreneurs. Others become exasperated with the rebuffs or perceived injustices at the hands of superiors in large organizations and leave in disgust to start their own businesses.

In a more positive vein, prospective entrepreneurs may unexpectedly stumble across business opportunities. A friend may offer, for example, to sponsor an individual as an Amway distributor. Or a relative may suggest that the individual leave a salaried position and take over a family business or other small firm.

Many prospective entrepreneurs, of course, simply plan for and seek out independent business opportunities. There is little in the way of a "precipitating event" involved in their decision to become entrepreneurs. We cannot say what proportion of new entrepreneurs make their move because of some particular event. However, many who launch new firms or otherwise go into business for themselves are obviously helped along by precipitating events.[19]

Self-Evaluation for Entrepreneurship

A number of questionnaires have been developed over the years to permit individuals to assess their aptitude for entrepreneurship. These questionnaires may be useful in that they encourage individuals to reflect on their personal values and to evaluate their strengths and weaknesses. And such questionnaires can be interesting, perhaps even fun, to complete. Unfortunately, they do not yet provide a reliable guide for individual decision making.

The questionnaire shown in Figure 1–8 was developed on the basis of a study of 500 entrepreneurs by Dr. Alan Jacobowitz, a psychology professor at Trenton State College, Trenton, NJ. The entrepreneurial image conveyed by the Jacobowitz questionnaire is that of a restless, independent individual who tends to be a loner and somewhat arrogant. Intuitively, we can think of some entrepreneurs who match that stereotype very well. Futhermore, some research seems to support such a picture of the entrepreneurial personality.[20] Research evidence is mixed, however. The truth is that no one yet knows how to predict prospects for entrepreneurial success very accurately. Consequently, you may find some confirmation of your entrepreneurial inclinations in a questionnaire, but you should not allow a negative evaluation to deter you. Although there is much that is unknown about entrepreneurs, we do know that they are a very diverse lot!

Figure 1–8 Entrepreneurial Personality Quiz

Are you tough enough to be an entrepreneur? Do you have what it takes to start up your own business? We've put together a list of questions, based on Alan Jacobowitz's theory of entrepreneurial personality, that you can try to measure up against.

1. Were your parents, close relatives, or close friends entrepreneurs?
2. Did any of that business carry over into your home when you were growing up?
3. Did you have a lemonade stand or a paper route as a kid?
4. Was your academic record in school less than outstanding?
5. Did you feel like an outsider among peers at school?
6. Were you often reprimanded for your school behavior?
7. Do you have difficulty attaining satisfaction from any job with a large firm?
8. Do you often feel that you could do a better job than your boss?
9. Would you rather play sports than watch them on television?
10. Do you prefer nonfiction to fiction?
11. Have you ever been fired from a job or left one under pressure?
12. Do you never lose sleep at night over your work or personal business?
13. Would you rather jump into a project than plan one?
14. Would you consider yourself decisive, a good thinker on your feet?
15. Are you active in community affairs?

If you answered yes to 12 or more of these questions and you are not an entrepreneur already, you may be missing your big chance. If you answered yes to fewer than 12 and you already are an entrepreneur...well, good luck!

Source: Neil Cohen, "The Five Ages of the Entrepreneur," *Venture*, Vol. 2, No. 7 (July, 1980), p. 40. Reproduced with permission.

ENTREPRENEURIAL ROLES, VENTURES, AND STYLES

The field of small business encompasses a great variety of entrepreneurial roles, ventures, and styles. *Entrepreneurial roles* refer to the type of activity in which entrepreneurs are involved. *Entrepreneurial ventures* refer to types of businesses in terms of their potential for growth and profits. Different *entrepreneurial styles* usually result from the varied personal backgrounds of entrepreneurs.

Types of Entrepreneurial Roles

Although categories tend to overlap, entrepreneurial roles may be classified into three types: founders, general managers, and franchisees.

Founding Entrepreneurs   Generally considered to be the "pure" entrepreneurs, **founders** may be inventors who initiate businesses on the basis of new or improved products or services. They may also be craftsmen who develop skills and then start their own firms. Or they may be enterprising individuals, often with marketing backgrounds, who draw upon the ideas of others in starting new firms. Whether acting as individuals or in groups, these people bring firms into existence by surveying the market, raising funds, and arranging for the necessary facilities. After the firm is launched, the founding entrepreneur may preside over the subsequent growth of the business.

General Managers   As new firms become well-established, founders become less innovators and more administrators. Thus, we recognize another class of entrepreneurs called **general managers**. General managers preside over the operation of successful ongoing business firms. They manage the week-to-week and month-to-month production, marketing, and financial functions of small firms. The distinction between founders and general managers is often hazy. In some cases, small firms grow rapidly, and their orientation is more akin to the founding than to the management process. Nevertheless, it is helpful to distinguish those entrepreneurs who found and substantially change firms (the "movers" and "shakers") from those who direct the continuing operations of established firms.

Franchisees   It is helpful to recognize a third category of entrepreneurial role—that of the franchisee. Franchisees differ from general managers in the degree of their independence. Because of the constraints and guidance provided by contractual relationships with franchising organizations, franchisees function as limited entrepreneurs. Chapter 6 presents more information about franchisees.

Types of Entrepreneurial Ventures

Small-business ventures differ greatly in terms of their potential for growth and profits. To account for such variation, Patrick R. Liles has suggested the following categories: marginal firms, attractive small companies, and high-potential ventures.[21] In thinking about small business, however, one can easily fall into the trap of considering only one end of the spectrum. Some writers treat only the tiny, marginal firms whose owners barely survive, while others focus entirely on high-growth, high-technology firms. A balanced view must recognize the entire range of ventures with the varied problems and rewards presented by each point on the spectrum.

Marginal Firms   The very small dry cleaners, independent garages, beauty shops, service stations, appliance repair shops, and other small firms which provide a very modest return to their owners are the *marginal firms*. We do not call them "marginal" because they are in danger of bankruptcy. Some marginal firms, it is true, are on "thin ice" financially, but their distinguishing feature is their limited ability to generate significant profits. Entrepreneurs devote personal effort to such ventures and receive a profit return that does little more than compensate them for their time. Part-time businesses typically fall into this category of marginal firms.

ACTION REPORT
Polly Reilly's Part-Time Business—One Type of Marginal Firm

Polly Reilly of Westfield, NJ, discovered a business opportunity in a personal hobby. A wife and mother, she enrolled in an evening art class and was soon making tissue-paper collages, pressed-flower pictures, and pinecone candle holders. When friends bought them, she began selling them in local specialty shops. In November, 1968, she invited three fellow crafts enthusiasts to join her in a Christmas boutique in her home. The sale lasted three days and was highly successful.

A few years later, Mrs. Reilly employed a sales representative, and her ornaments were sold in fine stores throughout the country, including Bloomingdale's and Lord & Taylor's in New York. In 1979, she began to market her designs at craft shows on the Eastern seaboard, and she had plans to initiate a mail-order business.

In spite of success and growth, Mrs. Reilly continues to operate the business from her home. She described her home work area as follows:

> Even though I like my privacy, I am a gregarious soul at heart. I had an extension phone installed by my side, so I could talk to friends while I painted. A television set was placed on a nearby table so I could keep abreast of news and entertainment programs. Talk shows became my favorites, but I had to concentrate on the fact that only one of the glasses on my desk contained coffee. When one is absorbed in her work *and* Stanley Siegel, it's easy to gulp down a container of red paint.

Source: Polly Reilly, "How My Hobby Became a Business," *McCall's*, Vol. 107 (September, 1980), p. 106. Reprinted by permission of the McCall Publishing Company.

Attractive Small Companies   In contrast to marginal firms, numerous *attractive small firms* offer substantial rewards to their owners. Entrepreneurial income from these ventures may easily range from $50,000 to $200,000 annually. These are the strong segment of small business—the "good" firms which can provide rewarding careers even to well-educated young people. One example of such a business is a restaurant established in the late 1970s with a waterfront atmosphere and motif. This business has thrived with customers waiting in line at peak periods, and its owners' net income easily exceeds $100,000 per year.

High-Potential Ventures   A few firms have such great prospects for growth that they may be called *high-potential ventures*. Frequently these are also high-technology ventures. At the time of the firm's founding, the owners often anticipate rapid growth, a possible merger, or "going public" within a few years. Some of the more spectacular examples within recent years include Digital Equipment Corporation, Polaroid, Amway Corporation, Wendy's, and Word, Inc. In addition to such widely recognized successes, there are at any time thousands of less-well-known ventures being launched and experiencing rapid growth. Entrepreneurial ventures of this type appeal to many engineers, professional managers, and venture capitalists who see the potential rewards and exciting prospects.

Types of Entrepreneurial Styles

Perhaps because of their varied backgrounds, entrepreneurs display great variation in their styles of doing business. They analyze problems and approach decision making in drastically different ways. Norman R. Smith has suggested two basic entrepreneurial patterns: craftsman entrepreneurs and opportunistic entrepreneurs.[22]

The Craftsman Entrepreneur   According to Smith, the education of the **craftsman entrepreneur** is limited to technical training. Such entrepreneurs have technical job experience, but they lack good communications skills. Their approach to business decision making is characterized by the following features:

1. They are paternalistic. (This means they direct their businesses much as they might direct their own families.)
2. They are reluctant to delegate authority.
3. They use few (one or two) capital sources to create their firms.
4. They define marketing strategy in terms of the traditional price, quality, and company reputation.
5. Their sales efforts are primarily personal.
6. Their time orientation is short, with little planning for future growth or change.

The typical mechanic who starts an independent garage and the beautician who operates a beauty shop illustrate the craftsman entrepreneur.

The Opportunistic Entrepreneur   Smith's definition of the **opportunistic entrepreneur** is one who has supplemented technical education by studying such nontechnical subjects as economics, law, or English. Opportunistic entrepreneurs avoid paternalism, delegate authority as necessary for growth, employ various marketing strategies and types of sales efforts, obtain original capitalization from more than two sources, and plan for future growth. An example of the opportunistic entrepreneur is the small building contractor and developer who uses a relatively sophisticated approach to management. Because of the complexity of the industry, successful contractors use careful record keeping, proper budgeting, precise bidding, and systematic marketing research.

In Smith's model of entrepreneurial styles, we see two extremes of managerial approach. At the one end, we find a craftsman in an entrepreneurial position. At the other end, we find a well-educated and experienced manager. The former flies "by the seat of his pants," and the latter uses systematic management procedures and something resembling a scientific management approach. In practice, of course, the distribution of entrepreneurial styles is less polarized than suggested by the model, with entrepreneurs scattered along a continuum in terms of their managerial sophistication. This book is intended to help the student move toward the opportunistic end and away from the craftsman end of the continuum.

Entrepreneurial Teams

In the discussion thus far, we have assumed that entrepreneurs are individuals. And, of course, this is usually the case. However, the entrepreneurial team is another possibility that is becoming popular, particularly in ventures of substantial size. An **entrepreneurial team** is formed by bringing together two or more individuals to function in the capacity of entrepreneurs.

By forming a team, founders can secure a broader range of managerial talents than is otherwise possible. For example, a person with manufacturing experience can team up with a person who has marketing experience. The need for such diversified experience is particularly acute in creating new high-technology businesses.

One study of 890 company founders found that 39.1 percent had one or more full-time partners.[23] The authors recognized the fact that their sample underrepresented very small firms and businesses in the service industry. Even though the study, therefore, tends to overemphasize the use of entrepreneurial teams, it does suggest that founding teams are not unusual.

Looking Back

1. Entrepreneurial opportunities are unlimited, as evidenced by various dramatic success stories of successful entrepreneurs.
2. Entrepreneurial rewards include profits, independence, and a satisfying way of life.
3. Individuals who become entrepreneurs have a high need for achievement, a willingness to take moderate risks, and a high degree of self-confidence.
4. The period between a person's mid-twenties and mid-thirties is described as the "free-choice period" in which entry into entrepreneurial careers tends to be easiest. The specific step into many entrepreneurs' businesses is often triggered by a "precipitating event" such as losing a job. Entrepreneurship includes a variety of entrepreneurial roles (founding versus managing, for example); types of ventures (marginal firms versus high-potential ventures, for example); and management style (craftsman versus opportunistic entrepreneurs, for example). Another distinctive type of entrepreneurship is the entrepreneurial team, in contrast to the individual entrepreneur, which provides leadership for the firm.

DISCUSSION QUESTIONS

1. What is meant by the term *entrepreneur*?
2. When we read the outstanding success stories at the beginning of the chapter, we realize they are exceptions to the rule. What, then, is their significance in illustrating entrepreneurial opportunity? Are these stories misleading?
3. Some corporate executives receive annual compensation in excess of $3 million. Profits of most small businesses are much less. How, then, can profits constitute a meaningful incentive for entrepreneurs?
4. What is the most significant reason for following an independent business career by the entrepreneur whom you know best?
5. In view of the fact that entrepreneurs must satisfy customers, employees, bankers, and others, are they really independent? Explain the nature of their independence as a reward for self-employment.
6. What is shown by the studies of David C. McClelland regarding an entrepreneur's need for achievement?
7. What types of risks are faced by entrepreneurs, and what degree of risks do they prefer?
8. Explain the internal locus of control and its significance for entrepreneurship.
9. On the basis of your own knowledge, can you identify a "foreign refugee" who is an entrepreneur?

10. Why is the period from the mid-twenties to the mid-thirties considered to be the "free-choice period" for becoming an er

11. What is a precipitating event? Give some examples.

12. What is the difference between a marginal firm and a high-potential ventu.

13. Distinguish between a craftsman entrepreneur and an opportunistic entrepreneur.

14. What is the advantage of using an entrepreneurial team?

ENDNOTES

1. For an extended discussion of the nature of entrepreneurship, see Justin G. Longenecker and John E. Schoen, "The Essence of Entrepreneurship," *Journal of Small Business Management*, Vol. 13 (July, 1975), pp. 26–32.

2. This information is taken from a number of sources. One of the most thorough reviews of Fatjo's career is Craig R. Waters, "The Gospel According to Fatjo," *Inc.*, Vol. 4 (April, 1982), pp. 52–59.

3. Craig R. Waters, "Fleshing out an Empire," *Inc.*, Vol. 6 (October, 1984), pp. 53–61.

4. This story of Barbara Gardner Proctor is reported in Jill Bettner and Christine Donahue, "Now They're Not Laughing," *Forbes*, Vol. 132, No. 12 (November 21, 1983), p. 124.

5. The account given here is drawn from a number of different sources. One particularly helpful source is "Frederick W. Smith of Federal Express: He Didn't Get There Overnight," *Inc.*, Vol. 6, No. 4 (April, 1984), pp. 88–89.

6. "Red McCombs: Making Money's Fun," *Forbes*, Vol. 126 (September 15, 1980), p. 124.

7. Albert Shapero, "Taking Control," *In Business*, Vol. 5, No. 2 (March–April, 1983), p. 61.

8. Sabin Russell, "Being Your Own Boss in America," *Venture*, Vol. 6, No. 5 (May, 1984), p. 52.

9. *Ibid.*

10. Carol Rose Carey, "Mr. Considine Builds His Dream House," *Inc.*, Vol. 4, No. 3 (March, 1982), p. 113.

11. David C. McClelland, *The Achieving Society* (New York: The Free Press, 1961); see also David C. McClelland and David G. Winter, *Motivating Economic Achievement* (New York: The Free Press, 1969).

12. Norman R. Smith and John B. Miner, "Motivational Considerations in the Success of Technologically Innovative Entrepreneurs," in John A. Hornaday, *et al.* (eds.), *Frontiers of Entrepreneurial Research, 1984* (Wellesley, MA: Babson College), pp. 488–495.

13. Patrick R. Liles, "Who Are the Entrepreneurs?" *MSU Business Topics*, Vol. 22 (Winter, 1974), pp. 13–14.

14. McClelland, *The Achieving Society, op. cit.*, Chapter 6. See also Robert H. Brockhaus, Sr., "Risk-Taking Propensity of Entrepreneurs," *Academy of Management Journal*, Vol. 23 (September, 1980), pp. 509–520. He questions the extent to which entrepreneurial risk-taking propensities differ from those of managers and the general population.

15. See J. B. Rotter, "Generalized Expectancies for Internal Versus External Control of Reinforcement," *Psychological Monographs*, 1966a. A recent review is given in Robert H. Brockhaus, Sr., "The Psychology of the Entrepreneur," in Calvin A. Kent, Donald L. Sexton, and Karl H. Vesper (eds.), *Encyclopedia of Entrepreneurship* (Englewood Cliffs, NJ: Prentice-Hall, Inc., 1982), pp. 39–57.

16. Russell M. Knight, "Entrepreneurship in Canada," a paper presented at the Annual Conference of the International Council for Small Business, Asilomar, CA, June 22–25, 1980.

17. Carter Henderson, "An American Dream Fulfilled with Eggrolls," *In Business*, Vol. 6, No. 4 (July–August, 1984), pp. 20–23.

18. Charles E. Van Vorst, "Behind the White Line," *In Business*, Vol. 4 (March–April, 1982), pp. 25–26.

19. For a study of job dissatisfaction as a precipitating event, see Robert H. Brockhaus, Sr., "The Effect of Job Dissatisfaction on the Decision to Start a Business," *Journal of Small Business Management*, Vol. 18 (January, 1980), pp. 37–43.

20. See, for example, Orvis Collins and David G. Moore, *The Organization Makers: A Behavioral Study of Independent Entrepreneurs* (New York: Appleton-Century-Crofts, 1970). Conflicting evidence is presented in Arnold C. Cooper and William C. Dunkelberg, "Influences upon Entrepreneurship—A Large-Scale Study," a paper presented to the Academy of Management, San Diego, CA, August 4, 1981.

21. Patrick R. Liles, "Who Is the Entrepreneur?" *Wharton Quarterly*, Vol. 7 (Spring, 1974), pp. 14–31.

22. For a recent treatment, see Gary McCain and Norman R. Smith, "A Contemporary Model of Entrepreneurial Style," a paper presented at the Annual Conference of the International Council for Small Business, Asilomar, CA, June 22–25, 1980. A similar model was earlier presented in Norman R. Smith, *The Entrepreneur and His Firm: The Relationship Between Type of Man and Type of Company*, Occasional Paper (East Lansing: Division of Research, Graduate School of Business Administration, Michigan State University, 1967).

23. Arnold C. Cooper and William C. Dunkelberg, "Influences upon Entrepreneurship—A Large-Scale Study," paper presented to Academy of Management, San Diego, CA, August 4, 1981.

REFERENCES TO SMALL BUSINESS IN ACTION

Feinberg, Andrew. "Inside the Entrepreneur." *Venture*, Vol. 6, No. 5 (May, 1984), pp. 80–86.
    A psychological study of 77 individuals, all of whom ran businesses that gave them personal incomes of $90,000 or more, is reported.

Merwin, John. "Have You Got What It Takes?" *Forbes*, Vol.128, No. 3 (August 3, 1981), pp. 60–64.
    This article profiles a number of prosperous entrepreneurs and outlines the qualities that made them successful.

Nelton, Sharon. "The People Who Take the Plunge." *Nation's Business*, Vol. 72, No. 6 (June, 1984), pp. 22–26.
    Characteristics of entrepreneurs are illustrated by citing examples of specific individuals. The article also includes a test that purportedly measures the qualities of the successful entrepreneur.

"Women in Charge: Eight Who Made It." *U.S. News & World Report*, Vol. 88, No. 11 (March 24, 1980), pp. 64–66.

    Women often show great success as entrepreneurs. This article describes eight "winners" in such varied fields as asphalt paving, wire-rope sales, and construction.

"Wooden Wagon Is Back," *In Business*, Vol. 4 (November–December, 1982), p. 10.

    A craftsman entrepreneur who makes children's wooden wagons "the way they used to" is featured. The solid oak wagon with ball bearing wheels sells for $160.

CASE 1

Construction Equipment Dealership*

Weighing a career with IBM against running the family business

As Professor Alan Stone talked on the telephone, he watched his graduate assistant, Jerry Weston, shifting nervously in his chair. When Stone had completed his call, the following conversation with Jerry took place.

Professor: Sorry we were interrupted, Jerry! You said you have a problem. How can I help you?

Jerry: Dr. Stone, I'll be finishing my M.B.A. next month, and I still haven't been able to decide which job offer to accept. Two of the companies want answers next week, so I simply have to make some decisions.

Professor: Well, Jerry, you will have to make the final determination yourself, but we can certainly discuss the various alternatives. As a matter of curiosity, did any of the consulting work we did for IBM ever result in a job offer?

Jerry: Yes, sir! IBM has offered me a really intriguing project-planning job in their National Marketing Division in Atlanta at $32,800. I would have a lot of responsibility from the start, and I would be coordinating the efforts of personnel from several functional departments. If all went well, they have indicated I'd probably have a good chance to be the head of product development for the entire division. Of course, they would pay all moving expenses, and they really have a package of fringe benefits.

Professor: That sounds awfully good! What else do you have?

Jerry: Samsonite, Shell Development, and Boise Cascade. If my wife has her way, we'll go to San Francisco with Boise Cascade. My only question is, can two people live in San Francisco on $29,000 a year, particularly if one of them is my wife?

Professor: Say, what about the family business? Have you given up the idea of being the biggest construction equipment dealer in Billings, Montana?

Jerry: No, sir, not really! As a matter of fact, that's one of the complicating factors. I've been getting some pressure to go back to Billings.

Professor: How do you mean, Jerry?

Jerry: Well, I never really noticed how subtle Dad has been until I started thinking about it. As far as I can recall, he has never specifically said that he thought I should come into the business. But he always said that the opportunity was there if I wanted to take it. His classic statement is how good the business and Billings have been to the family, and I think it is fair to say he influenced me to go to Iowa State, his alma mater, and even to major in

*This case was prepared by John E. Schoen, Richards Equipment Company, Waco TX.

accounting. My uncle, who is the accountant in our company, is retiring this year, and I see now that I was probably being prepared all along for that position.

Professor: Does you mother voice an opinion?

Jerry: Yes, sir! She voices more than an opinion! To give you an idea, the last time I talked to her about some of the job offers, she burst into tears and said that it would break my father's heart if I didn't join the business. She said they built the business for me and that they hadn't worked all those years to turn it over to some stranger. Since my uncle has to retire because of his health, she accused me of turning my back on Dad just when he needs me the most. By the time she finished, she had me feeling confused, miserable, and mad!

Professor: Mad?

Jerry: Yeah! Mom made some statements about Carol, my wife. Mom thinks Carol is trying to persuade me not to go back to Billings because it's too small and I'd be too close to the family. I suppose I wouldn't have been so angry if it hadn't been partially the truth!

Professor: You mean your wife doesn't want to go to Billings?

Jerry: Oh, I'm sure she'll go if that's what I decide to do, but I think she'd greatly prefer San Francisco. She is from Seattle and likes all the bright lights and activity in big cities. In addition, she has a degree in interior design and the opportunities for employment and learning would be greater in San Francisco than any of the other places, particularly Billings. She has worked to help put me through school for the last two years, so I may owe this to her. She also believes it would be better for me to stand on my own two feet and asks why I went for an M.B.A. if all I was going to do was join the family business. She made me mad, too, last week when she said the worst thing she can imagine is being barefoot and pregnant and eating at my folks' house three times a week.

Professor: What about the Shell and the Samsonite offers?

Jerry: Oh, they're really just offers I've had. It is basically San Francisco, IBM, or home!

Professor: Well, Jerry, you do seem to have a problem. Can you compare the nature of the work in each job?

Jerry: Yes, sir! The IBM job looks very interesting, and the possibilities for advancement are good. Boise Cascade, on the other hand, has a typical cost accounting position. I suppose it would be all right for a couple of years while Carol does her thing and we see if we like San Francisco, but something else would have to come along eventually!

Professor: What about your work in the family business?

Jerry: That's the funny part of it! Everything about the IBM offer—the salary, fringes, authority, prestige, promotion possibilities, and so forth—appeals to me, but I like the family business, too. I mean I've grown up in the business; I know and like the employees, customers, and suppliers; and I really like Billings. Of course, I'd be working as an accountant for awhile; but I would eventually succeed my father, and I've always thought I'd like to run the business someday.

Professor: What about salary in the family business?

Jerry: That's a part I've forgotten to tell you! Last week, my uncle was in town, and even he was dropping broad hints about the family looking forward to our return to Billings and how he will give me a short orientation and then "get the heck outa Dodge." His parting comment was that he was certain Dad would match anything the big companies could do on starting salary.

Professor: Even $32,800?

Jerry: Apparently! Well, there it is, Dr. Stone! What do you think? I've got to let IBM know by the end of the month.

Professor: I don't know, Jerry. Could you go with IBM or Boise Cascade for a couple of years and then go back to the family business?

Jerry: I thought of that possibility, but I think that if I'm going to go with the family business, this is the right time. Uncle Phil is retiring, so there is a position; and I know Dad was a little hesitant about the M.B.A. versus getting experience in the family business. Dad is approaching 60, and the business is hitting all-time highs, so I believe he will try to sell it if I go somewhere else. No, I think it's now or never!

Professor: Well, you were right about one thing, Jerry. You do have a dilemma! This reminds me of the cases in management textbooks—no easy solution! Good luck, and let me know your decision.

Jerry: Thanks, Prof!

Questions

1. Does Jerry Weston have an obligation to the family to provide leadership for the family business?
2. What obligation does Jerry have to his wife in view of her background, education, and career interests?
3. Should Jerry simply do what he wants to do? Does he know what he wants to do?
4. In view of the conflict between Jerry's own interests and those of his wife, what should his career choice be?

2

The Family Business

Figure 2–1   The Komar Family

©*James Hamilton*

  A family business may involve several generations of a family. Such is the case with Charles Komar & Sons, a family firm in the garment-manufacturing industry. One writer states:

>   In the family, they already tell stories about Herman Komar's son, young Charlie. How at two he crawled up on to his great-aunt's lap to show her the picture he had crayoned—"My factory," he announced proudly. How at five he would sit in a garment bin while his father pulled him through their New Jersey plant, down the long rows of sewing machines, past the piles of lace and trim. Day after day he would hear the tales of his grandfather, an immigrant just eight years over from Russia, starting out back in 1908 on New York's Lower East Side with a few seamstresses and $500 borrowed from the Hebrew Free Loan Association. Even before he could read, Charlie would perch at the kitchen table with his dad, trying to decipher the day's CVO (cuts versus order)—the pulse beat of the family's lingerie-manfacturing business.

Source: Reprinted with permission, *Inc.* magazine, November, 1984. Copyright © 1984 by Inc. Publishing Company, 38 Commercial Wharf, Boston, MA 02110

Looking Ahead

Watch for the following important topics:

1. The way family and business interests overlap.
2. Special advantages and distinctive values deriving from family involvement.
3. Special concerns of nonfamily employees.
4. Roles of Dad, Mother, sons, daughters, in-laws, and others.
5. The process of succession—how the next generation takes over.

Many firms are readily recognized as "family businesses." The obvious implication is that a family is involved in some special way in the operation and decision-making processes of the business. In this chapter we look at the family business and the characteristics that make it unique in the world of small business.

THE FAMILY BUSINESS: A UNIQUE INSTITUTION

A number of features distinguish the family firm from other types of small businesses. In its decision making and culture, for example, we observe a congruence of family and business values. This section examines the family business as a unique type of institution.

What Is a Family Business?

To speak of a family business is to imply an involvement of the family in the life and functioning of that business. The nature and extent of that involvement varies. In some firms, family members may work full-time or part-time. In a small restaurant, for example, the entrepreneur may serve as host and manager, the spouse may keep the books, and the children may work in the kitchen or serve as waiters or waitresses.

The business also comes to be distinguished as a family business when it passes from one generation to another. For example, Thompson's Plumbing Supply may be headed by Bill Thompson, Jr., son of the founder who is now deceased. His son, Bill Thompson III, has started to work on the sales floor, after serving in the stockroom during his high school years. He seems to be the heir apparent who will some day replace his father. People in the community recognize Thompson's Plumbing Supply as a family business.

Most family businesses, and the type we are concerned with in this book, are small. However, family considerations may continue to be important even when these businesses become large corporations. Companies like DuPont, Levi Strauss and Company, Ford Motor Company, and Bechtel Corporation are still recognized, to some extent, as family businesses.

Family and Business Overlap

The family business is composed of both a family and a business. Although these are separate institutions—each with its own members, goals, and values—they are brought into a condition of overlap in the family firm.

Families and businesses exist for fundamentally different reasons.[1] The family's primary function relates to the care and nurture of family members, whereas the business is concerned with the production of goods and/or services. The family's goal is the fullest possible development of each member, regardless of limitations in ability, and the provision of equal opportunities and rewards for each member. The business goal is profitability and survival. There is a possibility for either harmony or conflict in these goals, but it is obvious that they are not identical. In the short run, what is best for the family may or may not be what is best for the business.

Figure 2–2   The Overlap of Family Concerns and Business Interests

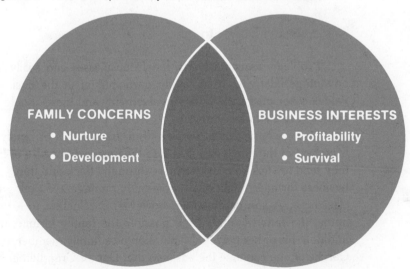

Business Decisions and Family Decisions

Family relationships complicate the management process of the family firm. Some *business* decisions are also *family* decisions, and nonfamily managers may be surprised at the way in which family interests influence business operations. Rene Plessner, whose executive search firm specializes in finding executives for family-owned companies, explains how family decisions dominate the business:

> In a family company, you may have the title and the responsibility, and one day you walk into the office and you don't know that two cousins, a brother-in-law, sister, and the Papa had dinner over the weekend and made a decision upsetting what you expected to do...Nobody was out to get you; it's simply, to be trite about it, blood is thicker than water. The family members talk among themselves. You have to be flexible enough to handle that.[2]

If the business is to survive, its interests cannot be unduly compromised to satisfy family wishes. Firms that grow must recognize the need for professional management and the necessary limitations on family concerns. An example is found in the experience of Pierre DuPont:

> As far as Pierre was concerned, the large firm did not have the obligation to provide the family with jobs; instead, it should ensure them of large dividends. Of course, when the firm expanded, there would be increased employment opportunities for younger relatives. Family traditions were meaningful to Pierre, and he saw the family as playing a different role rather than being forgotten.[3]

The health and survival of the family business, therefore, requires a proper balancing of business and family interests. Otherwise, results will be unsatisfactory to both the business and the family.

Advantages of Family Involvement in the Business

Problems associated with family businesses can easily blind us to the advantages deriving from family participation in the business. There *are* values associated with family involvement, and these should be recognized and used in the family firm.

One primary benefit derives from the strength of family relationships. Members of the family are drawn to the business because of family ties, and they tend to stick with the business through "thick and thin." A downturn in business fortunes might cause nonfamily managers to seek greener pastures elsewhere. A son or daughter, however, is reluctant to leave. The family name, the family welfare, and possibly the family fortune are at stake. In addition, his or her personal reputation as a family member may be at stake. Can he or she continue the business that Dad or Grandfather built?

ACTION REPORT
Business Benefits from Family Relationships

One benefit deriving from family relationships is the willingness of family members to "help out" when needed. When Angus Wurtele attended Stanford Business School in 1961, he aspired to run a rapidly growing electronics firm like Hewlett-Packard or Control Data.

However, Minnesota Paints Company, an unglamorous paint manufacturer founded by a great-uncle in 1870, needed a helping hand after the death of its company president. Wurtele reluctantly agreed to help "for a while" after graduation. Rather than moving on quickly, however, he stayed with the company (now Valspar Corporation), acquired other paint companies, and made the firm the industry's profit leader.

Source: "Bargain Hunter," *Forbes*, Vol. 133 (June 4, 1984), pp. 177–178.

Family members may also sacrifice income needed in the business. Rather than draw large salaries or high dividends, they permit such resources to remain in the business for current needs. Many families have gone without a new car or new furniture long enough to let the new business get started or to get through a period of financial stress.

Family firms also possess certain features that can contribute to superior business decision making. To achieve their full potential, family businesses must develop some key advantages. According to Peter Davis, three such advantages are the following:[4]

1. *Preserving the humanity of the workplace.* A family business can easily demonstrate higher levels of concern and caring for individuals than are found in the typical corporation.
2. *Focusing on the long run.* A family business can take the long-run view more easily than corporate managers who are being judged on year-to-year results.
3. *Emphasizing quality.* Family businesses have long maintained a tradition of providing quality and value to the consumer.

The Culture of the Family Business

The imprint of its founder is often evident in the family firm. The founder may emphasize values which become part of the business and family code. Observance of such values becomes a matter of family pride. Of course, the founder cannot merely foist his or her values upon the organization. As Stein has pointed out, these basic assumptions can become part of the culture only if they work and become accepted by the group.[5]

The founder, for example, may develop the business by catering to customer needs in a special way. Customer service becomes a guiding principle for the business, and legends may be passed on to illustrate the extreme measures taken by the founder to satisfy customer needs. Any business operates according to some set of values, but the family business follows with special diligence those values clearly emphasized by the founding family.

Knowledge of family business values is not limited to employees and managers. Even the general public perceives the family firm as possessing characteristics that distinguish it from nonfamily enterprises. Research has shown, for example, that the public believes that family firms have higher ethical standards and that they show greater concern for customers than do nonfamily firms.[6]

Nonfamily Members in a Family Firm

Even those employees who are not family members are nevertheless affected by family considerations. In some cases their opportunities for promotion are circumscribed by the presence of family members who seem to have the "inside track" for promotion. What father is going to promote an outsider over a competent son who is being groomed for future leadership? The potential for advancement of nonfamily members, therefore, may be limited.

The extent of such limitation will depend on the number of family members active in the business and the number of managerial or professional positions in the business to which a nonfamily member might aspire. It will also depend on the extent to which the owner demands competence in management and maintains an atmosphere of fairness in supervision. To avoid a stifling atmosphere, the owner should make clear the extent of opportunity that does exist for the nonfamily member and identify the positions, if any, that are reserved for family members.

Nonfamily members may also be caught in the crossfire between family members who are competing with each other. Family feuds in family businesses make it difficult for outsiders to maintain strict neutrality. If a nonfamily employee is perceived as siding with one contender, he or she will lose the support of other family members. Some hard-working employees no doubt feel they deserve hazard pay for working in a firm plagued by an unusual amount of family conflict.

ACTION REPORT
Son-in-Law Marvin

Promoting family members of a business, according to the following report, should be handled in a manner that will minimize anxiety among nonfamily members:

Marvin was sharp, ambitious, and a graduate of a good business school. When Ruthie married Marvin, the family beamed with delight. And when his father-in-law, the president, offered Marvin the vice-presidency after a one-year apprenticeship, it was not true that he had gotten a job he didn't deserve.

Of course, he got it sooner than he might have otherwise. But he worked hard, and he was competent.

What, then, was the problem? As I found when I ran across this situation in a company we once considered for acquisition, the problem was disgruntlement in the ranks.

Marvin's job, with its prestige and fat salary, was a plum sought after by a whole field of contenders. When Marvin won out, the inevitable conclusion was that he had been smiled upon not because of his ability, but because he had married the boss's daughter. What followed was an exodus of talented managers and seething bitterness among many who remained. One of them summed up the feelings of all: "The only way to get ahead in this outfit is to marry into the family."

Care must always be taken in promoting family members. In this case, management should have tried for two objectives. One was to get the message across that, son-in-law or not, Marvin was good for the firm.

At the same time, management should have made it clear that you did not have to be a relative to get ahead in the company. It is important to design an attractive management development and advancement program that includes nonfamily members as well as those in the family.

Source: Robert E. Levinson, "What to Do about Relatives on the Payroll," *Nation's Business*, Vol. 64 (October, 1976), p. 56

FAMILY ROLES AND RELATIONSHIPS

As noted earlier, a family business involves the overlapping of two institutions—a family and a business. This fact makes the family firm incredibly difficult to manage. In this section we examine a few of the numerous possible family roles and relationships that contribute to the complexity of such a firm.

Mom or Dad, the Founder

A common figure in the family business is the man or woman who founds the firm and plans to pass it on to a son or a daughter. In most cases, the business and the family grow simultaneously. Some founders achieve a delicate balance between their business and family responsibilities. In other situations, parents must exert great diligence to squeeze out time for weekends and vacation time with the children. In some cases, business pressures are such that the family suffers neglect. In any event, parents generally experience tension in trying to reconcile business demands and family responsibilities.

Entrepreneurs who have sons and daughters typically think in terms of passing the business on to the next generation of the family. Parental concerns in this process include the following:

1. Does my son or daughter possess the temperament and ability necessary for business leadership?
2. How can I, the founder, motivate my son or daughter to take an interest in the business?
3. What type of education and experience will be most helpful in preparing my son or daughter for leadership?
4. What timetable should I follow in employing and promoting my son or daughter?
5. How can I avoid favoritism in managing and developing my son or daughter?
6. How can I prevent the business relationship from damaging or destroying the parent–child relationship?

Of all relationships in the family business, the parent–child relationship (especially the father–son relationship) has been most sensitive and troublesome. The issue and problem have been recognized informally for generations. In more recent years, counseling has developed, seminars have been created, and books have been written about such relationships. In spite of an abundant literature, however, the parent–child relationship continues to perplex numerous families involved in family businesses.

Couples in Business

Some family businesses involve husband–wife teams. Their roles may vary depending on their backgrounds and expertise. In some cases, the husband serves as general manager and the wife runs the office. In other cases, the wife functions as operations manager and the husband keeps the books. Whatever the arrangement, both parties are an integral part of the business.

An interesting example is found in a New Hampshire country store operated by Richard and Jane Kokel.[7] Kokel, an escapee from corporate life as a chemical engineer, bought the store and adjoining apartment in 1978 for about $110,000, using money from the sale of their house as a down payment. The store is set up as a partnership between Richard and Jane, with Jane helping in the store three hours a day and caring for their two-year-old son the rest of the time.

A potential advantage of the husband-wife team is the opportunity it provides for them to share more of their life. Richard Kokel enjoys having the family together in the rural environment of New Hampshire. "It's been great for our son," he adds. "He gets a lot of attention from the customers."[8]

For some couples, the potential benefits tend to become eclipsed by problems related to the business. Differences of opinion about business matters may carry over into family life. And the energies of both parties may be so dissipated by their work in a struggling family firm that little zest remains for a strong family life.

Sons and Daughters

Should sons and daughters be groomed for the family business, or should they pursue careers of their own choosing? This is a basic question facing the entrepreneurial family. A natural tendency is to think in terms of a family business career and to push the son or daughter, either openly or subtly, in that direction. Little thought, indeed, may be given to the basic issues involved.

One question is that of talent, aptitude, and temperament. The offspring may be a "chip off the old block," but the offspring may also be an individual with different bents and aspirations. The son or daughter may prefer music or medicine to what he or she perceives to be the mundane world of business. He or she may fit the business mold very poorly. It is also possible that the abilities of the son or daughter may simply be insufficient for the leadership role. (Of course, a child's talents may be underestimated by parents simply because there has been little opportunity for development.)

A second issue is that of freedom. We live in a society that values the rights of individuals to choose their own careers and way of life. If the entrepreneur wishes to recognize this value—a value that is typically embraced by the son or daughter—that son or daughter must be granted the freedom to select a career of his or her own choosing.

The son or daughter may feel a need to go outside the family business, for a time at least, to prove that "I can make it on my own." To build self-esteem, the young person may wish to operate independently of the family. Going back to the family business immediately may seem stifling— "continuing to feel like a little kid with Dad telling me what to do."

If the family business is profitable, it does provide opportunities. The son or daughter may well give serious consideration to accepting such a challenge. If the relationship is to be satisfactory, however, family pressure must be minimized. And both parties must recognize the choice as a business decision, as well as a family decision—a decision that may conceivably be reversed.

Sibling Cooperation—Sibling Rivalry

In families having a number of children, two or more of them may become involved in the family firm. This depends, of course, on the interests of the individual children. In some cases, parents feel themselves fortunate if even one child elects to stay with the family firm. Nevertheless, it is not unusual for two or more, sometimes all, of the children to take positions in the family business. Even those who do not work in the business may be more than casual observers on the sidelines because of their stake as heirs or partial owners.

At best, the children work as a smoothly functioning team, each contributing services according to his or her respective abilities. Just as some families experience excellent cooperation and unity in their family relationships, so family businesses can benefit from effective collaboration among brothers and sisters.

But just as there are squabbles within the family, so can there also be sibling rivalry within the business. Business issues tend to generate competition internally (within the firm), as well as externally (in the marketplace), and this affects family as well as nonfamily members. Two sons, for example, may disagree about business policy or about their respective roles in the business.

One older son, Howard, described a power struggle that developed between him and his younger brother, Charles, over which one would run the company after their father relinquished control:

> In his mid-twenties, when I was about thirty-five, Charles let me know he planned to succeed Dad in the top spot. Years before, when he was in high school, I had assured him I envisioned him taking the company's lead. But the passing of time and my own grasp on power made that memory very dim. Now, sitting in my office, his words bombed me:
> "Howard, what are your long-range plans?"
> "I don't know," I said. "One day at a time."
> "We've got to think about the future," he said, "and if I'm going to stay, then I'm going to be in charge. Leadership can't work undefined."
> I spat out my answer. If words could be flames, mine would have burned up that desktop.
> "Well, I don't plan to leave."
> Charles insisted on knowing precisely who was in command. He refused to work under a part-time brother as a boss. He demanded our company hierarchy be spelled out.[9]

After reacting furiously to his younger brother's challenge, Howard reflected more calmly on his own interests and the overall welfare of the family and the business. Eventually, he agreed that leadership should be assumed by the younger brother and, as he expressed it, "a family mess turned into a family miracle."[10]

In-Laws in and out of the Business

As sons and daughters marry, the sons-in-law and daughters-in-law become significant actors in the family business drama. Some of them may be directly involved when one, a son-in-law, for example, is employed in the family firm. If a son or daughter is also employed in the same firm, the potential for rivalry and conflict is present. How are the performance and progress of a son-in-law to be rewarded equitably as compared with the performance and progress of a son or daughter?

For a time, effective collaboration may be achieved by assigning family members to different branches or roles within the company. Eventually, the competition for top leadership will require decisions that distinguish among sons, daughters, sons-in-law, and daughters-in-law employed in the business. Being fair and retaining family loyalty become difficult as the number of family employees increases.

Sons, daughters, sons-in-law, and daughters-in-law who are on the sidelines are also participants with an important stake in the business. For example, they may be daughters-in-law whose husbands are employed, or husbands of daughters who are on the family payroll. Whatever the relationship, the view from the sideline has both a family and a business dimension. A decision by Dad affecting one member is seen from the sideline as a family *and* a business decision. Dad is giving the nod to a son or a son-in-law, and that is more than merely changing another employee in a business. Both the business and the family come to involve highly sensitive relationships.

The Entrepreneur's Spouse

One of the most critical roles in the family business drama is that of the entrepreneur's spouse. Traditionally and typically, this is the entrepreneur's wife and mother of his children. As wife, she plays a supporting role to her husband's career; as mother, she monitors the socialization of their children for careers in the family business.

In many respects, the spouse's support of the entrepreneur is similar to that of any spouse of an employed mate. One difference is the tendency of the family business to spill over into family time and to permeate life at home, as well as life at the shop or office. This leads to a need for communication between spouse and entrepreneur. The spouse can contribute by being a good listener. To do so, the spouse needs to hear what's going on in the business;

otherwise, the spouse feels detached and must compete for attention. The spouse can offer understanding and act as a sounding board only if there is communication on matters of such obvious importance to them both individually and as a family.

It is easy for the spouse to function as "worrier" for the family business. This is particularly true if there is insufficient communication about business matters. One spouse said:

> I've told my husband that I have an active imagination—very active. If he doesn't tell me what's going on in the business, well, then I'm going to imagine what's going on and blow it all out of proportion. When things are looking dark, I'd rather know the worst than know nothing.[11]

ACTION REPORT
Letter from an Entrepreneur's Spouse

The spouse of an entrepreneur is often a victim of poor communication. Following is a letter to an entrepreneur-husband expressing such concerns:

Dear Mr. President:

I have just a few questions I've always wanted to ask, but didn't because I either didn't want to bother you, or I was afraid you wouldn't answer. I should have asked them long ago.

*Why is it that when you have a business "concern" you wait until it is a full-blown "problem" before you share it with me? If we discussed the "concern," we might be able to solve it before it becomes a "problem."

*Why is it that our children have to be given all the hard, dirty jobs just because their Dad is The Boss?

*Why is it that when I make a business suggestion, you smile and ignore it; then in two weeks you come up with the same idea and think it's great?

*Why is it that you think my day as a homemaker consists only of TV, baby sitting, and coffee with the girls?

*Why is it that our son-in-law, who has already held a responsible job outside our business, has to start at the bottom and be treated as an outsider?

*Why is it you don't tell me when money is tight? You'd be surprised how adaptable I can be if you'd just be honest with me.

*Why can't I find a way to tell you that I'm not comfortable with your lawyer and that if something happens to you I want a lawyer I can relate to?

*Why is it I can be elected to set up and administer the budget for the Art Museum, yet you feel my ideas on finance aren't worth your time?

*Why do you tell me, "Don't worry; if something happens to me, John the Banker will take good care of you"? I'd rather you'd share your plans with me.

*Why is it that I work full time for you without a salary?

*Why can't you discuss with me the business problems you're having with our children, instead of closing me out and trying to solve them yourself?

*Why don't you take the time to share your dream with our daughter-in-law, who just can't understand why you work her husband so hard and long?

*And when are you going to plan a long weekend with no business—just us?

I have more, but these might be good for starters...

Love,
Your Willing Partner,
Katy

Source: Katy Danco, *From the Other Side of the Bed: A Woman Looks at Life in the Family Business* (Cleveland: The Center for Family Business, 1981), pp. 25–27. Reproduced with permission.

The spouse also serves as mediator in relationships between the entrepreneur and his children. Comments such as the following may illustrate the nature of this function:

1. "John, don't you think that Junior may have worked long enough as a stockboy in the warehouse?"
2. "Junior, your father is going to be very disappointed if you don't come back to the business after your graduation."
3. "John, do you really think it is fair to move Stanley into that new office? After all, Junior is older and has been working a year longer."
4. "Junior, what did you say to your father today that upset him?"

Ideally, the entrepreneur and spouse form a team committed to the success of both the family and the family business. They share with each other in the processes that affect the fortunes of each. Since such teamwork does not occur automatically, it requires a collaborative effort by both parties to the marriage.

THE PROCESS OF SUCCESSION

The task of preparing family members for careers and turning the business over to them is difficult and sometimes frustrating. Professional and managerial requirements tend to become intertwined with family feelings and interests. In this section we look at the development and transfer process and some of the difficulties associated with it.

Available Family Talent

A stream can rise no higher than its source, and the family firm can be no more brilliant than its leader. The business is dependent, therefore, upon the quality of leadership talent provided by the family. If the available talent is deficient, the entrepreneur must provide other, outside leadership or supplement family talent in some way. Otherwise, the business will suffer decline under the leadership of the second- or third-generation family members.

In some family businesses, key positions are reserved for family members. They may be retained in key positions because of their family relationship, even though they are professionally weak. One family entrepreneur's attempt to correct a lack of management skill is described below:

> In one case the founder's son, who was in command, diagnosed the business' problem as a lack of specialized talent. His solution was to become the firm's all-purpose expert—lawyer, accountant, and personnel specialist all wrapped into one. And to implement his solution, he went to night school. Little did he know that hiring someone outside the family who already had the necessary knowledge would have been better. His choice had several negative consequences, including his own physical exhaustion. The lesson here is that, when the money is available or the need is critical, there is no substitute for genuine expertise.[12]

Thus, decisions which sacrifice efficiency in the interest of preserving family interests can easily destroy the vitality of the family firm's management.

The question of competency of family members presents both a critical and delicate issue. With experience, individuals can improve their abilities; so, younger people cannot be judged too harshly too early. Furthermore, potential successors may be held back by the reluctance of a parent–owner to delegate realistically to them.

Perhaps the most appropriate philosophy is to recognize the right of family members to prove themselves. A period of testing may occur either in the family business or in another organization. As children show themselves to be capable, they earn the right to increased leadership responsibility. If the fairly judged leadership abilities of potential successors are inadequate, preservation of the family business and even the welfare of family members demand that they be passed over for promotion. The appointment of competent outsiders to these jobs, if necessary, increases the value of the firm to all family members who have an ownership interest in it.

Stages in the Process of Succession

Sons or daughters do not typically assume leadership of a family firm in a moment of time. Dad or Mom does not step down on Friday with the son or daughter taking over Monday morning. Instead, a long, drawn-out process of preparation and transition is customary—a process that extends over years and often decades. We may visualize this process as a series of stages as portrayed in Figure 2–3.[13]

Pre-Business Stage   In Stage I, the successor becomes acquainted with the business as a part of growing up. He or she accompanies the parent to the office or store or warehouse, or plays with equipment related to the business. There is no formal planning of the youngster's preparation in this early period in which he or she might be only four or five years of age. This first stage forms a boundary that precedes the more deliberate process of socialization.

Introductory Stage   Stage II includes experiences that occur before the successor is old enough to begin part-time work in the family business. It differs from Stage I in that family members deliberately introduce the child to certain people associated directly or indirectly with the firm and to other aspects of the business. The parent explains the difference between a front loader and a backhoe or introduces the child to the firm's banker.

Introductory Functional Stage   In Stage III, the son or daughter begins to function as a part-time employee. This often occurs during vacation periods or after the school day is completed. During this time, the son or daughter develops an acquaintance with some of the key individuals employed in the firm. Often, such work begins in the warehouse or office or production department and may involve assignments in various functional areas as time goes on. The introductory functional stage includes the educational preparation and the experience the son or daughter gains in other organizations.

Functional Stage   Stage IV begins when the successor enters full-time employment, typically following the completion of an educational program. Prior to moving into a management position, the successor may work as an accountant, a salesperson, or an inventory clerk and possibly gain experience in a number of such positions.

Advanced Functional Stage   As the successor assumes supervisory duties, he or she enters the advanced functional stage, or Stage V. The management positions in this stage involve directing the work of others but not the overall management of the firm.

Early Succession Stage   In Stage VI, the son or daughter is named president or general manager of the business. At this point, he or she presumably exercises overall direction of the business, but the parent is still in the background. The leadership role of an organization does not transfer as easily or absolutely as does the leadership title. The successor has not necessarily mastered the complexities of the presidency, and the predecessor may be reluctant to give up all decision making.

Mature Succession Stage   Stage VII is reached when the transition process is complete. The successor is leader in fact as well as in name. In some cases,

Figure 2-3   A Model of Succession in a Family Business

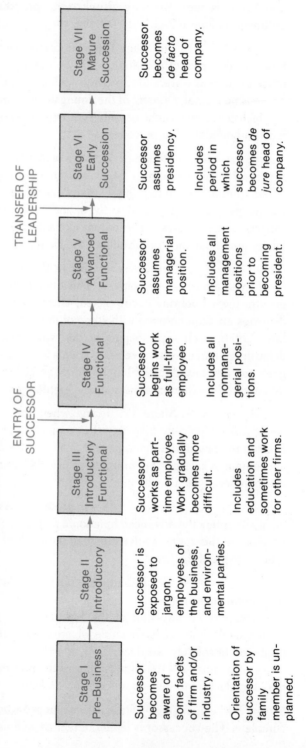

this does not occur until the predecessor dies. Perhaps optimistically, we assume progress on the part of the successor and regard Stage VII as beginning two years after the successor assumes the presidency of the firm.

Reluctant Fathers and Ambitious Sons

Let us assume the business founder is preparing his son to take over the family firm. The founder's attachment to the business must not be underestimated. Not only is he tied to the firm financially—it is probably his primary if not his only major investment—but he is also tied to it emotionally. The business is "his baby," and he is understandably reluctant to entrust its future to one who is immature and unproven. (Unfortunately, fathers often have a way of seeing their children as immature long after their years of adolescence.)

The son may be ambitious, possibly well-educated, and insightful regarding the business. His tendency to push ahead—to try something new—often conflicts with his father's caution. As a result, he may see his father as excessively conservative, stubborn, and unwilling to change.

ACTION REPORT
Father–Son Relationships in a Family Firm

Inadequate communication often leads to rough spots in the relationships between fathers and sons in the family business. The following account identifies some of the difficulties in family relationships at Welders Supply Inc. of Dallas, TX.

Just as hard as deciding to join the business is sticking with it. Welders' Terry Squibb admits to a period of unhappiness when there was just not enough communication between him and his brother, Randy, the firm's sales manager, and their father, Charley.

"My dad had told us he was going to retire in 1985," recalls Squibb. "I didn't think I was being prepared to take over. I wasn't sure he would teach us what we needed to learn." There was uneasiness between the brothers about who would succeed their father and how the stock would be shared.

The family obtained outside help by attending seminars on the family business and worked out a solution which preserved peace in the family.

Source: Sharon Nelton, "Shaky about Joining the Family Firm?" *Nation's Business*, Vol. 71, No. 11 (November, 1983), pp. 58–60.

At the root of many such difficulties is a lack of a clear understanding between father and son. They work together without a map showing where they are going. Sons, and also their wives, may have expectations about progress that, in terms of the founder's thinking, are totally unrealistic. The successor tends to sense such problems much more acutely than does his father. But much of the problem could be avoided if a full discussion about the development process took place. The problem is highlighted in the following comments:

> Where Dad means to be open and generous, his children tend to see him as stubborn and inconsistent. As far as they can see, he refuses to move on anything even slightly important. When he does move, his decisions seem to vary day to day—and they rarely seem to be in the successor's favor.
>
> Where the successors are trying to do their jobs (as they see them) by pushing for changes, investment, and a little more risk, Dad sees them as spendthrift and economically naive. Where the successors' spouses only want to make sure their own families are on the right track, Dad sees them as uncommitted and disloyal.
>
> Each of these perceptions, real though they may seem, are seldom true. They're seldom even close. Yet everybody operates on them—their individual versions of reality.[14]

Transferring Ownership

A final and often complex step in the succession process is the transfer of ownership in the family firm.[15] Questions of inheritance affect not only the successor or potential successor in management, but also other family members with no involvement in the family business. In distributing their family estate, parents typically wish to treat all their children fairly, both those involved in the business and those on the outside.

One of the most difficult decisions is that of determining the future ownership of the business. If there are several children, for example, should they all receive equal shares? On the surface, this seems to be the fairest approach. However, such an arrangement may play havoc with the future functioning of the business. Suppose that each of five children receives a 20 percent ownership share when only one of them is active in the business. The child active in the business—the successor—becomes a minority stockholder completely at the mercy of relatives on the outside.

Ideally, the entrepreneur is able to arrange his or her personal holdings so that he or she creates wealth outside the business as well as within it. In this way, he or she may be able to bequeath comparable shares to all heirs while allowing business control to remain with the child or children active in the business.

Tax considerations are relevant, of course, and they tend to favor gradual transfer of ownership to all heirs. As noted above, however, this arrangement may be inconsistent with the future of efficient operation of the business. Tax laws cannot be allowed to dominate decisions about transferring ownership without regard for these other practical considerations.

Planning and discussing the transfer of ownership is not easy, but such action is recommended. Over a period of time, the owner must reflect seriously on family talents and interests as they relate to the future of the firm. The plan for transfer of ownership can then be "firmed up" and modified as necessary when it is discussed with the children or other potential heirs.

Leon A. Danco describes an arrangement worked out by a warehouse distributor in the tire industry.[16] The distributor's son and probable successor was active in the business, but his daughter was married to a college professor in a small southern university. Believing the business to be their most valuable asset, the owner and his wife were concerned that both the daughter and the son receive a fair share. Initially, the parents decided to give the real estate to the daughter and the business itself to the son, who would then pay rent to his sister. After discussing the matter with both children, however, they developed a better plan whereby the business property and the business itself would both go to the son. The daughter would receive all *nonbusiness* assets plus an instrument of debt by the son to his sister which was intended to balance the monetary values. In this way, they devised a plan that was not only fair, but also workable in terms of the operation and management of the firm.

Good Management in the Process of Succession

Good management is necessary for the success of any business, and the family firm is no exception. Significant deviations for family reasons from what we might call good management practices, therefore, will only serve to weaken the firm. Such a course of action would run counter to the interests of both the firm and the family. In concluding this discussion of succession, we should recall and emphasize those management concepts which are particularly relevant to the family firm.

The first concept relates to the competence of professional and managerial personnel. A family firm cannot afford to accept and support family members who are incompetent or who lack the potential for development.

Second, the extent of opportunities for nonfamily members and any limitations on those opportunities should be spelled out. They should know and not have to wonder whether they can aspire to promotion to key positions in the firm.

Third, favoritism in personnel decisions must be avoided. If possible, the evaluation of family members should involve the judgment of nonfamily members—those in supervisory positions, outside members of the board of directors, or managers of other companies in which family members work for a time.

Fourth, plans for succession, steps in professional development, and intentions regarding changes in ownership should be developed and discussed openly.[17] Founders who recognize the need for managing the process of succession can work out plans carefully rather than drift haphazardly. Lack of knowledge regarding plans and intentions of key participants creates uncertainty and possible suspicion. This planning process can begin as the founder or the presiding family member shares his or her dream for the family firm and family participation in it. Outside advisors may be used by the founder if impartial assistance is needed or desired in planning the transition.

The family firm is a business—a competitive business. The observance of these and other fundamental precepts of management will help the business to thrive and permit the family to function as a family. Disregard of such considerations will pose a threat to the business and impose strains on family relationships.

Looking Back

1. A family business is one in which the family has a special involvement. Such a business involves an overlapping of business interests (production and profitability) and family interests (care and nurture).

2. A family business often benefits from the strong commitment of family members to the welfare of the business and the ability of management to focus on human potential, quality, and long-run decisions. Potential weaknesses include a tendency to place family interests before business interests.

3. It is difficult to provide strong motivation for nonfamily employees whose promotional opportunities are limited. This problem can be minimized by open communication concerning the extent of these opportunities.

4. A primary family relationship is that between the founder and the son or daughter who may succeed the founder in the business. Sons, daughters, in-laws, and sometimes other relatives have the possibility for collaboration or conflict with the founder and among themselves in the operation of the business. The role of the founder's spouse is especially important, often as a mediator between other family members.

5. Succession is typically a long-term process starting early in the successor's life. Tension often exists between the founder and the successor as the latter gains experience and becomes qualified to make business decisions independently. Transfer of ownership involves issues of placing control in the hands of the successor, being fair to all heirs, and facing tax consequences. A carefully formulated plan is helpful in the proper resolution of these issues.

DISCUSSION QUESTIONS

1. How would you define a *family business*? How does the size of the business affect your definition?
2. Suppose that an entrepreneur's son is employed in the family firm. What conflict might possibly occur in the son's career regarding family interests and business interests?
3. To what extent should business interests be compromised or sacrificed because of family considerations?
4. What benefits result from family involvement in a business?
5. On the basis of your own observations, describe a founder–son or founder–daughter relationship in a family business. What strengths or weaknesses do you see in that relationship?
6. Does the involvement of both husband and wife in a family business strengthen or weaken their family relationship? Can you cite any situations you have observed to support your answer?
7. Should a son or daughter feel an obligation to carry on a family business?
8. Identify and describe the stages outlined in the model of succession shown in Figure 2–3 on page 44.
9. What steps can be taken to minimize conflict between parent and child in family business decisions?
10. Should estate tax laws or other factors be given the greatest weight in decisions about transferring ownership of a family business from one generation to another?

ENDNOTES

1. This distinction between family and business is carefully examined in Ivan Lansberg S., "Managing Human Resources in Family Firms: The Problem of Institutional Overlap," *Organizational Dynamics*, Vol. 12 (Summer, 1983), pp. 39–46, and Elaine Kepner, "The Family and the Firm: A Coevolutionary Perspective," *Organizational Dynamics*, Vol. 12 (Summer, 1983), pp. 57–70.

2. Priscilla Anne Schwab, "Matchmaker Discourages Love at First Sight," *Nation's Business*, Vol. 69 (January, 1981), p. 64.

3. Pat B. Alcorn, *Success and Survival in the Family Owned Business* (New York: McGraw-Hill Book Company, 1982), p. 107.

4. Peter Davis, "Realizing the Potential of the Family Business," *Organizational Dynamics*, Vol. 12 (Summer, 1983), pp. 53–54.

5. Edgar H. Schein, "The Role of the Founder in Creating Organizational Culture," *Organizational Dynamics*, Vol. 12 (Summer, 1983), pp. 13–28.

6. Justin G. Longenecker and Carlos W. Moore, "Consumer Perceptions of the Family Business: An Exploratory Study," paper presented at the International Council for Small Business, Chicago, IL, June 12, 1984.

7. Neil Cohen, "Leaving the Rat Race for the Good Life," *Venture*, Vol. 1 (December, 1979), pp. 39–44.

8. *Ibid.*, p. 42.

9. Howard Butt, *The Velvet Covered Brick* (New York: Harper and Row, Publishers, 1973), pp. 5–6.

10. *Ibid.*, p. 9.

11. Katy Danco, *From the Other Side of the Bed: A Woman Looks at Life in the Family Business* (Cleveland: The Center for Family Business, 1981), p. 21.

12. Elmer H. Burack and Thomas M. Calero, "Seven Perils of the Family Firm," *Nation's Business*, Vol. 69 (January, 1981), p. 63.

13. For an earlier, extended treatment of this topic, see Justin G. Longenecker and John E. Schoen, "Management Succession in the Family Business," *Journal of Small Business Management*, Vol. 16 (July, 1978), pp. 1–6.

14. Donald Jonovic, *The Second-Generation Boss* (Cleveland: The Center for Family Business, 1982), p. 85.

15. Transfer of ownership is discussed by a specialist in tax accounting in Irving L. Blackman, "A Financial Guide to Turning over the Helm," *Nation's Business*, Vol. 74, No. 1 (January, 1986), pp. 40–42.

16. Leon A. Danco, *Inside the Family Business* (Cleveland: The Center for Family Business, 1980), pp. 198–199.

17. An excellent treatment of this topic appears in Richard Beckhard and W. Gibb Dyer, Jr., "Managing Continuity in the Family Owned Business," *Organizational Dynamics*, Vol. 12 (Summer, 1983), pp. 5–12.

REFERENCES TO SMALL BUSINESS IN ACTION

Goldstein, Nora. "When Brothers Run the Show." *In Business*, Vol. 5 (May–June, 1983), pp. 29–31.

The nature of family relationships in a business is discussed in this report on a family firm involving four brothers and one sister, with the prospect of still more relatives to come.

Hempstead, John E. "A 'Freeze' That Can Put the IRS out in the Cold." *Nation's Business*, Vol. 72 (November, 1984), pp. 48–50.

In this article, the owner of a family firm explores a way to pass ownership of his business on to his daughter without creating a huge burden of estate taxes.

"Letters: Rocky Road for Partners." *Inc.*, Vol. 6 (June, 1984), pp. 7–10.

Four letters to the editor present viewpoints of a university researcher, two consultants, and an attorney on family strains in family businesses.

Merwin, John. "Pushing Cars in Corn Country." *Forbes*, Vol. 134 (July 16, 1984), pp. 96–102.

This article describes an auto dealership in Illinois which functions as a family business. The four retail outlets—three Chevy dealerships and a Toyota agency—are run by the owner's two sons, a daughter, and a son-in-law.

CASE 2

The Woodward Well Company*

The rise and fall of a family business

The Woodward Well Company had a very inauspicious beginning a few years before the United States entered World War I. Chester Woodward was a farmer in Illinois and, like many farmers unable to afford skilled artisans for every job, he became a sort of fix-it man himself. This involved fixing the pump that supplied water to the farm. Other farmers less skilled with their hands heard of Chester's prowess, and soon he was cleaning and repairing his neighbors' wells. As more and more people sought his advice and services, Chester thought more about business and less about farming. He hired a few people and began drilling wells and installing pumps, and the Woodward Well Company was formed.

At the time the business was founded, Chester's brother, Jacob, was the sales manager for a pump-manufacturing company in Chicago. Some 20 years later, during the mid-Depression years, Chester became physically unable to handle the well-drilling business, and Jacob took over the management of his brother's firm while still managing his own pump-sales organization. As the business grew, Jacob began to devote more and more of his time to the water well contracting business. It was after this time that the Woodward legend grew. Beginning with two locations—one in Chicago and one in Joliet—the entire operation was finally moved to Joliet, where it began to climb to a $6 million a year water well business.

Jacob Woodward was a driving entrepreneur. The familiar "business-is-life" syndrome took over, and all social life faded into the background. He worked seven days a week to expand his business to include all phases of the development of ground water, including the water and waste treatment fields. In fact, it was commonly said that Jacob Woodward could sell oil to the Arabs.

Many businesspeople climbing to the top leave a trail of bodies behind them. Not so with Jacob Woodward. Although he built an empire that towered above others in the industry, he managed to hold on to the friendship and respect of his competitors. On many occasions, competitors beat Woodward on contract bids but called on him for help when they found the jobs over their heads. He always sent crews and machinery to assist them.

The quintessential self-made man, Jacob ran the business in a patriarchal manner. If he needed machinery for a job, he ordered it and informed the "purchasing department" by memo. He made all decisions and interviewed

*This case is taken from Pat B. Alcorn, *Success and Survival in the Family-Owned Business* (New York: McGraw-Hill Book Company, 1982), pp. 3–5. Reproduced with permission.

all prospective employees, even down to the level of mechanics' assistants. The business was a "family" operation at all levels. Most company personnel came from the families of current employees. Many of the drill rigs were operated by father-and-son teams or at least by crew members who were related to one another. The employees were thus fiercely loyal to Jacob Woodward and he to them.

By this time, hard-driving-father-with-up-and-coming-son problems began to emerge. Jacob's son, Warren, studied business management in college, did a stint in the Air Force, and then came into his father's business, beginning as a helper on a drill rig. He was ultimately promoted to vice-president of the company; but with his father making all the decisions, Warren felt more like an office boy with a title than a responsible executive. Not feeling that he was sharing in the growth of the company, he thought often of seeking employment elsewhere, but this was far from easy to do. Prospective employers whose slots he would have loved to fill shied away because they felt he would ultimately return to his father's business. Thus, Warren devoted more time to his family than his father had ever devoted to his. But he still increased in stature in the water well industry. Although Jacob was proud of his son, there were frictions. Jacob was furious when he was introduced as "Warren Woodward's father"; he was accustomed to hearing Warren introduced as "Jacob Woodward's son."

By the 1960s, Woodward Well Company was the largest privately owned water well business in the industry. A staff of 60 at the Joliet headquarters supported 125 permanent employees and over 20 drill rigs in the field. In addition to its basic business of providing safe and efficient water systems for industrial and municipal users, the company was constantly involved in new and innovative ventures. Woodward pioneered the development of well water for air cooling; it installed a system of vertical and horizontal wells at beaches to provide crystal-clear water for swimming pools; it established a state-approved laboratory for biological and chemical testing of water—a laboratory staffed by three graduate chemists and assistants.

The mushrooming growth of Woodward Well Company had been a source of concern to its financial backers for some time, but things continued to work out, most people said, because of the genius of Jacob Woodward. But recession struck in the 1970s, and there was a general decline in business.

It was the beginning of the end for the company, but Jacob Woodward insisted that he had weathered many storms and could weather this one. He refused to lay off loyal employees and sent drillers earning over $9 an hour out to polish their equipment. Soon, payroll expenses and overhead were far outstripping revenue. Finally, 60 employees were laid off, but it was too late. The bank called in a loan. State and federal taxes were overdue, and the government tax collector seized the business assets. The remaining equipment was sold at auction. The combination home and business empire that Jacob Woodward built had fallen.

But life goes on, even when the business collapses, and Jacob did not admit defeat. He began a career as a consultant—in his eighties! His own man for the first time, Warren opened a new business, Warren Woodward Associates, and announced that he would continue to be an active participant in—what else?—the water well industry.

Questions

1. Evaluate Jacob Woodward as an entrepreneur.
2. Evaluate Jacob Woodward as a family man. Was he a better father or a better entrepreneur?
3. Did Warren Woodward do as well as possible with his career? Should he have acted differently in any way?
4. Was failure of the firm necessary? What might have prevented it?
5. How do you interpret the actions of both Jacob Woodward and Warren Woodward after the collapse of the family business?

3

Small Business: Vital Component of the Economy

Figure 3–1   Stew Leonard

B. L. Ochman Public Relations

As this chapter explains, small business operates in a highly competitive economy—an economy that includes big corporations, middle-size businesses, and small firms. To succeed in such an economy, small businesses must demonstrate competence, even superiority. A splendid example of a vigorously competitive small firm—the "Disneyland of Dairy Stores"—is described by Tom Peters and Nancy Austin in their discussion of a "passion for excellence."

Stew Leonard grossed $80 million in his one location last year. Average grocery store sales run a bit over $350 per square foot. Stew Leonard cashes in at about $3,000 a square foot. The trick? He's made it a delight to shop for chicken, cheese, eggs, and other foods. He has a petting zoo for kids. Two robot dogs sing country music, and a robot cow and farmer sing nursery rhymes. The egg department features a mechanical chicken, "the world's fastest egg layer." On one wall there are about 1,000 pictures of Stew's customers displaying the store's shopping bags. He happens now to have a picture taken under water of a customer with a bag on a deep-sea dive, another of a Leonard regular atop the Great Wall of China.

Stew solicits his people's ideas regularly. One unique way is via regular visits to other stores. There aren't many stores that compete with Stew across the board, but sometimes he will come across an interesting department like one of his (for example, bakery goods) or an interesting store in another business. When he does, even if it's 300 or 400 miles away, he's likely to grab 15 of his people (including hourly people, even very recent hires) and hop into the 15-person van that he uses for such occasions.

Source: Tom Peters and Nancy Austin, "A Passion for Excellence," *Fortune,* Vol. 111 (May 13, 1985), p. 30. Copyright by Random House, Inc. Reprinted with permission.

Looking Ahead

Watch for the following important topics:

1. The definition of small business—that is, what types of firms may be classified as small businesses.
2. The types of industry in which small businesses operate.
3. The proportion of all business activity accounted for by small businesses.
4. Unique contributions of small businesses.

It is easy to overestimate the importance of big business because of its greater visibility. Small businesses seem dwarfed by such corporate giants as General Motors (748,000 employees), Bank of America ($95 billion deposits), Prudential Life Insurance Company ($533 billion worth of insurance in force), and IBM (over $6 billion annual profits). Yet small firms, even though less conspicuous, are a vital component of our economy. In this chapter, we not only examine the extent of small-business activity but also the unique contributions of small businesses that help preserve our economic well-being. But first, we need to look at the criteria used to define small business.

DEFINITION OF SMALL BUSINESS

Specifying any size standard to define small business is necessarily arbitrary because people adopt different standards for different purposes. Legislators, for example, may exclude small firms from certain regulations and specify ten employees as the cutoff point. Moreover, a business may be described as "small" when compared to larger firms, but "large" when compared to smaller ones. Most people, for example, would classify independently owned gasoline stations, neighborhood restaurants, and locally owned retail stores as small businesses. Similarly, most would agree that the major automobile manufacturers are big businesses.[1] And firms of in-between sizes would be classified as large or small on the basis of individual viewpoints.

Even the criteria used to measure the size of businesses vary. Some criteria are applicable to all industrial areas, while others are relevant only to certain types of business. Examples of criteria used to measure size are:

1. Number of employees.
2. Sales volume.
3. Asset size.
4. Insurance in force.
5. Volume of deposits.

Although the first criterion listed above—number of employees—is the most widely used yardstick, the best criterion in any given case depends upon the user's purpose.

Another complicating factor in deciding what is small is the variation among industries. In capital-intensive industries, such as steel making, the typical business is very large. In some types of service businesses, such as beauty shops, the typical firm is quite small.

SBA Standards

The Small Business Administration (SBA) establishes size standards which determine eligibility for SBA loans and for special consideration in bidding on government contracts. In 1984, the SBA issued a revised set of standards, some of which are stated in terms of number of employees and others of which are stated in terms of sales volume. Some of these standards are shown in Table 3-1. Size standards for most nonmanufacturing industries are now expressed in terms of annual receipts. As you can see, $3.5 million is a common upper limit in the service and retail areas in which small business is strong. In mining and manufacturing, however, the SBA classifies firms with fewer than 500 employees as small.

Size Standards Used in This Book

To provide a clearer image of the small firm discussed in this book, we suggest the following general criteria for defining a small business:

Table 3-1   Examples of SBA Size Standards

Type of Business	Number of Employees or Sales Dollars
Advertising agencies	$ 3.5 million
Copper ores mining	500 employees
Employment agencies	$ 3.5 million
Furniture stores	$ 3.5 million
General contractors—single-family houses	$17.0 million
Insurance agents, brokers, and service	$ 3.5 million
Metal can manufacturing	1,000 employees
Mobile home dealers	$ 6.5 million
Newspaper publishing and printing	500 employees
Poultry dressing plants	500 employees
Radio and television repair shops	$ 3.5 million
Radio broadcasting	$ 3.5 million

Source: Small Business Size Standards, SBA Rules and Regulations, Part 121, published by the Small Business Administration, February 9, 1984.

1. Financing of the business is supplied by one individual or a small group. Only in a rare case would the business have more than 15 or 20 owners.
2. Except for its marketing function, the firm's operations are geographically localized.
3. Compared to the biggest firms in the industry, the business is small.
4. The number of employees in the business is usually fewer than 100.

Obviously, some small firms fail to meet *all* of the above standards. For example, a small executive search firm—a firm that helps corporate clients recruit managers from other organizations—may operate in many sections of the country and thereby fail to meet the second criterion. Nevertheless, the discussion of management concepts in this book is aimed primarily at the type of firm that fits the general pattern described above.

SMALL BUSINESS IN THE MAJOR INDUSTRIES

Small firms operate in all industries, but they differ greatly in their nature and importance from industry to industry. In thinking about their economic contribution, therefore, we need first to identify the eight major industries and to note the types of small firms that function in these industries. These eight major industries are: wholesale trade; contract construction; retail trade; services; finance, insurance, and real estate; mining; transportation and other public utilities; and manufacturing.

Wholesale Trade

The wholesaler's primary function is to act as an intermediary between manufacturers and retailers or industrial users by assembling, storing, and distributing products. Small firms are dominant in the area of wholesaling. They sell a wide range of products such as drugs, groceries, hardware, fruits and vegetables, grain and farm produce, farm implements and supplies, machinery, industrial supplies, and electrical appliances. Petroleum bulk stations are also considered to be wholesale businesses, as are agents and brokers who buy or sell raw materials or manufactured products for the account of others.

Contract Construction

General contractors who erect skyscrapers and mammoth factory buildings are big-business firms. But there are also thousands of small firms serving as general contractors on a more modest scale. In addition to general contracting, small firms play an important role in contracting for work in such specialized fields as electrical, plumbing, and painting jobs. Even public-construction contractors, such as those who build streets, bridges, and sewers, many times are small businesses.

Retail Trade

Examples of small businesses abound in the field of retailing. Among these are drugstores, independent grocery and meat markets, clothing stores, shoe stores, variety stores, auto accessories dealers, appliance dealers, bookstores, music stores, service stations, and restaurants. Other examples include jewelry stores, hardware stores, record shops, sporting goods stores, toy stores, furniture stores, and vending machine businesses. While most small retailers operate as single-unit firms, others function successfully as small chains.

Service Industries

Any attempt to catalog service firms immediately reveals their diversity. For example, there are business services such as accounting firms, advertising

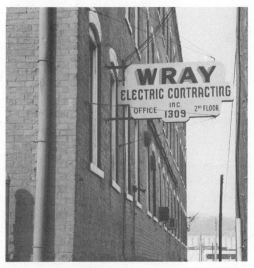

agencies, private employment agencies, blueprint services, and managerial consultants. Personal services include barber and beauty shops, dry cleaners, photographic studios, funeral homes, travel agencies, and so on. Then there are automobile repair services, entertainment and recreational services, hotels, and motels.

Finance, Insurance, and Real Estate

Small banks, loan companies, pawnbrokers, real estate brokerage firms, and insurance agencies illustrate the types of small firms which operate in the industrial category of finance, insurance, and real estate. The insurance agency, for example, is an independent business which sells insurance policies for large insurance companies. Insurance and real estate brokerage services are often combined in the same organization.

Mining

Small-scale mining involves many types of minerals. There are thousands of small bituminous coal mines, for example. Some of them are strip mines operated with only a few employees. There are also many small companies providing services in mining and oil and gas extraction industries. Some small quarries and sand and gravel companies also belong to the mining industry.

Transportation and Other Public Utilities

The required investment is so great in the industry of transportation and other public utilities that big business is dominant in this field. Even so, some small firms find a niche in which to operate. Examples of such firms include taxicab companies, local bus lines, privately owned water systems, chartered flight services, local radio and television stations, and community newspaper publishers.

ACTION REPORT
Small Business in a Big-Business Industry

Although railroading is big business, some small lines are operated as individual or family businesses. An example is the Willamina and Grande Ronde Railroad Company. One of 16 short-line operations in Oregon alone, W&GR uses a 35-year-old diesel locomotive to transport lumber to the Southern Pacific Railroad at Willamina—a 17-mile round trip. The railroad was acquired in 1980 by the Root family, with the help of relatives and friends. Michael Root is general manager, vice-president, engineer, and owner of one eighth of the stock. In addition to Root, W&GR employs an engineer, a section foreman, a section man, and a part-time freight agent and office manager.

Source: "Little Engines That Could—And Will Again," *Venture*, Vol. 3, No. 2 (February, 1981), pp. 70–72.

Manufacturing

Although big business overshadows small business in the manufacturing industry, there are nonetheless hundreds of thousands of small firms in this field. They include bakeries, sawmills, toy factories, job printing shops, shoe factories, bookbinding plants, ice cream plants, and soft-drink bottling works. Small machine shops, ironworks, ready-mixed concrete plants, cabinet shops, furniture manufacturing plants, and clothing manufacturing plants also fit this category.

SMALL-BUSINESS STRENGTH IN NUMBERS

A number of measures can be used to evaluate the relative numerical strength of small business. One of these classifies business firms in terms of the number of employees on their payroll.[2] Figure 3–3 shows the percentage of paid employees working in small business—that is, in firms with fewer than 100 employees. Using this criterion, we can see that small-business firms employ almost 40 percent of all employees in all industries. In some fields, of course, small business is much stronger. Figure 3–3 shows that small firms account for 73 percent of all employees in wholesale trade, 71.8 percent of all employees in contract construction, 54.4 percent of all employees in retail trade, and 50.3 percent of all employees in the services industry.

Again, using 100 employees as the upper limit for being small is obviously arbitrary. Many firms that have 200 or 300 employees are regarded as small by their owners. These firms operate in one locality, obtain their capital from one or a few individuals, and are much smaller than other firms in their industries. Thus, if we used a larger size criterion, we would find that a larger percentage of business is classified as small. Regardless of the exact point at which one draws the line, it is apparent that much—roughly 40 to 50 percent—of American business may be classed as small.

The most rapid growth is occurring in nonmanufacturing industries—industries such as services, retailing, insurance, and real estate.[3] Someone has called it the "new economy of services and high technology." Although both large and small firms exist in each industrial area, the shift appears basically favorable to small business—with more rapid expansion occurring in areas of traditional strength for small firms.

SPECIAL CONTRIBUTIONS OF SMALL BUSINESS

As part of the business community, small firms unquestionably contribute to our nation's economic welfare. They produce a substantial portion of our total goods and services. Thus, their general economic contribution is similar to that of big business. Small firms, however, possess some qualities which make them more than miniature versions of big business corporations. They provide new jobs, introduce innovations, stimulate competition, aid big business, and produce goods and services efficiently.

Figure 3-3   Percentage of Total Employees in Big Business and Small Business (Firms
with Fewer Than 100 Employees)

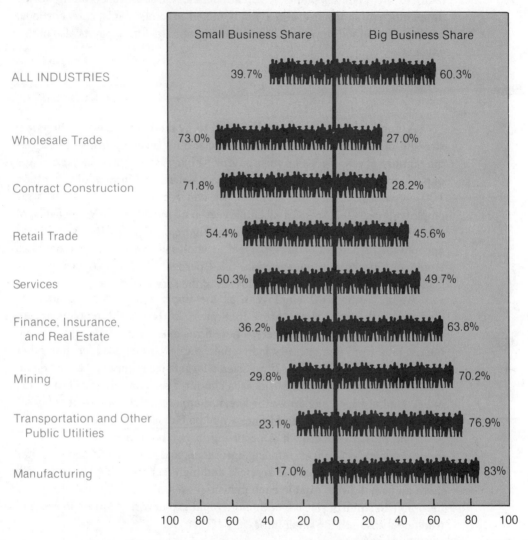

Source: U.S. Department of Commerce, Bureau of the Census, *County Business Patterns*, 1977:
Enterprise Statistics (Washington: U.S. Government Printing Office, 1979), Table 2.

Providing New Jobs

As the population and the economy grow, small businesses must provide
many of the new job opportunities. It seems clear, indeed, that small business
must produce the "lion's share" of the new jobs.

Recent studies have revealed the special contributions of new and small
firms to growth of employment. The best known analyses are those of MIT

economist David Birch who estimates the share of jobs created by businesses with 100 or fewer employees to range from 50 to 80 percent of all new jobs.[4] On a year-to-year basis, Birch points out that the proportion varies depending on the performance of large businesses—whether they are expanding or shrinking. Even so, the percentage of jobs created by small firms is usually significantly higher than their corresponding share of employment in the economy.

Data released by the Office of Advocacy, Small Business Administration, show clearly the special contribution of small firms in expansion of employment. As you can see in Figure 3–4, small firms were the leaders in adding jobs between 1976 and 1982, particularly firms with fewer than 20 employees.

Of course, as newer firms grow in employment size, they become part of the big-business sector. We should also note that all small firms do not grow at an even rate. Birch concludes that 12 to 15 percent of all small enterprises create most of the growth.

> It is thus incorrect to speak of small enterprises as a uniformly expanding and active group. It is better to think of them as a large collection of seeds, a few of which sprout and become large plants. Their job-creating powers flow from the few, not the many.[5]

Figure 3–4   Employment Growth by Employee Size of Firm, 1976–1982

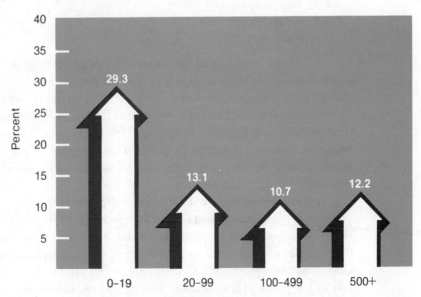

Source: *The State of Small Business,* A Report of the President to the Congress, May, 1985, p. 108; U.S. Small Business Administration, Office of Advocacy, Small Business Data Base, unpublished data.

New jobs, therefore, come from the birth of new firms and their subsequent expansion. Also, some growth in employment comes from large corporations which expand and create additional jobs. The statistics reported above, however, reveal the unique, disproportionate contribution of small business to the creation of new jobs.

Introducing Innovation

New products which originate in the research laboratories of big business make a valuable contribution to our standard of living. There is a question, however, as to the relative importance of big business in achieving the truly significant innovations. The record shows that many scientific breakthroughs originated with independent inventors and small organizations. Below are some twentieth-century examples of new products created by small firms:

1. Xerography.
2. Insulin.
3. Vacuum tube.
4. Penicillin.
5. Cottonpicker.
6. Zipper.
7. Automatic transmission.
8. Jet engine.
9. Helicopter.
10. Power steering.
11. Kodachrome.
12. Ball-point pen.

A current example of an innovative product originating outside the laboratories of big business is a device which permits quadriplegics to operate motorized wheelchairs by voice commands.[6] The device was developed by Marvin Herscher and Phillips Scott, whose company, Threshold Technology, is a pioneer in the field of voice recognition equipment. The machine can be trained to understand a person's words in any language. This innovation from small business is obviously beneficial to society and particularly to certain physically handicapped persons.

It is interesting to note that research departments of big business tend to emphasize the improvement of existing products. In fact, it is quite likely that some ideas generated by personnel in big business are sidetracked because they are not related to existing products or because of their unusual nature. Unfortunately, preoccupation with an existing product can sometimes blind one to the value of a *new* idea. The jet engine, for example, had difficulty securing consideration by those who were accustomed to internal combustion engines.

Studies of innovation have shown the greater effectiveness of small firms in research and development. Figure 3-5, based on a study by Edwards and Gordon, shows that small firms are superior innovators in both increasing-employment and decreasing-employment industries. Others believe that small companies are somewhere between 1.8 and 2.8 times as innovative per employee as large companies.[7]

Innovation contributes to productivity by providing better products and better methods of production. A slowing of innovation has been blamed for our nation's recent sluggish rate of growth in productivity.[8] The millions of small firms that provide the centers of initiative and sources of innovation are thus in a position to help improve American productivity.

Figure 3-5   Innovations per Million Employees by Employment Size of Firm, 1982

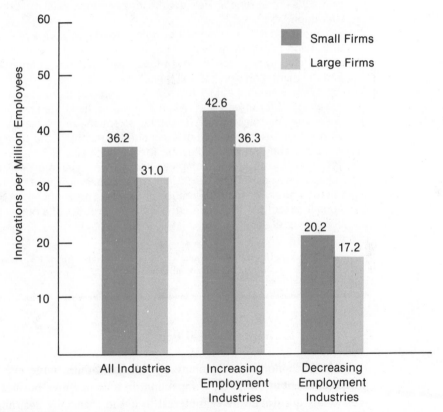

Note: Small firms are defined here as firms with fewer than 500 employees.

Source: The State of Small Business, A Report of the President transmitted to the Congress, May, 1985, p. 128; Keith L. Edwards and Theodore J. Gordon, "Characterization of Innovations Introduced on the U.S. Market in 1982" (Glastonbury, CT: prepared for the U.S. Small Business Administration, Office of Advocacy, under award no. SBA-6050-OA-82, March 1984), p. 46.

ACTION REPORT
Small Business Innovation in Scientific Instruments

In 1985, Robert Allington of Lincoln, NE, was selected by an SBA panel of judges as the "National Small Business Person of the Year." Product innovation was one factor affecting this selection. Allington has achieved a brilliant record as an entrepreneurial innovator in designing and producing scientific instruments.

Allington is responsible for more than 100 of his firm's (ISCO, Inc.) patents, but he is more than an inventor. He developed the instruments and brought them to the point of successful usage in the marketplace. Stanley Liberty, dean of the College of Engineering at the University of Nebraska, praised Allington's achievements as follows: "He's the entrepreneur's entrepreneur. He's got the ideas and the ability to bring them to fruition."

Allington is described as having a "broad knowledge of the scientific fields in which he works, an innovative mind, the management capabilities to produce his inventions, the resources to finance them, and the marketing savvy to sell them."

While a student at MIT in 1955, Allington contracted polio and was hospitalized for three years. While recovering, he started repairing and designing instruments for university scientists—instruments, for example, to measure the area of a leaf and the acidity in the stomach of a live cow. The first profitable year for the business, 1962, saw sales of $142,000. By 1985, the company had grown to employ 400 people, achieved a sales volume of $20 million, and become one of the 10 major manufacturers of instruments for chemists! These numerous innovations in scientific instrumentation were the product of a highly innovative entrepreneur.

Source: Adapted from Frederic Hron, "Flying on Instruments," *Nation's Business*, Vol. 73 (July, 1985), pp. 46–48. Reproduced with permission.

Stimulating Economic Competition

Many economists, beginning with Adam Smith, have expounded the values inherent in economic competition. In a competitive business situation, individuals are driven by self-interest to act in a socially desirable manner. Competition acts as the regulator which transforms their selfishness into service.

When producers consist of only a few big businesses, however, the customer is at their mercy. They may set exorbitant prices, withhold technological developments, exclude new competitors, or otherwise abuse their position of power. If competition is to have a "cutting edge," there is need for small firms.

Even socialist economies such as that of China tolerate and encourage the formation of small businesses as a means of stimulating economic growth. As China's leaders have in recent years introduced elements of capitalism, including privately owned businesses, the country has experienced a dramatic rise in living standards.[9] Once-scarce bicycles, radios, and watches have become commonplace, and higher-income families now hope to acquire refrigerators, washing machines, and motorcycles. Chinese policy makers recognize the importance of entrepreneurial activity to a vigorous economy. "For the past three decades, the Chinese people have been deprived of their creativeness," says Jing Shuping, a former capitalist and unofficial economic advisor to Premier Zhao Ziyang. "Now we will unleash that energy."[10]

Not every competitive effort of small firms is successful, but big business may be kept on its toes by small business. Some entrepreneurs have no qualms about competing with giant corporations. For example, in Winchester, KY, a small soft-drink producer is marketing a ginger-ale-like product that outsells Coke, Pepsi, RC, and Dr Pepper in its home territory. And the younger member of the firm's family management team, Frank "Buddy" Rogers III, is quoted as saying, "My goal is to make Coca-Cola the No. 2 soft-drink company in this country."[11]

However, there is no guarantee of competition in numbers alone. Many tiny firms may be no match for one large firm or even for several firms that dominate an industry. Nevertheless, the existence of many healthy small businesses in an industry may be viewed as a desirable bulwark of the American capitalistic system.

Aiding Big Business

The fact that some functions are more expertly performed by small business enables small firms to contribute to the success of larger ones. If small businesses were suddenly removed from the contemporary scene, big businesses would find themselves saddled with a myriad of activities that they could only inefficiently perform. Two functions which small business can perform more efficiently than big business are the distribution function and the supply function.

Distribution Function Few large manufacturers of inexpensive consumer products find it desirable to own wholesale and retail outlets. Take, for example, the successful small-business operation of Genesco retail cast-offs.[12] Genesco, Inc., a $1 billion manufacturer of footwear and clothing, sold off a number of its lackluster retail divisions to entrepreneurs who changed them into thriving businesses. One of its retail divisions—Gidding Jenny, a fashionable women's store in Cincinnati, OH—was sold in July, 1978, to Barry Miller, a former executive with Federated Department Stores. Genesco's main problem, according to Miller, was that "they couldn't adjust to stores that were atypical, that served a select trade."

Supply Function   Small businesses act as suppliers and subcontractors for large firms. General Motors, for example, purchases goods and services from more than 25,000 small businesses. Approximately three-fourths of these small firms employ fewer than 100 persons.

ACTION REPORT
Small Business as Supplier

An interesting example of a highly successful small supplier is provided by Zero Corporation of Burbank, CA. In 1951, Jack Gilbert bought the business, which had about ten employees, from Herman Zierold. (After receiving so many letters addressed to the Zero Corporation, Gilbert finally changed the name.) The business is devoted to the production of aluminum boxes, which are used for such purposes as covering electronic gadgets. The firm simply produces aluminum boxes in standard sizes. If an order is received for a fairly standard box, Gilbert absorbs the cost of building a die. Although he merely breaks even on the original order, he then owns the die and can profit from additional orders for boxes of that size. To illustrate Zero's type of relationship with big business, consider Digital Equipment Corporation, which produces thousands of computer printers each year. "But Digital Equipment can't be bothered building the stands the printers rest on. Enter Zero, which produces the simple stand for about $40. Digital Equipment writes the book, so to speak; Zero, the cover."

Source: "Getting Rich on Little Nothings," *Forbes,* Vol. 126 (November 1, 1980), pp. 104–109.

In addition to supplying services directly to large corporations, small firms provide services to customers of big business. For example, they service automobiles, repair appliances, and clean carpets produced by large manufacturers.

Producing Goods and Services Efficiently

In considering the contributions of small business, we are concerned with an underlying question of small-business efficiency. Common sense tells us that the efficient size of business varies with the industry. We can easily recognize, for example, that big business is better in manufacturing automobiles but that small business is better in repairing them.

The continued existence of small business in a competitive economic system is in itself evidence of efficient small-business operation. If small firms were hopelessly inefficient and making no useful contribution, they would be forced out of business quickly by stronger competitors.

Additional evidence for the operating efficiency of small business is found in some studies of profitability. These studies compare small firms and large firms according to profits earned per dollar of assets. We expect highly efficient companies to earn higher profits than less efficient companies from dollars invested in plant, equipment, and inventory. And according to Table 3-2, small firms have significantly better earnings than larger firms.[13] In manufacturing, for example, the smallest firms earned 49 cents per dollar of assets. In fact, smaller companies have higher earnings in every industry group. Contrary to a common misconception, therefore, earnings per dollar of assets are inversely related to size of firm. This supports the conclusion that small business contributes in a special way to the economic welfare of our society.

Table 3-2   Earnings, Including Compensation of Officers, per Dollar of Assets for Corporations with and without Net Income, by Asset Class, 1972

Asset Class (Thousands of Dollars)	Earnings per Dollar of Assets				Wholesale and Retail Trade
	Manufacturing	Services	Construction	Trans.	
Under $25	$0.49	$2.42	$0.85	$0.42	$0.49
$25–$50	.39	1.03	.53	.26	.34
$50–$100	.35	.53	.40	.26	.29
$100–$250	.28	.29	.30	.23	.24
$250–$500	.24	.19	.23	.18	.21
$500–$1,000	.22	.13	.19	.15	.20
$1,000–$2,500	.18	.11	.16	.13	.17
$2,500–$10,000	.16	.09	.13	.11	.15
$10,000–$25,000	.14	.09	.09	.10	.12
$25,000–$100,000	.12	.09	.08	.08	.12
Over $100,000	.10	.07	.05	.05	.09

Note: *Income = Total receipts − (Total deductions + Officers' compensation + Charitable contributions)*

Source: U.S. Congress, Senate, Joint Hearing before the Select Committee on Small Business and the Joint Economic Committee, *The Role of Small Business in the Economy: Tax and Financial Problems,* 94th Congress, 1st Session, November 21, 1975, p. 39. (Primary source: Office of Tax Analysis, Office of the Secretary of the Treasury.)

Looking Back

1. Definitions of small business are necessarily arbitrary and differ according to purpose. Although there are exceptions, we generally think of a business as small when it has one or a small group of investors, operates in a geographically restricted area, is small compared to the biggest firms in the industry, and has fewer than 100 employees. Size standards issued by the Small Business Administration relate to eligibility for SBA loans and to considerations in bidding for government contracts.

2. Small firms operate in all industrial areas but are particularly dominant—in terms of number of employees on their payroll—in the fields of wholesale trade, contract construction, retail trade, and personal services.

3. The proportion of total business activity accounted for by small business ranges from 40 percent to 50 percent.

4. Small businesses make several unique contributions to our economy. They provide employment for millions of employees and play a special role in generating an unusually large share of new jobs needed for a growing labor force. They are responsible for introducing many innovations and originating such scientific breakthroughs as xerography and insulin. Small firms act as vigorous economic competitors and perform some business functions (such as distribution and supply) more expertly than large firms in many ways. Small firms can also produce goods and services efficiently as evidenced by a study that shows the superiority of small firms when measured in terms of earnings per dollar of assets.

DISCUSSION QUESTIONS

1. In view of the numerous definitions of small business, how can you decide which definition is correct?

2. Of the businesses with which you are acquainted, which is the largest that you consider to be in the small-business category? Does it conform to the size standards used in this book?

3. On the basis of your acquaintance with small-business firms, give an example of a specific small firm in the field of transportation and other public utilities.

4. What generalizations can you make about the relative importance of large and small business in the United States?

5. In which sectors of the economy is small business most important? What accounts for its strength in these areas?

6. What special contribution is made by small business in providing jobs?

7. How can you explain the unique contributions of small business to product innovation?

8. In what way does small business serve as a bulwark of the capitalistic system?

9. If all small businesses could be merged into large firms in some way, what would be the impact on industrial efficiency and on our standard of living? Why?

10. What is shown by Table 3–2 about the apparent relative efficiency of large and small firms? What might account for the relatively large amount of earnings reported for the smallest firms in services?

ENDNOTES

1. In 1966, the Small Business Administration classified American Motors, the nation's 63d largest company with more than 28,000 employees, as a small business. This decision permitted American Motors to enjoy special advantages in bidding on government contracts. It also illustrated the arbitrary nature of such definitions and the unusual classifications that are possible.

2. One weakness of this payroll criterion is that it overlooks the contributions of proprietors, partners, and unpaid family help who are not on the payroll.

3. A brief, nontechnical summary of recent development is given in "New Jobs—Where, When and at What Pay?" *Forbes*, Vol. 135 (April 29, 1985), pp. 49–50.

4. *The Contribution of Small Enterprise to Growth and Employment* (Cambridge, MA: Program on Neighborhood and Regional Change, Massachusetts Institute of Technology, undated), p. 9. Although Birch's conclusions have been challenged to some extent by a Brookings Institution study, many apparent differences have subsequently been explained with the conclusion regarding small firms' disproportionate contribution to job creation being acknowledged by both studies. For an excellent review of this research, see Tom Richman, "What America Needs Is a Few Good Failures," *Inc.*, Vol. 5, No. 9 (September, 1983), pp. 63–72.

5. *The Contribution of Small Enterprise to Growth and Employment, op. cit.*, p. 10.

6. "Small Business Innovation: Eight Who Innovate," *Inc.*, Vol. 3 (August, 1981), p. 41.

7. Tom Richman and Susan Benner, "Stanley Mason Is Growing Oil on Trees," *Inc.*, Vol. 3 (August, 1981), p. 34. Also see a National Science Foundation study (which overstated the advantage of small business), U.S. Congress, Senate, Joint Hearings before the Select Committee on Small Business and other committees, *Small Business and Innovation*, August 9–10, 1978, p. 7.

8. See "The Sad State of Innovation," *Time* (October 22, 1979), pp. 70–71; and "A Diminished Thrust from Innovation," *Business Week*, No. 2643 (June 30, 1980), pp. 60–61.

9. "Capitalism in China," *Business Week*, No. 2876 (January 14, 1985), pp. 53–59.

10. *Ibid.*, p. 53.

11. "Going after Coke," *Fortune*, Vol. 101, No. 8 (April 21, 1980), p. 19.

12. "Revamping Genesco's Cast-Offs," *Venture*, Vol. 2, No. 11 (November, 1980), pp. 14–16.

13. For a discussion of small-firm profitability, including the rationale for including officer compensation in earnings, see Stahrl W. Edmunds, "Performance Measures for Small Businesses," *Harvard Business Review*, Vol. 57, No. 1 (January–February, 1979), pp. 172–176.

REFERENCES TO SMALL BUSINESS IN ACTION

Kahn, Joseph P. "Bucking the System." *Inc.*, Vol. 5 (August, 1983), pp. 71–72.
   Buck Wilson is an innovative entrepreneur. This story tells how he even sold one recording device *before* he had invented it! Other innovations are also described.

"Small Is Beautiful Now in Manufacturing." *Business Week*, No. 2865 (October 22, 1984), pp. 152–156.
   Contrary to conventional wisdom, many corporations are discovering that large plants involve "diseconomies of scale." This report on the movement among large corporations toward smaller manufacturing plants suggests opportunities for small business efficiency in manufacturing.

"Small Railroads on a Fast Track." *In Business*, Vol. 7 (May–June, 1985), p. 33–36.
   Transportation, particularly railroads, is generally regarded as a big-business industry. This article reports on many small firms which thrive in this area.

"The New Entrepreneurs." *Business Week*, No. 2786 (April 18, 1983), pp. 78–82.
   This article describes newly organized companies and the ways in which they are giving the United States a competitive edge.

CASE 3

Frost Jewelry Store
Can the smallest jewelry store in a large shopping mall survive?

The Monday morning coffee break during football season is a popular time for college professors to gather in faculty lounges for "Monday morning quarterbacking." On one particular occasion, Professor Charles Morris, a long-time marketing professor, was visiting with Professor Mike Agee, who was recently employed to teach accounting. After Saturday's game had been replayed, Charles learned that Mike and his wife Jean operated a business. Charles was interested in the small-business area and began to inquire into their business experiences. The ensuing conversation ran as follows:

Mike: My wife Jean and I operate a very small jewelry store in Fort Collins, Colorado. It's located in the city's biggest mall. It occupies a very small space—only about 450 square feet.

Charles: How did you get into that particular business?

Mike: I saw a little ad in the newspaper one day. I was teaching accounting in Fort Collins at the time. I had been looking for something—kind of wanted to see if I could make a profit. The ad didn't name the business. After answering the ad, I learned where it was and recognized the store name—Frost Jewelry Store.

Charles: I don't believe I've heard of that name.

Mike: It started out as a franchise. It seems the franchisor owners lost interest and got into some other things, but they still have the lease on the mall space. I have a sublease with them. However, I am not operating as a franchise, and my contract with them gives me control over renewing the lease.

Charles: How did you finally decide to make the purchase?

Mike: Let me give you a little background. The previous owner who ran the ad wanted to leave Fort Collins and go back home to Louisiana. Also, his wife was not in very good health. He was the sole owner. I knew his accountant and, with the owner's permission of course, got three years' sales figures on the business. Sales in the past year (1979) had dipped considerably from the previous years. The accountant was sure that the owner had been skimming (not reporting cash income). In fact, the owner had actually told us he was skimming. We figured about $15,000 in cash had been taken in the last part of the year. When we compared the last-quarter figures of 1979 with those for 1977 and 1978, it was pretty obvious.

Charles: Did this almost scare you away from the deal?

Mike: No, not really. We certainly planned to operate the business honestly, and other factors made the deal look good. David Jones, a friend of mine, and his wife decided to join Jean and me in buying the business as a partnership.

The financing was no problem. We went to the bank which had the loan with the previous owner. We took over during the last week of March, 1980.

Charles: Tell me more about the store.

Mike: My wife's first impression of the store was that it had junk. She never went in there. It was just sort of a cheapie earring-type place. She was a little bit surprised when we did go in and look at it and saw the amount of 14-karat gold stuff they had. We, of course, bought his inventory. We have changed the inventory mix and gotten much more costume jewelry and much lower priced merchandise. Currently costume jewelry accounts for about 50 percent of our sales. We also sell gift items such as belt buckles, plastic trays, combs, hairbrushes, and mirrors. Most of these items can be personalized, which we send out to have done. Gift items probably account for 30 percent of our business. Most of our jewelry and gift items are relatively inexpensive. We do have some 14-karat gold items that run up to $60. These sell to customers who go to May D&F, a department store, and stop and shop with us. However, most of our customers tend to be of the lower middle class. Also, we still do ear piercing. In fact, it accounts for almost 20 percent of our business. It's the number-one place in the county for ear piercing. We have days where we've done as high as 40 on a Saturday. You get all kinds—we've had a few guys, too.

Charles: Does your store have a good location in the mall?

Mike: The ad said this was the best location in the mall. And that's probably true. You go in the main entrance, then you go straight back; there's a fountain and a May D&F store, which is a fine department store. We are next to May D&F on the corner, with an entrance open from two sides. On the other corner is Flowerama, a shop which sells live plants.

Charles: How is the partnership working out?

Mike: I forgot to mention it's no longer a partnership. A partnership is just not like owning your own business. We were leaving Fort Collins to come here, and so we all decided to sell. Toward the end of 1980, we put the store up for sale. We had a number of people talk to us about it. One party seemed to be pretty serious about it and asked us to try to clarify the lease arrangement. This person wanted to be sure she wouldn't have any problems renewing the lease in three years when it expires. My partner sent a letter asking the property managers, located in Boston, to give us some encouragement. The reply was a little upsetting to us. (See Figure 3–6.)

Charles: What was in the letter?

Mike: It referred to a decrease in sales from 1979 to 1980 but overlooked the fact that we generated $80,000 in the 9 months and 1 week of 1980 that we were owners. If the previous owner had been up to par for the first 2 months and 3 weeks, we probably would have had an increase over 1979. Also, we have spent a considerable amount of money on the appearance of the store with new paint, carpet, and display cases. We have had some new signs and different things made, and we got a lot of favorable comments from people, including the manager of the mall. I don't believe the property managers looked at anything but the computer printout showing sales and the square footage of the store. I've heard some of the mall people say they would like to see a franchise store selling nuts in my location. A store like that would probably make more revenue per square foot. I suspect that, at the end of the lease, people will be after that space. I'll show you a copy of the letter sometime.

Charles: How are lease payments arranged?

Mike: There is a minimum monthly rent paid to the mall, and I cannot remember exactly what it is. It's either the minimum or 8 percent of sales. Now, this means that we have to sell about $96,000 a year, or close to that, before we have to pay more than the minimum. There are some additional bills, such as utilities and taxes, which are prorated to tenants based on their square footage. Anyway, to make a long story short, Jean and I decided to keep the store. So, we made an offer to our partners and they accepted.

Charles: What are you going to do about the lease when the time comes for renewal?

Mike: A very good question!

Figure 3-6   Letter Received from the Mall's Property Managers

March 4, 1981

Dear Mr. Agee

We received your letter of February 23 asking for an extension of your lease for the purpose of making a sale of the business. This is a most unusual request at this time, but we do understand your concern.

We have, therefore, reviewed the sales performance of this store so that we can make some kind of sensible decision. In doing so, we have discovered that, for the calendar year of 1980, the store produced approximately $90,000 in volume, which was a decrease of 1.6% from the previous year. You should be aware that there was a general overall increase in the mall during that calendar year. Further, in the category of jewelry, you have the smallest store which has the lowest sales per square foot of all the stores in the category. Normally the smallest store would have the highest sales per square foot.

The general appearance of the store does not seem to fit the standard of better costume jewelry stores that we have seen in various parts of the country. Based on these assessments, there does not seem to be any reason for us to extend the lease as per your request. It seems to us that both Landlord and Tenant should seriously consider whether this is the proper use for this space.

Very truly yours

Property Managers
Fort Collins Mall

Questions

1. Assess the bargaining position of Professor Mike Agee in dealing with the property management firm. How does the smallness of the store affect its bargaining power?
2. How would you respond to the property managers' criticisms regarding decreased sales volume and low sales per square foot? Is it too early for Professor Agee to worry about the lease?
3. What alternatives are available to Professor Agee if he cannot obtain a lease extension? Evaluate the alternatives you have suggested.
4. Of what significance is the jewelry store's location next to the May D&F department store?
5. What is the nature of "skimming" as described as Professor Agee? What are its implications in assessing the health of this business and its prospects for the future?

PART II
STARTING THE SMALL BUSINESS

4 – Creating a New Venture and Preparing a Business Plan

5 – Analyzing the Market

6 – Franchising or Buying an Existing Business

7 – Selecting a Location and Physical Facilities

8 – Initial Financial Planning

9 – Legal Aspects of the Business

4

Creating a New Venture and Preparing a Business Plan

Figure 4–1   Pansy Ellen Essman

©Pansy Ellen Essman

Venture creation, the subject of this chapter, involves a wide range of people and ideas. Sometimes, the inspiration for a new business comes from the frustrations of daily life. A 42-year-old grandmother, Pansy Ellen Essman, found it difficult to hold her squealing, squirming granddaughter while bathing her in a tub.

What to do? "I took the problem to bed with me and dreamt I was bathing her in this sponge pillow," she recalls. "The dream was so vivid I couldn't get it out of my mind." She awoke in the middle of the night with an idea for a sponge product to cradle a child in the bath, freeing the mother's hands so she could easily clean her baby. Since that dream, Essman, now chairman of $5 million (sales) Atlanta-based Pansy Ellen Products, Inc., has sold at least 10 million bath aids.

The product line has expanded to include nursery lamps, baby food organizers, and an imported line of high chairs, strollers, and hook-on baby seats. Pansy Ellen Essman obviously discovered a real need (opportunity) and created a successful business to meet that need.

Source: "It Scared the Bejeebers out of Me," *Forbes*, Vol. 131, No. 3 (January 31, 1983), p. 48. Reproduced with permission.

Looking Ahead

Watch for the following important topics:

1. Sources of ideas for creating new ventures.
2. Benefits of preparing a written new-venture plan.
3. Features of new-venture plans which make them attractive or unattractive to investors.
4. Items to be included in business plans.

This chapter talks about starting a business. To get into a business of your own, you must find a business opportunity and plan an effective way to exploit it. Accordingly, this chapter begins by explaining how you find a new venture idea. It then points out the importance of a new-venture plan or business plan and explains how you prepare such a plan. Bankers, venture capitalists, and others acquainted with the entrepreneurial process widely recognize the decided advantage provided by a sound business plan and the contribution it can make to the success of a new business.

CREATING A NEW VENTURE

Reasons for starting new ventures rather than buying existing firms include the following:

1. Invention of a new product or service that necessitates a new type of business.
2. Freedom to select the ideal location, equipment, products or services, employees, suppliers, and bankers.
3. Avoidance of undesirable precedents, policies, procedures, and legal commitments of existing firms.

Regardless of the reason, the would-be entrepreneur should ask the following questions before deciding to implement the venture concept: Have I found a genuine business opportunity? What sources of new-venture ideas are available? Have I refined the idea? Do I have the necessary education and experience for this type of venture?

Find a Genuine Business Opportunity

The opportunities portrayed in Figure 4–2 may be visualized as alternative routes to successful new-business ventures. Note that the opportu-

Figure 4–2 Routes to New-Business Ventures

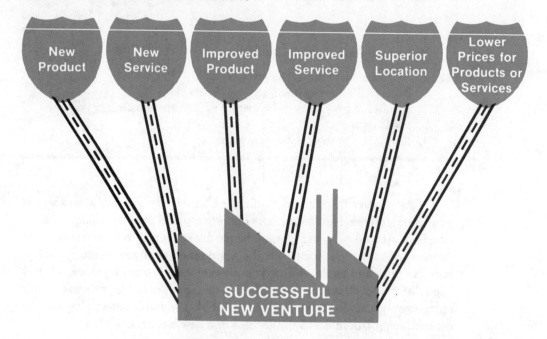

nity may involve an entirely new product or service. More frequently, however, the opportunity involves a market not adequately served by existing businesses.

Whatever type of business opportunity is involved, it must be genuine. This means that the new business must have some type of advantage that will provide a competitive edge. This special edge is necessary because the marketplace generally does not welcome a new competitor. As Karl Vesper has pointed out, the newcomer needs an "entry wedge."[1] The prospective entrepreneur must visualize some new product or service or location or "angle" that will not only "get the foot in the door" but keep it there.

Some apparent opportunities are insufficient for the long-term success of a new venture. For example, an influx of population during the construction of a large power plant or dam may provide a sizable market now but an inadequate market later because of the population decline when construction is completed. Of course, in this situation one could purposely go into business—for instance, a mobile food service—with plans for temporary operation, large profits, and closure or relocation when the "boom" is over.

Identify Sources of New-Venture Ideas

Since the new venture starts with an idea, let's consider the circumstances which tend to spawn such new ideas. Some of the numerous possibilities discussed below are: work experience, invention of a new product, hobbies, accidental discovery, and deliberate search.

Work Experience   One basis for new-venture ideas is work experience. From the knowledge of their present or recent jobs, some employees see possibilities in modifying an existing product, improving a service, or duplicating a business concept in a different location. For example, a furniture salesperson may see the possibility of opening a new furniture store in a different area of the city. The new store may follow the business strategy of the existing store, or it may feature different, restricted, or expanded lines of merchandise. It may also adopt credit or delivery policies which are more appealing to customers in that area.

Work experience may well be the most productive of all venture-idea sources. After studying the histories of approximately 100 highly successful entrepreneurs, Karl Vesper summarized his findings as follows:

> The pattern of close connection between prior work and new-venture ideas was common to a large majority of the successful start-ups—between 60% and 90%, depending on the industry—the correlation being highest in advanced-technology areas like computers and medical instruments and lowest in enterprises of a relatively unspecialized nature such as nursing homes, fast-food franchises, and other consumer-oriented businesses.[2]

Invention of a New Product   Another idea which can grow into a business involves the invention of a new product. The entrepreneur may invent a product or acquire an invention from the original inventor. An invention may be acquired, for example, by consulting *Venture/Product Digest* which was originated by General Electric Company and is now published by Genium Publishing Company. Each monthly issue lists products and processes that are available for acquisition or licensing.

Hobbies   Sometimes hobbies grow beyond their stature as hobbies to become businesses. For example, a coin collector who buys and sells coins to build a personal collection may easily become a coin dealer. Recall the story of Polly Reilly, related in Chapter 1, whose artwork evolved into a successful business venture.

Accidental Discovery   As a source of new-venture ideas, accidental discovery involves something we call **serendipity**—the faculty for making desirable discoveries by accident. Any person may stumble across a useful idea in the ordinary course of day-to-day living. This was true of Jim and Betty Smulian whose search for lighting fixtures, recounted below, led to the creation of their own business, Trimble House, in Atlanta, GA.

> When Betty Smulian was redecorating her home in Atlanta, she began shopping around for a candle chandelier. None of the stores had exactly what she wanted. Neither did the catalogs featuring specialty lighting items.

ACTION REPORT
Students Launch New Ventures

Students frequently develop ideas for new ventures and implement them while they are still pursuing their degrees. Three such student ventures are described below.

Scott Burns, a business student, noticed that many parking lots in front of Waco stores needed cleaning. So, he bought a mechanical sweeping machine and contracted with store owners to provide such a service. "Wherever there is a parking lot, there's a potential market," he says. His business prospered, and he acquired customers not only in Waco but also in other nearby cities.

Another business student, Karen Adams, founded Baylor Balloons with a friend, using the slogan "Flowers are nice, but balloons are fun." They delivered bouquets of balloons to customers in the university area. Karen later became sole owner of the business and eventually sold it as a flourishing concern.

Brent Pennington designed a safety switch which automatically cuts off a home cooling and heating system in the event of a fire. A fusible link in the device melts when the house temperature reaches a certain level. Brent assembled the switches in his apartment and was hard-pressed to meet the demand from builders and electrical contractors!

Source: Adapted from Alan Hunt, "Practicing Private Enterprise...Baylor Style," *Baylor University Report*, Vol. 1, No. 32 (April 17, 1981), pp. 2–3.

Most homeowners would have given up at that point and settled for a conventional chandelier. But Betty, a design engineer, created her own fixture. And her husband, Jim, a mechanical engineer, fabricated the fixture in their basement, using Betty's precise design drawing.

When friends and neighbors saw the chandelier, they oohed and aahed. They each wanted one of their own. And so a multimillion-dollar lighting fixture business was born about 20 years ago.[3]

Deliberate Search   A new business may also emerge from a prospective entrepreneur's **deliberate search**—a purposeful exploration to find a new-venture idea. M. L. Gimpl suggests two approaches to this search: an inside-out approach and an outside-in approach. When an **inside-out approach** is used, entrepreneurs first survey their own capabilities and then look at the new products or services they are capable of producing. When entrepreneurs follow an **outside-in approach**, they first look for needs in the marketplace and then relate those needs to their own existing or potential capabilities.[4]

The outside-in (or market first) thinking has apparently produced more successful ventures, especially in the field of consumer goods and services. To explore the marketplace, prospective entrepreneurs can reflect upon the changing life-styles and markets in the world around them and then talk to consumers, salespersons, attorneys, engineers, business owners, and so on, who may provide ideas.

ACTION REPORT
New Business Idea from a Market Search

The "outside-in" search for a new venture idea begins with a study of the market and its needs. An example of a firm started in this way is Concept, Inc., a small medical products company in Clearwater, FL. Terry F. Tanner, a 36-year-old country doctor, knew that he wanted to be in the medical supply business, but he didn't know what he wanted to supply. He found his product by asking doctors and dentists for ideas.

"I invited 15 or so doctor and dentist friends for a brainstorming session," Tanner recalls. "I wanted to see what the medical world was waiting for. Our first product came from an idea from a dentist who complained that he was always running out of batteries for the flashlight he used during examinations. He said, 'Why don't you make a flashlight you can throw away when the batteries are gone?'"

Other products were added in the same way. Doctors would tell Tanner of a need, and the company would fill it.

Source: Paul B. Brown, "We Can't Afford Failures," *Forbes,* Vol. 132, No. 1 (July 4, 1983), pp. 68–69. Reproduced with permission.

A deliberate search also helps in a general way by stimulating a readiness of mind. If a prospective entrepreneur thinks seriously about new-business ideas, he or she will be more receptive to new ideas from any source.

Since a truly creative person may find useful ideas in many different ways, the sources of new-venture ideas mentioned above are suggestive, not exhaustive. We encourage you to seek and reflect upon new-venture ideas in whatever circumstances you find yourself.

Refine a New-Venture Idea

A new-venture idea often requires an extended period of time for refinement and testing. This is particularly true for original inventions which necessitate developmental work to make them operational. The need for refining a new idea is not limited to high-technology ventures, however. Almost any idea for a new business deserves careful study and typically requires modification as the aspiring entrepreneur moves toward opening day for the new business.

An example is found in the case of John Morse, who founded Fratelli's Ice Cream in Seattle. A course with Karl Vesper at the University of Washington required him to bring some practicality to his abstract ideas for this business.

> "When I first mentioned the ice cream idea to Karl, he told me I was crazy. He pointed out that we had experience bordering on weeks, no contacts, and that we'd be up against big hitters," says Morse. "The idea was 99% inspiration and 1% thought. Karl forced me to think it through." Responding to Vesper's challenges over the next two years, Morse finally signed an agreement with a local dairy to produce Fratelli's ice cream. "They had 76 years of experience—and connections," he says. Today he annually sells $1 million of ice cream in three states.[5]

The process of preparing a business plan, as discussed later in this chapter, helps the individual to think through an idea and to consider all aspects of a proposed business. Outside experts can be used to review the business plan, and their questions and suggestions can help to improve the plan. Jeffry Timmons reported the case of the founders of a rotary-drill venture whose initial strategy was to price its products below the competition even though they had a superior product innovation in a growing market.[6] Outside experts persuaded them to price 10 percent over the competition, and this decision contributed significantly to later profits.

Evaluate Your Education and Experience

A successful start-up calls not only for a sound business idea, but also for some minimum amount of entrepreneurial education and experience. Even so, it is impossible to prescribe exacting requirements. Fabulously successful exceptions will always exist.

It is a matter of record, however, that many business failures are the result of *avoidable* inadequacies on the part of the entrepreneur. In a study of manufacturing failures, William Hoad and Peter Rosko discovered that deficiencies in education and experience were associated with those failures. Of 36 entrepreneurs who failed, 11 were deficient in education, 11 in experience, and 11 in both. Only three of the failing entrepreneurs possessed the appropriate combination of training and experience.[7]

Incompetence, a cause of many failures, frequently reflects inadequate educational preparation. Today a high school education is a virtual necessity for business ownership. A college education with graduate study in business might be recommended as the ideal academic preparation.

Academic education is no substitute for experience, however. Lack of experience in the industry, lack of managerial experience, and lack of general experience in production, marketing, and finance are all common causes of failure. Naturally, the length of desirable experience varies from one type of enterprise and/or person to another. Individuals contemplating a business of their own typically do well to consider several years of employment in a similar business. Preferably this experience should be such as to bring them into contact with the full range of activities and problems associated with the given type of business.

We must temper our remarks about entrepreneurial qualifications by recognizing that the necessary blend of education and experience varies with the nature of the business. This is apparent in the Vesper study cited earlier. Vesper found that nearly all entrepreneurs involved in starting successful high-technology companies had earned one or more college degrees, while most entrepreneurs who started successful machining businesses had worked in machine shops but not attended college.[8]

Much work is required—some of it tedious, much of it exciting—to go from the idea stage to the operation stage. The effort expended during this preoperating period is extremely important in laying the foundation for a successful start-up. The remainder of this chapter discusses the planning necessary in the preoperating period.

PREPARING A NEW-VENTURE PLAN

In preparing to launch a new venture, the prospective entrepreneur should prepare a *written* business plan. The **new-venture plan** describes the new-venture idea and projects the marketing, operational, and financial aspects of the proposed business for the first three to five years. Its preparation permits analysis of the proposal and helps the prospective entrepreneur avoid a downhill path which leads from wild enthusiasm to disillusionment to failure. Although we will explain the planning process and present an outline for a business plan in this chapter, we wish to make it clear that you should use the ideas presented throughout this book and particularly those in Chapters 5 through 9 when preparing such a plan.

Benefits of Preparing a Written Plan

Any activity that is initiated without adequate preparation tends to be haphazard and unsuccessful. This is particularly true of such a complex process as initiating a new business. Although planning is a mental process, it must go beyond the realm of thought. Thinking about a proposed business becomes more rigorous as rough ideas must be crystallized and quantified on paper. The written plan is essential to assure the systematic coverage of all important features of the new business.

One benefit derived from preparing a formal written plan is the discipline provided for the prospective entrepreneur. For example, in order to prepare a written statement about marketing strategy, the prospective entrepreneur must perform some market research. Likewise, a study of financing requirements is necessary. In commenting on a venture which never quite succeeded, Ted Harwood stressed the crucial importance of the written business plan as follows:

> It [the business plan] forces a useful discipline in thinking about how each stage of the venture will proceed and especially about how to anticipate expenditures and revenues month by month. Even with a good product, unanticipated negative cash balances can kill a venture despite the fact that orders are coming in and sales growing.[9]

Thus, preparing a written plan forces the prospective entrepreneur to exercise the discipline that good managers must possess.

Another benefit of the written plan is that it may be used by the new entrepreneur as an initial operating plan. The written new-venture plan provides direction for the early decisions to be made, and it establishes standards for evaluating business performance during the early months of operation.

Perhaps an even more important benefit of the written new-venture plan lies in its use by outside parties. Practically every new entrepreneur faces the task of raising financial resources to supplement personal savings. Unless the entrepreneur has relatives who will supply funds, he or she must appeal to individual investors, bankers, venture capitalists, the Small Business Administration, or other outsiders. Such parties will typically want to review the new-business plan before participating in the new venture.

Tendency to Neglect Initial Planning

Prospective entrepreneurs tend to neglect the planning stage of a new venture. They are eager to get started, and they do not always realize the

ACTION REPORT
Venture Capitalist Comments on New-Venture Plan

Citicorp Venture Capital, Ltd., is an investment company which invests risk capital in new ventures. Its president, Rick Roesch (a University of California MBA), was asked what might improve the chances of an applicant for new-business financing. His answer stressed the importance of a well-thought-out, persuasive, *written* business plan.

The most successful entrepreneurs have thought through their business plans. They know their strengths and weaknesses. They know what the competition is offering.... The entrepreneur is doing himself a disservice to think he can go in eye-to-eye with a prospective investor and simply sell his company. It's safe to say that if it is not on paper, it is not well enough thought out for a venture capitalist to consider it.

Source: Sam Adams, "What a Venture Capitalist Looks For," *MBA*, Vol. 7 (June–July, 1973), p. 9.

importance of a written plan. They may also lack sufficient funds or necessary expertise to conduct an adequate feasibility study. Of course, sometimes they are forced to engage in a minimum of planning in order to gain a hearing from venture capitalists—the potential investors in their business.

The neglect of initial planning is evident from a study by G. M. Naidu of business start-ups in Wisconsin.[10] For example, Naidu found that:

1. 63 percent of the new entrepreneurs did not evaluate the location of the business.
2. 72 percent did not conduct a trade-area analysis.
3. 52 percent did not evaluate their competition.
4. Almost 25 percent did not even estimate revenues and expenses.

Failure to prepare an initial written plan for a new venture undoubtedly contributes to the early failure of some firms.

Reports Which Attract Investors

As stated earlier, one reason for preparing a business plan is to attract investment funds. As a result, the plan must be presented in a manner which appeals to prospective investors. This means that the plan should not be extremely long or encyclopedic in detail. Such plans should seldom exceed 50 pages in length. Those who work with venture capitalists have reported their tendency to go for brief reports and to avoid those which take too long to read. It follows also that the general appearance of the report should be attractive and that it should be well-organized with numbered pages and a table of contents.

Venture capitalists are more market-oriented than product-oriented, and there is a reason for this orientation. They realize that most inventions, even those patented, never earn a dime for the inventors. It is desirable for budding entrepreneurs to join them in their concern about market prospects (see Figure 4–3).

Factors which presumably "turn on" investors are the following:[11]

- Evidence of customer acceptance of the venture's product or service.
- An appreciation of investors' needs, through recognition of their particular financial-return goals.
- Evidence of focus, through concentration on only a limited number of products or services.
- Proprietary position, as expressed in the form of patents, copyrights, and trademarks.

Prospective investors may also be "turned off" by a business plan. Some of the features that create unfavorable reactions are the following:[12]

- Infatuation with the product or service rather than familiarity with and awareness of marketplace needs.
- Financial projections at odds with accepted industry ranges.
- Growth projections out of touch with reality.
- Custom or applications engineering, which make substantial growth difficult.

Content of the New-Venture Plan

A prospective entrepreneur needs a guide for the preparation of a new-venture plan. Figure 4–4 presents such a guide. It outlines the type of information that should be included in a business plan and suggests a pattern for organizing the material.[13] However, you should recognize that there is no single format for such plans. No sample plans are included here, partly because of space limitations. There is also a danger, because of the unique aspects of any specific business venture, in attempting to follow a suggested plan by merely changing the numbers.[14]

In the next few pages, we present brief comments on the various areas of the business plan outlined in Figure 4–4. The discussion does not treat each item in detail but rather points out general investor concerns related to the broad areas of the outline.

Figure 4-3   Plans That Succeed

Based on their experience with the MIT Enterprise Forum, Stanley R. Rich and David E. Gumpert have identified the type of plan that wins funding. (The MIT Enterprise Forum sponsors sessions in which prospective entrepreneurs present business plans to panels of venture capitalists, bankers, marketing specialists, and other experts.) Following are the "winning" features:

- It must be arranged appropriately, with an executive summary, a table of contents, and its chapters in the right order.
- It must be the right length and have the right appearance—not too long and not too short, not too fancy and not too plain.
- It must give a sense of what the founders and the company expect to accomplish three to seven years into the future.
- It must explain in quantitative and qualitative terms the benefit to the user of the company's products or services.
- It must present hard evidence of the marketability of the products or services.
- It must justify financially the means chosen to sell the products or services.
- It must explain and justify the level of product development which has been achieved and describe in appropriate detail the manufacturing process and associated costs.
- It must portray the partners as a team of experienced managers with complementary business skills.
- It must suggest as high an overall "rating" as possible of the venture's product development and team sophistication.
- It must contain believable financial projections, with the key data explained and documented.
- It must show how investors can cash out in three to seven years, with appropriate capital appreciation.
- It must be presented to the most potentially receptive financiers possible to avoid wasting precious time as company funds dwindle.
- It must be easily and concisely explainable in a well-orchestrated oral presentation.

Source: "Plans That Succeed" (pp. 2–3) and dialogue on pp. 126–127 from BUSINESS PLANS THAT WIN $$$: Lessons from the MIT Enterprise Forum by Stanley R. Rich and David E. Gumpert. Copyright © 1985 by Stanley R. Rich and David E. Gumpert. Reprinted by permission of Harper & Row, Publishers, Inc.

The Product and Marketing Issues   Following an introductory section that summarizes the project, the business plan should describe the product or service to be offered to customers. If a physical product is involved and a working model or prototype is available, a photograph should be included.

Figure 4–4   Outline for Preparing a Business Plan

I. INTRODUCTION
   A. General statement of purpose and objectives
   B. Overview of the industry
II. PRODUCTS/SERVICES
   A. Description
   B. Proprietary features
   C. Patent or copyright protection
   D. Quality level
   E. Breadth of product line
III. MARKET RESEARCH
   A. Description of market to be served
   B. Market size and segments
   C. Market trends
   D. Customers—type and locations
   E. Competition—strengths and weaknesses
   F. Sales forecast
IV. MARKETING PLAN
   A. Overall marketing strategy
   B. Channels of distribution
   C. Personal selling
   D. Advertising and promotion
   E. Pricing
   F. Service and warranty policies
V. OPERATIONS
   A. Location
   B. Facilities
   C. Raw materials
   D. Inventory control
   E. Quality control
   F. Production control
   G. Staffing
   H. Research and development
VI. ORGANIZATION AND MANAGEMENT
   A. Legal form of organization
   B. Managerial organization—roles and relationships
   C. Key management personnel
   D. Management compensation and ownership
   E. Board of directors
   F. Outside professional services
VII. FINANCIAL PLAN
   A. Initial financial requirements
   B. Profit-and-loss forecast
   C. Cash-flow forecast
   D. Break-even analysis
   E. Projected source of funds
   F. Projected balance sheet
   G. Ownership interests
   H. Risks and contingency plans

Some products must be carried through a long period of development— proceeding from a conceptual stage to building a prototype to refinement of an operating model. Investors will naturally show greatest interest in products which have been developed, tested, and found to be functional. Any innovative features should be identified and patent protection, if any, explained. (Product strategies are discussed in more detail in Chapter 10.)

As stated earlier, prospective investors and lenders attach a high priority to market considerations. A product may be well-engineered but unwanted by customers. The business plan, therefore, must proceed quickly to identify the user benefit and the type of market that exists.

Depending on the type of product or service, you may be able not only to identify but also to quantify the user's financial benefit. The plan may show cost benefits—for example, how quickly a user can recover the cost of the product through savings in operating cost. Of course, benefits may also take the form of convenience, time saving, greater attractiveness, better health, and so on, and some of these are difficult to quantify.

The business plan should follow the establishment of user benefit by documenting the existence of customer interest, showing that a market exists and that customers are ready to buy the product or service. (Market analysis will be discussed at some length in Chapter 5.) The market analysis must be carried to the point that a reasonable estimate of demand can be achieved because this is a key element of the financial projections contained in the plan. Such estimates of demand must be analytically sound and be more than assumptions if they are to be accepted as credible by prospective investors or serve as a proper basis for the commitment of the entrepreneur to the proposed venture. For example, vague statements saying that the market is growing rapidly should be avoided.

Market analysis must consider the existence of competitive products or services. In this connection, the prospective entrepreneur may be able to identify a market niche that permits him or her to distinguish the new venture in some way from existing businesses. (The idea of a special niche is explored in Chapters 5 and 14.)

As you can see in the outline of the business plan in Figure 4-4, the entrepreneur must also describe the marketing plan. This includes the overall marketing strategy, channels of distribution, advertising, selling approaches, and related considerations. (Chapters 10-12 relate to these topics.)

Operations and Management   Sections V and VI of the business plan, as outlined in Figure 4-4, treat the basic operations or production process and the management plan. It may seem that discussion of these factors should precede the review of marketing issues. However, this order is deliberate because we wish to maintain a marketing orientation. Nevertheless, the plan must also explain how you will manufacture the product or perform the service.

The operating plans requiring analysis include such items as location and facilities—how much manufacturing space you will need and what type of capital equipment you will require. (These topics are treated more fully in Chapter 7.) The explanation should also cover inventory control, quality control, production control, and other items of this nature explained in Chapters 17 and 18. The importance and nature of these operating plans obviously differ from venture to venture, but most are important for firms providing services as well as for those producing products. The operating plans should detail the proposed approach to assuring production quality, the extent to which subcontracting will be used, and any special needs or problems related to raw materials.

Prospective investors look for well-managed companies. Unfortunately, the ability to formulate an idea for a new venture is no guarantee of managerial ability. The plan, therefore, should detail the organizational arrangements and the backgrounds of those who will fill key positions in the proposed firm.

Ideally, investors desire to see a well-balanced management team. They wish to find financial and marketing expertise, as well as production experience and inventive talent. Managerial experience in related enterprises and in other start-up situations is particularly valuable in the eyes of outsiders reading the business plan.

Financial Plan   The financial analysis constitutes a crucial section of the business plan. In it, the prospective entrepreneur must present projections of revenues and profits and reveal the basic financial structure of the firm. In order to maintain a broad perspective of the overall plan, we shall mention only the most significant statements that form part of the financial plan. Detailed treatment of the content and preparation of these statements must be postponed until later chapters. At this point, therefore, you should concentrate on the general content and purpose of these statements, leaving procedural considerations until later.

The projected income statement is obviously designed to show the profitability of the venture, and it should project these profits (or losses) not only for the first year of operation but for five years or more. In fact, projections should be prepared monthly for the first year and quarterly for the second and third years. (Preparation of the income statement is explained in Chapter 19.)

A sales forecast provides the starting point for the income statement, and it must be realistic if the income statement is to have meaning. Any assumptions made in its preparation should be carefully explained. Those starting new firms tend toward extreme optimism in anticipating financial results. As a consequence, the projected income statement typically errs on the side of overestimating revenues and underestimating expenses. This is

ACTION REPORT
One-Man Bands

Since investors place value on a well-balanced managerial team, they are suspicious of ventures in which management appears to be "thin." Following is an account of a review panel's discussion with the proprietor of a three-year-old company that produced circuit boards. The proprietor sought advice on how he could get sales out of the $50,000 to $100,000 range where they seemed to be stuck.

"Who is the chief executive officer?" a panelist asked.
"I am," the entrepreneur answered.
"Who is the chief financial officer?"
"I am."
"Who is head of engineering?"
"I am."
"Who is the sales manager?"
"I am."
"How much of your time do you devote to sales?" the same panelist asked.
"About 10%," came the answer.
To which the panelist responded, "If you had someone putting 100% of their time into sales, it's almost certain your company's revenues could increase to between $500,000 and $1 million."
The owner took the panelist's advice, and his company has since begun to live up to its promise.

Source: "Plans That Succeed" (pp. 2–3) and dialogue on pp. 126–127 from BUSINESS PLANS THAT WIN $$$: Lessons from the MIT Enterprise Forum by Stanley R. Rich and David E. Gumpert. Copyright © 1985 by Stanley R. Rich and David E. Gumpert. Reprinted by permission of Harper & Row, Publishers, Inc.

understandable, since pessimists seldom start businesses. Nevertheless, one preparing the business plan should strive for realism in estimates and proceed as rationally as possible in making them. (Methods of forecasting are discussed in Chapter 5.)

The pro-forma balance sheet for a new venture shows the intended financial structure. The listed assets reveal the proposed configuration of the firm's resources—how much of the money will be devoted to equipment, inventory, and so on. It also shows the proposed sources of funds—how much will be borrowed and how much invested. (Estimating financial needs and finding sources of funds are discussed in Chapter 8. Preparation of the balance sheet is covered in Chapter 19.)

The cash flow forecast, a third important statement, is related to, but not the same as, the income statement. (Its preparation is discussed in Chapter 20.) A business may be profitable but still fail to produce a positive cash flow.

Sales may increase but cash may decline, for example, as dollars are tied up in growing accounts receivable and inventory. This statement shows when money comes in and when it goes out and presents a plan to guarantee an adequate amount of cash on a month-by-month or quarter-by-quarter basis.

One additional element of the financial plan is a break-even analysis on the venture. This analysis, discussed in Chapter 11, shows the relationship between revenues and costs at various volume levels. The **break-even point** is that point at which total sales revenue equals total costs. A break-even chart, therefore, shows the volume level that will be necessary for the new venture to avoid losses and begin to earn profits.

Computer-Aided Business Planning

The computer may be used to reduce the clerical work and calculations associated with the preparation of a financial plan. Since the various parts of a financial plan are interwoven in many ways, a change in one item—sales volume or interest rate or cost of equipment, for example—will cause ripples to run through the entire plan. If the planner wishes to check out a number of assumptions, this requires a long, tedious set of calculations.

By using a computer simulation, the planner can accomplish this work electronically. Such a program is available in Terry S. Maness, *Small-Business Management Using Lotus 1-2-3* (Cincinnati: South-Western Publishing Company, 1987). That publication, designed for use with this text, provides a program for developing a complete financial plan. By using this type of simulation, a planner can experiment with various scenarios and quickly ascertain their impact on cash flow and operating profits.

Uses of the Business Plan

As stated earlier in the chapter, the business plan has multiple uses. One of these is its function as an operating document in programming the new firm's initial activities. Having outlined the intended plan of operations, then, the entrepreneur can proceed to implement the plan.

If the entrepreneur also wishes to use the business plan to solicit funds, he or she must then seek out the most appropriate type of funds source—banker, private investor, venture capitalist, or other source. Even among venture capitalists, there is a wide variety in terms of their specialization and geographical area. Some of them consider only high-technology investments, while others invest in consumer-oriented fields such as restaurants and retail stores.

In most cases, the entrepreneur must supplement the written plan with an oral presentation. During this presentation, probably less than an hour in length, potential investors attempt to size up intangible factors such as the entrepreneur's integrity, flexibility, and ability. They also try to assess the merit of the proposed venture. By preparing a sound written plan and supporting it with a carefully prepared oral presentation, the entrepreneur can maximize chances for successful funding.

Looking Back

1. Ideas for new ventures come from many different sources, including work experience, inventions, hobbies, accidental discovery, and deliberate search. Such ideas require study and refinement before the business is launched.
2. Preparing a written new-venture plan is beneficial in that it stimulates a careful study of the new venture, provides an initial operating plan, and explains the venture to bankers and other outside parties.
3. To be attractive to investors, business plans should be long enough to provide a thorough analysis of the venture but not too long (not over 50 pages). They should also show a market orientation and avoid financial projections that are at odds with industry ranges and/or out of touch with reality.
4. Business plans should provide a systematic treatment of all aspects of the proposed venture. In particular, they should include a marketing analysis, an explanation of the product or service and plan of operation, a review of the organization structure and managerial talent, and financial projections.

DISCUSSION QUESTIONS

1. Why should an entrepreneur prefer to launch an entirely new venture rather than buy an existing firm?
2. Can you identify a business that grew out of the entrepreneur's hobby and one that resulted from the entrepreneur's work experience?
3. Can you suggest a product or a service not currently available that might lead to a new small business? How safe would it be to launch a new small business depending solely on that one new product or service? Why?
4. What is the difference between an "inside-out" approach and an "outside-in" approach in seeking new-venture ideas? Explain.
5. What benefits are associated with the preparation of a written new-venture plan? Who uses it?

6. Venture capitalists were described as being more market-oriented than product-oriented. What does this mean? What is the logic behind this orientation?

7. Why shouldn't longer business plans be better than shorter ones in view of the fact that more data and supporting analysis can be included?

8. In selling a new type of production tool, how might you quantify user benefit?

9. The founders of Apple Computer, Inc., eventually left or were forced out of the company's management. What implications does this have for the organization and management section of a business plan?

10. If the income statement in a business plan shows the business will be profitable, what is the need for a cash flow forecast?

ENDNOTES

1. Karl H. Vesper, *New Venture Strategies* (Englewood Cliffs, NJ: Prentice-Hall, Inc., 1980), p. 176.

2. Karl H. Vesper, "New-Venture Ideas: Do Not Overlook the Experience Factor," *Harvard Business Review*, Vol. 57, No. 4 (July–August, 1979), p. 165.

3. "The Entrepreneurs: For Want of a Lamp...a Flourishing Firm," *Nation's Business*, Vol. 69, No. 3 (March, 1981), p. 18.

4. M. L. Gimpl, "Obtaining Ideas for New Products and Ventures," *Journal of Small Business Management*, Vol. 16, No. 4 (October, 1978), pp. 21–26.

5. Stephen Robinett, "What Schools Can Teach Entrepreneurs," *Venture*, Vol. 7, No. 2 (February, 1985), p. 58.

6. Jeffry A. Timmons, "A Business Plan Is More Than a Financing Device," *Harvard Business Review*, Vol. 58, No. 2 (March–April, 1980), p. 30.

7. William M. Hoad and Peter Rosko, *Management Factors Contribute to the Success or Failure of New Small Manufacturers*, Michigan Business Report No. 44 (Ann Arbor: Bureau of Business Research, Graduate School of Business Administration, University of Michigan, 1964), Table 47.

An entrepreneur with more than five years' experience as owner-manager or manager of the same or a similar kind of business was classified as "experienced." An entrepreneur with formal education of one or more years beyond high school was classified as "educated."

8. Vesper, "New-Venture Ideas," *loc. cit.*

9. Ted Harwood, "A Venture Is Not a Game," *In Business*, Vol. 2 (November–December, 1980), p. 45.

10. G. M. Naidu, "Problems and Perceptions of Emerging Businesses in Wisconsin: Some Implications," a paper presented at the International Council for Small Business Conference, Western Carolina University, Cullowhee, NC, June, 1978.

11. Stanley R. Rich and David E. Gumpert, *Business Plans That Win $$$* (New York: Harper and Row, Publishers, 1985), p. 22.

12. *Ibid.*, p. 23.

13. For other examples of planning outlines, see Jeffry A. Timmons, "A Business Plan Is More Than a Financing Device," *Harvard Business Review*, Vol. 58, No. 2 (March–April, 1980), p. 34; Bank of America, "Financing Small Business," *Small Business Reporter*, Vol.

14 (1980), p. 19; *Raising Venture Capital: An Entrepreneur's Guidebook*, a pamphlet published by Deloitte, Haskins and Sells, 1982.

14. You can find sample plans in: Seymour Jones and M. Bruce Cohen, *The Emerging Business: Managing for Growth* (New York: John Wiley and Sons, 1983); Joseph R. Mancuso, *How To Prepare and Present a Business Plan* (Englewood Cliffs, NJ: Prentice-Hall, Inc., 1983).

REFERENCES TO SMALL BUSINESS IN ACTION

"He Retired to a 70-Hour Week." *Nation's Business*, Vol. 70, No. 10 (October, 1982), p. 96.
   After retiring at age 55, Carl G. Sontheimer created a new business to keep from being bored. This article tells how he found a new type of food processor in France and built Cuisinarts, Inc.

"How to Start a Sideline Business." *Business Week*, No. 2597 (August 6, 1979), pp. 94–97.
   Many small firms begin as sidelines of entrepreneurs whose principal livelihood comes from other sources. A number of sideline ventures are described, and some of their special problems are explained.

Kent, Nita Sue. "The Icewoman Cometh in a Pinch." *In Business*, Vol. 6, No. 2 (April, 1984), pp. 40–42.
   Forced into self-sufficiency by divorce, a Texas woman built a successful business with quick delivery of ice to restaurants. Her experiences in launching this new type of business are described.

Rhodes, Lucien. "Winning Is a State of Mind at Nike." *Inc.*, Vol. 3, No. 8 (August, 1981), pp. 52–57.
   This article describes the origin of Nike, Inc. in a student paper and its growth to a major producer and marketer of athletic shoes.

CASE 4

Asphera Lens Company
Launching a new venture with a new product

The Asphera Lens Company was organized on the basis of an invention related to aspheric optical lenses.

Nature of the Invention

The invention that formed the basis for this venture was a method and/or machine for manufacturing aspheric lenses. The concept of an aspheric lens is not new. Scientists in the field of optics have long known of its potential superiority. A conventional spheric spectacle lens, for example, produces accurate vision at its center but involves some distortion of vision in peripheral areas. A person who threads a needle while wearing such glasses must position the needle at just the right place relative to the center of the lenses. An aspheric lens, in contrast, can give visual acuity even in peripheral areas.

The problem in the past has been the lack of a method for accurately and economically producing an aspheric lens surface. The inventor, with a Ph.D. in physics, had learned of the problem while temporarily employed by a lens manufacturer several years earlier. After leaving that company, this person continued to work on the problem and eventually devised a solution.

Market Assessment Problems

In considering market prospects, the first question was concerned with the industrial area to be studied. The possibilities were numerous. Production of ophthalmic lenses (prescription spectacle and contact lenses) was one possibility. Photographic lenses, rifle sights, and instrument lenses were also investigated. In addition, the invention's concept had possible applications in solar energy, military research, and even nonlens areas. It was difficult to specify the application in which an aspheric lens might have the greatest advantage or face the least intensive competition.

Somewhat arbitrarily, but partially because of market size, the inventor selected the field of ophthalmic lens production for further study. The inventor knew, for example, that more than 50 percent of the United States population wore prescription lenses. However, there was no certainty as to the segment of this market in which the aspheric lens would be applicable. While it seemed clear that the aspheric lens would have value for cataract patients and others using extremely strong lenses, its potential value for the average person wearing glasses was unknown. Doctors of ophthalmology explained that individuals could adapt themselves to various types of lenses. It was possible, however, that the average wearer might experience less discomfort and tiredness by using aspheric lenses. In fact, even individuals wearing nonprescription sunglasses might find aspheric lenses more comfortable.

More detailed data on the production and sale of ophthalmic lenses were unavailable. Several apparently related trade associations disclaimed knowledge, many of them responding to inquiries by referring the inventor to someone else. After completing this circle to no avail, the inventor decided that a substantial market did exist, provided the manufacturing process and the resultant lenses lived up to expectations. Admittedly, the range of potential volume was great, but the business could break even on only a tiny percentage (less than 1 percent) of the total potential market.

Financing Problems

The search for capital sources began with the preparation of a crude prospectus. In addition, discussions were held with technically oriented people—ophthalmologists, optometrists, opticians, operators of optical laboratories, and optical engineers—and with other individuals who might be interested as investors. However, the difficulty in understanding the concept of the aspheric lens and in appreciating its potential represented one impediment in these discussions. Some who apparently grasped the idea in an abstract way evidenced little excitement about its possibilities. Ophthalmologists were cautious and seemed to perceive themselves as medical scientists whose major concern was the proper functioning of the human eye. They regarded lenses as "hardware" items to be produced by subprofessional tradespeople and sold by hucksters. The reaction from optometrists was typically more encouraging. Their interest was evident as they began to discuss the usefulness of aspheric ophthalmic lenses.

Understanding the aspheric lens principle, however, did not guarantee recognition of the value of this specific invention. Believing in its merits called for a considerable measure of faith, if not credulity. There was no patent, and no formal patent application had yet been filed. The inventor was reluctant to divulge any secrets to strangers, and most potential investors were unqualified to assess the quality of the invention even if they read its technical description.

Two entrepreneurially oriented optometrists eventually agreed to invest in the business. They recognized the tremendous potential of the invention and were not so exclusively professional that they were afraid to act like businesspeople. The total amount of approximately $50,000, including additional smaller sums invested by others, was quite limited relative to anticipated needs. However, it would finance the building of the first machine, thereby demonstrating the practicality of the invention. It was hoped that additional investors would become interested as progress became evident.

The volume of equity capital was not sufficient for rapid development of the machine. This was clear at the beginning, but it became even more obvious as time went on and original cost estimates proved to be unrealistic. At the time, the principals had seemingly faced a choice of either starting "on a shoestring" or not starting at all, and so had chosen the former.

As additional cash was required, the principals sought help from friendly local bankers. The principals' efforts in obtaining bank assistance were less fruitful than one would have anticipated from the bank's advertising jingles. However, the bank eventually agreed to a modest loan as long as the note was properly authorized by the corporation and further guaranteed by the personal signature of each of the principals—any one of whom could have repaid the loan many times. As a further reflection of their willingness to go the second mile with a new venture, the bank specified an interest rate substantially above the prime rate.

The problem of inadequate financing continued. Although there appeared to be attractive opportunities and genuine interest on the part of potential investors, the next step was difficult. The new firm's bank account approached zero at a time when cash was needed for market studies, preparation of a prospectus, further development of the machine, payment of patent attorneys, conferences with prospective investors, and living expenses of the inventor. The investors were unwilling to accept a major dilution of ownership for anything less than a substantial infusion of capital. In the meantime, they hung on, confident that a big breakthrough was just around the corner.

Incorporation of the Business

Incorporation of the business was necessary for a number of reasons, including limitation of liability for investors. This process of incorporation was complicated by the nature of the invention. Legal documents were drawn to transfer ownership of the invention to the corporation with provision for reversion of ownership to the inventor in case of corporate failure. Provisions also covered the amount of royalty to be paid to the inventor, the extent of the inventor's stock ownership, and the extent of the inventor's services during further development of the invention.

Another agreement was formulated to protect minority stockholders. This voting agreement, in effect, required general agreement of most minority stockholders on corporate decisions during an initial period or until the ownership base was broadened.

Invention Protection Problems

Having little prior knowledge of patent law, the inventor experienced some uncertainties regarding the extent of protection. The first step taken by the patent attorney was a patent search, which showed no prior conflicting patents, and a patent disclosure statement to the U.S. Patent Office. The latter document apparently gave official notice of this idea, without divulging details, and guaranteed a period of two years to file a formal application. Delaying the formal application as long as possible seemed desirable because competitors could not pick up key ideas of the invention until they obtained the information contained in the formal application.

The inventor was aware that a patent would yield incomplete protection at best. If someone were to steal the idea, the inventor would be hard pressed to find enough money for adequate legal defense. Furthermore, one novel idea may, in turn, generate another which is not covered by the original patent. The inventor spent many days and weeks developing background materials and working with the legal and technical staff of the attorney. The amount of time could have been reduced if additional technical support had been available. Lack of money precluded any search for a qualified engineer or designer who could have provided such assistance.

Production/Operations Problems

The beginning step of production was to build a prototype model of a surfacing machine. Most of the problems in doing this were related to the financial limitations described earlier. As an economy measure, the inventor turned over the machine design process to a designer employed by a major manufacturer who did the necessary design work on a "moonlighting" basis. Some delays occurred as a result of preparing the drawings on a part-time basis. A more serious problem involved design errors that became evident. It seemed likely the design deficiencies might have been reduced if better engineering and design consulting services had been used.

The decision was made to use a relatively new local shop that promised superior quality of workmanship. Relationships with the machine shop vacillated between "cooperative" and "strained." In production scheduling, the machine shop tended to give higher priority to other orders, thereby delaying work on the new machine far beyond the anticipated completion date. To some extent, these delays were occasioned by design changes that were necessary during the machine-shop work.

Another irritant was related to financing of the machine-shop work. The contract called for payment as invoices were provided from time to time, covering both purchased component parts and work by the shop. Money was short and payments were sometimes delayed. The result was a strain in the relationship as well as a delay in building the machine.

Original cost estimates, as no doubt might have been predicted by an experienced analyst, were grossly out of line. Cost estimates had been prepared in cooperation with the machine-shop owner, using a full set of working drawings. As the actual cost almost doubled, the thin financing and the good nature of both parties stretched almost to the breaking point. Eventually the machine was completed and the bill paid, with the process being twice as long, twice as expensive, and twice as hectic as planned.

Future Plans

The lack of additional funds meant that further development must proceed very slowly. It appeared to the inventor that the future availability of funds would determine the time period within which this concept would get its market test.

Questions

1. Evaluate the market assessment carried out by the inventor. Was it adequate for starting the business?
2. Evaluate the financing plan developed by the inventor, including both stockholder investment and bank borrowing.
3. How could the inventor have improved the invention protection process?
4. What mistakes, if any, were made in the beginning production stage of building the machine?
5. What course of action should be followed by the owners in view of the present lull in the new business?

5

Analyzing the Market

Figure 5-1   Brian S. Peskin

©Dan Ford Connolly/Gamma Liaison

Finding a market niche where there is little or no competition is how Brian S. Peskin is "cleaning up" with his Ultra Wash business. Peskin, 28, is an electrical engineer who left the large corporation scene to start his own business of on-site, truck fleet cleaning based in Houston, TX.

Peskin has successfully segmented a market of fleet operators who want to avoid the time and expense of going to a truck wash. Last year client contracts totaled more than $400,000.

Source: Reprinted from the January, 1985 issue of *Venture*, The Magazine for Entrepreneurs, by special permission. © 1985 Venture Magazine, Inc., 521 Fifth Ave., New York, NY 10175.

A small business can be successful only if a market exists for its product or service. Therefore, one would expect every entrepreneur to be knowledgeable about his or her market. To find out if this is true, simply ask the manager of a small firm to describe that firm's market. Be prepared for vague generalities! Surprisingly enough, you will find how little thought small-business managers give to understanding their markets.

Analyzing a market is particularly important prior to starting a business. Without it, the entrepreneur enters the marketplace much like a high diver who leaves the board without checking the depth of the water. Many types of information from numerous sources are required for a market analysis. Proper techniques for gathering market information must be understood. Therefore, marketing research methods and forecasting techniques are explained in this chapter also. With an understanding of these marketing tools, an entrepreneur will be better prepared to develop the business plan and operate the business venture.

DEFINITIONS OF A MARKET

The term *market* means different things to different people. Sometimes it simply refers to a location where buying and selling take place, as when we hear, "She went to the market." On other occasions the term is used to describe selling efforts, as when business managers say, "We must market this product aggressively." Still another meaning is the one we use in this chapter. We define a market as a group of *customers* or potential customers who have *purchasing power* and *unsatisfied needs*.

Notice carefully the three components of our definition of a market. First, a market must have a buying unit, or customers. These units may be individuals or business entities. For example, consumer products are sold to individuals and industrial products are bought for use by businesses. Thus, a market is more than a geographic area. It must contain potential customers.

Second, customers in a market must have purchasing power. Assessing the level of purchasing power in a potential market is very important. Customers who have unsatisfied needs but who lack the money and/or credit are poor markets because they have nothing to offer in exchange for a product or service. In such a situation, no transactions can occur.

Third, a market must contain buying units with unsatisfied needs. Final consumers, for instance, will not buy unless they are motivated to do so. Motivation can occur only when an individual has unsatisfied needs. It would be difficult, for example, to sell tent dehumidifiers to desert nomads!

In light of our definition of a market, therefore, analyzing a market is the process of locating and investigating buying units that have purchasing power and needs that can be satisfied with the product or service that the entrepreneur can offer.

THE PROCESS OF MARKET ANALYSIS

A good market analysis is predicated on certain key concepts. Three of these concepts are: marketing management philosophies, market segmentation strategies, and consumer behavior. Since consumer behavior affects all marketing efforts—including pricing, promotion, and distribution—the discussion of this concept in this book is reserved for Chapter 10.

Understanding Marketing Management Philosophies

A person's philosophy will naturally influence the tactics used to achieve a particular goal. For example, consider the football coach who believes in "three yards and a cloud of dust." This coach overlooks neither passing nor the role of the defense. But success begins with the ground game, so the running attack is used as the major tool. Similarly, the small-business manager can subscribe to a particular philosophy. The type of market analysis performed depends on the marketing management philosophy selected.

Types of Marketing Management Philosophies Three distinct philosophies are evident among small firms. These are commonly referred to as production-oriented, sales-oriented, and consumer-oriented philosophies. A consumer-oriented philosophy is the essence of what is called the **marketing concept.**

Over a period of time from the late nineteenth century to the present, big business has shifted its marketing emphasis from production to sales to consumer satisfaction. The production-oriented philosophy associated with the Industrial Revolution created a period of very limited "marketing." Later, emphasis was placed on sales, so marketing managers concentrated on personal selling and advertising as the major marketing activities. Finally, businesses turned to the marketing concept, which required marketing activities to discover customer needs and preferences before making and trying to sell products.[1]

What can the small-business manager learn from this brief history lesson? Is this evolution limited to large businesses? The answer is no. It need not be. Indeed, it should not be. Is one philosophy more consistent with success? The answer is yes. In the long run nothing is better than consumer orientation.[2]

Factors That Influence a Marketing Management Philosophy   Why have some firms failed to adopt the marketing concept? The answer lies in three crucial factors which strongly influence a firm's marketing philosophy. First, *the state of competition for providing a bundle of satisfaction largely determines a firm's orientation.* If there is little or no competition and if demand exceeds supply, a firm's emphasis naturally turns to production efficiency. On the other hand, an increase in competition forces the firm to emphasize consumer-based marketing activities for the potential edge that these can provide in the marketplace.

Second, *small-business managers show an enormous range of interest and ability in gathering market-related information and interpreting consumer characteristics.* For example, some small-business managers are strongest in production and weakest in sales. Therefore, production considerations receive the majority of their attention. Surely it is difficult to be aggressive in areas of weak personal expertise.

Third, *a specific orientation may exist because of the manager's shortsightedness.* A sales-oriented philosophy, for example, is a shortsighted approach to marketing. Emphasis on "moving" merchandise can often create customer dissatisfaction if high-pressure selling is used with little regard for customers' needs. On the other hand, the marketing concept contributes to a long-range survival by emphasizing customer satisfaction.

If these three factors are inconsistent with the marketing concept, a production-oriented or sales-oriented philosophy will likely emerge. Such philosophies may permit success. However, the marketing concept is preferable because it not only recognizes production-efficiency goals and professional selling, but also adds concern for the customer's satisfaction. In effect, a firm that adopts the marketing concept considers the consumer as the beginning and the end for its exchange transactions.

Understanding Market Segmentation Strategies

Even though all people are similar, market segmentation is built on the premise that differences exist among them. Formally defined, market segmentation is the process of analyzing one market to find out if it should be viewed as more than one market. A small business may view its market in either general or specific terms. It may consider its market as all women or as only the 24-to-35-year-old single women living in the eastern United States. In the latter case, the firm is segmenting its market. "The main mistake made in start-up situations is heading off in all directions," says Grid Systems Corporation of Santa Clara, California. "The key thing is to identify the market."[3]

The Need for Market Segmentation   If a business had control of the only known water supply in the world, its sales volume would be huge. This business would not be concerned about differences in personal preferences for taste, color, or temperature. It would consider its customers to be *one* market. As long as the water product was "wet," it would satisfy everyone. However, if someone else discovered a second water supply, the view of the market would change. The first business might discover that sales were drying up and turn to a modified strategy. The new approach could well emerge from an understanding of consumer behavior.

In the real world, a number of preferences for liquid drinks exist. What may seem to be a homogeneous market is actually heterogeneous. The different preferences may take a number of forms. Some preferences may relate to the way consumers react to the taste or to the container. Other preferences may relate to the price of the liquid drink or to the availability of "specials." Preferences might also be uncovered with respect to different distribution strategies or to certain promotional tones and techniques. In other words, markets may actually be composed of several submarkets.

Types of Market Segmentation Strategies   The three types of market segmentation strategies discussed in this text can best be illustrated by using an example of a hypothetical firm—the Community Writing Company. These strategies are the unsegmented approach, the multisegmentation approach, and the single-segmentation approach.

The Unsegmented Strategy   When a business defines the total market as its target market, it is following an **unsegmented strategy**. This strategy can be successful occasionally, but it assumes that all buying units desire the same general benefit from the product or service. This may hold true for water but probably not for shoes, which satisfy numerous needs through many styles, prices, colors, and sizes. With an unsegmented strategy, the firm would develop a single marketing mix, which means one combination of the product, price, promotion, and distribution plan. For the unsegmented strategy of Community Writing Company, see Figure 5-2. Community Writing Company's product is a lead pencil which is sold at the one price of 79 cents and is communicated with a single promotional and distribution plan. Notice how the marketing mix is aimed at everybody. With this strategy only one sales forecast is required.

Figure 5–2   An Unsegmented Market Strategy with Its Single Marketing Mix

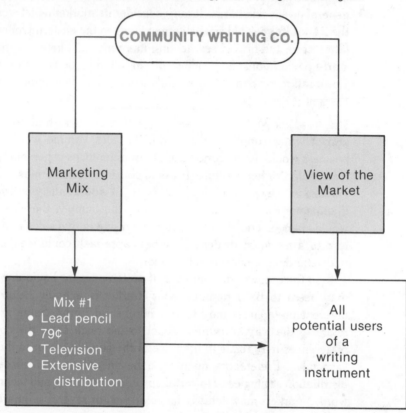

The Multisegmentation Strategy With a view of the market which recognizes individual segments that have different preferences, a firm is in a position to tailor-make different strategies. If a firm feels that two or more homogeneous market segments can be profitable, it will be following a *multisegmentation strategy* if it develops a unique marketing mix for each segment.

Let us now assume that Community Writing Company has discovered three separate market segments: students, professors, and executives. Following the multisegmentation approach, the company develops three mixes, which might be based on differences in pricing, promotion, distribution, or the product itself, as shown in Figure 5–3. Mix #1 consists of selling felt-tip pens to students through vending machines at the slightly higher-than-normal price of $1.00 and supporting this effort with a promotional campaign in campus newspapers. With Mix #2 the company might market the same pen to universities for use by professors. Personal selling is the only promotion used in this mix, distribution is direct from the factory, and the product price of 49 cents is extremely low. Finally, with Mix #3, which is aimed at executives of companies of the Fortune 500 type, the product is a solid gold ink-writing instrument sold only in exclusive department stores. It is promoted in prestigious magazines and carries the extremely high price of $50. Although students might conceivably buy the solid gold pens for classroom writing, they are not viewed as members of this target market.

Figure 5-3   A Segmented Market Strategy with Multiple Marketing Mixes

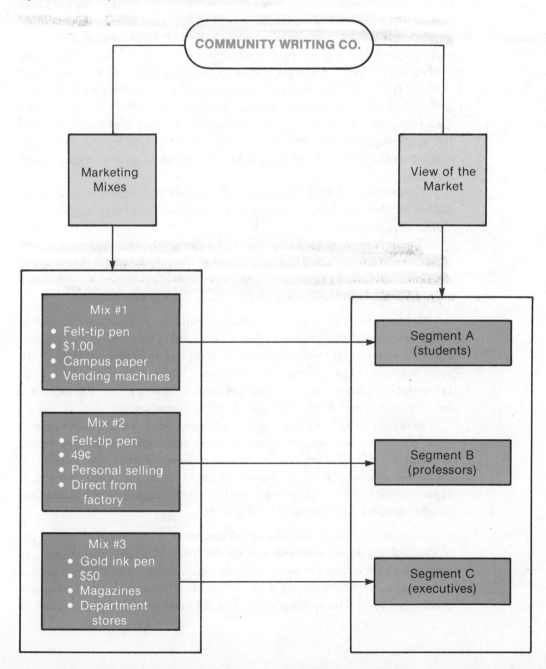

Notice the dramatic differences in the three marketing mixes. Small businesses, however, tend to postpone the use of multisegmentation strategies because of the risk of spreading resources too thinly among several marketing efforts.

The Single-Segmentation Strategy   When a firm recognizes that several distinct market segments exist but chooses to concentrate on reaching only one segment, it is following a **single-segmentation strategy**. The segment selected will be one which the business feels will be most profitable. One real-life example is a quick-service alteration shop called ASAP (Alter Soon As Possible). Beverly and Paul Malham opened their first store in 1984 in an Atlanta, GA, mall after deciding to concentrate on a relatively small but very profitable market. Its target market, about 60% of sales, are stores in the mall who prefer not to do alterations themselves.[4] The Malhams have used the single-segmentation strategy to build a reputation among the target market which they feel will spread to other markets as they expand their services.

Community Writing Company, our hypothetical example, selects the student market segment when pursuing a single-segmentation approach, as shown in Figure 5-4.

The single-segmentation approach is probably the best strategy for small businesses during initial marketing efforts. This approach allows them to specialize and make better use of their more limited resources. Then, when a reputation has been built, it is easier for them to enter new markets.

Segmentation Variables   A firm's market could be defined very simply as "anyone who is alive"! However, this is too broad to be useful even for a firm that follows an unsegmented approach. With any type of market analysis, some degree of segmentation must be made. Notice in Figure 5-2 on page 108, which represents an unsegmented market strategy, that the market is not everyone in the universe but rather only potential users.

In order to divide the total market into appropriate segments, a business must consider segmentation variables. Basically, **segmentation variables** are labels which identify the particular dimensions that are thought to distinguish one form of market demand from another. Two particular sets of segmentation variables which represent the major dimensions of a market are benefit variables and demographic variables.

Benefit Variables   Our earlier definition of a market highlighted the unsatisfied needs of customers. **Benefit variables** are related to this dimension in that they are used to divide and identify segments of a market according to the benefits sought by customers. For example, the toothpaste market has several benefit segments. The principal benefit to parents may be

Figure 5-4   A Segmented Market Strategy with a Single Marketing Mix

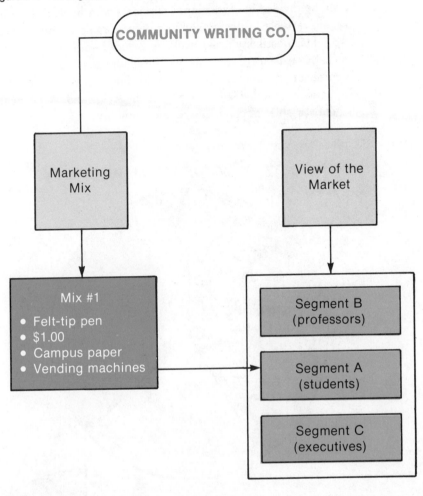

cavity prevention for their young children. On the other hand, the principal benefit to a teenager might be freshness. In both cases toothpaste is the product, but it has two different markets.

Demographic Variables   Benefit variables alone are insufficient for market analysis. It is impossible to implement forecasting and marketing strategy without defining the market further. Therefore, small businesses commonly use demographics as part of market segmentation. Typical demographics are age, marital status, sex, occupation, and income. Remember again our definition of a market—customers with purchasing power and unsatisfied needs. Thus, **demographic variables** refer to certain characteristics which describe customers and their purchasing power.

The market scenario for Segment A in Figure 5–3 on page 109 can easily be divided into additional segments with benefit variables and demographic variables. (Occupation as a demographic variable was used in Figure 5–3.) This possibility is illustrated in Figure 5–5. Notice that the Segment A market, consisting of students, can be subdivided into Segments A-1 and A-2 according to the demographic variable of marital status. In addition, Segment A-1 can be subdivided into Segments A-11 and A-12 according to the benefit variables of convenience and economy.

Figure 5–5   Combined Demographic and Benefit Segmentation Variables

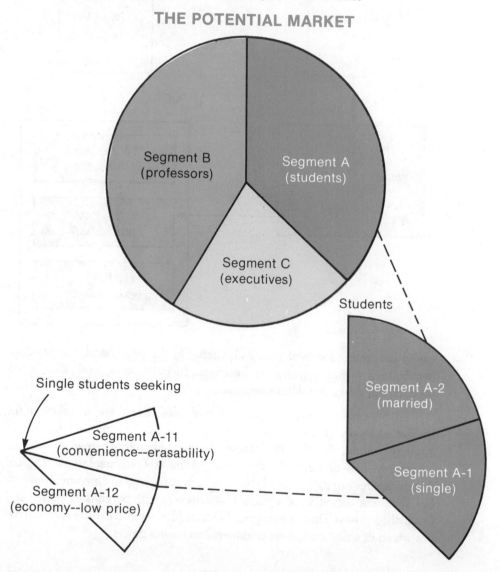

THE POTENTIAL MARKET

Segment B (professors)

Segment A (students)

Segment C (executives)

Students

Segment A-2 (married)

Segment A-1 (single)

Single students seeking

Segment A-11 (convenience--erasability)

Segment A-12 (economy--low price)

Based on this hypothetical case, a sales forecast for a single-segmentation approach could be structured and included in the business plan. The single-segmentation strategy could aim at the number of people in a geographic market who are single students looking mainly for convenience features in the writing instruments they purchase. Such precision in market delineation makes sales forecasting easier.

Benefits of a Market Analysis

A market analysis benefits the entrepreneur in several ways. It helps to conceptualize further the product idea or the service idea. After examining the market for cosmetics, for example, one business decided that it was really selling "hope" rather than cosmetic ingredients! This gave an added dimension to the marketing effect. A market analysis also aids in other decisions such as pricing, packaging, and store location.

The most immediate benefit of a market analysis, however, is the prediction of sales. The sales forecast is probably the most critical measure for assessing the feasibility of a new venture within the business plan. If the market is insufficient, the business is destined for failure. The sales forecast is also useful in other areas of business planning. Production schedules, inventory policies, and personnel decisions—to name a few—all start with the sales forecast. Obviously, forecasts can never be perfect. Furthermore, the entrepreneur should remember that forecasts can be in error in either of two ways—an underestimation or an overestimation of potential sales.

MARKETING RESEARCH

Marketing managers can make marketing decisions based on intuition alone, or they can supplement their judgment with good marketing information. More often than not, a manager welcomes more information for decision making. The availability of research information in no way guarantees a good decision, but it is a major ingredient.

Neglect of Marketing Research

Many entrepreneurs avoid marketing research, not fully understanding what it can do for them. Five common misconceptions related to marketing research are described by one author as myths:[5]

1. *The "big decision" myth.* You turn to marketing research only when you have a major decision to make; otherwise it has little to do with the details of day-to-day decision making.

2. *The "survey myopia" myth.* With its random samples, question-naires, questionnaires, computer printouts, and statistical analyses, marketing research is synonymous with field survey research.
3. *The "big bucks" myth.* Marketing research is so expensive that it can only be used by the wealthiest organizations, and then only for their major decisions.
4. *The "sophisticated researcher" myth.* Since research involves complex and advanced technology, only trained experts can and should pursue it.
5. *The "most research is not read" myth.* A very high proportion of marketing research is irrelevant to managers or is simply confirming what they already know.

The entrepreneur should recognize these myths and thereby be more open to gathering marketing information.

ACTION REPORT
Is It Worth It?

Entrepreneurs are widely known to prefer their own "gut feel" over hard, research facts. But this appears to be changing! One reason for the trend is the number of success stories among those who have used market research. Also, there is increasing pressure from suppliers of funding to include research in an entrepreneur's business plan.

- Julius Jensen, with Copley Venture Capital in Boston, says his firm does not even bother these days with companies that have no hard market research data to support their gut feeling about a product.
- John Werner had a vision. He decided to translate an Asian nut-coating process into a gourmet peanut business in his Connecticut home state. He came up with a loose business plan but after a year was persuaded to put his vision to the test with market research. The research showed him his original plan would not work.
- Kevin Callaghan, the Director of Marketing for DioLight Technology Inc., of Pontiac, MI, did some of his own research when targeting a new market niche for its long-lasting light bulb. He visited office buildings to count the number of exit signs needing bulbs. "We learned that the industrial institutional market, rather than the consumer market, was definitely the place to go."
- Polygon Software Corp. in New York has learned the value of research the hard way. Regarding the introduction of its first software package, George Cushner, co-founder, says "...we made too many assumptions about the market, relying on our own views rather than going out and evaluating..." As a result, the software package has sold poorly. But Cushner believes his company has learned its lesson. The company is spending about $20,000 in marketing research prior to introducing its newest product.

Source: Reprinted from the October, 1985 issue of *Venture*, The Magazine for Entrepreneurs, by special permission. © 1985 Venture Magazine, Inc., 521 Fifth Ave., New York, NY 10175.

Nature of Marketing Research for Small Businesses

Marketing research may be defined as the gathering, processing, reporting, and interpreting of marketing information. A small business typically conducts less marketing research than a big business.

"In a small company like ours, we don't have the luxury of brand managers or research managers," says Richard Denning, Vice-President for Sales and Marketing at T. Marzetti, Co., in Columbus, OH. His firm makes salad dressing and chip dip, but conducts little formal research. "We rely on our own experience," he says, "and if the product fails, we've spread the risk among ourselves."[6]

Part of the reason for this situation is cost. Another factor is a lack of understanding of the marketing research process. Our coverage of marketing research will emphasize the more widely used practical techniques that small-business firms can use as they analyze their market and make other operating decisions.

Evaluating the cost of research against the expected benefits is another step that the small-business manager should consider. Although this is a difficult task, some basic logic will show that marketing research can be conducted within resource limits.[7]

Steps in the Marketing Research Procedure

A knowledge of good research procedures benefits the small-business manager. It helps in evaluating the validity of research done by others and in guiding the manager's own efforts. The various steps in the marketing research procedure include: identifying the problem, searching for secondary data and primary data, and interpreting and reporting the information gathered.

Identify the Problem   The first step in the marketing research procedure is to define precisely the informational requirements of the decision to be made. Although this may seem too obvious to mention, the fact is that needs are too often identified without sufficient probing. If the problem is not defined clearly, the information gathered will be useless. For example, a sales decline may be only a symptom of the true problem, which is the sudden resignation of key salespeople.

Search for Secondary Data   Information that has already been compiled is known as **secondary data**. Generally speaking, secondary data are less expensive to gather than new, or primary data. The small business should exhaust all the available sources of secondary data before going further into the research process. Marketing decisions often can be made entirely with secondary data.

Secondary data may be internal or external. *Internal* secondary data consist of information which exists within the small business. The records of the business, for example, may contain useful information of the decision to be made. *External* secondary data abound in numerous periodicals, trade associations, private informational services, and government publications. A particularly excellent source for the small business is the Small Business Administration. This agency publishes extensive bibliographies relating to many decision areas, including market analysis.

Unfortunately several problems accompany the use of secondary data. One problem is that such data may be outdated and, therefore, less useful. Another problem is that the units of measure in the secondary data may not fit the current problem. For example, a firm's market might consist of individuals with incomes between $20,000 and $25,000, while the secondary data show the number of individuals with incomes between $15,000 and $25,000. Finally, the question of trust is always present. Some sources of secondary data are less trustworthy than others. Publication of the data does not in itself make the data valid and reliable!

Search for Primary Data   If the secondary data are insufficient, a search for new information, or **primary data**, is the next step. Several techniques can be used in accumulating primary data. These techniques are often classified as observational methods and questioning methods. Observational methods avoid contact with respondents, while questioning methods involve respondents in varying degrees.

Observational Methods   Observation is probably the oldest form of research in existence. Indeed, learning by observing is quite a common occurrence. Thus, it is hardly surprising that observation can provide useful information for small businesses, too. Observational methods can be used very economically. Further, they avoid a potential bias that results from a respondent's awareness of his or her participation under questioning methods.

Observation can be conducted by a human or a mechanical observer. The small-firm manager can easily use the less sophisticated personal observation method. For example, a restaurant manager can observe the preferences of customers as they order items from the menu. The major kinds of mechanical observation devices, which are usually beyond the budget of most small businesses, are eye-camera equipment, pupilometers, and the Audimeter used by A.C. Nielsen Co. A major disadvantage of observational methods, however, is that they are limited to descriptive studies.

Questioning Methods   Both surveys and experimentation are questioning methods that involve contact with respondents.[8] Surveys include contact by mail, telephone, and personal interviews. Mail surveys are often used when respondents are widely dispersed; however, these are characterized by low response rates. Telephone surveys and personal interview surveys involve verbal communication with respondents and provide higher response rates. Personal interview surveys, however, are more expensive than mail and telephone surveys. Moreover, individuals often are reluctant to grant personal interviews because they feel that a sales pitch is forthcoming.

ACTION REPORT
Survey Kindles Cold Idea

A Wendy's International Inc. spokesman says, "He could make a fortune." The reference is to 23-year-old Richard A. Gilbertson, a recent college student turned dropout largely due to the results of a marketing research study conducted at Indiana University. A survey of 400 students was conducted after a fellow student had the idea to deliver McDonald's hamburgers and Taco Bell burritos to the 13,000 college students.

The quick survey showed that students liked the fast-food Mexican food and hamburgers over other fast-food items such as pizza. McDonald's Big Mac was identified by the survey as the preferred hamburger—so much so that survey respondents indicated a willingness to pay about $1 above the regular price for dorm delivery.

The survey also discovered that students had strong preferences against certain dorm menus. "We can look at the dorm menu and predict how many drivers we'll need that night," says Mr. Gilbertson.

Student reaction to the service, named Fast Breaks, has been outstanding. Any customer who is unhappy with the delivery is allowed another order free.

The business idea was given the cold shoulder by the university's Entrepreneurial Club which evaluated it before the market survey.

Source: Reprinted by permission of *The Wall Street Journal,* © Dow Jones & Company, Inc., 1984. All Rights Reserved.

Experimentation is a form of research that concentrates on investigating cause-and-effect relationships. The goal of experimentation is to establish the effect which an experimental variable has on a dependent variable. For example, the problem might be defined as: What effect will a price change have on sales? Here the price is the experimental variable, and sales volume is the dependent variable. Measuring the relationship between these two variables would not be difficult if it were not for the many other variables which confound the true relationship. For example, rain, a new display, and different packaging all could distort an experiment attempting to measure the effect of a lower price on sales of umbrellas. A properly designed experiment will control those confounding variables so that the actual effect of the experiment can be measured.

Developing a Questionnaire   A questionnaire is the basic instrument for guiding the researcher and the respondent when surveys are being taken. The questionnaire should be developed carefully and pretested before it is used in the market. Several major considerations in designing a questionnaire are listed below:

1. Ask questions that relate to the decision under consideration. An "interesting" question may not be relevant. Assume an answer to each question, and then ask yourself how you would use that information. This provides a good test of relevance.
2. Select a form of question that is appropriate for the subject and the conditions of the survey. Open-ended and multiple-choice questions are two popular styles.
3. Carefully consider the order of the questions. The wrong sequence can cause biases in answers to later questions.
4. Ask the more sensitive questions near the end of the questionnaire. Age and income, for example, are usually sensitive subjects.
5. Carefully select the words of each question. They should be as simple and clear as possible.

Figure 5–6 shows a one-page questionnaire developed for a small business by one of the authors of this textbook. The firm's research problem was to assess the market potential for its new product—wooden pallets. Potential users of wooden pallets were identified and mailed the one-page questionnaire. Notice the use of both multiple-choice and open-ended questions in this questionnaire. Responses to Item 6 were particularly useful for this firm.

Interpret and Report the Information   After the necessary data have been accumulated, they should be transformed into usable information. Large quantities of data are only facts without a home. They must be organized and molded into meaningful information. Numerous methods of summarizing and simplifying information for users include tables, charts, and other graphic methods. Descriptive statistics, such as the mean, mode, and median, are most helpful during this step in the research procedure.

Marketing-Information Systems

Marketing-information systems refer to an organized way of gathering market-related information for the purpose of providing useful information on a regular basis. These systems emerge when managers realize the repetitive nature of their informational needs. A formal marketing-information system helps them stay in contact with the firm's changing market profile.

Figure 5-6   Questionnaire for a Mail Survey

QUESTIONNAIRE

Special Note. If you would like to receive information on our wooden pallets once production is started, please check the square below and write in your current mailing address.

I would like to receive this information ☐
Address: _____
_____
_____

1. Does your business currently use wooden pallets?   Yes_____ (1.1)
    (If *No*, skip to Question 7.)   No_____   (1.2)

2. What percentage of your wooden pallet needs require *Expendable Pallets*
    (pallets used only one time)?
                                                         0-25%_____   (2.1)
                                                         26-50%_____   (2.2)
                                                         51-75%_____   (2.3)
                                                         76-100%_____   (2.4)

3. For each of the following types of wooden pallets, please indicate the
    approximate quantity you require each year.

Type	*Quantity*	
Pallet Bins (All Sizes)......................._____		(5-10)
Pallet Bases (All Sizes)......................._____		(15-20)
Other (Please Specify)......................._____		(25-30)
_____	_____	(35-40)
_____	_____	(45-50)
_____	_____	

4. Please indicate which one of the following statements best describes your firm's buying patterns
    for wooden pallets. (Please check only one.)
    Purchase each month............................... _____ (60.1)
    Purchase about twice a year .... _____ (61.1)
    Purchase only once a year .... _____ (62.1)

5. Approximately how close to your business site is your major supplier of wooden pallets?
    Less than 20 miles .... _____ (63.1)
    20 to 50 miles .... _____ (63.2)
    51 to 80 miles .... _____ (63.3)
    81 to 120 miles .... _____ (63.4)
    121 to 150 miles .... _____ (63.5)
    Over 150 miles .... _____ (63.6)

6. What suggestions would you make to help us provide wooden pallets to better meet your needs?
    _____
    _____
    _____

7. Please indicate the major products of your firm.
    _____
    _____

Please mail the questionnaire in the enclosed self-addressed envelope.

THANK YOU FOR YOUR COOPERATION!!!

The marketing-information system should be tailored to reflect a consumer orientation. This may require extension beyond the traditional sources of information for marketing-information systems. For example, a small business might conceivably use a consumer advisory board consisting of representative customers in order to keep in touch with market needs and problems. Also, the small business can structure a consumer communication system for hearing consumer complaints and questions. Some businesses have referred to this system as a "cool-line." Much of the information received through this approach can be used for decision making.[9]

Most people associate marketing-information systems with computerized systems. However, a marketing-information system does not necessarily require computers. In a very small business, the needed information flow may not justify the cost of computers. Furthermore, collecting marketing information is not as magical as some small-business people believe. Once they have done it, or seen it done, many of their reservations about it are removed.[10]

SALES FORECASTING

It is difficult enough to document the past, much less forecast the future. Nevertheless, businesses engage in forecasting to reap the benefits of "knowing" what lies ahead. A knowledge of possible future sales levels is particularly valuable to the new business.

A recent survey of sales executives among small companies found the following:[11]

- About 40 percent of the respondents estimated that their sales forecasts were 75–89 percent accurate; 23 percent said they were 90–94 percent accurate.
- Over 90 percent stated that no consultants were used in sales forecasting.
- Secondary purposes for their sales forecast were budget preparation, setting quotas for salespeople, determining advertising and sales promotion expenditures, hiring personnel, advance purchasing of raw materials and parts, and making cash forecasts.

The Sales Forecast

Formally defined, a **sales forecast** is the prediction of how much of a product or service will be purchased by a market for a defined time period. The sales forecast can be stated in terms of dollars and/or units.

Notice that a sales forecast revolves around a specific market. This means that the market should be defined as precisely as possible. The market description forms the forecasting boundary. For example, consider the sales forecast for a manual shaving device. If the market for this product is described simply as "men," the potential sales forecast would be extremely large. Alternatively, a more precise definition, such as "men between the ages of 15 and 25 who are dissatisfied with electric shavers," will result in a smaller but more useful forecast.

Also note that the sales forecast implies a defined time period. One sales forecast may cover a year or less, while another extends over several, maybe five years. Both the short-term and the long-term forecasts are needed in the entrepreneur's business plan.

Limitations to Forecasting

For a number of practical reasons, forecasting is used more successfully by large firms than by small companies. First, the typical small-business manager is unable to use or to appreciate the methods of quantitative analysis.[12] This is not to say that all forecasting must be quantitatively oriented. Qualitative forecasting is helpful and may be sufficient. However, quantitative methods have proven their value in forecasting over and over again.

Second, the small-business entrepreneur is not familiar with the forecasting process, and it is unlikely that the small firm employs a forecaster. To overcome these deficiencies, some small firms attempt to keep in touch with industry trends through contacts with their trade association. From the standpoint of its professional staff members, the trade association is frequently better qualified to engage in business forecasting. Also, small-business entrepreneurs provide themselves with current information about business trends by regularly reading trade publications and economic newsletters such as the *Kiplinger Washington Letter*, *Business Week*, and *The Wall Street Journal*. Figure 5-7 shows a typical forecast from one of these sources. This information would be useful in developing the sales forecast for the business plan of an entrepreneur entering the videodisc market.

Government publications, such as *Survey of Current Business*, *Federal Reserve Bulletin*, and *Monthly Labor Review*, are also of interest in a general way. Then there is the possibility of subscribing to professional forecasting services, which provide forecasts of general business conditions or specific forecasts for given industries.

Third, the entrepreneur's forecasting circumstances are unique. Inexperience coupled with a new idea represents the most difficult forecasting situation, as depicted in Figure 5-8. An ongoing business which needs only

Figure 5-7 Forecast of Sales for Videodisc Players

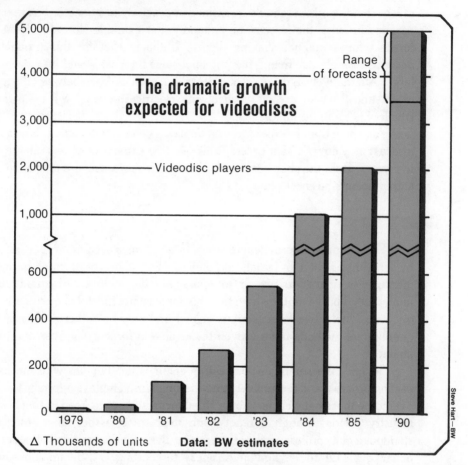

an updated forecast for its existing product is in the most favorable forecasting position.

Yet the small business should not slight the forecasting task because of its limitations. Remember how important the sales outlook is to the business plan when obtaining financing! The statement "We can sell as many as we can produce" does not satisfy the information requirements of potential investors.

Steps in the Forecasting Process

Estimating market demand with a sales forecast is a multistep process. Typically, the sales forecast is a composite of several individual forecasts.

Figure 5-8   Dimensions of Forecasting Difficulty

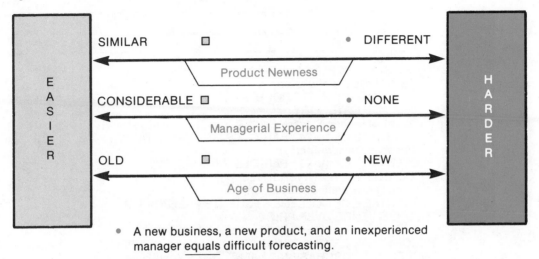

- A new business, a new product, and an inexperienced manager equals difficult forecasting.

☐ An existing business, an existing product, and an experienced manager equals less difficult forecasting.

The process of sales forecasting then must merge the individual forecasts properly.

The forecasting process can be characterized by two important dimensions: (1) the point at which the process is started, and (2) the nature of the predicting variable. The starting point is usually designated by the terms *breakdown process* or *buildup process*. The nature of the predicting variable is denoted by either *direct* forecasting or *indirect* forecasting.

The Starting Point   The **breakdown process**, sometimes called a "chain-ratio" method, begins with a macro-level variable and systematically works down to the sales forecast. This method is frequently used for consumer products forecasting. The starting point might be a population figure for the targeted market. By using percentages, the appropriate link is built to generate the sales forecast. For example, consider the market segment identified by our hypothetical company, Community Writing Co., in Figure 5-5 on page 112. The targeted market is single students seeking convenience in their writing instrument. Furthermore, assume the initial geographic target is the state of Idaho. Table 5-1 outlines the chain-ratio approach. Possible sources for each number are shown in parentheses. Obviously, the more "links" in the forecasting chain, the greater the potential for error.

The *buildup process* calls for identifying all potential buyers in a market's submarkets and then adding up the estimated demand. This method is especially helpful for industrial goods forecasting. Census of Manufacturers

Table 5-1   Sales Forecasting with the Breakdown Approach

Sales Forecast Components	
TOTAL STATE POPULATION—IDAHO (U.S. Census of Population)	1,000,000
PERCENTAGE OF STATE POPULATION IN 18–24 AGE CATEGORY (Survey of Buying Power—*Sales & Marketing Management*)	12%
PERCENTAGE OF 18–24 YEAR-OLDS WHO ARE SINGLE (*American Demographics*)	50%
PERCENTAGE OF 18–24 YEAR-OLD SINGLES IN COLLEGES AND UNIVERSITIES (Idaho Department of Education)	80%
PERCENTAGE OF COLLEGE STUDENTS PREFERRING CONVENIENCE OVER PRICE (Student Survey from Marketing Research Class)	35%
PERCENTAGE OF "CONVENIENCE-ORIENTED" STUDENTS LIKELY TO PURCHASE NEW FELT-TIP PEN WITHIN NEXT MONTH (Personal Telephone Interviews)	75%
PERCENTAGE OF PEOPLE LIKELY TO PURCHASE WHO ACTUALLY BUY (*Journal of Consumer Research*)	35%

Sales Forecast for 1987

$1,000,000 \times .12 \times .50 \times .80 \times .35 \times .75 \times .35 = 4,410$ units

data are often used to estimate potential. The information can be segmented with the Standard Industrial Classification (SIC) code. This classification system identifies potential industrial customers by SIC code, allowing the forecaster to locate information on number of establishments, location, number of employees, and annual sales. By summing this information for several relevant SIC codes, a sales potential can be constructed.

The Predicting Variable In *direct forecasting*, sales is used as the predicting variable. This is the simplest form of forecasting. Many times, however, sales cannot be predicted directly. In this case other variables related to sales must be forecasted. *Indirect forecasting* takes place when the other forecasts are used to project the sales forecast. For example, a firm may lack information about industry sales of baby cribs but may have data on births. The figures for births can help forecast an industry sales estimate for baby cribs.

Forecasting Techniques

Many forecasting techniques can be used in a small business. Some techniques are simple, while others are extremely complex. But do not assume that the most complex are necessarily the best! A simple method can be just as accurate as a complex method. If you want to know the number of new homes which will be constructed on the north side of town, for example, a drive in the area may give you the correct figure. Conversely, you might consider a complex model incorporating a statistical forecast of several key factors such as interest rates and building-material costs.

Forecasting techniques are classified in many ways. Most classifications make distinctions based on the complexity of quantitative methods, the amount of available information, and the source of the information. The **time series techniques**, for example, rely on historical data and on quantitative tools. For a new venture, a time series technique could be used with an indirect forecasting process even though no historical sales data for the specific firm exist.

Generally, it is preferable to state the sales forecast as a range of possible sales levels. For example, a forecast of $50,000 to $65,000 in sales is better than a forecast of $57,500. In the final analysis, however, the entrepreneur must judge the validity of the sales forecast.

Looking Back

1. The three major marketing management philosophies are production-oriented, sales-oriented, and consumer-oriented. The consumer-oriented philosophy is the essence of the marketing concept.
2. Market segmentation is the process of analyzing a market to decide if it should be considered as more than one market. There are three types of market segmentation strategies: the unsegmented strategy, the multi-segmentation strategy, and the single-segmentation strategy.
3. The first step in the marketing research procedure is to identify accurately the problem to be solved. The second step is to search for secondary and primary data, which are two forms of marketing information. Data are collected by observational and questioning methods. Finally, the data are interpreted and reported to the appropriate people.
4. Marketing-information systems refer to an organized way of gathering marketing information so as to obtain the needed data on a regular basis.
5. Estimating market demand with a sales forecast involves a multistep process. The starting point of the sales forecast can be designated as a buildup process or a breakdown process. Direct forecasting and indirect forecasting are two basic forms of forecasting sales. Forecasting techniques are usually classified in two ways: qualitative techniques and quantitative techniques.

DISCUSSION QUESTIONS

1. Explain why the three components in our definition of a market must be viewed as having a multiplicative relationship rather than an additive relationship.
2. Why is it so important to understand the target market? What difference would it make if the entrepreneur simply ignored the characteristics of market customers?
3. How do the three marketing management philosophies differ? Select a consumer product and discuss your marketing tactics for each philosophy.
4. How does a multisegmentation view of the market differ from a single-segmentation approach? Be specific.
5. Assume your instructor desired to design this course using benefit variables. What various types of benefits do you believe exist for your classmates (consumers)? How would this influence your instructor's course requirements?
6. Assume you are planning to market a new facial tissue product. Write a detailed market profile of your target customers. Use benefit and demographic variables in your profile. Redefine one or more of these variables. How would this change the marketing mix?
7. What research methods would you use to measure the number of blond males at your school?
8. What research method would you use to determine if a warranty helped product sales? Be specific.
9. What is the basic difference between marketing research and marketing-information systems?
10. Distinguish between direct sales forecasting and indirect sales forecasting. Give examples.

ENDNOTES

1. For a more complete discussion of these different eras, see E. Jerome McCarthy and William D. Perreault, Jr., *Basic Marketing: A Managerial Approach* (8th ed.; Homewood: Richard D. Irwin, Inc., 1984), Ch. 2.

2. This is naturally a generalization. Ultimately, it is the firm's individual circumstances which dictate its philosophy.

3. Dave Kemp, "Who Wants Your New Product?" *Inc.*, Vol. 3, No. 11 (November, 1981), p. 161

4. Patricia Winters, "Alteration Shops Sew Up Mall Market," *Venture*, Vol. 7, No. 9 (September, 1985), p. 14.

5. Alan R. Andreasen, "Cost-Conscious Marketing Research," *Harvard Business Review*, Vol. 61, No. 4 (July–August, 1983), p. 74.

6. Richard Kreisman, "Buy the Numbers," *Inc.*, Vol. 7, No. 3 (March, 1985), p. 110.

7. See Paul D. Boughton, "Marketing Research and Small Business: Pitfalls and Potential," *Journal of Small Business Management*, Vol. 21, No. 3 (July, 1983), pp. 36–42.

8. Another form of questioning is focus group research. This is described in Charles Keown, "Focus Group Research: Tool for the Retailer," *Journal of Small Business Management*, Vol. 21, No. 2 (April, 1983), pp. 59–65.

9. Priscilla A. La Barbera and Larry J. Rosenberg, "How Marketers Can Better Understand Consumers," *MSU Business Topics*, Vol. 28, No. 1 (Winter, 1980), pp. 29–36.

10. For a concise presentation of a practical approach to a market information system, see D. Michael Werner, "Market Research Made Easy," *In Business*, Vol. 6, No. 2 (April, 1984), pp. 46–48.

11. Excerpted from Harry R. White, *Sales Forecasting Timesaving and Profit-Making Strategies That Work* (Glenview, IL: Scott, Foresman and Company, 1984), Ch. 3.

12. Students who have a special interest in forecasting can refer to Spyros Makridakis and Steven C. Wheelwright, editors, *The Handbook of Forecasting: A Manager's Guide* (New York: John Wiley & Sons, 1982).

REFERENCES TO SMALL BUSINESS IN ACTION

Grossman, John. "Resurrecting Auto Graveyards." *Inc.*, Vol. 5, No. 3 (March, 1983), pp. 71–80.
  A consultant entrepreneur to the automobile salvage industry is profiled by this article. His story is an example of recognizing a need—expertise for modernizing a junkyard image—and meeting that need with a consulting service.

Kelleher, JoAnne. "Getting to Know Your Market." *Venture*, Vol. 5, No. 5 (May, 1983), pp. 70–74.
  The first-hand experiences of numerous entrepreneurs' use of marketing research is related in this article. The development of computerized data bases is emphasized as a major development in analyzing markets.

Persinos, John F. "Reaping Profit in the Heartland." *Inc.*, Vol. 5, No. 1 (January, 1983), pp. 65–66.
  A strong customer orientation is the philosophy of the small manufacturer described in this article. His approach has enabled the small farm machinery company to compete successfully in a depressed agricultural economy.

Schumer, Fern. "The New Magicians of Market Research." *Fortune*, Vol. 108, No. 2 (July 25, 1983), pp. 72–74.
  This article describes how a small research firm has developed a forecasting service for new products which is being used by several major consumer product companies.

CASE 5

HOT Magazine*
Researching market potential

Kate Johnson, director of public information for a social-service organization in Waco, TX, was scanning the newspaper at lunch with her friend Susan Baldwin, an advertising account representative for the *Waco Tribune Herald*.

"Did you see this story about the city magazine the Waco Chamber of Commerce may start?" asked Kate.

"Yeah, sounds interesting. They'd probably have to hire an editor. Would you be interested? You've had a lot of experience with publications."

"I just don't know, Sue. I think Waco is ripe for a city magazine, but I just can't get excited about a chamber of commerce publication. They're all so boring."

"You're right about that. But what do you expect? The editors don't have much freedom, having to answer to the business establishment," Susan added.

"I really think Waco needs a city magazine. We've got a lot going on here, and we're virtually ignored by *Texas Monthly* and the special-interest magazines. They've all written us off as a small town," Kate said. "What we really need is a high-quality, independent city magazine like *D, the Magazine of Dallas* or *Philadelphia*."

"Do you really think a magazine like that would go in Waco?"

"I know it would, and I think we're the ones who could pull it off, Sue," Kate replied.

"There would be quite a risk involved, and we'd have to quit our jobs," Susan commented.

"Well, I don't want to be an employee and a public servant all my life. I'm ready for something new and challenging, something on my own," said Kate.

"A city magazine would certainly be a challenge, Kate."

Background of the Would-Be Entrepreneurs

Kate, who was 35 years old, had worked in public affairs positions for local, regional, and state organizations during the past 13 years, editing a variety of organizational newsletters, magazines, and brochures. In addition, she had been editor of both a small-town newspaper and a special-interest publication about music. Kate's longest tenure in any of the jobs was less than

*This case was prepared by Minette E. Drumwright, Lecturer in Marketing at Baylor University.

three years. As soon as she mastered a job, she would begin looking around for a new challenge. Kate had lived in Waco a total of 11 years, including the time she spent studying journalism at Baylor University.

Although the Waco Chamber of Commerce eventually abandoned the idea of sponsoring a city magazine, Kate held tenaciously to her aspirations for an independent city magazine. She persuaded her 30-year-old sister, Debra Lunsford, and Susan Baldwin, who was 23 years old, to join her in the venture. Although Susan had been out of college for only 2 years, she had worked for the newspaper in her hometown since she was 16 years old. Debra was the vice-president and business manager of a shipping company in Houston. The three women would form the full-time staff of the publication with Kate serving as editor. Susan would be the advertising sales director, and Debra would be the business manager. All the stories, photography, and graphics would be contracted on a free-lance basis, providing local artists a showcase for their work.

The *HOT* Idea

Kate proposed to call the publication *HOT*, which was a commonly used abbreviation for "Heart of Texas." *HOT* would include an entertainment guide, features on local personalities, and a variety of stories focusing on social, economic, and political trends of the locality. The target audience would be central Texans between the ages of 25 and 55 years with annual incomes ranging from $18,000 to $50,000.

The percentage of advertising in each issue is a key variable for any publication, representing the primary source of revenue. Susan projected that the initial advertising-to-editorial contents ratio would be 60:40 and that eventually a 70:30 ratio would be attained.

Debra determined that an initial investment of $400,000 would need to be contributed by local investors to launch the magazine. The $400,000 would be used to sustain the magazine through the initial periods of loss, providing for salaries, free-lance work, promotion, and production.

Together, the 3 entrepreneurs interested James Jenkins, a 32-year-old accountant, in the magazine idea. James, who was from an established Waco family, was president of Downtown Waco, Inc., a group of retail merchants with a vested interest in reviving the downtown area. His family owned and operated one of the city's highly successful specialty retail businesses.

Before approaching potential investors about the city magazine, James insisted that the entrepreneurs substantiate their feelings that the magazine would be a success. In an effort to get the necessary information, Kate called a professor specializing in marketing research at Baylor University's Hankamer School of Business. The professor referred the entrepreneurs to two graduate students in his seminar in marketing research.

The Research

The graduate students set out to develop a profile of independent city magazines to determine the feasibility of initiating a successful venture in Waco. Using a structured, undisguised questionnaire, they surveyed city-magazine publishers throughout the nation. The sample included the publishers of all the city magazines with complete listings in Standard Rate and Data Service. Participants were asked to enclose a recent issue of their magazine along with the completed questionnaires. A $2 incentive was enclosed to defray the cost of the magazine and the mailing expense. The following were among the survey questions:

General Information

1. How many employees do you have?

   In editorial   _____

   In advertising   _____

   Other   _____

2. On the average, what percentage of the stories are written by free-lance writers?

   _____

3. What is your production cost per issue?

   _____ less than $25,000   _____ $40,001–$50,000

   _____ $25,000–$30,000   _____ more than $50,000

   _____ $30,001–$40,000

Advertising

4. What was the approximate ratio of advertising to editorial contents...

	Advertising		Editorial
in the first issue	_____	to	_____
after a year of issues	_____	to	_____
currently	_____	to	_____

5. What was the advertising revenue during the magazine's first year?

   _____ less than $100,000   _____ $500,001–$1,000,000

   _____ $100,000–$500,000   _____ more than $1,000,000

6. What was the advertising revenue last year? (Please omit this question if last year was your first year of publication.)

_____ less than $100,000   _____ $500,001–$1,000,000

_____ $100,000–$500,000   _____ more than $1,000,000

7. What businesses are your major advertisers in?

_____

_____

Subscriptions

8. At the time of the first issue, what was the total circulation of the magazine?

_____ less than 5,000   _____ 10,001–15,000   _____ 25,001–40,000

_____ 5,000–10,000   _____ 15,001–25,000   _____ more than 40,000

9. When the first issue was published, how many paid subscriptions did the magazine have?

_____ less than 5,000   _____ 10,001–15,000   _____ 25,001–40,000

_____ 5,000–10,000   _____ 15,001–25,000   _____ more than 40,000

10. What is the average income bracket of your readership?

_____ less than $15,000   _____ $30,001–$50,000   _____ more than $75,000

_____ $15,000–$30,000   _____ $50,001–$75,000   _____ don't know

11. What is the average age of your readership?

_____ less than 25 years   _____ 36–45 years   _____ 56–65 years

_____ 25–35 years   _____ 46–55 years   _____ more than 65 years

12. Please rank in priority order the subject matter your readers prefer. Let a "1" represent the most preferred topic and a "5" represent the least preferred topic.

_____ local politics   _____ local news analysis   _____ business news

_____ entertainment   _____ local personalities

13. What adjectives would you use to describe your readership?

_____

14. What advice would you give to someone interested in starting a city magazine?

_____

_____

Analysis of the Questionnaire

The response rate to the survey was 63 percent. As the questionnaires were returned, the data were analyzed with a computer using a variety of procedures. The means for some of the quantitative variables are listed below:

Percentage of stories written by free-lance writers	59.4%
Percentage of advertising in the first issue	40.3%
Percentage of advertising after one year of issues	45.5%
Percentage of advertising currently	49.5%
Promotion expenditure before publication	$29,000
Promotion expenditure during the first year	$39,958
SMSA population*	671,924
Circulation**	59,178
Newsstand price***	$1.80

*The population of the Standard Metropolitan Statistical Areas (SMSA) in which the magazines were located were taken from the *1980 Census of Population and Housing: United States Summary.*
**The circulations were listed in consumer magazines and farm publications published by Standard Rate and Data Service, Inc.
***The issue prices were taken from the covers of the sample issues submitted by participants.

Readership Profile   Ninety percent of the participants responded to the open-ended question asking them to describe their readerships with the word "affluent." Ninety-six percent of the readership had an annual income greater than $30,000, and more than 80 percent ranged from 36 to 45 years of age. Participants ranked the subjects their readers preferred in the following order: (1) feature stories on local personalities, (2) entertainment, (3) local news analysis, (4) local politics and (5) business news.

Major Sources of Advertising   Participants were asked to list the businesses of their major advertisers to permit an analysis of the primary sources of advertising in city magazines. Eighty-eight percent of the respondents listed retail businesses, while 38 percent included restaurants and banks in their lists. Nineteen percent mentioned real estate companies.

National advertising appeared in the lists of only two respondents, and one of the two specified that the national ads were "occasional." The respondent who indicated that national advertising was a frequent source of revenue was the publisher of a magazine in an SMSA with a population exceeding 3,000,000.

Profile of Waco SMSA (McLennan County)[1]

Population	172,800
Population ranking in the United States	194
Number of households	63,000
Total effective buying income (in thousands of dollars)	$1,189,402
Retail sales	$840,358,000
Retail sales per household	$13,381
Age groups:	
18–24	24,000
25–34	23,000
35–49	27,000
50–64	28,000
65 or older	23,000
Undetermined	1,000
Median age	44
Income Distribution of Adult Population:	
Under $10,000	37,000
$10,000–$19,999	38,000
$20,000 or more	51,000
Median income	$16,800

Questions

1. Do you see any flaws in the sample selection that would create a bias toward larger, metropolitan areas?
2. What other questions should have been included in the questionnaire?
3. Do the survey data support the entrepreneur's plans for the advertising-to-editorial ratio?
4. What additional information about the Waco market is needed by the entrepreneurs?
5. Given the research findings, do you recommend that a city-magazine venture be initiated in Waco? Why or why not?

Case Endnote

1. This abbreviated profile was obtained from federal government Census publications.

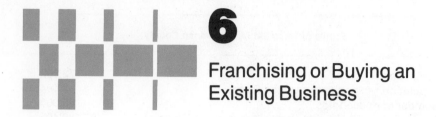

6

Franchising or Buying an Existing Business

Figure 6–1   Winston Alleyne

©Judith Pszenica

Motivations for buying and operating a franchise are quite varied. Some franchise purchasers find franchising to be a quick and easy way to break from the corporate world of big business. Such was the circumstance of Winston Alleyne when he lost his job as assistant corporate secretary at General Host Corporation. A company reorganization eliminating his job became the motivation for Winston to use his severance pay to buy a yogurt bar franchise named Everything Yogurt, and an orange juice stand named Bananas. Winston chose the franchising route primarily because "the franchisor had experience that made up for my lack of experience in retailing." His stores brought in sales of $80,000 in the first quarter of the year.

Source: Reprinted from the September, 1985 issue of *Venture*, The Magazine for Entrepreneurs, by special permission. © 1985 Venture Magazine, Inc., 521 Fifth Ave., New York, NY 10175.

Looking Ahead

Watch for the following important topics:

1. Types of franchising systems.
2. Advantages and limitations of franchising.
3. Considerations in evaluating a franchise.
4. Reasons for buying an existing business.
5. How to determine the value of a business being considered for purchase.

In Chapter 4 we explained the steps involved in launching a new business. In this chapter, we examine franchising and buying an existing business—two alternatives to starting an independent business from scratch.

SCOPE AND DEVELOPMENT OF FRANCHISING

Franchising offers an attractive option for starting a small business. The franchising concept helps thousands of entrepreneurs realize their business-ownership dreams each year. Initially, let us examine the language and structure of franchising and also some of its history.

Franchising Terminology

The term *franchising* is defined in many ways. In this text, we use a broad definition to encompass its wide diversity. **Franchising** is a marketing system revolving around a two-party legal agreement whereby one party (the **franchisee**) is granted the privilege to conduct business as an individual owner but is required to operate according to methods and terms specified by the other party (the **franchisor**). The legal agreement is known as the **franchise contract** and the privileges it contains are called the **franchise**.

The potential value of any franchising arrangement is determined by the rights contained in the franchise contract, and the extent and importance of these rights are quite varied. For example, a potential franchisee may desire the right to use a widely recognized name. Alternatively, the potential franchisee may need an entire marketing system. Regardless of the specific need, a franchise provides an attractive start-up mechanism for an independently owned business.

ACTION REPORT
The Sweet Smell of Success

The Krön family name has been associated with fine chocolates even before Thomas Krön sold his first franchise in 1975. Tom's father set up a small chocolate shop in America in the 1950s after fleeing the 1956 Hungarian uprising. The shop soon failed due to a lack of understanding of American marketing methods.

Tom revived the business in 1972, after attending medical school for several years. When Krön began to think about expansion a few years later, he was approached by a Florida businessman whom he liked and trusted. "I didn't even know what franchising was," said Krön. But the proposal sounded inviting.

It would allow him to increase his sales and reach a brand new market without raising capital or selling out. With the franchise fee he would have enough cash to keep production ahead of increased demand. He could control the manufacturing and quality, and the franchise would build a business of its own around a proven product line, a distinctive image, and a reputation that had begun to spread.

Krön sold the Florida franchise for $12,000. He asked for no royalty payments and had no minimum sales or inventory requirements. Today his Krön Chocolatier costs up to $75,000, and the franchise purchaser must be able to lease a prime retail location and provide start-up capital of $100,000. The newest franchise contract requires royalties up to 5 percent.

By the end of 1981, Krön had 12 outlets, all in prime locations. Sales have grown from $250,000 worth of chocolate his first year to an estimated $3 million in revenues in 1981.

Source: Reprinted with permission, *Inc.* magazine, July, 1982. Copyright © 1982 by Inc. Publishing Company, 38 Commercial Wharf, Boston, MA 02110.

Types of Franchising Systems

Three types, or levels, of franchising systems offer opportunities for entrepreneurs. Figure 6–2 depicts each of these systems and provides examples. In *System A*, the producer/creator (the franchisor) grants a franchise to a wholesaler (the franchisee). This system is often used in the soft-drink industry. Dr Pepper and Coca-Cola are examples of System A franchisors.

In the second level, designated as *System B*, the wholesaler is the franchisor. This system prevails among supermarkets and general merchandising stores. Ben Franklin, Gamble-Skogmo, and Ace Hardware are examples of System B franchisors.

Figure 6–2   Alternative Franchising Systems

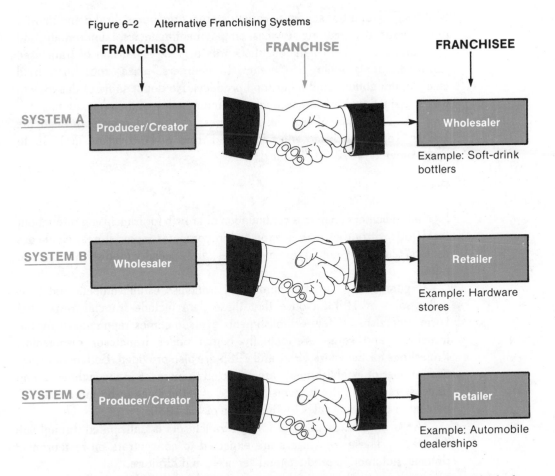

The third type, *System C*, is the most widely used. This system finds the producer/creator as franchisor and the retailer as franchisee. Automobile dealerships and gasoline service stations are prototypes of this system. In recent years, this system also has been used successfully by many fast-food outlets and printing services. Notable examples of System C franchisors are Burger Chef and Kwik-Kopy.

Early Franchising

One of the first franchise arrangements involved a relationship between Singer Sewing Machine Company and its dealers during the nineteenth century. In the early part of this century, other types of franchising were primarily associated with the sale of automobiles, soft drinks, and gasoline.

The post-World War II franchise boom was based on the expansion of the franchising principle into many different types of businesses. Some of these are franchised motels, beauty parlors, equipment-renting outlets, bookkeeping and tax services, variety stores, drugstores, brake and muffler repair shops, dry cleaning services, employment agencies, laundromats, and car-rental services. In addition, there was a great expansion of franchised fast-food outlets selling ice cream, hamburgers, pizza, root beer, fried chicken, doughnuts, and other food products. No doubt some of this growth was explained by the increased income and mobility of the population.[1]

The expansion of franchised business continued rapidly through the 1970s. Total franchised sales increased from $116.5 billion in 1970 to approximately $313.3 billion in 1979.[2]

Franchising in the Eighties

All indicators point to a continuation of growth for franchising throughout the 1980s. Strong growth is expected in computer repair stores, child-care centers, temporary employment agencies, and specialty food shops, to name a few.[3]

Figure 6–3 shows the number of franchise establishments and their dollar sales in 1983. Notice that these data include franchisor-operated businesses also. (A few establishments are sometimes repurchased by the franchisor and some are actually begun under franchisor ownership.) Projections for the years 1984 and 1985 are also provided. Both dollar sales and number of establishments are expected to increase in the eighties. Some forecasters project the franchising share of retail sales to be more than 50 percent of total retail sales by the middle of the 1980s.[4]

An even greater influx of foreign franchisors is anticipated throughout the 1980s. These franchisors are expected to concentrate on restaurants, clothing, automotive products and services, and furniture.

BUYING A FRANCHISE

"Look before you leap" is an old adage which should be heeded by potential franchisees. Entrepreneurial enthusiasm should not cloud the eyes to the realities, both good and bad, of franchising. We shall first look at the advantages of buying a franchise and then examine the weaknesses of this decision. Study these topics carefully, and remember them when you are evaluating a franchise.

Franchising vs. Starting an Independent Business

One way to compare the advantages of franchising with the alternative of launching an independent business is to look at a side-by-side comparison.

Figure 6-3   Total Franchise Sales and Number of Establishments

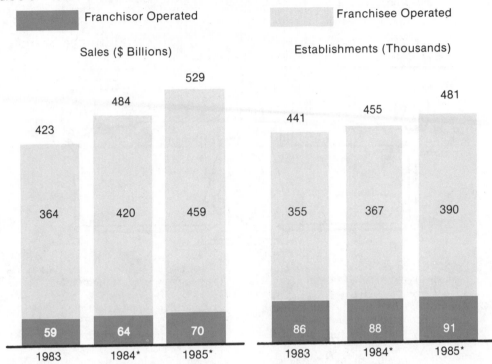

*Estimated by Respondents

Source: U.S. Department of Commerce, *Franchising in the Economy: 1983–1985* (Washington: U.S. Government Printing Office, 1985), Chart 1.

Figure 6-4 profiles eight major differences between buying a franchise and starting an independent business. Neither approach is a winner in all cases. However, in their particular circumstances, many people find the franchise form of business to be better.

Advantages of Franchising

A franchise is attractive for many good reasons. Three advantages in particular warrant further analysis. A franchise can offer (1) formal training, (2) financial assistance, and (3) marketing and management benefits. Naturally, all franchises may not be equally strong on all these points. But it is these advantages which motivate many persons to consider the franchise arrangement.

Formal Training   The importance of formal training received from the franchisor is underlined by the generally glaring managerial weakness of

Figure 6–4   Major Considerations in Deciding Between a Franchise and Starting an
Independent Business

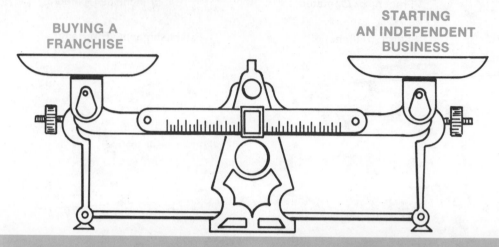

BUYING A FRANCHISE

1. Right to use a known trademark or brand with established public acceptance.
2. Availability of operational training usually provided by franchisor.
3. Possibility that sales territory is restricted by franchisor.
4. Benefits from the franchisor's advertising program.
5. More accurate forecasts of financial needs and greater ease in obtaining initial capital.
6. Franchisor often the sole source of supplies.
7. Fixtures, equipment, and other premise-related assets often specified by franchisor.
8. Possible restrictions in contract on franchisee's decisions to sell or to expand.

STARTING AN INDEPENDENT BUSINESS

1. Requires time, effort, and cost to establish a new name in the market.
2. Managerial ability based on entrepreneur's expertise.
3. Sales territory as large as entrepreneur can serve.
4. Advertising load carried by entrepreneur but permits freedom in advertising.
5. More difficult to plan and obtain financing needs.
6. May obtain supplies anywhere at the best available prices.
7. Freedom to develop the store image that entrepreneur feels is most appropriate.
8. Total freedom to operate as entrepreneur sees fit.

Source: Adapted with permission from *Buying a Franchise* (Montreal, Quebec: Federal Business Development Bank, 1979), p. 3.

small entrepreneurs. To the extent that this weakness can be overcome, therefore, the training program offered by the franchisor constitutes a major benefit.

The value and the effectiveness of training are evident from the records of business failures, a large majority of which are caused by deficiencies in management. For example, franchisors such as McDonald's and Kentucky Fried Chicken have reputedly never experienced a failure. Some franchisors admit to purchasing a weak operating franchisee to keep it from going under, thereby maintaining its image. However, there appears to be little question that the failure rate for independent small businesses in general is much higher than for franchised businesses in particular.

Operating as a franchisee, however, in no way guarantees success. A particular franchisor may offer unsatisfactory training, or the franchisee may not apply the training correctly or fail for some other reason.

Initial Training Training by the franchisor often begins with an initial period of a few days or a few weeks at a central training school or at another established location. For example, the Holiday Inn franchise chain operates the hotel industry's largest training center, Holiday Inn University, which was built in 1972 at a cost of $5 million.

ACTION REPORT
Hamburger Homework

Applications for Burger King franchises run about 1,000 a year. About 10 percent of the applicants become franchisees. Burger King is not looking for someone who knows food but rather for someone who knows how to follow instructions. Applicants who can provide the liquid assets required by Burger King spend over eight weeks in training. The first week is spent in an existing restaurant, followed by six weeks of basic training at a regional center. The final nine days of training are conducted at Burger King University, the company's training center in Miami, FL.

Source: Lee Smith, "Burger King Puts Down Its Dukes," *Fortune,* Vol. 101, No. 12 (June 16, 1980), p. 96.

Figure 6–5 shows a training session for franchisees conducted by T-Shirts Plus. (The founder, Ken Johnson, is holding the shirt in the photograph.) Initial training programs cover not only the operating procedures to be used by the business, but also broader topics such as record keeping, inventory control, insurance, and human relations.

The Mister Donut franchise requires an initial training course of four weeks, including such topics as doughnut making, accounting and controls, advertising and merchandising, scheduling of labor and production, purchasing, and so on. Naturally, the nature of the product and the type of business affect the amount and type of training required in the franchised business. In most cases, training constitutes a potent advantage of the franchising system and permits individuals who are deficient in training and education to start and succeed in businesses of their own.

Figure 6-5   Training Session at T-Shirts Plus

Continuing Guidance   Initial training is ordinarily supplemented with subsequent continued training and guidance. This may involve refresher courses
and/or training by a traveling representative who visits the franchisee's
business from time to time. The franchisee may also receive manuals and
other printed materials that provide guidance for the business. However,
guidance shades into control so that in particular cases it may be difficult to
distinguish the two. The franchisor normally places a considerable emphasis
upon observing strict controls. Still, much of the continued training goes far
beyond the application of controls. While some franchising systems have
developed excellent training programs, this is by no means universal. Some
unscrupulous promoters falsely promise satisfactory training.

Financial Assistance   The costs of starting an independent business are often
high and the prospective entrepreneur's sources of capital quite limited. The
entrepreneur's standing as a prospective borrower is weakest at this point.
But by teaming up with a franchising organization, the aspiring franchisee
may enhance the likelihood of obtaining financial assistance.

If the franchising organization considers the applicant to be a suitable prospect with a high probability of success, it frequently extends a helping hand financially. For example, the franchisee seldom is required to pay the complete cost of establishing the business. In addition, the beginning franchisee is normally given a payment schedule that can be met through successful operation. Also, the franchisor may permit delay in payments for products or supplies obtained from the parent organization, thus increasing the franchisee's working capital.

Association with a well-established franchisor may also improve the new franchisee's credit standing with a bank. The reputation of the franchising organization and the managerial and financial controls that it provides serve to recommend the new franchisee to a banker. Also, the franchisor frequently will cosign notes with a local bank, thus guaranteeing the franchisee's loan.

Marketing and Management Benefits   Most franchised products and services are widely known and accepted. For example, customers will readily buy McDonald's hamburgers or Baskin-Robbins ice cream because they know the reputation of these products. Or travellers who recognize a restaurant or a motel because of its name, type of roof, or some other feature may turn into a Denny's Restaurant or a Holiday Inn motel because of their previous experience and the knowledge that they can depend upon the food and service that these outlets provide. Thus, franchising offers both a proven successful line of business and product identification.

The entrepreneur who enters a franchising agreement acquires the right to use the franchisor's nationally advertised trademark or brand name. This serves to identify the local enterprise with the widely recognized product or service. Of course, the value of product identification differs with the type of product or service and the extent to which it has received widespread promotion. In any case, the franchisor maintains the value of its name by continued advertising and promotion.

In addition to offering a proven successful line of business and readily identifiable products or services, franchisors have developed and tested their methods of marketing and management. The standard operating manuals and procedures they supply have permitted other entrepreneurs to operate successfully. This is one reason why franchisors insist upon the observance of standardized methods of operation and performance. If some franchises were allowed to operate at substandard levels, they could easily destroy the customer's confidence in the entire system.

The existence of proven products and methods, however, does not guarantee that a franchised business will succeed. For example, what appeared to be a satisfactory location as a result of the franchisor's marketing research techniques may turn out to be inferior. Or the franchisee may lack ambition or perseverance. Yet the fact that a franchisor can show a record of successful operation proves that the system can work and has worked elsewhere.

Limitations of Franchising

Franchising is like a coin—it has two sides. We have examined the positive side of franchising, but we must look on the other side of the coin and examine the negative side of franchising. In particular, three shortcomings permeate the franchise form of business. These are: the cost of a franchise, the restrictions on growth which can accompany a franchise contract, and the inherent loss of absolute independence on the part of the franchisee.

Cost of a Franchise   The total franchise cost consists of several components. Only after all of these cost components have been examined can a realistic picture be drawn. The cost of a franchise begins with the franchise fee. Generally speaking, higher fees will be required by the well-known franchisors.

Other costs include royalty payments, promotion costs, inventory and supplies costs, and building and equipment costs. When these costs are considered with the franchise fee, the total investment may look surprisingly large. The individual who acquires a McDonald's franchise must make an initial investment of approximately $300,000.[5] But Augie's Inc., an industrial catering service, requires only $1,000 in investment capital.[6] If entrepreneurs could earn the same income independently, they would save the amount of these fees and some of the other costs. However, this is not a valid objection if the franchisor provides the benefits previously described. In that case, franchisees are merely paying for the advantages of their relationship with the franchisor. And this may be a good investment, indeed.

Restrictions on Growth   A basic way to achieve business growth is to expand the existing sales territory. However, many franchise contracts restrict the franchisee to a defined sales territory, thereby eliminating this form of growth. Usually, the franchisor agrees not to grant another franchise to operate within the same territory. The potential franchisee, therefore, should weigh territorial limitation against the advantages cited earlier.

Loss of Absolute Independence   Frequently, individuals leave salaried employment for entrepreneurship because they dislike working under the direct supervision and control of others. By entering into a franchise relationship, such individuals may simply find that a different pattern of close control over personal endeavors has taken over. The franchisee does surrender a considerable amount of independence upon signing a franchise agreement.

Even though the franchisor's regulation of business operations may be helpful in assuring success, it may be unpleasant to an entrepreneur who cherishes independence. In addition, some franchise contracts go to extremes by covering unimportant details or specifying practices that are more helpful to others in the chain than to the local operation. Thus, as an operator of a franchised business, the entrepreneur occupies the position of a semi-independent businessperson.

EVALUATING FRANCHISE OPPORTUNITIES

Once an interest in becoming a franchisee emerges, much remains to be done before the dream materializes. The prospective franchisee must locate the right opportunity, investigate a franchise offer for possible fraud, and examine the franchise contract carefully.

Locate the Right Franchise Opportunity

With the proliferation of franchising over the years, the task of locating the most suitable opportunities has become difficult. Sources of franchise opportunities are not always obvious. Yet one source that is readily available to anyone is the advertisements in newspapers and trade publications. For example, in any issue of *The Wall Street Journal* numerous franchise opportunities are advertised (see Figure 6–6). *Franchising Today* and *Venture* magazines also include information on many franchise opportunities. In following up these advertisements, the prospective franchisee needs to beware of advertising claims that are misleading or that promise more than is warranted.

Other helpful guides in locating franchise opportunities are the following:

1. *Franchise Opportunities Handbook* published by the U.S. Department of Commerce. This handbook contains a comprehensive listing of franchisors with a brief statement about the nature and requirements of each franchise. It also cites many other sources of franchising information and assistance and is updated frequently. The handbook may be purchased from the Government Printing Office, Washington, DC 20402.
2. *Pilot Books*, 347 Fifth Avenue, New York, NY 10016, publishes several franchising guides. One of its publications is *The 1984 Directory of Franchising Organizations*, which lists over 700 leading franchise firms.

Figure 6–6 Franchise Opportunities Advertisement

HOME INSPECTION SERVICE

Valerie Bradley owns and successfully operates a HouseMaster of America franchise in Pennsylvania.

"I run the business fulltime, while my husband, who's a teacher, helps out occasionally. We both love it. And we've had no trouble hiring qualified engineers to perform the professional HouseMaster inspections."

It's a great opportunity for men and women alike!

CALL: 800–526–3939

HouseMaster of America
BOUND BROOK, N.J. 08805

JACK IN THE BOX FRANCHISES

PROVEN RESTAURANTS NEED OWNERS TO MATCH, MULTIPLE UNITS AND EXPANSION ARE POSSIBILITIES – DALLAS, SAN ANTONIO, FORT WORTH.

You'll need a net worth of $190,000 with liquid of $140,000 per restaurant, plus your own proven track record of success.

ALSO AVAILABLE: EXCLUSIVE TERRITORY AGREEMENTS FOR AMARILLO, LUBBOCK, MIDLAND, ODESSA, AND OTHER AREAS.

FOODMAKER, INC.
(619) 571-2200

SHOP OUR FRANCHISE LAST.

30 years of experience make us a leader in our field with **over 600 units** worldwide.

Explore what we offer vs. any other franchise you may be considering.

Our **service business** is **virtually recession-proof**...involves **minimal inventory** and **no receivables**...is **ideal for absentee ownership**...and **requires no background** in our industry.

Have other operations you've looked at all those advantages?

We provide **full startup assistance** and **full ongoing support.** Single unit cash requirements start **as low as $50,000.** (The average licensee of more than five years standing has increased his holdings—often via reinvested profits—to 6 units.)

Do alternative opportunities hold as much personal growth potential?

Get all the details. Call Mr. Norman Bander collect at **516-334-8400.** Or write CutCo Industries, Inc., Box 265, Jericho, NY 11753.

After you've other franchises to compare us to.

SHOP OUR FRANCHISE LAST.

YOU CAN MAKE IT HAPPEN COTTMAN TRANSMISSION

over 140 franchise centers, has excellent opportunities in many areas including Florida and the Southwest for those who realize the tremendous potential of the automotive repair industry.

No mechanical experience needed.
- Real estate support
- Complete training
- Continuous guidance
- Excellent advertising
- Financing assistance
- 78% growth past 4 yrs.
- Multi-units possible
- Approx. $35,000 required
- 20 year track record

If you desire the rewards and independence of your own business call L. Edelman

Toll Free **1-800-233-5515**
Pa. call (215) 643-5885

COTTMAN TRANSMISSION SYSTEMS, INC.
575 Virginia Drive
Fort Washington, Pa 19034

This Offering Is Made By Prospectus Only

HI·TECH HEALTH™

WELLNESS CENTER FRANCHISE

State-of-the-art computer technology, all-natural products, disease prevention/life extension programs, weight control, smoking cessation and nutrition... as well as programs focusing on stress reduction, PMS, allergy, natural cleansing and coronary risk.

– the income and investment opportunity with the eye on the future.

Retail, wholesale and network marketing.

Estimated investment:
Individual units $15 to $25,000.
Master Franchises from $75,000.

Financing available.
4416 N. Scottsdale Road
Scottsdale, Arizona 85251
Call COLLECT (602) 991-2904

Successful Franchise Opportunity.
Own an Insty-Prints® Printing Center

Excellent sites available in the Sunbelt. $10M down plus $17M in working capital — with below-market-rates on financing available on the balance. Full corporate support. Comprehensive training. Low royalty fees.

Call 1-800-228-6714 now. Or write us at **417 North 5th Street, Minneapolis, MN 55401.**

insty-prints
Printing Centers

CALL YOUR OWN SHOTS

If you'd rather take charge than take orders, owning an American Speedy Printing Center is the unlimited opportunity you're looking for.

CALL 1-800-521-4002
Financing available to qualified candidates.

AMERICAN SPEEDY PRINTING CENTERS™

32100 Telegraph, Birmingham MI

Franchise
BE IN BUSINESS FOR YOURSELF, BUT NOT BY YOURSELF

DEBIT ONE THE MOBILE BOOKKEEPING SERVICE

Outstanding opportunity for growth and income potential. No retail store or inventory necessary. We will assist you in hiring the right professionals. Accountants or investors welcome. Single or multi-unit franchise available. Low investment, high return, unique concept. For more information on one of the fastest growing franchise opportunities call:

1-800-331-2491

TACO MAYO ®

GET IN ON THE EXCITEMENT of owning a fast food Mexican restaurant. Taco Mayo Franchise Systems, Inc. offers you the opportunity to own a Franchise. For more information contact: Director of Franchise Sales, 405/691-8226, 10405 Green Briar Pl., Suite B, Oklahoma City, Oklahoma 73159.

Let us put a lid on your printing budget.

BUDGET PRINTING CENTERS

Own an instant printing center without the high cost of other printing programs

NO FEES
INITIAL INVESTMENT $12,500

Contact:
BUDGET INSTANT PRINT CENTERS
4133 Presidential SW
Lafayette Hill, Pa. 19444
Call Collect
(215) 836-5215

WANTED! ACQUISITIONS & FRANCHISEES

Nat'l temporary help services firm aggressively seeks acquisitions and existing temp owners as franchisees. Cash incentive for current temp owners. Attractive terms plus payrolling of temp payroll also available.

EMPLOYERS OVERLOAD
Joe Hansen, 1-800-854-2345

BE THE BOSS

Own a Sir Speedy Printing Center franchise. Over 500 others have, ask them.

Call today for free information.

Sir Speedy®
Printing Centers

892 W. 16th Street
Newport Beach, CA 92663
CALL 1-800-854-3321
INSIDE CALIFORNIA
COLLECT (714) 642-9470

Source: An Advertisement in *The Wall Street Journal*, September 12, 1985, p. 39.

3. International Franchise Association, 1025 Connecticut Avenue, NW, Suite 707, Washington, DC 20036 is a trade association which sponsors legal and government affairs symposiums, franchise management workshops, franchisor–franchisee relations seminars, and trade shows.

Information concerning franchise opportunities may also be obtained from the franchisors themselves. For example, the Jack 'N' Jill franchisor provides the information sheet shown in Figure 6–7.

In recent years, franchise consultants have appeared and now offer their services to individuals in seeking and evaluating franchise opportunities. As in choosing any type of consultant, the prospective franchisee needs to select a reputable, rather than a fly-by-night, consultant. This is not always easy in view of the newness of this consulting field.

Investigate the Franchise Offer

The nature of the commitment required in franchising justifies a careful investigation inasmuch as a franchised business typically involves a substantial investment, possibly many thousands of dollars. Furthermore, the business relationship is one that may be expected to continue over a period of years.

Ordinarily, the investigation process is a two-way effort. The franchisor wishes to investigate the franchisee, and the franchisee obviously wishes to evaluate the franchisor and the type of opportunity offered. Time is required for this kind of investigation. One should be skeptical of a franchisor who pressures a franchisee to sign at once without allowing for proper investigation.

Examine the Franchise Contract

The basic features of the relationship between the franchisor and the franchisee are embodied in the franchise contract. Since 1978, the Federal Trade Commission has required fuller disclosure of information provided by a franchisor to prospective franchisees. Twenty of the required types of information are listed below:[7]

1. The franchisor and its affiliates, and their business experience.
2. The business experience of each of the franchisor's officers, directors, and management personnel responsible for franchise services, training, and other aspects of the program.
3. Lawsuits involving the franchisor and its officers, directors, and management personnel.

Figure 6-7   Steps to Opening Your Jack 'N' Jill Donut Shop

10 STEPS TO OPENING YOUR
JACK 'N' JILL DONUT SHOP

1)   YOU'VE TAKEN THE FIRST STEP by requesting our information package. After reviewing the material, you should have an idea of what is involved.

2)   FILL OUT THE PERSONAL INFORMATION AND FINANCIAL STATEMENTS and return to us. This will indicate your willingness to explore the possibilities further. Your information will be held in strict confidence and will not obligate you in any manner.

3)   IT'S TIME FOR A MEETING. After we have reviewed your personal and financial data, an appointment will be made between you and a JACK 'N' JILL representative. If a mutual interest exists at that time, a franchise offering will be made. All necessary documents and cost figures will be made at that time.

4)   YOUR DEPOSIT DEMONSTRATES FURTHER INTEREST. If you have finally decided you want a JACK 'N' JILL shop, you will remit a deposit to JACK 'N' JILL. JACK 'N' JILL will then help you select a site for your business. Upon signing of the final franchise, your deposit will be applied to your franchise fee.

5)   SEARCH FOR LOCATION. An intensive search will begin for the best possible location for your business. JACK 'N' JILL will utilize its experience and knowledge to provide you the best site available.

6)   FINANCING. JACK 'N' JILL will help you gather and complete all the data necessary for you to obtain financing. Upon obtaining satisfactory financing, you will present JACK 'N' JILL a letter of confirmation from the lending institution.

7)   SIGNING OF THE FRANCHISE. After the site has been selected and financing has been obtained, you will sign the franchise agreement and remit the franchise fee to JACK 'N' JILL.

8)   BUILDING PERIOD. Construction of your building will begin if necessary and JACK 'N' JILL will supply all assistance necessary to see the project brought to a successful conclusion.

9)   TRAINING. Two to four weeks before your store opens, you will receive two weeks training in all phases of operation in JACK 'N' JILL's training facility.

10)   OPENING. This is the time you've waited for. JACK 'N' JILL representatives will help you with all phases including advertising.

Source: Jack 'N' Jill Donut Flour Company, Waco, TX. Reproduced with permission.

4. Previous bankruptcies involving the franchisor and its officers, directors, and management personnel.
5. The initial franchise fee and other initial payments required to obtain the franchise.
6. Continuing payments required from franchisees after the franchise opens.
7. Restrictions on the quality of goods and services used in the franchise and where they may be purchased.
8. Any financial assistance available from the franchisor or its affiliates.
9. Limits on the goods or services franchisees are permitted to sell.
10. Restrictions on the customers with whom franchisees may deal.
11. Territorial protections granted to the franchisee.
12. Conditions under which the franchise may be repurchased or refused renewal by the franchisor, transferred to a third party by the franchisee, and terminated or modified by either party.
13. Training programs.
14. The involvement of any celebrities or public figures in the franchise.
15. Site selection assistance.
16. Present and projected future number of franchises, and number of franchises terminated, not renewed, and repurchased in the past.
17. Franchisor's financial statements.
18. The extent to which franchisees must personally participate in the franchise's operations.
19. The basis for any earnings claims made to the franchisee, including the percentage of existing franchises that actually achieved those results.
20. Names and addresses of other franchisees.

The contract is typically a complex document, often running to several pages. Because of its extreme importance in furnishing the legal basis for the franchised business, no franchise contract should ever be signed by the franchisee without legal counsel. As a matter of fact, many reputable franchisors insist that the franchisee have legal counsel before signing the agreement. An attorney would be useful in anticipating trouble and in noting objectionable features of the franchise contract.

In addition to consulting an attorney, you as a prospective franchisee should use as many other sources of help as possible. In particular, you should discuss the franchise proposal with a banker, going over it in as much detail as possible. You should also obtain the services of a professional accounting firm in examining the franchisor's statements of projected sales, operating expenses, and net income. The accountant can be of invaluable help in evaluating the quality of these estimates and in discovering projections which may be unlikely to occur.

One of the most important features of the contract is the provision relating to termination and transfer of the franchise. Some franchisors have been accused of devising agreements that permit arbitrary cancellation. Of course, it is reasonable for the franchisor to have legal protection in the event that a franchisee fails to obtain a satisfactory level of operation or to maintain satisfactory quality standards. However, the prospective franchisee should avoid contract provisions that contain overly strict cancellation policies. Similarly, the rights of the franchisee to sell the business to a third party should be clearly stipulated. Any franchisor who can restrict the sale of the business to a third party can assume ownership of the business at an unreasonable price. The right of the franchisee to renew the contract after the business has been built up to a successful operating level should also be clearly stated in the contract.

Beware of Franchising Frauds

Every industry has its share of shady operations, and franchising is no exception. Unscrupulous fast-buck artists offer a wide variety of fraudulent schemes to attract the investment of unsuspecting individuals. The franchisor in such cases is merely interested in obtaining the capital investment of the franchisee and not in a continuing relationship.

The possibility of such fraudulent schemes requires alertness on the part of prospective franchisees. Only careful investigation of the company and the product can distinguish between fraudulent operators and legitimate franchising opportunities. Mark J. Klein, a Kansas City, MO, lawyer says, "Sometimes the best advice a lawyer can give a client is to stay away from a particular franchiser."[8] Certainly visits to, and discussion with, other franchisees operating in the same field are mandatory. Finally, a formal checklist, such as that provided in Appendix A at the end of this textbook, can be an extremely helpful tool.

SELLING A FRANCHISE

Franchising contains opportunities on both sides of the fence. We have already presented the franchising story from the viewpoint of the potential franchisee. Now we shall look through the eyes of the potential franchisor.

Why would a businessperson wish to become a franchisor? At least three general benefits may be identified. An American Marketing Association study sees these advantages as follows:[9]

1. *Source of capital.* The firm involved in franchising, in effect, through fee and royalty arrangements, borrows capital from the franchisee for channel development and thus has lower capital requirements than does the wholly owned chain.
2. *Increased motivation through franchising.* The franchisee as an independent businessperson is probably more highly motivated than salaried employees because of profit incentives and growth opportunities.
3. *Less susceptibility to labor organization.* Since franchising is decentralized, the franchisor is less susceptible to labor-organizing efforts than centralized organizations.

Amid the older and highly successful large franchisors, such as McDonald's, are many small businesses which are finding success as franchisors. In fact, some of them begin as franchisors rather than evolve into franchisors by adding franchised outlets to an already established operation (see Action Report below). Regardless of when the franchise program is developed, it should be planned well.

ACTION REPORT
Lighting the Franchise Candle

The idea of Wicks 'N' Sticks was born as Harold R. Otto was strolling around in a shopping center. At that time, Otto was a salesperson for an electrical equipment company. His plans were to begin operation with one store, and the initial financing was achieved routinely. About two months before the grand opening, Otto was asked to "share ideas" about a candle shop with a couple who wanted to get into business. The mall developer, who had contacted Otto on behalf of the couple, was amazed when Otto said, "I'll tell you what I'll do. We'll sell them a franchise." And that's what happened. For a fee of $2,500 and a 5 percent royalty, Wicks 'N' Sticks sold its first franchise. Otto has since opened several corporate-owned stores along with franchised outlets.

Cash problems besieged the business in the early 1970s. Analysis of unit profits showed that the franchising stores were doing better than the corporate-owned stores. By emphasizing franchising outlets, Wicks 'N' Sticks began to recover. Otto is now a strong supporter of what actually marked the beginning of Wicks 'N' Sticks—franchising. He says, "It took several years to understand, but now I'm a 100 percent believer in franchising."

Source: "The House of Wax," *Forbes* (November 10, 1980), pp. 100–105.

Some entrepreneurs are finding that one key to building a successful franchise system is perfecting a prototype. By developing a model unit, franchisors are able to show potential franchisees how a well-planned and managed unit can run. After only one year of franchising Entre Computers, Steven B. Heller, 43, and James J. Edgette, 42, have sold over 200 franchises and they continue to sell at the rate of 10 per month. They say, "A prototype will enable you to do a tremendously refined job of opening a center."[10]

Franchising has undoubtedly enabled many individuals to enter business who otherwise would never have escaped the necessity of salaried employment. Thus, franchising has contributed to the development of many successful small businesses.

BUYING AN EXISTING BUSINESS

Would-be entrepreneurs can choose to buy an existing business as an alternative to buying a franchise or starting from scratch with a new venture. This decision should be made only after careful consideration of the advantages and disadvantages of buying an established business.

Reasons for Buying an Existing Business

All decisions in life have pros and cons. The decision to buy an existing business is no exception. An extensive listing of these pros and cons is provided below.[11]

Pros

1. Prior successful operation of a business increases your chances of success with the same business.
2. Prior successful operation provides the location of the business previously selected and in use.
3. If the business has been profitable or is headed toward profit, you will be profitable sooner than if you start up your own business.
4. The amount of planning that may be necessary for an ongoing business will probably be less than that for a new business.
5. You will already have established customers or clientele.
6. You will already have established suppliers and will not have to look for them.
7. You may already have inventory on hand and will not lose the time necessary for selecting, ordering, and waiting for the order to arrive before you can make your first sales.

8. Necessary equipment is probably already on hand.
9. Financing will be necessary for the single transaction of purchasing the business.
10. You may be able to buy the business at a bargain price.
11. You will acquire the benefit of the experience of the prior owner.
12. Much of the hard work of start-up is avoided, including finding the location, purchasing the equipment, and so forth.
13. If employees are on board, they are probably already experienced in the business.
14. You may be able to finance all or part of the purchase price through a note to the owner.
15. Existing records of the business may help you and guide you in running the business.

Cons

1. You will inherit any bad will that exists because of the way the business has been managed.
2. The employees who are currently working for the company may not be the best or the best for you and the way you manage.
3. The image of the business is already established. If it is a poor image, it will be difficult to change.
4. Precedents have already been set by the previous owners. They may be difficult to change.
5. Modernization may be needed.
6. The purchase price may create a burden on future cash flow and profitability.
7. It is possible that you can overpay due to misrepresentation or an inaccurate appraisal of what the business is worth.
8. The business location may be a drawback.

The above listing of the pros and cons of buying an existing business can be condensed into three reasons: (1) reduction of uncertainties, (2) acquisition of ongoing operations and relationships, and (3) a bargain price. These reasons capture the main considerations in the decision to purchase an existing business. We will examine each of these in more detail.

Reduction of Uncertainties   A successful going concern has demonstrated an ability to attract customers, to control costs, and to make a profit. Although future operations may be different, the firm's past record shows what it can do under actual market conditions. For example, the satisfactory location of a going concern eliminates one major uncertainty. Although traffic counts are useful in assessing the potential value of a location, the acid test comes when a business opens its doors at that location. And this test has already been met in the case of an existing firm, with the results available in the form of sales and profit data.

Acquisition of Ongoing Operations and Relationships   The buyer of an existing business typically acquires its personnel, inventories, physical facilities, established banking connections, and ongoing relationships with trade suppliers. Consider the time and effort otherwise required in acquiring them "from scratch." Of course, this situation is an advantage only under certain conditions. For example, the firm's skilled, experienced employees constitute a valuable asset only if they will continue to work for the new owner. The physical facilities must not be obsolete, and the relationships with banks and suppliers must be healthy.

A Bargain Price   A going business may become available at what seems to be a low price. Whether it is actually a "good buy" must be determined by the prospective new owner. The price may appear low, but several factors could make the "bargain price" anything but a bargain. For example, the business may be losing money; the location may be deteriorating; or the seller may intend to reopen another business as a competitor. However, the business may indeed be a bargain and turn out to be a wise investment.

Finding a Business to Buy

Frequently in the course of day-to-day living and business contacts, a would-be buyer comes across an opportunity to buy an existing business. For example, a sales representative for a manufacturer or a wholesaler may be offered an opportunity to buy a customer's retail business. In other cases, the would-be buyer may need to search for a business to buy.

Other sources of business leads include suppliers, distributors, trade associations, and even bankers, who may know of business firms available for purchase. Also, realtors—particularly those who specialize in the sale of business firms and business properties—can provide leads. In addition, there are specialized brokers, called "matchmakers," who handle all the arrangements in closing a buyout. "Now about 1,000 to 1,500 matchmakers are handling mergers and acquisitions of companies with sales under $75 million," reports Jerome S. Siebert, head of Siebert Associates.[12]

Investigating and Evaluating the Existing Business

Regardless of the source of business leads, each opportunity requires a background investigation and careful evaluation. As a preliminary step, the buyer needs to acquire information about the business. Some of this information can be obtained through personal observation or discussion with the seller. Also important is the need to talk with other parties such as suppliers, bankers, and possibly customers of the business. Although some of this investigation requires personal checking, the buyer can also seek the help of outside experts. The two most valuable sources of assistance in this regard are accountants and lawyers.

The seller's real reasons for selling a going business may or may not be disclosed. Robert Haas, general partner of Intercapco, a venture capital firm, expresses this concern by saying, "When somebody puts a company on the market, you wonder why they are trying to get rid of it. Either the company is not doing well, or it has a skeleton in the closet that will affect its future performance."[13]

The buyer must be wary, therefore, of taking the seller's explanations at face value. Here, for example, are some of the most common reasons why owners offer their businesses for sale:

1. Old age or illness.
2. Desire to relocate in a different section of the country.
3. Decision to accept a position with another company.
4. Unprofitability of the business.
5. Discontinuance of an exclusive sales franchise.

The buyer will also be interested in the history of the business and the direction in which it is moving. To form a clear idea of the firm's value, however, the buyer must eventually examine the financial data pertaining to its operation. Although valuation is not a science, the entrepreneur must decide "how much" the business is worth. A logical starting point is an independent audit of the firm offered for sale.

The Independent Audit   The major purpose of an independent audit is to reveal the accuracy and completeness of the financial statements of the business. It also determines whether the seller has used acceptable accounting procedures in depreciating equipment and in valuing inventory. If financial statements are available for the past five or ten years, or even longer, the buyer can obtain some idea of trends for the business.

Adjustment of Audited Statements   Even audited statements may be misleading and require "normalizing" to obtain a realistic picture of the business. For example, business owners sometimes understate business income by failing to report some cash receipts as taxable income. Adjustment may also be required if the pricing of goods and/or services is abnormally low—lower than necessary to attract a satisfactory volume of business.

Other items that may need adjustment include personal or family expenses and wage or salary payments. For example, costs related to the family use of business vehicles frequently appear as a business expense. And in some situations, family members receive excessive compensation or none at all. "I don't touch 80% of the businesses...even when you have the books and records, it's a fiction...the owners hide the perks," cautions Stanley

Salmore, a Beverly Hills business broker.[14] All items must be examined carefully to be sure that they relate to the business and are realistic. Figure 6-8 shows an income statement which has been adjusted by a prospective buyer. Notice carefully the reasons for the adjustments which have been made. Naturally, there are many other adjustments which can be performed.

The buyer should also scrutinize the seller's balance sheet to see whether asset book values are realistic. Property often appreciates in value after it is recorded on the books.[15] In other cases, physical facilities or inventory or receivables decline in value so that their actual worth is less than their inflated book value.

Valuation of the Business   A word of caution is needed for those who see the valuation process as simple. It is not easy or exact. Officers of Corporate Investment Business Brokers describe the situation as follows:

> A lot of them [small businesses] are still run out of shoe boxes...What to do? Ask to examine federal tax returns and state sales tax statements...You can gain a better fix on the business by looking through invoices and receipts with both customers and suppliers, as well as bank statements.[16]

Even with accurately adjusted financial statements, the business valuation process is difficult. Each of several valuation methods focuses on different elements of value, but none is without its unique limitations. There are four common approaches to business valuation based on the following: (1) market value, (2) replacement cost, (3) liquidation value, and (4) earnings. In this section we describe these approaches and provide a calculated example of how to apply the earnings approach.

The Market Value Approach   The **market value approach** relies on previous sales of similar businesses. These transactions establish the value of the one currently being appraised. Obviously, successful application of this method depends on the similarity of the businesses and the recency of the sales. If good data can be obtained, this approach is highly desirable because it is simple and reflects market values. Real estate appraisals rely extensively on this method.

The Replacement Cost Approach   The **replacement cost approach** to business valuation is one of several asset-based methods. A buyer following this approach tries to find the replacement value of property being purchased. A practical starting point is the most recent balance sheet of the business. Replacement cost would then be determined for all assets contributing to the business; some balance-sheet assets may be obsolete and of no continuing value to operations. Although this method of valuation usually ignores nontangible assets, it can increase the accuracy of asset values shown on the unadjusted balance sheet. This method is also difficult to use when a small

Figure 6–8   Income Statement as Adjusted by Prospective Buyer

	Original Income Statement		Required Adjustments	Adjusted Income Statement	
Estimated sales	$172,000			$172,000	
Cost of goods sold	84,240			84,240	
Gross profit	$87,760			$ 87,760	
Operating expenses:					
Rent	$20,000		Rental agreement will expire in six months; Rent is expected to increase 20 percent.	$ 24,000	
Salaries	19,860			19,860	
Telephone	990			990	
Advertising	11,285			11,285	
Utilities	2,580			2,580	
Insurance	1,200		Property is underinsured; Adequate coverage will double present cost.	2,400	
Professional services	1,200			1,200	
Credit card expense	1,860		Amount of credit card expense appears unreasonably large; Buyer assumes that approximately $1,400 of this amount may be better classified as personal expense.	460	
Miscellaneous	1,250	60,225		1,250	$64,025
Net income		$27,535			$23,735

business has been operating out of a "cigar box" and has no formal financial statements.

The Liquidation Value Approach   The **liquidation value approach** is another asset-based method of establishing value. The value of the business is equated with the salvage value of the business if operations ceased. Although liquidation is not the typical goal of the entrepreneur, this method does provide a minimum value of the business under a "worst scenario" assumption.

The Earnings Approach   The **earnings approach** centers on estimating the amount of potential income that may be produced by the business in the next year. A desired rate of return is then applied to the income estimate. The amount of investment equating these two factors is the estimated value of the business. This method is a practical approach consistent with the entrepreneur's desire to reap the operating benefits of the business.

The earnings approach can be further refined by incorporating year-by-year estimates of future income and "discounting" their value to determine current value. This refinement accounts for the greater value of a certain sum of money today compared to some time in the future. We develop the "discounting" concept much more fully in Chapter 20.

Because of the popularity and usefulness of valuation based on earnings, we wish to elaborate on this approach with a calculated example. We will use adjusted net income as our measure of earnings. According to David W. Nicholas, a vice-president of American Appraisal of New York, this method is the best valuation approach for entrepreneurs.[17] Valuation based on net income requires the use of a process known as **capitalization of profit**. Using this process, the buyer first estimates the dollars of profit that may be expected and then determines the dollar amount of investment which should logically earn the estimated dollars of profit. The dollar amount of investment constitutes the value of the business.

To illustrate, suppose that the adjusted income statement of a business shows that its annual net income is $60,000. What should a buyer be willing to pay for such a business? To answer this question, the buyer should follow four steps:

Step 1: Estimate the probable future profit for next year on the basis of past profit data. In doing this, the buyer must adjust past profit figures to eliminate nonrecurring gains or losses—for example, a loss from a fire. The buyer must ask himself or herself what operating profit the business can be expected to earn in the future.

Step 2: Allow for personal time invested in the business. In the case of a proprietorship, see whether the expenses shown on the income statement include a proper salary for the owner–manager. If no allowance has been made for the owner–manager's salary, a reasonable amount should be deducted before capitalizing the profit. Of course, this assumes that the buyer intends to devote personal time to the business—time that might otherwise be spent productively elsewhere. In the case of both proprietorships and partnerships, the "salary" for a proprietor or partner is not identified as an expense but is included as part of the firm's net profit.

Step 3: Estimate the degree of risk involved in the business. One might expect a 30 to 40 percent return on investment in businesses that entail considerable risk; in a less hazardous venture, 20 or 25 percent might be quite satisfactory.

Step 4: Determine the existence and amount of goodwill, if any. Goodwill derives from the loyalty of customers or other advantages that cause earnings to be exceptionally high in view of the physical resources involved. Goodwill tends to be less durable than other assets and thus is worth proportionately less to the buyer.

Following the four steps noted above, let us now calculate the value of that business whose annual income we estimated to be $60,000. According to Step 1, we must decide whether the $60,000 can be expected to continue in the future. An examination of the income statement may show no unusual expense or income items. A general review of business prospects, moreover, may suggest no drastic changes in the foreseeable future. We might assume, therefore, that the $60,000 constitutes a reasonable prediction of future profit.

Following Step 2, we may find that no salary expense has been shown for the owner–manager in arriving at the $60,000 profit. If the buyer places a value of $25,000 on personal time and effort, this amount should be deducted from the $60,000, leaving $35,000 to be capitalized. This $35,000 is the profit which will compensate the buyer for the dollars invested in the business.

When estimating the degree of risk involved in the business as prescribed in Step 3, we assume that the buyer considers the business to be moderately safe and feels that a 20 percent profit would be a good return on investment (ROI) in comparison with alternative investment opportunities. We can then calculate the value of the business as follows, assuming that no goodwill exists:

$$\text{Value of business} \times \text{Desired rate of return} = \text{Net profit}$$
$$\text{Value of business} \times 20\% = \$35,000$$
$$\text{Value of business} = \$35,000 \div 0.20$$
$$\text{Value of business} = \$175,000$$

Thus, the $175,000 provides a benchmark for use in negotiating the purchase price of the business.

In following Step 4, the buyer inquires about the existence of goodwill. If the profit is unreasonably high in view of the physical resources of the business, the buyer will be purchasing goodwill along with the physical assets of the business. And if a substantial amount of the firm's profit is attributable to goodwill, the buyer should value the firm more conservatively due to the intangible and somewhat fragile nature of goodwill. Under these circumstances, the buyer needs to use a higher rate for capitalizing the profit. Assuming that the higher rate, adjusted for goodwill, is 30 percent rather than 20 percent, the value of the business can then be calculated as follows:

$$\text{Value of business} \times \text{Desired rate of return} = \text{Net profit}$$
$$\text{Value of business} \times 30\% = \$35,000$$
$$\text{Value of business} = \$35,000 \div 0.30$$
$$\text{Value of business} = \$116,667$$

Clearly, the estimated value of the business is lower when we assume that we are paying for goodwill, which may soon disappear.

Other Factors to Evaluate   A number of other factors remain to be explored when evaluating an existing business. Some of these are:

1. *Competition.* The prospective buyer should look into the extent, intensity, and location of competing businesses. In particular, the buyer should check to see whether the business in question is gaining or losing in the race with competitors.
2. *Market.* The adequacy of the market to maintain all competing business units, including the one to be purchased, should be determined. This entails market research, study of census data, and personal, on-the-spot observation at each competitor's place of business.
3. *Future community developments.* Examples of community developments planned for the future include:
   a. Changes in zoning ordinances already enacted but not yet in effect.
   b. Land condemnation suits for construction of a public building, municipally operated parking lot, or a public park.
   c. Change from two-way traffic flow to one-way traffic.
   d. Discontinuance of bus routes that will eliminate public transportation for customers and employees.
4. *Legal commitments.* These may include contingent liabilities, unsettled lawsuits, delinquent tax payments, missed payrolls, overdue rent or installment payments, and mortgages of record against any of the real property acquired.
5. *Union contracts.* The prospective buyer should determine what type of labor agreement, if any, is in force, as well as the quality of the firm's employee relations.

6. *Buildings.* The quality of the buildings housing the business, particularly the fire hazard involved, should be checked. In addition, the buyer should determine if there are restrictions on access to the building. For example, is there access to the building without crossing the property of another? If necessary, a right of way should be negotiated before the purchase contract is closed.

7. *Future national emergencies.* The buyer should determine the potential impact of possible future national emergencies such as price and wage controls, energy shortages, human-resources shortages, raw-material shortages, and the like.

8. *Product prices.* The prospective owner should compare the prices of the seller's products with manufacturers' or wholesalers' catalogs or prices of competing products in the locality. This is necessary to assure full and fair pricing of goods whose sales are reported on the seller's financial statements.

ACTION REPORT
Let's Make a Deal

Cash up front is not always the preferred method in a buy-out deal. More sophisticated deals involve royalties, annuities, and separate payments for assets. Consider the transaction between a buyer and the owner of a manufacturing company as described by Richard M. Rudnick, Chairman of Geneva Corporation, a Santa Ana, California, broker:

> The buyer...didn't want to pay more than the $3.2 million book value of the business. And the owner was worried that if he got all of the money at once, he would have to pay a lot of income tax...The deal was structured to include separate payments for the assets, for the owner to be a consultant to the business...the seller got $1 million at the closing of the deal...the seller will collect annual payments of $200,000 for 20 years, and, as inflation protection, lump sums of $500,000, $1 million, and $1.5 million payable, respectively, 5, 10, and 20 years after the sale. In all, he gets $8 million.

The deal, however, keeps the cost to the buyer at $3.2 million. How can this be? The buyer...spent $1.4 million for an annuity that pays the seller $200,000 yearly for 20 years. And for $800,000, the buyer purchased zero-coupon bonds with 5, 10, and 20-year maturities to provide the three lump sums due the seller.

The buyer can treat the bond cost and annuity as a business expense. Where there is a will there is a way!

Source: Reprinted by permission of *The Wall Street Journal,* © Dow Jones & Company, Inc., 1985. All Rights Reserved.

Negotiating the Purchase Price and Terms

The purchase price of the business is determined by negotiation between buyer and seller. Although the calculated value is not the price of the business, it gives the buyer an estimated value to use in negotiating price. Typically, the buyer tries to purchase the firm for something less than the full estimated value. Likewise, the seller tries to get more than the estimated value.

An important part of this negotiation is the terms of purchase. In many cases, the buyer is unable to pay the full price in cash and must seek extended terms. The seller may also be concerned about taxes on the profit from the sale. Terms may be more attractive to the buyer and seller as the amount of the down payment is reduced and/or the length of the repayment period is extended.

Closing the Deal

As in the purchase of real estate, the purchase of a business is closed at a specific time. The closing may be handled, for example, by a title company or an attorney. Preferably the closing should occur under the direction of an independent third party. If the seller's attorney is suggested as the closing agent, the buyer should exercise caution. Regardless of the closing arrangements, the buyer should never go through a closing without extensive consultation with a qualified attorney.

A number of important documents are completed during the closing. These include a bill of sale, certifications as to taxing and other governmental authorities, and agreements pertaining to future payments and related guarantees to the seller.

Looking Back

1. Three basic types of franchising systems are: System A, where the producer is the franchisor and the wholesaler is the franchisee; System B, where the wholesaler is the franchisor and the retailer is the franchisee; and System C, where the producer is the franchisor and the retailer is the franchisee. The most widely used is System C.

2. Franchising provides three main advantages to the franchisee. These are: formal training, financial assistance, and marketing and managerial expertise—all provided by the franchisor.

3. Three shortcomings permeate the franchise form of business. These are: the cost of a franchise, the restrictions on growth which can accompany a franchise contract, and the inherent loss of absolute independence on the part of the franchisee.

4. A number of reasons exist for buying a business. Fewer uncertainties are involved than in launching an entirely new firm. Also, the facilities, personnel, and other elements of a going business are already assembled. The business may also be available at a bargain price.

5. After corrected financial statements are available, a buyer can estimate the value of the business by: the market value approach, the replacement cost approach, the liquidation value approach, or the earnings approach.

DISCUSSION QUESTIONS

1. What makes franchising different from other forms of business? Be specific.
2. Explain the three types of franchising systems. Which is most widely used?
3. Briefly recount franchising changes from a historical perspective.
4. Evaluate the marketing benefits derived from a franchise.
5. Evaluate "loss of control" as a disadvantage of franchising.
6. What reasons for buying an existing business, in contrast to starting from scratch, appear most important?
7. Is uncertainty eliminated or merely minimized when an existing business is purchased? Explain.
8. What is the significance of the seller's real reasons for selling? How might you discover them?
9. How should a buyer determine the estimated profit and rate of return to use in capitalizing business profits?
10. Suppose that a business firm available for purchase has shown an average net profit of $40,000 for the past 5 years. During these years, the amount of profit fluctuated between $20,000 and $60,000. State your assumptions and then calculate the value that you might use in negotiating the purchase price.

ENDNOTES

1. A more detailed history of franchising for the period preceding 1970 can be found in Donald W. Hackett, *Franchising: The State of the Art* (Chicago: American Marketing Association, 1977).

2. U.S. Department of Commerce, *Franchising in the Economy: 1983–1985* (Washington: U.S. Government Printing Office, 1985), Tables 4 and 7.

3. William Celis III, "Franchises Can Be Profitable, But Which One?" *The Wall Street Journal*, Vol. LXXV, No. 70 (April 10, 1985), p. 27.

4. Tom West, "Starting up the Franchise Way," *In Business*, Vol. 7, No. 1 (February, 1983), p. 28.

5. Celis, *op.cit.*

6. Teri Agins, "Owning Franchises Has Pluses But Wealth Isn't Guaranteed," *The Wall Street Journal*, Vol. LXXIV, No. 79 (October 22, 1984), p. 33.

7. Meg Whittemore and Carol Steinberg, "Guide to Franchising," *Venture*, Vol. 7, No. 7 (July, 1985), p. 88.

8. Agins, *op.cit.*

9. Hackett, *op.cit.*, p. 14.

10. Kevin Farrell, "Franchise Prototypes," *Venture*, Vol. 6, No. 1 (January, 1984), p. 38.

11. William A. Cohen, *The Entrepreneur and Small Business Problem Solver* (New York: John Wiley & Sons, 1983), pp. 126–127.

12. "Selling Your Small Company," *Business Week*, No. 2879 (February 4, 1985), p. 101.

13. Ronald Tanner, "When It's Better to Buy," *Venture*, Vol. 6, No. 6 (June, 1984), p. 76.

14. Stanford L. Jacobs, "Asian Immigrants Build Fortune in U.S. by Buying Cash Firms," *The Wall Street Journal*, Vol. LXXIV, No. 64 (October 1, 1984), p. 29.

15. Standard accounting practice requires land, for example, to be recorded at cost. No adjustments are subsequently made to recognize its increasing or decreasing value. When real estate values are changing substantially, therefore, the amounts shown on the books do not correspond with reality.

16. John A. Byrne, "The Business of Businesses, " *Forbes*, Vol. 134, No. 4 (August 13, 1984), p. 112.

17. William Meyers, "Determining a Value," *Venture*, Vol. 7, No. 1 (January, 1985), p. 35.

REFERENCES TO SMALL BUSINESS IN ACTION

Cooper, Glen. "How Much Is Your Business Worth?" *In Business*, Vol. 6, No. 5 (September–October, 1984), pp. 50–54.

    An in-depth look at business valuation is provided by the author. An actual appraisal with somewhat involved computations is included.

Gupta, Udayan. "A Question of Equality." *Venture*, Vol. 6, No. 9 (September, 1984), pp. 92–97.

    The movement by minority groups to enter business through franchising and some of their problems are examined in this article. Many of the issues confronting franchisors and minorities are focused upon.

Johnson, Alan W. "How To Measure Your Company's Value." *Nation's Business*, Vol. 71, No. 4 (April, 1983), pp. 68–70.

    Three basic approaches to business valuation are described in easy-to-understand language. A few calculations are also included.

Justis, Robert. "Franchisors: Have You Hugged Your Franchisee Today?" *Nation's Business*, Vol. 73, No. 2 (February, 1985), pp. 46–49.

    This article is a special report on unique efforts in cultivating ongoing frachisor–franchisee relationships. Numerous franchises are used as examples of franchise advisory councils, regional and national seminars, and other formalized ways of structuring the relationship.

O'Donnell, Thomas. "No Entrepreneurs Need Apply." *Forbes*, Vol. 134, No. 13 (December 3, 1984), pp. 124–130.

    Some of the typical problems between franchisees and franchisors are examined with recent examples from the "real world."

CASE 6

Al's Car-Care
Evaluating a franchise opportunity

During most of his college career, Al Mendez had taken a full academic load. However, during the current semester he had reduced his class schedule to a part-time level in order to work as the manager of a local car-care business operating as a Tidy Car franchise. The prospects for this business seemed so attractive that Al was giving some thought to obtaining his own franchise for another area of the city.

Al's Background and Personal Ambitions

Al was an enterprising young man who had earned most of his way through college. Some of his experience was entrepreneurial in nature. For example, he and his brother had contracted with the owner of an apartment house to perform all of the maintenance work for the apartment. By taking projects on a contract basis, he had been able to work efficiently and to earn a much higher hourly income than would have been possible in salaried employment.

Al was also an industrious student—earning mostly A's. In some classes, he had performed so well that, even as an undergraduate, he had been made a student assistant. In fact, he had been given responsibility for conducting some classes on his own for brief periods of time.

Another part of Al's experience was centered in leadership of youth activities in religious and camp settings. During two summers, for example, he worked in a youth camp, carrying responsibility for directing a major segment for the camp's activities.

Although Al expressed general confidence in entering business, he did admit to some concerns. He said:

> The concerns are a lack of experience with paperwork and not being able to afford an accountant right off. Also, I worry about the business involving a greater commitment than I want. That would mean becoming a workaholic, and I am trying to stay away from that. I easily fall into that trap.

Although Al had taken a number of college courses in business, he had not majored in business. Some of his business education had been acquired through personal study outside formal classes. Al explained his informal pattern of study as follows:

> I've always studied textbooks on the side. I didn't want to waste time getting a degree in business when I was going to end up being in my own business where I wouldn't have to impress anyone with a degree. As long as I could acquire the knowledge, I didn't care about the grades. Generally, when I got as much as I

wanted to learn, I'd end up with an A. But I didn't learn as much as I wanted to. It's been mainly just learning on my own.

During his college years, Al had given considerable thought to the possibility of getting into business for himself. As he expressed it, "I wanted to be my own boss." Working for others had been generally harmonious, but he had at times experienced dissatisfaction. Speaking of certain people he had worked for, he said: "I get frustrated a little bit at their incompetence. Sometimes it relates to things I have already learned. If they haven't learned it yet and they are supposed to be teaching me, I figure this just isn't the place I'm supposed to be."

Al's Problem of Priorities

Al had completed most of his bachelor's degree program at a nearby liberal arts college and could finish his program by taking one additional semester on a full-time basis. If he continued to manage the present franchise, he could finish in two semesters. If he were to take his own franchise, he would need to drop out of school until he could get the business established.

Part of the problem involved in combining a new franchise of his own with a continuation of his education lay in the location of the available franchise. It was located approximately 50 to 75 miles from his college. The distance involved would make it difficult to be at his best in both endeavors. Even after he started his own franchise, he would need to limit his further study to a part-time basis.

How a Tidy Car Franchise Operated

The Tidy Car franchise provided a protective finish to the exterior of automobiles. The finish was a silicone rather than an ordinary wax, and it was guaranteed to last for as long as the owner kept the car. It was applied by an orbital applicator developed by the same company. The applicator had two rotating heads that vibrated at the same time. An ordinary buffer would spin and could burn the paint. However, the orbital applicator would stop if too much pressure was applied. It heated sufficiently to establish the bond between the paint and the preservative finish, but not so much that it damaged the paint. Al planned to charge $114 for the exterior finish, and he would be charged a franchise fee of $2 for each such job.

The franchisor had also developed a product for preserving the interior finish of the car's upholstery. The upholstery was first cleaned with a dry cleaning process, and then a protective coating was applied. After the coating was applied, liquids which were spilled would not stain the fabric but could be easily removed. This coating, like the exterior finish, was designed to last as long as the owner kept the automobile.

Franchises were issued on the basis of one franchise for each area with a population of 20,000. The available franchise that Al was considering was located in an affluent area of the city. It seemed to Al that people living there, especially those who owned such cars as Porsches and Audis, would be willing to pay for proper car care.

In contrast to a franchised operation, Al had also given some thought to operating a "detail" shop which would give various types of car care— reupholstering, reshining rims, cleaning engines, or other treatments related to the surface of automobiles. He would simply try to operate as an "appearance specialist." However, he assumed that the franchise would offer credibility and an advertising program that he could use. Also, Al was impressed with the quality of the products that had been developed by the Tidy Car organization.

How Al Could Become a Franchisee

The cost of starting as a Tidy Car franchisee would run as much as $5,000. This amount included $1,400 for the orbital applicator, a vacuum cleaner, and an inventory of supplies. Al thought that he could obtain the necessary capital.

Two ways of conducting the business were possible: to operate as a mobile unit or to establish a central business shop. Al would need to own a van, small truck, or other vehicle if he were to operate as a mobile unit. The equipment could be carried in the trunk of a car, so there were no necessary large investment costs involved for transportation. Al already owned a car that could be used for this purpose or be traded for one slightly more suitable. Establishing a central business shop, on the other hand, would entail much more operating expense. In the long run, however, a suitable location would give the business a measure of credibility.

In the short run, Al thought he could begin by keeping his investment at a minimum if he operated a mobile unit. He felt that such a venture would involve very little overhead and had the possibility of producing many thousands of dollars in profits. Prospects were attractive for getting contracts with auto rental organizations and other businesses having many autos to maintain. Al thought he might be able to earn as much as $6,000 per month by employing 3 persons. Obviously this was an optimistic estimate. Much of the business would be generated by recommendations of satisfied customers, and Al planned to stress quality to the point that his work produced many referrals.

Questions

1. Evaluate Al Mendez's potential for successful entrepreneurship. What are his greatest strengths? What are his most crucial weaknesses?
2. Evaluate the prospects for Al as a Tidy Car franchisee.
3. In this case, what are the relative merits of acquiring a franchise in contrast to going into business on his own? Which alternative would you recommend?
4. What additional steps do you recommend that Al should take before he commits himself to this franchise?
5. How should Al resolve the conflict between the exciting prospects for a successful business venture and his own educational program?

7

Selecting a Location and Physical Facilities

Figure 7-1   Bakery Becomes Manufacturing Site

©1984 Randa Bishop

Four entrepreneurs have used an old bakery building to house their manufacturing operation which produces medical testing kits. The beautiful tile walls and maple floors attracted the partners to the Portland, ME facility but their chief criteria were "a cheap location that would have a reputable medical center, proximity to Boston, good transportation, and an attractive quality of life...." At first they only rented 2,700 square feet of the 80,000 square foot bakery.

Source: Reprinted from the December, 1984 issue of *Venture*, The Magazine for Entrepreneurs, by special permission. © 1984 Venture Magazine, Inc., 521 Fifth Ave., New York, NY 10175.

Looking Ahead

Watch for the following important topics:

1. Considerations in choosing a location.
2. Sources of information about locations.
3. Spatial, functional, and structural requirements for the building housing the business.
4. Efficient layouts for small factories and retail stores.
5. Equipment and tooling needs of small factories and retail stores.

Every business needs a base of operations, be it a million-dollar plant or just a suitcase. The emergence of a business facility should be more than a chance happening. Locating and designing the physical facility deserve careful analysis. Although individual venture circumstances will determine the eventual business location and facility design, most entrepreneurs can benefit from evaluating certain factors that commonly influence decisions about these matters. These factors are discussed in this chapter.

IMPORTANCE OF A WELL-CHOSEN LOCATION

For most small businesses, a location decision is made only when the business is first established or purchased. Occasionally, however, a business considers relocation to reduce operating costs, get closer to its customers, or gain other advantages. Also, as a business expands, it sometimes becomes desirable to begin additional operations at other locations. The owner of a custom drapery shop, for example, may decide to open a second unit in another section of the same city or even in another city.

It is not the frequency but the lasting effects of location decisions that make them so important. Once the business is established, it is costly and often impractical, if not impossible, to "pull up stakes" and move. If the business depends upon a heavy flow of customer traffic, a shrewdly selected site that produces maximum sales will increase profits throughout its existence at that location. In contrast, a site with light traffic will reduce sales volume throughout the life of the business. If the choice is particularly poor, the business may never be able to "get off the ground," even with adequate financing and superior ability in purchasing and selling merchandise. This enduring effect is so clearly recognized by national chain-store organizations that they spend thousands of dollars investigating sites before establishing new stores.

The choice of a location is much more vital to some businesses than to others. For example, the site chosen for a dress shop can make or break it. In contrast, the exact location of a painting contractor is of relatively minor importance. Even painting contractors, however, may suffer from certain locational disadvantages. All cities have buildings that need painting, but property is kept in better repair and painted more frequently in some communities than in others.

CONSIDERATIONS IN SELECTING A LOCATION

It is possible that more than one location is satisfactory. An automobile garage may do an equal amount of business at either of two corner buildings. On the other hand, many undesirable locations appear satisfactory on the surface. Only careful investigation will reveal the good and bad features of any particular location.

General Considerations

Large business firms have professionally qualified personnel whose analysis and advice are invaluable in evaluating prospective locations. In contrast, the small-business entrepreneur must personally do the major part of the investigational work. Four general factors are important in this investigation. These factors are: personal preference, environmental conditions, resource availability, and customer accessibility. In a particular situation, one factor may have a stronger pull than the others, but each always has an influence. These factors and their impact on location decisions are depicted in Figure 7–2. Notice that the compass needle is influenced by all four factors, moving restlessly and unable to point to the best location until specific venture circumstances are provided.

Personal Preference   All too often, a prospective entrepreneur considers only the home community for locating the business. Frequently, the possibility of locating elsewhere never enters one's mind. Home community preference, of course, is not the only personal factor influencing location. The owner may, for example, wish to locate in an area of the country that offers warm weather, fishing opportunities, or a desired religious or social atmosphere.

Choosing one's hometown for personal reasons is not necessarily an illogical decision. In fact, there are certain advantages. For one thing, the individual generally accepts and appreciates the atmosphere of the home community, whether it is a small town or a large city. From a practical business standpoint, the entrepreneur can more easily establish credit. The hometown banker can be dealt with more confidently, and other business-

Figure 7-2 Location Compass for a Small Business

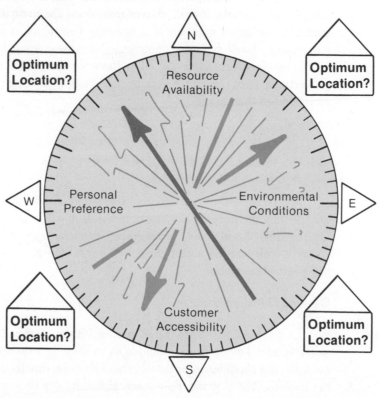

persons may be of great service in helping evaluate a given opportunity. If customers come from the same locality, the prospective entrepreneur would probably have a better idea of their tastes and peculiarities than an outsider would have. Relatives and friends may also be one's first customers and may help to advertise one's services. The establishment of a beauty shop in the home community would illustrate a number of these advantages.

Personal preferences, however, should not be allowed to cancel out location weaknesses even though such preferences may logically be a primary factor. Just because an individual has always lived in a given town does not automatically make it a satisfactory business location!

Environmental Conditions   A small business must operate within the environmental conditions of its location. These conditions can hinder or promote success. For example, weather is an environmental factor which has traditionally influenced location decisions. In recent years the harsh winters of the northern United States have moved businesses further south. One business owner justifies his preference for a southern coastal state by saying, "You can swim in December, pick oranges virtually year-round, and go to the beach on your lunch hour."[1] Other environmental conditions, such as competition, laws, and citizens' attitudes, to name a few, are all part of the business environment. The time to evaluate all these environmental conditions is prior to making a location decision.

Resource Availability   Resources associated with the location site and the ongoing operation of a business are an important factor to consider when selecting a location. Land, water supply, labor supply, and waste disposal are just a few of the many site-related resources that have a bearing on site costs.

Raw materials and labor supply are particularly critical considerations to the location of a manufacturing business. A wholesale business is also dependent on a convenient location to receive the goods for redistribution to its customers. The location compass in Figure 7–3 symbolizes the prominent role of resource availability to manufacturers and wholesalers. The compass needle has settled considerably and now points in one general direction—a

Figure 7–3   Location Compass for a Small Manufacturing/Wholesaling Business

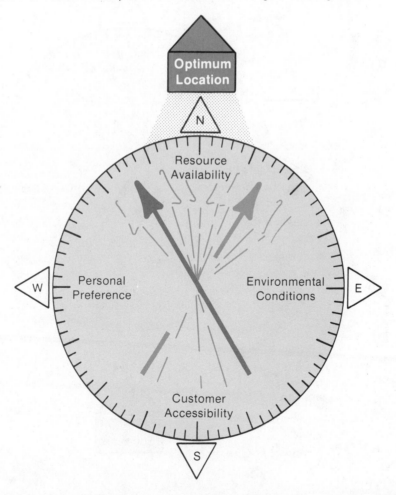

location that favors resource availability. However, personal preference or environmental conditions may exert a stronger influence on the final location decision and thus sacrifice some resource advantage.

Customer Accessibility   Sometimes the foremost consideration in selecting a location is customer accessibility. Retail outlets and service firms are typical examples of businesses that must be located conveniently to customers. Figure 7–4 shows the compass needle settling in the general direction of the customer-accessibility variable, reflecting its importance in locating service/ retail businesses. Once again, the precise location may be influenced more strongly by the variables of personal preference or environmental conditions.

Figure 7–4   Location Compass for a Small Service/Retail Business

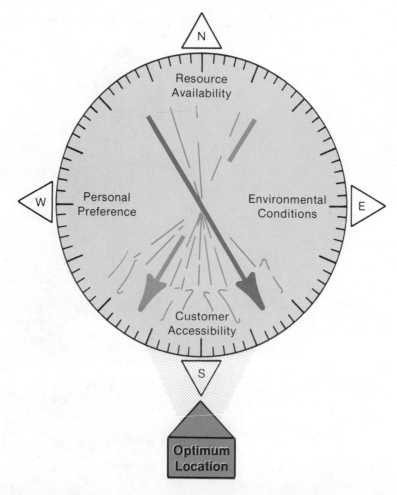

Specific Considerations in Evaluating Geographical Locations

For some businesses—a barbershop or drugstore, for example—the choice of a geographical area is simple. These businesses can operate successfully in most areas of the country. Personal preference is their major consideration. Other types of small businesses, however, need to analyze the problem of geographical location with extreme care. Their location decision need not be played entirely by chance as in the Monopoly game in Figure 7–5. A logical step-by-step process in evaluating the region, city, or actual site for the business can aid the entrepreneur in making this decision.

Figure 7–5   Location Decisions Based on Chance

"I'm putting two hotels on Park Place, a house on Boardwalk and a McDonald's on Marvin Gardens."

Source: *The Saturday Evening Post*, Vol. 253, No. 3 (April, 1981), p. 38. Reprinted with permission from The Saturday Evening Post Company, © 1981.

Choice of Region   Some markets for goods and services are restricted to certain regions. The following examples will make this point clear:

1. A ski lodge is practical only in an area with slopes and snow.
2. A boat repair service must locate near the water.
3. Stores selling home air conditioners have a larger market potential in the southern states than in the northern states.
4. Subcontractors to aircraft manufacturers produce parts for use in nearby production plants.

Several basic considerations that enter into evaluations concerning a regional choice, particularly for manufacturing businesses, are: nearness to the market, availability of raw materials, and adequacy of labor supply.[2]

Nearness to the Market   Locating near the center of the market is clearly desirable if other factors are approximately equal. This is especially true of industries in which the cost of shipping the finished product is high relative to its value. For example, bricks and soft drinks require production facilities that are close to the consuming markets. And even though toy manufacturers are able to serve both national and international markets, they must think in terms of their heaviest concentration of customer orders.

Availability of Raw Materials   If the raw materials required by the business are not abundantly available throughout the country, then the region in which these materials abound would offer locational advantages. Bulky or heavy raw materials that lose much of their bulk or weight in the manufacturing process are powerful forces that affect location. The sawmill is an example of a plant which must stay close to its raw materials in order to operate economically.

ACTION REPORT
Exceptions to the Rule

The personal preferences of an entrepreneur can sometimes overshadow location considerations, such as being near your customers. The Western Fair, founded by Judge R. W. Hailey, who is now deceased, is an excellent example of how there are exceptions to every rule.

The Fair is a specialty western store located in Lott, TX, a small town of around 900 people. The store's appeal to high-quality merchandise at a low price brings customers from all over the U.S. Some days Lott will see five or six times its population in the Western Fair store. The outside appearance of the store is plain and the inside is stacked with merchandise.

The owner's grandson, Bert Hailey, manages the store, which has grown from a sales volume in 1956 of $750,000 to $5.5 million in 1985. Bert concedes that their operation isn't always run by the textbook, but things have seemed to work out okay.

Source: Personal conversation with Dr. Helen Ligon, daughter of the Western Fair founder.

Adequacy of Labor Supply   A manufacturer's labor requirements depend upon the nature of its production process. In some cases the need is for semiskilled or unskilled labor, and the problem is to locate in a surplus labor area. Other firms find it desirable to seek a pool of highly skilled labor—the highly skilled machine trade of New England is a well-known example of such a labor supply. In addition, wage rates, labor productivity, and a history of peaceful industrial relations are particularly important considerations for labor-intensive firms. Information about these factors is readily available. *Inc.* magazine, for example, publishes an annual report which ranks the 50 states on several factors, including labor, which contribute to location decisions.[3]

Choice of City   For several decades many cities have tried to attract new industry. Much of this effort has been directed toward obtaining new manufacturing plants, but other types of business are welcomed also. In the last few years, however, the drive for environmental protection and the emphasis on the quality of life for residents have led some cities to reduce or abandon their attempts. This seems especially true where suburban, rather than central-city, locations are contemplated.

ACTION REPORT
Going to the Labor

In certain manufacturing industries, labor is the most critical factor. This is particularly true where raw materials and the finished product can be transported easily. Pencils and pens, for example, are transported with little difficulty. Therefore, a pencil and pen factory can be located with labor as the prominent consideration.

The Blackfeet Indian Writing Company in Browning, MT, provides 300,000 pencils and 100,000 ballpoint pens each day to office-supply dealers in all 50 states. This business is located in a 1.5 million-acre reservation adjoining Canada.

The entrepreneurial force behind the business is Chief Earl Old Person. He says, "The tribe has oil and gas resources, but unemployment is chronic...We are trying to market their skills." The pencil factory is a business where "the work is labor-intensive...and a labor force was available."

Source: "We Want Your Business, Not Help," *Nation's Business*, Vol. 69, No. 1 (January, 1981), p. 16.

Growth or Decline of a City   Some cities are on the upgrade. They are growing in both population and business activity, and the income levels of their citizens are advancing. In contrast, other cities are expanding slowly or even declining in population. Economic factors, such as shifts in markets, technological changes, and transportation advantages, apparently favor some cities at the expense of others.[4]

Extent of Local Competition   Most small businesses are concerned about the nature and the amount of local competition. Manufacturers who serve a national market are an exception to this rule, and there are perhaps others. But overcrowding can occur in the majority of small-business fields. The quality of competition also affects the desirability of a location. If existing businesses are not aggressive and do not offer the type of service reasonably expected by the customer, there is likely to be room for a newcomer.

Published data can sometimes be used to shed light upon this particular problem. The average population required to support a given type of business can frequently be determined on a national or a regional basis. By comparing the situation in the given city with these averages, it is possible to get a better picture of the intensity of local competition.

Unfortunately, objective data of this type seldom produce unequivocal answers. The population's income level and nearness to other shopping centers might account for certain discrepancies. There is no substitute for personal observation. In addition, the entrepreneur will do well to seek the opinion of those well acquainted with local business conditions. Wholesalers frequently have an excellent notion of the potential for additional retail establishments in a given line of business.

Other Factors   As in the choice of region, the supply of skilled labor may be a significant factor in the choice of city. The city of Portsmouth, OH, has an adequate supply of skilled shoe workers, while Detroit and Flint in Michigan have a large pool of auto workers. The prevailing wage scale is particularly important for manufacturers competing with other firms who have lower wage costs.

The amount and the character of industry in a given city are likewise significant. A one-industry town is often subject to severe seasonal and cyclical business fluctuations in contrast to a city of diversified industries. In addition, the necessary customers and suppliers of essential services should be available.

Local government can help or hinder a new business. In choosing a city, the prospective entrepreneur should be assured of satisfactory police and fire protection, streets, water and other utilities, street drainage, and public transportation. Unreasonably high local taxes or severely restrictive local ordinances are to be avoided.

Finally, the city might also qualify with respect to civic, cultural, religious, and recreational affairs that make it a better place in which to live and do business.

Choice of Actual Site   After the entrepreneur chooses a region and a city in which to locate, the next step is to select a specific site for the business. Some critical factors to consider at this stage include costs, customer accessibility, amount of customer traffic, neighborhood conditions, and the trend toward suburban development.

Costs   Some firms stress the operating costs and purchasing costs associated with a specific business site. Examples of these firms are most manufacturers, wholesalers, bookkeeping services, plumbing contractors, and painting contractors. It would be foolish for these firms to pay high rent for locations in central business districts. However, other types of businesses are finding that downtown business locations are a good buy. Several states are encouraging downtown revitalization plans by funding programs which provide low interest rate loans and special investment tax credits.[5]

Cost considerations have attracted some firms to what are called incubator facilities. Small-business incubators, located in many different areas of the country, provide physical space by allowing small-business tenants to lease a small area of a large building. In addition, they provide a range of services such as assistance in obtaining loans, accounting services, and secretarial help. These incubators are both publicly and privately sponsored. By reducing initial operational costs, the new enterprise is in a reduced-risk environment. It was estimated that over 150 of these facilities would be operational by 1986.[6]

Customer Accessibility   Earlier we recognized customer accessibility as a general consideration in selecting a location. This factor becomes even more critical when evaluating a specific site for certain retail stores. For example, a shoe store or a drugstore may fail simply because it is on the wrong side of the street. On the other hand, a store that sells a specialty good—such as pianos—has greater freedom in selecting a site. Furthermore, some restaurants have achieved such distinction that customers drive for miles to patronize them in spite of their relatively inaccessible locations.

Unless one has a product or a service sufficiently powerful to attract the customer, however, one must locate where the customer wants to buy. In the case of motels and service stations, this means a location convenient to many motorists. For clothing stores and variety stores, it probably means a suburban shopping center location. For some drugstores and food stores, it means a location in or close to the residential areas.

Amount of Customer Traffic   Customer traffic is recognized and discussed more frequently than it is measured. To make a count of pedestrian traffic, the investigator is stationed in front of the potential site and records the number of passersby. This may be done at alternate half-hour intervals during the day for enough different days to get a representative sample of the traffic. The results should be compared with the amount of traffic at other available sites and at sites known to be successful. Naturally, the traffic must also be evaluated carefully to tell whether it includes prospective customers for the particular business. A ladies' shoe store, for example, will profit little from a high flow of pedestrian traffic that is primarily male.

Of course, other factors in addition to amount of traffic must be taken into consideration. The general location must be in keeping with the prestige of the product or service. Business neighbors may likewise contribute to making a given site either desirable or undesirable. To illustrate, a high-class restaurant generally could not successfully locate in a low-income neighborhood. Neither would it locate next to a laundry.

Neighborhood Conditions   We pointed out earlier that certain cities are on the decline while others are growing more or less rapidly. What is true of cities is also true of sections within cities. City growth occurs in a given direction, and that section thrives as a result of the development. Older sections of the city are blighted and display the picture of a past more prosperous than their present. Small retail firms and, to some extent, small service businesses must consider this factor in the selection of a business site. However, since blight can be eliminated, the small retailer should also consider the impact of urban renewal programs on site values in or close to renewal areas.

ACTION REPORT
Not a Nice Neighborhood, But It's Home

Ed Alago is the founder of Alago Sales and Manufacturing Corporation which sells panel-cutting machines produced in its Brooklyn plant. Ed grew up in the Williamsburg neighborhood where his company is located. Many businesses have moved out of the area because of crime. A New York City detective, Nelson Arroyo, describes the area of Ed's business this way:

> We have lots of junkies and robberies around here, and many homicides as well...He (Ed) knows the score, and he's a survivor. He lets people know that they can't mess with him and get away with it. No one is going to make him move his company.

One incident referred to by detective Arroyo involved a "punk" who broke into Ed's car which was parked in front of his business. Ed and an employee chased him down the street. After a few knocks on the thief's head, he was released to never bother them again. Ed, who is Puerto Rican-born, describes the incident just as "a typical business day." For Ed it's personal preference which dictates his company's location.

Source: Reprinted with permission, *Inc.* magazine, July, 1984. Copyright © 1984 by Inc. Publishing Company, 38 Commercial Wharf, Boston, MA 02110.

Suburban Development   The trend toward suburban shopping centers has been an impressive development of recent decades. Increasing suburban population, greater use of the family car, traffic congestion and lack of parking space downtown, and other factors have contributed to the relative decline of central business district activity in many cities. Suburbanites who find it difficult or unpleasant to shop downtown turn to shopping centers located nearer the residential areas.

This shift in business has created problems in the downtown area, as well as offered opportunities in the suburbs. For the small retail business, an opportunity is often presented by the shopping center or other suburban location that has a greater future than a downtown spot.

Significant Considerations for Special Types of Small Businesses

Small wholesalers, retailers, service firms, and manufacturers face the same sequence of location choices as to region, city, and actual site. For each of these types of businesses, however, certain factors are more significant than others.

The Small Wholesaler   Perhaps the most significant geographical consideration for the small wholesaler and the industrial distributor is the selection of a city. The wholesaler of consumer goods is particularly interested in the volume of retail sales, both for the separate lines of goods that will be sold and for the total. Certain cities serve as wholesaling centers, and the wholesaler's market includes not only the central city but also the surrounding towns. The small wholesaler must discover which city is the wholesaling center and measure the intensity of local competition in considering any given city.

In addition, specialized types of wholesalers perform functions that dictate particular locations. For example, a resident buyer of clothing must locate in a major city, but an assembler of farm products must locate in a rural area.

Small wholesalers considering specific sites for their warehouses often must choose between locations within and outside the central wholesale district. The warehouses should be near the center of the trading area to be served, while remaining accessible to highways and railways. Locations within the central wholesale district command higher rent or provide less space for a given amount of rent. Locations outside the district, but still accessible to railways and highways and having suitable loading and unloading facilities, will often mean lower rent, more space, lower operating expenses, and faster deliveries—and possibly newer and more attractive quarters and parking facilities (see Figure 7-6).

Figure 7–6   Wholesaler's Business Location

The Small Retailer   The suburban areas of cities provide excellent opportunities for many small retailers. In contrast, the older areas of a city are generally less preferable than the new, expanding areas. The retailer's specific site must attract the customers who patronize it, and parking facilities must be adequate.[7] In reference to a retail automotive parts store, Samuel Downey, chief executive officer of Downey Automotive Inc., in Chattanooga, TN, says:

> Every store should be on the going-home side of traffic flow. People buy auto parts in the afternoon, on the way home from work. And in residential areas, free-standing buildings are best—they're conspicuous. We also try to be near our competition. People have to see the difference in us.[8]

Each individual form of retailing has unique location problems. The special location considerations pertinent to restaurants are shown in Figure 7–7.

The Small Service Firm   The location problem of most small service firms is much like that of small retailers. A convenient location is imperative, except in the case of those firms that can build reputations for such high-quality or unique service that customers will seek them out. For example, barbershops, beauty shops, and photographic studios are visited by their customers and

Figure 7-7   A Summary of Special Location Problems for a Restaurant

---

Picking a Location

It has been said that being at the right place at the right time is essential to success. That certainly applies to the selection of a restaurant site. However, finding the right place requires considerable study. Much time should be devoted to the search since, in the final analysis, the restaurant isn't likely to prove any better than its location.

A wise person doesn't open a restaurant in the first vacant building discovered. All the factors affecting restaurant location must be weighed and analyzed. First, the prospective restaurant owner usually decides the kind of eating establishment he or she prefers to operate. Attention should be turned to the neighborhood desired. What is its character? Is it a business locality? Industrial? Residential? Is it on the way up?

Studying the Neighborhood

Many conditions that might appear comparatively unimportant can have a great influence on successful restaurant operation. For instance:

- Neighborhoods should be avoided if they harbor loafers, have an unpleasant odor, or are noisy. Restaurants seldom are popular when located in or near undertaking homes, hospitals, or cemeteries. In addition, churches and schools do not make good restaurant neighbors. They may alter conditions or liquor licenses and quite often cause congestion on the sidewalks, noise, or other disturbing factors.
- Parking facilities are a factor, too. A water hydrant at the front of a restaurant prevents parking, slows down food deliveries, and is very often responsible for puddles of water and congestion near the entrance. On the other hand, value may be increased immeasurably by such a simple thing as an abutting alley. The alley will provide delivery facilities not always available on the thoroughfare.
- Competition must be studied. Is there ample opportunity for the business in the area, or is it already overcrowded with eating places? Are the other restaurants making a profit? What is their history? To determine whether the area can use another eating place, it is necessary to ascertain the success of existing places and the types of patronage they are receiving. And it is wise to know whether or not the community is growing.
- It will be important to know the population in surrounding businesses, hotels, apartments, and the like. Changing conditions in the area will have a bearing on the value of the location. Just as construction work in the neighborhood causes traffic congestion that often temporarily drives away business, so new buildings on the opposite side of the street may deprive a restaurant of customers. It is a fact that the general public favors the side of the street having new buildings.
- Being on a busy thoroughfare often enhances the value of a restaurant, but value of the traffic cannot always be determined by counting the people as they pass. It is necessary to know where the traffic is going and the type of persons riding. Many people may pass the restaurant, but the type of eating place planned may not necessarily appeal to sufficient numbers of them.

Figure 7–7 (Continued)

- The new restaurant must be planned to suit the pocketbooks and the likes and dislikes of its potential customers, for the people who live and work around it are the ones who will eventually decide whether it is to succeed. The new restaurant owner will want to know where the customers come from, the kind of transportation they will use, what they will want to eat, how much they will be willing to spend, group potential, whether they will want quality or quantity, and types of service to be offered.
- If the location is in a residential section, the prospective restaurant owner must realize that luncheon trade will be light and should consider evening trade. The very nature of the neighborhood will determine whether customers will come in singly, in couples, or in family groups. Such information may be obtained through talks with other persons operating small-business houses in the area or with some of the older and representative residents of the neighborhood.
- A restaurant located in an industrial area presents a special problem. Since much of its business will stem from the surrounding plants, it will be necessary to know whether the plants operate their own lunchrooms, how many persons they employ, the hours they work, and the percentage of persons who bring their own lunch. The type of work the employees do and the wages they receive will have much to do with the kind of food they want and the amount of money they will be willing to spend on their meals. Here, of course, a convenient location is vital as workers will not travel far for the noon meal. Also, in an industrial neighborhood the problem is to serve large portions at a reasonable figure. The best source of information will be the workers themselves. Why not ask them?
- Regardless of the type of eating place, good transportation facilities are of prime importance. A corner location at intersecting public transportation lines may attract persons leaving buses or waiting to board them.
- A roadside restaurant or cafe has still other problems. It should be on a main highway, preferably just on the outskirts of a city. Plenty of parking space should be provided, and the place should have an attractive exterior if it is to catch the eye.
- It is important to keep in mind that the restaurant should be in a neighborhood adequately supplied with gas, electricity, or other forms of fuel and water.

Source: Adapted from the National Cash Register Company, Merchants Service Department, *Success in the Restaurant Business,* undated pamphlet, pp. 16–17.

must be located conveniently for them. On the other hand, plumbers or television repairers are seldom visited by customers. Calls for their services are typically received by telephone. Consequently, such firms can be located in their owners' homes or in some low-rent area. Their location problem is more cost-oriented than customer-oriented.

The Small Manufacturer   While costs are an important location factor even for the small retail business, they are the very crux of the problem for the cost-oriented small manufacturer. This means that the small manufacturer should analyze the major cost factors on a comparative basis. Figure 7–8 shows the major cost factors to be analyzed. For any one business, however, other significant costs may require serious study.[9] The small manufacturer must recognize that the process of cost comparison and analysis can become extremely involved and difficult. Some location problems are sufficiently complex as to justify the use of professional help.

Figure 7–8   Manufacturer's Comparative Cost Analysis Form

MANUFACTURER'S COMPARATIVE COST ANALYSIS FORM			
Cost Element	Location A	Location B	Location C

MATERIALS
  Raw Materials
  Fuels			

OPERATING COSTS
  Labor
  Rent (or Depreciation)
  Power and Heat
  Other Utilities
  Insurance			

TAXES
  Property
  Income
  Payroll
  Other			

TRANSPORTATION
  Raw Materials
  Finished Goods			

Sources of Information about Locations

A knowledge of local business conditions and the history of given sites makes certain sources especially valuable in the choice of a business location. Some of these sources are:

1. *Bankers.* The contribution of bankers would be rather limited in the case of a business whose choice must be based on differences in costs and who has technical operating requirements. Many banks do have real estate departments that provide advice on proper locations.

2. *Chambers of commerce.* Although chambers of commerce may tend to oversell locations in the hope of attracting business, they can be of substantial aid in recommending desirable sites.

3. *Wholesalers and manufacturers.* With their experience and knowledge of the way products are currently marketed in a given location, wholesalers and manufacturers often know whether there is room for another aggressive business in a given line.

4. *Trade associations.* In a specific line of business, trade associations can often furnish valuable advice because of their close contact with and study of its peculiar problems.

5. *Government agencies.* The field offices of the Department of Commerce and the Small Business Administration can suggest an optimum location or provide leads that the prospective entrepreneur may follow up.

6. *Industrial parks.* The industrial park is a different type of source from those listed above. It is somewhat similar to an apartment building, with facilities and equipment already installed. A small manufacturing-type business may be able to occupy a unit of the industrial park without incurring excessive costs for street paving, sewage systems, building design and construction, railroad sidings, and the like.

7. *Professional area development groups.* More than 7,000 of these groups now operate in the United States. They provide information on wage and tax rates and help contact the "right people" for location information.[10]

8. *Railroads and power companies.* The typical data obtainable from these sources include (a) the cost and availability of raw materials; (b) available transportation and communication facilities in the area; (c) type, condition, and cost of buildings on given sites; (d) land costs; (e) adequacy of water, power, and fuel supplies; (f) size and skill level of the labor force; (g) existing tax rates, labor laws, and laws and ordinances regulating business activity; and (h) market possibilities.

THE BUILDING AND ITS LAYOUT

Starting a new business usually involves the purchase or lease of an existing building.[11] Only in rare cases would a new building need to be designed and constructed for a beginning business. Although buying an existing building has its advantages, it is often desirable for the new business to rent building space. Assuming suitable rented space is available, the entrepreneur would gain the following advantages by leasing:

1. A large cash outlay is avoided. This is extremely important for the new small firm, which typically lacks adequate financial resources.

2. Risk is reduced by avoiding substantial investment and by postponing commitments for building space until the success of the business is assured and the nature of building requirements is better known.

The suitability of the building would depend upon the spatial, functional, and structural requirements of the business being contemplated. Similarly, an efficient layout of the physical facilities would depend to a considerable extent upon the type of business.

Spatial Requirements

When planning the initial building requirements, the entrepreneur must avoid commitments for a building space that is too large or too luxurious. At the same time, the space should not be too small or too austere for efficient operation. Buildings do not produce profits directly. They merely house the operations and personnel which produce the profits. Therefore, the ideal building is practical but not pretentious. Many times the entrepreneur's home is the base of operations. It is estimated that more than ten million U.S. homes serve as headquarters for businesses.[12]

The amount of space required varies with both the type and size of business. The number of employees is one index of business size. Obviously a business employing 50 people will need more space than one employing 5 or 10. As to type of business, a drugstore requires less space than a furniture store because the latter must display heavy, bulky items. Similarly, a jewelry store requires less space than a supermarket.

Functional Requirements

The general suitability of a building for a given type of business operation relates to its functional character. For example, the floor space of a restaurant should normally be on one level. Other important factors to consider are the shape, age, and condition of the building; fire hazards; heating and air conditioning; lighting and restroom facilities; and entrances and exits. Obviously, these factors carry different weights for a factory operation as compared with a wholesale or retail operation. In any case, the comfort, convenience, and safety of employees and customers of the business must not be overlooked.

A desirable building should also have adequate aisles, traffic lanes, elevators, and stairs (or escalators) for moving customers and merchandise in the store or raw materials and goods-in-process in the factory. The internal transportation of merchandise or raw materials requires platforms and ramps for the loading and unloading of trucks. Chutes or conveyors may also be

ACTION REPORT
Beginning in the Basement

A new business must locate in an affordable building. Initial facilities are often makeshift and barely adequate. But with growth, building space can be improved.

Micro-Term, Inc., is a firm which was started in 1976 in the basement of a rented house. The founders—Robert Morley, David Scharon, and Thomas Monsees—were Washington University students who designed and built a homemade computer terminal to assist them in their class work. Instructors and fellow students were impressed with the terminal, so Morley, Scharon, and Monsees began producing and selling terminals.

By the end of the summer of 1976, the entrepreneurs had produced and delivered 50 computer terminals from the basement factory. This location soon proved too small, however, and the company eventually moved to a 33,000-square-foot production facility. By 1981, these quarters housed 95 full-time employees producing 1,000 terminals a month.

Source: Del Marth, "A Terminal Was the Beginning," *Nation's Business*, Vol. 69, No. 6 (June, 1981), p. 86.

required to transport materials to the receiving room. Other internal transportation facilities include hand trucks, dollies, pipelines, conveyors, hoists, cranes, and forklift trucks (see Figure 7–9).

General-purpose buildings are preferable to buildings that have features which limit their resale value. Although some types of business require specialized buildings, most can operate efficiently in less specialized structures. A standard prefabricated building typically is better than a custom-designed building for a new firm.

Expansion possibilities should also be considered when making the original building plan. For example, a building might provide excellent expansion opportunities by having a temporary wall on the side where there is vacant land.

Structural Requirements

A structurally sound building with a traditional appearance could imply stability and conservatism. However, its architecture may identify it with a bygone era—a matter that is more or less serious depending upon the type of business. Customers and others may identify old-fashioned architecture with

Figure 7-9   Materials Handling Equipment

outmoded, inefficient management. Other things being equal, most businesses find that modernization is highly desirable.

Factory floors should be capable of supporting heavy equipment. Concrete floors are often used, but they are hard on the feet. Store floors may require appropriate special finishes or carpeting.

Interior load-bearing walls and supporting columns must be adequate to carry the necessary load. Attention to this feature is particularly important for factories and other firms using heavy machinery in the production process. However, freestanding walls are extensively used today—and their use facilitates changes in plant layout.

Layouts

Layout refers to the logical arrangement of physical facilities in order to provide efficiency of business operations. To provide a concise treatment of layouts, we will limit our discussion to two very different layout problems—

layout for manufacturers (whose primary concern is production operations) and layout for retailers (whose primary concern is customer traffic).

Factory Layout   The factory layout presents a three-dimensional space problem. Overhead space may be utilized for power conduits, pipelines for exhaust systems, and the like. A proper design of storage areas and handling systems makes use of space near the ceiling. Space must be allowed also for the unobstructed movement of machine parts from one location to another.

The ideal manufacturing process would have a straight-line, forward movement of materials from receiving room to shipping room. If this ideal cannot be realized for a given process, backtracking, sidetracking, and long hauls of materials can at least be minimized. This will reduce production delays.

Two contrasting types of layout are used in industrial firms. One of these is called **process layout** and has similar machines grouped together. Drill presses, for example, are separated from lathes in a machine shop layout. The alternative to such a process layout is called a **product layout**. This is used for continuous-flow, mass production—usually conveyorized, with all machines needed for balanced production located beside the conveyor. Thus, similar machines are used at the same points on the different conveyor lines set up to process a given product.

In smaller plants which operate on a job-lot basis, a product layout cannot be used because it demands too high a degree of standardization of both product and process. Thus, small machine shops are generally arranged on a process layout basis. Small firms with highly standardized products, such as dairies, bakeries, and car wash firms, can use a product layout.

Retail Store Layout   The objectives for a retail store layout differ from those for a factory layout. Among the goals of the small retailer is the proper display of merchandise to maximize sales. A second objective is customer convenience and service. Normally, the convenience and attractiveness of the surroundings contribute to a customer's continued patronage. An efficient layout also contributes to operating economy. A final objective is the protection of the store's equipment and merchandise. In achieving all these objectives, the flow of customer traffic must be anticipated and planned. The **grid pattern** and **free-flow pattern** of store layout are the two most widely used layout designs.[13]

The grid pattern is the plainer and block-looking layout typical of supermarkets and hardware stores. It provides more merchandise exposure and simplifies security and cleaning. The free-flow pattern makes less efficient use of space but has greater visual appeal and allows customers to move in any direction at their own speed. The free-flow patterns result in curving aisles and greater flexibility in merchandise presentation.

Many retailers use a **self-service layout** which permits customers direct access to the merchandise. Not only does self-service reduce the selling expense, but it also permits shoppers to examine the goods before buying. Today practically all food merchandising follows this principle.

Some types of merchandise—for example, ladies' hosiery, cigarettes, magazines, and candy—are often purchased on an *impulse* basis. *Impulse goods* should be placed at points where customers can see them easily. Products which the customers will buy anyway and for which they come in specifically may be placed in less conspicuous spots.

Various areas of a retail store differ markedly in sales value. Customers typically turn to the right upon entering a store, and so the *right front* space is the most valuable. The second most valuable are the *center front* and *right middle* spaces. One department store places high-margin gift wares, cosmetics, and jewelry in these areas. The third most valuable are the *left front* and *center middle* spaces. And the *left middle* space is fourth in importance. Since the back areas are the least important so far as space value is concerned, most service facilities and the general office typically are found in the rear of a store. Certainly the best space should be given to departments or merchandise producing the greatest sales and profits. Finally, the *first floor* has greater space value than a second or higher floor in a multistory building. Generally the higher the floor, the lower its selling value.

EQUIPMENT AND TOOLING

The final step in arranging for physical facilities involves the purchase or lease of equipment and tooling. Here again, the types of equipment and tooling required obviously depend upon the nature of the business. We will also limit our discussion of equipment needs to the two diverse fields of manufacturing and retailing. Of course, even within these two areas there is great variation in the needed tools and equipment.

Factory Equipment

Machines in the factory may be either general-purpose or special-purpose in character. *General-purpose equipment* for metalworking includes lathes, drill presses, and milling machines. In a woodworking plant, general-purpose machines include ripsaws, planing mills, and lathes. In each case, jigs, fixtures, and other tooling items set up on the basic machine tools can be changed so that two or more shop operations can be accomplished. Bottling machines and automobile assembly-line equipment are examples of *special-purpose equipment*.

Advantages of General-Purpose Equipment   General-purpose equipment requires a minimum investment and is well-adapted to a varied type of operation. Small machine shops and cabinet shops, for example, utilize this type of equipment. General-purpose equipment also contributes the necessary flexibility in industries where the product is so new that the technology has not yet been well-determined or where there are frequent design changes in the product.

Advantages of Special-Purpose Equipment   Special-purpose equipment permits cost reduction where the technology is fully established and where a capacity operation is more or less assured by high sales volume. The large-volume production of automobiles, for example, justifies special-purpose equipment costing hundreds of thousands of dollars. Not all special-purpose equipment is that expensive, however. Even though it is used most in large-scale industry, the same principle can be applied on a more modest scale in many small manufacturing plants. A milking machine in a dairy illustrates specialized equipment used by small firms. Nevertheless, a small firm cannot ordinarily and economically use special-purpose equipment unless it makes a highly standardized product on a fairly large scale.

Specialized machines using permanently set up special-purpose tooling result in greater output per machine-hour operated. Hence, the labor cost per unit of product is lower. However, the initial cost of such equipment and tooling is much higher, and its scrap value is little or nothing due to its highly specialized function.

Retail Store Equipment

Small retailers must have merchandise display counters, storage racks, shelving, mirrors, seats for customers, customer push carts, cash registers (see Figure 7–10), and various items necessary to facilitate selling. Such equipment may be costly but is usually less expensive than equipment for a factory operation.

If the store attempts to serve a high-income market, its fixtures typically should display the elegance and beauty expected by such customers. Polished mahogany and bronze fittings of showcases will lend a richness of atmosphere. Indirect lighting, thick rugs on the floor, and big easy chairs will also make a contribution to the air of luxury. In contrast, a store that caters to lower income brackets would find luxurious fixtures a handicap in building an atmosphere of low prices. Therefore, such a store should concentrate on simplicity.

Figure 7-10   Modern Check-Out Equipment

Automated Equipment

Automation has come into use to a limited extent in small-business operations. It is quite well-developed in some general-office operations. However, some persons say that it is too expensive for the small business. Others disagree, saying that automation can be used on a small scale as well as on a large scale.

In a small plant, the major barrier to automation is found in short production runs which do not require the automated process to be in action most of the time. But if a small plant produces a given product in large volume, with infrequent changes in design, the owner should seriously consider the many benefits derived from automation. Among these are:

1. Operator errors are minimized.
2. Processing costs are lowered by speed of operation and machine efficiency.
3. Human resources are conserved while personnel skill requirements are upgraded.
4. Safety of manufacturing and handling operations is promoted.

5. Inventory requirements tend to be reduced because of faster processing.
6. Maintenance and inspection are improved by incorporating lubrication systems and devices in the automatic transfer machine.

ACTION REPORT
Automation Keeps Company Competitive

Jimmy Herndon, age 36, began his textile company in 1978 in Charlotte, NC. He started with one knitting machine producing 300 yards of fabric a week. The machine was located in his apartment and was powered by a small generator. In 1980, he decided to produce fitted sheets made on a knitting machine. The automated machine he purchased necessitated a move to a 3,000 square feet plant.

Today, Herndon, who is black, has a booming almost-fully automated plant running "15 hours a day, five days a week, and half a day on Saturday. When I set up my operations, I wanted low overhead, as well as the capability to make the goods cheaper and faster," Herndon explains.

By taking advantage of up-to-date technology, Metrolina Knitting Mills is competing successfully with cheaper imported goods.

Source: Bea Quirk, "Getting the Edge over Textile Imports," *In Business*, Vol. 5, No. 3 (May–June, 1983), pp. 26–28. Used by permission of *In Business* magazine.

Looking Back

1. In a given business, one of the four general considerations in selecting a location may have the greatest influence. Personal preferences should not be allowed to cancel out a location's weaknesses. Environmental conditions should be evaluated prior to making a location decision. The availability of raw materials, labor supply, and other resources affects the ongoing operation of a business. Customer accessibility can be the foremost consideration in some situations.

   Evaluating a geographical location is a step-by-step process. First, the region must be examined, then the city, and finally the actual site.

   For small wholesalers/industrial distributors, perhaps the most significant geographical consideration is the selection of a city. Small retailers and service firms, as a general rule, must locate in a convenient and attractive site. Location problems for small manufacturers are cost-oriented.

2. Information about various locations is available through such sources as bankers, local chambers of commerce, wholesalers and manufacturers, trade associations, government agencies, industrial parks, professional area development groups, railroads, and power companies.

3. Building requirements depend upon the nature of the business. In most cases, a new business should plan to lease rather than to buy building space.

4. Proper layout of building space also depends upon the type of business. Manufacturing firms use layout patterns that facilitate production operations and provide for the efficient flow of materials. Retailers lay out building space in terms of customer needs and the flow of customer traffic.

5. Most small manufacturing firms use general-purpose equipment, although some have sufficient volume and a standardized operation which permit the use of special-purpose equipment. The type of equipment and tooling in retail firms should be related to the general level and type of the business.

DISCUSSION QUESTIONS

1. Is the hometown of the business owner likely to be a good location? Why? Is it logical for an owner to allow personal preference to influence the decision on a business location? Why?

2. For the five small businesses which you know best, would you say that their locations were based upon the evaluation of location factors, chance, or something else?

3. In the selection of a region, what types of businesses should place greatest emphasis upon (a) markets, (b) raw materials, and (c) labor? Explain.

4. How may one measure the extent of existing competition in a given city? How is the quality of pedestrian traffic measured?

5. In the choice of specific sites, what types of businesses must show the greatest concern with customer accessibility? Why?

6. How do site factors differ for a wholesaler and a retailer?

7. What are "backtracking" and "sidetracking" as they apply to factory layout and materials movement? Do they affect operating costs? If so, how?

8. When should the small manufacturer utilize process layout, and when product layout? Explain.

9. Discuss the conditions under which a new small manufacturer should buy general-purpose and special-purpose equipment.

10. Describe the unique problems concerning store layout and merchandise display that confront a new small jeweler.

ENDNOTES

1. Glenn R. Singer, "An Entrepreneurial Place in the Sun," *Venture*, Vol. 4, No. 10 (October, 1982), p. 41.

2. One study showing the principal importance of these factors is described in Roger Schmenner, "How Firms Set Sights on Sites," *Nation's Business*, Vol. 69, No. 11 (November, 1981), pp. 14A–18A.

3. See, for an example, Bruce G. Posner, "Report on the States," *Inc.*, Vol. 6, No. 10 (October, 1984), pp. 108–113.

4. For an interesting discussion of how many towns are developing reputations as hospitable places for small businesses, see Margaret Coffey, "Towns Entrepreneurs Love," *Venture*, Vol. 4, No. 3 (March, 1982), pp. 34–40.

5. A further discussion can be found in Jeffrey T. Darbee, Judith B. Williams, and Howard F. Wise, "Doing It Downtown," *In Business*, Vol. 6, No. 1 (January–February, 1984), pp. 42–45.

6. For an in-depth analysis of the small-business incubator, see David N. Allen and Syedur Rahman, "Small Business Incubators: A Positive Environment for Entrepreneurship," *Journal of Small Business Management*, Vol. 23, No. 3 (July, 1985), pp. 12–22.

7. A more complete treatment of location analysis for a retailer is provided in William R. Davidson, Daniel J. Sweeney, and Ronald W. Stampfl, *Retailing Management* (5th ed., New York: John Wiley and Sons, 1984), ch. 7.

8. Bradford W. Ketchum, Jr., "The Auto Man's Empire," *Inc.*, Vol. 4, No. 8 (August, 1982), p. 84.

9. See Gerald J. Karaska and David F. Bramhall, *Locational Analysis for Manufacturing* (Cambridge, MA: The M.I.T. Press, 1969); James H. Thompson, *Methods of Plant Site Selection Available to Small Manufacturing Firms* (Morgantown: West Virginia University, 1961).

10. For further discussion, see Ted M. Levine, "Outsiders Can Ease the Site Selection Process," *Harvard Business Review*, Vol. 59, No. 3 (May–June, 1981), pp. 12–16.

11. For more information on facilities planning including a lease versus buy numerical example, see Marita Thomas, "Facilities Planning, Evaluation and Acquisition for Smaller Corporations," *Inc.*, Vol. 6, No. 9 (September, 1984), pp. 111–134.

12. "Home-Based Business," *In Business*, Vol. 6, No. 1 (January–February, 1984), p. 4.

13. A detailed discussion of these two layout patterns can be found in J. Barry Mason, Morris L. Mayer, and Hazel F. Ezell, *Foundations of Retailing* (2d ed., Plano, TX: Business Publications, Inc., 1984), Ch. 6.

REFERENCES TO SMALL BUSINESS IN ACTION

Knight, James H. "Moving: People Were the Best Reason—and the Biggest Problem." *Inc.*, Vol. 3, No. 3 (March, 1981), pp. 116–120.
    Various labor-related considerations are discussed by the president of a company which relocated.

Paris, Ellen. "The Revenge of the Podmalls." *Forbes*, Vol. 136, No. 2 (July 15, 1985), p. 33.
A brief but informative article on the value of site locations in strip centers—podmalls.

Quirk, Beatrice Taylor. "Gaining a Stronghold in the Billion Dollar Video Industry." *In Business*, Vol. 4, No. 6 (November–December, 1982), pp. 39–43.
This article describes the personal experiences of a husband-wife entrepreneurial team as lack of space forced a relocation from their home to an unused churchhouse.

Schultz, Leslie. "A Good Garage Is Hard to Find." *Inc.*, Vol. 5, No. 4 (April, 1983), pp. 91–97.
Picture after picture of garage-based businesses are included in this article. Each picture has a brief narrative discussing the business and the circumstances of its garage site.

Waters, Craig R. "There's a Robot in Your Future." *Inc.*, Vol. 4, No. 6 (June, 1982), pp. 64–74.
Robots are becoming a part of small-business manufacturing. Several specific examples of their use are described. Reference is also made to Japanese usage of robots.

CASE 7

The Fashion Attic*

Deciding on a new location threatens a partnership

Mary Lawrence and Jane Fitzgerald, two longtime friends, each invested $5,000 into a small, ladies' ready-to-wear boutique in Titusville, FL. Both young ladies were quite fashion-minded and, although neither had any retail background, they felt confident they could buy successfully for the 18- to 40-year old, well-dressed women of the area.

After carefully surveying the area, they decided upon a 500-square-foot store located on the outside of the major mall of the community. The rent of $7 per square foot was more attractive to their tight budget than the much higher price of an indoor-mall location. They opened with $8,000 retail inventory and used the rest of their monies to attractively lay out their store in an early 1900s decor and to set up an operating account.

The store, The Fashion Attic, opened with very little fanfare on a 10 am to 6 pm, six days a week operation. Business started very slowly, with many days not doing enough to pay for basic operating costs. However, within a three-month period it showed enough improvement to hire a part-time sales clerk and proceed with the next season's buying plans. At the end of the first year, sales were $38,436 with a net profit of $2,264. Neither partner took any draw against profits. Business continued to grow, and at the end of the second year the store showed the following profit-and-loss statement:

Sales		$48,701
Less Cost of Goods		25,900
Gross Profit		$22,801
Operating Expenses:		
Rent	$3,500	
Operating Supplies	655	
Salaries	3,073	
Advertising	433	
Insurance	186	
Taxes	2,076	(includes 4% sales tax)
Utilities	2,117	
Depreciation	775	
Travel	1,467	
Miscellaneous	767	
Accounting	295	
Total Operating Expenses		15,344
Net Profit		$ 7,457

---

*This case was prepared by James W. Halloran, an entrepreneur in Titusville, FL, and used with his permission.

Inventory had grown to $11,000 retail. The partners had withdrawn some net profit for compensation.

Based on their somewhat encouraging improvement, Mary proposed to Jane that they consider moving to an inside-the-mall location with more space. At the time there were two available spaces. The first store was 800 square feet, which leased for $8 per square foot or 6% of gross sales—whichever was higher. It was available on a three-year lease with a three-year option to renew, with a cost-of-living increase built into the base rent. This store would require total redecoration at a cost of $20 per square foot of sales area and $10 per square foot of stockroom space. Mary roughly figured that inventory would have to be doubled to accommodate the extra space and increased sales volume. She also figured that, at the new rent, she would have to sell a minimum of $72,000 to cover additional overhead. There would also be additional salaries of at least 80% due to the longer mall hours (10 am to 9 pm daily), and additional utilities of at least 50% since they would now be paying their share of airconditioning the mall. All other operating expenses and cost of goods sold should maintain approximately the same percentage level to sales as before.

The second store space was 1,750 square feet, which leased for $6.50 per square foot or 6% of gross sales. Like the first store, it was available on a three-year-lease. This store would also have to be redecorated, using the same cost basis as that for the other store. A store this size would require increasing inventory of approximately 400% over the current operation. Sales would need to be a minimum of $110,000 to cover additional overhead. In relation to their present operation, salaries would increase 300%; utilities, by 100%; and a more consistent advertising program of 3% of gross sales would be needed. As in the first store space being considered, Mary figured that all other operating expenses and cost of goods sold should be maintained at the same percentage level of sales.

Jane was not sure she wanted to take such a gamble. She told Mary, "If you want me to get interested, you'll have to show me three things: (1) estimated profit-and-loss statements for both locations, (2) a general store layout indicating basic decor, cash register area, dressing rooms, and stockroom space; and (3) some kind of general buying plan for the upcoming fall season. Right now I don't believe I am interested; and if you want to give me back my $5,000, you can have the whole thing."

Mary went to work on Jane's request, including the fall buying plans. She knew from past history that her sales were 7% of gross for September, 8% for October, 8% for November, and 16% for December. Using these percentages as guidelines and maintaining at least her minimum inventory as calculated for each location, she could come up with a basic dollar buying plan. She also made a note to remember to figure in her markdowns, which at that time of the year were 5% of gross sales per month.

Questions

1. Should Mary stay in her present location with her partner until she achieves a longer business history?
2. Should Mary expand to the 800-square-foot store or to the 1,750-square-foot store?
3. Should Mary end her partnership with Jane?

8
Initial Financial Planning

Figure 8–1   Scott Taylor

Courtesy of Bowler and Associates

Most entrepreneurs desire to be totally in charge of their business ventures—beginning with the development of the business plan. However, efforts to obtain financing sometimes require them to sacrifice control in return for assistance.

Scott Taylor, one of three founders of Pensa, Inc., in Portland, OR, couldn't even get an appointment with ordinary investors until he first contacted a venture capitalist. "It's no wonder," admits Scott, "because the marketing plan was unreasonable, and the president was a former basketball coach with little business knowledge." But Henry Hillman, Jr., of Hillman Company, a Pittsburgh venture capital firm, invested $250,000, rewrote the marketing plan, and reorganized management. In return, Hillman received 20 percent of Pensa's stock, a seat on the board of directors, and complete control of operations.

Source: Jon Levine, "Money for the Asking," *Venture*, Vol. 5, No. 6 (June, 1983), p. 35.

Looking Ahead

Watch for the following important topics:

1. Analyzing the nature of capital requirements of a new business.
2. Estimating the dollar amounts of initial capital requirements.
3. Individual investors and business suppliers as sources of funds.
4. Financial institutions as sources of funds.
5. Government-sponsored agencies as sources of funds.

Entrepreneurs can help prepare themselves for initial financial planning by recalling the activities surrounding traditional family vacations! There are many parallels between financing the new venture and planning a family vacation—some of them a bit unpleasant.

First, the initial vacation plans often must be trimmed when costs are estimated. Likewise, entrepreneurs often find it necessary to revise start-up plans after an initial financial budget is computed. Secondly, most family vacationers will admit that despite good planning they still spent more on their vacations than they estimated. The proverbial truth that "everything seems to cost more than we estimate" applies to a new business venture as well. Finally, most people agree that the least fun aspect of a family vacation is paying for it. Most entrepreneurs have a similar view of their business ventures. The excitement of "starting up" is temporarily suppressed while financial planning is conducted.

In this chapter, we examine certain financial considerations which can assist the entrepreneur in initial financial planning. Careful study and application of these ideas will reduce the number of financial "surprises" which create a cloud over the excitement and satisfaction associated with starting a new venture.

A new business must have funds mixed in the proper quantities to meet its different needs. Four basic questions must be answered during initial financial planning:

1. What are the financial requirements for my new business?
2. How can I estimate the amounts needed?
3. Where can I obtain the required funds?
4. What should my financing proposal include?

NATURE OF FINANCIAL REQUIREMENTS

The specific needs of a proposed business venture govern the nature of its initial financial requirements. If the firm is a food store, financial planning must provide for the store building, cash registers, shopping carts, inventory, office equipment, and other items required in this type of operation. An analysis of capital requirements for this or any other type of business must consider its needs for current-asset capital, fixed-asset capital, promotion-expense capital, and funds for personal expenses.

Current-Asset Capital

Current assets are the plus side of the working-capital equation.[1] Three current-asset items are cash, inventories, and accounts receivable. The term **circulating capital** is sometimes applied to these three items, emphasizing the constant cycle from cash to inventory to receivables to cash, and so on. Careful planning is needed to provide adequate current-asset capital for the new business.

Cash   Every firm must have the cash essential for current business operations. A reservoir of cash is needed because of the uneven flows of funds into the business (as income) and out of the business (as expense). The size of this reservoir is determined not only by the volume of sales, but also by the regularity of cash receipts and cash payments. Uncertainties exist because of unpredictable decisions by customers as to when they will pay their bills and because of emergencies that require substantial cash outlays. If an adequate cash balance is maintained, the firm can take such unexpected developments in stride.

Inventories   Although the relative importance of inventories differs considerably from one type of business to another, they often constitute a major part of the working capital. Seasonality of sales and production affects the size of the minimum inventory. Retail stores, for example, may find it desirable to carry a larger-than-normal inventory during the Christmas season.

Accounts Receivable   The firm's accounts receivable consist of payments due from its customers. If the firm expects to sell on a credit basis—and in many lines of business this is virtually imperative—provision must be made for financing receivables. The firm cannot afford to wait until its customers pay their bills before restocking its shelves.

Factoring is an option which makes cash available to the business *before* accounts receivable payments are received from customers. Under this option another firm, known as a **factor**, purchases the accounts receivable for their full value. The factor charges a servicing fee, usually 1 percent of the value of the receivables, and an interest charge on the money advanced. The interest charge may range from 2 percent to 3 percent above the **prime rate**, which is the interest rate that commercial banks charge their most credit-worthy customers.

Assume, for example, that the retailer sells products valued at $10,000 to a customer on 30-day credit terms. The $10,000 is listed as an account receivable on the retailer's books. Normally, the retailer would receive the $10,000 from the customer within 30 days. However, by selling the receivable to a factor, the retailer can receive $9,801 immediately. The $199 factoring cost includes the 1 percent servicing fee (1 percent of $10,000 = $100) and the interest charge (12 percent of $9,900 prorated for 30 days = $99). The 12 percent interest charge assumes a 9 percent prime rate plus a 3 percent factoring premium.

Of course, the proportion of cash sales to credit sales significantly affects the size of receivables, as do the terms of sale offered to credit customers. The size of the receivables is likewise affected by seasonality of sales and changes in business conditions, which influence promptness of payment by many customers.

Fixed-Asset Capital

Fixed assets are the relatively permanent assets that are intended for use in the business rather than for sale. For example, a delivery truck used by a grocer to deliver merchandise to customers is a fixed asset. In the case of an automobile dealer, however, a delivery truck to be sold would be part of the inventory and thus a current asset.

The types of fixed assets needed in a new business may include the following:

1. Tangible fixed assets—such as buildings, machinery, equipment, and land (including mineral rights, timber, and the like).
2. Intangible fixed assets—such as patents, copyrights, and goodwill. Many new firms have no intangible fixed assets.
3. Fixed security investments—such as stock of subsidiaries, pension funds, and contingency funds. In most cases a new business has no fixed security investments.

The nature and size of the fixed-asset investment are determined by the type of business operations. A modern beauty shop, for example, might be equipped for around $80,000, whereas a motel sometimes requires 50 or more times that amount. In any given kind of business, moreover, there is a minimum quantity or assortment of facilities needed for efficient operation. It would seldom be profitable, for example, to operate a motel with only one or two units. It is this principle, of course, that excludes small business from automobile manufacturing and other types of heavy industry.

A firm's flexibility is inversely related to its investment in fixed assets. Investments in land, buildings, and equipment involve long-term commitments. Equipment typically is specialized, and substantial losses and delays often occur in liquidation. The inflexibility inherent in fixed-asset investment underscores the importance of a realistic evaluation of fixed-asset needs.

Promotion-Expense Capital

Persons who expend time and money establishing or promoting a business expect repayment of their personal funds and payment for their services. Payment to these promoters may take the form of a cash fee or an ownership interest in the business. Of course, many new businesses come into being as proprietorships, with the entrepreneur acting as the promoter. In this case the proprietor must have sufficient funds to pay all necessary out-of-pocket promotional costs.

Funds for Personal Expenses

In the truly small business, financial provision must also be made for the owner's personal living expenses during an initial period of operation. Technically, this is not part of the business capitalization, but it should be considered in the business financial plan. Inadequate provision for personal expenses will inevitably lead to a diversion of business assets and a departure from the financial plan.

ESTIMATING FINANCIAL REQUIREMENTS

When estimating the magnitude of capital requirements for a small business, the entrepreneur quickly feels the need for a "crystal ball." The uncertainties surrounding an entirely new venture make estimation difficult.[2] But even for established businesses, forecasting is never exact. Nevertheless, when seeking initial capital, the entrepreneur must be ready to answer the question "How much?"

The amount of capital needed by various types of new businesses varies considerably. High-technology companies, such as computer manufacturers, designers of semiconductor chips, and gene-splicing companies, often require several million dollars in initial financing. Stephen A. Duzan, president of

Immunex Corp. of Seattle, WA, estimates that it takes $60 million to bring a new biotech company from development stages to the market.[3]

Most service businesses, on the other hand, require smaller amounts of initial capital. For example, Elsie Kelly started her temporary employment service with $70,000. Her initial facility consisted of a room with a card table and three telephones. Approximately 1 year after start-up, however, her company had 350 employees and expected sales of $300,000.[4]

The explanations that follow will show how a prospective entrepreneur may use a "double-barreled" approach to estimating capital requirements by (1) applying industry standard ratios to estimate dollar amounts, and (2) cross-checking the dollar amounts by empirical investigation. Dun & Bradstreet, Inc., banks, trade associations, and other organizations compile industry standard ratios for numerous types of businesses. If no standard data can be located, then estimating capital requirements inevitably involves educated guesswork.

Estimate the Sales Volume

As a first step in estimating capital needs, the volume of sales should be estimated. One approach to estimating sales is to select a desired profit figure and work backward from that figure to sales. For example, assume that the proposed business is a job printing shop and that its prospective owner hopes to earn annual profits of $40,000. If the industry standard ratio shows that job printers typically earn 5 percent on sales, the prospective owner must then achieve sales of $40,000/.05 = $800,000, or 20 times the expected profit.

The $800,000 sales figure now constitutes the minimum sales one must secure to make the venture sufficiently attractive. It does not prove, however, that the proposed business will guarantee this amount of sales. In fact, this figure should be cross-checked in as many ways as possible. In an existing business, past sales records should be compared with the estimated sales figures. In a new business, the sales records of other, somewhat similar firms may provide a benchmark for checking.

Calculate the Asset Requirements

Having arrived at a sales estimate as objectively as possible, the entrepreneur next must compute the dollar value of all assets consistent with the particular sales volume.

Cash Requirements Anticipated payments for labor, utilities, rent, supplies, and other expenses following the initiation of the firm must be studied in estimating cash requirements. A generous amount of cash must be set aside for those items, as well as for any unexpected expenses. For a new business, the standard amount of cash that is specified for the industry may be too small. Some additional cash may be needed for a margin of safety.

In many types of businesses, a cash balance adequate to pay one or two months' expenses is desirable. This is a good rule of thumb. But the prospective entrepreneur should realize that much subjective judgment is needed in estimating the desired cash balance for a particular business. Today banks and other financial institutions pay interest on checking accounts. This practice provides income to a small business from cash balances and provides an incentive to maintain somewhat larger checking-account balances.

Inventory Requirements   Adequate levels of inventory must be maintained. Industry ratios help estimate these levels. Suppose a retailer's estimated sales is $800,000 and the standard sales-to-inventory ratio is 8. This means that the retailer would need $800,000/8 = $100,000 worth of inventory to keep up with the industry ratio of 8.

In cross-checking inventory requirements through empirical investigation, the entrepreneur must consider the specific types and quantities of items to be kept in inventory. In the case of a clothing retailer, for example, the entrepreneur must make a distribution by sizes and styles of items to be sold to customers. The costs in stocking this merchandise can then be computed by reference to prices quoted by suppliers. Likewise, a prospective manufacturer would need to identify the types and quantities of raw materials to be kept on hand, considering the rate of usage, the location of suppliers, and the time required to replenish supplies.

Level of Accounts Receivable   Since accounts receivable, in effect, are loans to customers, these assets tie up capital. It is important to know how much capital will be involved in these assets. To estimate the amount of capital tied up in accounts receivable, we must first determine the estimated **average collection period** for the industry. (This period is the average length of time that a firm must wait before it receives cash from a credit sale.) The estimated level of accounts receivable may then be computed in two steps:

1. Divide annual credit sales by 360 to get the average daily credit sales.
2. Multiply the average daily credit sales by the average collection period for the industry.

Suppose that the average collection period for a particular type of retailing (that is, the average for the entire industry) is 36 days. Suppose, further, that a beginning retailer in this industry anticipates annual credit sales of $600,000. The level of accounts receivable that this retailer must maintain to conform to the industry standard may be calculated as follows:

Step 1. $\dfrac{\$600,000 \text{ (annual credit sales)}}{360 \text{ (days)}} = \$1,666 \text{ (average daily credit sales)}$

Step 2. $\$1,666$ (average daily credit sales)
$\underline{\times \quad 36 \text{ (average collection period)}}$
$\$60,000$

Fixed-Asset Requirement   The **fixed-asset turnover**, defined as the ratio of sales to fixed assets, can be used to calculate fixed-asset requirements. It measures the extent to which plant and equipment are being utilized productively. Suppose that the industry fixed-asset turnover is 4 in the case of the retailer with an estimated sales of $800,000. This means that the retailer would require $800,000/4 = $200,000 in fixed assets.

Cross-Check Asset Requirements with Break-Even Analysis

Ratio analysis is a useful approach for estimating asset requirements. Since its estimates are, however, closely tied to the estimate of sales, more than one sales level should be evaluated with the calculations. Also, these same sales levels should be cross-checked with break-even analysis to ascertain if they are above, below, or at the break-even level of sales. Potential investors are always eager to determine the break-even point for sales as this has a direct bearing on their investment decision.

Break-even can be explained either with graphs, by algebraic formulas, or by simple subtraction and division. The graphic presentation is included in Chapter 11 in connection with pricing. In this chapter we explain break-even with the simplest method—subtraction and division.

Break-even analysis is a method of showing the relationship between sales revenue and costs of producing that revenue. The focal point of the analysis is the *break-even point*—the particular sales volume where total costs will equal total revenue. At the break-even point a firm neither earns a profit nor sustains a loss.

In order to develop the application of break-even analysis to asset requirements, consider the following symbols and definitions:

P = Product unit selling price
V = Variable cost per unit (includes all costs which vary directly with the volume produced/sold)
F = Total fixed costs (includes all costs which are constant at various levels of production/sales)
CM = Contribution margin (the difference in product unit selling price and variable cost per unit, or P − V)
BEP = Break-even point (the point at which total costs equal total revenue)

The break-even relationship is expressed by the following equation:

$$F \div CM = BEP$$

Let's consider an entrepreneur selling a single product in a proposed retail outlet. After estimating initial asset requirements with ratio-analysis based on anticipated yearly sales of $800,000, break-even analysis can be used to discover when the venture will likely become profitable. Assume that total fixed costs are $400,000, variable cost is $6 per unit, and selling price is

$10 per unit. The break-even point is found by substituting the following numbers into the break-even equation.

$$F \div (P - V) = BEP$$
$$\$400,000 \div (\$10 - \$6) = 100,000 \text{ units}$$

Break-even revenue computes to be 100,000 units $\times$ $10 selling price = $1,000,000. This shows that the number of units forecasted to be sold—$800,000 $\div$ $10 = 80,000—is 20,000 units below the break-even point in the first year.

Break-even analysis helps evaluate the ratio-analysis estimates by putting them within the framework of the break-even point. In this hypothetical example, the break-even point will likely be reached in the second year of operation. If this appears realistic to investors, they will have more confidence in the ratio-analysis estimates. If not, further investigation is required.

Cross-Check Estimates by Empirical Investigation

Although break-even analysis is useful in cross-checking asset requirements, it should not be the only validation effort. The prospective entrepreneur should also make an independent, empirical investigation of capital needs.

For example, inventory requirements of a business should be checked with those who have experience in the same line of business. Similarly, cost estimates for land, building, and equipment may be compared with prices asked by sellers. If there are substantial discrepancies in estimates provided by the two different approaches, rechecking is necessary to decide which is more likely to be accurate.

Minimize Investment in Fixed Assets

The need for adequate working capital deserves special emphasis. A common weakness in small-business financing is the disproportionately small investment in current assets relative to fixed assets. In such weakly financed firms, too much of the money is tied up in assets that are difficult to convert to cash. Danger arises from the fact that the business depends upon daily receipts to meet obligations coming due from day to day. If there is a slump in sales or if there are unexpected expenses, creditors may force the firm into bankruptcy.

The lack of flexibility associated with the purchase of fixed assets suggests the desirability of minimizing this type of investment. Often, for example, there is a choice between renting or buying property. For perhaps the majority of new small firms, renting provides the better alternative. A rental arrangement not only reduces the capital requirement, but also provides the flexibility that is helpful if the business is more successful or less successful than anticipated. It also provides a tax-deductible operating expense.

LOCATING SOURCES OF FUNDS

We have examined the nature of capital needs and ways to estimate these requirements. Now we turn our attention to locating the sources of these funds and establishing the necessary financial arrangements to obtain them.

The initial financing of a small business is quite often patterned after the typical personal financing plan, as the following indicates:

> A prospective entrepreneur, inspired by a vision of success and profit, canvasses first his own means, then those of his immediate family, and finally more remote relatives. If he is a man well regarded by friends and neighbors, he may be able to secure supporting financing from them. His aspiration is to do well, repay family and friends with a generous garnish of profits, and then to live well. If the entrepreneur approaches the more formal channels of finance—banks and the like— his application for funds is likely to be treated in much the same terms as any personal loan.[5]

Every lender wants a feeling of confidence in the borrower and the borrower's idea. A well-prepared assessment of capital needs and sources of funds can help to win that confidence.

Types of Initial Capital

Initial capital consists of **owner capital** and **creditor capital**. Sometimes the terms *ownership equity* and *debt capital* are used, respectively. Traditionally owner capital in a new firm should be at least two-thirds of the total initial capital. This two-thirds dictum is quite conservative, and many small businesses are started with ownership equities that are smaller. Sometimes initial ownership equity is even nonexistent! However, many small firms fail every year due to inadequate ownership equity. The conservative approach thus provides the prospective entrepreneur with a margin of safety that the shoe-string operator lacks.

The sources of funds discussed in this chapter are particularly important in establishing the original financial structure of the new firm. Of course, the use of these and other sources of funds is not limited to initial financing. They can also be tapped to finance growing day-to-day operating requirements and business expansion. Figure 8–2 gives a visual overview of the funding sources discussed in this chapter.

Figure 8–2   Sources of Initial Financing for Small Business

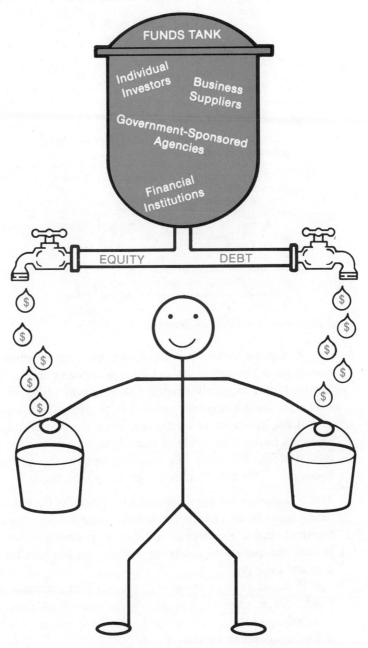

ACTION REPORT

Success Without Equity Financing

There are exceptions to most patterns. This is true of the initial financial structure of a business. On rare occasions, successful operation can begin with no equity financing. Some well-known examples are the following:

David H. McConnell started Avon with a $500 loan and no equity. Sales last year were $1.1 billion.

Ray Kroc, with no capital, was able to leverage, with a $2 million insurance company loan, the exclusive McDonald's franchise into a $2 billion business.

Frank Sieberling began operations at Goodyear Tire with a $13,500 debt and no equity. Current sales: $8.3 billion.

Joseph Campbell started Campbell Soup with absolutely no equity. Sales in 1979 were $2.2 billion.

Source: "Debt and Taxes, Part 2," by Richard Greene, *Forbes* (September 15, 1980), p. 88.

Individual Investors as Sources of Funds

A popular avenue for funding begins close to home. The entrepreneur invests his or her own funds and often persuades parents, relatives, and other acquaintances to supply capital. These investors typically make loans (debt capital) to the entrepreneur rather than provide equity capital.

If the entrepreneur so desires, he or she can also appeal to individual investors beyond the circle of close friends and relatives by offering to sell capital stock. By using this financing option, the entrepreneur can share ownership of the new company with many individuals.

Personal Savings   A financial plan which includes the entrepreneur's personal funds helps build confidence among potential investors. It is important, therefore, that the entrepreneur have some personal assets in the business. Indeed, the ownership equity for a beginning business typically comes from personal savings.

Personal savings invested in the business eliminate the requirement of fixed interest charges and a definite repayment date. If profits fail to materialize exactly as expected, the business is not strapped with an immediate drain on capital.

Funds from Friends, Relatives, and Local Investors   At times, loans from friends or relatives may be the only available source of new small-business financing. Friends and relatives can often be a shortcut to borrowing. Mr. Wells, a Dallas banker, says, "If Momma's got the money, get it from her.

ACTION REPORT
Friend or Foe?

Obtaining funds from friends and relatives has certain disadvantages. Sometimes these investors are too close to the business, disagreeing with decisions in the business and causing a strain on friendships.

Derek F. du Toit started an investment group in 1965. Friends and business associates made contributions to the business. At one point, 35 investors had supplied money to join as equal shareholders.

Investment risk was reduced by du Toit, who personally guaranteed each shareholder that he would be a "buyer of last resort" and pay the balance-sheet value of the shares if the shareholder wished to sell his or her interest in the business. This guaranteed friends against complete loss of investments. Many shareholders later decided to convert their investments into cash in order to make down payments on houses or cars. By July, 1969, the number of shareholders had dropped to approximately 13.

Differences in investment ideas between du Toit and the remaining shareholders resulted in a buy-out by du Toit. After the deal was consummated, du Toit commented, "The bonds of friendship from our previous relationships were irreparably broken. The shareholders discounted the financial reward they received because they felt I had virtually placed a shotgun at their heads to achieve my ambitions."

Source: Reprinted by permission of the *Harvard Business Review.* Excerpt from "Confessions of a Successful Entrepreneur" by Derek F. du Toit (November/December 1980). Copyright © 1980 by the President and Fellows of Harvard College; all rights reserved.

She loves you. She knows you're great, and her interest rate is low."[6] However, friends and relatives who provide capital loans feel that they have the right to interfere in the management of the business. Hard business times may also strain the bonds of friendship. If relatives and friends are indeed the only available source, the entrepreneur has no alternative. However, the financial plan should provide, if possible, for repayment within the first six months of operation.

Local capitalists—for example, lawyers, physicians, or others who wish to invest funds—are good sources of financing. But the small firm must compete with other investment opportunities for the resources of such financial "backers." Local capitalists are not inclined to invest money in a risky, small-business venture unless it bears the prospect of a significantly better rate of return than is available elsewhere. *Angels* is a term recently applied to these private investors. Consider Bob McCray who ran his own company for 26 years until he sold out for $50 million:

He's made four investments, each within 50 miles of his house. Like most angels, he invests anywhere from $10,000 to $100,000 in a deal, and usually brings other angels into the picture. In return, the average angel seeks 30% per annum return on any investment, fully aware that up to half the companies he backs will fold.[7]

Sale of Capital Stock   A third way to obtain capital is through the sale of stock to individual investors beyond the scope of one's immediate acquaintances. Periods of high interest rates turn entrepreneurs to this equity market. This is commonly called "going public."[8] Going public provides both benefits and drawbacks. These have been identified by one public accounting firm as:

Benefits

1. Future financing.
2. Merger and acquisition framework.
3. Enhanced corporate image.
4. Estate planning.

Drawbacks

1. Loss of control.
2. Sharing success potential.
3. Confidentiality.
4. Costs.
5. Periodic reporting requirements.[9]

Whether the owner is wise in declining to use outside equity financing depends upon the firm's long-range prospects. If there is an opportunity for substantial expansion on a continuing basis and if other sources are inadequate, the owner may decide logically to bring in other owners. Owning part of a larger business may be more profitable than owning all of a smaller business.

Private Placement   One way to sell capital stock is through **private placement**. This means that the firm's capital stock is sold to selected individuals who are most likely to be the firm's employees, the owner's acquaintances, local residents, customers, and suppliers. Private sale of stock is difficult because the new firm is not known and has no ready market for its securities. However, the entrepreneur avoids many requirements of the securities law when a stock sale is restricted to a private placement.

Public Sale   Some small firms make their stock available to the general public. These are typically the larger small-business firms. The reason often cited for a public sale is the need for additional working capital or, less frequently, for other capital needs. The personal financial objectives of owners may also enter into the reasoning behind the public sale of stock.

In undertaking the public sale of stock, the small firm subjects itself to greater public regulation. There are state regulations pertaining to the public sale of securities, and the Securities and Exchange Commission (SEC) also exercises surveillance over such offerings.[10] In 1982 the SEC adopted Regulation D in an effort to make public sale of stock even easier. This regulation allows companies to offer up to $500,000 worth of securities without meeting all filing requirements. However, only slightly more than one-half of the states have modified their state laws to reflect Regulation D.[11]

Common stock may also be sold to underwriters, who guarantee the sale of securities. The compensation and fees paid to underwriters typically make the sale of securities in this manner expensive. The fees themselves may range from 10 percent to 30 percent, with 18 percent to 25 percent being typical. In addition, there are options and other fees that may run the actual costs higher. The reason for the high expense is, of course, the element of uncertainty and risk associated with public offerings of stock of small, relatively unknown firms.

Studies of public sale of stock by small firms reveal the fact that small companies frequently make financial arrangements that are not sound. Indeed, the lack of knowledge on the part of small-firm owners often leads to arrangements with brokers or securities dealers that are not in the best interest of the small firms.

The condition of the financial markets at any given time has a direct bearing on the prospects for the sale of capital stock. Entrepreneurs found the early years of the 1980s to be strong for new-venture stock sales. For example, consider this quote from a 1980 article in *Venture*: "Today's venture market is so hot that if you had a corner hot dog stand, you could take it public. There is a push to take companies public."[12] Market conditions do change, however, and therefore must be studied carefully. Consider this quote from the same publication just five years later: "Money was tight in 1984. And 1985 doesn't promise much relief...the availability of all financing...currently giving entrepreneurs shivers."[13]

There are differences in opinion regarding initial public offerings (IPOs) for start-up companies. Some market professionals say IPOs should be avoided for new businesses because they lack operating histories.[14] In any case, it is only the rare case in which the new venture can make a successful initial public offering. Most new startups are simply too small and unimpressive at the beginning to attract serious public interest.

Business Suppliers as Sources of Funds

Companies with which a new firm has business dealings also represent a source of funds for the firm's merchandise inventory and equipment. Thus, both wholesalers and equipment manufacturers/suppliers can be used to provide trade credit or equipment loans and leases.

Trade Credit   Credit extended by suppliers is of unusual importance to the beginning entrepreneur. In fact, trade (or mercantile) credit is the small firm's most widely used source of short-term funds. Trade credit is of short duration—30 days being the customary credit period. Most commonly, this type of credit involves an unsecured, open-book account. The supplier (seller) sends merchandise to the purchasing firm and sets up an *account receivable*. The buying firm sets up an *account payable* for the amount of the purchase.

The amount of trade credit available to a new firm depends upon the type of business and the supplier's confidence in the firm. For example, shoe manufacturers provide business capital to retailers by granting extended payment dates on sales made at the start of a production season. The retailers, in turn, sell to their customers during the season and make the bulk of their payments to the manufacturers at or near the end of the season. If the retailer's rate of stock turnover is greater than the scheduled payment for the goods, cash from sales may be obtained even before paying for the shoes.

Suppliers are inclined to place greater confidence in a new firm and to extend credit more freely than bankers because of the former's interest in developing new customers. A bank might require financial statements and possibly a cash-flow budget. A supplier, on the other hand, may simply check the general credit standing of the purchaser and extend credit without requiring detailed financial statements. The supplier also tends to be less exacting than a banker or other lender in requiring strict observance of credit terms.

Costs of Failing to Use Trade Credit Properly   When considering the use of trade credit, one should give attention to the pertinent costs of failing to use it properly. For example, there is a cost involved if the buying firm makes payment before the required date. By paying unnecessarily early, the buying firm commits funds that might have been used for other purposes. The more critical cost, however, involves the failure to take an offered cash discount. Stated in terms of equivalent annual interest, the real cost of failing to take an offered cash discount is much higher than the nominal discount rate—a concept developed in Chapter 20.

Careful Selection of Trade Suppliers   Suppliers of merchandise or raw materials on credit should be selected carefully. A supplier should have a reputation for maintaining scheduled deliveries of materials or merchandise so that the buyer will neither lose sales nor experience operating delays because of late deliveries. The trade supplier who is willing to participate in the small firm's advertising is a boon to the small entrepreneur. Moreover, in times of unavoidable emergency, it is desirable for a firm to have a supplier who is willing to wait for payment and, in some cases, to extend direct financial assistance.

Equipment Loans and Leases   Some small businesses—for example, restaurants—utilize equipment that may be purchased on an installment basis. A down payment of 25 to 35 percent is ordinarily required, and the contract period normally runs from 3 to 5 years. The equipment manufacturer or supplier typically extends credit on the basis of a *conditional sales contract* (or mortgage) on the equipment. During the loan period, the equipment cannot serve as collateral for a bank loan.

The small-business firm should be aware of the danger in contracting for so much equipment that it becomes impossible to meet installment payments. It is a mark of real management ability to recognize the desirable limits in this type of borrowing.

Equipment leasing, a practice that has grown rapidly in recent years, provides an occasionally attractive alternative to equipment purchase. Cars, trucks, business equipment, and machinery used in manufacturing are examples of assets that may be leased. Possible advantages of equipment leasing include greater investment flexibility and smaller capital requirements. Offsetting these advantages is the typically higher total cost of leasing compared to the cost of purchasing. However, leasing may be desirable in cases where continuing specialized maintenance and protection against obsolescence are necessary—as with electronic computers, for example.

Financial Institutions as Sources of Funds

Two major financial institutions which supply beginning capital for new firms are banks and venture-capital companies. Historically, banks have provided a steady, though limited, source of start-up funds. On the other hand, venture-capital companies are in and out of start-up investments. Expansion financing typically accounts for most of the venture-capital investment portfolios. Their start-up investments were low in the mid-1970s, grew strongly in the early 1980s, and have continued at a high level into the middle 1980s.

Commercial Banks   Although commercial banks tend to limit their lending to working-capital needs of going concerns, some initial capital does come from this source. If the small firm is adequately financed in terms of equity capital and if the entrepreneur is of good character, the commercial bank may lend on the basis of signature only. Of course, this is less likely for the beginning firm than for the established one. In any event, collateral and/or personal guarantees are often required.

Collateral Arrangements   On some notes, the name of the cosigner provides adequate security to satisfy the bank. If the borrowing firm is a corporation, such an arrangement is often used to hold the principals personally liable. Assets such as life insurance policies, equipment, and real estate may also be pledged. Chattel mortgages and real estate mortgages are particularly useful in supporting longer term loan requests.

Line of Credit The entrepreneur should arrange for a line of credit in advance of actual need because banks extend credit only in situations about which they are well-informed. Obtaining a loan on a spur-of-the-moment basis, therefore, is virtually impossible. If the entrepreneur attempts this and fails, the business usually becomes bankrupt. When the line of credit is arranged prior to the beginning of operations, the entrepreneur should ask for the maximum amount likely to be needed as shown by projected business plans. And, when subsequently requesting a loan, he or she should be ready to demonstrate that the firm's current financial condition still provides an adequate basis for borrowing. In one recent survey of over 800 entrepreneurs which assessed satisfaction with commercial banks, the most satisfied group (56% of the respondents) had an average credit line of $30,000.[15]

Long-Term Loans Permanent working capital and fixed assets should be financed by ownership equity or long-term loans. It is often disastrous to finance a substantial portion of the fixed investment by short-term loans. This is because the debt matures before the fixed investment can be amortized from the income it yields.

Long-term borrowing actually is divided into intermediate-term and long-term. Intermediate-term loans mature in two to five years. Long-term loans mature after five years, and they are likely to be 10- to 25-year loans.

Unused Debt Capacity Initial financing should be carried out with an eye to the future. This means that initial commitments should not preclude financial moves that will become desirable or necessary later. If emergencies arise, the new firm may need additional capital to weather the storm. As the business becomes successful, it will also need additional capital to finance expansion. For these reasons, the firm should not totally exhaust its borrowing capacity at first.

Selection of a Bank The varied services provided by a bank make the choice of a bank important. For the typical small firm, the provision of checking-account facilities and the extension of short-term (and possibly long-term) loans are the two most important services of a bank. Normally loans are negotiated with the same bank in which the firm maintains its checking account. In addition, the firm may use the bank's safety deposit vault or its services in collecting notes or securing credit information. An experienced banker can also provide management counsel, particularly in financial matters, to the beginning entrepreneur.

The factor of location limits the range of choices possible for the small firm. For reasons of convenience in making deposits and in conferring with

ACTION REPORT
Strike One, Strike Two, Home Run

Putting together a financial package to purchase a business requires hard work and a commitment to keep on trying after missing one or two strikes. Three entrepreneurs who can attest to this are Bob Phillips, Gary Edman, and Charles Stewart. They successfully purchased the Chambers Belt Company of Phoenix, AZ, where they had worked as corporate vice-presidents, but only after several refusals from bankers who they felt wanted too much or simply didn't want to take the risk. They needed between four and five million dollars for the deal. Each of the three had no personal capital other than the equity they had in their homes. "We really didn't know what we were going to do," said Phillips. "We didn't know where to start, and we only had about two weeks to pull everything together."

As a team, they approached their first bank, which wouldn't consider the loan until the three could raise $500,000 of additional equity—beyond the value of their homes. They were also told that "...it would be impossible to get a loan approved without going through several layers of committees." Strike one...

At the next bank, they were also told they must have more personal equity. This bank recommended they seek another partner who could invest funds. Phillips remembers, "We found one person who wanted 51 percent of the company for investing less than $800,000." This was, of course, unacceptable. Strike two...

Finally, the team located a small bank in Phoenix which was willing to talk to them. Fully expecting the same type of questions which were asked by the first two banks, they were surprised when the business loan director wanted to know their marketing plans, details about their backgrounds, and how well they got along with each other. Within a few days, the $4-million package was put together. Home run...!

Source: Bruce G. Posner, "Belt Tightening," *Inc.*, Vol. 6, No. 9 (September, 1984), pp., 161–163.

the banker concerning loans and other matters, it is essential that the bank be located in the same vicinity as the firm. Any bank is also interested in its home community and therefore tends to be sympathetic to the needs of business firms in the area. Except in very small communities, however, two or more local banks are available, thus permitting some freedom of choice.

Some banks actively seek small-business accounts. The Bank of New Haven is one example:

Everything Bank of New Haven does is aimed at making small-business people feel that the bankers care about their business. Each account is handled by a senior officer, 'No games, no gifts, no gimmicks...just banking,' promised one newspaper ad.[16]

Lending policies of banks are not uniform. Some bankers are extremely conservative, while others are more venturesome in the risks they will accept. If a small firm's loan application is neither obviously strong nor obviously weak, its prospects for approval depend as much upon the bank as upon the borrowing firm. Such differences in willingness to lend have been clearly established by research studies, as well as by the practical experience of many business borrowers.

In addition to variations in their conservative or venturesome orientation, banks also differ in length of loans, interest rates, types of security required, and other such features. The bank's reputation for sticking with a firm in times of adversity is also pertinent. Some banks are more flexible than others in assisting a firm that is experiencing temporary difficulty. The beginning small business certainly needs a banker who is willing to make reasonable concessions in times of stress.[17]

Venture-Capital Companies Technically speaking, anyone investing in a new-business venture is a venture capitalist. However, the term **venture capitalist** is usually associated with those corporations or partnerships which operate as investment groups. Each year more venture-capital groups are being organized. The investment philosophy of many venture-capital companies is shown by the following quote:

> Technology Venture Investors (TVI) is a privately held venture-capital partnership organized in 1980 to make equity investments in businesses having the potential for extraordinary increases in value over the long term. We are patient, capital-gains-oriented investors; i.e., we have the same overall objectives as the entrepreneurs in whom we invest.
>
> Our interests run the gamut from start-ups to secondary stock purchases in mature venture companies. Indeed, our initial TVI investments have ranged from "two guys and an idea" to profitable growth companies who are seeking their first significant outside capital as a means to obtain help and counsel in guiding further rapid growth.[18]

Some venture-capital companies provide management assistance to the young business. They also can assist in later financing needs. One such venture-capital firm is Onset, based in Palo Alto, CA. Started in 1984, it had $5 million in capital two years later. It is what is called a seed or incubator fund. Entrepreneurs have access to capital, management skills, and product-design advice, all from one source.[19]

Special resource directories are available for the entrepreneur seeking venture capital. One such book, compiled by Stanley Pratt, lists over 500 venture-capital sources plus several informative articles written by venture capitalists.[20] Magazines such as *Venture* also publish a venture capital directory in some editions.

Government-Sponsored Agencies as Sources of Funds

The federal government has a long-standing reputation for helping new businesses get started. In this section we discuss some types of loans available through the Small Business Administration (SBA) and Small Business Investment Companies.

Small Business Administration Loans   In fiscal year 1985, SBA business loans numbered 16,864 and totaled $2.4 billion.[21] To qualify for an SBA loan, the prospective borrower must have been unable to obtain financing from private sources on reasonable terms. At the same time, the loan must be of such sound value or so secured that repayment is reasonably assured. These loans are normally secured by real estate mortgages or chattel mortgages, or by assignment of accounts receivable, life insurance policies, franchises, securities, and so forth. In addition, the Small Business Administration guarantees bank loans up to $350,000.

Different types of loans are provided by the Small Business Administration. **Direct loans** are made for a maximum amount of $150,000.[22] These generally provide for monthly payments with maturities up to 10 years, or 15 years on loans for new construction. The SBA also grants **participation loans**, which are made in cooperation with private banks and in which the degree of participation by the SBA ranges up to 90 percent. **Disaster relief loans**, examples of which are the loans extended to small businesses after devastating tornadoes, are one important phase of the SBA lending program. Finally, the SBA provides **economic opportunity loans** to minority and other disadvantaged groups. Management assistance is given as part of the economic opportunity loan program, and an effort is made to seek out deserving applicants in ghetto and other depressed areas.

Small Business Investment Companies (SBICs)   In 1958, Congress passed the Small Business Investment Act, which provides for the establishment of privately owned capital banks whose purpose is to provide long-term and/or equity capital to small businesses. SBICs are licensed and regulated by the Small Business Administration. They may obtain a substantial part of their capital from the SBA at attractive rates of interest.

Although SBICs may either lend funds or supply equity funds, the Act was intended to place a strong emphasis upon equity financing. The SBIC that provides equity financing may do so either by directly purchasing the small firm's stock or, quite commonly, by purchasing the small firm's convertible debentures (bonds), which may be converted into stock at the option of the SBIC.

The typical SBIC wishes to invest in companies that have rapid growth prospects. In addition, the cost of investigating investment opportunities makes it more profitable for the SBIC to concentrate its attention upon the bigger investments required by the larger small businesses. These considerations and the reluctance of many small-business owners to accept a dilution of equity have limited the use of SBICs by small-business firms that need long-term capital.

Many SBICs have provided not only funds but also counsel and advice to the small firms they have served. It is not uncommon for an SBIC to have a representative on the board of directors of the borrowing firm. The SBIC does not normally wish to assume operating control of a business, but it is often able to provide constructive advice, particularly of a financial nature. Some SBICs provide management counsel and advice on a fee basis, in addition to the unofficial counsel that accompanies the original investment or loan.

Miscellaneous Sources of Funds

Commercial finance companies lend money to small-business firms on a secured basis. Their loans may be backed by inventories, accounts receivable, equipment, or other items. They participate in floor-planning arrangements and also purchase installment paper from small firms. The interest rates charged by commercial finance companies tend to be higher than those charged by commercial banks.

Insurance companies have also made term loans available to small business. Although their major financing efforts have been directed toward big business, some insurance companies have established small-business loan departments. These companies place considerable emphasis on the submission of financial statements and projections by the borrowing company. Consequently, small businesses are often reluctant to subject themselves to such effort and evaluation.

Other financial institutions and groups that make financing available to small-business firms from time to time include: savings and loan associations, credit unions, mutual savings banks, factors, personal finance companies, universities, and investment bankers.

POINTS TO CONSIDER IN THE FINANCING PROPOSAL

Once the entrepreneur has determined what capital is needed, how much is needed, and the most likely sources of these funds, he or she must structure the financing proposal. A potential investor in the business wants something concrete to substantiate the entrepreneur's claims of profit and success! This "something concrete" is a document known as the financing proposal.

A *financing proposal* is constructed from, or is part of, the business plan outlined on page 90 in Chapter 4. The detailed financial section of that plan can be used to show the capital needs and the plans for funding these needs. Figures 8–3, 8–4, and 8–5 show typical *pro forma* financial statements— income statement, .cash budget, and balance sheet—included within a financing proposal. These particular statements were generated on a personal computer and cover only the first 12 months of operation of a business. Financial statements are discussed in Chapter 19, and a cash budget is developed in Chapter 20. Potential investors will also be interested in an abbreviated version of the other parts of the plan. The complete financing proposal should be as brief as possible, while still including the necessary information.

It is also desirable to discuss in the financing proposal some of the problems facing the proposed business. Most investors realize that business prospects are not all rosy. For example, venture capitalist Fred Adler says:

> The ideal (financing) proposal has a business plan and a market analysis, with a full explanation of how and why the plan will work. It discusses the problems— every company has problems—and tells how they will be overcome.... In short, we want proposals that give us precise information and are concise and candid about the company's problems as well as its successes.[23]

In order to prepare a financing proposal properly, the entrepreneur should analyze the informational needs of potential investors. If the entrepreneur is seeking funds from government-sponsored sources, banks, or venture-capital companies, he or she can easily learn their exact informational needs by telephoning or writing them.

A concluding word of advice for the new entrepreneur who is seeking start-up capital is expressed by one businessman who put together $3 million for a new venture. He says, "Don't be bashful. Tell your venture-capital guy your dream. He wants to believe you're the next Apple Computer or Xerox."[24] Remember, the potential investor is most interested in who you are, what your idea is, what you will do with the money, how much you want, and how it will be repaid.

Figure 8-3   Income Statement

	January	February	March	April	May	June	July	August	September	October	November	December
Sales	10000	15000	30000	50000	70000	75000	65000	80000	55000	40000	40000	55000
Cost of Goods Sold	7000	10500	21000	35000	49000	52500	45500	56000	38500	28000	28000	38500
Gross Margin	3000	4500	9000	15000	21000	22500	19500	24000	16500	12000	12000	16500
Operating Expenses												
Selling and Adm.	20000	15000	12000	12000	12000	12000	12000	12000	12000	12000	12000	12000
Depreciation	500	500	500	500	500	500	500	500	500	500	500	500
Inventory Charge	35	53	105	175	245	263	228	280	193	140	140	193
Operating Income	-17535	-11053	-3605	2325	8255	9738	6773	11220	3808	-640	-640	3808
Interest Expense	0	0	61	218	434	647	730	638	673	510	282	219
Earnings Before Tx	-17535	-11053	-3666	2107	7821	9090	6042	10582	3134	-1150	-922	3589
Taxes	-8768	-5526	-1833	1054	3911	4545	3021	5291	1567	-575	-461	1794
Net Income	-8768	-5526	-1833	1054	3911	4545	3021	5291	1567	-575	-461	1794

Source: Terry S. Maness, *Small-Business Management Using Lotus 1-2-3* (Cincinnati, OH: South-Western Publishing Co., 1987), Chapter 3.

Figure 8-4 Cash Budget

	January	February	March	April	May	June	July	August	September	October	November	December
Sales	10000	15000	30000	50000	70000	75000	65000	80000	55000	40000	40000	55000
Cash Receipts												
Cash Collections:												
Month of Sale	0	0	0	0	0	0	0	0	0	0	0	0
1 Month After	0	5000	7500	15000	25000	35000	37500	32500	40000	27500	20000	20000
2 Months After	0	0	5000	7500	15000	25000	35000	37500	32500	40000	27500	20000
3 Months After	0	0	0	0	0	0	0	0	0	0	0	0
Cash Receipts	0	5000	12500	22500	40000	60000	72500	70000	72500	67500	47500	40000
Cash Disbursements:												
Purchases	7000	10500	21000	35000	49000	52500	45500	56000	38500	28000	28000	38500
Selling and Adm.	20000	15000	12000	12000	12000	12000	12000	12000	12000	12000	12000	12000
Inventories	35	53	105	175	245	263	228	280	193	140	140	193
Interest Expense	0	0	61	218	434	647	730	638	673	510	282	219
Taxes	-8768	-5526	-1833	1054	3911	4545	3021	5291	1567	-575	-461	1794
Cap. Expenditure	0	0	0	0	0	0	0	0	0	0	0	0
Dividends	0	0	0	0	0	0	0	0	0	0	0	0
Cash Disbursement	18268	20026	31333	48446	65589	69955	61479	74209	52933	40075	39961	52706
Net Cash Flow	-18268	-15026	-18833	-25946	-25589	-9955	11021	-4209	19567	27425	7539	-12706
Beginning Cash Bal	30000	11733	4000	4000	4000	4000	4000	4000	4000	4000	4000	4000
Unadjusted Ending	11733	-3294	-14833	-21946	-21589	-5955	15021	-209	23567	31425	11539	-8706
Minimum Cash Bal	4000	4000	4000	4000	4000	4000	4000	4000	4000	4000	4000	4000
Borrow	0	7294	18833	25946	25589	9955	0	4209	0	0	0	12706
Repay	0	0	0	0	0	0	11021	0	19567	27425	7539	0
Ending Cash Bal	11733	4000	4000	4000	4000	4000	4000	4000	4000	4000	4000	4000

Source: Terry S. Maness, *Small-Business Management Using Lotus 1-2-3* (Cincinnati, OH: South-Western Publishing Co., 1987), Chapter 3.

Figure 8-5   Balance Sheet

	January	February	March	April	May	June	July	August	September	October	November	December
ASSETS:												
Cash	11733	4000	4000	4000	4000	4000	4000	4000	4000	4000	4000	4000
A/R	10000	20000	37500	65000	95000	110000	102500	112500	95000	67500	60000	75000
Inventory	10500	21000	35000	49000	52500	45500	56000	38500	28000	28000	38500	21000
Current	32233	45000	76500	118000	151500	159500	162500	155000	127000	99500	102500	100000
Fixed	20000	20000	20000	20000	20000	20000	20000	20000	20000	20000	20000	20000
(Acc.Depr)	500	1000	1500	2000	2500	3000	3500	4000	4500	5000	5500	6000
Net Fixed	19500	19000	18500	18000	17500	17000	16500	16000	15500	15000	14500	14000
Total Assets	51733	64000	95000	136000	169000	176500	179000	171000	142500	114500	117000	114000
LIABILITIES & EQUITY												
LIABILITIES:												
Trade Payables	10500	21000	35000	49000	52500	45500	56000	38500	28000	28000	38500	21000
S.T. Bank Notes	0	7294	26127	52073	77662	87617	76596	80805	61238	33813	26274	38980
Total Current	10500	28294	61127	101073	130162	133117	132596	119305	89238	61813	64774	59980
L.T. Debt	0	0	0	0	0	0	0	0	0	0	0	0
Total Liabilities	10500	28294	61127	101073	130162	133117	132596	119305	89238	61813	64774	59980
EQUITY:												
Common	50000	50000	50000	50000	50000	50000	50000	50000	50000	50000	50000	50000
Retained Earnings	−8768	−14294	−16127	−15073	−11162	−6617	−3596	1695	3262	2687	2226	4020
Total Equity	41233	35706	33873	34927	38838	43383	46404	51695	53262	52687	52226	54020
Total Liab. & Equity	51733	64000	95000	136000	169000	176500	179000	171000	142500	114500	117000	114000

Source: Terry S. Maness, *Small-Business Management Using Lotus 1-2-3* (Cincinnati, OH: South-Western Publishing Co., 1987), Chapter 3.

Looking Back

1. Current-asset capital, fixed-asset capital, promotion-expense capital, and funds for personal expenses constitute the capital requirements in starting a new business.
2. The dollar amounts of initial capital requirements can be estimated by using industry ratios and cross-checking with empirical investigation. A small business should be careful to avoid a disproportionately small investment in current assets relative to fixed assets.
3. Individual investors as sources of funds include the owner(s) of the business, friends, relatives, and local people. The capital stock of the business may be sold by private placement or by a public sale. The condition of the financial markets at any particular time has a direct bearing on the feasibility of a public sale of capital stock. Business suppliers as sources of funds include suppliers who provide trade credit and manufacturers/wholesalers who provide equipment loans and leases.
4. Commercial banks as sources of funds grant both short-term and long-term loans. The selection of a bank is of prime importance to the beginning entrepreneur. Venture-capital companies as sources of funds are usually corporations or partnerships which operate as investment groups. They provide both debt and equity capital and assist in later financing needs. They also provide management assistance to the young business.
5. Government-sponsored agencies as sources of funds include the Small Business Administration and Small Business Investment Companies (SBICs).

DISCUSSION QUESTIONS

1. Define working capital. What three items make up circulating capital? What is the typical cycle involving the three components of circulating capital?
2. Why should personal expenses be included in the initial financing planning?
3. Suppose that a retailer's estimated sales are $900,000 and the standard sales-to-inventory ratio is 6. What dollar amount of inventory would be estimated for the new business?
4. If the industry average collection period for accounts receivable is 72 days, what level of accounts receivable must be maintained with estimated sales of $900,000?
5. Distinguish between owner capital and creditor capital.
6. What are the major problems involved in obtaining loans from friends and relatives? How should they be repaid?

7. What are some of the major advantages and disadvantages of "going public"?

8. Explain how trade credit and equipment loans provide initial capital funding.

9. Discuss banks as a source of funds.

10. How does the federal government help with initial financing for a small business?

ENDNOTES

1. Current liabilities—debts which must be paid within the near future—represent the minus side of the working-capital equation. Accountants technically define working capital as the difference between current assets and current liabilities.

2. The subject of forecasting is discussed in Chapter 5 as a part of market analysis and sales estimation. Most sales forecasting techniques apply to forecasting in general.

3. Sally O'Neil, "Financing 'Ivory Tower' Companies," *Venture*, Vol. 6, No. 2 (February, 1984), p. 86.

4. Nancy J. White, "Supplying Temporary Help," *Venture*, Vol. 3, No. 2 (February, 1981), p. 28.

5. Roland I. Robinson, "The Franchising of Small Business in the United States," in *Small Business in American Life*, edited by Stuart W. Bruchey (New York: Columbia University Press, 1980), p. 280.

6. Sanford L. Jacobs, "Aspiring Entrepreneurs Learn Intricacies of Going It Alone," *The Wall Street Journal*, March 23, 1981, p. 23.

7. William Bryant Logan, "Finding Your Angel," *Venture*, Vol. 8, No. 3 (March, 1986), p. 39.

8. An excellent discussion of going public is contained in James M. Johnson and Robert E. Miller, "Going Public: Information for Small Business," *Journal of Small Business Management*, Vol. 23, No. 4 (October, 1985), pp. 38–44.

9. A booklet entitled *Deciding to Go Public*, Ernst & Whinney, 1984.

10. An excellent discussion of these security laws can be found in Raymond D. Watts, "Selling Stock to Finance a New Business," *In Business* (November–December, 1980), p. 17.

11. Kevin Farrell, "Not All States Are Eager to Adopt Reg D," *Venture*, Vol. 7, No. 1 (January, 1985), p. 98.

12. Loretta Kuklinsky Huerta, "The Ups and Downs of Going Public," *Venture*, Vol. 2, No. 11 (November, 1980), p. 22.

13. Stephen Robinett, "Blood from a Rock," *Venture*, Vol. 7, No. 1 (January, 1985), p. 38.

14. Francine Schwadel, "Stock Market Pros Offer Some Tips on Judging Initial Public Offerings," *The Wall Street Journal*, February 21, 1986, p. 21.

15. Nancy Madlin, "Can You Bank on Your Banker?" *Venture*, Vol. 7, No. 12 (December, 1985), p. 20.

16. Ashok Chandrasekhar, "New Haven Bank Targets Small Firms," *The Wall Street Journal*, September 21, 1984, p. 33.

17. For a more detailed discussion on choosing a bank, see James McNeill Stancill, "Getting the Most from Your Banking Relationship," *Harvard Business Review*, Vol. 58, No. 2 (March–April, 1980), pp. 20–28.

18. From a draft of a brochure for Technology Venture Investors provided by Burton J. McMurtry through personal correspondence.

19. Udayan Gupta, "California Venture Capitalists Take Earlier Role in Start-Ups," *The Wall Street Journal*, February 3, 1986, p. 14.

20. Stanley Pratt (ed.), *Guide to Venture Capital Sources* (6th ed.; Wellesley Hills, MA: Capital Publishing Company, 1982).

21. Stanford L. Jacobs, "Big-Firm Alumni Apt to Be Growth-Oriented Entrepreneurs," *The Wall Street Journal*, December 9, 1985, p. 25.

22. The agency can raise the ceiling to $350,000 for direct loans and $500,000 for guarantees for special "social policy purposes."

23. Burton W. Teague, "Venture Capital—Who Gets It, and Why?" *Inc.*, Vol. 2, No. 6 (June, 1980), p. 72.

24. Jacobs, *loc. cit.*

REFERENCES TO SMALL BUSINESS IN ACTION

Asinof, Lynn. "Begging for Money: Young Firms Find Venture Capital Harder to Get." *The Wall Street Journal*, April 1, 1985, p. 25.
The experiences of three firms with venture-capitalists are described.

Aspaklaria, Shelley. "Down But Not Out," *Venture*, Vol. 8, No. 3 (March, 1986), pp. 58–60.
Some of the financing efforts of entrepreneurs who have experienced business failures are presented in this article.

Greenwald, Judy. "'Home-Grown' Equity." *Venture*, Vol. 4, No. 5 (May, 1982), pp. 14–15.
This article describes how one family used a second mortgage on their home to obtain funds for a new business.

Halbrooks, John. "They Never Quit." *Inc.*, Vol. 3, No. 3 (March, 1981), pp. 58–62.
This article tells the story of a husband-and-wife team who, prior to marriage, pooled $2,000 in savings to start a new business venture. It describes how they went public, later were "capital-poor," and made personal sacrifices to reach their current $22 million sales level.

Linderff, Dave. "Investment Bankers Take the Venture Plunge." *Venture*, Vol. 3, No. 1 (January, 1981), pp. 42–47.
Numerous examples of small-business financing problems are provided in this article as it profiles the participation of investment bankers in the venture-capital market.

"One Day, at an Earthquake Party..." *Forbes*, Vol. 126, No. 8 (October 13, 1980), pp. 197–200.
The rise of a business initially financed by friends and relatives is the subject of this story. Later funding was raised from equipment manufacturers and bank loans.

CASE 8

Walker Machine Works*
Financing arrangements for a new venture

Jim Walker was a management consultant on a continuing but indefinite assignment with a medium-sized plastics company. He was also an M.B.A. candidate at a nearby university. He had thought that the consultant's position would be challenging and would add a dimension of practical experience to his academic background. But after several months Jim had become very disenchanted with his job. Although he seemed to have much freedom in his duties, he began to discover that his reports and suggestions could not be translated into meaningful results and solutions. He realized that the management was interested only in maintaining the status quo and that he was hired as a more or less token consultant. His efforts to help the company were largely ignored and overlooked. It seemed as if his job was quickly becoming nothing more than an exercise in futility.

Jim discussed the situation with a few friends, most of whom urged him to seek a more fulfilling position with another company. But he had another idea—why not start a small company of his own? He had toyed with this idea for the last couple of years, and there was no better time than the present to give it a try. At least it would be a real test of his management abilities.

After a few days and considerable thought, Jim had several potential ventures in mind. The most promising idea involved the establishment of a machine shop. Before entering college, he had worked two years as a general machinist and acquired diversified experience operating a variety of lathes, milling machines, presses, drills, grinders, and more. And he really enjoyed this sort of work. He guessed that making things on machines satisfied some sort of creative urge he felt.

After a very comprehensive and systematic research of the local market, it appeared that there was a definite need for a quality machine-shop operation. Thus, Jim's mind was made up. He was sure that he had an adequate knowledge of machining processes (and enough ambition to find out what he didn't know), and his general business education was also a valuable asset. The problem was money. The necessary machinery for a small shop would cost about $12,000, yet he had only about $3,000 in savings. Surely he could borrow the money or find someone willing to invest in his venture.

A visit to one of the local banks was something less than productive. The vice-president in charge of business investments was quite clear. "You

*This case was prepared by Richard L. Garman.

don't have a proven track record. It would be a big risk for us to lend so much money to someone with so little actual experience," the vice-president said. Jim was greatly disappointed but unwilling to give up yet. After all, there were six other banks in town, and one of them might be willing to lend him the money.

Financing Proposal #1

One possibility lay in a suggestion the banker had given Jim. He was told to contact Russ Williams, the president of a local hydraulics company. The banker felt that Russ might be interested in investing a little money in Jim's venture. It was certainly worth a try, so Jim called Russ and made an appointment to see him.

Russ had been involved in manufacturing for over 40 years. As a young man, he had begun his career as Jim had—in the machine shop. After several years of experience as a journeyman machinist, Russ was promoted to shop supervisor. Rising steadily through the ranks, Russ, now in his early sixties, had been promoted to president of the hydraulics company only two years ago.

Jim had never met Russ before and knew little about the man or his background. Nevertheless, Jim soon found Russ to be pleasant in nature and very easy to talk to. Jim spent about an hour presenting his business plan to Russ, who seemed impressed with the idea. Although Russ's time and energies were currently committed to an expansion project for the hydraulics company, he indicated that he might be interested in contributing both money and management. As Jim rose to leave, Russ proposed a 50-50 deal and asked Jim to think it over for a few days.

Financing Proposal #2

A few days later, Stan Thomas came by to see Jim. They had been good friends for about a year and had even roomed together as undergraduates. Stan had talked with his father about Jim's idea and perhaps had even glorified the possibilities a little. Stan's father was intrigued with the plan and offered to meet with Jim to discuss the possibility of a partnership.

Phil Thomas, Stan's father, was a real estate investor who owned his own agency. Although he had been in business only a few years, he was very successful and constantly looking for new investment prospects. He drove the 250 miles from his home to meet with Jim one Saturday. After looking over the business plan and some pro forma financial statements that Jim had prepared, he agreed that it might be a worthwhile venture. "I'll contribute all of the capital you need and give you a fair amount of freedom in running the business. I know that most investors would start out by giving you only 10 or

15 percent of the equity and then gradually increase your share, but I'll make you a better deal. I'll give you 40 percent right off the bat, and we'll let this be a sort of permanent arrangement," he said. Jim was a little unsure about that, so he said he'd think it over for a few days and then let him know.

Jim didn't know quite what to do. He had several options to choose from, and he wasn't sure which would be best. The sensible thing would be to talk to someone who could offer some good advice. So, he went to the business school to talk to a professor he knew fairly well.

Financing Proposal #3

Jim found Professor Wesley Davis in his office and described the situation to him. The professor was an associate dean and a marketing specialist. Although he had no actual manufacturing experience, he had edited some semitechnical publications for the Society of Manufacturing Engineers. Thus, he had at least a general knowledge of the machining processes involved in Jim's proposed business.

The professor had been aware of Jim's interest in starting a business and frequently inquired about the progress Jim was making. At the end of this discussion, Jim was surprised to hear the professor offer to help by investing some of his own money. "It sounds like you have an excellent idea, and I'd like to see you give it a try. Besides, a little 'real-world' experience might be good for an old academic type like me," said the professor. "And I would suggest bringing in Joe Winsett from the accounting department. I know neither one of us relishes keeping the books. Besides, Joe is a C.P.A. who could provide some valuable assistance. I'll talk to him if you like." The professor suggested that the equity be split into equal thirds, giving Jim the first option to increase his share of the equity.

Questions

1. Evaluate the backgrounds of the possible "partners" in terms of the business and management needs of the proposed firm.
2. Evaluate the three financing proposals from the standpoint of Jim Walker's control of the firm and the support or interference he may experience.
3. Compare Jim's equity position under each of the three proposals.
4. What are some important characteristics to look for in a prospective business partner?
5. Which option should Jim choose? What reasons can you give to defend your answer?

9

Legal Aspects of the Business

Figure 9-1   Jim Jaeger

© 1984 Arnold Zann/Black Star

The general partnership, one form of organization discussed in this chapter, has its weaknesses. One of these is illustrated by the experiences of Michael Valentine and Jim Jaeger who once were students at the University of Cincinnati and later partners in manufacturing and selling radar detectors. Their Cincinnati Microwave company, which distributed products exclusively through the mail, was managed by Valentine, and Jaeger supervised production. Prosperity brought problems over strategy. Eventually, the partnership was terminated. Jaeger and Valentine parted with a great deal of money but extremely hard feelings. Says Jaeger, "I think if the company had plodded along and we were making reasonable salaries, we'd still be fast friends."

Source: Barry Stavro, "A License to Speed," *Forbes*, Vol. 134, No. 6 (September 10, 1984), pp. 94–102. Reproduced with permission.

Looking Ahead

Watch for the following important topics:

1. Characteristics of the proprietorship.
2. Characteristics of the general partnership, the partnership agreement, and the limited partnership.
3. Characteristics of the corporation and the limited liability of stockholders.
4. Relevance of contracts, agency relationships, negotiable instruments, real property, trademarks, patents, copyright, and libelous acts to the small business.
5. How to choose an attorney for a small firm.

Should a new firm be organized as a proprietorship, a partnership, or a corporation? Anyone who buys or starts a business faces this question very early in the venture developmental process. Moreover, the problem reappears as a business grows. Firms begun as proprietorships later may find it desirable to become partnerships or corporations.

In this chapter we examine the major forms of business organization and also selected areas of law relevant to small business. In view of the need for legal counsel both in forming the organization and in dealing with various legal issues, we conclude the chapter by discussing the choice of an attorney for the small firm.

OPTIONS FOR LEGAL ORGANIZATION

Various legal forms of organization are available to organize small businesses. Several options are, however, appropriate for only very specialized applications. We confine our attention here to the forms widely used by small business. These forms are shown in Figure 9-2. At one level we have the proprietorship, the partnership, and the corporation. Within the partnership form, there are two basic types—the general partnership and the limited partnership. Also, in addition to the regular corporation there is a legal form known as a Subchapter S corporation.

The proprietorship is the most popular form of business organization among small businesses. This popularity exists across all industries. There are, however, many small businesses operating as partnerships and as corporations, suggesting that there are circumstances which favor these forms. In the next several sections, we will examine each of the more popular legal forms of organization.

Figure 9-2   Forms of Small-Business Legal Organization

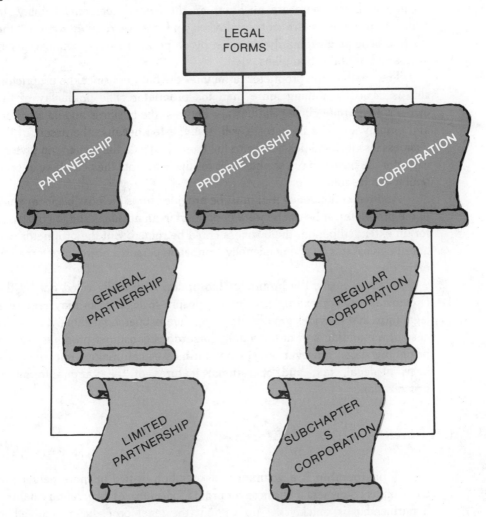

CHARACTERISTICS OF THE PROPRIETORSHIP

The **proprietorship** is a business owned and operated by one person. The individual proprietor has title to all business assets, subject to the claims of creditors. He or she receives all profits but must also assume all losses, bear all risks, and pay all debts of the business. Such a business can be established merely by starting operation and requires no legal documentation.[1] In view of this fact, the proprietorship is the simplest and cheapest way to start operation and is frequently the most appropriate form for a new business. In the proprietorship, the owner is free from interference by partners, shareholders, directors, and officers.

The proprietorship lacks some of the advantages of other legal forms. As noted above, there are no limits on the owner's personal liability. In addition, proprietors are not employees and cannot receive some of the tax-free benefits customarily provided by corporations—for example, insurance and hospitalization plans.

The death of the proprietor terminates the business since the proprietorship is basically nothing more than the proprietor. The possibility of the owner's death may cloud relationships between the business and its creditors and employees. The need for a will is suggested because the assets of the business less its liabilities belong to the heirs. In a will, the owner can give an executor the power to run the business for the heirs until they can take over or until it can be sold.

Another contingency that must be provided for is the possible incapacity of the proprietor. If he or she were badly hurt in an accident and unconscious for an extended period, the business could be ruined. But the proprietor can guard against this by giving a legally competent person a power of attorney to carry on.

In some cases, the proprietorship option is virtually ruled out by the circumstances. For example, a high exposure to legal risks may require a legal form that provides greater protection against personal liability, as in the case of a manufacturer of potentially hazardous consumer products. At the beginning stage, however, most small businesses can make a choice on the basis of legal, tax, and operational features of the various forms of organization.

CHARACTERISTICS OF THE PARTNERSHIP

A **partnership** is a voluntary "association of two or more persons to carry on as co-owners a business for profit."[2] Because of its voluntary nature, a partnership is quickly set up without the legal procedures involved in creating a corporation. A partnership pools the managerial talents and capital of those joining together as business partners.

Qualifications of Partners

Any person capable of contracting may legally become a business partner. Individuals may become partners without contributing to capital or sharing in the assets at the time of dissolution. Such persons are partners only as to management and profits.

Aside from legal aspects, however, partnership formation deserves serious study. A strong partnership requires partners who are honest, healthy, capable, and compatible.

One engineering and management consulting firm with four partners which has made a partnership work is Dynamic Systems. The founding partner in the business, David H. Bennet, expressed his views of the advantages of a partnership this way:

> You lower your own risk and required investment; you share the burden of decision-making and benefit from the strengths of each other; and you add one or more cooperative, hard-charging members to your team—members as highly motivated as yourself.
>
> A partnership is very much like a marriage... As you work with each other, you will get to know each other's strengths, limitations, idiosyncrasies, goals, values, skills, and behavior patterns. How well these human characteristics complement or conflict with one another and how much they help or harm a young company are the often-hidden forces that heavily influence long-term success.[3]

Rights and Duties of Partners

Partners' rights and duties should be stated explicitly in the **articles of partnership**. These articles should be drawn up during the pre-operating period and should cover the following items as a minimum:

1. Date of formation of the partnership.
2. Names and addresses of all partners.
3. Statement of fact of partnership.
4. Statement of business purpose(s).
5. Duration of the business.
6. Name and location of business.
7. Amount invested by each partner.
8. Sharing ratio for profits and losses.
9. Partners' rights, if any, for withdrawals of funds for personal use.
10. Provision for accounting records and their accessibility to partners.
11. Specific duties of each partner.
12. Provision for dissolution and for sharing the net assets.
13. Restraint on partners' assumption of special obligations, such as endorsing the note of another.
14. Provision for protection of surviving partners, decedent's estate, etc.

Unless specified otherwise in the articles, a partner is generally recognized as having certain implicit rights. For example, partners share profits or losses equally if they have not agreed on a profit-and-loss sharing ratio.

In a partnership each partner has **agency power**, which means that a partner can bind all members of the firm. Good faith, together with reasonable care in the exercise of management duties, is required of all partners in a business. Since their relationship is fiduciary in character, a partner cannot compete in business and remain a partner. Nor can a partner use business information solely for personal gain.

Termination of a Partnership

Death, incapacity, or withdrawal of a partner terminates a partnership and necessitates liquidation or reorganization of the business. Liquidation often results in substantial losses to all partners. It may be legally necessary, however, because a partnership is a close personal relationship of the parties that cannot be maintained against the will of any one of them.

This disadvantage may be partially overcome at the time a partnership is formed by stipulating in the articles of partnership that surviving partners can continue the business after buying the decedent's interest. This can be facilitated by having the partners carry mutual life insurance. Or the executor might act as a partner until the heirs become of age. In the latter case, the agreement should also provide for liquidation in the event of unprofitability or in the event of major disagreements with the executor as partner.

The Limited Partnership

A small business sometimes finds it desirable to use a special form of partnership called the **limited partnership**.[4] This form consists of at least one general partner and one or more limited partners. The **general partner** remains personally liable for the debts of the business, but all **limited partners** have limited personal liability as long as they do not take an active role in the management of the partnership. In other words, limited partners risk only the capital which they invest in the business.[5] Because of this feature, an individual with substantial personal assets can invest money in a limited partnership without exposing his or her total personal estate to liability claims that might arise through activities of the business.[6]

The limited partnership is frequently used to provide real estate tax shelters to the limited partners. For example, the limited partnership may acquire a piece of undeveloped real estate, apartment houses, or commercial buildings. Most of the interest and other costs of the partnership are prorated to the limited partners, who report them as tax-deductible expenditures on their personal income tax returns. (Of course, income from the property must likewise be reported on the partners' tax returns, but the costs frequently exceed revenue in the early going.) When the property is finally sold, it may produce a capital gain, which is taxed at a lower rate than ordinary income.

A special application of the limited partnership concept can be found in research and development ventures. These R&D limited partnerships are designed to foster the development of new techniques and services. These partnerships can range from a few people to a few hundred. Sometimes referred to as the "sponsor" company, the general partner assumes the associated risk obligations while the R&D limited partners have a tax

---

ACTION REPORT
Partnership "Marriage" Counseling

As in marriage, there are often rough times in partnership relationships. Donald L. Sexton, professor of entrepreneurship at Baylor University, says, "It's more common for partners not to get along than to get along."

Mardy Grothe and Peter Wylie are partners in counseling with small businesses which are trying to keep troubled partner relationships intact. Their fees for "patching up a partnership" can run up to $10,000.

The job of improving a partnership relationship is described by Wylie as a "difficult, painful process." Wylie points out that people change very slowly:

> It's like being 40 or 50 pounds overweight and making a commitment to get into shape. That's hard for someone to do. You will resist with every fiber of your being because it will cause anxiety. You'll get sweaty under your arms.

The best advice from Grothe and Wylie is to rate the potential partner on trust, respect, affection, and confidence. Then, base the "marriage" commitment on this overall score.

Source: Reprinted by permission of *The Wall Street Journal,* © Dow Jones & Company, Inc., 1985. All Rights Reserved.

---

deduction for research and development and a share in the new technology when and if it is developed.[7]

CHARACTERISTICS OF THE CORPORATION

In the Dartmouth College Case of 1819, Chief Justice John Marshall of the United States Supreme Court defined a **corporation** as "an artificial being, invisible, intangible, and existing only in contemplation of the law." By these words the court recognized the corporation as a **legal entity**. This means that a corporation can sue and be sued, hold and sell property, and engage in business operations stipulated in the corporate charter.

The corporation is a creature of the state, being chartered under its laws. Its length of life is independent of its owners' (stockholders) lives. It is the corporation, and not its owners, that is liable for debts contracted by it. Its directors and officers serve as agents to bind the corporation.

Rights and Status of Stockholders

Ownership in a corporation is evidenced by stock certificates, each of which stipulates the number of shares held by the given stockholder. An ownership interest does not confer a legal right to act for the firm or to share in its management. It does evidence the right to receive dividends in proportion to stockholdings—but only when they are properly declared by the board of directors. And it typically carries the right to buy new shares, in proportion to stock already owned, before the new stock is offered for public sale.

In the initial organization of a corporation, the owner does well to consider a type of stock known as **Section 1244 stock**. By issuing stock pursuant to Section 1244 of the Internal Revenue Code, the stockholder is somewhat protected in case of failure. If the stock becomes worthless, the loss (up to $100,000 on a joint return) may be treated as an ordinary tax-deductible loss.

A stockholder casts one vote per share in stockholders' meetings. Thus, the stockholder indirectly participates in management by helping elect the directors. The **board of directors** is the governing body for corporate activity. It elects the firm's officers, who manage the enterprise with the help of management specialists. The directors also set or approve management policies, receive and consider reports on operating results from the officers, and declare dividends (if any).

The legal status of stockholders and managers is fundamental, of course, but it may be overemphasized. In the case of many small corporations, the owners may also be directors and managing officers. The person who owns most of the stock can control the business as effectively as if it were a proprietorship. In such a case, this person can name his or her spouse and an outsider as fellow directors. The directors can meet only when legally required to do so, and they can elect the principal owner as president and general manager of the firm. This is not to imply that it is good business practice to ignore a board of directors but simply to point out that direction and control may be exercised as forcefully by a majority owner in a small corporation as by an individual proprietor. The corporate form is thus applicable to individual and family-owned businesses.

Major stockholders must be concerned with their working relationships, as well as their legal relationships, with other owners, particularly with those who are active in the business. Cooperation among the entire owner–manager team of a new corporation is necessary for its survival. Legal technicalities are important, but they provide an inadequate basis for successful collaboration by those who are in reality "partners" in the enterprise.

Limited Liability of Stockholders

One of the advantages of the corporate form of organization is the limited liability of its owners. However, new small-business corporations often are in somewhat shaky financial circumstances during the early years of operation. As a result, the stockholders, few in number and active in management, frequently asume personal liability for the firm's debts by endorsing its notes.

Death or Withdrawal of Stockholders

Unlike the partnership, ownership in a corporation is readily transferable. Exchange of shares of stock is all that is required to convey an ownership interest to a different individual.

In a large corporation, stock is being exchanged constantly without noticeable effect upon the operations of the business. In a small firm, however, the change of owners, though legally just as simple, may produce numerous complications. To illustrate, suppose that two of the three equal shareholders in a business for one reason or another sold their stock to an outsider. The remaining stockholder would then be at the mercy of the outsider, who might decide to remove the former from any managerial post he or she happened to hold. In fact, a minority stockholder may be legally ousted from the board of directors and have no voice whatsoever in the management of the business.

The death of the majority stockholder could be equally unfortunate. An heir, executor, or purchaser of the stock might well insist upon direct control, with possible adverse effects for the other stockholders. To prevent problems of this nature from arising, legal arrangements should be made at the time of incorporation to provide for management continuity by surviving stockholders, as well as for fair treatment of heirs of a decedent stockholder. As in the case of the partnership, mutual insurance may be carried to assure ability to buy out the decedent's interest. This arrangement would require an option for the corporation or surviving stockholders to: (1) purchase the decedent's stock ahead of outsiders, and (2) specify the method for determining the stock's price per share. A similar arrangement might be included to protect remaining stockholders if a given stockholder wished to retire from the business at any time.

The Corporate Charter

In most states, three or more persons are required to apply to the secretary of state for permission to incorporate. After preliminary steps, including required publicity and payment of the incorporation fee and initial franchise tax, the written application is approved by the secretary of state and becomes the corporation's charter. A **corporation charter** typically provides for the following:

1. Name of the company.
2. Formal statement of its formation.
3. Purposes and powers—that is, type of business.
4. Location of principal office in the state of incorporation.
5. Duration (perpetual existence, 50-year life and renewable charter, etc.).
6. Classes and preferences of classes of stock.
7. Number and par (or stated value) of shares of each class of stock authorized.
8. Voting privileges of each class of stock.
9. Names and addresses of incorporators and first year's directors.
10. Names and addresses of, and amounts subscribed by, each subscriber to capital stock.
11. Statement of limited liability of stockholders (required specifically by state law in many states).
12. Statement of alterations of directors' powers, if any, from the general corporation law of the state.

A corporation's charter should be brief, in accord with the law, and broad in the statement of the firm's powers. Details should be left to the bylaws. The charter application should be prepared by an attorney.

The Subchapter S Corporation

For many small firms the corporate income tax is a disadvantage of the corporate form of organization.[8] One solution in such cases is to organize as a **Subchapter S corporation**, an arrangement which allows stockholders to be taxed as partners and thus avoid the corporate income tax. Approximately 17 percent of the companies filing income tax returns do so as Subchapter S corporations.[9] The name of this type of corporation comes from Subchapter S of the Internal Revenue Code, which permits corporations to retain the limited-liability feature while being taxed as partnerships. During the early years of corporate life, the Subchapter S arrangement also permits corporate losses to flow through to stockholders, who can use them to offset other types of income on their tax returns.

A number of restrictions exist in the creation of Subchapter S corporations. For example, the number of stockholders is restricted to 35 or less. Various other restrictive features should be checked with an attorney at the time of organization, but the potential advantages of the Subchapter S corporate form are such as to justify its serious consideration.[10]

AREAS OF BUSINESS LAW RELEVANT TO THE SMALL BUSINESS

Some of the legal issues that affect small businesses are evident in the discussion of the various topics throughout this book. For example, in buying a business, reviewing a franchise contract, or incorporating, the need for legal counsel is clear. In addition, some broad areas of business law are relevant to small-business operation and need to be a part of the entrepreneur's planning as he or she starts a business.

Contracts

Managers of small firms frequently make agreements with employees, customers, suppliers, and others. In some of these agreements, called **contracts**, the parties intend to create mutual legal obligations. For a valid contract to exist, the following requirements must be met:

1. *Voluntary agreement.* A genuine offer must be accepted unconditionally by the buyer.
2. *Competent contracting parties.* Contracts with parties who are under legal age, insane, seriously intoxicated, or otherwise unable to understand the nature of the transaction are typically unenforceable.
3. *Legal act.* The subject of the agreement must not be in conflict with public policy, such as a contract to sell an illegal product.
4. *Consideration.* Something of value, or consideration, must be received by the seller.
5. *Form of contract.* Contracts may be written or oral. Some contracts must be in written form to be enforceable. Under the **statute of frauds**, sales transactions of $500 or more, sales of real estate, and contracts extending for more than 1 year must be in writing. The existence of an oral contract must be demonstrated in some way; otherwise it may prove difficult to establish.   .

If one party to a contract fails to perform in accordance with the contract, the injured party may have recourse to certain remedies. Occasionally, a court will require specific performance of a contract when money damages are not adequate. However, courts are generally reluctant to rule in this manner. In other cases, the injured party has the right to rescind, or cancel, the contract. The most frequently used remedy takes the form of money damages, which are intended to put the injured party in the same condition that he or she would have been in had the contract been performed. In many cases, a creditor–seller arranges for certain security devices so that he or she need not rely exclusively on the credit standing or ability of the debtor to pay.

Another claim against property that is quite important to some types of small businesses is the **mechanic's lien**. For example, materials suppliers or contractors who perform repair or construction would have a lien against the property if the property owner or tenant defaulted in payments for either materials or labor.

State laws that require creditors to be reasonably prompt in filing their claims are known as **statutes of limitations**. These laws are intended to protect debtors from claims in which the evidence is so old that the facts have become difficult to establish. Although time periods under the statute of limitations vary depending on the type of contract, an action for breach of contract on a sale of goods must be started within four or other state-specified number of years. For small creditors, this means that legal action should not be postponed indefinitely if there is any expectation of forcing payment.

Various states have enacted **bulk sales laws**, which effectively preclude a debtor from making a secret sale of an entire business before a creditor can take the necessary legal action to collect. In general, bulk sales laws provide that any debtor's sale of a business inventory down to the bare walls must be preceded by written notification to the creditors of the business. Otherwise, such bulk sales are fraudulent and void with respect to the creditors.

Agency Relationships

An **agency** is a relationship whereby one party, the *agent*, represents another party, the *principal*, in dealing with a third person. Examples of agents are: the manager of a branch office who acts as the agent of the firm, a partner who acts as an agent for the partnership, and real estate agents who represent buyers or sellers.

Agents, however, differ in the scope of their authority. The manager of a branch office is a general agent, whereas a real estate agent is a special agent with authority to act only in a particular transaction.

The principal is liable to a third party for the performance of contracts made by the agent acting within the scope of the agent's authority. A principal is also liable for fraudulent, negligent, and other wrongful acts of an agent which are executed within the scope of the agency relationship.

An agent has certain obligations to the principal. In general, the agent must accept the orders and instructions of the principal, act in good faith, and use prudence and care in the discharge of agency duties. Moreover, the agent is liable if he or she exceeds stipulated authority and causes damage to the third party as a result—unless the principal ratifies the act, whereupon the principal becomes liable.

It is apparent that the powers of agents can make the agency relationship a potentially dangerous one for small firms. For this reason, small firms should exercise care in selecting agents and clearly stipulate their authority and responsibility.

Negotiable Instruments

Credit instruments that can be transferred from one party to another in place of money are known as **negotiable instruments**. Examples of negotiable instruments are promissory notes, drafts, trade acceptances, and ordinary checks. When a negotiable instrument is in the possession of an individual known as a **holder in due course**, it is not subject to many of the defenses possible in the case of ordinary contracts. For this reason, the small-business firm should secure instruments that are prepared in such a way as to make them negotiable. In general, the requirements for negotiable instruments are:

1. There must be a written, signed, unconditional promise or order to pay.
2. The amount to be paid must be specified.
3. The instrument must provide for payment on demand, at a definite time, or at a determinable time.
4. The instrument must be payable to the bearer or to the order of some person.

Real Property

As distinguished from **personal property**, which refers to things that are movable in nature, **real property** consists of land and buildings and other installations permanently attached to land. Real property is also commonly called real estate.

When the ownership in real property is absolute, that property in a legal sense is known as an **estate in fee simple**. Absolute ownership implies that owners can do what they wish with the property except for any government restrictions imposed. For example, an owner can sell, rent, lease, or even give away the real property. A conveyance of real property must be in written form to be valid. Legal counsel is desirable to assure that transactions are legally correct and truly represent the desires of the contracting parties. The transfer of ownership is accomplished by the transfer of a deed, which should be recorded in the office of the county recorder.

A **lease** is an agreement whereby a property owner (the landlord) confers upon a tenant the right of possession and use of real property for which the tenant pays rent. Leases may be either oral or written. According to the laws of most states, leases for periods longer than one year must be written.

Tenancies may be either definite or indefinite with regard to the time period of a lease. Under a **tenancy at will**, the lease may be terminated at any time upon the request of either party. A few states require the party terminating such a lease to provide some notice of the impending termination.

Registration of Trademarks

A **trademark** is a word, figure, or other symbol used to distinguish a product sold by one manufacturer or merchant. Small manufacturers, in particular, often find it desirable to adopt a particular trademark and to feature it in advertising.

Before a name is adopted it should be researched carefully. Joseph W. Alsop, president of Data Language Corporation of Billerica, MA, thought its name for a computer software program, Progress, was cleared for use. A trademark application was initially rejected because another company was using the name to sell educational materials. An agreement was worked out allowing both firms to use the name. But later a Houston, TX, software company, not uncovered in the trademark search, was found to be using the Progress name. However, Data Language was able to work out still another agreement with the Houston firm.[11]

Common law recognizes a property right in the ownership of trademark. In addition, registration of trademarks is permitted under the federal Lanham Trademark Act—a step that generally makes protection easier if infringement is attempted.[12] A trademark registration lasts for 20 years and may be renewed for additional 20-year periods. Application for registration should be made to the U.S. Patent and Trademark Office. The different states also have trademark registration laws, although it is still the common law that provides the basic protection for the owner of the trademark. Full registration is recommended because the growth of a business firm may eventually make its trademark an extremely valuable asset. Even with proper registration, the trademark owner may be considered to have abandoned the trademark if extensive disregard of it is allowed.

Proper use of a trademark in the marketing efforts of the small business serves to protect the trademark. Two rules can help. One is to be sure the name is not carelessly used in place of the generic name. For example, the Xerox company never wants a person to say that he or she is "xeroxing" something. Second, the business should inform the public that the trademark is a trademark by labeling it with the symbol ®.

Application for Patents

A **patent** is the registered right of an inventor to make, use, and sell an invention. Items that may be patented include machines and products,

---

ACTION REPORT
No Monopoly on a Name

There is a tendency for a small business to be pushed around by the threat of a legal battle with "big brother." But when you think you are right, there is strength to carry you through the days and years of battle. Ralph Anspach is a case in point. Having consulted two trademark lawyers prior to naming his board game Anti-Monopoly, he was not about to change names when Parker Brothers, the marketer of Monopoly since 1935, sent threatening letters promising to sue.

Anspach, through his lawyers, offered several compromises—Anti-Monopolist, Anti-Monopoli, or Anti-Monopolism—but each was refused by Parker Brothers. For nine years the conflict continued over the name. Parker Brothers even offered to settle by buying out the name for $500,000. No deal, because Anspach believed he was going to win. His confidence was shaken when U.S. District Court Judge Spencer William twice ruled in favor of Parker Brothers. But later, in the U.S. Ninth Circuit Court of Appeals, the lower court's decision was overridden and on February 22, 1983, the U.S. Supreme Court declined to hear the case.

The impact of the U.S. Supreme Court action was to declare "Monopoly" to be a generic term; therefore, it is no longer a trademark.

Source: Reprinted with permission, *Inc.* magazine, September, 1983. Copyright © 1983 by Inc. Publishing Company, 38 Commercial Wharf, Boston, MA 02110.

---

improvements on machines and products, and new and original designs. Some small manufacturers have patented items which constitute the major part of their product line. Indeed, some businesses can trace their origin to a patented invention.

A patent attorney is often retained to act for a small-business applicant in preparing an application. In addition to an attorney's fees, a modest filing fee is required. When obtained, a patent is good for a period of 17 years and is not renewable. Since improvements may be patented, however, even a small-business firm obtaining an original patent may perpetuate control of the device through timely improvements or design changes.

Suits for patent infringements may be brought, but they are costly and should be avoided if possible.[13] Finding the money and legal talent with which to enforce one's legal rights is one of the major problems of patent protection in small business. Monetary damages and injunctions are available, however, · if an infringement can be proved.

ACTION REPORT
Protection for a Student Invention

The process of obtaining legal protection for original work can be both time-consuming and costly. Joe Bays, a defensive lineman for Southern Methodist University, grew tired of parking-lot dents inflicted on his blue Mercury Cougar. So, he devised a door protector which was invisible when not in use but which could be deployed in 30 seconds. Prior to marketing the invention, Bays decided to obtain both trademark and patent protection.

At a cost of $150, the trademark search identified 18 other firms already using in their names his tentative product name, "Bodyguard." He then came up with the name "SUPA" (an acronym for "Security Unit Protecting Automobiles"). This time, at the cost of another $150, the trademark cleared, and Bays filed the trademark for another $250.

Bays also submitted a patent application in May, 1978. The first application was returned after ten months by the U.S. Patent Office with a notation that a patent had been awarded earlier for a device to protect whitewall tires from curb abrasions. Bays realized his application may have been misunderstood, so he filed a second application in May, 1979. After later making a substantial improvement in the door protector, he invested in still another patent application. The new application, together with the trademark applications and already-pending patent application, ran his legal fees into the $4,000 to $5,000 range.

Source: Dave Clark, "Cockeyed Inventive Optimist," *Texas Business* (April, 1981), pp. 102–103.

Copyright Protection

A **copyright** is the registered right of a creator (author, composer, designer, or artist) to reproduce, publish, and sell the work which is the product of the intelligence and skill of that person. According to the Copyright Act of 1976, the creator of an original work that has been copyrighted receives protection for the duration of the creator's life plus 50 years.

Authors, to avoid loss of protection, must give notice of a copyright on all distributed materials. The notice consists of three elements (see the page following the title page of this textbook):

1. The symbol ©.
2. The year when the work was published.
3. The copyright owner's name.

The law provides that copyrighted, creative work cannot be reproduced by another person or persons without authorization. Even photocopying of such work is prohibited, although an individual may copy a limited amount of material for research purposes. A copyright holder can sue a copyright violator for damages.

Libelous Acts

Libel may be defined as printed defamation of one's reputation. Unless proper precautions are taken, there is a danger of including materials in credit correspondence that may be held by the court to be libelous. Even ordinary collection letters to a debtor have in some cases been held to be libelous by virture of being dictated by a creditor to a stenographer. This was held to constitute "publication" of the statement.

Under the Fair Debt Collection Act of 1977, it is a federal offense for debt collectors to do the following, among other things:

1. Threaten consumers with violence.
2. Use obscene language.
3. Publish "shame" lists.

Violators are liable for any actual damages, as well as additional civil damages, determined by the court up to $1,000.

CHOOSING AN ATTORNEY

A review of legal organizational forms and areas of business law makes evident the need for proper legal counsel. Unless the entrepreneur is trained in law, he or she cannot be·expected to know the law sufficiently well to avoid the use of professionals. Nor should the small business wait to establish a working relationship with a competent attorney until an emergency arises. The small firm's team of professional counselors should include an attorney, a CPA, a banker, and other specialists.

The small firm needs an attorney experienced in legal practice related to small business. Lawyers might be selected by using the Yellow Pages, reading an advertisement, or consulting a law directory, but an informed choice requires a recommendation based on some acquaintanceship with the legal profession. Suggestions of possible attorneys may be obtained from the firm's banker, CPA, or even from other business owners. Lawyers who practice in other areas of law or law school professors, for example, may also be in a position to make recommendations.

Following is one set of advice to consider when locating a good lawyer:

1. Begin by talking to other people in your community who own or operate a small business. Ask them about other lawyers that they've used. Word-of-mouth is an excellent means to size up a lawyer.
2. Friends, relatives, and business associates can also provide names of lawyers.
3. Shop around. It's certainly acceptable to look before you leap. You would spend time shopping for a new car, so why not for a lawyer with whom you will be spending just as much if not more time?
4. Check on the lawyer's experience. Lawyers specialize, and your needs may be very specific also.
5. Be sure you are comfortable with the lawyer. Evaluate his or her personality to be sure that the relationship has a chance to work.
6. Evaluate the accessibility of the lawyer. Determine if he or she is interested in you and your business.
7. Try to select a lawyer who is a doer! Excessive delays in taking action can be extremely costly to your business.
8. Talk about fees. Have a clear understanding of what services are included. Don't be afraid to negotiate the rates.[14]

The firm's relationship with its attorney is most effective when courtroom battles are unnecessary. Much of an attorney's contribution is made by providing information when specific questions arise, when contracts or other documents are reviewed, and when counseling is needed. The relationship should preferably be a continuing one. Once an attorney–client relationship is established, the client should utilize the attorney's services promptly whenever the need arises.

Lewis Burger, president of Nationwide Legal Services, Inc., of Hartsdale, NY, emphasizes this need to stay in contact even if it's only a regular phone call to discuss a planned decision. Burger says, "If people took the time to check with their attorneys, the huge sum of monies spent on legal fees could be drastically reduced, and 80 percent of the matters that wind up in court would not."[15]

Looking Back

1. In a proprietorship the owner receives all profits and bears all losses. The principal limitation of this form is the owner's unlimited liability.

2. A general partnership should be established on the basis of a partnership agreement. Partners can individually commit the partnership to binding contracts. In a limited partnership, general partners are personally liable for the debts of the business, while limited partners have limited personal liability as long as they do not take an active role in managing the business.

3. Corporations are particularly attractive because of their limited-liability feature. The fact that ownership is easily transferable makes them well-suited for combining the capital of numerous owners. Corporations whose total equity capital does not exceed $1 million may issue stock pursuant to Section 1244 of the Internal Revenue Code. If such stock becomes worthless, the loss may be treated as an ordinary tax-deductible loss.

4. Contracts are binding agreements for legal acts made by competent contracting parties and involve something of value for both parties. A small firm should exercise care in selecting its agents and clearly stipulate their authority and responsibility. Negotiable instruments permit the transfer of credit from one party to another. Real property—or real estate—consists of land, buildings, and other installations. Small firms may seek protection of their names and original work by registering their trademarks and applying for patents or copyrights. Libel refers to the printed defamation of one's reputation, so precautions should be taken to avoid libelous statements about others.

5. The small firm needs an attorney experienced in legal practice related to small business. The most important contributions of the attorney are typically made by providing counsel and reviewing legal documents rather than appearing in court for the firm, although the latter may be required occasionally.

DISCUSSION QUESTIONS

1. Discuss the relative importance of the three major legal forms of organization.
2. Suppose a partnership is set up and operated without formal articles of partnership. What problems might arise? Explain.
3. Explain why the agency status of business partners is of great importance.
4. What is a limited partnership, and how does it differ from a general partnership?

5. What is the advantage of Section 1244 stock in a small corporation?

6. What is a Subchapter S corporation, and what is its advantage?

7. Evaluate the three major forms of organization from the standpoint of management control by the owner and the sharing of the firm's profits.

8. Is degree of liability for debt ordinarily a significant factor in choosing the legal form of organization? Why? Is it ever possibly a factor of negligible concern in selecting the form of organization? Why?

9. Give the legal requirements that must be fulfilled to make a contract valid and binding.

10. Define the following: (a) statute of frauds, (b) mechanic's lien, and (c) statute of limitations.

ENDNOTES

1. This does not imply that there are no legal obligations, such as compliance with zoning and licensing laws, but merely states that no legal documents are necessary to create a proprietorship.

2. This is the definition given in the Uniform Partnership Act now adopted by most states. A copy of the act can be found in Ronald H. Anderson, Ivan Fox, and David P. Twomey, *Business Law* (12th ed.; Cincinnati, OH: South-Western Publishing Co., 1984).

3. David H. Bennet, "Making a Partnership Work," *Nation's Business*, Vol. 72, No. 5 (May, 1984), p. 66.

4. For an excellent discussion of the limited partnership, see W. K. Daugherty, "The Limited Partnership—A Financing Vehicle," *Journal of Small Business Management*, Vol. 18, No. 2 (April, 1980), pp. 55–60.

5. Even when a deal goes bad the limited partner can take some positive actions. See, for example, Richard Greene, "All Men Are Not Created Equal," *Forbes*, Vol. 133, No. 6 (March 12, 1984), p. 158.

6. For a more detailed treatment of the tax benefits, see "Limited-Liability Deals: 'Selling Like a Good 5-Cent Cigar'," *Business Week*, No. 2822 (December 26, 1983), pp. 157–161.

7. An excellent treatment of R&D partnerships including advantages, risk, documentation, tax considerations, and more is found in *Forming R&D Partnerships: An Entrepreneur's Guidebook*, a pamphlet published by Deloitte, Haskins & Sells, 1983.

8. The corporate income tax is not a disadvantage in all cases—for example, in a new firm which is not yet profitable.

9. John A. Byrne, "A Trap for the Unwary?" *Forbes*, Vol. 129, No. 6 (March 15, 1982), p. 52.

10. For a side-by-side comparison of a proprietorship, partnership, regular corporation, and Subchapter S corporation on 28 selected characteristics, see Table 2-1 in Carolyn M. Vella and John J. McGonagle, Jr., *Incorporating A Guide for Small-Business Owners* (New York: AMACOM, 1984), pp. 18–23.

11. Christine Quarembo, "Trademarking Your Name," *Venture*, Vol. 7, No. 6 (June, 1985), p. 34.

12. An easy-to-understand presentation of the requirements for registration can be found in Ira N. Bachrach, "How To Choose and Use A Trademark," *Nation's Business*, Vol. 71, No. 3 (March, 1983), pp. 70–72.

13. An excellent discussion of patent laws can be found in Louis W. Stern and Thomas L. Eovaldi, *Legal Aspects of Marketing Strategy, Antitrust and Consumer Protection Issues* (Englewood Cliffs, NJ: Prentice-Hall, Inc., 1984), Ch. 2.

14. Based on the material in Fred S. Steingold, *Legal Master Guide for Small Business* (Englewood Cliffs, NJ: Prentice-Hall, Inc., 1983), Ch. 29.

15. Sid Kane, "When a Lawyer Is Unnecessary," *Venture*, Vol. 6, No. 6 (June, 1984), p. 43.

REFERENCES TO SMALL BUSINESS IN ACTION

Easton, Nina. "The Art of Partnership Survival." *In Business*, Vol. 6, No. 3 (May–June, 1984), pp. 34–38.
> The four partners of Just Desserts, a successful bakery, discuss the lessons learned from their partnership relationship. Good communications helped the partnership work.

Kahn, Joseph P. "Whipped!" *Inc.*, Vol. 7, No. 2 (February, 1985), pp. 35–44.
> This article provides a detailed account of the battle of an independently owned company against Kraft Food over the name of a new salad dressing. This "Salad Bowl" battle had an extremely disruptive impact on the small business.

Kamoroff, Bernard. "Saving Taxes in a Family Business." *In Business*, Vol. 7, No. 1 (February, 1985), pp. 54–56.
> A detailed look at how legal structure of "mom-and-pop" firms can affect tax payments. A numerical example comparing a proprietorship with a partnership scenario is provided.

Mamis, Robert A. "Hoyle Schweitzer's Decade of Discontent." *Inc.*, Vol. 4, No. 2 (February, 1982), pp. 54–60.
> The story of an inventor who, after receiving a patent, later received a challenge that his sailboard had already been invented.

———. "Sparring Partners," *Inc.*, Vol. 6, No. 3 (March, 1984), pp. 43–50.
> Partnership feuds, fights, and failures are described in this article devoted entirely to case histories. The names are changed to protect the innocent.

CASE 9

"No Strain" Testers

An inventor seeks to obtain a patent on his own

Harvey Strain was an employee of a highly successful lithographic printing equipment manufacturer in Dallas, TX. He had worked more than 15 years as a "trouble-shooter" for the company, solving customers' problems with purchased printing presses. Harvey had always been interested in mechanical devices. During his teenage days, he was constantly working in the family garage modifying automobiles for drag racing. His creative skills had remained active. For example, at age 44, he finished building a custom-designed car from new and used parts.

The Invention

Recently Harvey turned his creative talents and mechanical skills toward an idea which had the potential to be a marketable product. His invention would be used with lithographic printing presses such as those produced by his employer. His invention was an automatic testing reservoir used in connection with dampening systems on those lithographic printing presses. Figure 9–3 shows promotional material designed by Harvey for his invention. The device maintained a constant alcohol solution level, continuously sampling the circulating solution to give an accurate, specific gravity reading. The product overcame the existing problems, time, and expense involved in maintaining the proper alcohol percentage with existing battery-type testers.

Harvey realized the potential value of a patent but was uncertain if he could handle the patenting process or whether he should turn it over to a lawyer. In a recent article of a trade magazine, *Machine Design*, he read some hints on how to market an invention. The article encouraged Harvey to "try it on his own." The article stated further that a patent could be obtained at a cost in the neighborhood of $1,000.

The Patenting Process

On December 22, 1975, Harvey wrote a privately owned Washington-based patent search company. Its response was cordial, requesting that he fill out the enclosed patent Protection Forms "…giving us as detailed a sketch of your invention as possible…" and offering to conduct a patentability search for $50. "In the meantime," the letter continued, "…no attempt should be made to sell your invention since under our present laws you have nothing to sell (no legal property) until an application for patent has actually been filed in the Patent Office and you have *PATENT PENDING*."

Figure 9–3   Promotional Material for Alcohol Testers

No Strain ® Alcohol Testers

FEATURES:

1. CONTINUOUS AND AUTOMATIC SPECIFIC GRAVITY AND TEMP READ OUT
2. SIMPLE DESIGN
3. LOW COST MODELS FOR ALL CIRCULATING SYSTEMS
4. EASY INSTALLATION

ALCOHOL PERCENTAGE AT A GLANCE

AVAILABLE AS OPTIONAL EXTRA ON DAHLGREN DAMPENING SYSTEMS

No Strain Products
715 E. Center
Duncanville, Texas 75116
AC 214 — 296-2214

REMOTE MOUNT MODEL
APPROXIMATELY
½ SCALE

On January 19, 1976, Harvey authorized the patent search, enclosing the completed Record of Disclosure and the $50 fee. On February 4, 1976, A. Mercedes, Managing Director for the Washington Patent Office Search Bureau, wrote Harvey saying, "We are pleased to report that your invention appears to be patentable." A. Mercedes urged Harvey to proceed with the preparation and filing of a patent application. He also offered his company's services in helping Harvey prepare the specifications, claims, and the Official United States Patent Office Drawing. The fee for this assistance would be $500 plus the $65 Official United States Government Filing Fee.

Harvey decided to "continue on his own." He prepared his own drawings and specifications. On February 16, 1976, he filed his Petition for Patent and other required documents. His letter of transmittal is shown in Figure 9–4.

Figure 9–4   A Letter of Transmittal

P.O. Box 3185
Irving, TX 75061
February 16, 1976

Commissioner of Patents
United States Patent Office
Washington, DC 20231

To the Commissioner of Patents

Enclosed are my Petition for Patent, Oath to Accompany my Petition, Abstract, Specifications, Claim, and a check in the amount of $65.00, which I understand is the initial filing fee.

The preliminary patentability search was completed by the Washington Patent Office Search Bureau, P.O. Box 7167, Washington, DC 20044, who reported that my invention appeared to be patentable.

I am unable to utilize their additional services or the services of a patent attorney and will appreciate your indulgence in considering the attached drawings and specifications which I have prepared.

Yours sincerely

(Sgd.) Harvey A. Strain

Six months later, Harvey received a letter from the Commissioner of Patents and Trademarks. Harvey quickly opened the letter. His application had been rejected. Although this was bad news, Harvey did not want to give up.

The rejection decision was based on three reasons, two of which were minor and one serious. One minor problem concerned the oath (or declaration) provided by Harvey in his letter of February 16, 1976. The form required to correct this problem was enclosed in the letter from the

Commissioner of Patents and Trademarks. The other minor problem involved errors in the drawings, which could be corrected by the Patent Office for $24. The serious problem was that the Patent Office claimed that Harvey's idea fell under the requirements that "A patent may not be obtained...if the differences between the subject matter sought to be patented and the prior art are such that the subject matter as a whole would have been obvious at the time the invention was made to a person having ordinary skill in the art to which said subject matter pertains." This pronouncement sounded very "final."

Questions

1. Would you have believed the magazine article about a patent for less than $1,000, or would you have gone to a lawyer? What difficulties are involved in being one's own attorney?
2. What do you think Harvey Strain should have done to get his patent? Be specific.
3. Do you believe Harvey should have forgotten the patent and marketed his product without patent protection? Why or why not?

PART III
SMALL-BUSINESS MARKETING

10 – Consumer Behavior and Product Strategies
11 – Distribution, Pricing, and Credit Policies
12 – Personal Selling, Advertising, and Sales Promotion

10
Consumer Behavior and Product Strategies

Figure 10–1   Michael Klein

Photo by Michael Keza, Nation's Business

Small firms can sometimes use the same marketing strategies as larger firms. Selecting the "best" color for a product is one such strategy used effectively by Michael Klein of Sentinel Consumer Products as he positioned his firm's "cotton" swabs against those of Johnson & Johnson and Procter & Gamble. He successfully introduced his swabs, which are actually made of rayon rather than cotton, in blue, yellow, and pastel pink. The pastel colors of Klein's swabs contrast his product with the all-white swabs of his major competitors.

Source: Sharon Nelton, "Adapting to a New Era in Marketing Strategy," *Nation's Business*, Vol. 72, No. 8 (August, 1984), p. 22. Reproduced with permission.

Looking Ahead

Watch for the following important topics:

1. Activities which are encompassed by small-business marketing.
2. Economic, psychological, and sociological concepts of consumer behavior.
3. Decision-making stages of consumer behavior.
4. Product strategy, product development, and the product life cycle.
5. How a firm can build a total product using branding, packaging, labeling, and warranties.

Ultimately the success of every business requires an acceptable level of sales. Those activities that have the most direct impact on achieving success in sales are marketing activities. It is vital, therefore, that small-business managers recognize the importance of marketing and understand how to develop good marketing strategies. A business cannot rely on a strong financial strategy, a tight accounting system, or a sound organizational plan as a substitute for good marketing.

In Chapter 5 we analyzed market segmentation, marketing research, and sales forecasting because of the close relationship of these marketing activities to starting the small business. Many additional activities are also necessary for ongoing, successful small-business marketing. Consumer behavior analysis and product strategies are examined in this chapter. Distribution, pricing, and credit policies are analyzed in Chapter 11. Personal selling, advertising, and sales promotion are discussed in Chapter 12.

Before discussing consumer behavior, we need to examine the scope of small-business marketing more closely. This will provide an overall perspective for the treatment of various marketing topics.

SCOPE OF MARKETING ACTIVITIES FOR SMALL BUSINESSES

Many years ago, marketing was defined as "the performance of business activities that affect the flow of goods and services from producer to consumer or user."[1] Notice that this definition emphasizes distribution. Many people continue to view marketing in this manner. Actually marketing is much more. Many marketing activities occur even before a product is produced! In an effort to portray the complete scope of marketing and to make our discussion useful for small business, we will propose a definition for small-business marketing which focuses on marketing activities. **Marketing** consists of those business activities which relate directly to determining target markets and preparing, communicating, and delivering a bundle of satisfaction to these markets. Every small business should initially engage in marketing to determine its target markets. Then, and only then, can final preparation of the "product" be achieved. Communication and delivery of the "product" are the remaining purposes of marketing.

From the definition of marketing given above, we can identify the marketing activities which are essential to every small business. These activities, called *core marketing activities*, are depicted in Figure 10–2. Notice that the core marketing activities have been appropriately matched with the key terms in our definition of marketing. The activities numbered 1 through 3 constitute the process of market analysis. The activities numbered 4 through 7 comprise a firm's marketing mix and are the focal points in Part III of this text.

Figure 10–2   Core Marketing Activities for Small Business

Key Terms from Our Definition of Marketing	Core Marketing Activities	
"...determining target markets..."	1. Market segmentation 2. Market research 3. Consumer behavior analysis	Market Analysis
"...preparing...a bundle of satisfaction...	4. Product strategy 5. Pricing	Marketing Mix
"...communicating...a bundle of satisfaction..."	6. Promotion	Marketing Mix
"...delivering a bundle of satisfaction..."	7. Distribution	

Obviously the sophistication of the marketing effort in a small business will vary from situation to situation. Financial conditions often restrict the resources devoted to these activities. However, these realities in no way lessen the importance of understanding the benefits of marketing activities.

CONCEPTS OF CONSUMER BEHAVIOR

Having adopted both the marketing concept and a market segmentation strategy, the small-business manager is started on the road to successful sales. Before proceeding to develop a marketing program, however, one must first understand the realities of consumer behavior. We will begin this analysis by touching on the economic, psychological, and sociological aspects of consumer behavior.

Traditional Economic Concepts

Traditional economic theories visualized the consumer as a rational buyer who possesses perfect information. *Rational* means that emotional buying factors are not considered. Maximization of value is an assumed goal for the consumer. Price, therefore, becomes the sole mediator between supply and demand. The entrepreneur should not totally ignore these economic theories because they can help explain types of behavior. For example, if a consumer sees a half-price special on a nationally branded grocery product, she or he may buy more at the lower price. This buying decision follows the classic economic theory of consumer behavior.

Another assumption of classic economic theory is the existence of a homogeneous market where consumers behave in a fairly similar manner. Recall the total-market approach in our earlier discussion on market segmentation in Chapter 5. The total-market view has roots in the economic concept of consumer behavior.

While recognizing the contribution of economic theories, the entrepreneur should bear in mind that they are overly restrictive and lacking in scope. There is much consumer behavior that cannot be captured by the traditional image of the "economic man." A fuller explanation is needed.

A Modern Consumer-Behavior Roadmap

The complexity of consumer behavior is staggering. An exploration of this world of behavior requires a model, or "roadmap." Many models exist in the literature of consumer behavior, but our version is intended for the small-business situation. The roadmap in Figure 10–3 has a psychological, a sociological, and a decision-making phase. Study it carefully. When the totality of the trip is first seen, each leg of the journey should then become clearer. We will examine each "roadsign" and show its relevance to consumer behavior.

Psychological Concepts   Psychological factors may be labeled as hypothetical because they cannot be seen or touched. By process of inference, however,

Figure 10–3 . Roadmap to Understanding Consumer Behavior

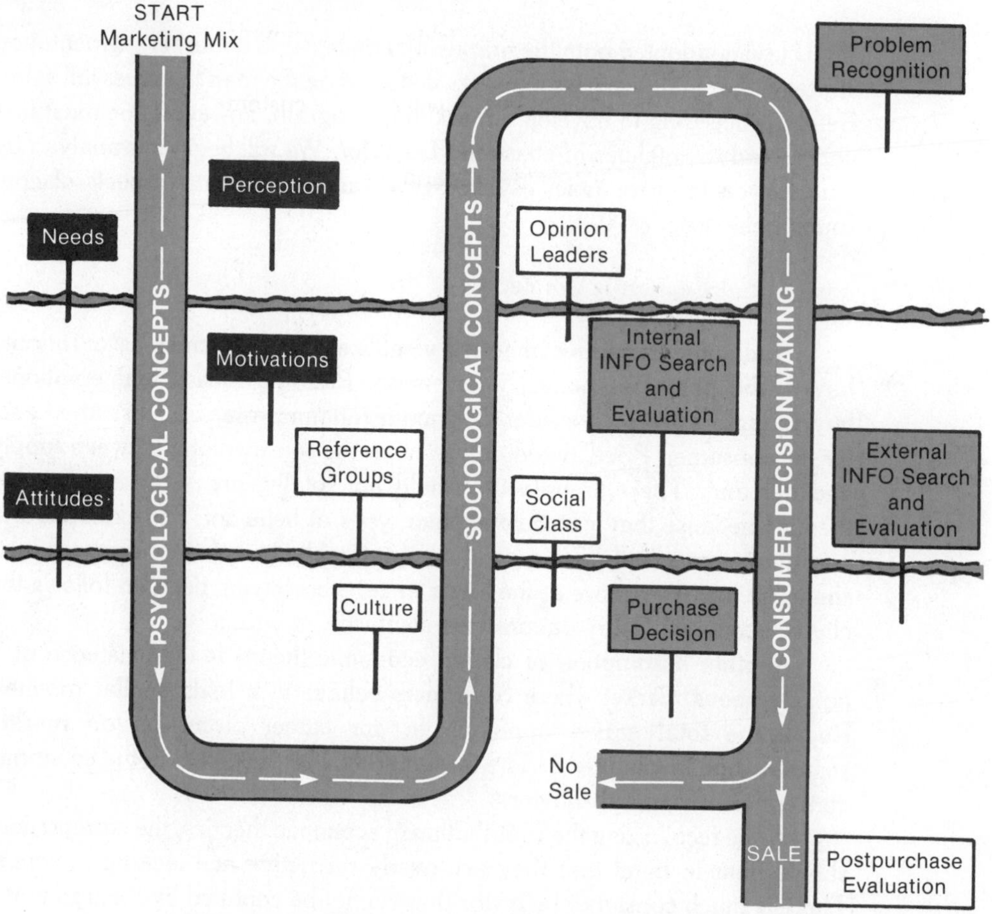

several factors have been "identified." The four factors that have the greatest relevance to small business are perception, needs, motivations, and attitudes.

Perception Our initial psychological roadsign in Figure 10–3 is perception. **Perception** describes those individual processes which ultimately give meaning to stimuli that confront consumers. The "meaning" is not easily understood, however. It may be severely distorted or entirely blocked. Perception by customers can screen a firm's marketing effort and make it ineffective.

Perception is a two-sided coin. It depends on the characteristics of both the stimulus and the perceiver. For example, it is known that consumers attempt to manage huge quantities of incoming stimuli by a process of **perceptual categorization**. This means that things which are similar are perceived as belonging together. If a small business attempts to position its product alongside an existing brand and to have it accepted as a comparable product, its marketing mix should reflect an awareness of perceptual categorization. A similar price can be used to communicate similar quality. A package design with a similar color scheme may also be used to convey the identical meaning. These techniques will help the customer fit the new product into the desired product category.

Firms that select a family brand name for a new product rely on perceptual categorization to "presell" the new product. On the other hand, if the new product is generically different or of a different quality, a unique brand name may be selected to avoid perceptual categorization.

If an individual has strong brand loyalty to a product, it is difficult for other brands to penetrate that person's perceptual barriers. Competing brands will likely experience distorted images because of the individual's attitude. The perceptual mood presents a unique communication challenge.

ACTION REPORT
Product "Look-Alikes"

A small business can use perceptual categorization to position its own brands against the brands of big business. Leon Levine uses this strategy with his Family Dollar brands in his variety discount stores in Charlotte, NC.

Levine uses packaging as one means of implementing the positioning strategy, as evidenced by the following comments:

> He points to a bottle of Family Dollar window cleaner that is next to bottles of Bristol-Myers' Windex. "Look familiar?" he asks. They do. The Family Dollar bottle looks like the Windex bottle. Is that on purpose? "I take the Fifth," he says, smiling.

Source: "The Leon and Al Show," *Forbes,* Vol. 126, No. 7 (September 29, 1980), pp. 52–56.

Needs   We will define **needs** as the basic seeds of (and the starting point for) all behavior. Without needs, there would be no behavior. There are many lists of consumer needs, but the major points we wish to convey do not require an extensive listing.[2] Needs are either physiological, social, psychological, or spiritual.

Needs are never completely satisfied. This favorable characteristic of needs assures the continued existence of business. An unfavorable characteristic of needs is the way they function together in generating behavior. In other words, various "seeds" (remember the definition) can blossom together.

This makes it more difficult to understand which need is being satisfied by a specific product or service. Nevertheless, a careful assessment of the need–behavior connection can be very helpful in developing marketing strategy. For example, many food products in supermarkets are purchased by consumers to satisfy physiological needs. But food is also selected in status restaurants to satisfy social and/or psychological needs. A need-based strategy would add a different flavor to the marketing strategy in each of these two situations.

Motivations Unsatisfied needs create tension within an individual. When this tension reaches a certain level, a person becomes uncomfortable and attempts to reduce the tension.

We are all familiar with "hunger pains." These are manifestations of tension created by an unsatisfied physiological need. What is it that directs a person to seek food so the "hunger pains" can be relieved? The answer is motivation. **Motivations** are goal-directed forces within humans which organize and give direction to tension caused by unsatisfied needs. Marketers cannot create needs, but they can create and offer unique motivations to consumers. If an acceptable reason for purchasing is provided, it will probably be internalized as a motivating force. The key for the marketer is to determine which motivation the consumer will perceive as an acceptable solution for the "hunger pains." The answer is found in analyzing the other consumer behavior variables.

For example, Slim-Fast, a meal replacement product, was first introduced in 1977 but was not promoted heavily until after the Cambridge Diet received nationwide attention in 1983. Slim-Fast was offered to the diet-conscious consumer as an alternative to appetite suppressants. The product was positioned to remove the tension associated with using the suppressants while also satisfying the motivation to lose weight.[3]

Each of the other three classes of needs is similarly connected to behavior via motivations. When a person's social needs create tension due to incomplete satisfaction, a firm may show how its product can fulfill those needs by providing acceptable social motivations to that person. For example, a campus clothing store can promote the styles which communicate that a college student has obtained group membership.

Understanding motivations is not easy. Several motives may be present in each situation. Many times the motivations are subconscious, but they must be investigated if the marketing effort is to have an improved chance for success.

Attitudes Like the other psychological variables, attitudes cannot be observed, but all persons know that they have attitudes even before these are defined. Do attitudes imply knowledge? Do they imply a feeling of good/bad or favorable/unfavorable? Does an attitude have a direct impact on behavior? Probably you answered "yes" to all these questions. If you did, you were correct each time. An **attitude** is a feeling toward an object organized around knowledge which regulates behavioral tendencies.

An attitude can be an obstacle or a catalyst in bringing a customer to your product. Armed with an understanding of the structure of an attitude, the marketer can approach the consumer more intelligently. One of the more popular structural views of an attitude is based on the original work of Martin Fishbein.[4] As adapted to a marketing situation, Fishbein's idea is that a person's attitude toward a brand results from the belief that the brand has certain attributes that are weighted by the importance of these attributes to that person. A more precise formulation is:

$$A_0 = \sum_{i=1}^{j} B_i I_i$$

where: A_0 = attitude toward an object (brand)
B = belief that the brand has a certain attribute
I = importance of the attribute to the individual
i = the particular attribute of concern
j = number of relevant attributes

Table 10-1 shows that two hypothetical market segments for a ballpoint pen have equal attitude scores but relatively different unfavorable attitudes. The strategies to improve these individual attitudes would be totally different. To improve the attitudes of consumers in Segment A, the seller needs to persuade them that the pen is attractive because attractiveness (importance rating of 7) is important to them. Currently they do not believe the pen is attractive (belief rating of 2). They recognize that the pen is inexpensive to buy (belief rating of 7), but this is obviously not very important to them (importance rating of 1). If the seller feels that price is a distinct marketing advantage, consumers need to be persuaded to place more importance on low price.

The company has a different problem with consumers in Segment B. How well the pen writes is very important to them. They see the pen as being attractive, but this attribute isn't important to them. Mathematically, you can see various possibilities for increasing their attitude score.

Sociological Concepts   Up to this point in our "trip," our roadmap has taken us past the psychological roadsigns. As we turn the corner in Figure 10-3, we are confronted with several social considerations. We cannot ignore the people around us and their influence on our actions. Among these social influences are culture, social class, reference groups, and opinion leaders.

Table 10-1   Attitude Structures of Two Market Segments

Object = Community Ballpoint Pen ®

SEGMENT A			SEGMENT B		
Attribute	**B_i***	**I_i***	**Attribute**	**B_i***	**I_i***
Attractive—	$2 \times 7 = 14$		Attractive—	$6 \times 1 = 6$	
High quality—	$3 \times 4 = 12$		High quality—	$5 \times 6 = 30$	
Writes well—	$5 \times 6 = 30$		Writes well—	$3 \times 7 = 21$	
Inexpensive—	$7 \times 1 = 7$		Inexpensive—	$2 \times 3 = 6$	
A_0	$= 63$		**A_0**	$= 63$	

---

*The scale ranges from 1 to 7, with a higher value meaning greater importance of the attribute to the individual or a greater belief that the attribute is present in the product.
**The most favorable attitude score would be 196.

Notice that each of the sociological concepts represents different degrees of people aggregation. Starting with culture, we see large masses of people. Then we see smaller groups—social classes and reference groups—until we find a single individual who exerts influence, the opinion leader.

Culture   Mankind's social heritage is called **culture**. This heritage has a tremendous impact on the purchase and use of products. Marketing managers will often overlook the cultural variable because its influences are so neatly concealed within the society. Cultural influence is somewhat like the presence of air. You really do not think about its function until you are in water over your head! Then you realize the role that air has played in your existence. On the other hand, international marketers who have experienced more than one culture can readily attest to the reality of cultural influence.

It is the prescriptive nature of culture which most concerns the marketing manager. Cultural norms create a range of product-related, acceptable behavior which tells consumers what they should buy or at least what they ought to buy. Culture does change, however. It adapts slowly to new situations. Therefore, what works today as a marketing strategy may not work a few years later.

An investigation of culture with a narrower definitional boundary, such as age, religious preference, ethnic orientation, or geographical location, is called **subcultural analysis**. Here, too, the unique patterns of behavior and social relationships concern the marketing manager. For example, the needs and motivations of the youth subculture are far different from those of the senior-citizen subculture. Certain food preferences are unique to Jewish culture. Cigarettes do not sell well among Mormons. If small-business managers familiarize themselves with cultures and subcultures, they can prepare better marketing mixes.

Innovative entrepreneurs can use what they know about local and cultural preferences to start successful businesses. One example is Alvin Copeland, the president and founder of Popeye's Famous Fried Chicken and Biscuits which began in New Orleans. He provided a menu emphasizing Cajun cuisine and super-spicy fried chicken which appealed to the taste preferences of Louisiana consumers. A tenth-grade dropout and native of New Orleans, he now drives a red Mercedes convertible with "SPICY" on his license plate.[5]

Social Class   Another sociological concept in consumer behavior is social class. **Social class** describes divisions in a society with different levels of social prestige. There are important implications for marketing in a social-class system. Different life-styles correlate with the different levels of social prestige, and products are often symbols of life-styles.

Unlike a caste system, a social-class system provides for upward mobility. It is not the status position of parents which permanently fixes the social class of their child. Occupation is probably the single most important determinant of social class. Other determinants that are used in social-class research include possessions, source of income, and education.

For some products, like consumer packaged goods, social-class analysis will probably not be very useful. For others, like home furnishings, it may help to explain variations in shopping and communication patterns.

Reference Groups   Although social class could, by definition, be considered to be a reference group, we are more generally concerned with small groups such as the family, the work group, a neighborhood group, or a recreational group. Not every group is a reference group. Reference groups are only those groups from which an individual allows influence to be exerted upon his or her behavior.

The existence of group influence is well-established.[6] The challenge to the marketer is to understand why this influence occurs and how the influence can be used to promote the sale of a product. Individuals tend to accept group influence for the benefits perceived. These perceived benefits allow the influencers to use various kinds of power. Bertram Raven and John French have classified these forms of power as reward, coercive, expert, referent, and legitimate. Each of these power forms is available to the marketer.

Reward power and **coercive power** relate to a group's ability to give and to withhold rewards. Rewards can be material or psychological. Recognition and praise are typical psychological rewards. A Tupperware party is a good example of a marketing technique which takes advantage of reward power and coercive power. The ever-present possibility of pleasing or displeasing the hostess–friend tends to encourage the guest to buy.

Referent power and **expert power** involve neither rewards nor punishments. These types of power exist because an individual attaches a unique importance to being like the group or perceives the group as being in a more knowledgeable position than the individual. Referent power causes consumers to conform to the group's behavior and to choose products selected by the group's members. Young children will often be influenced by referent power. Marketers can create a desire for products similar to those used by adults whom children seek to emulate. For example, young cowboys and young baseball players are now using a chewing gum product cleverly designed and packaged to look like chewing tobacco in packs. Figure 10–4 shows the wrapper of one of these products.

Legitimate power involves the sanction of what one ought to do. We saw legitimate power at the cultural level when we talked about the prescriptive nature of culture. This type of power can also be used at a smaller group level.

Opinion Leaders   The concept of opinion leaders is largely a communication idea. According to this concept, consumers receive a significant

Figure 10–4   Package Using Reference Group Appeal

amount of information through individuals called opinion leaders. Thus, an **opinion leader** is a group member playing a key communications role.

Generally speaking, opinion leaders are knowledgeable, visible, and exposed to the mass media. Small-business firms can enhance their own product and image by identifying with such leaders. For example, a farm-supply dealer may promote agricultural products in a community by arranging demonstrations on the farms of outstanding farmers. These farmers are the community's opinion leaders. Also, department stores may use attractive students as models in showing campus fashions.

Consumer Decision Making   Having passed the psychological and socio-logical roadsigns of consumer behavior, we will now examine those of consumer decision making. One theory about human-information processing holds that humans are problem-solvers. We will adopt this view for our discussion. Under this theory the stages of consumer decision making are:

1. Problem recognition.
2. Internal information search and evaluation.
3. External information search and evaluation.
4. Purchase decision.
5. Post-purchase evaluation.

The first roadsign of the consumer-decision phase of our roadmap tells us that the consumer must recognize a problem before making a purchase. This first stage cannot be circumvented. It is a mistake to concentrate on helping the consumer at later stages when, in reality, the consumer has not recognized a problem.

The time required for the second and third stages—internal and external information search and evaluation—varies with the product and the con-sumer. The scheduling of various communication strategies should reflect such time-dimension differences. The decision to buy a new product—the fourth stage—will naturally take longer than a decision involving a known product. For example, an industrial-equipment dealer may find it necessary to call on a prospective new customer over a period of months before making the first sale. Some decisions become routine and programmed; others do not.

The decision process does not terminate with a purchase. A small firm which desires repeat purchases from its customers should follow them into the post-purchase stage. A helpful concept for understanding the post-purchase process is **cognitive dissonance**, which takes the form of an uncomfortable psychological tension or a feeling of inequity. Cognitive dissonance tends to occur when a consumer has purchased one brand from among several which had attractive features. Second thoughts or doubts about the decision are bound to occur. The firm whose product was purchased should attempt to reduce the consumer's tension by communicating with that customer after the sale.

Consumers are complex creatures and will never be completely understood. However, the concepts we have presented are relevant to strategy development. Even a simple recognition of their existence, without a thorough understanding, can save a small business from serious mistakes. Too often these concepts are considered to be "big-business tools."

The ultimate benefit from what has been said so far in this chapter can be found by turning Figure 10–3 on page 264 so that "START" is in the top right-hand corner and "SALE" is in the lower left-hand corner. Do you see the big dollar sign? The most successful small-business manager will likely be the best student of consumer behavior.

DEFINITIONS OF PRODUCT TERMINOLOGY

In this book, **product strategy** describes the manner in which the product component of the marketing mix is used to achieve the objectives of a firm. A **product** is the total "bundle of satisfaction" which is offered to customers in an exchange transaction. The product can be tangible, like a watch, or intangible, like a tax service.

A product includes not only the main element of the "bundle," which is the physical product itself, but also complementary components such as packaging. Of course, the physical product is usually the most important component. But sometimes the main element of a product is perceived by customers to be like that of all other products. The complementary components can then become the most important features of the product. For example, a particular cake mix brand may be preferred by consumers, not because it is a better mix, but because of the toll-free telephone number on the package which can be called for baking hints.

A **product mix** is the collection of product lines within a firm's ownership and control. A **product line** is the sum of the individual product items that are related. The relationship is usually defined generically. Two brands of bar soap would be two product items in one product line. A **product item** is the lowest common denominator in a product mix. It is the individual item.

The more items in a product line, the more depth it has. The more product lines in a product mix, the greater the width of the product mix. Finally, **product mix consistency** refers to the closeness of the product lines. Closeness signifies the similarity of the product lines.

PRODUCT STRATEGIES FOR SMALL BUSINESS

Small-business managers are often weak in their understanding of product strategy. This creates ineffectiveness and conflict in the marketing effort. In order to provide a better understanding of product strategy in small business, we will now examine product strategy in greater detail.

Product Strategy Alternatives

The overall product strategy alternatives of a small business can be presented in eight categories. We identify these strategy alternatives as follows:

1. Current product/current market.
2. Current product/new market.
3. Modified product/current market.
4. Modified product/new market.
5. New similar product/current market.
6. New similar product/new market.
7. New unrelated product/current market.
8. New unrelated product/new market.

Each alternative represents a different approach to product strategy. Some strategies can be pursued concurrently. Usually, however, the small firm will find that it will adopt the alternatives in basically the order listed. Keep this premise in mind as you read about each one.

Current Product/Current Market   In the earliest stage of a new venture, the current product/current market product strategy is followed. Most entrepreneurs start with one product. Growth can be achieved under this strategy in three ways. First, current customers can be encouraged to use more of the product. Second, potential customers within the same market can be sold on the product. Third, current customers can be educated to use the existing product for additional purposes, thereby increasing demand. An example is Minnetonka's Softsoap, which was originally positioned as a replacement for bar soap. More recently, it has been promoted as a gift item and a skin-care product.

Current Product/New Market   An extension of the first alternative is the current product/new market product strategy. With a small additional commitment in resources, a current product can often be targeted to a new market. Taking a floor-cleaning compound from the commercial market into the home market would be an example of this strategy.

Modified Product/Current Market Customers seemingly anticipate the emergence of "new, improved" products. With the modified product/current market strategy, the existing product can be either replaced, gradually phased out, or left in the product mix. If the existing product is to be retained, the impact on sales of the modified product must be carefully assessed. It doesn't do much good to make an existing product obsolete unless the modified product has a larger profit margin. The product modification can involve a very minor change. For example, adding colored specks to a detergent can give the business a "new" and extremely sales-attractive product. Some people, of course, would question the social value of such "improvements."

Modified Product/New Market A modified product can also be used to reach a new market. The only difference in the modified product/new market strategy from the previous one is its appeal to a new market segment. For example, a furniture manufacturer currently selling finished furniture to customers might market unfinished furniture to the "do-it-yourself" market.

ACTION REPORT
Opening the Window to New Markets

Competition in an existing target market will often force a business to consider expansion of its product mix. This is exactly the motivation which led Efco Corporation of Monett, MO, to develop a commercial grade window to add to its residential-design window—an example of a modified product for a new market.

Efco started producing a residential window in the basement of a laundry in St. Louis, MO, in 1952. A price war was spawned by the entry of competitors and eventually Efco moved to Monett to escape the competition. However, as price cutting continued, Terry Fuldner, Efco's founder, did not find the solution to his problem by moving.

> Residential windows offered 'a frustrating future,' he says. 'We would make money one year and lose it the next.' Such cutthroat competition didn't exist in commercial windows, which were made then by a few companies.

Aided by a U.S. Government contract to supply commercial windows to an Air Force base, Efco expanded its product mix and quickly became entrenched in a new market. Efco later dropped its residential window production as the firm continued to extend the product mix. Efco now produces special windows for schools and hospitals.

Source: Reprinted by permission of *The Wall Street Journal,* © Dow Jones & Company, Inc., 1985. All Rights Reserved.

New Similar Product/Current Market   Current, satisfied customers make good markets for new additions to the product assortment of a small business. Many products can be added which are more than product modifications but are still similar to the existing products. These new products are considered to be similar when they have a generic relationship. For example, Celestial Seasonings, Inc., of Boulder, CO, has moved into a caffeine-free hot drink called Breakaway, which is a recent addition to its herb teas.[7] The new product is generically similar to the tea products. It is aimed at the same health-care market.

New Similar Product/New Market   Going after a different market with a new but similar product is still another product strategy. This approach is particularly appropriate when there is concern that the new product may reduce sales of the existing product in a current market. For example, a firm producing wood-burning stoves for home use might introduce a new gas-burning furnace targeted for use in office buildings.

New Unrelated Product/Current Market   A product strategy which includes a new product generically different from existing products can be very risky. However, the new unrelated product/current market strategy is sometimes used by small businesses, especially when the new product fits existing distribution and sales systems. For example, a local dealer selling Italian sewing machines may add a line of microwave ovens.

New Unrelated Product/New Market   The final product strategy occurs when a new unrelated product is added to the product mix to serve a new market. This strategy has the most risk among all the alternatives since the business is attempting to market an unfamiliar product to an unfamiliar market. For example, one electrical equipment service business added a private employment agency.

With this product strategy, however, a hedge can be built against volatile shifts in market demand. If the business is selling snowshoes and suntan lotion, it hopes that demand will be high in one market at all times.

Managing the Product Mix

The management of the firm's product mix is guided by many considerations. Competition, market demand, pricing flexibility—to name just a few—are important influences in this regard.

Two marketing concepts are extremely useful to the small-business manager in any efforts to control and develop the firm's product mix. These are the product development curve and the product life cycle. Both of these concepts provide concise summaries of activities or circumstances relating to the management of the product mix.

The Product Development Curve   A major responsibility of the entrepreneur is to recognize, prepare, and implement any of the product strategy alternatives discussed earlier. Many of these strategies require a structured mechanism for new-product development. In big business, committees or even entire departments are created for that purpose. In a small business this responsibility will usually rest with the entrepreneur.

The entrepreneur usually views new product development as a mountainous task. Therefore, we show the product development curve in Figure 10–5 in the form of a mountain. The left slope of the mountain represents the gathering of a large number of ideas. Beginning at the mountain peak, these ideas are screened as you move down the right slope until the base of the mountain—the retention of one product ready to be introduced into the marketplace—is reached.

Figure 10–5   The Product Development Curve

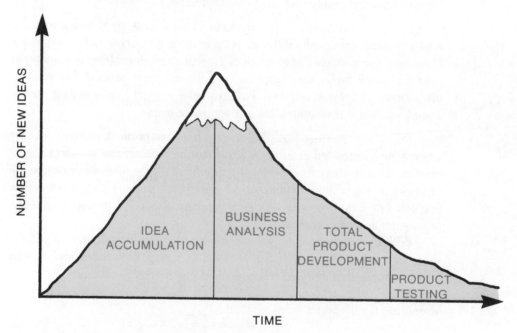

The first phase of the product development curve, labeled *Idea Accumulation*, shows the need to increase the number of ideas under consideration. New products start with new-product ideas, and these ideas have varied origins. Some of the many possible sources of ideas are:

1. Sales, engineering, or other personnel within the firm.
2. Government-owned patents, which are generally available on a royalty-free basis.

3. Privately owned patents listed in the Official Gazette of the U.S. Patent Office.
4. Other small companies which may be available for acquisition or merger.
5. Competitors' products and advertising.
6. Requests and suggestions from customers.

Business Analysis is the next stage in the process. Every new-product idea must be carefully analyzed in relation to several considerations.

Relationship to Existing Product Line   Any product to be added should be consistent with, or properly related to, the existing product line. For example, a new product may be designed to fill a gap in the company's product line or in the price range of the products it currently manufactures. If the product is completely new, it should normally have at least a family relationship to existing products. Otherwise, the new products may call for drastic and costly changes in manufacturing methods, distribution channels, type of promotion, or manner of personal selling.

Cost of Development and Introduction   One problem in adding new products is the cost of development and introduction. The capital outlays may be considerable. These include expenditures for design and development, market research to establish sales potential and company volume potential, advertising and sales promotion, patents, and the equipment and tooling that must be added. It may be from one to three years before profits may be realized on the sale of the contemplated new or altered product.

Personnel and Facilities   Obviously, having adequate skilled personnel, managers, and production equipment is better than having to add personnel and buy equipment. Hence, introducing new products is typically more logical if the personnel and the required equipment are already available.

Competition and Market Acceptance   Still another factor to be considered is the character of the market and the potential competition facing the proposed product. Competition must not be too severe. Some authorities, for example, think that new products can be introduced successfully only if a 5 percent share of the total market can be secured. The ideal solution, of course, is to offer a sufficiently different product or one in a cost and price bracket that avoids direct competition.

The next stage, *Total Product Development*, entails the planning for suitable branding, packaging, and other supporting efforts such as pricing and promotion. After these components are considered, many new-product ideas may be discarded.

The last step in the product development curve is *Product Testing*. This means that the physical product should be proven to perform correctly. While the product can be evaluated in a laboratory setting, a test of market reaction to the total product should also be conducted. This test can be performed only in the marketplace.[8]

The Product Life Cycle   Another valuable concept for managing the product mix is the product life cycle. Our portrayal of the product life cycle in Figure 10–6 takes the shape of a roller coaster ride. This is actually the way many entrepreneurs describe their experiences with the life cycle of their products. The initial stages are characterized by a slow and upward movement. The stay at the top is exciting but relatively brief. Then, suddenly the decline begins, and the movement down is fast.

The product life cycle gives the small-business manager a planning tool. Promotional, pricing, and distribution policies are a reflection of the curve. This gives the entrepreneur valuable insights into marketing mix modifications.[9]

When a small business is committed to the product development concept, it can look forward to expanding its product mix successfully and to staying above the nemesis of the "Roller-Coaster Ride" pictured in Figure 10–6.

Figure 10–6   The Product Life Cycle

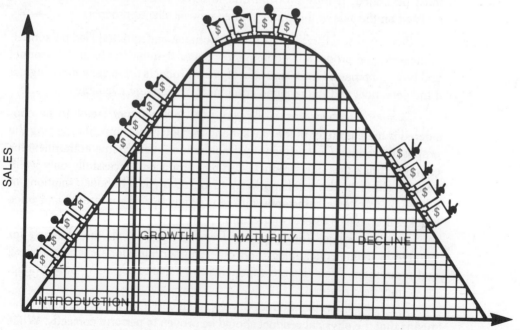

TIME

Building the Total Product

A major responsibility of marketing is to transform a basic product into a total product. An idea for a unique new writing pen which has already been developed into a physical reality is still not ready for the marketplace. The total product, in this example, would incorporate more than the materials molded into the shape of the new pen.[10] To be marketable, the basic product must be named, have a package, perhaps have a warranty, and be supported by many other product components. We will now examine a few of these components.

Branding   An identification for a product is termed a brand. A brand includes both the identification which can be verbalized and that which cannot. The name Xerox is a brand, as are the "golden arches" of a famous hamburger chain. A name and a trademark are important to the image of the business and its products. Therefore, considerable attention should be given to every decision in a branding strategy.

In general, there are five rules to follow in naming a product:

1. *Select a name which is easy to pronounce.* You want customers to remember your product. Help them with a name that can be spoken easily. An entrepreneur's own name should be carefully evaluated to be sure it is acceptable. The founder of a major fast-food chain used his daughter's name for the company. Her name? Wendy. The name of the business? Wendy's.

2. *Choose a descriptive name.* A name which is suggestive of the major benefit of the product can be extremely helpful. The name Elephant for a computer memory disk correctly suggests a desirable benefit. The name Rocky Road would be a poor selection for a mattress!

3. *Use a name which can have legal protection.* Be careful that you select a name that can be defended successfully. This is sometimes difficult, but do not risk litigation by intentionally copying someone else's brand name. A new soft drink named Prof. Pepper would likely be contested by the Dr Pepper company.

4. *Consider names that have promotional possibilities.* Exceedingly long names are not, for example, compatible for good copy design on billboards, where space is at such a premium. A competitor of the McDonald's hamburger chain is called Wuv's. This name will easily fit on any billboard.

5. *Select a name which can be used on several product lines of a similar nature.* Many times customer goodwill is lost when a name doesn't fit a new line. A company producing a furniture polish called Slick-Surface could not easily use the same name for its new sidewalk surfacing compound, which purports to increase traction.

A small business also should carefully select its trademark. The mark should be unique, easy to remember, and related to the product.[11]

Trademark registration for products in interstate commerce is handled through the U.S. Patent and Trademark Office under the authority of the Lanham Trademark Act. This Act also covers the registration of service marks, certification marks, and collective marks.

Once a trademark is selected by a small business, it is important to protect its use. Two rules can help. One is to be sure the name is not carelessly used in place of the generic name. For example, the Xerox company never wants a person to say that he or she is "xeroxing" something. Second, the business should inform the public that the brand is a brand by labeling it with the symbol ™. If the trademark is unusual or written in a special form, it is easier to protect.

Packaging   Packaging is another important part of the total product. In addition to protecting the basic product, packaging is also a significant tool for increasing the value of the total product. Consider for a moment some of the products you purchase. Do you buy them primarily because of preference for the package design and/or color?

Packaging is also used for promotional purposes. It is important for some food products, for example, to be visible through the package. The manager of Dryden & Palmer Co. in Norwalk, CT, which employs 30 people and produces rock candy, talks about the package for his product this way: "Basically you've got a round product that's put in a square box. Rock candy needs to be seen. It's really quite attractive."[12]

Packaging can also open the door to new markets. Sam Gallo, president of a small Baton Rouge company, has introduced coffee bags. Coffee bags have been tried before but failed due to packaging, which allowed the coffee to become stale. Mr. Gallo guarantees a nine-month shelf life for his product and calls it "Morning Treat."[13]

Labeling   Another part of the total product is its label. Labeling is particularly important to manufacturers who apply most labels. A label serves several purposes. It often shows the brand, particularly when branding the basic product would be undesirable. For example, a furniture brand is typically shown on a label and not on the basic product. On some products, visibility of the brand label is highly desirable. Calvin Klein jeans would probably not sell well with the name labeled only inside the jeans.

A label is also an important informative tool for the small business. It can include information on product care. It can inform consumers how to use the product correctly. It can even include information on how to dispose of the product.

Laws on labeling requirements should be consulted carefully.[14] Be innovative in your labeling information. Include information that goes beyond the specified minimum legal requirements.

Warranties   A **warranty** is simply a promise that a product will do certain things. It may be express (written) or implied. An *implied warranty* refers to the seller's clear title to the product and to its quality. An express warranty on a product is not always necessary. As a matter of fact, many firms operate without written warranties. They are concerned that a written warranty will only serve to confuse customers and make them suspicious. Figure 10–7 may be somewhat representative of this attitude among small businesses.

Figure 10–7   Satisfaction Guaranteed

"But we are completely satisfied with your money."

Source: *The Saturday Evening Post*, Vol. 253, No. 1 (January–February, 1981), p. 28. Reprinted with permission from The Saturday Evening Post Company, © 1981.

The Magnuson-Moss Warranty Act of 1974 has had an impact on warranty practices. This law covers several warranty areas, including warranty terminology. The most notable change in terminology is the use of the terms "Full" and "Limited" on an express warranty for a product that costs over $15.

Warranties are important for products which are innovative, relatively expensive, purchased infrequently, relatively complex to repair, and positioned as high-quality goods. The major considerations which help decide the merits of a warranty policy are:

1. Costs.
2. Service capability.
3. Competitive practices.
4. Customer perceptions.
5. Legal implications.

Looking Back

1. Marketing consists of those business activities which relate directly to determining target markets and preparing, communicating, and delivering a bundle of satisfaction to these markets. The core marketing activities are: market segmentation, marketing research, consumer-behavior analysis, product strategy, pricing, promotion, and distribution.

2. Traditional economic concepts of consumer behavior visualize the consumer as a rational buyer who possesses perfect information, and they assume the existence of a homogeneous market where consumers behave in a fairly similar way. Psychological concepts include perception, needs, motivations, and attitudes. Sociological concepts include culture, social class, reference groups, and opinion leaders.

3. The stages of consumer decision making include problem recognition, internal information search and evaluation, external information search and evaluation, the decision to purchase, and post-purchase evaluation.

4. The eight product strategy alternatives are: current product/current market, current product/new market, modified product/current market, modified product/new market, new similar product/current market, new similar product/new market, new unrelated product/current market, and new unrelated product/new market.

    Two concepts useful to the management of the product mix are the product development curve and the product life cycle. The product development curve consists of four phases: idea accumulation, business analysis, total product development, and product testing. The product life cycle consists of four stages: introduction, growth, maturity, and decline.

5. When choosing a good brand name, the entrepreneur should follow five basic rules. Packaging can be used for protection, promotion, and opening new markets. Labels are informative tools for the marketer. A warranty is simply a promise that a product will do certain things.

DISCUSSION QUESTIONS

1. Select a magazine advertisement and analyze it for the use of reference-group influence and cultural uniqueness.
2. Give some examples of the way in which legitimate power is used in marketing.
3. What kinds of consumer behavior occur in the post-purchase stage? Be specific.
4. What are the three ways to grow when using a current product/current market strategy?
5. How does the new similar product/new market strategy differ from the new unrelated product/new market strategy? Give examples.
6. A manufacturer of power lawn mowers is considering the addition of a line of home barbecue equipment. What factors would be important in a decision of this type?
7. List some of the major activities in the business analysis stage of the product development curve.
8. Select two product names and evaluate each with the five rules for naming a product listed in this chapter.
9. Would a small business desire to have its name considered to be the generic name for the product area? Defend your position.
10. For what type of firm is the packaging of products most important? For what firms is it unimportant?

ENDNOTES

1. Committee on Definitions, *Marketing Definitions: A Glossary of Marketing Terms* (Chicago: American Marketing Association, 1960), p. 15.

2. Several more complete listings can be found in Del I. Hawkins, Roger J. Best, and Kenneth A. Coney, *Consumer Behavior: Implications for Marketing Strategy* (Revised edition; Plano: Business Publications, Inc., 1983), Chapter 11.

3. "A Company That's Getting Fat Because America Wants to Be Thin," *Business Week*, No. 2869 (November 19, 1984), p. 70.

4. *Ibid.*, pp. 418–421.

5. Jo Ellen Davis, "Blackened Fish, Red Beans, and a Cake to Go, Please," *Business Week*, No. 2920 (November 11, 1985), pp. 66–67.

6. For a good discussion of social group influence, see Chapter 9 in David L. Loudon and Albert J. Della Bitta, *Consumer Behavior: Concepts and Applications* (2d edition; New York: McGraw-Hill Book Company, 1984).

7. "What's Brewing at Celestial," *Business Week*, No. 2679 (March 16, 1981), p. 138.

8. For a more detailed discussion of product development, see Carlton A. Maile and Donna M. Bialik, "New Product Management: In Search of Better Ideas," *The Journal of Small Business Management*, Vol. 22, No. 3 (July, 1984), pp. 40–48.

9. A detailed discussion of these changes is beyond the scope of this book. For more details, see Charles D. Schewe and Reuben M. Smith, *Marketing: Concepts and Applications* (2d edition; New York: McGraw-Hill Book Company, 1983), Chapter 10.

10. An intangible service is also a basic product that requires additional product development.

11. For more extensive treatment of trademarks, see Chapter 2 of Louis W. Stern and Thomas L. Eavaldi, *Legal Aspects of Marketing Strategy: Antitrust and Consumer Protection Issues* (Englewood Cliffs, NJ: Prentice-Hall, Inc., 1984).

12. Doron P. Levin, "Rock-Candy Maker Takes Its Licks: An Ailing Vestige of Simpler Times," *The Wall Street Journal*, June 17, 1981, p. 25.

13. "Morning Treat Tilts with Giants," *Sales and Marketing Management*, Vol. 122, No. 7 (May 14, 1979), p. 13.

14. Laws that affect packaging and labeling are treated in Joe L. Welch, *Marketing Law* (Tulsa, OK: The Petroleum Publishing Company, 1980), pp. 127–133.

REFERENCES TO SMALL BUSINESS IN ACTION

Blobaum, Roger. "Rural Energy Market Place." *In Business*, Vol. 4, No. 6 (November–December, 1982), pp. 36–38.
    A family-owned business finds the keys to selling in the farm market are service, trust, and reasonably priced goods. These entrepreneurs' common-sense understanding of consumer behavior has allowed them to serve their customers well.

Goldstein, Rill Ann. "Carving a Niche in Gourmet." *In Business*, Vol. 5, No. 1 (January–February, 1983), pp. 32–34.
    Two female entrepreneurs have found diversification to be a key ingredient in the success of their cuisine-oriented business.

Kahn, Joseph P. "Whipped!" *Inc.*, Vol. 7, No. 2 (February, 1985), pp. 35–44.
    A small firm battles Kraft, Inc. when Kraft contends the firm's Yogowhip trademark is in violation of its Miracle Whip brand.

Mamis, Robert A. "Name-Calling." *Inc.*, Vol. 6, No. 7 (July, 1984), pp. 67–74.
    Many examples of company and product names are used to demonstrate what a name may say about a business.

CASE 10

The Expectant Parent Center*

Linking consumer behavior with a new service business

In February, 1980, Mrs. Ramona Caliban started the first profit-oriented childbirth education center in Scranton, PA. On the basis of eight years' hospital experience as a registered nurse in obstetrics, Ramona made the decision to establish herself as an entrepreneur in the fast-growing service area of childbirth education.

Location and Facilities

Ramona conducted her first prenatal classes in the fellowship hall of her church, charging $20 per couple. She stated:

> At first my only clients were three ladies in the married's Sunday school class at church, so space and facilities were no problem. However, the popularity of my instruction and techniques soon grew to the point that I needed additional room and more professional facilities.

Ramona then rented a small office in a mini shopping center in May, 1980, and began operating as The Expectant Parent Center (EPC). She subsequently moved into a slightly larger facility in the same shopping center.

Nature and Growth of Services

The Expectant Parent Center provided childbirth preparation and instruction to expectant parents through four separate classes, as follows:

1. Childbirth preparation at $45 per couple (6 instructional sessions).
2. Prenatal hygienics and orientation at $20 per couple (2 sessions).
3. C-section at $50 per couple (5 sessions).
4. Prenatal and postpartum exercises at $25 per couple (5 sessions).

Ramona shared instructional duties with two other registered nurses (RNs), who were compensated on the basis of number of teaching contact hours and class size.

The Center had experienced steady growth in enrollments despite lack of advertising. Ramona commented, "We doubled enrollment from May, 1980, to January, 1981. Between January and August of 1981, we doubled once again, peaking at 35 couples per month. Enrollment figures for the last quarter of 1981 averaged 33 couples per month."

*This case was prepared by Steve R. Hardy and Professor Philip M. Van Auken of Baylor University.

Potential Demand

Ramona felt that the Center had only scratched the surface of demand for childbirth education in the Scranton area. She said:

> For a city with more than 100,000 people, I know we could be doing a great deal more business than we are. I have been so busy over the last year with teaching and managerial duties that I really haven't had much time for growth planning. However, I feel that we offer a service very much in demand by enlightened couples. There's no reason why we can't continue to grow at a healthy pace. We'll need larger facilities and more teachers, but that will all come in time.

Marketing Issues

Ramona characterized her marketing strategy as a "bewildering bundle of unanswered questions and unstated assumptions." In particular, she was confused about pricing and advertising. She claimed:

> I just don't know what the market will bear in paying for prenatal education. I'm not even sure what the market is here in Scranton—to whom I should target my services.
>
> Only 2 hospitals in town offer any alternative childbirth education, and they do it for $25 for 2 sessions. However, their classes are typically overcrowded, poorly taught, and offered only sporadically. There is no doubt that most expectant couples are willing to pay for better instruction, but I just don't know how high they are willing to go. Right now I'm pricing pretty much at break-even, at least from the looks of my latest profit-and-loss statement. Now that the business has established itself locally, I want to start turning a decent profit. Prices will definitely have to go up, but I just don't know how far.
>
> Neither am I sure how to best market my services. Obviously our clients are fairly well-educated and somewhat affluent, or they wouldn't be interested in paying for first-class prenatal care. Beyond this reference point, however, my customer profile is fuzzy. If I had a better feel for which people are most interested in the Expectant Parent Center, I would know how to promote and diversify my services better.

Product Line

In addition to its four areas of childbirth instruction, the Center sold a limited line of child-care books, equipment, and educational toys. Included in the products inventory was a back massager invented by Ramona to aid mothers during labor. She explained:

> The massager helps the mother to relax during labor and minimizes muscle spasms in and around the back. The thing has a simple design consisting of a handle with two attached wooden doorknobs. When rolled up and down the back, the wooden wheels greatly counteract muscle tension.
>
> I subcontract out the manufacturing at a cost of $2.40 a unit. I sell them at the Center for $7.00, and they go like hotcakes. I'm currently in the process of getting a manufacturer's rep to circulate them at medical trade shows. He thinks they have national potential if properly marketed.

Competitive Strength

Ramona summed up her perceived competitive edge as follows:

The Expectant Parent Center offers the very finest in childbirth education, presented with tender loving care. We have good facilities, top-notch instructors, auxiliary products, and an affordable price. Given the right marketing, the Center's growth should really explode. To use a bad pun, we're really in a growth business!

Questions

1. Evaluate Ramona Caliban's pricing concerns and her firm's name in the light of consumers' perceptions of marketing stimuli. Recommend an appropriate pricing strategy.
2. What social and cultural influences may impact on the demand for Ramona's services?
3. What types of social power can Ramona use if she begins to promote her services more actively? Be specific. Give an example.
4. How important do you think opinion leadership would be in "selling" Ramona's services? Why?
5. Would you recommend that Ramona continue to pursue the marketing of auxiliary products through the Center? Why or why not?

11

Distribution, Pricing, and Credit Policies

Figure 11–1   Ken Johnson's T-Shirts Plus Warehouse

The warehousing and physical distribution of products is always a vital link in an efficient marketing system. These functions are not characterized as "glamour" marketing activities because they require considerable physical labor and are conducted in an environment much less desirable than an air-conditioned retail store.

However, Ken Johnson, founder of T-Shirts Plus, recognizes the importance of warehousing and regularly checks on the operation of its 44,000-square-foot distribution center in Waco, TX. Starting with an initial investment of $25,000 in 1975, his T-shirt business, commonly referred to as the "McDonalds of the T-Shirt industry," has grown from one store to 225 stores.

Source: Personal conversation with Mr. Ken Johnson.

Looking Ahead

Watch for the following important topics:

1. Functions of intermediaries in a channel of distribution.
2. Considerations in choosing a distribution system.
3. Considerations for the small-business exporter.
4. Cost and demand considerations in pricing.
5. Managing credit in a small business.

A product is finally prepared for exchange with a customer when it is readied for delivery and priced; and, increasingly, pricing must be augmented by credit. Thus, distribution, pricing, and credit policies are critical activities to a complete small-business marketing program and are examined in this chapter.

DISTRIBUTION ACTIVITIES

The term **distribution** in marketing includes both the physical movement of products and the establishment of intermediary (middleman) relationships to guide and support the movement of the product. The physical movement activities form a special field called **physical distribution** or **logistics**. The intermediary system is called a **channel of distribution.**

Distribution is critical for both tangible and intangible goods. Since distribution activities are more visible for tangible goods, our discussion will concentrate on them. Most intangible goods (services) are delivered directly to the user. An income tax preparer, for example, serves a client directly. But even a person's labor can involve channel intermediaries as when, for example, an employment agency is used to find an employer.

Channels of Distribution

A channel of distribution can be either direct or indirect. If it is a *direct* channel, there are no intermediaries. The product goes directly from producer to user. If the channel is *indirect*, one or more intermediaries may exist between the producer and the user.

Figure 11–2 depicts the basic ABCs of options available for structuring a channel of distribution. Channel A has no intermediaries. Door-to-door

Figure 11–2   Alternative Channels of Distribution

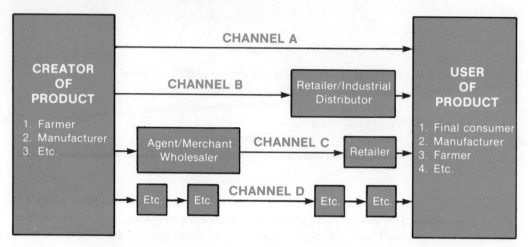

retailing and mail-order are familiar forms of this channel system for consumer goods.

Channel B incorporates one intermediary. The B-type channels are used for both consumer and industrial goods. As final consumers, we are all familiar with retailers. Industrial purchasers are equally familiar with industrial distributors. Channel C shows two levels of intermediaries. This is probably the most typical channel for small businesses that have a large geographic market. The last channel in Figure 11–2 is labeled D. This represents the many other extensions of Channel C. For example, there may be three or more separate intermediaries in the channel. It should be noted that a small business may operate with more than one channel of distribution. This is called **dual distribution.**

Justifying Channels of Distribution   The small-business manager is often puzzled over the use of intermediaries in a channel of distribution. Are they really necessary? What kinds of small businesses really need them? The answer to the first question is "yes," and to the second, "maybe yours."

Intermediaries exist to carry out marketing functions which must be performed and which they can perform better than the producer or the user of a product. Small businesses cannot always perform these necessary functions as well as the intermediaries. This is why intermediaries are necessary.

As an example of the need for intermediaries, consider small producers. The small producer can perform if the geographic market is extremely small, if customers' needs are highly specialized, and if risk levels are low. Otherwise, the producer may find intermediaries to be a more efficient means of performing distribution activities. Of course, many types of small firms also function as intermediaries—for example, retail stores. Four main functions of

---

ACTION REPORT
Dual Distribution Pays Off

What works today may not work tomorrow! This adage applies to many marketing decisions including distribution. The footwear industry is one particular industry which uses several alternative channels of distribution.

In the late 1970s, retail store orders for the shoes produced by E.T. Wright & Company of Rockland, MA, were decreasing. This decline was just a symptom of many underlying marketing problems—including distribution.

Wright made a bold move after a consultant identified its major distribution problem—clinging solely to a costly channel system targeted to independent shoe stores and department store chains. Wright recognized that changes had to be made. However, because of inventory costs, Wright did not want to open its own retail outlets, so it decided to try mail-order distribution. A mail-order system could be supplied with its current inventory. It hired a mail-order consultant and began the mail-order business in 1979. Now 25 percent of total sales are by mail.

Source: Reprinted by permission of *The Wall Street Journal* (July 29, 1985), © Dow Jones & Company, Inc. (1985). All rights reserved.

---

channel intermediaries are: breaking bulk, assorting, providing information, and shifting risks.

Breaking Bulk   Very few individual customers demand quantities which are equal to the amounts produced. Therefore, there must be channel activities which will take the larger quantities produced and prepare them for individual customers. **Breaking bulk** is the distribution term used to denote these activities. Wholesalers and retailers purchase large quantities from manufacturers, store these inventories, and sell them to customers in the quantities they desire.

Assorting   Customers' needs are diverse, requiring many different products to obtain satisfaction. Intermediaries facilitate shopping for a wide assortment of goods through the assorting process. **Assorting** consists of bringing together homogeneous lines of goods into a heterogeneous assortment. For example, a small business producing a special golf club can benefit from an intermediary who carries many other golf-related products and sells to a retail pro shop. It is much more convenient for the pro shop manager to buy from one supplier than from all the producers.

Providing Information   One of the major benefits of using an intermediary is information. Intermediaries can provide the producer with extremely helpful data on market size and pricing considerations.

Shifting Risks   By using intermediaries, the small-business manager can often share or totally shift business risks. This is possible by using **merchant middlemen**, who take title to the goods they distribute. Other intermediaries, such as **agents** and **brokers**, do not take title to the goods.

Choosing a Distribution System   One alternative for the small-business producer, as it decides on a distribution system, is to look at the competition. Some useful ideas about distribution are obtained from observing what others do. In all likelihood the competition will have made their decisions on the basis of practical considerations. At least a model of their distribution system can be used as a starting point.

Basically there are three main considerations in structuring a channel of distribution. We will call these the "three C's" of channel choice: costs, coverage, and control.

Costs   The small business must consider the cost of a channel carefully. A good beginning is to forget the idea that a direct channel is less expensive than an indirect channel. This idea is not inherently true. A small business may well be in a situation in which the less expensive channel is indirect. You should look at distribution costs as an investment. You have to spend money in order to make money. Ask yourself whether the money you would invest in intermediaries would get the job done if you used direct distribution.[1] And don't forget to cost your time fairly.

Coverage   Small businesses use indirect channels of distribution to increase market coverage. To illustrate this point, consider a small-business manufacturer whose sales force can make ten contacts a week. This direct channel provides ten contacts a week with the final users of the product. Now consider an indirect channel involving ten industrial distributors who (for convenience in illustration) each make ten contacts a week with the final users of the product. With this indirect channel, and no increase in the sales force, the small-business manufacturer is now able to expose the product to how many final users a week? If you said 100, you are correct!

Gary Serdel, vice-president of Utility Chemical Company in Paterson, NJ, briefly considered hiring the company's own sales force to reach new retail customers with its swimming pool chemicals and accessories. But "we had to find a low-cost way of opening up these markets," said Serdel. He finally decided on an indirect distribution plan where a sales representative, who was already selling cosmetics in a department store, would distribute his products.[2]

Control   A third consideration in choosing a distribution channel is control. Obviously there is more control in a direct channel of distribution. With indirect channels, products may not be marketed as intended. The small business must select intermediaries which provide the desired support.

The Scope of Physical Distribution

The main component of physical distribution is transportation. Additional components are storage, materials handling, delivery terms, and inventory management. In the following sections we will briefly examine all of these topics except inventory management, which is discussed in Chapter 18.

Transportation   The major decision regarding transportation concerns the mode to use. Alternative modes are traditionally classified as airplanes, trucks, railroads, pipelines, and waterways. Each mode has its unique advantages and disadvantages.[3]

Transportation intermediaries are of three types: common carriers, contract carriers, and private carriers. These are legal classifications which subject the first two types to regulations by federal and/or state agencies. **Common carriers** are available for hire to the general public, while **contract carriers** engage in individual contracts with shippers. Shippers who own their means of transport are called **private carriers**.

Storage   Space is a common problem for a small business because there is never enough. When the channel system uses merchant wholesalers, for example, title to the goods is transferred, as is the storage function. On other occasions, the small business must plan for its own warehousing. If a small business is too small to own a private warehouse, it can rent space in public warehouses. If storage requirements are simple and involve little special handling equipment, a public warehouse can provide an economical storage function.

Materials Handling   A product is worth little if it is in the right place at the right time but is damaged. Therefore, a physical distribution plan must consider materials-handling activities. Forklifts and special containers and packages are part of a materials-handling system. Tremendous improvements have been made through the years in materials-handling methods.

Delivery Terms   A small but important part of a physical distribution plan is the terms of delivery. Delivery terms specify the following:

1. Who pays the freight costs?
2. Who selects carriers?
3. Who bears the risk of damage in transit?
4. Who selects the modes of transport?

The simplest delivery term and the one most advantageous to a small-business seller is F.O.B. origin, freight collect. These terms shift all the responsibility for freight costs to the buyer.[4]

Distribution Abroad

Traditionally, small businesses have been hesitant to engage in exporting. The United States Department of Commerce has estimated that more than 25,000 small United States firms do not export even though they are producing exportable products. The primary reason for this reluctance appears to be unfamiliarity with the exporting process. Unfortunately, "foreign" market means "extraneous" market to many entrepreneurs.[5]

A small firm's interest in exporting can be heightened through an increased awareness in four areas—knowledge of international markets, sources of assistance available, alternative sales and distribution channels for exporting, and special financial incentives to exporters. We will briefly examine each of these in the next section.[6]

Understanding Foreign Markets   A foreign market becomes less foreign as a person learns more about it. An entrepreneur needs to study the cultural, political, and economic forces in the foreign market in order to understand why adjustments to domestic marketing strategies are required. When this is not done, costly mistakes will usually be made. For example, color and objects have different meanings in different cultures. The number *four* is a number symbolizing death in Japan. Unaware of this, a United States golfball manufacturer packaged its golfballs in sets of four for exporting to Japan. Sales were well below forecast.[7]

Sources of Assistance   Researching a foreign market should begin by exhausting as many secondary sources of information as possible. The United States government encourages exporting and offers an array of publications on methods of reaching foreign markets. Figure 11–3 lists some of these government sources and a sampling of their publications.

Universities and other private organizations also provide information on exporting. The national accounting firm of Deloitte Haskins & Sells is a good example. It publishes an excellent booklet entitled *Expanding Your Business Overseas: An Entrepreneur's Guidebook*.

Talking with a native of a foreign market or someone who has visited the foreign country can be a valuable method to learn about that market. Most universities have international students who can usually be contacted through faculty members who teach in the international area.

Sales and Distribution Channels   Channel options for foreign distribution are numerous. The channels can be direct or can involve intermediaries who work for commissions or who take title and assume all risks. Figure 11–4 shows the channels to foreign markets that are available to the small business. The export management companies (EMC) described in Figure 11–4 have been popular among entrepreneurs. According to Richard J. Singer, vice-president of marketing for Singer Products Company of Westbury, NY, "There is an EMC available for virtually any entrepreneur. The advantage for the entrepreneur is that we've built the goodwill necessary to do business in foreign countries."[8]

Figure 11–3   Foreign Trade Information Sources

U.S. FOREIGN TRADE SOURCES

Agencies

1. Director
   Bureau of Export Development
   U.S. Department of Commerce
   Washington, DC 20230
   202-377-5261

2. Export-Import Bank of the
   United States
   811 Vermont Avenue NW
   Washington, DC 20571
   Toll-free number:
   800-424-5201

3. Director
   Export Trade Services Division
   Foreign Agricultural Service
   U.S. Department of Agriculture
   Washington, DC 20250
   202-447-6343

4. Federal Trade Commission
   Public Reference Branch
   6th Street and Pennsylvania
      Avenue NW
   Room 130
   Washington, DC 20580
   202-523-3830

5. Department of the Treasury
   U.S. Customs Service
   1301 Constitution Avenue NW
   Washington, DC 20229
   202-566-8195

Publications

1. *Government and Business: A Joint Venture in International Trade* (free booklet published by the U.S. State Department's Office of Commercial Affairs)
   To order, write to:
   Office of Public
   Communication
   Bureau of Public Affairs
   U.S. State Department
   Room 48-27A
   Washington, DC 20520
   202-632-6575

2. *Guide to United Nations' Conference of Trade and Development (UNCTAD) Publications* (free catalog published by UNCTAD)
   To order, write to:
   United Nations Sales Section
   Editorial and Documents
      Section
   Palais Des Nations 1211
   Geneva 10, Switzerland

3. Lorna M. Daniells, *Business Information Sources* (Berkeley, CA: University of California Press, 1976), p. 258, list of reference data sources for exporters.

Figure 11-3 (Continued)

U.S. FOREIGN TRADE SOURCES

Agencies	Publications
6. Office of Commercial Affairs Bureau of Economic and Business Affairs Room 33-34 U.S. State Department Washington, DC 20520 202-632-8097	4. *Quarterly Economic Review* (London, England: Economist Intelligence Unit), reviews 45 countries quarterly. 5. *Foreign Economic Trends and Their Implications for the United States* (Washington, DC: U.S. Bureau of International Commerce), semi-annual. 6. *OECD Economic Surveys* (Paris, France: Organization for Economic Cooperation and Development), individual annual reviews listed by country. 7. *Investing, Licensing, and Trading Conditions Abroad* (New York, NY: Business International), two volumes.

Source: Reprinted by permission of the *Harvard Business Review.* Exhibit from "Systematic Approach to Finding Export Opportunities" by Changiz Pezeshkpur (September/October 1970). Copyright © 1979 by the President and Fellows of Harvard College; all rights reserved.

Figure 11-4   Foreign Market Channels of Distribution

Sales Representatives or Agents—A sales representative is the equivalent of a manufacturer's representative here in the United States. Product literature and samples are used to present the product to the potential buyer. He usually works on a commission basis, assumes no risk or responsibility, and is under contract for a definite period of time (renewable by mutual agreement). This contract defines territory, terms of sale, method of compensation, and other details. The sales representative may operate on either an exclusive or nonexclusive basis.

Distributor—The foreign distributor is a merchant who purchases merchandise from a U.S. manufacturer at the greatest possible discount and resells it for his profit. This would be the preferred arrangement if the product being sold requires periodic servicing. The prospective distributor should be willing to carry a sufficient supply of spare parts and maintain

Figure 11-4 (Continued)

adequate facilities and personnel to perform all normal servicing operations. Since the distributor buys in his name, it is easier for the U.S. manufacturer to establish a credit pattern so that more flexible or convenient payment terms can be offered. As with a sales representative, the length of association is established by contract, which is renewable if the arrangement proves satisfactory.

Foreign Retailer—Generally limited to the consumer line, this method relies mainly on direct contact by traveling sales representatives but, depending on the product, can also be accomplished by the mailing of catalogs, brochures, or other literature. However, even though it would eliminate commissions and traveling expenses, the U.S. manufacturer who uses the direct mail approach could suffer because his proposal may not receive proper consideration.

Selling Direct to the End-User—This is quite limited and again depends on the product. Opportunities often arise from advertisements in magazines receiving overseas distribution. Many times this can create difficulties because casual inquirers may not be fully cognizant of their country's foreign trade regulations. For several reasons they may not be able to receive the merchandise upon arrival, thus causing it to be impounded and possibly sold at public auction, or returned on a freight-collect basis that could prove costly.

State Controlled Trading Companies—This term applies to countries that have state trading monopolies, where business is conducted by a few government-sanctioned and controlled trading entities. Because of worldwide changes in foreign policy and their effect on trade between countries, these areas can become important future markets. For the time being, however, most opportunities will be limited to such items as raw materials, agricultural machinery, manufacturing equipment, and technical instruments, rather than consumer or household goods. This is due to the shortage of foreign exchange and the emphasis on self-sufficiency.

New Product Information Service (NPIS)—This special service, offered by the Department of Commerce, can facilitate your direct selling effort to potential overseas customers. It enables U.S. companies interested in selling a new product overseas to submit appropriate data through Commerce Department District Offices for placement in the Department's publication, *Commercial News USA*, which is distributed exclusively abroad through 240 U.S. Foreign Service posts. The new product data are extracted and reprinted in individual post newsletters that are tailored to local markets. Selected product information also is broadcast abroad by the International Communication Agency's (formerly the U.S. Information Agency) Voice of America.

Commission Agents—Commission or buying agents are "finders" for foreign firms wanting to purchase U.S. products. These purchasing agents obtain the desired equipment at the lowest possible price. A commission is paid to them by their foreign clients.

Country Controlled Buying Agents—These are foreign government agencies or quasi-governmental firms empowered to locate and purchase desired goods.

Export Management Companies—EMCs, as they are called, act as the export department for several manufacturers of noncompetitive products.

Figure 11-4 (Continued)

They solicit and transact business in the name of the manufacturers they represent for a commission, salary, or retainer plus commission. Many EMCs also will carry the financing for export sales, assuring immediate payment for the manufacturer's products.

This can be an exceptionally fine arrangement for small firms that do not have the time, personnel, or money to develop foreign markets, but wish to establish a corporate and product identity internationally.

Export Merchants—The export merchant purchases products direct from the manufacturer and has them packed and marked to his specifications. He then sells overseas through his contacts, in his own name, and assumes all risks for his account.

Export Agents—The export agent operates in the same manner as a manufacturer's representative, but the risk of loss remains with the manufacturer.

In transactions with export merchants and export agents the seller is faced with the possible disadvantage of giving up control over the marketing and promotion of the product, which could have an adverse effect on future success.

Source: U.S. Department of Commerce, *A Basic Guide to Exporting* (Washington: U.S. Government Printing Office, 1979), pp. 3–4.

Financial Incentives   There are a number of direct and indirect financial incentives taking various forms which help the small firm view foreign markets more favorably. We will call attention to a few of these.

Foreign Sales Corporation (FSC)   In 1971, the Domestic International Sales Corporation (DISC) was created by the federal government as a special entity to route foreign sales so participants could receive special tax deferrals. But United States trading partners in the General Agreement on Tariffs and Trade (GATT) insisted that a DISC involved an illegal subsidy. Largely because of GATT's position, the DISC has been replaced by the Foreign Sales Corporation (FSC). FSC attempts to provide similar benefits to participants. Although the jury is still out on FSCs, they may appease our trading partners while assisting small businesses.

Export Trading Company Act (ETCA)   Passed in 1982, this legislation encourages export businesses to band together to achieve economies of scale. The Export Trading Companies created by this Act can obtain special low-interest loans and special waivers of antitrust laws.

Foreign Trade Zone (FTZ)   FTZs operate in many countries throughout the world. They are sites located in a country which are exempt from customs duty. These "free" ports allow foreign shipments to be received duty-free. FTZs exist in the United States as well.[9]

ACTION REPORT
Exporter of the Year

"You have come a long way..." accurately describes the business accomplishments of Elizabeth Gould who, with a biology degree from college, returned to her family firm, created an international department in the business, and worked her way to the 1985 Small Business Administration award as Exporter of the Year. Her accomplishments stand as a model for all small businesses who view export sales as nothing but a pipe dream.

Gould is a strong advocate for small business exports. "We must learn to meet the competition on their home ground before they meet us on ours...because then it will be too late," she argues. "There's never a perfect time for anything, and if your product has a market overseas, start laying the groundwork now."

She emphasizes the importance of learning about exporting and channels of distribution. The simple but effective distribution system adopted by Gould for her National Graphics firm in St. Louis, MO, has contributed significantly to the 24 percent of company gross sales derived from exporting its photographic supplies. Gould worked out arrangements with foreign distributors rather than establishing its own sales force abroad. According to Gould, "They (the distributors) could handle their own sales presentations, service, advertising, importing and financing. Considering language differences, distance and all, it was felt they could do these things better and cheaper than National Graphics."

Source: Henry Eason, "Taking on the Giants in Trade Abroad," *Nation's Business*, Vol. 73, No. 7 (July, 1985), pp. 51–52.

PRICING ACTIVITIES

The price of a product is the seller's measure of what he or she is willing to receive from a buyer in exchange for ownership or use of that product. **Pricing** is the systematic determination of the "right" price for a product. While setting a price is easy, pricing is complex and difficult. Before we examine the process of product pricing for the small business, let us first consider why this process is important.

Importance of Pricing

The revenue of a small business is a direct reflection of two components: sales quantity and product price. In a real sense, then, the product price is half of the revenue figure. Yet a small change in price can drastically influence total revenue. For emphasis, consider the following situations.[10]

Situation 1

Quantity sold $\times$ Price per unit $=$ Revenue
500,000 $\times$ $10 $=$ $5,000,000

Situation 2

Quantity sold $\times$ Price per unit $=$ Revenue
500,000 $\times$ $9.90 $=$ $4,950,000

The price per unit in Situation 2 is only ten cents lower than in Situation 1. However, the total reduction in revenue is $50,000! Thus, a small business can lose revenue unnecessarily if a price is too low.

Another reason pricing is important is that a price has an indirect impact on sales quantity. In the examples above, quantity sold was assumed to be independent of price—which it may well be for a change in price from $10.00 to $9.90. However, a larger change, up or down, from $10.00 might change the quantity sold.

Pricing, therefore, has a double impact on total sales. It is important *directly* as one part of the revenue equation and *indirectly* through its impact on quantity demanded.

Cost Considerations in Pricing

In a successful business, price must be adequate to cover total cost plus some margin of profit. **Total cost** includes three elements. The first is the cost of goods (or services) offered for sale. An appliance dealer, for example, must include in the price the cost of the appliance and freight charges. The second element is the selling cost. This includes the direct cost of the salesperson's time as well as the cost of advertising and sales promotion. The third element is the general overhead cost applicable to the given product. Included in this cost are such items as office supplies, utilities, taxes, office salaries, and management salaries. Profit is the necessary payment for entrepreneurial services and the risk of doing business.

Another cost consideration concerns the way costs behave as the quantity marketed increases or decreases. **Total variable costs** are those costs that increase as the quantity marketed increases. Sales commission costs and material costs for production are typical variable costs. These are incurred as a product is made and sold. **Total fixed costs** are those costs that remain constant at different levels of quantity sold. An advertising campaign expenditure and factory equipment cost would be fixed costs. These are incurred even without production or sales.

By understanding these different kinds of costs, a small-business manager can keep from pricing too low to meet costs. If all costs are considered to behave in the same way, pricing can be inappropriate. Small businesses will often disregard fixed and variable costs and treat them identically for pricing. An approach called average pricing is an example of this disregard. **Average pricing** occurs when the total cost over a previous period is divided by the quantity sold in that period. The resulting **average cost** is then used to set the current price. Such a procedure overlooks the reality of a higher average cost at a lower sales level. This is, of course, due to a constant fixed cost spread over fewer units.

Demand Considerations in Pricing

Cost considerations provide a floor below which a price would not be set for normal pricing purposes. Cost analysis does not tell the small-business manager how far the "right" price should exceed that minimum figure. Only after considering the nature of demand can this be determined.

Demand Factors Several factors make up the demand consideration. One is the appeal of the product itself. If consumers perceive the product as an important solution to their unsatisfied needs, there will be demand.

Only in rare cases are identical "packages" of products and services offered by competing firms. In many cases the products are dissimilar in some way. Even when products are similar, the accompanying services typically differ. Speed of service, credit terms, delivery arrangements, personal attention by a top executive, and willingness to stand behind the product or service are but a few of the areas that distinguish one business from another. The pricing implications depend on whether the small firm is inferior or superior in these respects to its competitors. Certainly, there is no absolute imperative for the small business to conform slavishly to the prices of others. Its unique combination of goods and services may well justify a premium price.

Another factor that affects demand for a product is the marketing effort. Good promotion and distribution, for example, build demand. Currently several entrepreneurs are entering the water business by selling bottled water. "Demand for water has exploded in today's market," says water lawyer Raphael J. Moses, whose firm deals with water rights. Others in the business characterize the product demand as a *created* demand. "Water today is pure marketing."[11]

ACTION REPORT
Status Pricing

Status is a visible motivator for many consumers. These consumers will pay high prices to purchase status symbols.

S.T. Dupont Co. relies on these kinds of motivations to sell its products, which are priced accordingly. It markets $65 million of luxury goods a year to the rich. The company's newest addition is "the most luxurious fountain pen ever manufactured." It will retail for around $400!

The Dupont fountain pen is carved from a solid block of brass and is covered with five coats of lacquer from the sap of the rhus tree, which grows in China. The new pen is priced well above the typical $1 to $2 pens but is actually below a German firm's $9,000 platinum pen.

Dupont is appealing to the same motivations which sell its $150 to $400 cigarette lighters. The Dupont lighter "makes a recognizably different ringing sound that labels it to the discerning" when a smoker snaps open the lighter.

Source: Reprinted by permission of *The Wall Street Journal* (June 12, 1981), © Dow Jones & Company, Inc. (1981). All rights reserved.

The third factor which has a major influence on demand is the product price itself, as mentioned earlier. This influence varies from market to market. Higher-income-level markets are less sensitive to prices than lower-income groups. For example, Gary Klein of Chehalis, WA, manufactures bicycles which sell for up to $6,600.[12] Therefore, each market must be examined individually.

Elasticity of Demand   The effect that a change in price has on the quantity demanded is called **elasticity of demand**.[13] If a change in price produces a significant change in the quantity demanded, the product is said to have an **elastic demand**. On the other hand, if a price change does not bring about a significant difference in the quantity demanded, the product is considered to have **inelastic demand**.

Consider the simplest hand-held calculator, which retailed for about $45 in the early 1970s. When its price was reduced by about 50 percent, consumers responded with substantially higher orders. Salt, however, is a product with inelastic demand. Regardless of its price, the demand will not change significantly because consumers generally use a fixed amount of salt.

Break-Even Analysis in Pricing

Break-even analysis entails a formal comparison of cost and demand for the purposes of determining the acceptability of alternative prices. There are two stages of a complete break-even analysis: cost break-even and cost-adjusted break-even. Break-even analysis can be explained via formulas or graphs. We will use the graphic presentation.

Cost Break-Even Stage   The objective of the cost break-even stage is to determine the quantity at which the product, with an assumed price, will generate enough revenue to start earning a profit. Figure 11–5(a) presents a simple cost break-even chart. Total fixed costs are portrayed as a horizontal section in view of the fact that they do not change with the volume of production. The variable-cost section slants upward, however, because of the direct relationship of total variable costs with output. The area between the slanting total cost line and the horizontal base line thus represents the combination of fixed and variable costs. The area between the revenue and total cost lines reveals the profit or loss position of the company at any level of sales. The intersection of these two lines is called the **break-even point** because sales revenue equals total cost at this point.

Additional revenue lines at other prices can be charted on the break-even graph to evaluate new break-even points. This gives a flexible break-even chart as shown on Figure 11–5(b). The assumed higher price of $18.00 in Figure 11–5(b) plots a more steeply sloped revenue line, resulting in an earlier break-even point. Similarly, the lower price of $7.00 produces a "flatter" revenue line, increasing the break-even point. Additional sales revenue lines could be plotted to evaluate proposed prices.

The cost break-even chart implies that quantity sold can increase continually (as shown by the larger and larger profit area to the right). This is misleading and can be clarified by adjusting the cost break-even analysis with demand data.

Cost-Adjusted Break-Even Stage   The indirect impact of price on quantity sold is a confounding problem for pricing decisions. Occasionally more of a product is demanded as its price increases. This was the situation with a small poodle-grooming service. Business was slow with the original pricing. A friend suggested an increase in price. The owner heeded the advice and business grew immediately. Usually, however, a smaller quantity is demanded at higher prices.

Break-even analysis can incorporate the estimated demand and greatly increase its usefulness. A cost-adjusted break-even chart is built by using the cost break-even data and adding a demand curve. A demand schedule showing the estimated number of units demanded and total revenue at various prices is listed below and is used to plot the demand curve in Figure 11–5(c).

Price	Demand (Units)	Revenue ($)
$ 7	90	$630
12	60	720
18	15	270

Figure 11-5   Break-Even Charts for Pricing

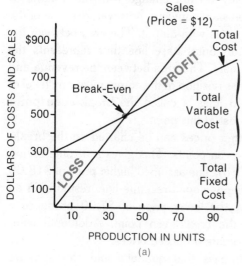

(a)

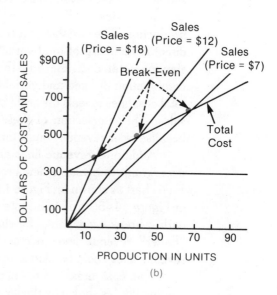

(b)

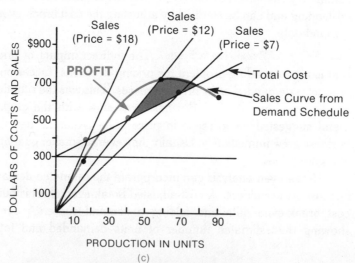

(c)

When this demand schedule is plotted on a flexible break-even chart, a more realistic profit area is identified, as shown in Figure 11-5(c). The break-even point in Figure 11-5(c) for an $18.00 unit price corresponds to sales quantities which cannot be reached at the assumed price. Therefore, the optimum of the 3 prices in Figure 11-5(c) is $12.00. This price shows the greatest profit potential as indicated by the shaded profit area in Figure 11-5(c).

Special Considerations in Pricing

Additional pricing considerations for the small business are: price-cutting, variable pricing, flexible pricing, price lining, and what the traffic will bear. These are discussed below.

Price-Cutting   Once a product is produced and efforts to sell it are under way, the price may have to be lowered. The probable reaction of competitors is a critical factor in determining whether to cut prices below a prevailing level. A small business in competition with larger firms seldom is in a position to consider itself the price leader. If competitors view the small firm's pricing as relatively unimportant, they may permit a price differential. This may well be the reaction if the price-cutting firm is sufficiently small. On the other hand, established firms may view a smaller price-cutter as a direct threat and counter with reductions of their own. In such a case, the smaller price-cutter accomplishes very little.

Variable Pricing   In some lines of business, the selling firm makes price concessions to individual customers even though it advertises a uniform price. Concessions are made for various reasons, one of which is the customer's knowledge and bargaining strength. In some fields of business, therefore, pricing decisions involve two parts: a stipulated "list price" and a range of price concessions to particular buyers.

Flexible Pricing   Although many firms use total cost as a point of resistance, most of them take into consideration special market conditions and practices of competitors in arriving at their prices. The following cases illustrate this point:

1. *Contractor A* estimates the full cost of building a house, but he modifies the price to meet market conditions. Even his concept of cost reflects variable estimates of the opportunity costs of his time. His time is less valuable in the winter, when business is slack, than at other seasons; he adjusts his estimates of cost accordingly. He also shaves price on a cash sale of a house, recognizing the avoidance of a risk as compared with sales involving complicated financing. Thus, the stress on full cost does not mean inattention to demand.

2. *Printing Company B* also pays considerable attention to full-cost estimates. While the management insists that prices should be kept on a full-cost basis, actual practice is more flexible. The managers are critical of "rate cutters," who, they claim, are responsible for the low industry profits, but they themselves show some willingness to adjust to market conditions when the necessity arises.

3. *Furniture Company C* starts with a cost estimate, including an allocation of indirect labor and factory overhead. But the management modifies the target return to meet market conditions.

On certain occasions it may be logical to price at less than total cost. For example, if the facilities of a business are idle, some costs may be continuing. In any case, the price should cover all marginal or incremental costs—that is, those costs specifically incurred to get the added business. In the long run, however, all overhead costs must be covered as well.

Price Lining   A **price line** is a range of several distinct prices at which merchandise is offered for sale. For example, men's suits might be sold at $150.00, $200.00, or $250.00. The general level of the different lines would depend on the income level and buying desires of a store's customers. Price lining has the advantage of simplifying choice for the customer and reducing the necessary minimum inventory.

What the Traffic Will Bear   The policy of pricing on the basis of what the traffic will bear can be used only when the seller has little or no competition. Obviously, this policy will work only for nonstandardized products. For example, a food store might offer egg roll wrappers which the competitors do not carry. Busy consumers who want to fix egg rolls but who have neither the time nor the knowledge to prepare the wrappers will buy them at any reasonable price.

Calculating the Selling Price

In calculating the selling price for a particular item, retailers, wholesalers, and even manufacturers must add a markup percentage to cover the following:

1. Operating expenses.
2. Profit.
3. Subsequent price reductions—for example, markdowns and employee discounts.

Markups may be expressed as a percentage of either the *selling price* or the *cost*. For example, if an item costs $6.00 and is selling at $10.00, the markup of $4.00 would be 40 percent of the selling price or 66 2/3 percent of the cost. Although either method is correct, consistency demands that the same method be used in considering the components entering into the markup. If operating expenses amount to 35 percent of sales and a profit of 5 percent of sales is desired, the markup (assuming no markdown) must be 40 percent of selling price. This is clearly different from 40 percent markup based on cost. In fact, an incorrect application of the 40 percent figure to cost would produce a markup amounting to less than 29 percent of sales, which is not enough to cover operating expenses. Table 11-1 presents simple formulas for markup calculations.

Table 11-1   Formulas for Markup Calculations

Cost + Markup = Selling price
Cost   = Selling price − Markup
Markup   = Selling price − Cost

$$\frac{\text{Markup}}{\text{Selling price}} \times 100 = \text{Markup expressed as a percent of selling price}$$

$$\frac{\text{Markup}}{\text{Cost}} \times 100 = \text{Markup expressed as a percent of cost}$$

If a seller wishes to translate markup as a percent of selling price into a percent of cost, or vice versa, the two formulas below are useful:

$$\frac{\text{Markup as a percent of selling price}}{100\% - \text{Markup as a percent of selling price}} \times 100 = \text{Markup as a percent of cost}$$

$$\frac{\text{Markup as a percent of cost}}{100\% + \text{Markup as a percent of cost}} \times 100 = \text{Markup as a percent of selling price}$$

CREDIT IN SMALL BUSINESS

Credit involves a sale on the basis of trust. In a credit sale, the seller conveys goods or services to the buyer in return for the buyer's promise to pay. The major objective in granting credit is an expansion of sales by attracting new customers and an increase in volume and regularity of purchases by existing customers. Some retail firms—furniture stores, for example—cater to newcomers in the city, newly married couples, and others by inviting the credit business of individuals with established credit ratings. In addition, credit records may be used for purposes of sales promotion by direct mail appeals to credit customers. Adjustments and exchanges of goods are also facilitated through credit operations.

Benefits of Credit to Sellers and Buyers

If credit buying and selling did not benefit both parties to the transaction, its use would cease. Firms extend credit to customers because they can obtain increased sales volume in this way. They expect the increased revenue to more than offset credit costs so that profits will increase.

Buyers also benefit from the use of credit. Their most obvious advantage is the deferred-payment privilege. Small firms, in particular, benefit from the judicious extension of credit by suppliers. Credit supplies the small firm with working capital and also permits continuation of marginal businesses that might otherwise expire. Buyers also find credit to be a convenience in many cases. Ultimate consumers need not carry large amounts of cash, and business buyers need not become involved in the cumbersome process of delivering cash prior to shipment of purchased goods.

Kinds of Credit

There are two broad classes of credit: consumer credit and trade credit. **Consumer credit** is granted by retailers to final consumers who purchase for personal or family use. **Trade credit** is extended by nonfinancial firms, such as manufacturers or wholesalers, to customers which are other business firms.

Consumer credit and trade credit differ as to types of credit instruments used and sources for financing receivables. Another important distinction is the availability of credit insurance for trade credit only. They also differ markedly as to terms of sale.

Consumer Credit   The four major kinds of consumer-credit accounts are: ordinary charge accounts, installment accounts, budget accounts, and revolving credit accounts. Many variations of these are also used.

Charge Accounts   Under the **ordinary charge account**, the customer obtains possession of goods (or services) when purchased, with payment due when billed. Stated terms typically call for payment at the end of the month, but customary practice allows a longer period for payment than that stated. The charge account is best used for recurring family expenses. Small accounts at department stores are a good example of such use.

Three types of credit cards are issued today by business organizations. One type is issued by major department stores and oil companies to customers with proved credit standings. Another type is issued by businesses engaged in the area of travel and entertainment such as American Express Company. Other popular credit cards are VISA and MASTER CARD, which are issued by a network of franchise-holding banks and can be used for virtually any good or service. In the case of VISA and MASTER CARD, the bank collects from the card-holding consumer and remits the amount to the participating retailer, less commission. Participating retailers also pay certain fees for joining, cash accommodation, merchant membership advertising, and rental for imprinting machines. The advantages of participation are increased sales volume and elimination of some record-keeping costs.

Installment Accounts   The **installment account** is the vehicle of long-term consumer credit. A down payment is normally required, and finance charges can be 15 percent or more of the purchase price. Finance charges must be disclosed in accordance with the Truth-in-Lending Act. The most common payment periods are from 12 to 36 months, although in recent years automobile dealers have extended payment periods to 60 months. An installment account is useful for large purchases such as automobiles, washing machines, and television sets.

The seller must also determine, in view of the different state laws, whether the credit should be secured by a conditional sales contract or a chattel mortgage. Under a **conditional sales contract**, legal title to the product does not pass until the customer makes the last payment; immediate repossession is possible in case a payment is defaulted. When a **chattel mortgage** is used, legal title passes when the sale is made but is subject to the seller's lien. When a payment is defaulted, the seller can take court action to repossess and resell the goods.

Budget Accounts   The **budget account**, sometimes called a Major Purchase Account (MPA), might be defined as a short-term installment account. It results from charge purchases in amounts typically ranging from $200.00 to $400.00, and payment is ordinarily spread over a period of three months. A consumer may purchase a power lawn mower or a set of tires, for example, in this way. Budget accounts are readily extended by many small merchants, but a service charge normally is added to the price when payments are deferred over 90 days. Monthly statements are usually not sent; this eliminates billing cost and places the responsibility for adhering to payment schedules on the customers.

Revolving Credit Accounts   The **revolving credit account** is another variation of the installment account. The seller may grant a line of credit up to $400.00 or $500.00, for example, and the customer may then charge purchases at any time if purchases do not exceed this credit limit. A specified percentage of the outstanding balance must be paid monthly, which forces the customer to budget and limits the amount of debt that can be carried. Finance charges are computed on the unpaid balance at the end of the month.

Trade Credit   Business firms may sell goods subject to specified terms of sale, such as 2/10, n/30. This means that a 2 percent discount is given by the seller if the buyer pays within 10 days of the invoice date. Failure to take this discount makes the full amount of the invoice due in 30 days. Other discount arrangements in common use are shown in Table 11-2.

Table 11–2   Trade-Credit Terms

Sales Term	Explanation
3/10, 1/15, n/60	Three percent discount for first 10 days; one percent discount for 15 days; net on 60th day.
E.O.M.	Billing at end of month, covering all credit purchases of that month.
C.O.D.	Amount of bill will be collected upon delivery of the goods.
2/10, n/30, R.O.G.	Two percent discount for 10 days; net on 30th day—but both discount period and 30 days start from the date of delivery of the goods.
2/10, n/30, E.O.M.	Two percent discount for 10 days; net on 30th day—but both periods start from the end of the month in which the sale was made.

Sales terms in trade credit depend on the kind of product sold and the buyer's and seller's circumstances. The credit period often varies directly with the length of the buyer's turnover period, which obviously depends on the type of product sold. The larger the order and the higher the credit rating of the buyer, the better the sales terms that can be granted if individual sales terms are fixed for each customer. The greater the financial strength and the more adequate and liquid the working capital of the seller, the more generous the seller's sales terms can be. Of course, no business can afford to allow competitors to outdo it in reasonable generosity of sales terms. In many lines of business, credit terms are so firmly set by tradition that a unique policy is difficult, if not impossible.

The Decision to Sell on Credit

Nearly all small businesses can sell on credit if they wish, and so the entrepreneur must decide whether to sell for cash or on credit. In some cases this is reduced to the question, "Can the granting of credit to customers be avoided?" Credit selling is standard trade practice in many lines of business, and in other businesses credit-selling competitors will always outsell the cash-selling firm.

Factors That Affect the Credit Decision   Numerous factors bear on the decision concerning credit extension. The seller always hopes to increase profits by credit sales, but each firm must also consider its own particular circumstances and environment.

Type of Business   Retailers of durable goods, for example, typically grant credit more freely than small grocers who sell perishables. Indeed, most consumers find it necessary to buy big-ticket items on an installment basis, and the product's life makes installment selling possible.

Credit Policy of Competitors   Unless a firm offers some compensating advantage, it is expected to be as generous as its competitors in extending credit. Wholesale hardware companies and retail furniture stores are businesses that face stiff competition from credit sellers.

Income Level of Customers   The income level of customers is a significant factor in determining a retailer's credit policy. Consider, for example, a corner drugstore adjacent to a city high school. High school students are typically unsatisfactory credit customers because of their lack of maturity and income.

Availability of Adequate Working Capital   There is no denying the fact that credit sales increase the amount of working capital needed by the business. Money that the business has tied up in open-credit and installment accounts cannot be used to pay business expenses.

The Four C's of Credit   In evaluating the credit standing of applicants, the entrepreneur must answer the following questions:

1. Can the buyer pay as promised?
2. Will the buyer pay?
3. If so, when will the buyer pay?
4. If not, can the buyer be forced to pay?

Before credit is approved, the answers to questions 1, 2, and 4 must be "yes"; to question 3, "on schedule." The answers depend in part on the amount of credit requested and in part on the seller's estimate of the buyer's ability and willingness to pay. Such an estimate constitutes a judgment of the buyer's inherent credit worth.

Every credit applicant possesses credit worth in some degree so that extended credit is not necessarily a gift to the applicant. Instead, a decision to grant credit merely recognizes the buyer's earned credit standing. But the seller faces a possible inability or unwillingness to pay on the buyer's part. In making credit decisions, therefore, the seller decides the degree of risk of nonpayment that must be assumed.

Willingness to pay is evaluated in terms of the four C's of credit: character, capital, capacity, and conditions.[14] *Character* refers to the fundamental integrity and honesty which should underlie all human and business relationships. In the case of a business customer, it takes shape in the business policies and ethical practices of the firm. Individual customers who apply for credit must also be known to be morally responsible persons. *Capital* consists of the cash and other assets owned by the business or individual customer. In the case of a business customer, this means capital sufficient to underwrite planned operations, including adequate owner capital. *Capacity* refers to the business customer's ability to conserve assets and faithfully and efficiently follow financial plans. The business customer with capacity utilizes the invested capital of the business firm wisely and capitalizes to the fullest extent on business opportunities. *Conditions* refer to such factors as business cycles and changes in price levels which may be either favorable or unfavorable to the payment of debts. Other adverse factors which might limit a customer's ability to pay include fires and other natural disasters, new legislation, strong new competition, or labor problems.

Credit Investigation of Applicants   In most retail stores, the first step in credit investigation is the completion of an application form. The information obtained on this form is used as the basis for examining the applicant's financial responsibility.

Nonretailing firms should similarly investigate credit applicants. One small clothing manufacturer has every sales order reviewed by a Dun & Bradstreet-trained credit manager who maintains a complete file of D&B credit reports on thousands of customers. Recent financial statements of dealer-customers are filed also. These, together with the dealer's accounts-receivable card, are the basis for decisions on credit sales, with major emphasis on the D&B credit reports.

Credit Limits   Perhaps the most important factor in determining a customer's credit limits is the customer's ability to pay the obligation when it becomes due. This in turn requires an evaluation of the customer's financial resources, debt position, and income level.

The amount of credit required by the customer is the second factor that requires consideration. Customers of a drugstore need only small amounts of credit. On the other hand, business customers of wholesalers and manufacturers typically expect larger amounts of credit. In the special case of installment selling, the amount of credit should not exceed the repossession value of the goods sold. Automobile dealers follow this rule as a general practice.

Sources of Credit Information   One of the most important and frequently neglected sources of credit information is found in the seller's accounts-receivable records. Properly analyzed, these records show whether the customer regularly takes cash discounts and, if not, whether the customer's account is typically slow.

Manufacturers and wholesalers frequently can use the financial statements submitted by firms applying for credit as an additional source of information. Obtaining maximum value from financial statements requires a careful ratio analysis which will reveal a firm's working-capital position, profit-making potential, and general financial health.

Pertinent data may also be obtained from outsiders. For example, arrangements may be made with other suppliers to exchange credit data. Such credit interchange reports are quite useful in learning about the sales and payment experiences of others with one's own credit customers or applicants.

Another source of credit data, on commercial accounts particularly, is the customer's banker. Some bankers are glad to supply credit information about their depositors, considering this a service in helping them obtain credit in amounts they can successfully handle. Other bankers feel that credit information is confidential and should not be disclosed in this way.

Organizations that may be consulted with reference to credit standings are trade-credit agencies and local credit bureaus. **Trade-credit agencies** are privately owned and operated organizations which collect credit information on business firms. After they analyze and evaluate the data, they make credit ratings available to client companies for a fee. These agencies are concerned with trade-credit ratings only, having nothing to do with consumer credit. Dun & Bradstreet, Inc., is a general trade-credit agency serving the nation. Manufacturers and wholesalers are especially interested in its reference book and credit reports. The reference book covers all United States businesses and shows credit rating, financial strength, and other key credit information. It is available to subscribers only.

A **credit bureau** serves its members—retailers and other firms in a given community—by summarizing their credit experience with particular individuals. A local bureau can also broaden its service by affiliation with either the National Retail Credit Association or the Associated Credit Bureaus of America. This makes possible the exchange of credit information on persons who move from one city to another. A business firm need not be a member of some bureaus in order to get a credit report. The fee charged to nonmembers, however, is considerably higher than that charged to members.

Collection of Past-Due Accounts

Slow credit accounts are a problem because they tie up the seller's working capital, prevent further sales to the slow-paying customer, and lead to losses from bad debts. Even if the slow-paying customer is not lost, relations with this customer are strained for a time at least.

Inadequate records and collection procedures often fail to alert the small firm in time to permit prompt collections. Also, the personal acquaintance of seller and customer sometimes tempts the seller to be less than businesslike in extending further credit and collecting overdue accounts. Conceding the seriousness of the problem, the small firm must know what steps to take and how far to go in collecting past-due accounts. It must decide whether to undertake the job directly or to turn it over to an attorney or a collection agency.

Collection Procedure   Perhaps the most effective weapon in collecting past-due accounts is the debtors' knowledge of possible impairment of their credit standing. This impairment is certain if an account is turned over to a collection agency. Delinquent customers who foresee continued solvency will typically attempt to avoid damage to their credit standing, particularly when it would be known to the business community generally. It is this knowledge that lies behind and strengthens the various collection efforts of the business.

Most business firms have found that the most effective collection procedure consists of a series of steps, each of which is somewhat more forceful than the preceding one.[15] Although these typically begin with a gentle written reminder, they may include additional letters, telephone calls, registered letters, personal contacts, and referrals to collection agencies or attorneys. The timing of these steps may be carefully standardized so that step two automatically follows step one in a specified number of days, with subsequent steps similarly spaced.[16]

The Bad-Debt Ratio   In controlling expenses associated with credit sales, it is possible to use various expense ratios. The best known and most widely used ratio is the **bad-debt ratio**, which is computed by dividing the amount of bad debts by the total credit sales.

The bad-debt ratio reflects the efficiency of credit policies and procedures. A small firm may thus compare the effectiveness of its credit management with that of other firms. There is a relationship between the bad-debt ratio on the one hand and the type of business, profitability, and size of firm on the other. Small profitable retailers have a much higher loss ratio than large profitable retailers. The bad-debt losses of all small-business firms, however, range from a fraction of one percent of net sales to percentages large enough to put them out of business!

Looking Back

1. The four main functions of channel intermediaries are breaking bulk, assorting, providing information, and risk taking. A channel of distribution with no intermediaries is a direct channel. An indirect channel is one that uses intermediaries such as retailers, industrial distributors, agents, or merchant wholesalers.

2. Choosing a distribution system involves considerations of costs, coverage, and control. The main components of physical distribution are transportation, storage, materials handling, delivery terms, and inventory management.

3. Small business is becoming more and more involved in exporting. The small business can learn about foreign markets through available publications, personal visits to the country, and talks with people who have visited the market. Numerous channel options are available to exporters.

4. Cost considerations in pricing involve an understanding of the components of total variable costs and of total fixed costs. Demand considerations involve such factors as product appeal, marketing effort, and product price, all of which exert an influence on demand. An understanding of elastic demand and inelastic demand is also important. Break-even analysis in pricing entails a formal comparison of cost and demand for purposes of determining the acceptability of alternative prices. Fixed and variable costs are used to construct a cost break-even chart. Demand factors can be incorporated to construct a cost-adjusted break-even chart.

5. By extending credit, sellers can increase sales volume and expect the increased revenue to more than offset credit costs so that their profits will increase. Benefits from the use of credit by buyers consist of deferred-payment privileges, convenience, and a supply of working capital. Before deciding to sell on credit, the small business should consider several factors such as the type of business, the credit policy of competitors, the income level of customers, and the availability of adequate working capital. It should evaluate the credit standing of applicants in terms of the four C's of credit—character, capital, capacity, and conditions.

DISCUSSION QUESTIONS

1. How does physical distribution differ from a channel of distribution?
2. Discuss the major considerations in structuring a channel of distribution.
3. What are the major components of a physical distribution system?
4. If a small business has conducted its break-even analysis properly and finds break-even at a price of $10.00 to be 10,000 units, should it price its product at $10.00? Discuss.
5. What is the psychology behind price lining?
6. What is the difference between consumer credit and trade credit?
7. What is meant by the terms 2/10, n/30? Does it pay to take discounts?
8. If the small-business owner has adequate investment to cover all working-capital needs, does it cost as much to sell on credit as it costs to borrow? Why?

9. Which of the "four C's" seems most important in considering extension of credit to an ultimate consumer? Is the same true in extending credit to a manufacturer or wholesaler?

10. Does the fact that a business is small make personal contact superior to letters in collecting past-due accounts?

ENDNOTES

1. The reduction in product price given an intermediary is the investment cost to which we refer.

2. Carol Rose Carey, "A Low-Cost Way to Find Top Salespeople," *Inc.*, Vol. 4, No. 3 (March, 1982), p. 119.

3. A good basic discussion of each of these modes of transportation is found in Chapter 14 of Charles D. Schewe and Reuben M. Smith, *Marketing: Concepts and Applications* (New York: McGraw-Hill Book Company, 1983).

4. For a more detailed discusion of various delivery terms, see Lynn Edward Gill, "Delivery Terms—Important Element of Physical Distribution," *Journal of Business Logistics*, Vol. 1, No. 2 (Spring, 1979), pp. 60–82.

5. Some of the challenges and rewards of international marketing by small business are discussed in Grant C. Moon, "International Enterprise: A Small Business Challenge," *Journal of Small Business Management*, Vol. 19, No. 2 (April, 1981), pp. 1-6.

6. A much more extensive discussion of these and other areas can be found in Vern Terpstra, *International Marketing* (3d ed.; Chicago: The Dryden Press, 1983).

7. Jacques Koppel, "The QUIRKS of Exporting," *In Business*, Vol. 5, No. 2 (March–April, 1983), p. 27.

8. Kevin Farrell, "Exports," *Venture*, Vol. 5, No. 3 (March, 1983), p. 63.

9. For an excellent discussion of Foreign Trade Zones, see "Trade: A Global Update," *Texas Business*, Vol. X, No. 7 (January, 1986), special insert.

10. Perfectly inelastic demand is assumed to emphasize the point. Other demand situations are analyzed in a later section of the chapter.

11. Phil Fitzell, "The Emerging Water Industry," *Venture*, Vol. 3, No. 8 (August, 1981), pp. 72–76.

12. Sanford L. Jacobs, "$6,600 May Seem High for a Bicycle, but at Least the Frame Won't Bend," *The Wall Street Journal*, June 25, 1981, p. 25.

13. Methods of estimating price elasticity for products of small firms are suggested in William J. Kehoe, "Demand Curve Estimation and the Small Business Manager," *Journal of Small Business Management*, Vol. 10, No. 3 (July, 1972), pp. 29-31.

14. Around the turn of the century, a noted financier and venture capitalist said that he would provide anyone having CHARACTER and CAPACITY with the necessary capital for launching a business, thus suggesting that only two factors are really needed. However, the borrower's capital position and the prevailing economic conditions would either facilitate payment or make it difficult.

15. A collection of several creative tactics are discussed in William G. Shepherd Jr., "Collecting Bad Receivables," *Venture*, Vol. 8, No. 1 (January, 1986), p. 28.

16. An excellent article on managing accounts receivable is Steven D. Popell, "Effectively Manage Receivables to Cut Costs," *Harvard Business Review*, Vol. 59, No. 1 (January–February, 1981), pp. 58–64.

REFERENCES TO SMALL BUSINESS IN ACTION

Buckley, Jerry. "Timesharing, 1980's Style." *Venture*, Vol. 2, No. 8 (August 1980), pp. 32–36.

> The time-sharing of resort condominiums is rooted in the price escalation of construction. Several pricing plans are included in this report of a new venture.

Gupta, Udayan. "A New Breed of Sales Rep." *Venture*, Vol. 3, No. 3 (March, 1981), pp. 57–58.

> The experiences of several women sales representatives are related in this report. Some advantages of starting a sales organization are included in the discussion.

Marion, Larry. "Exporting without Tears." *Forbes*, Vol. 127, No. 8 (April 13, 1981), pp. 62–66.

> Interesting accounts of the exporting experiences of four small businesses are provided in this article.

Rose, Carol. "Extending and Collecting—Exercises in Credit." *In Business*, Vol. 3, No. 2 (March–April, 1981), pp. 44–45.

> The collection experiences of several small businesses are related in this article, which also describes the use of collection services.

CASE 11

The Jordan Construction Account*
Extending credit and collecting receivables

Bob McFarland was the president and principal stockholder of Iowa Tractor Supply Company, a farm and construction equipment distributor located in Marshalltown, IA. The firm employed 27 persons, and in 1981 sales and net profit after taxes reached all-time highs of $3.4 million and $81,500, respectively. The ending net worth for 1981 was slightly in excess of $478,000.

Bob was highly gratified by these figures as 1981 was the first full year since he had appointed Barry Stockton as general manager. Although the company had been in operation since 1957, it had prospered only from the time Bob had purchased it in 1969. Having been a territorial sales manager for the John Deere Company, he was able to obtain that account for Iowa Tractor, and it typically contributed two-thirds or more of the annual sales volume. After struggling successfully for 10 years to build Iowa Tractor into a profitable firm, he decided that it was time to take things a little easier. Accordingly, he promoted Barry and delegated many of his day-to-day duties to him. Fortunately, Barry seemed to do an outstanding job, and during the summer of 1982, Bob felt secure enough to spend six weeks in Europe with his wife.

One day shortly after Bob returned to work, he looked up from his desk and saw his accountant, Marvin Richter, approaching with several ledger cards in his hand. Marvin entered the office, carefully closed the door, and began to speak earnestly. Marvin said:

> Mr. McFarland, I think you should look at these accounts receivable, particularly Jordan Construction. I've been telling Barry to watch out for Jordan for two months, but he just says they're good for it eventually. I got the latest Dun & Bradstreet monthly report today which didn't look very good, so I've called Standifer Equipment in Ames and the Caterpillar branch at Cedar Rapids. Jordan seems to have run up some pretty good bills with both of them, and Carter at Standifer said some of the contractors in Des Moines think that the two jobs Jordan got on Interstate 80 are just too big for them to handle. If Jordan can't finish those jobs, we are going to be in trouble! Carter says they're probably going to put them on C.O.D. and call in the rental equipment.

Bob examined the data for a few minutes, asked Marvin several questions before dismissing him, and then summoned Barry to his office. The following dialogue took place between Bob and Barry:

*This case was prepared by John E. Schoen, Richards Equipment Company, Waco, TX.

Bob: Barry, I've just been looking over the sheets on Jordan and the amount really scares me. Apparently they are over 90 days on nearly $21,000, between 30 and 90 days on another $17,000, and the total due is more than $45,000. Payments on their account have been dropping off since April, and last month they barely covered the interest on the amount outstanding.

Barry: I know, Bob. I've been over to talk to old man Jordan twice in the last three weeks. He admits they are having some trouble with those jobs on the Interstate, but he claims it is only temporary. I hate to push him too hard because he has bought a lot of equipment from us over the years.

Bob: That's right, Barry, but we're talking about $45,000! At this rate, we'll soon have more money in Jordan's business than he does! I'm not so sure we shouldn't put Jordan on C.O.D. until he makes some substantial payments on their account.

Barry: I don't think so, Bob! Old man Jordan has a real mean streak, and the first time I went over there he really cussed me out for even questioning his account. He reminded me that he had been a good customer for more than 10 years, and he threatened to cut us off if we put any pressure on him.

Bob: Yes, but you've heard that before, Barry. Here we are contributing capital to his business involuntarily; we never get a share of his profits if he succeeds, but we sure get a share of the losses if he goes "belly-up." Barry, I don't want any $45,000 losses!

Barry: Well, I won't say that Jordan doesn't have some problems, but Harry thinks they'll be all right. It's just that if we put them on C.O.D. or pick up the rental equipment and they make it, I'm sure they'll never spend another dollar in here.

Bob: Harry thinks they'll be O.K.?

Barry: Yes, sir.

Bob: Get Harry in here!

In a few minutes Barry returned with Harry Reiser, the sales manager for Iowa Tractor. The following dialogue took place between Bob and Harry:

Harry: Barry says you wanted to talk to me?

Bob: That's right, Harry. We've just been discussing Jordan Construction, and I'd like to get any information you have on them.

Harry: Well, they're pretty good customers, of course. I rented them two tractor-backhoes last month. There are some rumors about their Interstate jobs, but I don't think there is much to it because Jordan was talking about buying a couple of crawler tractors last Friday. I think we have a good chance to get those crawlers if that joker over at Ames doesn't sell his below cost.

Bob: Just a minute. You rented them some backhoes last month?

Harry: Yes, sir, two model 310-A's.

Bob: How much are we getting for those units?

Harry: $1,400 a month each, and I think we have a good chance to convert them to a sale if Jordan gets 6 months' rent into them.

Bob: Did you check with anybody before you put those units out with Jordan?

Harry: Well, I think I asked Barry. No, I think he was busy that day. I'm really not certain, but Jordan Construction is one of our best accounts, isn't it?

Bob: That's what we are trying to determine, Harry. Did you know that their accounts receivable is over $45,000?

Harry: No! That's great! I knew we'd really been selling them. I'm sure those rumors...

Bob: And did you know that $38,000 of the $45,000 is past due and that $21,000 is over 90 days?

Harry: Oh!

Then Bob turned to Barry and said:

Barry, I think we've established what Harry knows about Jordan. Why don't we get Marvin in here and see what information he has. Then I think the four of us need to decide the best approach to getting as much of our money back as soon as possible.

Questions

1. Evaluate the quality of the information provided Bob McFarland by each of his subordinates.
2. Evaluate the alternatives in solving the Jordan situation.
3. What action should Bob take regarding the Jordan account?
4. How could Bob improve the credit and collections procedure of Iowa Tractor to minimize problems of this nature?
5. Evaluate the performance of Marvin Richter, Barry Stockton, and Harry Reiser in handling the Jordan account. Do the circumstances warrant any type of disciplinary action?

12

Personal Selling, Advertising, and Sales Promotion

Figure 12–1   Jimmy Spradley

© 1984 Michael G. Borum, Nashville, TN

How can a small firm with a small advertising budget compete against a big firm with its huge advertising expenditures? One young entrepreneur, Jimmy Spradley, has two recommendations. First, avoid copying the big business by simply scaling down its promotional strategy. Second, devise your own unique promotional strategy.

Spradley, president of Standard Candy of Nashville, TN, has taken his firm nationally. For most of its life, the company marketed locally. Recently it has expanded to cover 23 states. Its major product is the Goo Goo Cluster—a candy cluster of chocolate, peanuts, caramel, and marshmallow. Spradley's advertising budget is only $125,000, compared to Hershey's budget of $68 million. "To make advertising effective, we'd have to buy a lot of it, and we can only afford a little," says Spradley.

Therefore, the company is gaining recognition by other promotional tactics. It has made arrangements with Delta Air Lines to supply its candy bar as a snack for in-flight travelers. Also, a deal has been made to supply Goo Goo's to Bloomingdale's and Marshall Field & Company, two prestigious department stores. Spradley believes, "Being on their shelves gets attention, and people start talking about us."

Source: Reprinted with permission, *Inc.* Magazine, May, 1984. Copyright © 1984 by Inc. Publishing Company, 38 Commercial Wharf, Boston, MA 02110.

Looking Ahead

Watch for the following important topics:

1. Considerations in developing a promotional mix.
2. Methods of determining promotional expenditures.
3. Preparing and making a sales presentation.
4. Advertising options for the small business.
5. Types of sales promotional tools.

Belief in the old adage, "Build a better mousetrap and the world will beat a path to your door," does not eliminate the entrepreneur's need for promotion. Why? Because potential customers must be informed of the new, improved "mousetrap" and how to get to the door! They may even need to be persuaded that the mousetrap is better. This process of informing and persuading is essentially communication. Therefore, we view **promotion** as communication between the small business and its target market.

Naturally, small businesses use promotion in varying degrees. Any given firm can use all or some of the many available promotional tools. The three groupings of promotional methods presented in this chapter are personal selling, advertising, and sales promotion.

PROMOTIONAL PLANNING

Small businesses sometimes stand in awe of promotional planning. They are confused by rate schedules, reach, and frequency terminology, as well as the numerous options which are available. Promotion is admittedly a complex area, and most entrepreneurs are not "turned" in that direction. But you can begin to understand promotion by realizing the simple fact that promotion is largely communication. In fact, promotion is worthless unless it communicates. Let's briefly look at the communication process and see how promotion needs to be built on these concepts.

The Communication Process

All of us communicate each day. However, we may not have stopped to analyze our communications to realize that communication is a process with identifiable components. Figure 12–2 depicts the various components of communication. Part A in the figure represents a personal communication. Part B represents a small-business communication (promotion).

Figure 12–2   An Analogy of Personal and Small-Business Communication

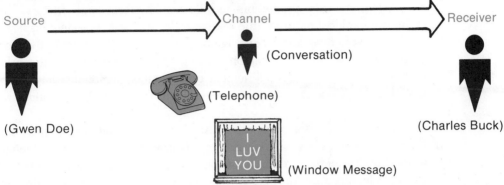

PART A: A PERSONAL COMMUNICATION

Source

Channel

Receiver

(Conversation)

(Telephone)

(Gwen Doe)

I LUV YOU

(Window Message)

(Charles Buck)

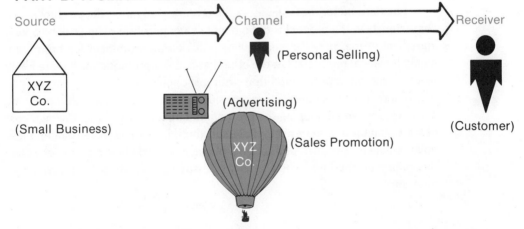

PART B: A SMALL-BUSINESS COMMUNICATION

Source

Channel

Receiver

(Personal Selling)

XYZ Co.

(Advertising)

(Small Business)

XYZ Co.

(Sales Promotion)

(Customer)

As you can see, the differences between Parts A and B in Figure 12–2 are in form, not in basic structure. Each communication involves a source, a channel, and a receiver. In Part B the receiver for the small-business communication from the XYZ Company is the customer. The receiver for Gwen Doe's personal communication is Charles Buck. She has used three different channels for her message: personal conversation, the telephone, and a special window message. The XYZ Company has used similar message channels: face-to-face communication (personal selling), the radio (advertising), and a hot-air balloon circling the city (sales promotional tool).

At this point your understanding of promotion and its roots in personal communication should be clearer. We now will turn to the particulars of molding a strong promotional plan. A good promotional plan must consider three major topics: which promotional tools to mix together, how much to spend, and how to create the messages.

The Promotional Mix

The mixture of the various promotional methods—personal selling, advertising, and sales promotion—is influenced by three major factors. First is the geographical nature of the market to be reached. A widely dispersed market tends to favor mass coverage by advertising, in contrast to the more costly individual contacts of personal selling. On the other hand, if the market is local with a relatively small number of customers, personal selling will be more feasible. Personal selling is more widely used for marketing to industrial customers.

Secondly, a small business must also understand (as discussed in Chapter 5) who its customers are. It is expensive to use shotgun promotion, which "hits" potential customers and nonpotential customers alike. This error can be minimized by knowing media audiences. The media are extremely helpful in profiling their audiences. But a small business cannot obtain a media *match* until it has specified its target market carefully.

The third factor that influences the promotional mix is the product's own characteristics. If a product is of high unit value, personal selling will be a vital ingredient in the mix. Personal selling will also be prominent for promoting highly technical products. On the other hand, sales promotion will more likely be used with an impulse good than with a shopping good.

There are of course other considerations which must ultimately be considered when developing the promotional mix. For example, the high cost of the optimum mix may necessitate substitution of a less expensive and less optimum alternative. But promotional planning should always try to determine the optimum mix and then make cost-saving adjustments if absolutely necessary.

Methods of Determining Promotional Expenditures

There is no formula to answer the question, "How much should a small business spend on promotion?" There are, however, some helpful approaches to solving the problem. The most common methods of earmarking funds for promotion are:

1. A percentage of sales (APS).
2. What can be spared (WCS).
3. As much as competition spends (ACS).
4. What it takes to do the job (WTDJ).

A Percentage of Sales (APS)   Earmarking promotional dollars based on a percentage of sales is a simple method for a small business to use. A company's own past experiences are evaluated to establish a promotional-sales ratio. If 2 percent of sales, for example, has historically been spent on promotion, the business would budget 2 percent of forecasted sales. Secondary data can be checked to locate industry ratio averages for comparison.

The major shortcoming of this method is its inherent tendency to spend more dollars when sales are increasing and less when they are declining.[1] If promotion stimulates sales, the reverse would seem desirable.

What Can Be Spared (WCS)   The most widely used approach to promotional funding is to spend what is left over when all other activities have been completed. Or a budget may be nonexistent and spending determined only when a media representative sells the entrepreneur on a special deal. Such a piecemeal approach to promotional spending should be avoided.

As Much as Competition Spends (ACS)   If the small business can duplicate the promotional mix of close competitors, it will be spending approximately as much as the competition. If a competitor is a large business, such as was the situation faced by Standard Candy described at the beginning of this chapter, this approach is not feasible. However, it can be used to react to a special short-run effort by close competitors.

What It Takes to Do the Job (WTDJ)   The preferred approach to estimating promotional expenditures is to decide what it takes to do the job. This method requires a complete analysis of the market and promotional alternatives. Assuming reasonably accurate estimates, this approach determines the amount that truly needs to be spent.

Our recommendation to a small business for estimating promotional expenditures incorporates all four approaches. This idea is represented by the flowchart in Figure 12–3. Start with an estimate of what it takes to do the job (WTDJ). If this estimate is equal to or smaller than any of the other three estimates, proceed to invest that amount in promotion. If the WTDJ estimate is larger than any of the others, compute the average of the four estimates [(WTDJ + APS + WCS + ACS)/4]. Then compare the WCS estimate with this average. If WCS equals or exceeds the average estimate, proceed to develop the promotion at the average estimate. On the other hand, if the WCS is less than the average, additional funds for promotion should be sought.

Sources of Promotional Expertise

Most small businesses must rely on others' expertise in creating promotional messages. There are several sources for this specialized assistance: the advertising agency, suppliers, trade associations, and the advertising media.

Figure 12-3   A Flowchart for Comparing Alternative Promotion Expense Estimates

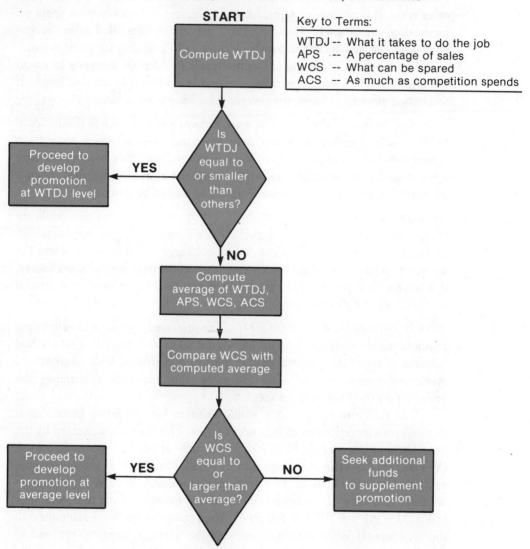

Some of the services that advertising agencies provide are:

1. To furnish design, artwork, and copy for specific advertisements and/or commercials.
2. To evaluate and recommend the advertising media with the greatest "pulling power."
3. To evaluate the effectiveness of different advertising appeals.
4. To advise on sales promotions and merchandise displays.
5. To make market-sampling studies for evaluating product acceptance or area sales potentials and to furnish mailing lists.

Since an advertising agency may charge a fee for its services, the advertiser must make sure that the return from those services will be greater than the fees paid. Only a competent agency can be of real assistance to the advertiser.

Other outside sources may also provide assistance in formulating and carrying out promotional programs. Suppliers often furnish display aids and even complete advertising programs to their dealers. Trade associations also are active in this area. Finally, the advertising media can provide some of the same services offered by an ad agency.

PERSONAL SELLING

Many products require personal selling. **Personal selling** is promotion delivered in a one-on-one environment. It includes the activities of both the inside salespersons of retail, wholesale, and service establishments and the outside sales representatives who call on business establishments and ultimate consumers.

Importance of Product Knowledge

Effective selling must be built upon a foundation of product knowledge. If a salesperson knows the product's advantages, uses, and limitations, she or he can educate the customers and successfully meet their objections. Most customers look to the salesperson for such information—whether the product is a camera, a suit of clothes, an automobile, paint, a machine tool, or an office machine. Customers seldom are specialists in the products they buy; however, they immediately sense the salesperson's knowledge or ignorance. The significance of product knowledge is revealed by the fact that personal selling degenerates into mere order-taking where such knowledge is not possessed by the salesperson.

The Sales Presentation

The heart of personal selling is the sales presentation to the prospective customer. At this crucial point the order is either secured or lost. The first step in preparing an effective sales presentation is **prospecting**, a systematic process of continually looking for new customers. The time to look is before you need them.[2]

Techniques of Prospecting   One of the most efficient techniques of prospecting is through *personal* referrals. Such referrals come from friends, customers, and other businesses. The initial contact with a potential customer is greatly facilitated by the ability to mention that, "You were referred to me by...."

Another technique of prospecting is through *impersonal* referrals. Examples of impersonal referrals are media publications, public records, and directories. Newspapers and magazines, particularly trade magazines, also help identify prospects. These publications report on new companies entering the market, as well as on new products. Prospects can be derived from this information. For example, wedding announcements in the newspaper are impersonal referrals for a local bridal shop.

Public records of property transactions and building permits can also provide prospects. For example, a garbage pick-up service might find prospective customers from those who are planning to build houses or apartments.

Prospects can be identified without referrals through *marketer-initiated contacts*. Telephone calls or mail surveys, for example, isolate prospects. One market survey conducted for a small business by an author of this text used a mail questionnaire to identify prospects. The questionnaire, which asked technical questions about a service, concluded with the following statement: "If you would be interested in a service of this nature, please check the appropriate space below and your name will be added to the mailing list."

Finally, prospects can also be identified by recording *customer-initiated contacts*. Inquiries by a potential customer which do not conclude in a sale would classify that person as a "hot" prospect. Small furniture stores will often require their salespeople to create a card for each person visiting the retail store. These prospects are then systematically contacted over the telephone, and records of these contacts are updated periodically.

Harvey Anderson, chief executive officer of Servamatic, a company selling solar heaters, has developed an elaborate prospecting system which has helped his sales force achieve a 25 percent closing rate. They identify potential customers by visually covering the target market area. Next they screen the potential customers by telephone. Finally, they give the "hot" prospects an in-home sales presentation.[3]

Practicing The old saying that "practice makes perfect" applies to the salesperson prior to making the sales presentations. If you are a salesperson, make the presentation to your spouse, a mirror, or a tape recorder. You may feel a little silly the first few times, but this method will improve your success rate. One sales textbook emphasizes the importance of practice with the following comments:

> *Prepare*...A Houston salesman accepted the challenge to spend as much as twice the time preparing for his sales presentation as he had been spending on making the presentation. He reported that he cut his selling time in front of the prospect from an hour and a half to eight minutes! Plus, he increased the size of the sale by over 50 percent.[4]

The salesperson should also be aware of possible objections and should prepare to handle them. Experience is the best teacher here; however, there are ten frequently used techniques which have proven helpful.[5] These are listed and briefly discussed below.

1. *Product comparison.* When the prospect is mentally comparing a product being used now or a competing product with the salesperson's product, the salesperson may make a complete comparison of the two. The salesperson lists the advantages and disadvantages of each product.

2. *Relating a case history.* Here the salesperson describes the experiences of another prospect similar to the prospect to whom he or she is talking.

3. *Demonstration.* A product demonstration gives a quite convincing answer to a product objection because the salesperson lets the product itself overcome the opposition.

4. *Giving guarantees.* Often a guarantee will remove resistance from the prospect's mind. Guarantees assure prospects that they cannot lose by purchasing. The caution, of course, is that guarantees must be meaningful and must provide for some recourse on the part of the prospect if the product does not live up to the guarantee.

5. *Asking questions.* The "why" question is of value in separating excuses from genuine objections and in probing for hidden resistance. The same question is useful in disposing of objections. Probing or exploratory questions are excellent in handling silent resistance. They can be worded and asked in a manner that appeals to the prospect's ego. In making the prospect do some thinking to convince the salesperson, questions of a probing nature get the prospect's full attention.

6. *Showing what delay costs.* A common experience of salespeople is to obtain seemingly sincere agreements to the buying decisions concerning need, product, source, and price, only to find that the prospect wants to wait some time before buying it. In such cases, the salesperson can sometimes take pencil and paper to show conclusively that delay of the purchase is expensive.

7. *Admitting and counterbalancing.* Sometimes the prospect's objection is completely valid because of some limitation in the salesperson's product. The only course of action in this case is for the salesperson to agree that the product does have the disadvantage to which the prospect is obviously objecting. Immediately after the acknowledgment, however, the salesperson should direct the prospect's attention to the advantages which overshadow the limitation of the product.

8. *Hearing the prospect out.* Some prospects object mainly for the opportunity to describe how they were once victimized. The

technique recommended for this type of resistance is that of sympathetic listening.

9. *Making the objection boomerang.* Once in a while the salesperson can take a prospect's reason for not buying and convert it into a reason for buying. This takes expert handling. Suppose the prospect says, "I'm too busy to see you." The salesperson might reply, "That's why you should see me—I can save you time."

10. *The "Yes, but" technique.* The best technique for handling most resistance is the indirect answer known as the "Yes, but" method. Here are two examples of what salespeople might say when using this technique: (1) "Yes, I can understand that attitude, but there is another angle for you to consider." (2) "Yes, you have a point there, but in your particular circumstances, other points are involved, too." The "Yes, but" method avoids argument and friction. It respects the prospect's opinions, attitudes, and thinking, and operates well where the prospect's point does not apply in a particular case.

Making the Sales Presentation   Salespersons must adapt their sales approach to the customer's needs. A "canned" sales talk will not succeed with most buyers. For example, the salesperson of bookkeeping machines must demonstrate the capacity of the equipment to solve a customer's particular bookkeeping problems. Similarly, a boat salesperson must understand the special interests of particular individuals in boating and talk the customer's language. Every sales objection must be answered explicitly and adequately.

There is considerable psychology in successful selling. The salesperson, as a psychologist, must know that some degree of personal enthusiasm, friendliness, and persistence is required. Perhaps 20 percent of all salespersons secure as much as 80 percent of all sales made. This is because they are the 20 percent who persist and who bring enthusiasm and friendliness to the task of selling.

Some salespersons have special sales "gimmicks" which they use with success. One automobile salesperson, for example, offered free driving lessons to people who had never taken a driver's training course or who needed a few more lessons before they felt confident enough to take the required driving tests. When such customers were ready to take the driving tests, this salesperson accompanied them to the driver examination grounds for moral support. Needless to say, these special efforts could hardly be turned down by new drivers who were in the market for cars.

Cost Control in Personal Selling

There are both economic and wasteful methods of achieving the same volume of sales. For example, the efficient routing of traveling salespersons and the making of appointments prior to arrival can conserve time and transportation expense. The cost of an outside sales call on a customer may be considerable—perhaps $80 or more. This emphasizes the need for efficient, intelligent scheduling. Moreover, the salesperson for a manufacturing firm can contribute to cost economy by stressing products which most need selling in order to give the factory a balanced run of production.

Profitability is increased to the extent that sales are made on the basis of quality and service rather than price-cutting. All products do not have the same margin of profit, however, and the salesperson can maximize profits by emphasizing high-margin lines.

ACTION REPORT
Personal Selling Through 1-800-686-2377

Telemarketing is a growing method of selling. One aspect of telemarketing is the use of special toll-free 800 numbers called *anagram numbers*—phone numbers that spell out a product or company's name. Examples are 800-IBM-PCJR and 800-NABISCO.

Many marketing experts believe that this form of anagrams is an effective promotional technique. Greg Griswold of Madison, WI, used 1-800-BEEHIVE to help take his beekeeping supply house from sales of $480,000 to $3.2 million in two years. "If you hear the 'number' once, you remember it for life, and that can be a tremendous marketing edge," says Griswold. He is so convinced of their merit that he has asked AT&T for over 5,000 anagram numbers which he hopes to re-sell to other businesses.

Other marketing people, such as Ernan Roman of Campaign Communications Institute of America, Inc., New York City, say that "There's absolutely no conclusive data to suggest that anagram numbers out-perform easy-to-remember regular numbers."

What do you think? Can you dial the telephone number in the title of this Action Report without looking at it again? What if you now know that the anagram for the number is 1-800-NUMBERS?

Source: Reprinted with permission, *Inc.* Magazine, July, 1983. Copyright © 1983 by Inc. Publishing Company, 38 Commercial Wharf, Boston, MA 02110.

Compensating the Salespeople

Salespeople are compensated in two ways for their efforts: financially and nonfinancially. Creating an effective compensation program must begin by recognizing that salespeople's goals may be different from the entrepreneur's goals. For example, the entrepreneur may be seeking nonfinancial goals, but the salespeople may not. A good compensation program will allow its participants to work for both forms of rewards.

Nonfinancial Rewards   Personal recognition and the satisfaction of reaching a sales quota are examples of nonfinancial rewards. A person can be motivated by these goals. Many retail small businesses will post the photograph of the top salesperson of the week on the bulletin board for all to see. Plaques are also used for a more permanent record of sales achievements.

Financial Rewards   Nonfinancial compensation is important to salespeople, but it doesn't put bread on the table. Financial compensation is typically the more critical issue. There are two basic plans of financial compensation: commissions and straight salary. Each has specific advantages and limitations.

Most small businesses would prefer to use a commission plan of compensation, which is simple and directly related to productivity. Typically a certain percentage of the sales generated is the salesperson's commission. A commission plan incorporates a strong incentive into the selling activities—no sale, no income! With this type of plan, there is no drain on cash flow until there is a sale.

With the straight salary form of compensation, salespeople have more security because their level of compensation is assured regardless of personal sales made. However, this method can tend to make a salesperson lazy.

A combination of the two forms of compensation can give the small business the "best of two worlds." It is a common practice to structure the combination plans so that salary represents the larger part for new salespeople. As the salesperson gains experience, the ratio is adjusted to provide a greater share from commissions and less from salary.

Building Customer Goodwill

The salesperson must look beyond the immediate sale to build customer goodwill and to create satisfied customers who will patronize the company in the future. One way to accomplish this is to preserve a good appearance, display a pleasant personality, and demonstrate good habits in all contacts with the customer. One can also help build goodwill by understanding the customer's point of view. Courtesy, attention to details, and genuine friendliness will help to gain acceptance with the customer.

Of course, high ethical standards are of primary importance in creating customer goodwill. This rules out misrepresentation and calls for confidential treatment of a customer's plans. Certainly the salesperson who receives secret information from a firm should preserve the confidence of that customer.

ADVERTISING

Advertising is the impersonal presentation of an idea which is identified with a business sponsor and is projected through mass media. Common media include television, radio, magazines, newspapers, and billboards. Advertising is a vital part of every small-business operation. As Steuart Henderson Britt has expressed it, "Doing business without advertising is like winking at a girl in the dark." You know what you are doing, but no one else does!

Objectives of Advertising

A primary goal of advertising is to draw attention to the existence or superiority of a firm's product or service. To be successful, it must rest upon a foundation of product quality and efficient service. Advertising can bring no more than temporary success to an inferior product. Advertising must always be viewed as a complement to a good product and never as a replacement for a bad product. This is the attitude of Frank Perdue, a highly successful marketer of chicken. He says:

> ...the quality of the product is number one; our advertising is number two....In advertising, you have to tell people why [they should buy the product]. That means "you have to have a product that's better than most—if possible, the best in your field...too many people take a mediocre product and fail. Eighty percent of all newly advertised products fail. The manufacturers decide the consumer is a fool. That's why it fails. They think advertising is a cure-all. But when you advertise something, you stick it in the consumer's mind that [your product] is better. They expect something a little more."[6]

The entrepreneur should not create false expectations with advertising. This can reduce customer satisfaction. Advertising may also accentuate a trend in the sale of an item or product line, but it seldom has the power to reverse such a trend. It must, consequently, be closely related to change in customer needs and preferences.

Used superficially, advertising may appear to be a waste of money. It seems expensive, while adding little utility to the product. Nevertheless, the major alternative is personal solicitation of potential customers, which is often more expensive and time-consuming.

Types of Advertising

There are two basic types of advertising—product advertising and institutional advertising. **Product advertising** is designed to make potential customers aware of a particular product or service and of their need for it.

Institutional advertising, on the other hand, conveys an idea regarding the business establishment. It is intended to keep the public conscious of the company and of its good reputation.[7] Figures 12–4 and 12–5 illustrate the differences between product advertising and institutional advertising.

No doubt the majority of small-business advertising is of the product type. Retailers' advertisements, for example, stress products almost exclusively, whether those of a supermarket featuring weekend specials or a women's shop focusing upon sportswear. At times the same advertisement carries both product and institutional themes. Furthermore, the same firm may stress product advertising in newspapers and, at the same time, use institutional appeals in the Yellow Pages of the telephone book. Decisions regarding the type of advertising used should be based upon the nature of the business, industry practice, media used, and objectives of the firm.

Figure 12–4   Example of Product Advertising

Source: Bryan-College Station Eagle (Texas), 25 August 1985.

Figure 12–5   Example of Institutional Advertising

Source: Bryan-College Station Eagle (Texas), 25 August 1985.

How Often to Advertise

Frequency of advertising is an important question for the small business. Advertising should be done regularly. Attempts to stimulate interest in a company's products or services should be part of a continuous advertising program. One-shot advertisements which are not part of a well-planned advertising effort lose much of their effectiveness in a short period.

Some noncontinuous advertising, of course, may be justified. This is true, for example, of advertising to prepare consumers for acceptance of a new product. Similarly, special advertising may be employed to suggest to customers new uses for established products. This is true also in advertising special sales.

Where to Advertise

Most small firms are restricted in their advertising efforts either geographically or by class of customer. Advertising media should reach—but not overreach—the present or desired market. From among the many media available, the small-business entrepreneur must choose those that will provide the greatest return for the advertising dollar.

The selection of the right combination of advertising media depends upon the type of business and its governing circumstances. A real estate sales firm, for example, may rely almost exclusively upon classified advertisements in a local newspaper, supplementing these with listings in the Yellow Pages of the telephone book. A transfer and storage firm may use a combination of radio, billboards, and telephone directory advertising to reach individuals planning to move household furniture. A small toy manufacturer may place greatest emphasis on television advertisements and participation in trade fairs. A local retail store may concentrate upon display advertisements in a local newspaper. The selection should be made not only on the basis of tradition but also upon an evaluation of the various ways to cover the particular market.

The best way to build a media mix is to talk with representatives from each medium. The small-business manager will usually find these representatives willing to recommend an assortment of media and not just the one they represent. Before you meet with these representatives, study as much as possible about advertising so you will know both the weaknesses and the strengths of each medium. Pages 338–339 give a concise summary of several important facts about media.[8] Study these pages carefully. Note particularly the advantages and disadvantages of each medium. Recognize that time and space costs vary from place to place and will change over time.

SALES PROMOTION

Sales promotion is promotion which serves as an inducement to perform a certain act while also offering value to recipients. The term *sales* *promotion* includes all promotional techniques which are neither personal selling nor advertising.

When to Use Sales Promotion

The small firm can use sales promotion to accomplish varied objectives. For example, small-business manufacturers can use sales promotion to stimulate commitments among channel intermediaries to market their product. Wholesalers can use sales promotion to induce retailers to buy inventories earlier than normally needed. Finally, with varied sales promotional tools, retailers can induce final consumers to make a purchase.

Sales Promotional Tools

Sales promotion should never represent the entire promotional effort of a small business. It should always be interlaced with advertising and personal selling. A partial list of sales promotional tools is given below:

1. Specialties.
2. Publicity.
3. Exhibits.
4. Sampling.
5. Coupons.
6. Premiums.
7. Contests.
8. Point-of-purchase displays.
9. Cooperative advertising.
10. Free merchandise.

The scope of this book does not allow us to comment on each of the sales promotional tools listed above. However, we will examine the first three on the list—specialties, publicity, and exhibits.

Specialties   The most distinguishing characteristic of specialties is their enduring nature and tangible value. Specialties are referred to as the "lasting medium." As functional products they are also worth something to recipients.

The most widely used specialty item is the calendar. Other examples are pens, key chains, and shirts. Actually, almost anything can be used as a specialty promotion. Every specialty item will be imprinted with the firm's name or other identifying slogan.

Specialties can be used to promote a product directly or to create company goodwill. Specialties also are excellent reminder promotions. For example, a small appliance repair shop can position its name and telephone number at the customer's phone with a specialty item related to dialing.

Medium	Market Coverage	Type of Audience	Sample Time/Space Costs
Daily Newspaper	Single community or entire metro area; zoned editions sometimes available.	General; tends more toward men, older age group, slightly higher income and education.	Per agate line, weekday; open rate: Circ: 8,700: $ .20 19,600: $ .35 46,200: $ .60 203,800: $ 1.60
Weekly Newspaper	Single community usually; sometimes a metro area.	General; usually residents of a smaller community.	Per agate line; open rate: Circ: 3,000: $ .35 8,900: $ .50 17,100: $ .75
Shopper	Most households in a single community; chain shoppers can cover a metro area.	Consumer households.	Per agate line; open rate: Circ: 10,000: $ .20 147,000: $ 2.00 300,000: $ 3.20
Telephone Directories	Geographic area or occupational field served by the directory.	Active shoppers for goods or services.	Yellow Pages, per half column; per month: Pop: 14-18,000: $ 15.00 110-135,000: $ 35.00 700-950,000: $ 100.00
Direct Mail	Controlled by the advertiser.	Controlled by the advertiser through use of demographic lists.	Production and mailing cost of an 8½″ × 11″ 2-color brochure; 4-page, 2-color letter; order card and reply envelope; label addressed; third class mail: $.33 each in quantities of 50,000.
Radio	Definable market area surrounding the station's location.	Selected audiences provided by stations with distinct programming formats.	Per 60-second morning drive-time spot; one time: Pop: 400,000: $ 35.00 1,100,000: $ 90.00 3,500,000: $ 150.00 13,000,000: $ 300.00
Television	Definable market area surrounding the station's location.	Varies with the time of day; tends toward younger age group, less print-oriented.	Per 30-second daytime spot; one time; nonpreemptible status: Pop: 400,000: $ 100.00 1,100,000: $ 300.00 3,500,000: $ 500.00 13,000,000: $ 600.00
Transit	Urban or metro community served by transit system; may be limited to a few transit routes.	Transit riders, especially wage earners and shoppers; pedestrians.	Inside 11″ × 28″ cards; per month: 50 buses: $ 125.00 400 buses: $1,000.00 Outside 21″ × 88″ posters; per month: 25 buses: $ 1,850.00 100 buses: $ 7,400.00
Outdoor	Entire metro area or single neighborhood.	General; especially auto drivers.	Per 12′ × 25′ poster; 100 GRP* per month: Pop: 21,800: $ 125.00 386,000: $ 135.00 628,900: $ 150.00
Local Magazine	Entire metro area or region; zoned editions sometimes available.	General; tends toward better educated, more affluent.	Per one-sixth page, black and white; open rate: Circ: 25,000: $ 310.00 80,000: $ 520.00

*Several boards must be purchased for these GRPs.

Particular Suitability	Major Advantage	Major Disadvantage
All general retailers.	Wide circulation.	Nonselective audience.
Retailers who service a strictly local market.	Local identification.	Limited readership.
Neighborhood retailers and service businesses.	Consumer orientation.	A giveaway and not always read.
Services, retailers of brand-name items, highly specialized retailers.	Users are in the market for goods or services.	Limited to active shoppers.
New and expanding businesses; those using coupon returns or catalogs.	Personalized approach to an audience of good prospects.	High CPM.
Businesses catering to identifiable groups; teens, commuters, housewives.	Market selectivity, wide market coverage.	Must be bought consistently to be of value.
Sellers of products or services with wide appeal.	Dramatic impact, wide market coverage.	High cost of time and production.
Businesses along transit routes, especially those appealing to wage earners.	Repetition and length of exposure.	Limited audience.
Amusements, tourist businesses, brand-name retailers.	Dominant size, frequency of exposure.	Clutter of many signs reduces effectiveness of each one.
Restaurants, entertainments, specialty shops, mail-order businesses.	Delivery of a loyal, special-interest audience.	Limited audience.

Finally, specialties are personal. They are distributed directly to the consumer in a personal way, they are items which can be used personally, and they have a personal message. Since the small business needs to retain its personal image, entrepreneurs can use specialties to achieve this objective.

ACTION REPORT
Advertising Specialties Create Warm Relationships

There is a very special restaurant located in the small town of Barrow, Alaska. The restaurant's name is Pepe's North of the Border, and it specializes in Mexican–American cuisine. Its owner is Fran Tate who started the business in 1978 in a remodelled two-bedroom house. Today, it serves about 400 customers daily.

Three facts make this restaurant special. First, it is located in the northernmost inhabited region in North America where the average winter temperature on the Fahrenheit scale is 50 to 60 below zero. Secondly, it's the only restaurant in the area and does not need to use promotion. Thirdly, Pepe's does use promotion!

Tate puts it this way, "Let's face it...I really don't need to advertise. Everyone who knows I'm here is *here*." Nevertheless, Tate uses specialties to create and maintain friendly communication between her and customers. She uses Pepe's T-shirts, caps, tote bags, thermometers, and many other items to say thank you to customers.

Tate has also used specialty items to overcome negative reactions of customers to somewhat high prices, which are necessitated by high shipping costs for some of her food items. For example, if Pepe's weekly tortilla bill is $500, the freight will be about $450.

The specialty advertising gifts are also used to smooth over the inconvenience of power failures. "The gifts are one way of showing that we really do care about them and regret any inconvenience they may experience while dining," according to Tate.

Source: Reprinted with permission from IMPRINT, copyright 1986, Advertising Specialty Institute, Langhorne, PA 19047.

Publicity   Of particular importance to retailers because of their high visibility is the type of promotion called publicity. Publicity can be used to promote both a product and a firm's image and is a vital part of good public relations for the small business. A good publicity program must maintain regular contacts with the news media.

Although publicity is considered to be "free" advertising, this is not always an accurate profile of this type of promotion. A cost is associated with this effort. Examples of publicity efforts which entail considerable expense are involvements with school yearbooks or summer baseball programs. While the benefits are difficult to measure, publicity is nevertheless important to a small business and should be exploited.

ACTION REPORT
Public Opinion Tips Coffee Shop

Small business can benefit from public opinion. Publicity can be instrumental in building a favorable or unfavorable image.

Barry Warfel attributes the loss of his small business to bad publicity. Business at his Roseland, NJ, coffee shop was "perking" until a competitor set up business. The competitor was aggressive and often insulted Warfel's food and prices. But Warfel fought back. He chased the competitor from his coffee shop entrance and even turned him in to the local health inspector.

The public reacted negatively to Warfel's tactics. "People shunned his coffee shop, sales plunged, the Warfel family got nasty phone calls. 'I knew I couldn't stay,' Mr. Warfel says. He sold his shop. Today he manages a fast-food outlet in another town."

The competitor became a hero and last year received an award at the White House Conference on Small Business. By the way, Warfel's competitor operated his business in a red wagon outside Warfel's coffee shop. The competitor's name was Billy. He was 11 years old.

Source: Reprinted by permission of *The Wall Street Journal* (June 15, 1981), © Dow Jones & Company, Inc. (1981). All rights reserved.

Exhibits   The use of exhibits permits product demonstrations, or "hands-on" experience with a product. The customer's place of business is not always the best environment for product demonstrations in normal personal selling efforts. And advertising cannot always substitute for try-out experiences with a product.

Exhibits are of particular value to manufacturers. The greatest benefit of exhibits is its potential cost savings over personal selling. Trade-show groups claim that the cost of exhibits is less than half the cost of a sales call.[9] Small manufacturers also view exhibits as offering a savings over advertising. For example, Virginia V. Ness, owner of a small company in San Rafael, CA, says, "You might not write many orders, but this sure costs less than advertising as a way of making the product known in the industry."[10]

ACTION REPORT
Consumers "Dig" Contest

The most successful contests are those which generate excitement. An attractive prize is one way to stimulate enthusiasm and excitement.

The promotion manager of the *Ottawa Citizen* newspaper, Ben Babelowsky, knows how this can be done. He organized a "gold rush" contest in which the prize was gold wafers valued at over $4,000. The contest instructions were, "The gold is in a public place, and it isn't necessary to dig or damage anything to find it."

The contest inspired several escapades:

- A hunter who was convinced the gold was in a bird's nest checked every tree along the city's seven-mile canal.
- Jailkeepers had to call police to clear the district jail of treasure hunters after a newspaper drawing indicated the prison might be a hiding place.
- Police headquarters also was a target. Before searchers were cleared from there, they had pulled insulation from the crevices of the building's exterior walls.

Where were the golden wafers? They were found in a tree near a cross-country snow trail. But before the contest ended, the newspaper was selling 1,500 more copies a day!

Source: Reprinted by permission of *The Wall Street Journal* (March 3, 1981), © Dow Jones & Company, Inc. (1981). All rights reserved.

Looking Back

1. The promotional mix includes personal selling, advertising, and sales promotion. The exact mixture is influenced by the nature of the market and the nature of the product. The optimum promotional mix may be modified because of cost limitations.
2. The four techniques used to estimate promotional funding needs are: a percentage of sales, what can be spared, as much as competition spends, and what it takes to do the job.
3. The two major steps in preparing for a sales presentation are prospecting and practicing. In making the sales presentation, salespersons must adapt their sales approach to the customer's needs and must show some degree of enthusiasm, friendliness, and persistence.
4. The two general types of advertising are product advertising and institutional advertising. Each available form of advertising has certain advantages and disadvantages. The majority of small-business advertising is product advertising.

5. Sales promotion can be used (1) by the manufacturer to stimulate commitments among channel intermediaries to market its product, (2) by the wholesaler to induce retailers to buy inventories earlier than normally needed, and (3) by the retailer to induce final consumers to make a purchase. Some sales promotional tools are specialties, publicity, and exhibits.

DISCUSSION QUESTIONS

1. Outline a promotional mix which you believe would be appropriate to help market this textbook to college bookstores. Which promotional element do you feel is the most essential to your mix?
2. What problems, if any, do you see in selecting television to promote dental laboratory services to dentists' clients? Be specific.
3. Discuss the advantages and the disadvantages of each of the methods of earmarking funds for promotion.
4. Outline a system of prospecting which could be used by a small camera store. Incorporate all the techniques presented in the chapter.
5. Why are the salesperson's techniques for handling objections so important to a successful sales presentation?
6. What are the advantages and disadvantages of compensating salespeople by salary? By commission? What is an acceptable compromise?
7. Refer to pages 338–339 and list five media that would give the small business the most precise selectivity. Be prepared to substantiate your list.
8. How does sales promotion differ from advertising and personal selling?
9. How do specialties differ from other sales promotional tools? Be specific.
10. Comment on the statement that "publicity is free advertising."

ENDNOTES

1. A strong case for maintaining or increasing advertising efforts in times of business downturns is made in J. Wesley Rosberg, "Is a Recession on the Way? It's No time to Cut Ad Budgets," *Industrial Marketing*, Vol. 64, No. 4 (April, 1979), pp. 64–79.

2. For an interesting analysis of the importance of "setting the stage" in a sales presentation, see "Why First Impressions Count," *Industrial Distribution*, Vol. 70, No. 1 (January, 1980), pp. 79–80.

3. Mark K. Metzger, "Once Is Not Enough," *Inc.*, Vol. 7, No. 2 (February, 1985), p. 118.

4. James F. Robeson, H. Lee Mathews, and Carl G. Stevens, *Selling* (Homewood, IL: Richard D. Irwin, Inc., 1978), pp. 85–86.

5. Charles A. Kirkpatrick and Frederick A. Russ, *Effective Selling* (7th ed.; Cincinnati, OH: South-Western Publishing Co., 1981), pp. 254–255. Reproduced with permission.

6. Robert A. Mamis, "Frank Perdue," *Inc.*, Vol. 6, No. 2 (February, 1984), pp. 21–22.

7. Some practical advice for creating newspaper advertising consistent with store image is found in L. Lee Manzer, R. Duane Ireland, and Philip M. Van Auken, "Image Creation in Small Business Retailing: Applications of Newspaper Advertising," *Journal of Small Business Management*, Vol. 18, No. 2 (April, 1980), pp. 18–23.

8. Reprinted with permission from Bank of America, NT&SA, "Advertising Small Business," *Small Business Reporter*, Vol. 15, No. 2, Copyright 1976, 1978, 1981.

9. See Bob Donath, "Show and Sell by the Numbers," *Industrial Marketing*, Vol. 65, No. 3 (March, 1980), p. 70.

10. Thomas J. Lueck, "Innovators Vie for Attention at Trade Shows," *The Wall Street Journal*, July 20, 1981, p. 19.

REFERENCES TO SMALL BUSINESS IN ACTION

Adler, Jack. "Staging an Exposition." *Venture*, Vol. 2, No. 4 (April, 1980), pp. 18–19.
    This article tells how an entrepreneur organizes an exposition, and it describes his promotional budget and "prospecting" strategy.

Carey, Carol Rose. "Techniques for Ringing up Orders." *Inc.*, Vol. 4, No. 11 (November, 1982), pp. 137–140.
    Using the telephone to sell is the subject of this article. Eleven key techniques for effective telephone sales are described by an entrepreneur marketing ladies' wigs.

Hartman, Curtis. "Selling the Brooklyn Bridge." *Inc.*, Vol. 5, No. 11 (November, 1983), pp. 58–70.
    This article shares the success story of several public relations campaigns developed by one firm for its small-business clients.

Post, David. "How to Sell to Big Companies." *Inc.*, Vol. 3, No. 3 (March, 1981), pp. 66–70.
    A young entrepreneur outlines what it takes to get started with a business. His personal sales presentation is described as a key ingredient.

Shapiro, Irv. "Solving an Ad Riddle." *In Business*, Vol. 3, No. 2 (March–April, 1981), pp. 40–41.
    In this article the simple and inexpensive direct mail campaign of a small delicatessen is described along with the promotional program of a furniture store.

CASE 12

Mitchell Interiors
Developing a promotional strategy

Joyce Mitchell, age 38 and married for 20 years, was a native Texan with 2 children. Her husband Joe, age 40, had recently taken a 20-year retirement from his firefighter's job in Dallas, TX. Together, Joyce and Joe operated an interior decorating business located on North Main Street in Corsicana, TX, a town of approximately 25,000 people.

Joyce's Background

During her early years of marriage, Joyce tried several jobs but was mainly a housewife. She was not content at being a housewife because, as she said, "I have a tendency to get everything done. I'm usually a pretty good organizer, and I just didn't feel fulfilled." When her children were older, she went back to school to pursue a home economics degree. During this time, she accepted a kindergarten teaching job at a private school.

Joyce soon found out she was not cut out to be a teacher. In her words, "I cannot train people. You know how some people play piano by ear—well, I'm that way. I feel I know how to do something, so why shouldn't you? So, teaching was frustrating to me." About this time, Joe and Joyce decided to move south of Dallas into the country. Joyce happily gave up her teaching.

Joe and Joyce decided to personally build their house on the land they purchased in Navarro County about 12 miles west of Corsicana. Therefore, the first year after Joyce had left teaching, she was busy helping with the construction project. "If I wasn't busy with a hammer and nails, wallpaper, or helping the plumber, I was running back and forth to Corsicana picking out interior decorations."

Working for a Large Chain

Joyce began helping her friends with their decorating. A large chain store in Corsicana was a place Joyce would go for her decorating purchases. The store manager was always impressed by the well-organized clippings and folders that she would bring into the store. One day the manager offered Joyce an opportunity to work with the store in a newly created interior decorating job. This chain was just getting into this type of business activity. Joyce was not interested at that time because she had enrolled for 18 credit hours at a local college. The manager persisted, "I've been watching you for four months, and I know you are what I need." Finally, Joyce consented to work on Saturdays beginning in December after the semester concluded. The manager agreed, and Joyce continued for two months under this arrangement. Then, in January, she began working full time and set up the interior design department. During the next 5 years, she was highly successful and reached the point where she was earning more than $1,500 a month from salary and commissions. For the Corsicana area, this was a high income and an excellent supplement to Joe's salary.

One day Joyce realized she was "working around the clock for another company." She would get up at 5 a.m. to figure bids, report to the store at 8 a.m., oversee installations, and then come home to figure more bids at night. "I really had too many clients," she recalled. She was overloaded and uncomfortable with carrying heavy carpet samples and wallpaper samples in and out of clients' houses. The weight of these samples was also wearing on her personal car. Finally, she requested a company van to carry these samples. The request was received favorably, but the company never did buy the van.

Joyce was also being asked to train interior decorators from other stores in the chain organization. "I was also getting behind in my other work. It was a nice compliment from the store, but I got to looking at it and decided they would have to compensate me or get me some help. I decided to resign." Later, Joyce was told the company was about to promote her to regional supervisor. This would have meant she would be teaching even more, something she didn't enjoy. Joyce decided, "I like decorating because that's my talent. That's the talent God gave me, so I'm going to stay with it."

Beginning Her Own Business

Since the lack of a van to transport decorating samples to clients' homes was a key issue in Joyce's departure from the chain store, Joe and Joyce decided to begin their own business with a used Dodge Motor Home. Mitchell Interiors was thus born in 1978. The business began smoothly. All of Joyce's suppliers were eager to help because they had observed her success with the large chain store. She had no trouble opening accounts with them because they knew she could sell.

After nine months, the van became crowded. Joyce told Joe, "If we are going to do this, let's do it big." So they bought a 28-foot Winnebago and Joyce personally designed a plush interior. Joe built the interior, and they had a decorating studio on wheels. "The type of clients I want need to see what you can do the minute they step into your place," Joyce commented. "I want them to think, 'If she can do this to a van, she can do my home to please me.'"

Opening the Mitchell Interiors Store

The Mitchell Interiors store opened in November, 1980. It was located in Corsicana and occupied 2,000 square feet of store and warehouse space. The store allowed for increased display of many items which were also for sale to walk-in customers. The location was leased and had three neighbor tenants: Prestige Realty, Clint's Jewelers, and Pat Walkers (a reducing salon). All these four businesses catered to the same type of clientele.

Joyce still used the Winnebago for travel to clients' homes. Business had been good. In fact, Joyce said, "I am so busy, I cannot take everything which comes in off the street. The first question I ask is: Have you been recommended? I cannot physically get to all the potential business. Therefore, I consider only those jobs I know I can get. I am really wasting time going out to bid on a job if they don't know whether they want me to do it or not."

Joyce was a strong believer in bringing the personal touch to a business. She always tried to bring this to her clients. Even Joe, who installed all drapes and supervised carpet installation, believed in the personal touch. Joyce said, "I hope our business never gets so big that we cannot personally oversee all our jobs."

The Product/Service Mix

Contract sales provided about 75 percent of the total business volume of Mitchell Interiors. Contract sales were those sales made to interior decorating clients—individual homeowners or business owners. Joyce occasionally contracted with builders for the decorating of new houses. Recently, however, because of high interest rates, there was little speculative building in the area. The main products which sold in contract jobs were carpet, vinyl floor covering, draperies, and wallpaper. Drapery sales constituted 60 percent of the contract sales, and Joyce was happy with this situation because of the higher markup associated with draperies. Since competition was much greater in carpeting and vinyls, these products produced a much lower markup. The remaining 25 percent of the business volume came from in-store sales of tables, lamps, ceiling fans, and other decorative accessories.

Joyce saw her customers as upper-middle class and upper class, 35 to 50 years old, both in Corsicana and in surrounding towns.

Promotional Practices

Most of Joyce's promotion had been accomplished through the recommendations of satisfied customers. Customers who had known Joyce when she worked for the chain store recommended her to their friends. When Mitchell Interiors was initially "garaged" at Joe and Joyce's home, few people who had a cursory interest would call because of the long-distance telephone charges. Joyce would advertise such things as a drapery sale in the newspaper or on some other special occasion such as Mother's Day. Joyce also used radio advertising on the local FM country-western radio station. Joyce had done all the design work for the firm's stationery and for print advertising.

Joyce used direct mail advertising, too. She felt very strongly that this was an effective medium for her business. These mail-outs were primarily a reminder that her store was there and that she was available. The mailing lists came mainly from an internal file of satisfied customers. This file was updated to remove customers who had not visited the store after about three mail-outs. Additional names were solicited from employees, the Corsicana telephone directory, new residents in the more elite parts of town, and listings of doctors and lawyers.

Yearly promotional expenditures were planned by Joyce at the beginning of the year when the master budget was finalized. Joyce forecasted the expenses and the sales needed to meet these expenses. Break-even sales were around $20,000 per month. In the master budget Joyce included an advertising budget because she believed that advertising was important. In 1981, she allowed approximately $300 of the total budget per month for promotion on newspaper advertising, radio, direct mail, business gifts, and specialty advertising. Most of her promotion emphasized accessory items. Joyce reasoned, "I want people to come in and buy accessories. I want people to get used to having a store like this in Corsicana."

The Store Employees

The business had only one full-time employee and four part-time helpers. According to Joyce, "Joe is the only person besides me who gets outside the business and works with clients." Joyce wanted to remain as the designer–buyer for the store but was willing to take on another designer. She was also looking for someone to manage the accessories area at the store. She wanted the manager to pre-interview other employees, but she wished to make the final hiring decisions.

Questions

1. What other types of promotion would "fit" Joyce Mitchell's customers?
2. Evaluate the promotional practices of Mitchell Interiors.
3. Should Joyce continue to advertise when she already has more business than she can handle? Why or why not?
4. How can Mitchell Interiors grow and also retain the personal touch that is so important to Joyce?

PART IV
MANAGING SMALL-BUSINESS OPERATIONS

13 – The Process of Management

14 – Objectives, Strategy, and Operational Planning

15 – Organizing the Small Firm

16 – Managing Human Resources in Small Firms

17 – Operations Management

18 – Purchasing and Managing Inventory

13

The Process of Management

Figure 13–1   Steven Herrick and Steven Kirby

A tension between entrepreneurial and professional management often occurs in small firms when the founding entrepreneur's original free-wheeling management style gives way to more systematic approaches. An example of such a transition is found in SBH Corporation, where the entrepreneur, Steven Herrick, brought in a professional manager, Steven Kirby, who had been vice-president of marketing for a large auto parts distributor.

Since joining SBH, Kirby has found that "an entrepreneurial company tends to be a very one-person centered business with everyone waiting for the entrepreneur to assist in making decisions." For Kirby it's been an uphill struggle introducing a corporate management style to SBH employees. "It's hard for them now to accept responsibilities and make decisions on their own. There's been some resentment," he says.

Also, Kirby acknowledges that it has been hard for the entrepreneur, Steven Herrick, to let go. In the long run, he believes it should work out. "I plan to bring in a professional management style," says Kirby, "which should allow Steve to get back to being an entrepreneur."

Source: Ronald Tanner, "Picking a President." Reprinted from the July, 1983 issue of *Venture*, The Magazine for Entrepreneurs, by special permission. © 1983 Venture Magazine, Inc., 521 Fifth Ave., New York, N.Y. 10175.

Looking Ahead

Watch for the following important topics:

1. The nature of management functions in small firms.
2. The relationship of the management process to the growth cycle of a small business.
3. Special management characteristics of small entrepreneurial firms.
4. Effective use of managerial time.
5. Sources of management assistance.

To some extent, the management processes of large and small businesses are similar. Both require managerial direction and coordination of work activities. There are differences, however, in the sophistication of management methods and in the nature of challenges facing small-business managers. This chapter will focus on some of these unique aspects of managing the smaller enterprise.

MANAGEMENT FUNCTIONS IN SMALL BUSINESS

As a beginning step, let us review briefly the nature of management and management activities common to all forms of organized endeavor. We can then observe those elements or problems that are especially significant in small businesses.

Broadly speaking, **management** consists of all activities undertaken to secure the accomplishment of work through the efforts of other people. Those managerial activities are often referred to as **management functions** and, according to one widely used pattern, they include planning, organizing, leading/motivating, and controlling.

Planning

Planning requires decisions about a future course of action. As implied by this statement, planning involves goal setting. However, it also includes related decisions concerning "who" and "when" and "how." The following are part of the manager's overall planning functions:

1. Setting company objectives.
2. Devising a strategy for reaching objectives.
3. Formulating policies and procedures.

4. Outlining operating plans for each area of business activity.

5. Drawing up budgets for the various segments of the business.

Since planning is primarily a thinking process, action-oriented entrepreneurs sometimes postpone it in favor of activities more directly related to operations. Because of the great importance of planning in small business, Chapter 4 treats the preparation of the initial business plan and Chapter 14 explains the role of planning in the going concern.

Organizing

Organizing involves the assignment of functions and tasks to departmental components and to individual employees. It includes the delegation of authority to subordinate managers and operating employees so that they can properly carry out their duties. Thus, organizing establishes the pattern of relationships observed by all members of the organization.

A formal statement of structure ordinarily takes the form of an organization chart that shows all the managerial levels and positions. An example of an organization chart is presented in Figure 13-2. Some companies also prepare an organizational manual and/or job descriptions to show the detailed functions assigned to each member of the management team.

Preparation of an organization chart can clarify organizational arrangements that may otherwise be hazy in the minds of employees. Whether the organization structure is reduced to writing or not, it is desirable that relationships among members of the organization be logically conceived and thoroughly understood by all. In the very small business, of course, this may be satisfactorily accomplished without a formal organization chart or manual.

For the typical small business, the management group may, and probably will, consist of very few persons. It will grow as the small business itself grows. Chapter 15 expands on the different forms of organization structure that the small firm may assume.

Leading and Motivating

An entrepreneur activates an organization to accomplish business plans by **leading and motivating** subordinate managers and other employees. In the performance of this function, he or she directs and inspires those who are part of the organization.

Hard-working, high-performing employees can make the difference between an average and a superior firm. Through leadership, the manager gains the cooperation of others. And through motivation, managers encourage employees to strive persistently for high job performance.

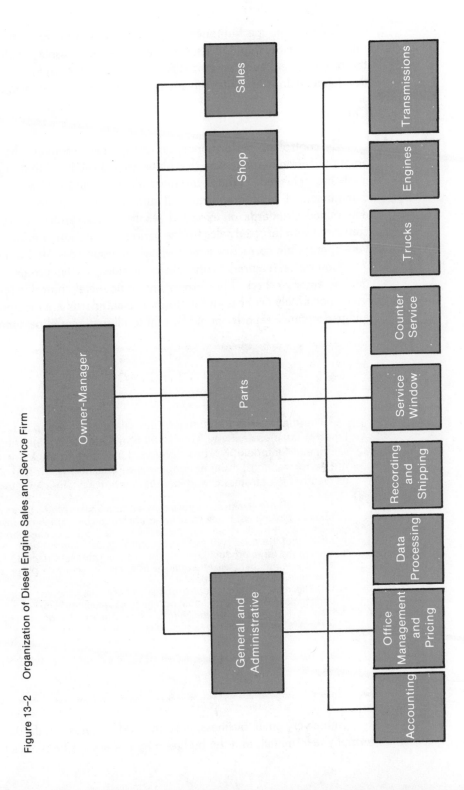

Figure 13-2   Organization of Diesel Engine Sales and Service Firm

Enthusiastic performance is thus an indicator and result of good managerial leadership. Occasionally, entrepreneurs display such a vision for the business and such an empathy for others in the organization that they develop a zealous and intensely loyal attitude among employees.

Controlling

By controlling performance, an entrepreneur monitors the activities of an organization to make sure that plans are followed and that organizational goals are achieved. Perhaps the most obvious feature of **controlling** is the comparison of both organizational and individual performance with predetermined standards or expected results. Sales results, for example, are compared with targeted sales for the period. The manager must evaluate and take appropriate corrective action whenever results deviate from standards.

Control is required in the areas of sales, costs, profits, output, and quality, among others. The cornerstone of financial control is the budget, in which accurately set cost and performance standards are incorporated. Cost and performance reports should be sent to all managerial personnel.

ACTION REPORT
Controlling Performance of Sales Representatives

The managerial function of controlling can be applied to many types of business activity. One small firm, Dranetz Engineering Laboratories of Plainfield, NJ, has developed a system to track and control the performance of independent sales representatives (reps) who sell its electronic instruments and instrumentation systems. A writer notes:

Graphs are also used to track reps' performances. After a quota is set for each rep, the projected sales levels are plotted on a graph to provide a base line for tracking sales in the next year. At the end of each month, a member of the sales staff plots the month's actual sales for each rep for each of the three product lines. As the year progresses, Orlacchio [sales vice-president] can tell at a glance how closely a rep is progressing towards his quota in each product line.

The reps get photocopies of their charts each month, along with comments from Orlacchio about how he thinks each rep is doing. If one of them is significantly off his quota, Orlacchio or one of his regional managers contacts the rep to try to discover the reasons.

Source: David De Long, "Track Sales to Control Company Growth," *Inc.*, Vol. 2, No. 5 (May, 1980), p. 80.

In the very small business, cost and performance standards may not be formally determined, and the budget may not always be reduced to writing.

Nevertheless, the efficient manager will know what cost and performance should be, keep track of actual results, and investigate—looking toward prompt remedial action—whenever the actual results vary from what they should be.

DISTINCTIVE FEATURES OF SMALL-FIRM MANAGEMENT

Even though managers in both large and small companies perform similar management functions, their jobs as managers are somewhat different. This is readily recognized by a manager who moves from a large corporation to a small firm. He or she encounters an entirely different business atmosphere. Furthermore, the small firm experiences constant change in its organizational and managerial needs as it moves from point zero, its launching, to the point where it can employ a full staff of professional managers. In this section we shall examine a number of these special features that serve to challenge managers of small firms.

Traditional Weaknesses in Small Firms

Although some large corporations experience poor management, small business seems particularly vulnerable to this weakness. Managerial inefficiency prevails in tens, or even hundreds, of thousands of small firms. Many small firms are marginal or unprofitable businesses, struggling to survive from day to day and month to month. At best, they earn only a pittance for their owners. The reason for their condition is at once apparent to one who examines their operations. They "run," but it is an exaggeration to say that they are "managed."

Weak management shows up in the service observed and received by customers. For example, consider the following comments made about hotel service:

> My guess, simply as one traveling man, is that the secret is primarily a secret of management. Capital may have something to do with it, of course; architecture, interior decoration, location, the nature of the clientele—all these doubtless figure into the equation. At bottom, I suspect, the difference between a poor hotel/motel and a good one lies in the experience, the attitude, and the personal attention of the man or woman who runs the place. If a manager does a good job of training the maids, and pays them tolerable wages, and treats them with dignity, and praises them for doing well, that manager's rooms will be comfortable rooms—for the maids will have checked the light bulbs and tried the TV before they leave. If a manager insists upon friendly courtesy on the part of his desk clerks, he can get it—or he can get some new desk clerks.[1]

Even though management weakness is prevalent in small business, it is not universal. More important, poor management is by no means inevitable just because a firm is small.

Constraints on Management in Small Firms

Managers of small firms, particularly new and growing companies, are constrained by conditions that do not trouble the average corporate executive. They do not have enough money and enough talented people. They must face the grim reality of small bank accounts and limited managerial staff. These limitations are sufficiently real that large-firm managers experience real difficulty in making the transition to small-firm management. One writer says:

> You cannot realize how lavish big business is until you try making the transition to small business. For example, a marketing man moving from a big company to a small one usually discovers, to his horror, that his new employer has no market surveys, and the sum of his research is a two-year-old article clipped from a trade magazine. Making bad matters worse, the little company desperately needs a four-color brochure for the salesmen. You can't sell without sales literature, now can you?
>
> In big business there is no question about it; you get these tools, and a major skill the new employee brings with him is knowledge of how to use the tools. In small business the new employee will likely be told by the company president, "We can't afford research. We can't afford surveys and probably don't need them anyway. As far as that brochure is concerned, if we really need one, there is always Jiffy Printing across the street. They can whip something out for $600. Nothing fancy, mind you. And ask 'em not to bill us 'til September."[2]

Thomas P. Murphy has cited the conflict between an entrepreneur and a Harvard Business School-trained senior executive whom the entrepreneur had hired.[3] The new executive had concluded that a $100,000 stainless-steel mold for making plastic extrusions was a far better investment than a $10,000 aluminum mold that wouldn't last as long. The analysis was correct, but the business did not have $100,000. The entrepreneur explained that he was more concerned about staying alive in the short run than having the best long-run solution, but this was difficult for the new executive to understand.

In a small firm, the entrepreneur also typically lacks adequate specialized staff. Most managers are generalists, and they lack the support of experienced staff in market research, financial analysis, advertising, human resources management, and other areas. The entrepreneur must make decisions involving these areas without the advice and guidance that is available in a larger business. Later in this chapter, we see that this limitation may be partially overcome by use of outside management consultants. Nevertheless, the shortage of immediately available talent is a part of the reality of the entrepreneurial firm.

ACTION REPORT
A Cadillac Dealer Runs Short of Cash

During the oil crisis of the 1970s, a young Cadillac dealer in Illinois, Rob Mancuso, learned the hard way about controlling costs. After the business started losing money and checks began to bounce, Mancuso began managing in a way that reflected these financial realities.

"In all the years I'd been at my father's store, I'd never heard the word 'overdraft,'" Mancuso admits. "I quickly learned how to turn frozen assets into liquid assets. We bailed out of used cars, sent new cars back to the factory, and cut back on parts to the point where, if a guy came in for a tune-up, we'd have to run down to K mart for spark plugs."

These were desperate measures, but the business survived and went on to prosper under Mancuso's imaginative leadership.

Source: Reprinted with permission, Inc. magazine, June, 1984. Copyright © 1984 by *Inc.* Publishing Company, 38 Commercial Wharf, Boston, MA 02110.

Stages of Growth and Implications for Management

As a newly formed business becomes established and grows, its organization and pattern of management change. To some extent, management must adapt to growth and change in any organization. However, the changes involved as business moves through periods of "childhood" and "adolescence" are much more extensive than those that occur with the growth of a relatively mature business.

As shown in Figure 13–3, a new firm passes through four stages of growth. Subordinates are employed and layers of management are added as it moves from Stage 1 to Stage 4.

In Stage 1, the firm is simply a one-person operation. Of course, not all firms begin at this level, but this situation is by no means rare. In Stage 2, the entrepreneur becomes a player-coach, which implies extensive participation in the operations of the business. In additon to performing the basic work—whether it be production, sales, writing checks, or record keeping—the entrepreneur must also coordinate the efforts of others.

In Stage 3, a major milestone is reached when an intermediate level of supervision is added. In many ways this is a difficult, dangerous point for the small firm because the entrepreneur must rise above direct, hands-on management and work through an intermediate level of management.

Stage 4, the stage of formal organization, involves more than increased size and multilayered organization. The formalization of management

Figure 13-3   Stages of Small-Business Growth

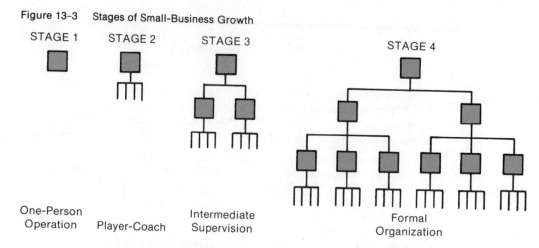

STAGE 1   STAGE 2   STAGE 3   STAGE 4

One-Person   Intermediate   Formal
Operation   Player-Coach   Supervision   Organization

involves the adoption of written policies, preparation of plans and budgets, standardization of personnel practices, computerization of records, preparation of organization charts and job descriptions, scheduling of training conferences, institution of control procedures, and so on.

Some formal management practices may be adopted prior to Stage 4 of the firm's growth. Nevertheless, the stages of management growth describe a typical pattern of development for successful firms. The early flexibility and informality may be functional at the beginning, but growth necessitates greater formality in planning and control. A tension often develops as the traditional easy-going patterns of management become dysfunctional. Great managerial skill is required to preserve the "family" atmosphere while introducing professional management.

Changing Skill Requirements

As a firm moves from Stage 1 to Stage 4, the pattern of entrepreneurial activities changes. The entrepreneur becomes less of a doer and more of a manager, as shown in Figure 13–4.

Firms that are overly hesitant to move through these organizational stages and to provide the necessary management limit their rate of growth. On the other hand, a small business may attempt to become a big business too quickly. The entrepreneur's primary strength may lie in product development or selling, for example, and a quick push into Stage 4 may saddle the entrepreneur with managerial duties and rob the organization of those valuable entrepreneurial talents.

Thomas P. Murphy has pointed out the significant nonmanagerial role played by many entrepreneurs:

Figure 13–4   Managerial Functions and Stages of Growth

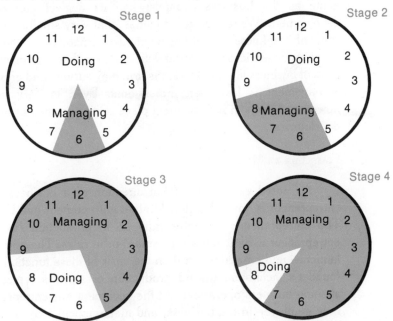

Having already set management science back to the dark ages, let me add a final heresy—the role of the boss is not to become the serene orchestra conductor while others tootle the instruments. Fine for larger companies. But small businesses are generally founded on an individual's special strength—the boss is a gifted engineer or an excellent salesman. Relegate him or her too early to the orchestra-leader role and you remove the basic strength of the business and replace it with a frustrated administrator.[4]

Murphy described a small company whose venture capitalists wanted to make it into a "real" company quickly.[5] To do so, they pulled the chief executive officer, who was also making half of the company's sales, back into the office and hired three new salesmen. However, the new salesmen failed to sell, the new financing was lost, and the venture capitalists walked away in disgust, leaving the company to sink. But it did not sink! The chief executive fired the salesmen who didn't sell, went back to selling—which he did very well—and watched the firm evolve into the "real" company the venture capitalists had tried to develop prematurely.

A tension exists, therefore, between the "doing" and "managing" roles of the entrepreneur. Care must be taken to capitalize on the special or unique "doing" strengths brought into the venture by the entrepreneur. The importance of these strengths obviously varies with the entrepreneur and the enterprise.

At the same time, the need for effective management becomes more acute as the business expands; and its neglect can retard the firm's development. We recognize, of course, that very small firms often survive in spite of weakness in management. To some extent, the quality of their products or services may offset deficiencies in their management. In the early days of business life, therefore, the firm may survive and grow even though its management is less than professional. Even in very small businesses, however, defects in management place strains on the business and retard its development.

Founders as Managers

As noted earlier, the initial direction of a business by the founding entrepreneur is uniquely related to that entrepreneur and his or her interests. The entrepreneur's strengths may lie in production (in some cases the entrepreneur is basically a tradesman) or in sales. The new business is often launched and carried forward on the basis of these functional strengths. The founder's inclination toward production or sales is typically influential in shaping business operations. At the beginning, the entrepreneur may be the only employee in the business, and management may be largely self-management.

Moreover, those who create new firms—the pure entrepreneurs—are not always good organization members. As we saw in Chapter 1, they are creative, innovative, risk-taking individuals who have the courage to strike out on their own. Indeed, they are often propelled into entrepreneurship by precipitating events, some of which involve a difficulty in fitting into conventional organizational roles. As a consequence, management and organizational precepts and practices are often secondary concerns of entrepreneurs who are caught up in the excitement of creating a new business.

Founders differ from professional managers in terms of their ownership and intense commitment to the businesses they found. In many subtle ways, the orientation of founders differs from that of professional managers. Edgar H. Schein has identified many of these differences, as shown in Figure 13-5. These variations show the founder as being more self-oriented and willing to take risks in contrast to the professional manager's greater organizational concern.

As a business grows, the founder sometimes finds himself or herself in conflict with those who recognize the importance of increasing the emphasis on professional management. If the business experiences special "growing pains," the pressure grows, sometimes to the point of squeezing the founder out of the business he or she has founded. One of many such examples is found in the experience of Jon Birck, founder of Northwest Instrument

Figure 13–5   How Do Founder/Owners Differ from "Professional Managers"?

Entrepreneurs/founders/owners are	Professional managers are

Motivation and Emotional Orientation

Oriented toward creating, building.	Oriented toward consolidating, surviving, growing.
Achievement-oriented.	Power- and influence-oriented.
Self-oriented, worried about own image; need for "glory" high.	Organization-oriented, worried about company image.
Jealous of own prerogatives, need for autonomy high.	Interested in developing the organization and subordinates.
Loyal to own company, "local."	Loyal to profession of management, "cosmopolitan."
Willing and able to take moderate risks on own authority.	Able to take risks, but more cautious and in need of support.

Analytical Orientation

Primarily intuitive, trusting of own intuitions.	Primarily analytical, more cautious about intuitions.
Long-range time horizon.	Short-range time horizon.
Holistic; able to see total picture, patterns.	Specific; able to see details and their consequences.

Interpersonal Orientation

"Particularistic," in the sense of seeing individuals as individuals.	"Universalistic," in the sense of seeing individuals as members of categories like employees, customers, suppliers, and so on.
Personal, political, involved.	Impersonal, rational, uninvolved.
Centralist, autocratic.	Participative, delegation-oriented.
Family ties count.	Family ties are irrelevant.
Emotional, impatient, easily bored.	Unemotional, patient, persistent.

Structural/Positional Differences

Have the privileges and risks of ownership.	Have minimal ownership, hence fewer privileges and risks.
Have secure position by virtue of ownership.	Have less secure position, must constantly prove themselves.
Are generally highly visible and get close attention.	Are often invisible and do not get much attention.
Have the support of family members in the business.	Function alone or with the support of nonfamily members.

Figure 13–5 (Continued)

Entrepreneurs/founders/owners are	Professional managers are
Have the obligation of dealing with family members and deciding on the priorities family issues should have relative to company issues.	Do not have to worry about family issues at all, which are by definition irrelevant.
Have weak bosses, Boards that are under their own control.	Have strong bosses, Boards that are not under their own control.

Source: Reprinted, by permission of the publisher, from "The Role of the Founder in Creating Organizational Culture," by Edgar H. Schein, ORGANIZATIONAL DYNAMICS, Summer, 1983, p. 26 © 1983 Periodicals Division, American Management Associations, New York. All rights reserved.

Systems.[6] Birck founded the business in 1979 and went through several rounds of financing by venture capitalists. Professional managers were brought in, at the suggestion of the venture capitalists, and in 1984 they suggested that Birck should resign.

Avoidance of such extreme conflict in managerial philosophy calls for the founder to add sufficient professional management to enable the organization to grow and remain adaptive to its environment. If the founder can do this while retaining the most important elements of his or her own values, he or she can provide a strong foundation for a growing business.

Managers and Decision Making

A manager constantly faces the necessity of making decisions. Proper guidance of the enterprise requires decisions on business objectives, scale of operation, marketing policies, products and product cost, product quality, work assignments, pay rates, and employee grievances, among many others. Virtually every managerial activity involves a choice among alternatives, thereby requiring a decision by the manager.

In making decisions, the business manager is often tempted to rely upon intuition. Indeed, one may be forced to do so because of the intangibles involved or the absence of necessary information. The intuitive decision may be criticized, however, if it disregards factual information that is already available or that is easy to obtain. Another basis for decisions is past experience, which has both strength and weakness. There is an important element of practicality that comes from experience; but at the same time, past experience is no sure guide to the future. In making decisions, therefore, the manager should have a healthy respect for factual data and should utilize them as extensively as possible.

TIME MANAGEMENT

Much of an owner-manager's time during the working day is spent on the firing line—meeting customers, solving problems, listening to employee complaints, talking with suppliers, and the like. The manager of a small firm tackles management problems with the assistance of only a small staff. All of this means that the manager's energies and activities are diffused more than those of managers in large firms. It also means that time is often the manager's scarcest resource.

Problem of Time Pressure

Many entrepreneurs and key managers in small firms work from 60 to 80 hours per week. A frequent and unfortunate result of such a schedule is the inefficient performance of their work. They are too busy to see sales representatives who can supply market information on new products and processes. They are too busy to read technical or trade literature in order to discover what others are doing and what improvements might be adapted to their own use. They are too busy to listen carefully to employees' opinions and grievances. They are too busy to give instructions properly and to teach employees how to do their jobs correctly.

Time-Savers for Busy Managers

One important answer to the problem of lack of time is a good organization of work. This means delegating duties to subordinates, who are then permitted to discharge those duties without close supervision. Of course, this requires the proper selection and training of individuals to. assume responsibility for the delegated functions.

Perhaps the greatest time-saver of all is the effective use of time. If an individual flits from one task to another and back again, it is likely that little will be accomplished. The first step in planning one's use of time should be a survey of time normally spent on various activities. Relying on general impressions is unscientific and is likely to involve considerable error. For a period of several days, or preferably several weeks, the manager should record the time spent on various types of activities during the day. An analysis of these figures will reveal the pattern of activities, those projects and tasks involving the greatest time expenditure, and factors responsible for waste of time. It will also reveal chronic waste of time caused by excessive socializing, work on trivial matters, coffee breaks, and so on.

After eliminating practices that cause unnecessary waste of time, a manager can plan carefully the use of available time. A planned approach to a day's work or week's work is much more effective than a haphazard do-whatever-comes-up-first approach. This is true even for those small-firm managers whose schedules are often interrupted in unanticipated ways.

Many specialists in time management recommend the use of a daily written plan of work activities. This may simply be an informal listing of activities on a note pad, but it should include an establishment of priorities. By classifying duties as first-, second-, and third-level of priority, the manager can identify the most crucial tasks. That manager's attention should then be focused primarily on tasks carrying the highest priority.

Effective time management requires self-discipline. It is easy to begin with good intentions and later lapse into habitual practices of devoting time to whatever one finds to do at the moment. Procrastination is a frequent thief of time. Most of us delay unpleasant and difficult tasks. We often retreat to trivial or less threatening activities by rationalizing that we are getting those items out of the way in order to concentrate later on the important tasks.

Some managers devote much time to meetings with subordinates. Often these meetings just happen and drag on without any serious attempt to control them. The manager should prepare an agenda for such meetings, set starting and ending times, limit the conferences to the subjects to be discussed, and assign the necessary follow-through to specific subordinates. In this way the effectiveness of business conferences may be maximized and the manager's own time conserved, along with that of subordinates.

OUTSIDE MANAGEMENT ASSISTANCE

In view of the managerial deficiencies discussed earlier in this chapter, the entrepreneur should give careful consideration to the use of outside management assistance. Such outside assistance can supplement the busy owner–manager's personal knowledge and the expertise of the few staff specialists on the company's payroll.

The Need for Outside Assistance

Not only is the typical entrepreneur deficient in managerial skills, but also he or she lacks the opportunity to share ideas with managerial colleagues. Although entrepreneurs can confide, to some extent, in subordinates, many of them experience loneliness. A survey of 210 owners revealed that 52 percent of them "frequently felt a sense of loneliness."[7] Moreover, this same group reported a much higher incidence of stress symptoms than those who said they did not feel lonely.

By using consultants, entrepreneurs can overcome some of their management deficiencies and reduce the sense of isolation they experience. Furthermore, an "insider" directly involved in a business problem often "cannot see the forest for the trees." To offset this limitation, the consultant brings an objective point of view and new ideas, supported by a broad knowledge of proven, successful, cost-saving methods. The consultant also can help the manager improve decision making through better organization of fact-gathering and the introduction of scientific techniques of analysis. Ideally the consultant should have an "on call" relationship with the small business so that improved methods may be put into use as the need arises.

Sources of Management Assistance

The sources of management assistance given here are by no means exhaustive. No doubt there are numerous, less obvious sources of management knowledge and approaches to seeking needed help. For example, owner-managers may increase their own skills by consulting public and university libraries, attending evening college, or considering suggestions of friends and customers.

Small Business Institute (SBI) Programs   In 1972, the Small Business Administration implemented the **Small Business Institute (SBI)** program to make the consulting resources of universities available to small-business firms.[8] SBI teams of upper-division and graduate students, under the direction of a faculty member, work with owners of small firms in analyzing their business problems and devising solutions. The primary users of such SBI consulting assistance are applicants for SBA loans, although the services are not restricted to such firms.

The program has been one of mutual benefit in providing students with a practical view of business management and in finding answers to the problems of small firms. Students from small-business, business-policy, or similar courses are typically combined in teams that provide a diversity of academic backgrounds. Individual teams, for example, may have different members specializing in management, marketing, accounting, and finance. There has been an evident enthusiasm on the part of those participating in the program, and many feel it has been one of the most successful consulting programs for small business.

ACTION REPORT
SBI Students Salvage a Small Business

Although there is no way of evaluating the overall effectiveness of the SBI student consulting program, a few teams have produced sensational results. One team which received national attention consisted of students at the University of North Florida under the direction of their faculty project director, Dr. Lowell M. Salter.

The client firm, a building contractor, was in serious trouble. His bills were delinquent, his contractor's license was revoked, and the IRS was threatening to close his business.

Dr. Salter assigned two graduate business students as the SBI counseling team. Within four weeks, the business was turned around. Within ten weeks, payments were current, including obligations to the IRS. Within six months, the business had tripled.

How did the students do it? First, they generated $22,000 worth of business for their client. Then they managed to have his license restored, and they helped him recruit some qualified personnel. Dr. Salter appraised the team as follows: "We not only saved this man from going on welfare, we also helped him employ jobless people. He would not be in business today if it were not for the students."

Source: Small Business Administration, "SBI Story Brings Deluge of Calls, Letters to Director," *Insight*, Vol. 4, No. 1 (August, 1976), p. 6.

Service Corps of Retired Executives (SCORE)   Small-business managers can obtain free management advice from a group called the **Service Corps of Retired Executives (SCORE)** by appealing to any Small Business Administration field office. SCORE is an organization of retired business executives who will consult on current problems with small-business managers. Functioning under the sponsorship of the Small Business Administration, this group provides an opportunity for retired executives to be useful to society, and it helps small-business managers solve their problems. Hence, the relationship is mutually beneficial. It may also encourage entrepreneurs to utilize paid consultants as their firms grow by demonstrating the worth of consulting service.

There are numerous stories of successful SCORE assistance to small firms. A race car driver, for example, went into the tire business but experienced problems with poor records and inadequate credit control. The SCORE counselor, a retired tire manufacturer and district sales manager, provided suggestions that led to an immediate increase in profits. Another firm, a small manufacturer, established a cost reduction/profit improvement program with the aid of a SCORE counselor. The enthusiastic owner reported increased sales volume, higher-than-industry profits, and improved financial standing.

Certified Public Accounting (CPA) Firms   CPA firms, both large and small, provide a range of financial and management services to small businesses. Deloitte Haskins and Sells, one of the major CPA firms, offers the services listed in Figure 13-6.

Figure 13-6   Financial and Management Services Offered to Small Businesses

---

Accounting and Reporting Systems

1. Developing basic accounting systems and forms, and establishing related office procedures.
2. Designing and installing cost accounting systems.
3. Designing and installing systems for the control of production and inventories.
4. Designing financial reports.
5. Planning and coordinating the use of outside computer services.
6. Assisting in recruiting, training, and evaluating accounting and clerical personnel.

Audit Services

1. Conducting a general audit of the financial statements.
2. Evaluating systems and procedures for internal control.
3. Assisting in various filings with the Securities and Exchange Commission and other regulatory agencies.

Budgets and Forecasts

1. Preparing monthly and annual operating budgets.
2. Developing long-range operating plans.
3. Installing cash-flow and other specialized forecasting systems.
4. Computing material, labor, and overhead rates for use in bidding and pricing.

Consulting

Consulting with management on the various aspects of:
1. Capital needs and alternative methods of financing business growth.
2. Credit and collection policies, dividend policies, compensation plans, and insurance.
3. Changes in products, methods, facilities, markets, and product pricing.
4. Accounting for pension and profit-sharing plans, stock-option plans, and other contracts.
5. Applying for loans and credit.
6. Preparing government reports.
7. Preparing contract bids and proposals.

Figure 13-6 (Continued)

Financial Statements

1. Assisting in the preparation of unaudited interim and year-end financial statements.
2. Assisting management in the interpretation of interim and year-end financial statements.

Taxes

1. Preparing annual income tax returns.
2. Advising on tax planning for the organization, the individual, and the individual's estate.
3. Training personnel to prepare payroll, sales and use, and similar tax returns due throughout the year.

Source: Services to Small and Growing Businesses (Deloitte Haskins and Sells, 1978), pp. 7–9.

Management Consultants General management consultants serve small-business firms as well as large corporations. The entrepreneur should regard the service of a competent management consultant as an investment in cost reduction. Many small firms could save as much as 10 to 20 percent of annual operating costs. The inherent advantage in the use of able consultants is suggested by the existence of thousands of consulting firms. They range from large, long-established firms to small one- or two-person operations. Two broad areas of service rendered by management consultants are:

1. To help a client get out of trouble.
2. To help prevent trouble by anticipating and eliminating its causes.

Business firms have traditionally used consultants to help solve problems they could not handle alone.[9] But an even greater service that management consultants provide is their daily observation and analysis, which keep problems from becoming "big." This view of the role of consultants greatly enlarges their service potential. Figure 13-7 shows a diagnostic checklist to determine whether or not the small business has a need for consultants.

Networks of Entrepreneurs

Entrepreneurs also gain informal management assistance through **networking**—the process of developing and engaging in mutually beneficial relationships with peers. As business owners meet other business owners, they experience a commonality of interests that leads to an exchange of ideas and experiences. The setting for such relationships may be a trade association,

Figure 13-7   Diagnostic Checklist to Determine Need for Consultants

---

The questions below may be used by owners to determine the need for management assistance and by students and other consultants who wish to "size up" a particular firm as an initial step in providing management assistance.

Management

_____ 1. Does the firm have specific objectives?
_____ 2. Are its objectives written?
_____ 3. Does it have written long-range and short-range plans?
_____ 4. Are there clear position descriptions for all key jobs?
_____ 5. Are relationships among positions and departments well-defined?
_____ 6. Does it have an organization chart?
_____ 7. Are its controls adequate for decision making?

Marketing

_____ 1. What has been the sales trend for the past five years?
_____ 2. Does the firm have a seasonal sales pattern?
_____ 3. Has the potential market been analyzed?
_____ 4. Is the nature of the firm's customers changing?
_____ 5. What share of the market does it hold?
_____ 6. Is its market share growing or declining?
_____ 7. Have its product lines been defined?
_____ 8. Does it explore new lines and delete less effective ones?
_____ 9. Does it prepare sales forecasts?
_____ 10. Does it compare sales results to sales quotas or forecasts?
_____ 11. Has the firm analyzed the effectiveness of its advertising?
_____ 12. Are its personal selling practices satisfactory?
_____ 13. Does it use appropriate sales promotion methods?
_____ 14. Does it measure customer satisfaction?
_____ 15. Does it price its products competitively?
_____ 16. Are credit accounts offered to its customers in line with industry practices?

Product/Operations

_____ 1. Is the firm's product design suitable for efficient production?
_____ 2. Is its production equipment technologically adequate and in good condition?
_____ 3. Does its physical layout contribute to operating efficiency?
_____ 4. If it is a marketing firm, does its physical layout encourage sales?
_____ 5. Is there extensive idle time for either machines or personnel?

Figure 13-7 (Continued)

_____ 6. Can the handling and storage of raw materials, work in process, or finished goods be significantly improved?

_____ 7. Does it control quality adequately?

_____ 8. At what points does it check for quality?

_____ 9. Are its production operations scheduled carefully?

_____ 10. Is its plant housekeeping adequate?

Purchasing and Inventory Control

_____ 1. Does the firm buy the desired quality at the best price?

_____ 2. Does it use the best sources of supply?

_____ 3. Does it have a minimum of dead stock?

_____ 4. Is its inventory truly current and usable?

_____ 5. Does it use an effective inventory control system?

_____ 6. Does it experience frequent stock-outs?

_____ 7. Is its inventory turnover rate adequate?

_____ 8. How does it determine its reorder point?

_____ 9. How does it determine its minimum ordering quantities?

Personnel

_____ 1. What sources does the firm use for recruiting personnel?

_____ 2. Are its selection methods adequate to assure properly qualified personnel?

_____ 3. Does it provide sufficient training for its personnel?

_____ 4. What types of training does it use?

_____ 5. Are its compensation levels and fringe benefits competitive?

_____ 6. How does its personnel turnover rate compare with that of the industry?

_____ 7. Has it prepared written personnel policies?

Finance

_____ 1. What is the firm's rate of return on equity?

_____ 2. What is its debt-equity ratio?

_____ 3. What is its current ratio?

_____ 4. What is its acid-test ratio?

_____ 5. Are its cash balances and working capital adequate for its sales volume?

_____ 6. Are its financial statements prepared regularly? By whom?

_____ 7. Does its accounting system provide current information on accounts payable and accounts receivable?

_____ 8. Does it use an operating budget?

_____ 9. Are its operating results compared with budgeted amounts?

_____ 10. Does it use a cash budget?

_____ 11. Does it take all available cash discounts in purchasing?

Figure 13-7 (Continued)

_____   12. Does it pay its current obligations promptly?
_____   13. Does it use the services of an outside CPA?
_____   14. Are its operating expenses in line for its type of firm?
_____   15. Are its credit applicants properly investigated before they are granted credit?
_____   16. Are its bad-debt losses in line with those of the industry?
_____   17. Are its accounts receivable aged as a part of credit control?
_____   18. Has it made an analysis to determine which expenses are fixed and which are variable?
_____   19. Has it prepared a break-even chart?

Risk Management

_____   1. Have the major risks facing the firm been identified and analyzed?
_____   2. What are its major risks?
_____   3. Does its insurance program adequately cover the major insurable risks?
_____   4. Are its insured amounts in line with present values?
_____   5. Can it possibly reduce major risks in any significant way?

---

civic club, fraternal organization, or some other situation that brings the parties into contact with one another. Of course, the personal network of an entrepreneur is not limited to other entrepreneurs, but those individuals are typically a significant part of that network.

An example of entrepreneurial networking is found in this report:

> Alan, for example, finds his involvement with the Smaller Business Association of New England very satisfying: "Anytime you go to an SBANE meeting, you'll find people talking—not about their skiing or flying, but about business. Everybody just loves to have the chance to talk to somebody else who's not a threat. There's no concern about confidentiality or anything like that. I do a lot of talking and it helps."[10]

Networks of entrepreneurs involve a variety of ties—*instrumental, affective,* and *moral.* An **instrumental tie** means that the parties find the relationship mutually rewarding—for example, exchanging useful ideas about certain business problems. An **affective tie** relates to emotional sentiments— for example, the sharing of joint vision about the role of small business in doing battle with giant competitors or with the government. A **moral tie** involves some type of obligation—for example, a mutual commitment to the principle of private enterprise or the importance of integrity in business transactions.

In personal networks of entrepreneurs, affective and moral commitments are believed to dominate those which are instrumental.[11] This suggests that a sense of identity and self-respect may be a significant product of the entrepreneur's network.

Networking has been particularly helpful to some women entrepreneurs. In the New York area, a group of ten women business owners meet monthly to help one another with business problems. They own and operate companies with annual sales of between $1 million and $10 million. One participant was quoted as saying, "The roundtable gives me the opportunity to hear what someone else has to say. They are much more capable of analyzing a problem sometimes because I am too close to it."[12]

Cost of Consulting Services

Management consultants may be hired on a fixed-fee basis (such as $100 per hour) or on a retainer basis (such as $500 per month). Retained consultants are "on call" to the small firms that have contracted for their services, thus assuring their clients of regular assistance.

The direct cost of consulting service often appears high. While the cost savings may not be immediately measurable, a benefit should be realized if competent counsel is obtained. Moreover, the small-business manager may propose a fee contingent upon demonstrable results (in the form of lower costs and higher profits, for example). This involves a hazard, however, in that a consultant might cut costs in the short run but damage the company in the long run.

Selection of a Consultant

Management consultants may be located by talking with business friends, accountants, attorneys, bankers, and trade associations. Firms which have used a particular consultant may share their opinions and provide recommendations or warnings. By talking with these firms, it is possible to evaluate this consultant's work. To check a consultant's reputation, furthermore, the prospective user can request a list of firms for whom similar projects have been completed by this consultant.

The small business may well be wary of firms that use "high-pressure" approaches. An ethical consulting firm will not engage in offensive self-promotion any more than it will haggle over fees. It is also well to learn some things about the consultant such as length of time engaged in business, training and experience, and financial status. Fees to be paid and time stipulated for the accomplishment of results should be contractually specified. And both consultant and client should require a clear definition of the consultant's task.

Cooperation between client and consultant is important. The small-business manager can contribute to the improvement of the consultant's service by throwing open the establishment and its business records to the consultant. Data requested should be promptly and accurately furnished—with no pertinent facts withheld. Problems noted by either client or consultant should be promptly called to the other's attention and full exploration made so that a solution may be found quickly. Promptness in taking remedial action reduces the scope and impact of many problems.

ACTION REPORT
A Good Small Business Consultant

A small business owner has reported the following positive experience with a management consultant:

> The consultant I remember best was the first one I ever used. The company I worked for had a problem handling incoming orders—sorting, processing, recording statistics, etc. My experience was mainly in editing. But because we had so few managers, I took over the job of directing subscription processing. I had enough trouble organizing the flow of papers on my desk, so I clearly needed some help organizing a system that covered mail opening through billing. That's when Jerry Hoffman came along.
>
> Jerry had the qualities needed in an outstanding consultant—a good teacher, a careful listener and quick analyst, a hands-on practitioner, and, perhaps most of all, the confidence to develop simple, understandable solutions for not-so-complex needs.
>
> I worked with Jerry for about 10 years, starting with a design for sorting racks, a billing system that involved perforated cards, and eventually the more sophisticated transition from a manual to a computerized in-house system. The dollars we spent on Jerry were returned many times over to the company, and each of us who worked with him became more efficient managers.
>
> Over the years, I've since worked with a number of other consultants. Some have approached Jerry's performance, but many exhibited the worst of the breed—a put-down attitude to persons whom they advise; a determination to force-fit a "model" approach; and a greater determination to establish a beachhead to become long-term residents.
>
> These experiences overall have made me cautious about consultants—and even more so, doubly appreciative of the ones who remind me of Jerry Hoffman.

Source: Nora Goldstein, "How to Find the Right Consultant," *In Business*, Vol. 5, No. 1 (January–February, 1983), p. 35. Reproduced with permission.

Common Criticisms of Consultants

One frequent criticism of management consultants is that even among the reputable ones there are charlatans who claim a background of skill and experience they don't possess. While this criticism may be valid occasionally, it does not warrant suspicion of able, ethical consulting firms. Instead, it calls for care in the selection of a consultant.

Another criticism is that management consultants, unlike doctors and public accountants, need not be licensed by the state to practice and are not subject to ejection from the profession in the event of unethical practice. There are, however, several associations whose members subscribe to a code of professional practice and ethics.

A third charge against management consultants is that they may insert themselves unduly into management and take over its responsibilities. Fulfillment of responsibilities is up to the managers themselves. They cannot be forced to turn responsibilities over to a consultant. Hence, if responsibilities shift from manager to consultant, it is the manager's own fault.

A fourth common criticism concerns lack of ability. Information on percentage of satisfied clients, like that on frequency of repeat engagements, is difficult to obtain. The growth of consulting services, however, makes it obvious that consultants have many satisfied customers.

Looking Back

1. The management functions of planning, organizing, leading/motivating, and controlling are performed by all managers of both small and big businesses.

2. A large proportion of small businesses is characterized by weak management. In part, this results from the lack of managerial expertise by entrepreneurs whose primary focus is creating a new business rather than managing.

3. In many ways, the management process in small firms is unique. Certain constraints, particularly in financial resources and specialized staff, limit the entrepreneur. Founders typically differ in a number of ways from professional managers, and difficulties are experienced as the firm grows. As the firm grows, the founder becomes more a manager and less a doer and moves in the direction of becoming a professional manager or bringing in professional management.

4. Small-business managers who have difficulty finding time to perform managerial tasks efficiently should learn to delegate some duties to subordinates and to organize their use of time by careful planning.

5. Outside management assistance is provided by many types of consultants, including SBI student consultants, SCORE (retired executives), CPA firms, general management consultants, and various others, as well as networking. The use of management consultants may be thought of as an investment in cost reduction. They may be employed for single projects or they may be retained on a continuing basis for use as necessary.

DISCUSSION QUESTIONS

1. What are the general functions of management? Briefly describe the nature of each.
2. Is a budget more closely related to the function of planning than to the function of controlling?
3. What are the activities involved in the function of leading/motivating?
4. What are the four stages of small-business growth outlined in this chapter? How do the managerial requirements change as the firm moves through these stages?
5. Is it likely that the quality of management is relatively uniform throughout the many types of small businesses? What might account for any differences noted?
6. Evaluate founders as managers. Why is there a tendency toward managerial weakness in those who create new firms?
7. What practices can a small-business manager utilize to conserve time?
8. Is it reasonable to believe that an outsider coming into a business could propose procedures or policies superior to those of the manager who is intimately acquainted with operations? Why?
9. Explain the nature of the SBI student consulting program. Is this program of primary benefit to the client firm or to the students?
10. What is networking, and how can an entrepreneur use it to improve management within a small firm?

ENDNOTES

1. James J. Kilpatrick, "Making Life More Bearable for the Traveler," *Nation's Business*, Vol. 65, No. 12 (December, 1977), p. 12.

2. Thomas P. Murphy, "From Eagles to Turkeys," *Forbes*, Vol. 134, No. 4 (August 13, 1984), p. 136.

3. *Ibid.*

4. Thomas P. Murphy, "The Role of the Boss," *Forbes*, Vol. 130, No. 12 (December 6, 1982), p. 246.

5. *Ibid.*

6. "Dear Jon," *Inc.*, Vol. 7, No. 2 (February, 1985), pp. 79–86.

7. David E. Gumpert and David P. Boyd, "The Loneliness of the Small Business Owner," *Harvard Business Review*, Vol. 62, No. 6 (November–December, 1984), p. 19.

8. A series of articles on the Small Business Institute program appears in the *Journal of Small Business Management*, Vol. 15, No. 2 (April, 1977).

9. Professor Herbert E. Kierulff of Seattle Pacific University has described a three-phase "turnaround" process successfully used by a consulting firm in helping more than 200 smaller companies. See Herbert E. Kierulff, "Turnaround vs. Bankruptcies," *In Business*, Vol. 3, No. 3 (May–June, 1981), pp. 37–38. This shows how consultants help small firms get out of trouble.

10. David E. Gumpert and David P. Boyd, "The Loneliness of the Small Business Owner," *op. cit.*, p. 24.

11. Bengt Johannisson and Rein Peterson, "The Personal Networks of Entrepreneurs," paper appearing in conference proceedings, Third Canadian Conference, International Council for Small Business—Canada, Toronto, Canada, May 23-25, 1984.

12. "Women Chief Executives Help Each Other with Frank Advice," *The Wall Street Journal* (July 2, 1984), p. 19.

REFERENCES TO SMALL BUSINESS IN ACTION

Kahn, Joseph P. "A Good Word about Consultants." *Inc.*, Vol. 6, No. 1 (January, 1984), pp. 57-60.

> The article describes a very small consulting firm, basically a one-man operation, which has provided practical outside management assistance to small businesses in the New Jersey area.

Kane, Sid. "Your Company... or Yourself." *Venture*, Vol. 7, No. 6 (June, 1985), pp. 98-100.

> A number of small high-tech firms have changed from management by founder to management by professionals. Many of the changes were brought about at the insistence of venture capitalists who were investing in the firms.

"What Makes Tandem Run." *Business Week*, No. 2645 (July 14, 1980), pp. 73-74.

> Tandem Computers, Inc., using a highly unorthodox management style, has grown rapidly and has prospered. Its people-oriented approach features Friday afternoon parties, flexible hours, a swimming pool open between 6 A.M. and 8 P.M., and a sabbatical for employees every four years.

"You've Got to Blow Your Horn." *Forbes*, Vol. 125, No. 3 (February 4, 1980), pp. 94-95.

> Carl G. Sontheimer, inventor and marketer of the Cuisinart food-processing machine, has been highly successful. However, the firm has grown to the point that the entrepreneur's personal involvement in the details of the business is proving inadequate as a basis for effective management.

CASE 13

Central Engineering

How the entrepreneur's managerial practices hampered decision making

Henry and Jami Wolfram, a husband-and-wife team, owned and operated Central Engineering, a heating and air-conditioning firm located in Huntsville, AL. The business prospered during the six years they owned it, and it served both residential and commercial accounts.

Organizational Structure

Henry served as general operations manager. (Figure 13–8 shows the simple organization structure of the firm.) As the business grew, more and more responsibility fell on Henry's shoulders. Although Jami assumed some of the burden by acting as treasurer and supervising the office work, Henry was personally involved in most of the key decisions. Henry's son, Jeff Wolfram, had started work on an installation crew. Later he moved into the position of estimator–salesman and acted as manager on those occasions when his father was away.

Figure 13–8   Organization Structure of Central Engineering

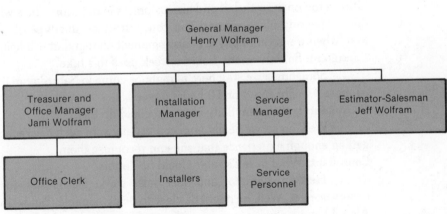

The Bottleneck

An unfortunate consequence of Henry's growing work load was the creation of a bottleneck at the very top of the business. Since he was a key person, his judgment seemed indispensable in many actions. As a result, decisions were sometimes delayed while waiting for his attention. Others in the organization sometimes found themselves waiting in line to get a chance to talk with him. And Henry found himself rushed, with insufficient time to think carefully about some aspects of the business. In addition, he would have liked to devote a little more time to family, church, and personal interests.

Review of Customer Billing

One task that required Henry's attention was his personal review of bills before they were sent to customers. When a management consultant asked why this was necessary, the following dialogue took place:

Henry: I really need to take a last look before bills are sent out. For example, on construction jobs there may be additions or extras that were included after we had made the original bid.

Consultant: On regular service calls, is there a similar chance of an error?

Henry: That's right. For instance, maybe the worker has left something off the work order. The worker may say he has done this and this and this, but over here on the material list he has some items that don't match up or that are missing from what he said he's done.

Consultant: Can you tell me how many hours in a day or week are required for this?

Henry: Well, it cuts into a lot of time. This is part of another problem. The office is too open, with Jeff and his customers in the same office with me. I just don't have any place where I can concentrate on this type of work. I think that, when we get that physical arrangement changed, it will help some.

Consultant: So, how many hours a week does this take?

Henry: Sometimes we stay here at night or come in Saturday to do this. But I suppose it might run 8 or 10 hours a week.

Consultant: Is there anybody else who could do this?

Henry: Well, on service calls Jami can usually spot such discrepancies. She is getting enough experience that she can recognize them.

Consultant: What is Jeff's role? Could he do this?

Henry: He's an estimator and does sales work. He doesn't quite have the experience yet. Well, he might be close to being capable. But he's pretty busy. Also, I have a service manager who could catch a lot of this when the orders are turned in. But he does not manage that carefully. I have a more aggressive manager in installation who is better at catching things like this.

The general theme in Henry's discussion with the management consultant was the difficulty of resolving the time-management problem. Henry recognized the burden this placed on him personally and on the business, but there seemed to be no obvious answer at this stage in the life of the firm.

Review of Accounts Payable

Henry also tried to look over all payments being made on trade accounts payable. His discussion with the management consultant regarding this function ran as follows:

Henry: These payments need to be checked over because we may be charged too much on some bills.

Consultant: How does this happen?

Henry: On particular jobs we may get special pricing. Say I'm working on a bid. I may pick up a phone and say to the supplier, "We need some special pricing. Here's what we're up against, and we need the special pricing to get this job." And if they give us the special pricing, we should pay accordingly.

Consultant: And you can't depend on them to bill you at that special price?

Henry: I don't think it is anything intentional. But they give it to their clerks to bill, and they may overlook the special pricing that was promised. So, if we don't catch it, we would lose it.

Henry's Dilemma

The responsibilities relative to accounts receivable and accounts payable were typical of the overall situation. In many aspects of the business, Henry felt compelled to give his personal attention to the issues and the decisions which needed to be made. In a sense he felt trapped by the very success and work that accompanied the operation of the business. He enjoyed the work, every minute of it, but occasionally he wondered why there was no obvious solution to his dilemma.

Questions

1. Is Henry Wolfram's personal involvement in the various specific aspects of the business necessary, or is it a matter of habit or of simply enjoying doing business that way?
2. What changes would be necessary to extricate Henry from the checking of customer bills before they are mailed?
3. If you were the consultant, what changes would you recommend?

14

Objectives, Strategy, and Operational Planning

Figure 14-1   Michael W. Rice

Photo by Blair Seitz

Small-business owners differ in the importance they attach to business growth. Conservative operators are content to maintain a given sales level or merely to keep up with growth in their industries.

When Michael W. Rice succeeded his father as president of Utz Quality Foods, a potato chip and pretzel company in Hanover, PA, he decided he wanted more rapid growth. By 1986, eight years after taking over, he had stepped up growth from the earlier annual rate of 5 to 10 percent to more than 20 percent.

Acceleration of growth was accomplished by careful attention to business strategy. Key elements of the successful strategy were as follows:

1. Expansion of the company's geographical market from Baltimore, Washington, D.C., and south-central Pennsylvania to encompass Virginia.
2. Addition of new products including corn chips and other corn snacks.
3. Increased marketing efforts.
4. Continuation of the company's dedication to high-quality foods.

Source: Sharon Nelton, "Strategies for Family Firms," *Nation's Business*, vol. 74, No. 6 (June, 1986), p. 20.

Looking Ahead

Watch for the following important topics:

1. Nature of profit, marketing, and growth objectives.
2. Social responsibilities and ethical standards of small firms.
3. Formulating strategy and finding a strategic niche.
4. The planning process in small business.
5. Quantitative tools to aid planning, and their limitations.

Someone has said, "If you don't know where you're going, any path will get you there." Unfortunately that statement describes many small firms—they don't know where they are going. This chapter directs attention to the planning process of deciding on objectives, formulating strategy, developing operating plans, and using quantitative tools to aid planning. The planning process enables the small firm to know *where* it is going and *how* it is going to get there.

In Chapter 4, we described the preparation of the original business plan—the plan used to secure financing prior to starting operations. Although that plan can serve as a launching pad for a business, its usefulness is limited to the period of starting the new venture. This chapter, in contrast, is concerned with the recurring cycle of planning that is important for any going concern, regardless of its age.

SMALL-BUSINESS OBJECTIVES AND RESPONSIBILITIES

All privately owned businesses, large or small, are presumed to have at least three main objectives: (1) to earn a profit, (2) to provide an economic good or service, and (3) to grow. In addition to these primary objectives, small firms also have a more general objective involving social responsibilities to the community.

Profit Objective

An important goal of every privately owned business is profit. Profits must be earned to reward the entrepreneur's acceptance of business risks and to assure business continuity. Without profit, a business firm can make no long-run contribution to employees, suppliers, customers, or the community.

Profit making is not a short-range concern but rather a matter of long-range significance. Hence, the owner cannot be unduly concerned with the net profit reported on the income statement each month, each quarter, or each year unless this is part of a long-run trend or condition. Profit maximization over the long run should be the major goal, with the periodic income statement regarded as a progress report.

Profit goals must be made specific if they are to be useful. These goals are part of the operational plans described on pages 394–404 of this chapter. In these plans, the profit objective must be specified in terms of so many dollars of profit in a particular year, quarter, or month.

Marketing Objective

Rendering economic service to the community means providing a flow of goods and/or services to the public. Providing such service is necessary to earn the profits desired by the owner. In a broader sense, the marketing objective is also an obligation of the privately owned firm to the society which permits its existence.

The customer is the focal point of the marketing objective. The crucial importance of customer service has been highlighted in the widely acclaimed book, *In Search of Excellence*.[1] Its authors argue that superior customer service is one key to corporate success. Although superior service is possible for businesses of any size, it is especially relevant to smaller firms. As Tom Peters has pointed out, the magic of large companies they hold up as excellent examples (such as Dana, 3M, and Hewlett-Packard) is that "they have all retained a much higher share of their 'small company' simplicity and vitality than their less effective competitors have."[2] This reasoning suggests that a strong marketing objective—going to great lengths to satisfy customers—can contribute directly to the achievement of a profit objective.

The marketing goals of a business firm must be modified as consumer tastes change and as competitive products and services are developed. The most basic marketing objectives are part of a firm's strategy, which is discussed on pages 389–394. In the process of formulating strategy, the entrepreneur must contemplate the basic mission of the firm and the extent to which it will be similar to or different from competitors in serving customers.

Growth Objective

A business philosophy concerned with profit making and economic service must also be concerned with enterprise growth. Some persons have gone so far as to suggest that a business must either grow or die. In an expanding company, growth is normal for a healthy, successful business. Growth envisions the need for additional operating facilities and calls for retained earnings or new investment by the owners. Growth demands an awareness of technological advances.

The importance attached to growth varies from firm to firm. Some entrepreneurs launch what they expect to be high-growth (often high-tech) firms and attract venture capital based on that premise. Federal Express, which was described in Chapter 1, was such a venture. Other managers are inclined to accept the status quo and to feel little need for growth. The entrepreneur's age is an example of one variable that may affect the attitude toward growth. There are undoubtedly other factors, some of which are rooted in the personalities of individuals. One research study of a small sample of business firms suggests the following three viewpoints concerning growth:

1. The *conservative operator's* major goal is survival. Growth in terms of production, revenue, or profit is not an objective. This person believes that the best way to remain relatively stable is to maintain the status quo.
2. The *industry stalwart's* goal is to seek an *acceptable* rather than an optimum rate of profit. This person merely strives to keep up with the industry.
3. The *aggressive, innovating operator's* goal is to maximize profit. This person views production and revenue growth as the means to this end.[3]

There is a danger in the assumption that all growth is good. Some owner–managers tend to prize growth for growth's sake without evaluating its impact on the profits of the business. Growth in sales volume, however, is no panacea for all business problems. It must be accompanied by careful control of costs if the firm is to attain growth in profits as well as volume.

Growth objectives become specific as particular goals are built into the operating plans for the business. Plans may be developed, for example, to call for a doubling of sales volume over the next five years.

Social Responsibilities

In recent years, public attention has been focused on the social obligations of business organizations. These feelings of concern are rooted in a new awareness of the role of business in modern society. In a sense, managers now occupy a "trusteeship" position and must act accordingly to protect the new interests of suppliers, employees, customers, and the general public, along with making a profit for the owners of the business.

Social Obligations and Profit Making   Small firms, as well as large corporations, must reconcile their social responsibilities with their need to earn profits. It is easy to think that only the large corporation can afford to be civic-minded. A corporate leader, George Weissman, argues otherwise, however:

> You don't have to be a giant company to participate. Even the tiniest firm can return a portion of what it takes *from* the community *back* to the community. Social responsibility has got to be a shared function of all business men and women, regardless of the size of their enterprises, if enterprise is to survive.[4]

Managers of small businesses recognize the same responsibility clearly, if not always as eloquently, as those who speak for big business. In fact, many independent entrepreneurs speak of their satisfaction in serving the community as one of the major rewards from their businesses. Of course, this does not mean that all firms share this philosophy; some fail to sense or refuse to recognize any obligation beyond the minimum necessary to produce a profit.

A sense of social responsibility may be perfectly consistent with the firm's long-run profit objective. Urban problems, for example, sometimes require small firms to take part in community projects more as a means of survival than altruism. In the 1970s, a group of local business owners on Cleveland's southeast side headed by John Young, owner of a pest exterminating business, formed an organization to deal with the urban deterioration surrounding their businesses.[5] This organization, Old Brooklyn Community Development Corporation, financed by dues and donations, has planted trees and flowers, thrown parties for the neighborhood kids, created a residents' forum, started a garden club, opened a community theater, and organized an auxiliary police unit.

The firm which consistently fulfills certain obligations makes itself a desirable member of the community and may attract patronage. Conversely, the firm which scorns social responsibilities may find itself the object of restrictive legislation and may discover its employees to be lacking in loyalty. It seems likely, however, that the typical independent entrepreneur contributes to the community and other groups because it is a duty and a privilege to do so, and not merely because the profit potential in each such move has been cunningly calculated.

Recognition of a social responsibility does not change a profit-seeking business into a charitable organization. Earning a profit is absolutely essential. Without profits, the firm is in no position to recognize social responsibilities toward anyone. The point is that profits, although essential, are not the only factor of importance.

Environmentalism and Small Business   In recent decades the deterioration of the environment has become a matter of widespread concern. One source of pollution has been business firms that discharge waste into streams, contaminants into the air, and noise into areas surrounding their operations. Efforts to preserve and redeem the environment thus directly affect business organizations, including small-business firms.

The interests of small-business owners and environmentalists are not necessarily or uniformly in conflict. Some business leaders, including those in small business, have worked and acted for the cause of conservation. For example, many small firms have taken steps to remove eyesores and to landscape and otherwise improve plant facilities. Others have modernized their equipment and changed their procedures to reduce air and water pollution. In a few cases, small business has been in a position to benefit from the emphasis on ecology. Those companies whose products are harmless to the environment gain an edge over competitive products that pollute. Also, small firms are involved in servicing pollution-control equipment. The auto repair shop, for example, services pollution-control devices on automobile engines.

Some small firms are adversely affected by efforts to protect the environment. Livestock feeding lots, cement plants, pet-food processors, and iron foundries are representative of industries that are especially vulnerable to extensive regulation. The cost impact on businesses of this type is often severe. Indeed, the required improvements can force the closure of some businesses.

ACTION REPORT
Environmentalism and Small Business

Regulations on the control of hazardous waste have created special, costly problems for some small firms. Potter Paint Company of Indiana is a family business which found itself penalized for the actions of another company, Enviro Chem Corporation. At one time, Enviro Chem collected dirty solvent used to scour paint-mixing tanks at Potter Paint and delivered clean, recycled solvent in its place.

Enviro Chem was licensed by Indiana as a waste recycler and was considered to be a model facility. However, an inspection at one time found the site in disarray, and the company was consequently closed. Eventually the EPA named it as one of the so-called Superfund sites in need of immediate attention. As one of the "waste generators" (that is, a producer of the dirty solvent), Potter Paint Company was held responsible for some of the damage and eventually paid $12,000—$10,000 for the cleanup and $2,000 for legal costs.

Source: Reproduced by permission of *The Wall Street Journal,* © Dow Jones & Company, Inc., 1983. All Rights Reserved.

The ability to pass higher costs on to customers is dependent upon the market situation and is ordinarily quite difficult for the small firm. Resulting economic hardships on small business must, therefore, be recognized as a cost of pollution control and evaluated accordingly. In some instances the controls are hardest on the small, marginal firm with obsolete equipment. Environmental regulation may merely hasten the inevitable demise of the firm.

The level of government regulation poses another potential problem for small business. Legislation, whether state or local, may prove discriminatory by forcing higher costs on a local firm than on competitive firms outside the regulated territory. The immediate self-interest of a small firm, therefore, is served by regulations that operate at the highest or most general level. A federal regulation, for example, applies to all United States firms and thereby precludes competitive advantages to low-cost polluters in other states.

Consumerism and Small Business   At one time the accepted philosophy was expressed as "let the buyer beware." In contrast, today's newer philosophy says "let the seller beware." Today's sophisticated buyers feel that they should be able to purchase products that are safe, reliable, durable, and honestly advertised. This theme has influenced various types of consumer legislation. The Magnuson-Moss Warranty Act, for example, imposes special restrictions on sellers such as requiring warranties to be available for inspection rather than be hidden inside a package.

Small firms are directly involved in the consumerism movement. To some extent, they stand to gain from it. Attention to customer needs and flexibility in meeting these needs have traditionally been strong assets of small firms. Their managers have been close to customers and thus able to know and respond easily to their needs. To the extent that these potential features have been realized in practice, the position of small business has been strengthened. And to the extent that small firms can continue to capitalize upon customer desires for excellent service, they can reap rewards from the consumerism movement.

Consumerism also carries threats to small business. It is hard to build a completely safe product and to avoid all errors in service. Moreover, the growing complexity of products makes their servicing more difficult. The mechanic or repairer must know a great deal more to render satisfactory service today than was needed two or three decades earlier. Rising consumer expectations, therefore, provide a measure of danger as well as opportunity for small firms. The quality of management will determine the extent to which opportunities are realized and dangers avoided.

Ethical Practices and Small Business   Although our competitive system and governmental action are both policing forces that tend to regulate business conduct, they are not enough. Society needs entrepreneurs who voluntarily observe ethical standards which exceed the requirements of the law.

Only the naive would argue that small business is pure in terms of ethical conduct. In fact, there is widespread recognition of unethical and even illegal activity. There is no way of measuring the extent of unethical conduct, of course, but there is an obvious need for improvement in small, as well as big, businesses.

One glaring example of poor ethics practiced by many small businesses is fraudulent reporting of income and expenses for income-tax purposes. This conduct includes "skimming" of income (that is, keeping some income off the record) as well as improperly claiming certain business expenses. The following account illustrates the nature of these practices:

> To countless small businesses, cheating Uncle Sam is as routine as making the payroll and marketing the product.
> For a Georgia cafeteria owner, it involved skimming at least $100 a day from the cash register before recording his receipts on the ledger. On the docks in Massachusetts, seafood buyers carry briefcases full of cash so their suppliers don't have to account for checks. A fashion designer refurbished his suburban Philadelphia mansion as a tax-deductible corporate expense.
> The government pressed charges in these cases, but most income-tax chiseling by small business goes undetected by overworked tax agents and accountants unable to probe deep enough to find it.[6]

Development of Business Ethics   Even though we can see ethical flaws in small businesses, we believe that some progress has been made. There is a growing recognition that business must act in the interest of its customers, employees, suppliers, and others affected by its operations, while also acting in its own interest.

In part, this moral progress has been fostered by competition. Ethical business practices, in other words, have been found to be good business. Enlightened self-interest has thus no doubt motivated much ethical behavior. It is true also that the government, through pure food and drug laws, Federal Trade Commission activities, and the like, has made a contribution to better business morals.

Nevertheless, much remains to be done. Our concern is not primarily with illegal practices. Legal conduct is assumed as the bare minimum for ethical behavior. In addition, management must be concerned with the borderline areas of ethical behavior. For example, the salesperson's expense account tends to become a "swindle sheet." Purchasing agents may accept expensive gifts from order-seeking firms. Unquestionably, this imposes some sense of obligation on their part and may create a conflict of loyalties.

Consistency in Business Ethics   A manager cannot be honest in big things and dishonest in little things. The cumulative effect of little dishonesties will pervert one's perspective of life and management. A manager is often tempted to engage in small violations of ethical practice for immediate gain. But taking advantage of others in the small case may lead to greater moral irresponsibility and improper use of managerial power.

It is indeed remarkable how those employed by a firm can sense its manager's moral code. Insincerity and a lack of integrity cannot long be concealed from subordinates. The manager's moral code must have a sound basis so that fair play and honesty in all relationships with workers, customers, and others become instinctive acts. The crux of the matter is that restraint cannot come entirely from law but requires conscience in the management of business. When self-imposed restraints fail, people turn to the government for a restraint which the collective conscience failed to provide.

Formal Code of Ethics   In some industrial and professional fields, group action has been taken to adopt formal codes of ethics. Doctors, lawyers, and public accountants are typical examples of professional groups that are closely regulated by self-imposed ethical codes. A few years ago, owners of automobile repair shops in a small city met and formulated a code of ethics stressing the principle of fair play with employees and good service for customers. This is significant as an attempt to do something constructive about ethics in the business field and raise it to a professional level.

A special reference should be made to the work of trade associations and the Federal Trade Commission, often acting cooperatively, in formulating ethical codes for various industrial fields. The Federal Trade Commission sponsors trade-practice conferences in which representative business leaders attempt to develop codes to prevent unfair methods of competition. They are encouraged to discuss openly the practices and problems of their industries in arriving at codes of fair competition.

Ethical Advertising   Unethical business behavior has perhaps been more apparent in advertising than in any other area. The public has the right to expect ethical advertising, however, because of its importance to the individual and its great persuasive power in the economy. Advertising is a form of communication, and untruthfulness or other breaches of ethical behavior are as objectionable here as they are elsewhere.

Because of advertising's far-reaching influence, the advertiser must assume some social responsibility and must abide by ideals of honesty, reliability, and integrity. Advertising must be truthful without omitting material facts. For example, if only one or two items are being offered at a reduced price, this fact should be clearly stated. The claim that a soft drink is healthful would be unreliable advertising if there are *any* ill effects. Merchandise represented as "formerly $10.98" should have been sold by the advertiser at that price for a period of time if the advertiser has integrity.

There is also the question of good and bad taste in advertising. Advertisements bordering on the vulgar and immoral should certainly be avoided. Advertisements which reflect adversely on religious beliefs or minority groups should also be avoided because they tend to create resentment toward both the company and the product which it advertises.

Better Business Bureaus   Better Business Bureaus have been established by privately owned business firms in many cities to promote ethical conduct on the part of all business firms in the community. Specifically, a Better Business Bureau's function is twofold: (1) it provides free buying guidelines and information about a company that the consumer should know *prior* to completing a business transaction, and (2) it attempts to solve questions or disputes concerning purchases. As a result, business swindles often decline in a community served by a Better Business Bureau. Figure 14-2 presents a small section from a code of advertising ethics developed by the Better Business Bureaus.

SMALL-BUSINESS STRATEGY

Planning for the small firm's future should begin with a basic strategy— an overall plan that relates the firm's products and/or services to the needs of the marketplace and the offerings of competitors. Entrepreneurs formulate strategy by sizing up the general situation pertaining to the business as a whole and deciding upon necessary changes of a fundamental nature.

Formulating Strategy

Business strategy is concerned with decisions which shape the very nature of the firm. Decisions affecting such issues as breadth of product line, geographical expansion, quality level, and orientation toward growth are strategic decisions. A restaurant's strategy, for example, is determined by its decisions regarding menu (steaks vs. hamburgers), motif (modern coffee shop vs. old waterfront theme), location (shopping center vs. resort· area), and other choices of this type. Small-business strategy may just "happen," or it may result from careful thought about the mission of the firm. The latter is obviously preferable in building a profitable business.

The process of strategic decision making is depicted in Figure 14-3. The beginning step involves an identification of environmental opportunities and risks. The world constantly changes, and the changes provide challenges and opportunities. If the business location begins to deteriorate, for example, the entrepreneur must decide how to adapt to the changing situation. Environ-

Figure 14-2 Better Business Bureau Code of Advertising

Bait Advertising and Selling

A "bait" offer is an alluring but insincere offer to sell a product or service which the advertiser does not intend to sell. Its purpose is to switch consumers from buying the advertised merchandise or service in order to sell something else, usually at a higher price or on a basis more advantageous to the advertiser.

a. No advertisement should be published unless it is a bona fide offer to sell the advertised merchandise or service.

b. The advertising should not create a false impression about the product or service being offered in order to lay the foundation for a later "switch" to other, more expensive products or services, or products of a lesser quality at the same price.

c. Subsequent full disclosure by the advertiser of all other facts about the advertised article does not preclude the existence of a bait scheme.

d. An advertiser should not use nor permit the use of the following scheme practices:

- refusing to show or demonstrate the advertised merchandise or service;
- disparaging the advertised merchandise or service, its warranty, availability, services and parts, credit terms, etc.;
- selling the advertised merchandise or service and thereafter "unselling" the customer to make a switch to other merchandise or service;
- refusing to take orders for the advertised merchandise or service or to deliver it within a reasonable time;
- demonstrating or showing a defective sample of the advertised merchandise; or
- having a sales compensation plan designed to penalize salespersons who sell the advertised merchandise or service.

e. An advertiser should have on hand a sufficient quantity of advertised merchandise to meet reasonably anticipated demands, unless the advertisement discloses the number of items available. If items are available only at certain branches, their specific locations should be disclosed. The use of "rainchecks" is no justification for inadequate estimates of reasonably anticipated demand.

f. Actual sales of the advertised merchandise or service may not preclude the existence of a bait scheme since this may be merely an attempt to create an aura of legitimacy. A key factor in determining the existence of "bait" is the number of times the merchandise or service was advertised compared to the number of actual sales of the merchandise or service.

Source: Council of Better Business Bureaus, Inc., *Code of Advertising (1985),* pp. 8–9. Reproduced with permission.

Figure 14–3   Strategic Decision Making

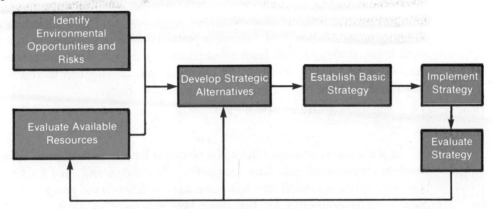

Source: Justin G. Longenecker and Charles D. Pringle, *Management* (5th ed.; Columbus, OH: Charles E. Merrill Publishing Company, 1981), p. 72. Reproduced with permission.

mental changes may be either positive or negative, and they may occur either slowly or quickly.

The evaluation of resources, another important part of strategic decision making, is concerned with the firm's strengths and weaknesses and the extent to which its resources are committed to long-term projects. Firms with little debt and a strong line of credit, for example, have superior resources for expansion. The depth of managerial and professional talent is another significant variable which affects the resources of the business.

ACTION REPORT
Environmental Opportunities for Jelly Beans

Environmental change is often subtle and gradual, but occasionally it is swift and dramatic. The election of President Ronald Reagan created a tremendous change in the market for one small firm. Herman Goelitz, Inc., a 59-year-old family-owned company in Oakland, CA, is the supplier of the President's favorite jelly beans.

According to Herman Rowland, 40, manager of the firm, the undelivered backlog skyrocketed in 1981 to 300,000 cases versus an average 15,000 cases before the inauguration. Sales were expected to double in 1981. To meet the need, Rowland installed $600,000 worth of new production equipment and hired 80 more employees. Although Rowland kept many customers on allocation, he continued to ship 60 cases per month to his steady client in the White House.

Source: "In the News (Jelly Boon)," *Fortune*, Vol. 103, No. 11 (June, 1981), p. 10.

After examining opportunities, risks, and resources, the strategist must then develop alternatives and select a basic strategy. Following the adoption of the strategy, the entrepreneur must implement and then periodically evaluate the strategy in a new round of strategic decision making. In many small firms, strategy results from management by default. The entrepreneur can act professionally, however, by devoting specific attention to strategy rather than reacting haphazardly to environmental change.

Finding a Strategic Niche

In a pluralistic economy there is a place for both large and small firms. Head-on competition with large competitors is difficult and may be fatal, however, unless the small firm has some natural advantages going for it. If possible, it is preferable for the small firm to capitalize on its potential strengths and to operate in the crack between larger firms.

ACTION REPORT
Strategic Niche for Farmers

The concept of the strategic niche is applicable even in the highly competitive world of farming. Note the way in which farmers find special areas for operation:

Some farmers are targeting regional niches, supplying products for fast-growing ethnic and upscale urban communities. For example, a small green vegetable called a tomatillo is widely consumed by Mexican-Americans, and new uses for garlic are making that herb more popular among yuppies. Larger operators generally bypass these products because of the relatively small market for them, and because the farmers may already be committed to long-term contracts to grow different crops. "It is, in a sense, something born out of survival," says Tom Haller, executive secretary of the California Association of Family Farmers.

Source: Reprinted with permission, *Inc.* magazine, April, 1985. Copyright © 1985 by Inc. Publishing Company, 38 Commercial Wharf, Boston, MA 02110.

The small firm should look for and emphasize the special niche it can best fill. If it can get a corner on the market for a particular specialized product, it will be in an unusually advantageous position. For example, some retailers specialize in children's clothing, fashions for tall people, formal wear, maternity clothes, blue jeans, or discount apparel. Some restaurants likewise specialize in baked potatoes, health foods, salads, spaghetti, Chinese food, Korean food, Greek food, and so on. By selecting the right specialty, a small firm can often compete effectively with large chain organizations.

Finding the Appropriate Starting Point

Getting started with a study of strategy often seems difficult, and the owner–manager may find the experience frustrating! Being unaccustomed to systematic investigation of this type, the entrepreneur has difficulty finding an appropriate starting point. One approach is to begin by asking a number of fundamental questions about the firm and then thoughtfully answering these questions. The questions in Figure 14–4 have been proposed by Frank F. Gilmore as a framework for small-business strategic planning sessions.

Figure 14–4   Questions to Use in Formulating Strategy

1. *Record current strategy:*
   a. What is the current strategy?
   b. What kind of business does management want to operate (considering such management values as desired return on investment, growth rate, share of market, stability, flexibility, character of the business, and climate)?
   c. What kind of business does management feel it ought to operate (considering management's concepts of social responsibility and obligations to stockholders, employees, community, competitors, customers, suppliers, government, and the like)?
2. *Identify problems with the current strategy:*
   a. Are trends discernible in the environment that may become threats and/or missed opportunities if the current strategy is continued?
   b. Is the company having difficulty implementing the current strategy?
   c. Is the attempt to carry out the current strategy disclosing significant weaknesses and/or unutilized strengths in the company?
   d. Are there other concerns with respect to the validity of the current strategy?
   e. Is the current strategy no longer valid?
3. *Discover the core of the strategy problem:*
   a. Does the current strategy require greater competence and/or resources than the company possesses?
   b. Does it fail to exploit adequately the company's distinctive competence?
   c. Does it lack sufficient competitive advantage?
   d. Will it fail to exploit opportunities and/or meet threats in the environment, now or in the future?
   e. Are the various elements of the strategy internally inconsistent?
   f. Are there other considerations with respect to the core of the strategy problem?
   g. What, then, is the real core of the strategy problem?
4. *Formulate alternative new strategies:*
   a. What possible alternatives exist for solving the strategy problem?
   b. To what extent do the company's competence and resources limit the number of alternatives that should be considered?

Figure 14-4 (Continued)

    c. To what extent do management's preferences limit the alternatives?

    d. To what extent does management's sense of social responsibility limit the alternatives?

    e. What strategic alternatives are acceptable?

5. *Evaluate alternative new strategies:*

    a. Which alternative *best* solves the strategy problem?

    b. Which alternative offers the *best* match with the company's competence and resources?

    c. Which alternative offers the *greatest* competitive advantage?

    d. Which alternative *best* satisfies management's preferences?

    e. Which alternative *best* meets management's sense of social responsibility?

    f. Which alternative *minimizes* the creation of new problems?

6. *Choose a new strategy:*

    a. What is the *relative significance* of each of the preceding considerations?

    b. What should the new strategy be?

Source: Frank F. Gilmore, "Formulating Strategy in Smaller Companies," *Harvard Business Review*, Vol. 49, No. 3 (May–June, 1971), p. 80. Reproduced with permission.

Strategic decisions should be reduced to writing to insure completion of the strategy-determination process and to provide a basis for subsequent planning. The firm's strategy, moreover, should be incorporated into more specific plans of action. Periodic review and evaluation sessions could be devoted to measuring progress in following strategic guidelines and to dealing with problems that might emerge.

OPERATIONAL PLANNING IN SMALL FIRMS

Decisions about objectives and strategy, as explained earlier in this chapter, constitute the first stage of the planning process. Let us now turn to operational plans, policies, and procedures for the small business.

Neglect of Planning

Sometimes the entrepreneur neglects the planning function as a result of severe business pressures. If he or she becomes too entangled in day-to-day operations, it becomes easy to put off the policy making and planning that is so essential to continuing success. For example, when a choice is to be made between getting out an order and planning operations for the next six months, the owner usually attends to the order. As a result, the time left for reflecting upon the future course of the business is reduced. In this case, a lack of appreciation of planning may be coupled with the limited time available. Planning becomes "postponable" and may not appear to be an absolute necessity. This situation is dangerous because failure to plan results in ineffective, undirected action.

Meaningful planning requires a commitment by the entrepreneur to devote time and energy to the planning process. According to Van Auken and Ireland:

> As a result of making the commitment to engage actively in planning, the small-business manager is ready to set aside and carefully preside over a specified time period for developing business plans. Nagging interruptions must be guarded against or "Gresham's law of planning" will inevitably prevail: daily brushfires push aside planning until it is forgotten altogether.[7]

Need for Formal Planning

Most small-business owners and managers plan to some degree. Such planning, however, tends to be spotty and unsystematic—dealing with how much inventory to purchase, whether to buy a new piece of equipment, and other questions of this type. The importance of systematic, formal planning varies with the nature of the business.[8] If the firm is very small, the manager may do most of the planning in his or her head with very little paperwork. Such informal planning may work satisfactorily if there is little complexity in the business itself. A low-technology firm with a simple product or process may be able to get by and even prosper with minimal formal planning.

Other variables affecting the need for formal planning are the degree of competition and the level of uncertainty. A small firm facing stiff competition needs to plan and monitor its operations closely. Although few companies face great certainty, there are differences in the degree of uncertainty that they face. If there is much uncertainty, planning can help the entrepreneur to grasp the nature of the challenges facing the firm.

Still another factor affecting the need for formal planning is the entrepreneur's experience and background. Those who are highly capable, who understand the various aspects of the business, and who are willing to involve themselves in the details of the business can do more of the planning in their heads and reduce the paperwork of formal planning. It should be obvious that such highly personalized management eventually acts as a constraint to growth by centering its planning around one or two individuals.

Employee Participation in Planning

The small-business owner is directly and personally responsible for planning. Typically, he or she does not have, and cannot have, a full-time

ACTION REPORT
Strategy and Planning by a Small Manufacturer

In 1973, Oliver O. Ward and three colleagues purchased the germanium division of an electronics manufacturer and began producing germanium-based semiconductors. The new company, Germanium Power Devices Corporation (GPD), succeeded and grew even though the big semiconductor manufacturers switched from using germanium to using silicon, a cheaper material. GPD's special success is apparently linked to its strategy and planning, described by a writer as follows:

GPD's Strategy

After he [Ward] and his co-founders had looked at the marketplace, they did some long-range planning. The strategy they proposed was to get an increasing share of the declining market by acquiring germanium divisions as the big companies got out of the business.

Ward and his colleagues also felt that new fields might open up for germanium.

GPD's Planning

To make that future as successful as possible, Ward and his three colleagues sit down once a week for an informal planning session. And they do a minimum of four days of long-range planning a year, which Ward considers invaluable. "When we sit down for two days each in the spring and the fall, we're trying to take a much broader view. In any area—whether it's a family or a business—it doesn't do any harm to sit back and take an objective look at where you are, where you're going, how you're going to get there, and what your needs and problems are."

Source: Susan E. Currier, "This Rare Bird Prospers in a Declining Market," *Inc.*, Vol. 2, No. 5 (May, 1980), pp. 93–98.

planning staff such as many large firms have. Neither the money nor the personnel are available for such a staff. Consequently, the owner must do the planning, and a great proportion of the owner's time will be spent in it. Nevertheless, this responsibility may be delegated to some extent because some planning is required of all the members of the enterprise. If the organization is of any size at all, the owner can hardly specify in detail the program for each department. Furthermore, there is a need for some factual information which can be supplied only by other members of the organization.

The concept that the boss does the thinking and the employee does the work is rather misleading. Progressive management has discovered that employees' ideas are often helpful in developing solutions to company problems. The salesperson, for example, is closer to the customer and usually best able to evaluate the customer's reactions. It is not enough for employees to call attention to problems—they must also turn up recommendations and solutions.

The practical use of participation in planning is apparently quite limited. A survey by *Venture* magazine revealed that 51 percent of their 1,090 respondents sought planning input solely from top management.[9] And only 24 percent disseminated their plans below the department-head level.

The value of such contributions by subordinates is clearly dependent on their ability. If subordinate managers and other key people lack ability and experience, they can contribute little to the firm's planning. Not all employees possess the capacity or even the motivation for planning.

Kinds of Plans

Business plans may be classified in several ways. When classified according to the time period for which they are established, they are called *long-range plans* or *short-range plans*. When classified according to their frequency of use, they are known as *standing plans* (such as policies and procedures) or *single-use plans* (such as special projects and budgets). More detailed functional plans are also developed in production, marketing, finance, and other areas.

Long-Range and Short-Range Plans   To make decisions intelligently, a manager must know what a firm will be doing several years in the future. Without some contemplation of the distant future, the business may find itself on a "dead-end street." The basic objectives and broad strategies discussed earlier in this chapter are examples of long-range plans.

One of the best-known and most used short-range, single-use plans is the budget. A **budget** is a device for expressing future plans in monetary terms. It is usually prepared for one year in advance, with a breakdown by quarters or months. As a plan of action, the budget provides a set of yardsticks by which operations can be controlled. To be effective, the budget must be based on a realistic estimate of sales volume, with appropriate expense levels determined accordingly. The budget is discussed in greater detail in Chapter 19.

Policies   **Business policies** are defined as fundamental statements which serve as guides to management practice. Some policies are *general* in that they affect the whole business, while other policies affect only particular departments or portions of the operation. In a small manufacturing firm there are product policies, sales policies, manufacturing policies, financial policies, expansion policies, personnel policies, and credit policies, among others. For example, any small firm establishes a personnel policy when it determines the amount of vacation to which its employees are entitled. Similarly, sales policy is established when a firm determines the geographical scope of its market and the type of customer it will seek.

An already-decided policy permits a prompt decision on a specific problem. This does not mean that the policy dictates the decision—a policy should allow a certain latitude for judgment in individual cases. Nevertheless, an established policy makes it unnecessary for the manager to analyze a specific problem each time it arises. For example, an employer need not decide each year the amount of vacation each employee should receive. The general statement of vacation policy is simply applied to individual cases.

Saving time is only one of the advantages in the use of definite policies in a small firm. Policies are established on the basis of a careful consideration of all pertinent factors and are thus arrived at logically. Without policy in particular areas, the manager is forced to make decisions under pressure and without the opportunity to think through the implications of those decisions. Finally, policies also provide consistency of action from one time to another. This is a matter of value to both customers and employees of the firm.

Procedures A standard operating procedure is similar to a policy in that it is a standing or continuing plan. Once a method of work or a procedure is worked out, it may be standardized and referred to as a *standard operating procedure*. For example, the steps involved in taking a credit application, investigating the applicant, approving or disapproving the request, and subsequent authorizations of particular purchases by approved customers may be completely standardized.

Steps in Planning

The steps in planning may be thought of as steps in problem solving. This series of steps includes: recognizing the problem, collecting and analyzing the facts, making a tentative decision among the possible alternatives, testing the practicality of the tentative plan, and selecting and announcing the final plan.

Recognizing the Problem Until the issue at hand is clear, it is impossible to develop a sound plan which will provide an adequate solution. Although this sounds easy, the true nature of a problem is not always evident on the surface. For example, a complaint about wages may be completely misleading and only a camouflage for another grievance. To assume that wages is the problem might lead to a plan that misses the mark completely.

Not all planning is problem-centered, however. For example, the mere act of carrying out organizational objectives requires planning. The first step in opening a restaurant, for example, would involve recognition of a need to plan the location, physical facilities, personnel requirements, financial structure, operating procedures, and so on. After the restaurant is under way, the manager would recognize a need to plan menus, purchasing, and replacement of equipment even though these matters are not visualized as "problems."

Collecting and Analyzing the Facts   The second step in planning involves the collection and analysis of pertinent facts. Not all facts are significant to particular issues and, therefore, to particular planning activities. In this preliminary analysis, the entrepreneur must distinguish the significant facts, classify them, and note causal relationships. Moreover, gaps in the available data must be noted and arrangements made to secure the needed facts. However, time and cost pressures, among other factors, may make it difficult or impossible to obtain these additional pertinent facts.

In planning the purchase of new equipment for a restaurant, for example, the entrepreneur would investigate the types of equipment available and the various possibilities for its arrangement. Some of this information would no doubt be derived from past experience and supplemented by discussions with equipment suppliers, visits to other restaurants, contacts with a trade association, and the reading of the trade publications. From these various sources, detailed information regarding the initial cost, durability, operating cost, efficiency, appearance, and size of the different types of equipment might be obtained. The effects of and demands for various types of equipment would be particularly noted, as would the types of financial arrangements available. For example, a particular unit might provide exceptional convenience of operation for personnel and require a down payment of one-half its total cost.

Making a Tentative Decision among Possible Alternatives   As factual information is collected and examined, various possible courses of action begin to suggest themselves. If planning is thorough, each of the major practical solutions or courses of action will be carefully identified. Here again, the process seems simple, but creative thinking is required to visualize possibilities that are not immediately apparent. Many times the obvious solution is not the best one.

Returning to our example of the restaurant, no doubt many alternatives exist with regard to the physical equipment that might be installed. Possible hypothetical alternatives might be:

1. Purchase of new Type A equipment from Supplier A at a cost of $1,500.
2. Purchase of new Type A equipment from Supplier B at a cost of $1,450 but with slower delivery.
3. Purchase of new Type B equipment from either supplier for $2,200.
4. Purchase of used Type A equipment from Supplier C for $950.

It should be clear that the possible alternative actions existing in other situations would be numerous. Only the most likely possibilities should be retained for further consideration.

Testing the Practicality of the Tentative Plan   Research and experimentation may sometimes be used to see what would happen under given circumstances. Insofar as experimentation can be utilized, it is well to do so because it will save hours of analysis and discussion, much of which might prove fruitless. For example, the prospective restaurant owner might be able to visit another restaurant, observe Type B equipment in operation, and talk with its operator. Of course, if research and experimentation are too costly or simply cannot be undertaken, one is thrown back upon the discussion of the pros and cons of the situation and upon analysis by mental trial and error.

Selecting and Announcing the Final Plan   The final step in planning is twofold: (1) selecting one of the alternatives after reflecting upon all the tangible and intangible factors in the case, and (2) announcing the final plan and its effective date to all concerned. The entrepreneur cannot postpone decisions merely because uncertainties and unknowns exist.

The final step in planning should flow naturally from the preceding steps. If alternatives have been clearly stated and carefully examined, the most desirable choice is usually apparent. Applying this step to our example of planning to buy new restaurant equipment, it is at this point that the entrepreneur would decide, perhaps, to buy Type B equipment.

QUANTITATIVE TOOLS TO AID PLANNING

In both large and small businesses, quantitative tools may be utilized to improve decision making. Most owners of independent businesses associate these quantitative tools with big business, considering them quite inapplicable to small firms. However, the potential usefulness of quantitative tools to the small firm should not be overlooked.

Value of Quantitative Methods

Many decisions in small firms can be improved by adopting quantitative decision-making techniques. Unfortunately, most small-business owners lack an awareness of the power of such techniques. Much of their decision making reflects personal experience—what they have learned through trial and error—and they fail to realize that such decisions can be made more rational. Reliance on intuitive approaches can be reduced by the analytical processes that are a part of management science.

In advocating careful planning in this chapter, we have argued for a rational approach to small-business management. The use of quantitative methods, where applicable, can extend this quest for rationality. It permits the decision maker to apply analytic methods to the solution of some problems which cannot be solved well by intuition.

As a practical matter, few managers of small firms have sufficient knowledge of advanced mathematics and statistics to apply these tools personally. A consideration of these tools is pertinent, however, for at least two reasons. First, the small-business owner should know that such tools exist and that assistance can be obtained from individuals qualified in the use of quantitative methods. Second, the growing use of these techniques points up the need for increased training in quantitative methods on the part of small-business managers. Even though an individual lacks the necessary technical knowledge for using the tools, it is desirable that he or she appreciate their possibilities, advantages, and limitations.

The variety and complexity of quantitative methods make it impossible to provide an extensive review of them in this book. Because of space limitations, only a few such approaches can be explained.[10]

Statistical Inference

By means of statistical analysis, one can use quantitative data to arrive at conclusions that are useful in managing a small business. Suppose, for example, that you wish to judge the quality of a large production run without inspecting each item or that you wish to understand your market without surveying each individual customer. You may accomplish these objectives by *sampling* the population and then applying **statistical inference**, that is, inferring something about a large group on the basis of facts known about a smaller group.

Although sampling is not the only tool which uses statistical inference, it illustrates its practical application in small business. In sampling, the manager wishes to obtain a sample that is truly representative of the underlying population. A sample is *representative* when it is like the population in all important respects. To assure this condition, the researcher will often use a *random sample* in which every item in the population has a known chance of being included. The sample should also be *adequate*, that is, large enough to yield a dependable answer.

Sampling is essential for the simple reason that the entire population of data can seldom be investigated. Cost and time pressure make this prohibitive.

Mathematical Programming

Several types of mathematical programming are available such as *integer programming, quadratic programming, goal programming, dynamic programming,* and *linear programming.* They can be applied to the solution of such varied problems as resource allocation, inventory management, production planning, advertising media selection, and capital budgeting.

Linear programming, the most widely used variety of mathematical programming, involves the use of mathematical algorithms for evaluating the results from several alternative courses of action, each of which contains a number of variables. This tool is used to discover the exact solution that will minimize costs or maximize gains. It is beyond the scope of this text to illustrate advanced mathematical theories in solving problems by linear programming. Suffice it to say that this tool can be used to analyze manufacturing problems that involve the production of several products for which basic, but scarce, raw materials are used. Linear programming could determine the following information for such a problem:

1. The amount of each raw material needed for each product.
2. The profit per unit for each product.
3. Which product or combination of products to produce in order to maximize profits.
4. How much of each product should be produced.
5. How much of a low-profit product to produce in order to "take care" of certain loyal customers.

Applied Probability Models

A number of applied probability models, including *queuing models, Markov chain models,* and *inventory models* are applicable to various types of business problems. We shall limit the present discussion to queuing models.

Queuing theory is waiting-line theory. It consists of the use of calculated probabilities for determining the number of persons who will stand in a line. Examples of problems that may be solved by applying this theory might include the number of depositors who will stand in line for service at a bank teller's window, customers who will stand in line at checkout counters in a supermarket, or car owners who will wait in line at car wash establishments.

Take the case of a barber facing retirement at age 65 in order to draw a social security pension. The alternatives considered were: (1) to sell out, (2) to trade the two-chair shop for a one-chair shop to be operated on weekends only, and (3) to keep the two-chair shop open on Fridays and Saturdays only. Using the queuing theory for Alternative No. 2 showed that the barber would work continuously, without rest breaks or meals, from 8:00 A.M. to 10:00 P.M. if all arriving customers waited until served—even though the shop was locked for an hour at noon and after 5:00 P.M. Because this was untenable, the possibilities of Alternative No. 3 were simulated. This alternative proved to be workable, except that the barber would still make too much money to be legally entitled to the social security checks. Hence, the waiting-line simulations suggested a different solution: The barber sold out and contracted to work for another barber on Fridays and Saturdays only, taking full pay for services up to the limiting monthly amount and letting the shop owner take everything over that figure. This case exemplifies the application of waiting-line theory for the guidance of a small-business owner's decision to sell out.

Simulation Technique

Experience can be a good teacher, but experience is costly and time-consuming. This is true of managerial decision making as it is elsewhere. **Simulation** permits the decision maker to gain experience in something resembling the actual business situation without taking the risk existing in that situation. The basic idea in simulation is the creation of a model that acts like the system it represents. Manufacturers, for example, test products in laboratories which simulate the environment in which those products are used. A model must contain the parameters which exist in the real-life situation if it is to produce results comparable to those that would emerge in real life.

Even in a small business, the manager can occasionally create a model of a problem that requires a solution. The model will typically express the problem in mathematical terms and be structured for solution by use of a computer. By having a mathematical, computerized model available, the decision maker can easily and quickly experiment with alternative actions in reaching a sound decision. When a particular decision is fed into the computer, the computer calculates its effects. Thus, the manager can immediately determine the consequences of that decision and also alternative decisions.

Simulation can be used for such problems as determining the number of loading docks to build and the number of people to hire for a warehouse where the amount of time between truck arrivals is random. In a different context, simulation can help in deciding how many products to order for a special sale in which leftover products must be sold at a loss. There are also other types of problems in which simulation can be used, but these examples should demonstrate its possible application to practical problems in the small firm.

Forecasting

Forecasts are necessary for many types of business decisions. Managers of small firms must decide how much to buy, how many employees to hire, how many products to produce, and how much money to borrow by predicting the demand for their products. In Chapters 4 and 5, we stressed the importance of a credible forecast when preparing a business plan.

Some forecasts are merely "guesstimates," or products of entrepreneurial intuition. However, management science offers quantitative tools to assist in preparing reliable forecasts. They vary in degree of sophistication and in their usefulness in particular situations. They include such methods as *moving averages, exponential smoothing,* and *multiple regression models,* among others.

Limitations of Quantitative Tools

Quantitative tools do not preclude the exercise of managerial judgment, which is definitely required because of the human factor in any problem situation. The tools are a means to an end, not the end itself. The manager's judgment remains the decisive factor in planning.

Neither does the use of quantitative tools preclude the requirement of feedback. Any information about operating results must be fed back to the planner so that plans, programs, and instructions may be modified when necessary. For example, when feedback reports describe deviations from an existing budget, the budget may have to be modified as a means of corrective action.

It must be emphasized that quantitative tools are just that—they are tools, and no more. When used properly, they tend to improve managerial decision making. These decision-making tools do not eliminate business risk totally. *Risk* is inherent in the use of present resources and production facilities for the creation of new goods. It is inherent also in the purchase of merchandise for resale. Decision-making tools are designed merely to minimize risk by providing a rational approach to business problems.

Looking Back

1. The main objectives of a privately owned business are: profit, economic service, and growth. Profits must be earned to reward the entrepreneur's acceptance of business risks and to assure continuity of the business. The marketing objective must be modified as consumer tastes change and as competitive products and services are developed. The growth objective envisions the need for additional operating facilities and calls for retained earnings or new investment by the owners.

2. A sense of social responsibility characterizes many modern business leaders. Entrepreneurs, in particular, often speak of their service to the community as one of the major rewards of their business activity. Consistency and sincerity in adherence to ethical codes are obligatory if ethical business practices are to remain effective. Ethical advertising is especially important, and local Better Business Bureaus have been established to advise consumers about unethical advertising and other objectionable business practices.

3. In strategic planning, entrepreneurs identify environmental opportunities and risks, evaluate the firm's resources, and make necessary changes in the basic nature of business operations. The small firm can maximize its competitive strength by avoiding head-on competition with big business, emphasizing its natural advantages, and finding a strategic niche.

4. The various kinds of plans include long-range and short-range plans, policies, and standard operating procedures. The steps in planning include: recognizing the problem, collecting and analyzing the facts, making a tentative decision among possible alternatives, testing the practicality of the tentative plan, and selecting and announcing the final plan.

5. Quantitative tools useful for the improvement of decision making include methods of statistical inference such as sampling, mathematical programming, applied probability models including queuing theory, simulation, and forecasting. The limitations of quantitative tools should be known to the entrepreneur. As tools, they assist in reaching a decision but do not preclude the use of personal judgment.

DISCUSSION QUESTIONS

1. What stake do the employees of a small firm have in the attainment of its profit objective?

2. Why must a business firm recognize and fulfill its marketing objective? Is this equally true in all types of businesses? Is the marketing objective as important as the firm's profit objective, or subordinate to it?

3. A men's clothing store has been opened by an extremely ambitious young person who is strongly growth-oriented. How might this orientation toward growth affect the operating methods and policies of the business?

4. Is it necessary for the entrepreneur to be a philanthropist to some degree in order to adhere to the social objectives of the business? Why?

5. Suppose that a used car dealer has just made an oral commitment to sell a car at a particular price. Before the deal is completed, another customer indicates a willingness to pay a substantially higher price. What is the ethical thing to do? Is it also practical and good business?

6. Give some examples of strategic moves that might be made by an independently owned gasoline service station.

7. What is the concept of the "strategic niche," and what are its values for the small firm?

8. Do small firms too often neglect the managerial function of planning? If so, what accounts for this neglect?

9. What major blunders might result from a lack of long-range planning on the part of a small manufacturing firm?

10. To what extent are sophisticated, quantitative decision-making tools actually applicable to small-business management?

ENDNOTES

1. Thomas J. Peters and Robert H. Waterman, Jr., *In Search of Excellence* (New York: Harper and Row, 1982).

2. Tom Peters, "An Excellent Question," *Inc.*, Vol. 6, No. 12 (December, 1984), p. 156.

3. Adapted from Chapter 5 of F. Parker Fowler, Jr., and E. W. Sandberg, *The Relationship of Management Decision Making to Small Business Growth*, Small Business Management Research Report. Prepared by Colorado State University Research Foundation under a grant from the Small Business Administration, Washington, DC, 1964.

4. George Weissman, "The Art of Responsibility: Corporations, Arts, and Economic Development," Address to Citizens for Business and Industry in North Carolina, March 14, 1984.

5. Tom Richman, "Not Everyone Can Move to Southern California, You Know," *Inc.*, Vol. 5, No. 5 (May, 1983), pp. 115–118.

6. Sanford L. Jacobs, "Hide and Sneak," *The Wall Street Journal*, May 20, 1985, p. 13c.

7. Philip M. Van Auken and R. Duane Ireland, "An Input-Output Approach to Practical Small Business Planning," *Journal of Small Business Management*, Vol. 18, No. 1 (January, 1980), p. 45.

8. Some of the variables affecting formal planning in small firms are identified in Philip H. Thurston, "Should Smaller Companies Make Formal Plans?" *Harvard Business Review*, Vol. 61, No. 5 (September–October, 1983), pp. 162–188.

9. "The Venture Survey: Sticking to Business Plans," *Venture*, Vol. 7, No. 4 (April, 1985), p. 25.

10. For a fuller discussion of such methods, see books on management science or operations management. One example is Israel Brosh, *Quantitative Techniques for Managerial Decision Making* (Reston, VA: Reston Publishing Company, Inc., 1985).

REFERENCES TO SMALL BUSINESS IN ACTION

"A Short-Haul Trucker Drives Hard to Expand." *Business Week*, No. 2651 (August 25, 1980), pp. 33–34.

A family-owned, short-haul trucking firm discovered opportunities for expansion as the Interstate Commerce Commission eased trucking rules. Careful planning is being used to exploit those opportunities.

Fouliard, Paul. "Profits by the Pound." *In Business*, Vol. 3, No. 4 (Autumn, 1981), pp. 28–29.

> A small family-owned, meat-packing firm changed its strategy by shifting from high volume and low prices to higher quality and higher prices.

Richman, Tom. "What Business Are You Really In?" *Inc.*, Vol. 5, No. 8 (August, 1983), pp. 77–86.

> This article reports on the self-examination by three small firms to decide the essential nature of their businesses—the most fundamental part of strategic planning.

Schifrin, Matthew. "Uncle Sam's Foot in the Door." *Forbes*, Vol. 133, No. 14 (June 18, 1984), p. 118.

> This article reports on the honesty of door-to-door marketers and on efforts by the Internal Revenue Service to make sure that all income is reported for tax purposes.

CASE 14

Emergency Filler Cap Case*
Ethical obligations related to products

Roller Sports, Inc., is a small manufacturing firm in Jacksonville, FL. It manufactures and sells for 35 cents each a small plastic adapter (see Figure 14–5) which it advertises as a funnel/emergency cap. This adapter can be put on the nozzle of a regular gas pump at the station to fill a car, designed to take unleaded gas, with regular leaded gas.

Figure 14–5   The Emergency Filler Cap

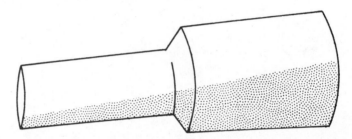

The question that immediately arises is whether or not it is illegal to put leaded fuel into an automobile designed for unleaded fuel. Environmental Protection Agency (EPA) regulations, as enacted by Congress, prohibit putting leaded fuel in a car designed for unleaded fuel by any *retailer* and his *employees* and *agents*.[1] Specifically, the Code of Federal Regulation states that:

> ... after July 1, 1974, no retailer or his employee or agent shall sell, dispense, or offer for sale gasoline represented to be unleaded unless such gasoline meets the defined requirements for unleaded gasoline in section 80.2 (g); nor shall he introduce, or cause or allow the introduction of, leaded gasoline into any motor vehicle which is labeled "UNLEADED GASOLINE ONLY," or which is equipped with a gasoline tank filler inlet which is designed for the introduction of unleaded gasoline.[2]

Conspicuously absent from the law, as defined by these regulations, is any action taken by a private individual to introduce leaded gasoline into an automobile designed to use unleaded gasoline only.

To understand how this glaring inconsistency in the law occurred, one must look to a historical perspective. "In 1973, virtually all gasoline was pumped by a service station attendant. Now over 70 percent is sold self-

*This case was prepared by Professor Daniel L. Harris of Seattle Pacific University with the research assistance of Steven Kessler.

service nationwide."[3] The EPA has not only come to realize the severity of the self-service station problem, but has even put forward as an option the closure of self-service gas stations.[4] It is interesting to note that this federal prohibition includes self-service stations as long as the attendant could reasonably be expected to be aware of the improper fueling. The law does provide that:

> ...in a bonafide emergency (such as when the gasoline tank of a vehicle is almost empty and no unleaded gasoline is available within a radius of several miles), the retailer or wholesaler purchaser/customer will not be deemed in violation, provided that the amount of leaded gasoline which was introduced into the vehicle was limited to no more than was reasonably required....[5]

This permissiveness in the emergency use of leaded fuel seems to conflict with the spirit of an EPA study which determined that even casual misfueling causes a 344 percent increase in baseline hydrocarbon emissions.[6]

The law provides a penalty of up to a $10,000 fine for the violation of the EPA regulations by a service station operator or employee, but no penalty in the case of an individual.[7] Some states have passed laws to deal with the individual violator. For example, the law in the state of Washington for using leaded fuel in a car designed for unleaded fuel states, "No person shall remove or render inoperable any devices or components of any systems on a motor vehicle installed as a requirement of federal law."[8] Thus, the state prohibits the individual from using leaded fuel in a car designed to use unleaded fuel. However, the penalty is unclear.

But what are the chances of getting caught? Very little, according to Betty Swan of the EPA. The EPA estimates that about 10 percent of all motorists are putting leaded gas into autos designed to burn unleaded gas. Other sources estimate that as many as 20 percent of all motorists are using leaded fuel in cars designed to use unleaded fuel.[9] In any case, the number of motorists using the filler cap are quite numerous.

Several questions must be asked. Why is such a large segment of our society bypassing the unleaded fuel requirement? To reduce pollution, our society has spent billions to develop and market unleaded fuel and to design cars that can burn it.[10] However, it is perfectly legal to produce or buy a filler cap, thus creating more pollution. What should be done? Should filler caps be made illegal? Is it unethical to produce, sell, and use a filler cap? Is Congress to blame because they failed to devise a practical way to make the achievement of a clean environment the responsibility of the citizens who own and use automobiles? Or should we take the view of Roller Sports, Inc., who has manufactured and sold to consumers 5.25 million filler caps since 1979, and answer the above questions by saying, "We manufacture a funnel; what you do with that funnel is entirely up to you."[11]

Questions

1. What are the ethical responsibilities, if any, of Roller Sports, Inc.? If the product is legal, is it also ethical?
2. Is there any conflict between the manufacturer's quest for profits and its ethical obligations? Can it afford to be ethical?
3. What can or should a self-service station do about the use of filler caps by customers?
4. What is the legal and ethical position of the motorist who uses the filler cap?

Case Endnotes

1. *Unleaded Gas...The Way to Go*, Environmental Protection Agency, September, 1978, OPH 148/8.

2. Title 40, Code of Federal Regulations, Part 80.22 (a).

3. Carol E. Curtis, "EPA's Next Hot Potato," *Forbes*, April 11, 1983, p. 42.

4. EPA Publications PB80-212780 80-04, PC A04/MF A01, "Analysis to Limit Air Quality Degradation Due to Misuse of Leaded Gasoline in Cars Equipped with Catalytic Converters."

5. Title 40, CFR, Part 80.23 (e) (2).

6. PB80-153950 MFAD1, "Casual Misfueling of Catalyst Equipped Vehicles."

7. Title 40, CFR, Part 80.5.

8. Title 18, Washington Administrative Code, Standards of Motor Vehicles, 18-24-040.

9. Carol E. Curtis, "EPA's Next Hot Potato," *op. cit.*, p. 43.

10. *Ibid.*

11. *Karl Scheufler*, Roller Sports, Inc.

15

Organizing the Small Firm

Figure 15-1   Sandy Brown

Courtesy of Sandy Brown

As small businesses grow, they experience "growing pains" in organizational relationships. The problems of Sandy Brown described here are typical:

> As owner and president of Rhode Island Welding Supply Co., Sandy Brown was used to overseeing every detail. He wooed customers, negotiated with the union, and even designed a new headquarters.
>
> But while his East Greenwich, RI, equipment-distribution company earned steady profits, "we weren't growing the way I knew we could," he says. "I was working from 7:00 A.M. to 7:00 P.M. and the business was running me. Doing everything, I had no time to think one day ahead."
>
> Mr. Brown finally decided to delegate authority to a new general manager. Telling employees they had a new boss was his toughest business decision, he says.

> Brown's reorganization paid off. Company sales nearly doubled (to about $5 million) in the two years after he began delegating.

Source: Reprinted by permission of *The Wall Street Journal*, © Dow Jones & Company, Inc., 1985. All Rights Reserved.

411

Looking Ahead

Watch for the following topics:

1. The unplanned organization structure.
2. Line-and-staff organization and the chain of command.
3. Informal organization.
4. Fundamentals of the organizing function.
5. Boards of directors in small corporations.

Figure 15-2   Getting Organized

This sign on a desk is intended to be facetious, but it expresses the real plight of many small firms. They are not well-organized, and they would like to do something about it. In this chapter, we will look at organizational relationships, both formal and informal, and the way in which these can best be structured for effectiveness and growth of the small firm.

TYPES OF FORMAL ORGANIZATION STRUCTURE

More than one type of organization structure is available to the small firm. The structures range from one that is unplanned to line organization and line-and-staff organization.

The Unplanned Structure

In small companies, the organization structure tends to evolve with little conscious planning. Certain employees begin performing particular functions when the firm is new and retain those functions as the company matures. Other functions remain diffused in a number of positions, even though they have gained importance as a result of company growth.

This natural evolution is not all bad. Generally, a strong element of practicality exists in organizational arrangements which evolve in this way. The structure is forged in the process of working and growing, not derived from a textbook. Unplanned structures are seldom perfect, however, and growth typically creates a need for organizational change. Periodically, therefore, the entrepreneur should examine structural relationships and make adjustments as needed for effective teamwork.

Assuming that the business is more than a one-person operation, the entrepreneur must decide whether a line organization is appropriate or whether a more complex form of organization is desirable.

Line Organization

In a **line organization** each person has one supervisor to whom he or she reports and looks for instructions. Thus, a single, specific chain of command exists. All employees are engaged directly in getting out the work—producing, selling, or arranging financial resources. Most very small firms—for example, those with fewer than ten employees—use this form of organization. A line organization is illustrated in Figure 15–3.

The term **chain of command** implies a superior–subordinate relationship with a downward flow of orders, but it involves much more. The chain of command is also a channel for two-way communication, although this does not mean that communication among employees at the same level is forbidden. Informal discussion among employees is inevitable. However, the chain is the *official, vertical channel of communication*. Even so, not all communication between superior and subordinate is official, and not all of the

Figure 15–3   Line Organization

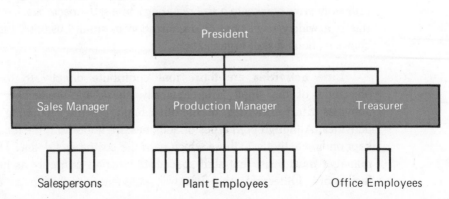

superior's statements are orders. There is normal social interaction, as well as order giving, between superior and subordinate. When orders are given, the subordinate's line of responsibility or obligation to the superior to carry out the orders becomes evident.

An organizational problem occurs when managers or employees ignore organization lines. In small firms, the climate of informality and flexibility makes it easy to short-circuit the formal chain. A president and founder of the business, for example, may get in a hurry and give instructions to salespersons or plant employees instead of going through the sales manager or the production manager. Similarly, an employee who has been with the entrepreneur from the beginning tends to maintain that direct person-to-person relationship rather than observe newly instituted channels of communication.

As a practical matter, adherence to the chain of command can never be complete. An organization in which the chain of command is rigid would be bureaucratic and inefficient. Nevertheless, frequent and flagrant disregard of the chain of command quickly undermines the position of the bypassed manager. This is a particular danger for the small firm, and only the entrepreneur can make sure that the integrity of the structure is maintained. Occasionally, for example, the entrepreneur may need to say, "Why don't you talk with your supervisor about that first?"

As a small business expands and hires additional employees, it outgrows the simple line organization. The need for specialized management assistance leads to the type of organization described in the next section.

Line-and-Staff Organization

The **line-and-staff organization** is similar to a line organization in that each person reports to a single supervisor. However, in a line-and-staff structure there are also staff specialists who perform specialized services or act as management advisers in special areas. Examples of staff specialists include a human resources manager, a production control technician, a quality control specialist, or an assistant to the president. Small firms ordinarily grow quickly to a size requiring some staff specialists. Consequently, this is a widely used type of organization in small business. Figure 15–4 shows a line-and-staff organization.

Line activities are those that contribute directly to the primary objectives of the small firm. Typically, these are production and sales activities. **Staff activities**, on the other hand, are the supporting or helping activities. Although both types of activities are important, the focus must be kept on line activities—those which earn the customer's dollar. The owner–manager must insist that staff specialists function primarily as helpers and facilitators. Otherwise, the firm will experience confusion as employees

Figure 15–4   Line-and-Staff Organization

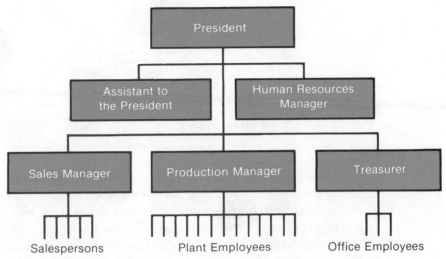

receive directions from a variety of supervisors and staff specialists. *Unity of command* would be destroyed.

Committee Organization

The **committee organization** is a variation of the line-and-staff structure. Superimposed on the line-and-staff organization is a set of committees such as executive and finance committees. Committees are designed to help managers reach necessary decisions by exploring the pros and cons of a given situation. In a very small firm, only the entrepreneur and perhaps one or two assistants are empowered to make major decisions. As a result, the extensive use of committees in small business is unnecessary and often inefficient.

INFORMAL ORGANIZATION

The types of organization structure previously discussed are concerned with formal relationships among members of an organization. In any organization, however, there are also informal groups that have something in common such as jobs, hobbies, carpools, age, or affiliations with civic associations. The dotted areas in Figure 15–5 represent informal groups in an organization.

Although informal groups are not a structural part of the formal organization, the manager should observe them and evaluate their effect on

Figure 15-5   Informal Relationships

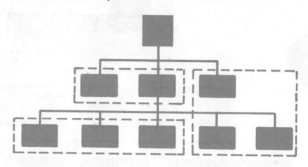

the functioning of the total organization. Ordinarily, no serious conflict arises between informal groups and the formal organization. It is probable, of course, that an informal leader or leaders will emerge who will influence employee behavior. The wise manager understands the potentially positive contribution of the informal groups and the inevitability of informal leadership. Of course, if a leader were to persist in influencing other employees to behave contrary to the wishes of management, it might become necessary to discharge such an individual.

Informal interaction among subordinates and managers can facilitate work performance and also can make life in the workplace more enjoyable for everyone. The value of compatible work groups to the individual became painfully clear to one college student who worked on a summer job and said:

> I was employed as a forklift driver for one long, frustrating summer. Soon after being introduced to my work group, I knew I was in trouble. A clique had formed and, for some reason, resented college students. During lunch breaks and work breaks, I spent the whole time by myself. Each morning I dreaded going to work. The job paid well, but I was miserable.

FUNDAMENTALS OF THE ORGANIZING FUNCTION

Several time-tested guidelines to promote effective organization and management are particularly applicable to the small business. These concepts are relevant not only to initial organizational decisions, but also to subsequent organizational changes.[1]

How People Affect Organization Design

At times, conflicts arise between organizational ideals and human considerations. Suppose some otherwise desirable employees have certain limitations which prevent the assignment of responsibility that they should theoretically bear. Must the manager dismiss such employees? There is, of course, no hard-and-fast answer. Although the manager cannot flagrantly disregard the important principles of organization, he or she will find it necessary to bend these principles at times in the interest of enabling the firm to operate effectively. The important thing is that departures from an ideal structure be supported by logical thinking and that they be recognized for what they are—temporary deviations from the theoretically desirable arrangement.

It is also well to recognize that some members of an organization have personal interests which can affect organizing decisions. Even in a small organization, managers may be guilty of "empire building" to enhance their own status. The entrepreneur needs to examine each organizational change to be sure it enhances the overall organizational effectiveness and not merely the welfare of one individual.

Departmentation—Grouping of Activities

In grouping activities into positions and departments, similarity of work provides a practical guiding principle. Obviously, production activities would be placed under a shop supervisor, while sales activities would be directed by a sales manager. Such homogeneous assignments of work facilitate effective operation.

As a small firm grows, other patterns of departmentation become possible. If the business has more than one location, for example, a geographic pattern may be used, with employees in each area reporting to a branch supervisor. Or, if the sales force expands sufficiently, sales personnel may be grouped according to product categories or geographic areas.

Delegation of Authority

Given a proper concept of **delegation of authority**, a superior will grant to subordinates, on the basis of competence, the right to act or to decide. By delegating authority, the superior can perform the more important tasks after turning over the less important functions to subordinates.

Failure to delegate may well be the weakest point in small-business organizations generally. Although the problem is found in all organizations, it is a special problem for the independent entrepreneur, whose background usually contributes to this situation. Frequently, the entrepreneur has organized the business and knows more about it than any other person in the firm. Thus, to protect the business, the owner is inclined to keep a firm hold on the reins of leadership.

Inability or unwillingness to delegate authority is manifested in numerous ways. For example, employees may find it necessary to "clear it with the boss" before making even a minor decision. A line of subordinates may be

ACTION REPORT
Learning to Delegate at Flambeau Corporation

Founders of business firms find it difficult to delegate authority, and Bill Sauey, founder of Flambeau Corporation, was no exception. Eventually he learned, however. "My biggest regret," he says, "is that I didn't do it sooner." The company, which manufactures plastic products, was started by Sauey in 1947. His single-handed control of the firm is described as follows:

> Sauey signed all the checks, bought all the plant equipment, interviewed all potential employees, and played a role in developing and selling all of Flambeau's products. The company was a testament to his persistence and his conviction that he could solve any business problem. So he continued to manage the company in his own tightly controlled way even though there were signs that this style wasn't working so well anymore.
>
> "My biggest weakness was my inability to listen," he says. "When I felt strongly about something, like my business, I wasn't really hearing what others were saying."

Sauey discouraged decision making by others by flying into a rage when others acted independently, as evidenced by the following:

> One manager remembers a typical incident back in 1975. Sauey was out of town when his company received an unusually large parts order from Chrysler. In his absence, the managers at the Baraboo, WI, plant reviewed their already tight production schedule and accepted only half the order. When Sauey returned and heard the news, he went wild. "No one turns down business around here except me," he shouted. "No matter what!"

When the work load became too heavy, Sauey simply made himself change and then found it worked better than expected. He said, "I feel more in control now than I ever did. The divisions are really separate companies now. I have very little direct control over them, and the surprise is, I like it!"

Source: David De Long, "They All Said Bill Sauey Couldn't Let Go," *Inc.*, Vol. 3, No. 5 (May, 1981), pp. 89–91.

constantly trying to get the attention of the owner to resolve some issue which the subordinates lack authority to settle. This keeps the owner exceptionally busy, rushing from assisting a salesperson to helping iron out a production bottleneck to setting up a new filing system.

Delegation of authority is important for the satisfactory operation of a small firm and is an absolute prerequisite for growth. This factor alone is the reason why many firms can never grow beyond the small size that can be directly supervised in detail by the owner. One owner of a small restaurant operated it with excellent profits. As a result of this success, the owner acquired a lease on another restaurant in the same area and proceeded to operate it for one year. During this time, the owner experienced constant "headaches" with the second restaurant. Working long hours and trying to supervise both restaurants finally led the owner to give up the job. This person had never learned to delegate authority.

By allowing others to participate in decision making, an entrepreneur develops their abilities and thereby builds an organization. However, a manager must delegate carefully, or subordinates may simply bring their problems back to the boss. One entrepreneur suggests the following way to analyze one's practices in delegating:

> Try analyzing your time and separating your work into two general categories: problems your employees "delegated" to you and your own activities. You will quickly learn how much control you have over your own problems versus how much control your employees have.[2]

If employees have too much control, the manager must encourage them to act independently and avoid doing all their work for them. Only by real delegation can the entrepreneur build an organization rather than merely run a business.

Equal Authority and Responsibility

A frequent criticism which relates to authority and responsibility is that the authority delegated is not equal to the responsibility assigned. A manager may expect the subordinate to produce or to achieve a given volume of sales but may limit the latter by unreasonable financial or personnel restrictions. Equity demands that the subordinate be held responsible only for that which is within the given range of authority.

Having acknowledged this ideal of equal responsibility and authority, we must realize that the ideal is seldom fully achieved. It is difficult to spell out authority in detail, and key employees are often expected to get a job completed without worrying about the precise degree of their authority. Moreover, a capable employee may gain cooperation from other employees by positive persuasion, as well as by wielding a stick. Nevertheless, substantial differences in authority and responsibility would contribute to poor morale.

Span of Control

The optimum **span of control** is the number of subordinates who can be effectively supervised by a manager. Although some authorities have stated that six to eight people are all that one individual can supervise effectively, the proper span of control actually is a variable depending upon a number of factors. Among these are the nature of the work and the superior's knowledge, energy, personality, and abilities. In addition, if the abilities of subordinates are greater than average, the span of control may be enlarged accordingly.

In a business organization there is a limit on the number of operative employees who can be effectively supervised. Of course, the span of control is greater in the case of personnel performing routine assignments than in the case of technical, professional, or administrative personnel.

As a very small firm grows and adds employees, the entrepreneur's span of control is extended. There is a tendency to stretch the span too far—to supervise not only the first 5 or 6 employees but later to supervise all 10 or 12 as they are added. Eventually a point is reached at which the attempted span exceeds the entrepreneur's reach—the time and ability he or she can devote to the business. It is at this point that the entrepreneur must establish intermediate levels of supervision, devoting more time to management and moving beyond the role of player–coach.

Organization Principles and Small-Business Success

A study of 20 Cuban-owned businesses in Miami, FL, was made to determine whether organization principles were related to business success. The principles examined were the following:

1. Unity of objectives.
2. Organizational balance.
3. Responsibility.
4. Flexibility.
5. Parity of authority and responsibility.
6. Unity of command.
7. Span of management.
8. Delegation of authority.
9. Stability.[3]

Overall, the study concluded that as a group these principles of organization did relate to business success, although some of them were not significantly related. This study lends support to our argument that the entrepreneur should devote careful attention to organizational relationships.

THE BOARD OF DIRECTORS IN SMALL CORPORATIONS

All too often, the majority stockholder (the entrepreneur) in a small corporation appoints a board of directors merely to fulfill a legal requirement.

Such owners make little or no use of directors in managing their companies. In fact, an entrepreneur may actively resent efforts of managerial assistance from directors. When appointing directors, the entrepreneur tends to select personal friends, relatives, or other managers who are too busy to analyze situations and are not inclined to argue. In directors' meetings, the entrepreneur and other directors may simply engage in long-winded, innocuous discussions of broad general policies, leaving no time for serious, constructive questions.[4] Some entrepreneurs, however, have found an active board to be both practical and beneficial.

Contribution of Directors

A properly assembled board of directors can bring supplementary knowledge and broad experience to corporate management. The board should meet regularly to provide maximum asistance to the chief executive. Such board meetings should be conferences in which ideas are debated, strategies determined, and the pros and cons of policies explored. In this way, the chief executive is assisted by the experience of all the board members. Their combined knowledge makes possible more intelligent decisions on major issues.

Utilizing the experience of a board of directors does not mean that the chief executive of a small corporation is abdicating active control of its operations. Instead, it means merely that the chief executive is consulting with, and seeking the advice of, the board's members in order to draw upon a larger pool of business knowledge.

An active board of directors serves management in several important ways. The first of these, of course, is the board's review of major policy decisions. But there is also the matter of advice on external business conditions and on proper reaction to the business cycle. Moreover, some directors are willing to provide individual advice informally, from time to time, on specific problems that arise.

Entrepreneurs responding to a survey by *Venture* magazine rated objectivity as the most valuable contribution of outside directors.[5] These respondents also valued their financial knowledge, ideas, management expertise, and connections.

Outside directors may also serve the small firm by scrutinizing and questioning its ethical standards. S. Kumar Jain notes that "operating executives, without outside directors to question them, may rationalize unethical or illegal behavior as being in the best interest of the company."[6] With a strong board, the small firm gains greater credibility with the public as well as with the business and financial community.

ACTION REPORT
A Director's Valuable Counsel

Directors of small firms are supposed to offer valuable counsel to management. Here is the story of one small company which received this type of assistance from a company director:

> In early 1978, Joseph D. Simons, chief executive officer of Badgerland Equipment Inc., of Waukesha, WI, faced a dilemma. Salesmen were pressuring him to reduce prices of the company's aerial work platforms and other high-reach equipment, leased or purchased by contractors to lift workers and supplies at construction sites. But Simons's late brother Peter, who had founded the firm in 1969, had built Badgerland by providing prompt, excellent service, which allowed the firm to charge 10% to 15% more than competitors. Simons's instincts told him to continue that policy, but he had doubts. One salesman, for instance, complained that Badgerland had lost a $40,000 contract because its prices were too high...
>
> When Simons faced his pricing strategy dilemma, he turned to John Komives, one of Badgerland's three outside advisers. If Badgerland cut prices, it would have to lower quality, Komives reasoned. And if it did that, the firm could destroy an image that had taken five years to establish. "Komives headed me off at the pass," says Simons. "I saw that it would be foolhardy not to keep our standards and our prices high."

Source: Bill Hendrickson, "Who Do You Turn to When You're the Boss?" *Inc.*, Vol. 3, No. 1 (January, 1981), pp. 69–74.

Selection of Board Members

Many sources are available to the owner attempting to assemble a cooperative, experienced, able group of directors. The firm's attorney, banker, accountant, other business executives, and local management consultants might all be considered as potential directors. Peter Drucker has questioned the independence of auditors and attorneys, however, in view of the fact that they are retained by the firm.[7] Thus, they may not be free to be as critical of management's policies as they should be.

The importance of selecting an independent board of directors is expressed in these comments by Drucker:

> Therefore, the small and medium-size company needs an effective board of directors even more than the big one and usually has one that is even less effective. If I were chief executive officer of a medium-size company, I would spend a fair amount of time thinking through what I want my board to do, what I need from a board—including, let me say, somebody who will look at my proposal and say flatly, "This is not good enough." One doesn't need a rubber stamp; one needs people on a board who can ask the right questions. You need people who can say, "Jim, you are moving into the toy business and you don't know a thing about it. Have you really thought it through? Or do you want to make this acquisition just because it's available at a good P-E ratio?"[8]

Business prominence in the community is not essential for the small-corporation director. Rather, it is desirable that this individual be one who really understands small business and sympathizes with its problems. Moreover, he or she should be interested in sharing knowledge and have the personality and ability to transmit knowledge to the chief executive.

Compensation of Directors

The amount of compensation paid to board members varies greatly, and some small firms pay no fees whatever. One survey of small-company director compensation reported the following compensation levels:

1. 45 percent of the responding companies offered no compensation to board members.
2. 15 percent paid annual retainers ranging from $600 to $5,000 and averaging $2,000.
3. 15 percent paid annual retainers ranging from $600 to $5,000 and averaging $1,900; in addition, they paid meeting fees ranging from $35 to $500 and averaging $275 per meeting.
4. 25 percent paid only meeting fees, which ranged from $25 to $500 and averaged $210 per meeting.[9]

The fact that many companies can attract directors without paying directors' fees indicates that money is not the only factor involved. This may be somewhat misleading, however, because compensation rates for outsiders and nonfamily members in the study exceeded the rates for insiders and family members. This tended to bring down the average compensation level that was reported. Nevertheless, the compensation levels appear modest, assuming that the directors provide a meaningful contribution to the management of the firm.

An Alternative: A Board of Advisors

In recent years, increased attention has been directed to the legal responsibilities of directors. Under the law, outside directors may be held responsible for illegal company action even though they are not directly involved in wrongdoing. As a result of such legal pressures, some individuals are now reluctant to accept directorships.

One alternative that is used by some small companies is a *board of advisors*. Rather than being elected as directors, qualified outsiders are asked to serve as advisors to the company. The group of outsiders then functions in much the same way as a board of directors does.

The following account illustrates the potential value of an advisory board:

In another case, a seven-year-old diversified manufacturing company incurred its first deficit, which the owner-manager deemed an exception that further growth would rectify. Council members noted, however, that many distant operations were out of control and apparently unprofitable. They persuaded the owner to shrink his business by more than one-half. Almost immediately, the business began generating profits. From its reduced scale, growth resumed—this time soundly planned, financed, and controlled.[10]

By virtue of its advisory nature, a board of advisors does not set policy and avoids certain legal obligations to critique executive performance. This type of board may, consequently, pose less of a threat to the owner and possibly work more cooperatively than a conventional board.

Looking Back

1. The unplanned structure refers to the organization structure of small firms which often evolves with little conscious planning. Some conscious planning is usually desirable to eliminate weaknesses that creep into such naturally evolving structures.

2. Line organization involves a single chain of command, and all employees and managers are expected to go through channels as much as possible. In a line-and-staff organization, specialists are added to help or advise line personnel.

3. Informal relationships in an organization arise spontaneously and supplement formally prescribed relationships. The wise manager understands the potentially positive contribution of the informal organization and informal leaders.

4. Among the basic organizational concepts that are relevant to the organizing function are human factors and organization design, departmentation, delegation of authority, equality of authority and responsibility, and span of control. It appears that business success is correlated with the use of good organizational principles.

5. Boards of directors can contribute to small corporations by offering counsel and assistance to their chief executives. To be most effective, selected members of the board must be properly qualified and be independent outsiders.

DISCUSSION QUESTIONS

1. How large must a small firm be before it encounters problems of organization? As it grows, do its problems become more difficult to solve? Explain.

2. What type of small firm might properly use the line type of organization? When should its type of structure require change? To what type? Why?

3. Is the chain of command more than a conduit for orders? Explain.

4. What are the reasons for, and the dangers in, going outside of formal channels of communication in small firms?

5. In a line-and-staff organization, which positions are line positions? What is the proper relationship between line departments and staff departments?

6. When one employee becomes the recognized leader of an informal organization and has goals at variance with those of management, what should the manager do to correct the situation?

7. Should a manager disregard human considerations when an ideal organization structure is threatened? Explain.

8. What are the two most likely causes of failure to delegate authority properly? Is delegation important? Why?

9. Explain the relationships, if any, between span of control and proper delegation.

10. How might a board of directors be of real value to management in a small corporation? What are the qualifications essential to a person chosen as a director in a small corporation? Is stock ownership in the firm a prerequisite?

ENDNOTES

1. Unfortunately, most organization theory has been developed in large organizations. See Thomas C. Dandridge, "Children Are Not 'Little Grown-Ups': Small Business Needs Its Own Organizational Theory," *Journal of Small Business Management*, Vol. 17, No. 2 (April, 1979), pp. 53–57

2. Glenn H. Matthews, "Growing Concerns: Run Your Business or Build an Organization?" *Harvard Business Review*, Vol. 62, No. 2 (March–April, 1984), p. 35.

3. Leonardo Rodriguez, "Organization Principles and Financial Measures of Success in Cuban-Owned Businesses in Miami, Florida," *American Journal of Small Business*, Vol. 1 (October, 1976), pp. 23–29.

4. For a review of this topic as it applies to business organizations in general, see Milton C. Lauenstein, "Preserving the Impotence of the Board," *Harvard Business Review*, Vol. 55, No. 4 (July–August, 1977), pp. 36–38, 42, 46.

5. "The Venture Survey: Who Sits on Your Board?" *Venture*, Vol. 6, No. 4 (April, 1984), p. 32.

6. S. Kumar Jain, "Look to Outsiders to Strengthen Small Business Boards," *Harvard Business Review*, Vol. 58, No. 4 (July–August, 1980), p. 166.

7. "Conversation with Peter F. Drucker," *Organizational Dynamics* (New York: AMACOM, a division of American Management Associations, Spring, 1974), p. 49.

8. *Ibid.*

9. Jain, *op. cit.*, p. 169.

10. Harold W. Fox, "Growing Concerns: Quasi-boards—Useful Small Business Confidants," *Harvard Business Review*, Vol. 60, No. 1 (January–February, 1982), p. 164.

REFERENCES TO SMALL BUSINESS IN ACTION

Churchill, Neil. "I Was an Expert on Small Companies (Until I Tried to Run One)." *Inc.*, Vol. 3, No. 2 (February, 1981), pp. 84–88.

> This article presents the experiences of a business professor who became the chief operating officer of a small business. He describes some of the organizational and managerial problems he encountered.

Fox, Harold W. "Quasi-Board Monitors Management." *In Business*, Vol. 4, No. 3 (May–June, 1982), pp. 22–24.

> Krizman, Inc., a small manufacturer of automobile parts in Mishawaka, IN, uses an advisory board as a sounding board of competent executives who are detached from day-to-day problems. Management believes the advisory board keeps them on their toes and increases their sophistication in management.

Posner, Bruce C. "A Board Even an Entrepreneur Could Love." *Inc.*, Vol. 5, No. 4 (April, 1983), pp. 73–87.

> Amtrol, Inc., a privately owned manufacturing company in West Warwick, RI, listens carefully to the advice of four outside directors and uses many of their ideas. The contributions of those directors have enabled the company to remain profitable and financially strong.

Rose, Carol. "Strong Managers Made His Business Bloom." *Inc.*, Vol. 3, No. 2 (February, 1981), pp. 79–82.

> Dick Hutton, manager of a family-owned nursery business, concluded that he was the company's biggest impediment because he was spending too much time solving his subordinates' problems. Hutton's solution to this situation is described.

Wojahn, Ellen. "Management by Walking Away." *Inc.*, Vol. 5, No. 10 (October, 1983), pp. 68–76.

> The managers of Quad/Graphics, Inc., have developed a work team that can virtually run itself. Delegation is the core of many of their management methods.

CASE 15

Fourt Furniture Incorporated*
Uncharted organizational relationships

Fourt Furniture Store was founded in 1965 by Mr. and Mrs. Millard Fourt. The original store occupied a space of 5,000 square feet and was operated by the Fourts and two employees. Ben Lonsberry joined the business in 1974 as the general manager and then was elected president in 1978.

Corporate Growth

In 1974, Fourt Furniture had a sales volume of $400,000 and operated with 5 employees, including the Fourts and Lonsberry. Merchandise was warehoused in a separation location where the firm leased 8,000 square feet of space. The business was incorporated in May, 1975, as a Subchapter S corporation. In June of 1979, it elected to become a regular corporation.

Construction began on a second store location to be named Lonsberry's Home Furnishings in August, 1978. This location opened for business on December 20, 1978. By November, 1979, all administrative and accounting offices had been moved to the new location and all paperwork was being processed at Lonsberry's. Together, the 2 store locations had a total of 60,000 square feet of sales space and 52,000 square feet of warehousing space. In addition to retail furniture and accessory sales, the business included an interior design sales division and a contract furniture sales division.

The total annual sales volume of Fourt Furniture Incorporated had grown from $400,000 in 1974 to $3,250,000 in 1980; and the number of employees had grown from 5 to 46 (including 8 part-time employees) in the same time period. The firm's departments and number of employees were as follows:

Department	Number of Employees
Sales	15
Design	7
Accounting	5
Warehousing	11
Administrative and Support	8

*This case was prepared by Professor Kenneth A. Middleton of Baylor University.

Organizational Structure

No formal organizational chart had been formulated for the firm. The lines of power, authority, and delegation were defined only in the minds of each employee. However, each employee realized that Ben Lonsberry was the president and chief executive officer and that all decision-making power came from him.

Ben hired Don Baker in September of 1978 as company manager and general merchandise manager. Prior to 1978, Don had been employed as an engineer in a high-technology electronics firm. Don's responsibility as company manager and general merchandise manager was to oversee daily operations and coordinate the purchase of inventory. A very good working relationship had existed between Ben and Don from the very beginning.

In 1978, when Ben was elected president and chief executive officer, Millard Fourt had retired from active management of the corporation due to ill health. Mrs. Fourt, however, retained her position as corporate secretary-treasurer. The principal stockholders of Fourt Furniture Incorporated were:

Stockholder	Position
Ben Lonsberry	President and Chief Executive Officer
Jane Fourt	Secretary-Treasurer
Ray Sands	Vice-President

Ray Sands, who held the position of corporate vice-president, had no active role in the daily operations of the company. He acted as a voting member of management only and was active in the operation of his own other businesses.

If a chart of the firm's organizational structure were drawn, it would resemble a hub-and-wheel configuration as illustrated in Figure 15–6.

Management Style

Ben Lonsberry retained total control of daily operations in all phases of the corporation. It was not uncommon to see him building merchandise displays, moving inventory on the sales floor, and loading delivery trucks on any given day. He actively participated in the sale of merchandise and in routine housekeeping duties. He also instructed new sales personnel in sales techniques and helped store designers in color and fabric coordination and display.

Don Baker participated in the selection of merchandise and coordinated its delivery to the display floors and warehouse. Don was also involved in the

Figure 15–6   Organizational Relationships at Fourt Furniture, Inc.

training of new sales personnel and all general corporate personnel. He would also be observed loading and unloading delivery trucks, moving displays, selling merchandise, and answering the phone.

It can be said that each of these managers became totally involved in each facet of daily operations and that each gave daily directions to the other employees. Ben and Don were the type of individuals who are motivated by self-competition and do not need outside feedback or reinforcement concerning their job performance.

Organizational Problems

The lack of a formal organizational chart created an overlap of power and authority centers within the firm. Employees were unable to identify who their immediate supervisors were and whose directions and instructions should be followed. One person employed as a merchandise stocker identified nine individuals who gave him job instructions. This situation was shown to exist at all levels within the organization. The impression of the majority of employees was that no one really knew to whom he or she was accountable.

Mrs. Lonsberry and Mrs. Baker, the wives of the managers, frequently visited the two store locations. When they visited, they would suggest methods of merchandise display and fabric coordination to the design administrator. They would tell the merchandise stockers what needed to be done and what displays were to be rearranged. They would also assist the sales personnel in the selling of merchandise and indicate which product lines should be promoted.

The employees within this organization did not know how their job performance was reviewed by top management (Ben and Don). No formal evaluation or job reviews were utilized, and little verbal feedback was given. This frustration was evident when Ben was asked how he viewed Leo (a top salesperson) and when Leo was asked about his perceived status within the organization. Their respective comments illustrated the situation when Ben said, "Leo is one of our best. I couldn't be more pleased. I hope that he'll be with us for a long time because we sure need him." And Leo's reply was, "I feel that if I made a mistake today—I'm gone. I try to do my job, and the money isn't bad. But I'm not sure if they like me. I'd like to know if I'm doing a good job or not. I may leave at the end of the month." It must be noted that this was not an isolated case because this situation existed at all levels within the organization.

Questions

1. Evaluate the overall performance of Fourt Furniture Incorporated. What does this show about the effectiveness of its management?
2. Identify the various organizational problems in this business. Which appears to be the most serious? Why?
3. What are the probable causes of Ben Lonsberry's practices regarding delegation of authority? As a consultant, what changes, if any, would you recommend? How would you suggest that these changes be effected?
4. Outline an organizational plan for the firm, and defend any changes you propose.

16

Managing Human Resources in Small Firms

Figure 16-1   Peter L. Sheeran

While small firms often find it difficult to pay competitive salaries, some have offered special financial incentives which enable them to attract talented personnel. Peter L. Sheeran, president of Sheeran Cleveland Architects, needed such a plan to reduce turnover among architects and designers.

"We wanted," Sheeran says, "to find a way to reward people, so that they knew the harder they worked, the more money they made. A profit-sharing plan seemed to fit the bill." That first year, Sheeran Cleveland's profit-sharing plan doled out a generous 50 percent of the firm's earnings to employees. In no time at all, productivity jumped. "People started working nights and coming in early," Sheeran recalls, "and they started taking on more responsibilities without the partners having to delegate it to them."

What's more, Sheeran Cleveland's turnover rate slowed down dramatically—almost to the vanishing point. And the firm found itself in the enviable position of being able to recruit architects and designers from competing firms. "Usually," Sheeran says, "partners want the profits for themselves. Our profit-sharing plan set us apart from those other firms."

Source: Donna Sammons Carpenter, "We're in the Money." Reprinted with permission, *Inc.* magazine (November, 1984). Copyright © (1984) by Inc. Publishing Company, 38 Commercial Wharf, Boston, MA 02110.

Looking Ahead

Watch for the following important topics:

1. Recruiting and selecting personnel.
2. Steps in evaluating job applicants.
3. Training and development.
4. Financial and nonfinancial compensation.
5. Effective human relationships in small firms.

Smallness creates a unique situation in the management of human resources. For example, the owner of a small retail store cannot adopt the human resources program of Sears, Roebuck and Company, which has 450,000 employees, by merely scaling it down. The atmosphere of a small firm also creates distinctive opportunities to develop strong relationships among its members. In view of the special employment characteristics associated with smallness, the entrepreneur needs to develop a human resources program which is directly applicable to a small firm.

RECRUITING AND SELECTING PERSONNEL

The initial step in a sound human resources program is the recruitment of capable employees. In recruiting, the small firm competes with both large and small businesses. It cannot afford to let competitors take the cream of the crop. Aggressive recruitment requires the employer to take the initiative in locating applicants and to search until enough applicants are available to permit a good choice.

Importance of People

Employing the right people and getting their enthusiastic performance are keys to business success. Financial resources and physical resources will eventually be insufficient if adequate human resources are lacking. In many small businesses, sales are directly related to the attitudes of employees and their ability to serve customer needs. The effective use of people is also crucial because payroll expense is one of the largest expense categories for most small firms.

Since people are important, the entrepreneur must give high priority to recruiting and selecting employees. This beginning step establishes the foundation for a firm's on-going human relationships. If talented, ambitious recruits can be obtained, the business will be able to build a strong human organization through effective management.

Sources of Employees

To recruit effectively, the small firm must know where and how to obtain qualified applicants. The sources are numerous, and one cannot generalize about the best source in view of the variations in personnel requirements and quality of sources from one locality to another. Some major sources of employees are discussed below.

Unsolicited Applicants A firm may receive any number of unsolicited applications from acceptable or unacceptable individuals of various backgrounds. If qualified applicants cannot be hired immediately, their applications should be kept on file for future reference. In the interest of good public relations, all applicants should be treated courteously whether or not they are offered jobs.

Schools Secondary schools, trade schools, colleges, and universities are desirable sources for certain classes of employees, particularly those who need no specific work experience. Secondary and trade schools provide applicants with a limited but useful educational background. Colleges and universities can supply candidates for positions in management and in various technical and scientific fields. In addition, many colleges are excellent sources of part-time employees.

Public Employment Offices State employment offices, which are affiliated with the United States Employment Service, offer, without cost, a supply of applicants who are actively seeking employment. These offices attempt to place applicants on the basis of work experience, education, and extensive psychological testing. Public employment offices are located in all major cities.

Private Employment Agencies Numerous private agencies offer their services as employment offices. In most cases an employer receives their services without cost because the applicant pays a fee to the agency. However, some firms pay the fee if the applicant is highly qualified. Whether or not private employment agencies can be used profitably depends upon their services and the quality of the applicants listed with them.

Employee Referrals If current employees are good employees, their recommendations may provide excellent prospects. Ordinarily, current employees will hesitate to recommend applicants thought to be inferior in ability. Many small-business owners say that this source provides more of their employees than any other source.

ACTION REPORT
Hiring Interns from a State University

Cleveland State University sponsors a cooperative education program which allows business firms to employ interns for three months of the year. Kalcor Coatings Company, a small manufacturer in Willoughby, OH, has found the program useful in obtaining short-term employees with technical training and also in sizing up students as prospects for subsequent full-time employment. A representative of Kalcor states:

> Since joining the program, we've employed five interns, with mixed results. Two students were downright lazy, one was mediocre, and two were excellent.
>
> Jack and Steve (the names are fictitious) both had a bad habit of sleeping on the job. Jack, however, was industrious—at avoiding work. He decided to test random samples at the quality control station and, at times, fudged the results on the rest. In his spare hours, he dozed, neglecting the R&D labs. Jack and Steve received poor evaluations for their efforts.
>
> Bill and Ellen, on the other hand, showed enough initiative to finish their scheduled work early and seek out work in other departments. Bill became a company "utility" person, helping out wherever he was needed. Ellen was so helpful in the lab that we hired her again for another term just to do lab work. We hope to hire her when she reaches the job market—we know what kind of worker we'd be getting.
>
> Overall, we're pleased with the results. The way we look at it, we got to look over five prospective employees without making any commitment. We were able to benefit from some fresh ideas and genuine enthusiasm. And we were able to see what kind of people are available while getting a glimpse of the training they are likely to receive.

Source: M. Cory Zucker, "School Interns Get High Marks from Us," *Inc.*, Vol. 2, No. 9 (September, 1980), p. 38.

Help-Wanted Advertising   The "Help Wanted" sign in the window of a business establishment is one form of recruiting used by small firms. More aggressive recruitment takes the form of advertisements in the classified pages of local newspapers. Although the effectiveness of this source has been questioned by some, the fact remains that many well-managed organizations recruit in this way. Advertising is particularly useful when there is a shortage of highly skilled personnel, scientists, or professional employees.

Selection Guidelines

The small-business manager should analyze the functions required by the business and determine the number and kinds of jobs to be filled. Knowing the job requirements and the capacities and characteristics of the individual applicants permits a more intelligent selection of persons for specific jobs. In particular, the small business should attempt to obtain individuals whose capacities and skills complement those of the owner–manager.

Certainly the owner–manager should not select personnel simply to fit a rigid specification of education, experience, or personal background. Rather, the employer must concentrate upon the ability of an individual to fill a particular position in the business.

Finally, some legal requirements must be met when selecting applicants for employment. Age, gender, minority status, and physical handicaps are employment factors that are covered by federal laws and, in many cases, state laws as well. An excellent outline of the basic requirements of the major federal employment rules and regulations appears in a publication of the Bank of America.[1]

ACTION REPORT
Equal Employment Opportunity Regulation

Small business faces many of the same employment regulations that apply to big business. According to one source:

> One Philadelphia area contractor, Dane DiGaetano, became a classic example when, with only three employees (one black), and a modest federal contract for $112,000, he was hounded by contract compliance officers for failure to fill in reports correctly, for not having separate toilets for women, and for failure to set a hiring goal for women. He finally had a "conciliation agreement" forced on him that puts the burden of proof on him, not the government, that he is obeying the law.

Source: Reprinted from the May 25, 1981 issue of *Business Week* by special permission, © 1981 by McGraw-Hill, Inc., New York, NY 10020. All rights reserved.

Recruiting Managerial and Professional Personnel

Personnel filling managerial and professional positions are obviously important in any business, especially in one that is small. Their recruitment, therefore, deserves special attention and also involves some special considerations.

Technical competence is necessary, as it is in a large business, but versatility may be an even more important virtue in the small-firm setting. "The day will come when that engineer has to go out and make sales calls. He had better be the sort that can do it. By the same token, the marketing people should be able to get a handle on a wrench. So you need versatility and flexibility."[2]

Finding capable, experienced key employees is often difficult. For this reason, some small firms, especially high-tech firms, turn to executive search firms (headhunters) to locate qualified candidates. Armos Corporation, a new scientifically oriented firm in San Francisco, is an example of a firm using this approach in filling top management positions.[3] Although the fee is equal to one-third of each person's salary, the founders of this firm feel it is worth the payment because of their own lack of time to engage in such a search.

Evaluation of Applicants

Many techniques for evaluating applicants are available to the small business. An uninformed, blind gamble on new employees may be avoided by following the series of steps described below.

Step 1—Use of Application Forms   The value of having an applicant complete an application form lies in its systematic collection of background data that might otherwise be overlooked. The information recorded on application forms is useful in sizing up an applicant and serves as a guide in making a more detailed investigation of the applicant's experience and character.

An application form need not be elaborate or lengthy. In fact, it need not even be a printed sheet. A simple application form is illustrated in Figure 16–2. In drawing up such a form, the employer should remember that questions concerning race or religion are prohibited by the Civil Rights Act of 1964. Even questions about education must be demonstrably job-related.

Step 2—Interviewing the Applicant   An employment interview permits the employer to get some idea of the applicant's appearance, job knowledge, intelligence, and personality. Any of these factors may be significant in the job to be filled. Although the interview is an important step in the process of selection, it should not be the only step. Some individuals have the mistaken idea that they are infallible judges of human nature on the basis of interviews alone.

The profitability of the interview depends upon the interviewer's skill and methods. Any interviewer can improve the quality of interviewing by following these generally accepted principles:

1. Determine the questions you want to ask before beginning the interview.
2. Conduct the interview in a quiet atmosphere.
3. Give your entire attention to the applicant.
4. Put the applicant at ease.
5. Never argue.
6. Keep the conversation at a level suited to the applicant.
7. Listen attentively.

Figure 16-2   Simplified Application Form

APPLICATION FORM

1. PERSONAL DATA

Name _____ Social Security No. _____

Address _____ Tel. No. _____

2. WORK EXPERIENCE

Present or last job:
Name and address of employer _____
Dates of employment _____
Title of your job _____
What kind of work did you perform? _____
_____
Why did you leave? _____

Next-to-last job:
Name and address of employer _____
Dates of employment _____
Title of your job _____
What kind of work did you perform? _____
_____
Why did you leave? _____

3. EDUCATION

High School:
Name and address of school _____
Did you graduate? _____ When? _____

College or Specialized School:
Name and address of school _____
Did you graduate? _____ When? _____
Nature of course _____

4. REFERENCES (List three references not mentioned above)

NAME	*ADDRESS*	*OCCUPATION*

---

8. Observe closely the applicant's speech, mannerisms, and attire if these characteristics are important to the job.
9. Try to avoid being unduly influenced by the applicant's trivial mannerisms or superficial resemblance to other people you know.

To avoid the possibility of running into legal problems with the Equal Employment Opportunity Commission (EEOC), the interviewer should refrain from:

1. Direct or indirect inquiries that will reveal the applicant's national, ethnic, or racial origin.
2. Questions to female applicants on marital status, number and age of children, pregnancy, or future child-bearing plans.
3. Inquiries about arrest or conviction records, unless such information is demonstrably job-related.

Step 3—Checking References and Further Investigation When contacted, most references listed on application forms give a rose-colored picture of the applicant's character and ability. Nevertheless, careful checking with former employers, school authorities, and other references can be most constructive. A written letter of inquiry to these references is probably the weakest form of checking because people hesitate to put damaging statements in writing. However, individuals who provide little useful information in response to a written request often speak more frankly when approached by telephone or in person.

For a fee, an applicant's history (financial, criminal, employment, and so on) may be supplied by personal investigation agencies or local credit bureaus. If an employer needs an investigative consumer report to establish the applicant's eligibility for employment, the Fair Credit Reporting Act requires that the applicant be notified in writing prior to the request for such a report.

Step 4—Testing the Applicant Many kinds of jobs lend themselves to performance testing. For example, a typist may be given some material to type to verify the typing speed and accuracy previously reported. With a little ingenuity, employers may improvise practical tests pertinent to most of the positions in their businesses.

Psychologial examinations may also be used by small-business firms, but the results can easily be misleading because of difficulty in interpretation or in adapting the tests to a particular business. In addition, the United States Supreme Court has approved the EEOC's requirement that *any* test used in making employment decisions must be job-related.

Step 5—Physical Examinations Though frequently neglected, physical examinations of applicants are of practical value to the small business. Few small firms have staff physicians, but arrangements can be made with a local doctor to administer the examinations. The employer, of course, should pay for the cost of the physical examination. In a few occupations, physical examinations are required by law; but even when they are not legally required, it is wise to discover physical limitations and possible contagious diseases of all new employees.

Leasing Employees

Leasing equipment or property has long been an accepted alternative to buying it. Leasing employees, as surprising as it may seem, is also an alternative to hiring one's own employees!

For temporary personnel needs, employers have turned to firms like Kelly Services, Manpower, and other private employment agencies. By paying a fee based upon the number of hours worked, a small firm can obtain qualified people on short notice to help with emergency projects or to fill in for vacationing employees. (In some cases, employers later hire on a full-time basis those temporary employees they find to be well-qualified.)

However, leasing employees is not limited to temporary personnel replacements. An estimated 275 leasing companies have emerged in recent years to lease personnel to thousands of small businesses.[4] For a fee of from 5 to 10 percent of payroll, the leasing company takes over all personnel paperwork. The small firms benefit by escaping the red tape related to payroll and employee records. However, they do not necessarily escape the tasks of recruitment and selection. Many leasing contracts simply involve shifting a small firm's employees to the leasing company's payroll at some specified date.

Many employees also like the leasing arrangement. Since leasing companies typically employ several hundred people, they can afford to offer benefits which are superior to those possible in most small firms.

TRAINING AND DEVELOPMENT

Once an employee has been recruited and added to the payroll, the process of training and development must begin. The new recruit is the "raw material," and the well-trained technician, salesperson, manager, or other employee, is the "finished product."

Purposes of Training and Development

One obvious purpose of training is to prepare the new recruit to perform the duties for which he or she has been employed. There are very few positions in industry for which no training is required. It would be a rare individual who had an adequate background when applying for employment. If the employer fails to provide training, the new employee must proceed by trial and error, frequently with a waste of time, materials, and money.

Training to improve skills and knowledge is not limited to newcomers. The performance of current employees may often be improved through additional training. In view of the constant change in products, technology, policies, and procedures in the world of business—even in a small business—training is necessary to update knowledge and skills. Only in this way can personnel be rendered capable of meeting the changing demands placed upon them.

Both employers and employees also have a stake in the advancement of personnel to higher level positions. Preparation for advancement usually involves developmental efforts—possibly of a different type than those needed to sharpen skills for current duties.

In view of the fact that personal development and advancement are prime concerns of able employees, the small business can profit from careful attention to this phase of the personnel program. If the opportunity to grow and move up in an organization exists, it not only improves the morale of current employees, but also offers an inducement for outsiders to accept employment.

Orientation for New Personnel

The developmental process begins with the employee's first two or three days on the job. It is at this point that a new person tends to feel "lost." Much is confusing—a new physical layout, different job title, unknown fellow employees, different type of supervision, changed hours or work schedule, and a unique set of personnel policies and procedures. Any surprises that conflict with the newcomer's expectations are interpreted in the light of his or her previous work experience, and these interpretations can foster a strong commitment to the new employer or lead to feelings of alienation.

At this point of great sensitivity of the new employee, the employer can contribute to a positive effect by proper orientation. Initial steps can be taken to help the newcomer adjust and to minimize feelings of uneasiness in the new setting.

In addition to explaining specific job duties, supervisors can outline the firm's policies and procedures in as much detail as possible. The new employee should be encouraged to ask questions, and time should be taken to provide careful answers. The employer may facilitate the orientation process by giving the recruit a written list of company procedures. These may include information about work hours, paydays, breaks, lunch hours, absences, holidays, names of supervisors, employee benefits, and so on.

Training Nonmanagerial Employees

For all classes of employees, more training is accomplished on the job than through any other method. The weakness of on-the-job training results from the use of haphazard learning in contrast to planned, controlled training programs. A system designed to make on-the-job training more effective is known as Job Instruction Training (JIT). The steps of this program, listed below, are intended to help the manager who is not a professional educator in "getting through" to the nonmanagerial employee.

1. *Prepare the employee.* Put the employee at ease. Find out what he or she already knows about the job. Get the employee interested in learning the job. Place the employee in an appropriate job.
2. *Present the operations.* Tell, show, illustrate, and question carefully and patiently. Stress key points. Instruct clearly and completely, taking up one point at a time—but no more than the employee can master.
3. *Try out performance.* Test the employee by having him or her perform the job. Have the employee tell, show, and explain key points. Ask questions and correct errors. Continue until the employee knows that he or she knows how to do the job.
4. *Follow up.* Check frequently. Designate to whom the employee should go for help. Encourage questions. Get the employee to look for the key points as he or she progresses. Taper off extra coaching and close follow-up.

Developing Managerial and Professional Employees

The small business faces a particularly serious need for developing managerial and professional employees. Depending on the size of the firm, there may be few or many key positions. Regardless of the number, individuals must be developed in or for these key positions if the business is to function most effectively. Incumbents should be developed to the point that they can adequately carry out the responsibilities assigned to them. Ideally, potential replacements should also be available for key individuals who retire or leave for other reasons. The entrepreneur often postpones grooming a personal replacement, but this step is likewise important in assuring a smooth transition in the management of a small firm.

In accomplishing management training, the manager should give serious consideration to the following factors:

1. *Determine the need for training.* What vacancies are expected? Who needs to be trained? What type of training and how much training does each of them need?
2. *Develop the plan for training.* How can the individuals be trained? Do they currently have enough responsibility to permit them to learn? Can they be assigned additional duties? Should they be given temporary assignments in other areas—for example, should they be shifted from production to sales? Would additional schooling be of benefit?

3. *Establish a timetable.* When should training be started? How much can be accomplished in the next six months or one year?

4. *Counsel with employees.* Do the individuals understand their need for training? Are they aware of the prospects for them in the firm? Has an understanding been reached as to the nature of training? Have the employees been consulted regularly about progress in their work and problems confronting them? Have they been given the benefit of the owner's experience and insights without having decisions made for them?

COMPENSATION AND INCENTIVES FOR SMALL-BUSINESS EMPLOYEES

Compensation and financial incentives are important to all employees, and the small firm must acknowledge the central role of the paycheck and any "extras" in attracting and motivating personnel. In addition, small firms can also offer several nonfinancial incentives which appeal to both managerial and nonmanagerial employees.

Wage or Salary Levels

In general, small firms find that they must be roughly competitive in wage or salary levels in order to attract well-qualified personnel. Wages or salaries paid to employees either are based on increments of time—such as an hour, a day, a month—or vary directly with their output. Compensation based on increments of time is commonly referred to as **daywork**. The daywork system is most appropriate for types of work where performance is not easily measurable. It is the most common compensation system in American industry and is easy to understand and administer.

Financial Incentives

Those firms that have good prospects for growth can offer applicants the opportunity to grow and share the prosperity of the business. For managerial and professional employees, stock options which are offered by growing firms serve as powerful inducements in recruiting.

In order to motivate nonmanagerial employees to increase their productivity, incentive systems have been devised. Incentive wages may constitute an employee's entire earnings or may supplement regular daywork wages. Some financial incentive plans are the *piecework system*, the *production bonus system*, and the *commission system*, which is widely used to compensate salespersons.

Other types of financial incentives which are less directly related to employee output consist of *profit-sharing plans* and *fringe benefits*. Profit sharing provides more direct work incentive in small companies than in large ones because the connection between individual performance and company success can be more easily understood and appreciated by employees in small firms. On the other hand, fringe benefits (which usually include vacations, holidays, group insurance, pensions, and severance pay) are expensive for the small firm. Obviously, the costs of these benefits add substantially to the direct wage costs, which may account for more than 50 percent of the small firm's operating expense. Nevertheless, the small firm cannot ignore fringe benefits if it is to compete effectively for good employees.

ACTION REPORT
Lavish Fringe Benefits

Throughout our business history, a few employers have provided lavish fringe benefits as part of their employee relations programs. Some were part of well-conceived compensation plans, some were fads, some represented crude attempts to buy employee loyalty, and some were highly paternalistic. One 69-year-old family firm which has prospered while successfully offering elaborate benefits is Fel-Pro, a highly profitable producer of gaskets and sealants for engines.

It is also renowned for some other things, such as the converted horse farm where employees can garden on weekends, or send their children to summer camp, or get married. Then there is the company-subsidized day-care center, not to mention the gym. At Fel-Pro, no holiday goes by without a gift for each worker: a box of chocolates on Valentine's Day, a canned ham on Easter, a tin of pistachio nuts on Thanksgiving, a turkey on Christmas. There are monetary gifts, too, for practically every event in the human life cycle: $100 for a birth, $500 for an adoption, and up to $5,000 for a child's college tuition. And, lest the spirit need elevating as well, the company has a half-time sculptor on the payroll, whose sole job is to create gasket art.

Source: Reprinted with permission, *Inc.* magazine (January, 1986). Copyright © (1986) by Inc. Publishing Company, 38 Commercial Wharf, Boston, MA 02110.

Nonfinancial Incentives

Although small firms must be competitive in levels of compensation, they can also emphasize their unique features as they attempt to attract well-qualified personnel. Not all of the recruiting advantages lie with large corporations. Small firms, particularly those which appear to be fast-growing, high-potential businesses, appeal to individuals who shun the stultifying atmosphere of bureaucratic corporations. M. Alison McGrath, assistant dean and director of placement for the Kellogg Graduate School of Management at Northwestern University, has said:

A growing number of our students want to work for a small business. They believe there will be fewer layers to the top than if they worked for a big corporation, and that they will have a better chance of ending up in a position of real responsibility.[5]

It should be obvious, of course, that the degree of opportunity depends on the management practices of a small firm. An entrepreneur who is reluctant to delegate authority does not provide the type of opportunity sought by these young people.

Some small firms, it should be made clear, do offer their professional and managerial personnel greater freedom than they would have in big business. According to one writer, the president of a small electronics company in California, Marshall Fitzgerald, has emphasized this advantage of the small firm as follows:

> Fitzgerald says he has managed to win in the Silicon Valley bidding wars not by offering more money than his better-financed rivals, but by better understanding what motivates and attracts the different kinds of employees his company needs.
>
> "We start by identifying an expert in a key area where we need superior talent," explains Fitzgerald. "We lure him into the company by offering him more freedom than he'll probably ever get in a large bureaucracy. And then we use him as a magnet to attract a supporting staff of people who want an opportunity to work with a superstar."
>
> "Good people are motivated as much by creative challenges, by a chance to learn and grow, as they are by paychecks," Fitzgerald adds. "Here's where a small company actually has an advantage over a large organization. We can give a person a job and let him run with it."[6]

In the small firm, key personnel may also have the opportunity for a more diversified type of experience. Their positions or assignments are often broader in scope, and their impact on the business is more evident. A vice-president of an international executive search firm, Kieran J. Hackett, has described the type of person who may be attracted to the smaller company as follows:

> The best small-company managers are entrepreneurial personalities—people who are willing to bank on themselves and their efforts. They don't want to turn around and blame somebody else if something goes wrong. The right kind of person likes doing things himself. He hates watching his plans filter through layers of management, and he hates carrying out other people's plans even more.[7]

In lower level positions, the advantages cited above are less persuasive, and wage rates are relatively more important. Even here, however, small-firm flexibility may be attractive.

Legislation Affecting Wages

Various external influences affect the setting of compensation levels for employees. For example, wages cannot be established on an individual basis when employees are represented by a union. Furthermore, the small firm cannot afford to pay more than its competitors unless the higher wage stimulates greater productivity. Perhaps the most important external influence on wage-setting is the applicable federal and state legislation.

Compensation levels are subject to various federal statutes. The most comprehensive law is the Fair Labor Standards Act, which establishes minimum wage rates and requires the payment of overtime rates for hours over 40 per week. The Equal Pay Act of 1963 specifies that women and men shall be paid at the same rate "for equal work on jobs requiring equal skill, effort, and responsibility which are performed under similar working conditions within the same establishment."

Many states have also legislated in the field of wages and hours, and those with comprehensive fair employment practice laws now include sex discrimination among the prohibitions. The minimum wage provisions of state laws, however, are generally lower than those of the Fair Labor Standards Act. In cases where state fair employment practice laws have been found to conflict with state "protective" laws prohibiting the employment of women in certain types of work and/or regulating the hours they work, the fair employment laws have been consistently upheld in both state and federal courts.

EFFECTIVE HUMAN RELATIONSHIPS IN THE SMALL FIRM

Satisfactory compensation, company picnics, and fringe benefits do not guarantee harmony in employer–employee relationships. These elements of a personnel program are only part of the total fabric of interpersonal relationships. Some of the more general concerns which are significant in building effective teamwork are discussed below.

Effective Communication

The key to healthy interpersonal relationships lies in effective communication. To be sure, much communication flows in the form of orders and instructions to employees. But communication is a two-way process, and it is difficult for employees to be either intelligent or enthusiastic teamworkers if they do not know the reasons for such orders and instructions. Furthermore, the opportunity to contribute ideas and opinions *before* the manager decides an issue adds dignity to the job in the eyes of most employees.

Other aspects leading to effective communication include telling employees where they stand, how the business is doing, and what plans are for the future. Negative feedback to employees may be necessary at times, but positive feedback is the primary tool for establishing good human relations.

Perhaps the most fundamental concept to keep in mind is that employees are people. They quickly detect insincerity, but they respond to honest efforts to treat them as mature, responsible individuals.

ACTION REPORT
Effective Two-Way Communication

Hope's Windows, Inc., is a custom manufacturer of steel and aluminum windows located in Jamestown, NY. In 1977, the company experienced a drop in orders in one of its key markets, forcing the layoff of 23 of 35 employees. The problem was caused by the bidding process, which produced bids that were consistently too high.

To solve the problem, Hope's management appealed to employees who made the windows. The company created a bidding committee made up of managers and production workers which proved successful in winning most of their subsequent bids. Dale Mansfield, a ten-year veteran at Hope's, commented as follows:

> In a lot of companies the managers act like they're too good to be speaking to a "nobody." Here they listen to people like me. No manager can do every job or understand every job. So how can he always know what needs to be done? I don't think managers are relinquishing anything by asking us what we think. We're just providing the information; management still has to make the decisions. But, with their ideas and our ideas, maybe we can come up with something that will really help the company.

Source: "Hope's Windows, Inc.: Surviving with the Workers' Help," *Inc.*, Vol. 3, No. 4 (April, 1981), pp. 82–84.

To go beyond good intentions in communicating, a small-firm manager may adopt some practical techniques of stimulating two-way communication. A few examples, by no means exhaustive, are the following:

1. Periodic performance review sessions as a time for discussing the employee's ideas, questions, complaints, and job expectations.
2. Bulletin boards to keep employees informed about developments affecting them and/or the company.
3. Suggestion boxes as a means of soliciting employee ideas.
4. Staff meetings for the discussion of problems and matters of general concern.

These methods can be used to supplement the most basic of all channels for communication—the day-to-day interaction between each employee and his or her supervisor.

Personal Contact Between Employees and Entrepreneur

Employees of a small firm get to know the owner–manager personally within a relatively short period of time. As the result of day-to-day contact, the owner–manager can be understanding when employees have personal problems. If the employer–employee relationship is good, the employee develops a strong feeling of personal loyalty to the employer, coupled with a stronger sense of responsibility than is likely in a large business. How could you feel deeply about the president of a large corporation whom you have never seen?

On the other hand, there is a danger in the reluctance of an employer to discipline those employees who are also friends. For example, Miss Ash, the owner of a small supermarket, employs an old acquaintance, Mrs. Gray. Miss Ash is aware of Mrs. Gray's acute need of a job. Mrs. Gray's main duty is to be the cashier. In performing her work, however, she is extremely choosy about what she will do. When there are no customers to be checked out, for instance, Mrs. Gray refuses to arrange stock on the shelves or perform other work. The long-suffering Miss Ash permits this situation to exist because of her sympathy for Mrs. Gray as a friend.

Informal Personnel Relationships

Most small firms do not have the written personnel policies and formalized procedures that are found in large companies. The advantage of the small firm's informality lies in the manager's ability to devise solutions to fit particular personnel problems. Individual considerations may be taken into account, and problems that do not fit a rule book may be solved in the most appropriate manner.

The danger inherent in the informal solution of personnel problems on a case-by-case basis is that solutions may be improvised without proper thought. The quick answer may not be the right answer, and precedents established might prove to be embarrassing later. Placing some minimal set of policies in writing is usually desirable as a safeguard against the dangers of excessive informality.

The Entrepreneur's Pervading Influence

A large firm may need years to educate lower-level supervisors who may misunderstand or even sabotage any new personnel philosophy that needs to be introduced into the business. In contrast, a weakness in personnel philosophy may be seen and corrected immediately by the owner–manager of a small firm. Suppose, for example, that the decision has been made to change from fighting a union to cooperating with it. If the owner–manager is the only manager in the business, the new philosophy can be adopted completely without delay. Even if there are additional managers, the new philosophy can be quickly explained to them and relayed in turn to all other employees.

This pervading influence of the owner–manager can be a disadvantage, however, when he or she has a specialized background in one functional area of business, say, production management. In day-to-day operations, there looms a diversity of pressing production problems, sales problems, and financial problems. Personnel problems, in contrast, appear less critical—at least in their early stages. As a result, the owner–manager may become so enmeshed in production, sales, or financial problems that human relations factors are inadvertently ignored.

Use of a Personnel Manager

A firm with only a few employees cannot afford a full-time specialist to deal with personnel problems. Some of the more involved personnel tools and techniques which are required in large businesses may be unnecessarily complicated for the small business. As it grows in size, however, its personnel problems will increase in both number and complexity.

The point at which it becomes logical to hire a personnel manager cannot be specified precisely. Each entrepreneur must decide whether the type and size of the business would make it profitable to employ a personnel specialist. Hiring a part-time personnel manager might be a logical first step in some instances.

Some conditions that encourage the appointment of a personnel manager in a small business are:

1. When there is a substantial number of employees. (What is "substantial" varies with the business, but 100 employees is suggested as a guide.)
2. When employees are represented by a union.
3. When the labor turnover rate is high.
4. When the need for skilled or professional personnel creates problems in recruitment or selection.
5. When supervisors or operative employees require considerable training.
6. When employee morale is unsatisfactory.
7. When competition for operative personnel is keen.

Labor Unions and Small Business

Most entrepreneurs prefer to operate independently and to avoid unionization. Indeed, most small businesses are not unionized. To some extent, this results from the predominance of small business in such areas as services, where unionization is less common than in manufacturing. Also, unions typically concentrate their primary attention on large companies.

This does not mean, of course, that labor unions are unknown in small firms. Many types of firms—building and electrical contractors, for example—negotiate labor contracts and employ unionized personnel. The need to work with a union formalizes and, to some extent, complicates the relationship between the small firm and its employees.

If employees wish to bargain collectively, the law requires the employer to participate in such bargaining. The demand for labor union representation may arise from labor dissatisfaction with the work environment and employment relationships. By following enlightened personnel policies, the small firm can minimize the likelihood of labor organization and/or contribute to healthy management–union relationships.[8]

Looking Back

1. To obtain capable employees, the small firm must take the initiative in seeking applicants. Sources include unsolicited applicants, schools, public and private employment agencies, friends and acquaintances of current employees, and advertising. The selection process must conform to legislation applying to the hiring of minorities and other special employment groups. Leasing employees is an alternative to hiring used by some firms.

2. Steps in the evaluation of applicants include the use of an application form, applicant interviewing, checking references and background investigation, testing, and physical examinations.

3. Both managerial and nonmanagerial employees of small firms require training to develop skill and knowledge in their jobs and to prepare them for promotion. The need for developing personnel at the managerial and professional levels is particularly acute.

4. Small firms must be competitive in wage and salary levels. They can also use both financial and nonfinancial incentives. As an example of the latter, freedom to operate with a minimum of bureaucratic control is appealing to many managerial and professional employees.

5. Effective teamwork in small firms can be developed by effective communication, close personal contact between the owner–manager and the employees, appropriate discipline, and informality in relationships. In some cases, the development of a personnel program also involves the use of a personnel manager and bargaining with a labor union.

DISCUSSION QUESTIONS

1. Discuss with the owner or manager of a small firm the sources that the firm uses for obtaining new employees. In particular, ask for the owner's opinion of the relative value of the available sources.

2. How might the manager of a small business be aggressive in recruiting new employees? Explain.

3. Do small firms that cannot afford elaborate employment procedures suffer a competitive disadvantage in comparison to larger companies? Why?

4. For what types of jobs would it be practical to inquire closely into the applicant's arrest and conviction record? Explain.

5. Consider the small business with which you are best acquainted. Has adequate provision been made to replace key management personnel? Is the firm using any form of executive development?

6. What problems are involved in using incentive wage systems in a small firm? Would the nature of the work affect management's decision concerning use or nonuse of wage incentives? Why?

7. Is the use of a profit-sharing system desirable in a small business? What major difficulties might be associated with its use when intended to provide greater employee motivation?

8. What types of nonfinancial incentives can be used by a small firm to attract highly qualified managers?

9. List the factors in small-business operation that encourage the appointment of a personnel manager. Should a personnel manager always be hired on a full-time basis? Why or why not?

10. It has been said that labor unions have been more successful in their organizing efforts in small manufacturing firms than in small merchandising firms. Why is this true?

ENDNOTES

1. See "Personnel Guidelines," *Small Business Reporter*, 1985, published by the Bank of America, San Francisco, CA.

2. Thomas P. Murphy, "Peopling a Business," *Forbes*, Vol. 130, No. 11 (November 22, 1982), p. 270.

3. Dave Lindorff, "Assembling Your Team," *Venture*, Vol. 3, No. 5 (May, 1981), p. 44.

4. "Employees Learn to Love Being Leased Out," *Fortune*, Vol. 111, No. 7 (April 1, 1985), p. 80.

5. Rita Stollman, "Jobs in Small Business," *Business Week's Guide to Careers*, Spring/Summer, 1984, p. 60.

6. James Fawcette, "Money Alone Can't Buy Top Talent," *Inc.*, Vol. 3, No. 3 (March, 1981), p. 92.

7. "Can a Small Company Attract Top Managers?" *Inc.*, Vol. 3, No. 5 (May, 1981), p. 138.

8. For a further discussion of this topic, see Linda A. Roxe, *Personnel Management for the Smaller Company* (New York: AMACOM, 1979), Chapter 10.

REFERENCES TO SMALL BUSINESS IN ACTION

"Entrepreneurial Trap." *Forbes*, Vol. 125, No. 7 (March 31, 1980), pp. 86–91.
> The founder of Lawter Chemicals experienced difficulty—but eventually succeeded—in hiring and delegating decision making to qualified professional assistants. However, he has still failed to designate a successor for his own position.

Kuntzleman, Charles T., and Dan Runyon. "Fitness for Ten Employees or Less." *In Business*, Vol. 4, No. 4 (July–August, 1982), pp. 58–59.
> Physical fitness programs provided by specific small firms are described. Smallness does not preclude the offering of this type of fringe benefit.

Sambul, Nathan J. "Fine Tune Your Training Program." *Inc.*, Vol. 2, No. 8 (August, 1980), pp. 74–76.
> The author describes the use of videotape equipment in the training programs of various small businesses.

Tanner, Ronald. "Picking a President." *Venture*, Vol. 5, No. 7 (July, 1983), pp. 46–48.
> The actions taken by several small firms to fill key management positions by recruiting personnel from *Fortune 500* companies are described.

Wood, Robert C. "How to Do Without Employees." *Inc.*, Vol. 5, No. 1 (January, 1983), pp. 81–82.
> This article describes the services provided by PayStaff, Inc., a new and growing firm which leases employees to 200 small businesses. Employee benefits received by the more than 1,000 employees are outlined.

CASE 16

The Case of the Dirty Washrooms*
Poor employee practices become a source of complaints

A supervisory workshop began to bog down as foremen expressed their gripes and their criticisms about inaction at higher management levels. The workshop leader eventually asked the foremen to write out specific complaints and agreed to act as moderator in discussing them in a future joint session of the foremen with the plant superintendent and the production manager.

The Company's Background

The company manufactured radius aluminum and glass window products and employed about 350 people, the majority of whom worked in the plant. The plant was an old building with a leaking roof and obstructed aisles. There was a great deal of noise and constant "hot item" interruptions on three production lines which were never running smoothly because of stockouts, conflicting orders, and many "reworks."

The majority of the plant employees were of Hispanic origin, and the present owner—the founder's son—perpetuated his father's "patrone" style of leadership. Management did not listen to employees' suggestions or grievances—which added to worker frustration and anger.

In November, 1977, the company had just had a $750,000 warehouse fire that left it with no raw materials. The workshop leader had been brought in to help the company get back into production during the peak selling season. There was a lot of confusion on the factory floor, with everyone from the president to the sales manager giving orders to the workers, and all orders getting a number 1 priority. Everyone was disgusted. The members of the executive committee were upset with low shipments, the production manager was hassled by materials problems, and the foremen were frustrated because of the stockouts, conflicting orders, and grumbling workers. The problem with the washrooms, however, antedated the fire.

The Joint Session on Complaints

A list of complaints had been compiled and provided to all plant personnel. The cooperation of the plant superintendent and the production manager was enlisted, and the complaints were prioritized so that they could be presented in the least threatening order.

*This case was prepared by Robert A. Blumenthal of Seattle Pacific University.

When the meeting was held, the agenda was followed closely and each item was discussed in its order. These items include complaints about hand tool availability, hiring practices, and the men's washrooms. The complaint about the washrooms was that the walls were covered with obscene graffiti, the floors were filthy and badly littered, and the toilets overflowed because of objects that were purposely jammed into them.

The foremen blamed the management for not keeping the washrooms clean. Management, however, claimed that it had actually just cleaned up the washrooms and painted the walls for the umpteenth time, yet the graffiti and paper and filth had reappeared by the following day. Daily attempts to clean up were unsuccessful.

As the discussion progressed, both groups of management (lower level foremen and upper level plant superintendent and production manager) suggested a variety of disciplinary steps:

1. Pencils, pens, and felt-tipped pens should be confiscated before anyone goes to the washroom.
2. Employees should be made to sign in and out of the washrooms.
3. Employees should ask their foremen permission to leave their work stations.

The above "rules" were dutifully written down. After a long list of other "rules" had been generated, a pall of utter hopelessness fell over everyone. Finally, Jose Gomez, a normally silent figure of strength among the foremen, said: "When I was younger, I wrote on the walls, on the rocks in the hills, on bridges...everywhere, and I didn't see anything wrong with it. You grow out of it."

The pall lifted. A silent feeling of agreement flowed among the foremen. The superintendent and the plant manager, both Anglos, looked surprised and totally perplexed. Then Edward Rodriguez said, "I come from East Los Angeles. They had that problem there, but they solved it." The foremen all nodded in agreement and again fell silent.

Questions

1. What do you think are the reasons for the graffiti and filth in these washrooms?
2. What evidences do you find of strengths and weaknesses in the management of this firm?
3. To what extent are recruitment and training practices a factor in this case?
4. How would you attempt to solve the washroom problem?

17

Operations Management

Courtesy of Frederick B. Sontag

Operations management, the subject of this chapter, involves day-to-day activities that crucially affect a firm's productivity. In many small firms, unfortunately, managers find it difficult to maximize productivity. Even when they know what needs to be done, they often lack the necessary resources to do it.

Unison Industries, Inc., a tiny manufacturer of industrial motors in Rockford, IL, is such a firm. It uses aging equipment strewn haphazardly across a 135,000-square-foot factory floor. Even on a new production line, all but 2 of 30 steps required to assemble motors are still performed by hand. Frederick B. Sontag, who purchased the plant in 1980, is struggling to improve its productivity. Although Sontag has excellent qualifications (including an M.B.A. degree from Harvard), he is limited in time and money. His frustrations are commonplace in small firms. "When you only have $400,000 to spend, you can't just order up a batch of $100,000 robots," he says.

Similarly, he has no industrial relations staff to set up quality circles or to lead discussions about work improvement. In spite of such limitations, this small firm improved productivity 9 percent in just 2 years. And it is continuing to make those changes which it can afford. By recognizing its need for improvement and by making "affordable" improvements, it is staying competitive and profitable.

Source: Reprinted by permission of *The Wall Street Journal,* © Dow Jones & Company, Inc., 1984. All Rights Reserved.

Looking Ahead

Watch for the following important topics:

1. Types of production processes and steps in control of operations.
2. Role of and types of maintenance.
3. Creating and controlling quality in products and services.
4. Methods of work improvement and measurement.
5. Industrial research for small plants.

In this chapter, we go to the very core of the enterprise—the management of its production/operations process. If a firm is to be profitable, it must carefully manage the various elements of this process which include production/operations control, maintenance, quality control, work improvement and measurement, and industrial research.

PRODUCTION/OPERATIONS CONTROL

Every business firm has some production or operations process. This is true whether it produces a physical product or an intangible service. The operations process, as pictured in Figure 17-2, is concerned with the conversion of inputs into outputs.

Inputs include money, raw materials, people, equipment, information, and energy—all of which are combined in varying proportions depending on the nature of the finished product or service. Both production and service-type businesses are concerned with processes which change inputs into outputs. Printing plants and toy manufacturers, for example, use inputs such as paper, ink, wood products, employees, printing presses, lathes, product designs, and electric power to produce printed material and toys. Car-wash facilities and motor freight firms, which are service businesses, also use operating systems to transform inputs into car-cleaning and freight-transporting services. Operations management deals with the planning and control of these basic processes, whatever their nature. Since most operations management techniques were developed in manufacturing, however, many of the examples in this chapter reflect that type of environment.

Kinds of Operations

There are many types of operations and operating systems. *Production operations*, for example, include manufacturing, converting raw materials

Figure 17–2 The Operations Process

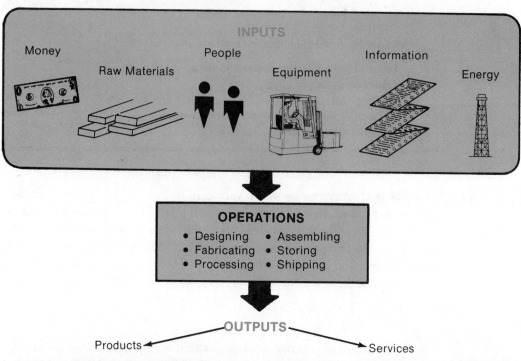

INPUTS

Money   People   Information

Raw Materials   Equipment   Energy

OPERATIONS
- Designing
- Fabricating
- Processing
- Assembling
- Storing
- Shipping

OUTPUTS

Products ←   → Services

(such as refining oil), and repairing. *Service operations* include protection (such as insurance), logistics (such as mass transit or motor freight), and services related to personal well-being (such as education and entertainment).

Operations may also be differentiated on a continuum according to the degree of repetitiveness and the quantity of goods or services produced at one time. Although some operations are performed only one time (such as building the company's plant), we can classify most operations as *intermittent* or *continuous*.

Intermittent Operations   Often described as *job-order production*, **intermittent operations** involve short production runs with only one or a few products being produced before shifting to a different production setup. General-purpose machines are used for this type of operations. Examples of businesses that use intermittent operations include print shops, machine shops, and automobile repair shops.

Continuous Operations   Firms that produce a standardized product or a relatively few standardized products use **continuous operations** which involve long production runs. Highly specialized equipment can be used. A soft-drink bottling plant is an example of a continuous operations process.

Figure 17-3 shows the layout of a small factory that produces a single, final product called ABC. This product is made from three machine parts: Part A, which is fabricated by the factory in three shop operations, and Parts B and C, which are purchased. The raw materials for Part A, as well as the purchased parts, flow to the plant from suppliers by rail and by truck. They are received, inspected, and then sent to the storeroom for subsequent issue.

To start a production run, the raw materials for Part A move lot by lot to the storage table and then to the machines for Shop Operation #1 through Shop Operation #3. Meanwhile, Parts B and C move by conveyor to the two assemblers near the end of the process. When each lot of Part A has passed inspection, it goes to the line loader, who places one part at a time on the conveyor going to Assembler #1. Parts A and B are joined by Assembler #1 to form subassembly AB. Then subassembly AB goes to Assembler #2, who joins Part C to subassembly AB to produce the finished product, ABC. Final inspection, storage, and shipping operations follow.

Steps in Production Control

Production control procedures have been developed most extensively in manufacturing. They consist of steps designed to achieve the orderly sequential flow of products through the plant at a rate commensurate with scheduled deliveries to customers. To attain this objective, it is essential to avoid work stoppages, to eliminate production bottlenecks when they occur, and to utilize machines and personnel efficiently.

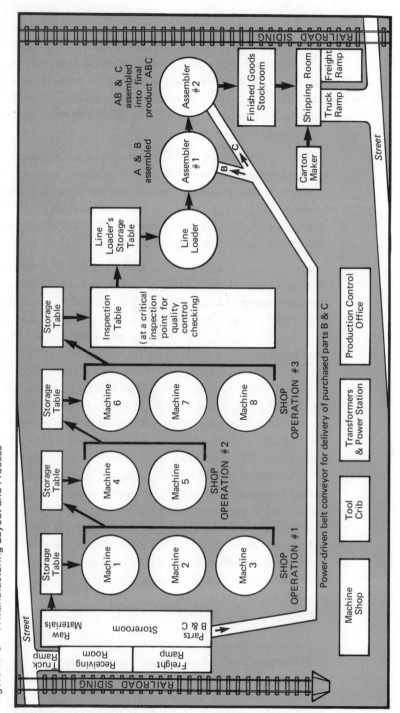

Figure 17-3   A Manufacturing Layout and Process

Simple, informal control procedures are frequently used in small plants. If a procedure is simple and the output small, the manager can keep things moving smoothly with a minimum of paperwork. Personal observation might even suffice. However, there comes a time in the growth of any manufacturing organization when formal procedures must be established to attain production efficiency. Each of the steps in formal production control is explained below.

Planning and Routing *Planning* involves the determination of the basic manufacturing data needed. Among the most important data needed are:

1. Kinds of raw materials and fabricated parts required.
2. Number of fabricated parts and amounts of material of each kind required per unit of finished product.
3. Best sequence of processing operations for making each product.
4. Number of machines and operators needed on each processing operation.
5. Number and kinds of tooling items needed to set up each machine.
6. Standard output rate of each machine.
7. Number of units of finished product that the plant can produce daily or yearly.

Once the manufacturing data are determined, two things can be prepared: (1) a *bill of materials* listing the raw materials, consumption standards, and other related information, and (2) a *route list* showing the sequence of processing operations and who will perform them.

In intermittent operations, machines are shut down rather frequently and retooled to produce a different product. Therefore, the basic manufacturing data are needed well in advance of the start of production. This allows management sufficient time to make any necessary changes in plant layout, to buy new tooling items required, and to train workers.

In continuous operations, most or all of the machines run without stopping for long periods of time. Advance planning is even more essential; for once the machinery is set up and operations have begun, changes are both difficult and costly.

Scheduling and Dispatching After a given process is planned and set up, timetables for each department and work center are established to control the flow of work. In continuous operations, which involve large-scale production and which are found in very few small factories, flow control is fairly simple and involves little paperwork. This is the case because continuous operations assure a steady flow of finished products off the final assembly line. The dispatcher must keep all lines (subassembly and final assembly) operating all the time. If delays occur, rescheduling or other adjustment is required.

In intermittent operations, which involve small- to medium-volume production where lots are produced one at a time, there are different flow-control techniques. Where a lot is in process for several days, or is slow-moving, it is possible to use *visual control boards* to reflect both work assignments and the progress of work toward completion. For fast-moving processes where a lot clears each machine quickly, the *block control* technique clears the oldest blocks first on each processing operation.

Supervising and Performance Follow-Up   Keeping the work moving on schedule is the major responsibility of the shop supervisor. *Schedule performance reports* and necessary *follow-up routines* are established. After an order is completed, the schedules are terminated, and the work records are filed for future use.

Balancing Sales Volume and Production Control

Planning, timing, and volume of output are all limited by the plant's capacity to produce. Typically the sales demand can be satisfied with production at less than capacity. However, an unexpected high sales volume may force a plant to produce at capacity. The plant then makes what it can when it can. Of course, if long-term increased sales are expected, the plant's capacity may be enlarged.

PLANT MAINTENANCE

According to Murphy's Law, if anything can go wrong, it will! In operating systems which make extensive use of tools and equipment, there is indeed much which can go wrong. The maintenance function is intended to correct malfunctions of equipment and, as far as possible, to prevent such breakdowns from occurring.

Role of Maintenance in Small Firms

The nature of maintenance work obviously depends upon the type of operations and the nature of the equipment being used. In an office, for example, the machines that require maintenance may simply include type-writers, office copiers, computers, and related office machines. Maintenance services are usually obtained on a contract basis—either by calling for repair personnel when a breakdown occurs or by contracting for periodic servicing and other maintenance when needed.

In manufacturing firms that use more complex and specialized equipment, the maintenance function is much more important. For all types of firms, maintenance includes plant housekeeping as well as equipment repair. Plant housekeeping contributes to effective performance, moreover, even in those operations that use simple facilities.

It is easy to underestimate the importance of maintenance. Managers often think of it as janitorial-type work and postpone it as much as possible in order to concentrate upon the production process. The increased use of expensive, complex equipment, however, has made the maintenance role a much greater factor in the firm's overall effectiveness. A major breakdown in production equipment, for example, can interfere with scheduled deliveries and cause labor costs to skyrocket as personnel are idled. Figure 17–4 pictures the type of equipment requiring maintenance in an ice cream production plant.

In small plants, maintenance work often is performed by regular production employees. As a firm expands its facilities, it may add specialized maintenance personnel and eventually create a maintenance department.

Figure 17-4   Production Equipment Requiring Maintenance

American Motors Corporation

Types of Maintenance

Plant maintenance activities fall into two categories. One is **corrective maintenance**, which includes both the major and minor repairs necessary to restore a facility to good condition. The other is **preventive maintenance**, which includes inspections and other activities intended to prevent machine breakdowns and damage to people and buildings.

Corrective Maintenance Major repairs are unpredictable as to time of occurrence, repair time required, loss of output, and cost of downtime. Because of these characteristics, some small manufacturers find it desirable to contract with other service firms for major repair work. In contrast, the regular occurrence of minor breakdowns makes the volume of minor repair work reasonably predictable. Minor repairs are completed easily, quickly, and economically. Therefore, many small plants use one or two of their own employees to perform such work.

Preventive Maintenance A small plant can ill afford to neglect preventive maintenance. If a machine is highly critical to the overall operation, it should be inspected and serviced regularly to preclude costly breakdowns. Also, the frequent checking of equipment reduces industrial accidents, and the installation of smoke alarms and/or automatic sprinkler systems minimizes the danger of fire damage.

Preventive maintenance of equipment need not involve elaborate controls. Some cleaning and lubricating is usually done as a matter of routine. But for preventive maintenance to work well, more systematic procedures are needed. A record card showing cost, acquisition date, periods of use and storage, and frequency of preventive maintenance inspections should be kept on each major piece of equipment. On any given day, the machinist is handed the set of cards covering that day's required inspections. The machinist inspects each piece of equipment, makes necessary notations on the cards, and replaces worn parts.

Good Housekeeping and Plant Safety

Good housekeeping facilitates production control, saves time in looking for tools, and keeps floor areas safe and free for production work. Disregard for good housekeeping practices is reflected in a plant's production record, for good workmanship and high output are hard to achieve in an ill-kept plant.

According to the Occupational Safety and Health Act of 1970 (OSHA), employers are required to provide a place of employment free from hazards which are likely to cause death or serious physical harm. This means that the building and equipment must be maintained in a way that minimizes safety and health hazards. Although very small firms have been relieved from some of OSHA's record-keeping requirements, they are still subject to the requirements of the law.[1]

As far as safety of the premises is concerned, not all small manufacturers require a sophisticated security system. However, all should be aware of the security problem and of available security devices. Such devices include the use of fences to help deter intruders, security guards, burglar-alarm systems, and gates or doors equipped with access controls which are activated only by identification cards or keys given to authorized personnel.

QUALITY CONTROL

Most consumers view quality subjectively as a single variable ranging from very bad to very good. The manufacturer knows, however, that there is a set of objectively measurable physical variables—such as length or diameter—which *together* determine how good or bad a product is. To approach perfection on even one variable is very costly. To make a product inferior to that of competitors, however, means that they will get the business. Thus, a product must be good enough so that it will be competitive, yet it must not be prohibitively expensive.

Building Quality into the Product

One company advertises, "The quality goes in before the label goes on." This slogan implies that quality does not originate with the inspection process that checks the finished product, but with the earlier production process. Quality of a product begins, in fact, with its design and the design of the manufacturing process.

Other factors that contribute to product quality include the quality of the raw materials used. Generally the finished product is better if a superior grade of raw material is used. A contractor who uses lumber of inferior grade in building a house produces a low-quality house.

In many types of businesses, an even more critical variable is found in the performance of employees. Employees who are careful in their work produce products of a better quality than those produced by careless employees. You have probably heard the admonition, "Never buy a car which was produced on Friday or Monday!" The central role of personnel in producing a quality product suggests the importance of human resources management—properly selecting, training, and motivating production personnel.

ACTION REPORT
Improving Management and Quality

Quality must be built into a product. It cannot be "inspected" into the product. It follows, therefore, that managers of operations must see to it that work processes result in products or services of a desired quality.

Hydro Optics Inc. is a small Hackensack, NJ, manufacturer of plastic air fresheners and controlled polymer products. This firm improved its quality by improving its operations management. According to a report:

> The basic problem of Hydro Optics was one of undersupervision. Kenneth Roth, company president, says as many as 50 workers reported to a single supervisor.
>
> When Hydro Optics' orders leaped to $5.5 million from $2.8 million within a year, the upsurge in production requirements "meant our production area had to be reorganized," explains Roth. The company imposed a supervisory structure where none previously existed. The 150 workers in 3 broad production areas were divided into groups of 5 or 6 workers. The most experienced member of each group was assigned as a leader and reported directly to a supervisor. Workers were told exactly what standard the company was after.
>
> Hydro Optics watched while internal rejects were reduced by about 30 percent, according to the company's own figures. "Our profits virtually doubled as a result of solving the quality problem," says Roth.

Source: Reprinted from the August, 1983 issue of VENTURE, The Magazine for Entrepreneurs, by special permission. © 1983 Venture Magazine, Inc., 521 Fifth Ave., New York, NY 10175.

Quality Circles

Quality circles, a Japanese innovation, are used in small business as well as big business. A **quality circle** consists of a group of employees, usually a dozen or fewer, performing similar or related work. They meet periodically, typically about once a week, to identify, analyze, and solve production problems, particularly those involving product or service quality. Supervisors often serve as circle leaders, but others may also be given this role.

The following example shows the type of improvement possible through quality circles:

> A circle at Benson Mfg. Corp., a 44-employee maker of wood and plastic products in Milwaukee, halved the number of times wood chipped during production of blades for old-fashioned ceiling fans. A $1,000 investment in a more reliable system proposed by the workers is expected to save the company $12,800 a year.[2]

For quality circles to function effectively, participating employees must be given appropriate training. Also, top management must give consistent support on a long-term basis. With such support, quality circles have the potential for tapping the often unused potential for enthusiastic contributions by employees.

Inspection: The Traditional Technique

Inspection consists of scrutinizing a part or a product to determine whether it is good or bad. An inspector typically uses gauges to evaluate the important quality variables. For effective quality control, the inspector must be honest, objective, and capable of resisting pressure from shop personnel to pass borderline cases.

Inspection Standards   In manufacturing, *inspection standards* consist of design tolerances that are set for every important quality variable. These tolerances show the limits of variation allowable above and below the desired dimension of the given quality variable. Tolerances must satisfy the requirements which customers will look for in finished products.

Points of Inspection   Traditionally, inspection occurs in the receiving room to check the condition and quantity of materials received from suppliers. Inspection is also customary at critical processing points—for example, *before* any operation that would conceal existing defects, or *after* any operation that produces an excessive amount of defectives. Of course, the final inspection of finished products is of utmost importance.

Reduction of Inspection Costs   To reduce costs, the manufacturer must be alert to possibilities for mechanization or automation of inspection. Automated inspection requires only first-piece inspection and periodic rechecks. So long as the setups remain satisfactory, the production run continues without other inspection.

100 Percent Inspection   When each item in every lot processed is inspected, this is called **100 percent inspection**. Supposedly it assures the elimination of all bad materials in process and all defective products prior to shipment to customers. Such goals are seldom reached, however. In addition, this method of inspection is not only time-consuming, but also costly. Furthermore, inspectors often make honest errors in judgment. A reinspection of lots that have been 100 percent inspected, for example, will show that inspectors err by placing good items in the scrap barrel, and bad items or rework items in the good-item barrel. Also, some types of inspection—for example, opening a can of vegetables—destroy the product, making 100 percent inspection impractical.

Statistical Quality Control

To avoid the cost and time of 100 percent inspection, small firms can use statistical methods to devise sampling procedures for quality control. In this way, the small firm can inspect a small number of items in a group and make an inductive decision about the quality level of the entire group.

Attributes Sampling Plans   Some products are judged to be either acceptable or unacceptable, good or bad. For example, a light bulb either lights up or it doesn't. Likewise, a manufactured part either falls within the tolerance size limits or it doesn't. In these cases, control of quality involves a measurement of *attributes*.

Suppose a small firm receives a shipment of 1,000 parts from a supplier. Rather than evaluating all 1,000 parts, the purchaser can check the acceptability of a small sample of parts and decide about the acceptability of the entire order. The size of the sample—for instance, a sample of 25 of the 1,000 parts—affects the discriminating power of an attributes sampling plan. The smaller the sample, the greater the danger of either accepting a defective lot or rejecting a good lot due to sampling error. A larger sample, on the other hand, reduces this danger but increases the inspection cost. An **attributes sampling plan** must strike a balance between these two forces, avoiding excessive inspection costs and simultaneously avoiding an unreasonable risk of accepting a bad lot or rejecting a good lot.

Variables Sampling Plans   A **variables sampling plan** measures many characteristics of an item, rather than simply judging the item as acceptable or unacceptable. If the characteristic being inspected is measured on a continuous basis, a variables sampling plan may be used. For example, the weight of a box of candy—which is being manufactured continuously throughout the day and week—may be measured in pounds and ounces. The process can be monitored to be sure it stays "in control." Periodic random samples are taken and plotted on a chart to discover if the process is out of control, thus requiring corrective action.

The variables control chart used for this purpose has lines denoting the upper and lower control limits. For example, a shop might produce wooden pieces averaging 42 inches in length. The upper control limit might be 43 inches and the lower control limit 41 inches. A signal of a lack of control would be given by a measurement falling outside either control limit, by a trend run of points upward or downward, or by various other indicators.

To establish a specific variables or attributes sampling plan, the small-business manager may consult more specialized publications in production/operations management or statistical quality control. Or, more likely, the manager may consult a specialist in quantitative methods for assistance in devising a sound sampling plan. The savings possible by using an efficient quality control method can easily justify the consulting fees required in devising a sound quality control plan.

Quality Control in Service Businesses

The discussion of quality control typically centers on a manufacturing process involving a tangible product which can be inspected or measured in some way. The need for quality control, however, is not limited to producers of physical products. Service businesses, such as motels, dry cleaners, accounting service firms, and automobile repair shops, also need to maintain an adequate control of quality. In fact, many firms offer a combination of a tangible product and intangible services and, ideally, wish to control quality in both areas.

Measurement problems are greater in assessing the quality of a service, however. One can measure the length of a piece of wood more easily than the quality level of motel accommodations. Nevertheless, methods can be devised for measuring the quality of services. Customers of an automobile repair shop, for example, may be sampled to determine their view of the service they received. And a motel can maintain a record of the number of "foul-ups" in travelers' reservations, complaints about cleanliness of rooms, and so on.

For some types of service firms, control of quality constitutes the single most important managerial responsibility. All that such firms sell is service, and the future of their businesses rests upon the quality of their service as perceived by customers.

WORK IMPROVEMENT AND MEASUREMENT

Work improvement means finding work methods that demand the least physical effort and the shortest execution time at the lowest possible cost. Most large manufacturing plants employ industrial engineers who specialize in work improvement methods. In the small plant, however, the manager may have to initiate and carry out a work improvement program with the help of shop supervisors.

Nature of Work Study

When conducted for the entire operation of a plant, **work study** involves an analysis of equipment and tooling, plant layout, working conditions, and individual jobs. It means finding the answers to such questions as:

1. Is the right machine being used?
2. Can one employee operate two or more machines?
3. Can automatic feeders or ejectors be utilized?
4. Can power tools replace hand tools?
5. Can the jigs and fixtures be improved?
6. Is the workplace properly arranged?
7. Is the operator's motion sequence effective?

To be successful, work improvement and measurement require the collaboration of employees and management. Figure 17–5 outlines the procedures to be followed in devising and installing new work methods. Note that two steps toward the end of the procedure—"sell" and "install"—call for convincing and training employees who must use the new methods.

Figure 17–5   Procedure for Developing and Installing New Work Methods

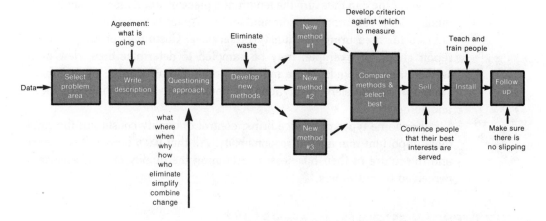

Source: Figure from MANAGING THE PRODUCTIVE PROCESS, by Joel Corman © 1974 General Learning Corporation. Reprinted by permission of Silver Burdett Company.

The competitive pressures on today's small-business firms provide the incentive for work improvement. Small firms can improve their productivity and stay competitive. To the extent that methods can actually be improved, there will be increasd output from the same effort (or even reduced effort) on the part of production employees.

Laws of Motion Economy

Underlying any work improvement program—whether it be for the overall operations of a plant or for a single task—are the **laws of motion**

economy. These laws concern work arrangement, the use of the human hands and body, and the design and use of tools. Some of these laws are:

1. If both hands start and stop their motion at the same time and are never idle during a work cycle, maximum performance is approached.
2. If motions are made simultaneously in opposite directions over similar paths, automaticity and rhythm develop naturally, and less fatigue is experienced.
3. The method requiring the fewest motions generally is the best for performance of a given task.
4. When motions are confined to the lowest practical classification, maximum performance and minimum fatigue are approached. *Lowest classification* means motions involving the fingers, hands, forearms, and trunk.

A knowledge of the laws of motion economy will suggest various ways to improve work. For example, materials and tools should be so placed as to minimize movement of the trunk and the extended arms.

Methods of Work Measurement

There are several ways to measure work in the interest of establishing a performance standard. **Motion study** consists of a detailed observation of all the actual motions that the observed worker makes to complete a job under a given set of physical conditions. From this study the skilled observer should be able to detect any wasted movements that can be corrected or eliminated. **Time study**, which normally follows motion study, involves timing and recording each elemental motion of a job on an observation sheet. **Micromotion study** is a refinement of the time study in that a motion-picture camera, rather than a stopwatch, is used to record the elemental motions, as well as the times.

As you can readily see, the methods of work measurement mentioned above require trained observers or analysts. Most small plants would find it impractical to utilize the costly methods of time study and micromotion study. A more practical method of work measurement, which provides little operating detail but estimates the ratio of actual working time and downtime, is **work sampling**. This method was originated in England by L. H. C. Tippett in 1934. Work sampling involves random observations in which the observer simply determines whether the observed worker is working or idle. The numbers of observations are tallied in "working" and "idle" classifications; the percentages of the tallies are estimates of the actual percent of time that the worker was working and idle.

INDUSTRIAL RESEARCH FOR SMALL PLANTS

In small companies, industrial research is aimed at improving manufacturing processes or products. Some small manufacturers, however, believe that research of this type is too expensive to undertake. And still others equate research with experimentation conducted in an expensively equipped laboratory, when sometimes all it requires is a questioning attitude which seeks to improve existing methods and products.

ACTION REPORT
Docutel's R&D Problems and Progress

To stay competitive, producers of high-technology products must maintain an active research and development program. Docutel Corporation, which introduced the first automatic bank teller machine in 1971, came close to losing out to its larger corporate competitors—Diebold, IBM, and NCR. Its weakness was technological sluggishness. As a result, "the tiny Dallas company was slow to incorporate technological advances into its machines and quickly lost its market dominance to powerful new entrants."

After losing ground to competitors, Docutel sought to correct its problems. It survived, in fact, by bringing out a low-cost retrofit unit for its aging machines. As of 1981, many bankers ranked Docutel's unit as the best on the market—a tribute to its revitalized research and development effort.

Source: Reprinted from the July 27, 1981 issue of *Business Week* by special permission, © 1981 by McGraw-Hill, Inc., New York, NY 10020. All rights reserved.

Problems of the Small Manufacturer

There is no question that industrial research requires the expenditure of both money and management time. Yet the small manufacturer cannot ignore it because competitive firms are continually introducing new products and processes which pose a challenge to existing ones. The money spent for productive research can easily be outweighed by the profits from successful new products or the cost savings from improvements achieved. And if a lack of management time is the problem, the manager can assign special responsibility for keeping abreast of research in the firm's area of interest to its most technically proficient employees. Such employees should review the current trade literature, attend professional and technical conferences, and contact suppliers who engage in research and development. Furthermore, the manager can utilize the following external resources:

1. Individual members of university faculties—as research consultants.
2. University research bureaus—for the completion of research projects.
3. Private research agencies—to which research problems can be referred.
4. Trade associations serving the given industry with a research program—in which participation through membership is open.

Possibilities for Research

The possibilities for industrial research and development are almost endless. Here are just a few of them:

1. Checking on old, but still useful, inventions which have been thrown open for use by the general public.
2. Reclamation of waste materials.
3. Recycling of already used materials.
4. Finding substitute raw materials for those that are scarce and in current use.
5. Devising equipment to control air and water pollution.

We might emphasize that the public awareness of air and water pollution is forcing today's small manufacturer to conduct research in this area.

Looking Back

1. Both production and service organizations use a production/operations process which converts inputs into products or services. Two basic types of processes are intermittent and continuous. Intermittent manufacturing involves short production runs, with only one or a few products being produced before shifting to a different production setup. Continuous manufacturing involves long production runs and is used by firms that produce one or a few standardized products. Production control provides for the orderly, efficient flow of production operations. It includes the steps of planning and routing, scheduling and dispatching, and supervising and follow-up.
2. The maintenance function is critical for firms that use complex and highly specialized equipment. Plant maintenance includes corrective maintenance to restore a facility to good condition and preventive maintenance to minimize breakdowns. Plant housekeeping and safety engineering are also part of the maintenance function.

3. Quality is built into a product during the production process, not at the inspection stage. The quality of a product is influenced by its design, the quality of raw materials used, and the performance of employees. Quality circles draw upon the thinking of employees by bringing them together periodically to identify and solve quality and other operating problems. Inspection is the method traditionally used to maintain control of quality. Modern quality control involves the use of two statistical techniques: attributes sampling and variables sampling plans. Quality control is important in service businesses as well as in manufacturing.

4. Work improvement and measurement are accomplished by the use of motion study, time study, work sampling, and other tools of industrial engineering.

5. Industrial research to improve products and processes is important for most small manufacturers in order to maintain a competitive position. Although such research is difficult for a small business, the methods may be adapted to fit its resources.

DISCUSSION QUESTIONS

1. What is the difference between intermittent manufacturing and continuous manufacturing?

2. What are the proper objectives of production planning and control in a small manufacturing establishment?

3. Explain the difference between preventive and corrective maintenance. Explain the relative importance of each of the above when (a) one or more major breakdowns have occurred in a small plant, and (b) shop operations are running smoothly and maintenance does not face any major repair jobs.

4. The breakdown of machines during their use is a result of failure to exercise preventive maintenance. Why should these breakdowns always be investigated promptly? What should be the outcome of such investigations? Are cost considerations or lost production of paramount importance in such situations? Why?

5. What is meant by the saying, "You can't inspect quality into a product"?

6. It is said that the major problems of manufacturing inspection are where to inspect, how much to inspect, and the cost of inspection. Explain each of these inspection problems concisely.

7. A small manufacturer does not believe that using statistical quality control charts and sampling plans would be useful. Can traditional methods suffice? Can 100 percent inspection by final inspectors eliminate all defectives? Why?

8. How can a service business, such as a dry cleaner, use the concept of quality control?

9. What is meant by the "laws of motion economy"?
10. Discuss the following concisely: (a) goals of industrial research in small industrial firms, (b) techniques available, and (c) types of research that can be done.

ENDNOTES

1. "Easing Regulatory Burdens on Small Business," *Business Week*, No. 2641 (June 16, 1980), pp. 156–159.

2. Robert C. Wood, "Squaring Off on Quality Circles," *Inc.*, Vol. 4, No. 8 (August, 1982), p. 98.

REFERENCES TO SMALL BUSINESS IN ACTION

Currier, Susan E. "After 81 Years, Pirsch & Sons Proves That Quality Pays." *Inc.*, Vol. 3, No. 8 (August, 1981), pp. 65–66.
  A small custom manufacturer of fire trucks builds about 100 trucks per year. The firm uses master craftsmen and follows a production process described in the article.

Fenn, Donna. "The Lord of Discipline." *Inc.*, Vol. 7, No. 11 (November, 1985), pp. 82–95.
  Oberg Industries is a small tool and die shop located in western Pennsylvania. Its tough management, exceptional maintenance, superior workmanship, and high standards are described.

Furstenberg, Mark. "In Search of Survival." *Inc.*, Vol. 6, No. 1 (January, 1984), pp. 67–74.
  A group of investors purchased an inefficient, marginal manufacturing plant in 1982. The article describes the efforts of management to make its operations profitable.

"Miss Enid Stays Put." *Forbes*, Vol. 126, No. 6 (September 15, 1980), p. 194.
  The Nacona Boot Company produces custom-made boots that can cost as much as $2,500. Some of its production process is standardized, but it also has expert craftsmen who will make specialty products for those willing to pay the price.

CASE 17

Concessionaire Trailers*
Production planning in trailer manufacturing

Concessionaire Trailers, a proprietorship, was owned and operated by Ty Bedmore since February, 1981. Located in Rock Island, IL (population 48,000), the firm custom-manufactured concession trailers for mobile refreshment stands used at carnivals, fairs, amusement parks and sporting events. Its manufacturing facilities consisted of 2 buildings (1,100 square feet and 650 square feet) which had a combined monthly rental cost of $475.

Production Operations in 1981

According to Ty, his first year in business seemed to be an unending succession of 12- to 16-hour days and 7-day weeks, shared with 2 other employees. Notable production achievements during the first year included narrowing down the product line to three basic trailer prototypes (with a variety of customized options), engineering standardized and interchangeable parts, and finalizing pricing parameters. Unfortunately, Ty was unable to establish an efficient production layout system during the first year, even though 30 trailers were produced.

Production Operations in 1982

Business picked up considerably for Concessionaire during 1982, with 66 trailers sold during the first 9 months alone. Sales orders for the fourth quarter of 1982 called for the production of an additional 32 trailers. Ty was also studying a contract offer from a major customer to produce 80 Concessionaires during the first quarter of 1983.

Some progress was made during the first three quarters of 1982 toward more efficiently systematizing the trailer manufacturing process. However, Ty recognized the need for futher work-flow improvements before large customer contracts could be accommodated. In the production set-up shown in Figure 17–6, trailers were built from the ground up on each of the three production stations. Assembly was done in the larger building (Building 1); and painting and finishing, in the smaller facility.

*This case was prepared by Steve R. Hardy and Professor Philip M. Van Auken of Baylor University.

Figure 17-6   Plant Layout of Concession Trailers

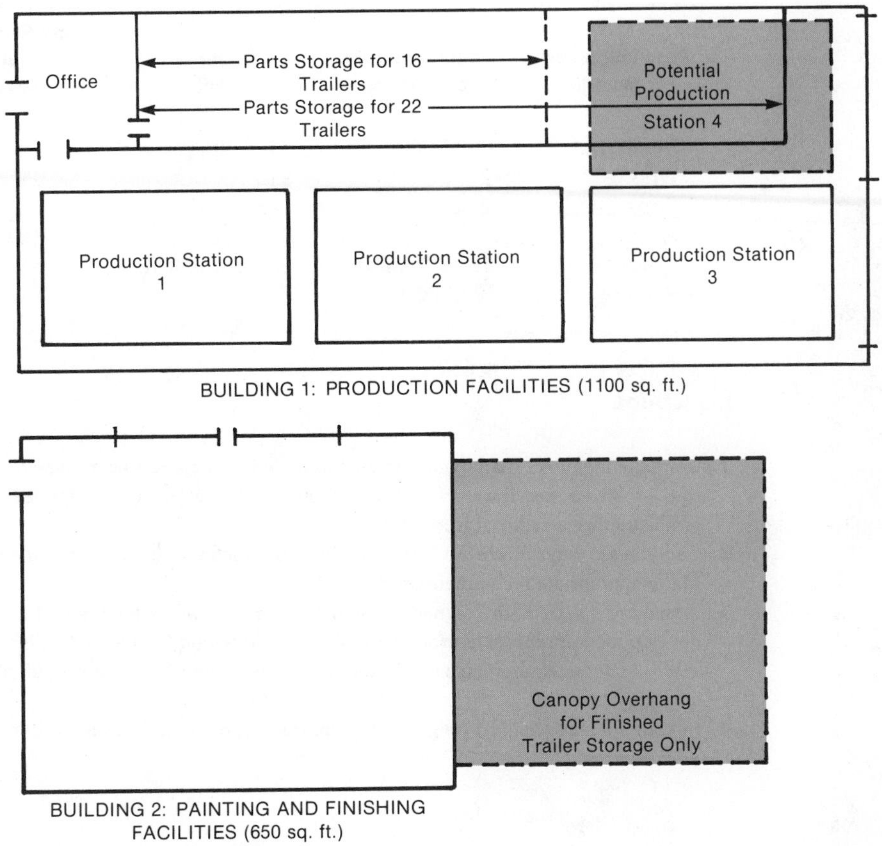

BUILDING 1: PRODUCTION FACILITIES (1100 sq. ft.)

BUILDING 2: PAINTING AND FINISHING
FACILITIES (650 sq. ft.)

Production Specifications

All three Concessionaire trailer models were constructed from the same materials: sheet metal, paint, wheels, tires, axles, and braces (see Exhibit 1). On the average, each trailer required a total production time of 48 labor hours. On extremely humid days (70 percent humidity or greater), paint-drying considerations necessitated operating at 75 percent capacity. Based on past experience, Ty estimated that humidity was a factor during 30 to 40 days annually, mainly during the spring and summer quarters.

Concessionaire's plant had raw-material storage facilities for 22 trailers. Six in-process or finished trailers could be inventoried. Ty felt that labor could be reduced from 48 hours per trailer to 36 if raw-material storage space were reduced to accommodate only 16 trailers. The freed-up floor space would be used to effect production-flow efficiencies, resulting in reduced labor hours per trailer.

Exhibit 1   Production Specifications for Concessionaire Trailers

Production Part or Material	Units Required per Trailer	Cost per Unit	Time Required for Delivery from Supplier
Sheet metal	600 lbs.	$1.45/lb.	5 weeks
Wheels	2	$10	6 weeks
Tires	2	$45	1 day
Axles	1	$200	2 days
Braces	16 (6 ft. each)	$0.15/linear ft.	5 weeks
Paint	2 gallons	$12	1 week

Questions

1. Compute the direct manufacturing cost of a Concessionaire trailer given an average labor rate of $6.15 per hour. How much would this cost be reduced if average hours of production were reduced from 48 to 36?

2. Can you see ways in which Concessionaire's production setup can be made more efficient? Make appropriate recommendations.

3. Assuming Ty Bedmore signed the contract for 80 trailers for the first quarter of 1983, develop a comprehensive production plan for the period September, 1982 through April, 1983. Include requirements for the following: raw materials, personnel, plant capacity, and inventory planning.

4. In your opinion, should Ty sign the first-quarter contract for 80 trailers? Explain and defend your reasoning.

18

Purchasing and Managing Inventory

Figure 18-1   Richard Downey

©Gerald Holly/Back Star

The goal of Downey Automotive Inc. of Chattanooga, TN, is to sell more auto parts than anyone else in Tennessee, Alabama, and Georgia. Achieving this goal requires competitive pricing as Richard Downey, founder and CEO, explains:

"Where it gets interesting is when a competitor goes under price in the market. You gotta go under him," Downey says. "If the guy starts selling shocks at $8.99, you sell 'em at $7.99—and promote it..."

To sell at such competitive prices, Downey must "buy right."

"I'll buy 52 trailers of antifreeze at one time," Downey boasts, "or 19 truckloads of batteries. I'll even buy do-it-yourself manuals by the car load."

This firm has consistently operated at a pretax profit margin of 6 percent—more than twice the industry average. Its success points up the vital role of purchasing and inventory control, the topics of this chapter.

Source: Reprinted with permission, *Inc.* magazine, August, 1982. Copyright © 1982 by Inc. Publishing Company, 38 Commercial Wharf, Boston, MA 02110.

Looking Ahead

Watch for the following important topics:

1. The purchasing cycle.
2. Purchasing policies.
3. Factors to consider in selecting suppliers.
4. Objectives of inventory control.
5. Control of inventory costs.
6. Methods of accounting for inventory.

A saying goes, "nothing ventured, nothing gained." The justification for this chapter is described by a slight modification of this phrase to "nothing bought, nothing sold." Raw materials and merchandise do not automatically appear in warehouses and stores. They must be purchased and managed. In this chapter, we explain how small firms should purchase and manage their inventories.

PURCHASING

The objective of purchasing activities is to obtain materials, merchandise, equipment, and services needed to meet production and/or marketing goals. Through effective purchasing, a firm secures all production factors except labor in the required quantity and quality, at the best price, and at the time needed for its operations.

Importance of Effective Purchasing

There is a direct correlation between the quality of finished products and the quality of the raw materials placed in process. For example, if tight tolerances are imposed on a manufacturer's product by design requirements, this in turn requires the acquisition of high-quality materials and component parts. Then, given an excellent process, excellent products will be produced. But even a superior process will not compensate for inferior materials or components. Therefore, purchasing is crucial in the manufacturing process. Similarly, the acquisition of quality merchandise makes a retailer's sales to customers easier and reduces the number of markdowns required.

It is also desirable that the delivery of goods be timed to meet the exact needs of the buyer. In a small factory, failure to receive materials, parts, or equipment on schedule is likely to cause costly interruptions in production operations. Machines and personnel are idled until the items on order are finally received. And in the retail business, failure to receive merchandise on schedule may mean the loss of one or more sales and, possibly, the permanent loss of disappointed customers.

Recent developments in our economy have placed even greater importance on purchasing and managing inventory. Shortages of materials, inflation, and high interest rates have forced the small business to emphasize purchasing and inventory activities.

ACTION REPORT
A Purchasing Yarn

Profitable selling for some firms requires purchasing raw materials at low prices. This is one key to success for Oneita Knitting, a family business which earns a return on investment comparable to or greater than that of larger competitors such as Levi Strauss and Spring Mills. Oneita's president, a third-generation family member, explains how Oneita keeps its sales prices low:

> The trick is to know when to buy yarn—that's our commodity....In 1971...I heard that there was a good, inexpensive yarn to be had in Portugal—the government there wanted to export it. So, I spent a month going through every yarn mill in Portugal and had the stuff shipped over here at a savings to us of about 20 percent over U.S. prices. I think we were the first U.S. firm to buy yarn in Portugal.

Efficient purchasing, along with other modern management practices, permits Oneita Knitting to price its products competitively and to retain four major firms as customers—Sears, K mart, J. C. Penney, and Montgomery Ward.

Source: "The Generation Syndrome," *Forbes*, Vol. 126, No. 3 (August 4, 1980), pp. 48–50.

The Purchasing Cycle

Purchasing is a process involving a number of steps as noted below. It is essential that all steps be followed in the proper sequence.

1. Receipt of a purchase request.
2. Locating a source of supply.
3. Issuance of the purchase order.
4. Maintenance of buying and warehousing records.
5. Follow-up of purchase order.
6. Receipt of goods.

Receipt of a Purchase Request   A **purchase requisition** is a formal, documented request from an employee or a manager of the firm for something to be bought for the business. In a small business, a purchase request is not always documented. But financial control is improved by purchasing only on the basis of purchase requests.

Locating a Source of Supply   Suitable suppliers can be located through sales representatives, advertisements, trade associations, word of mouth, and company records of past supplier performance. Price quotations are obtained, and, for major purchases, bids may be solicited from a number of potential sources. The importance of good relationships with suppliers is discussed later in this chapter.

Issuance of the Purchase Order   The next step in purchasing is the issuance of a **purchase order**. A standard form, such as that shown in Figure 18–2, should be used in all buying operations. When the signed order is accepted by a vendor (supplier), it becomes a binding contract. In the event of a serious violation, the written purchase order serves as the basis for adjustment.

Figure 18–2   A Purchase Order

PURCHASE ORDER THE RED WING COMPANY, INC. Fredonia, NY 14063-4925				No. 05202 SHOW THIS NUMBER ON INVOICE
June 27, 19-- DATE OF ORDER				
BYRON JACKSON & COMPANY 4998 Michigan Avenue Chicago, IL 60615-2218		SHIPPING INSTRUCTIONS: Mark purchase order number on each piece in shipment		

DELIVERY REQUIRED	F.O.B.	ROUTING		TERMS
July 24	Chicago	via NYC-Buffalo		2/10 net 30

ITEM	QUANTITY & UNIT	DESCRIPTION		PRICE & UNIT
622	35 each	Spring assembly		14.35 ea
230	200 each	Bearings		3.35 ea
272	70 each	Heavy duty relay 50V		7.50 ea
478	490 each	Screw set		.03 ea

ORIGINAL BILL OF LADING MUST ACCOMPANY ALL INVOICES FOR GOODS SHIPPED BY FREIGHT.
2% DISCOUNT FOR PAYMENT IN 10 DAYS WILL BE DEDUCTED FROM FACE OF INVOICE UNLESS OTHERWISE SPECIFIED.

INVOICE IN DUPLICATE   BY *J. Gromboski*
                                                            Purchasing Agent

Maintenance of Buying and Warehousing Records   Small firms should keep buying and warehousing records for all purchased items. As mentioned above, stores cards show the supply of each kind of raw material, purchased part, and supply item carried in the storeroom. Other records include the following:

1. Price quotations and credit terms—by suppliers and by kinds of materials or parts.
2. Purchase records showing outstanding orders and receipts from suppliers for each commodity.
3. Record of contract commitments.
4. Vendor quality and yield ratings.
5. Miscellaneous supplier records, showing such information as steps to inform the buying firm of new materials, cooperativeness in meeting delivery schedules, and improvement of quality control over purchased materials.

Purchase records should be so filed as to facilitate expediting of inbound shipments and to assure the prompt arrival of the goods or equipment orders. While price quotations received should be retained in a *price quote* file, the purchasing agent should obtain *price confirmations* before mailing any major purchase order. Some suppliers' prices are "subject to change without notice." Price confirmation avoids the receipt of a shipment and invoice at a higher unit price than expected.

Follow-Up of Purchase Order   The follow-up of purchase orders is necessary to assure delivery on schedule. Troublesome orders may take repeated checking to be sure materials or merchandise will be available when needed.

Receipt of Goods   The receiving clerks take physical custody of incoming materials and merchandise, check their general condition, and sign the carrier's release. Inspection follows to assure an accurate count and the proper quality and kind of items. The quality check may be performed on a sampling inspection basis by a representative of the firm's quality control department. Figure 18–3 shows a weekly or quarterly summary analysis of the quality of a given material.

Purchasing Policies

Purchasing policies can significantly affect the cost of purchasing, but they may be even more important for the preservation of good relationships with suppliers. Whenever possible, purchasing policies should be written. This will assure that the policies are understood and will eliminate the need for repetitive decisions.

Reciprocal Buying   Some firms try to sell to others from whom they also purchase. This policy of **reciprocal buying** is based on the premise that one company can secure additional orders by using its own purchasing requests as a bargaining weapon. Although the typical order of most small companies is not large enough to make this a potent weapon, there is a tendency for purchasers to grant some recognition to this factor. Of course, this policy

Figure 18–3   Materials Yield Summary

Materials Yield Summary
The Iowa Manufacturing Company

Stores Item _____   Week Ending _____

Stores Item Number _____   Quarter Ending _____

Supplier	Units of Product Put in Process	Allowance per Unit of Finished Product	Total Units Allowed	Actual Units Used	Usage as % of Units Allowed
1	2	3	4 = 3·2	5	6 = 5/4 (100) (Quotient) = %

Note: *The materials yield summary provides an analysis of the quality of the given material (or part), as supplied by each vendor, for the given week (or quarter). Both weekly and quarterly summaries are made for each major stores item, using this same form. Since the standard usage percent of units allowed = 100, actual percentages for each supplier afford the purchasing agent concrete evidence of which suppliers are good and which are bad.*

Percentages under 100 (given high-quality output) are favorable yield ratings; percentages over 100 are unfavorable.

would be damaging if it were allowed to obscure quality and price variations. Otherwise, there is probably little to be lost or gained from this policy.

Making or Buying   Whether to make or to buy component parts is a manufacturer's problem. The arguments in favor of *making* the component parts are:

1. Uses otherwise idle capacity, thus permitting more economical production.
2. Makes the buyer more independent of suppliers so that there are fewer delays and interruptions resulting from difficulties with suppliers.
3. Protects a secret design.
4. May be cheaper by avoiding payment of the supplier's selling expense and profit factors.

5. Permits closer coordination and control of total production operations, thus facilitating scheduling and quality control.
6. Permits better control over timing of design changes.

Some of the arguments for *buying* the component parts are:

1. May be cheaper, as shown by cost studies, due to the supplier's concentration on production of the given part, which makes possible specialized facilities, added know-how, and greater efficiency.
2. A shortage of space, equipment, personnel skills, and working capital may exist, thus precluding "in-plant" manufacture of the part.
3. Requirement of less diversified managerial experience and skills.
4. Greater flexibility; for example, seasonal production of a given item makes its manufacture risky.
5. Frees "in-plant" operations for concentration on firm's specialty (finished products).
6. Partial purchase of components serves to check the efficiency of one's own parts-fabricating operations.
7. The increasing impact of technological change enhances the risk of equipment obsolescence, making diversion of this risk to outsiders a sound procedure.

The decision to make or to buy may be expensive to reverse. It should certainly be based on long-run cost and profit optimization. The underlying cost differences need to be analyzed very carefully since small savings in buying or making may greatly affect profit margins.

The entrepreneur in a small firm should approach this policy decision with an open mind and should be receptive to the arguments on both sides of the question. In particular, the entrepreneur should be perceptive of the supplier's added costs (and profit factor) as compared with the buying firm's ability, capacity, and costs (overhead, administration, records and payroll, materials, design, tooling, equipment, and supervision). There is no definitive formula to guide one's decision.

Substituting Materials or Merchandise   New types of materials and merchandise are constantly being developed. Some of them may be both cheaper and better than older products. For example, certain upper leathers stretch just right to make shoes feel comfortable and last effectively, while others cannot possibly "last" without wrinkling the vamps. Nevertheless, the purchaser must consider not only the impact on the product and its cost but also the effect upon the process. A change in materials may alter the sequence of operations or may even cause the deletion or addition of one or more operations.

ACTION REPORT
Buy with Savvy

A good retail purchasing agent must first know what will sell and then must make a good buy. Leon Levine can do both. He is the founder and chief officer of Family Dollar Stores in North Carolina, which operates small self-service outlets selling "everything from soap to blue jeans to toys."

One of Levine's golden rules for good buying is expressed as follows:

> In order to buy well yourself, you must keep shopping the competition to see what they're carrying and for how much. One company manager put my pictures up in his stores....And I've been asked to leave some stores.

Levine is always alert to a good buy. One of his deals was:

> ...with this gentleman in Chicago, who had a plant in Mississippi.... He would go to General Motors and Ford plants and buy their carpet remnants for next to nothing to use for coat linings. And they were *warm*. We'd get them for $2 apiece and sell them for $2.99. Other stores would come in and buy them from us—48 and 60 at a time—to sell at $5 or $6. Finally, we had to limit the sales to two per customer to keep enough in stock for our regular customers.

Source: "The Leon and Al Show," *Forbes*, Vol. 126, No. 7 (September 29, 1980), pp. 52–56.

Purchasing policy should be sufficiently flexible to permit ready consideration of new or different materials or merchandise. Of course, a change must be based upon the possibility of producing or selling a better, cheaper product.

Taking All Purchase Discounts One argument in favor of taking all purchase discounts available is that this evidences financial strength to suppliers and tends to promote good relationships with them. Even more important is the fact that discounts provide a source of savings. If the discount is taken on terms of 2/10, n/30, the savings are equivalent to interest at the rate of 36 percent per year (under the banker's rule for interest calculation). This is such a good rate that it pays to borrow if necessary in order to take the discount.

Diversifying Sources of Supply In the purchase of a particular time, there is a question of whether it is desirable to use more than one supplier. Division of orders among several suppliers can be a form of insurance against difficulties with a sole supplier. For example, a strike or a fire might eliminate the supply for a time. The purchaser would then experience the delays involved in placing initial orders with a new source of supply. Another danger is the fact that failure to "shop" may result in a loss of the lower prices, better quality, and superior service offered by other suppliers.

Nevertheless, the arguments on this problem do not all favor diversification of sources of supply. With centralized buying from one firm, the purchaser may acquire the right to special quantity discounts and other favorable terms of purchase. Special service, such as prompt treatment of rush orders, is more readily granted to established customers. Moreover, the single source of supply may provide financial aid to the regular customer who encounters financial stress. It will also provide management advice and market information. It may even grant an exclusive franchise or dealership for the merchandising of certain branded goods.

Some firms follow a compromise policy by which they concentrate enough purchases to justify special treatment. At the same time, they diversify purchases sufficiently to provide alternative sources of supply.

Speculative Buying   Buying substantially in excess of quantities needed to meet actual use requirements is called **speculative buying**. This is done in the expectation that prices are going up. Price appreciation produces inventory profits. The great danger is that speculative buying entails gambling on the continued rise of prices. Broad price declines subsequent to heavy speculative buying could bankrupt the speculator. Unless one is very stable financially and very wise, speculative buying should be avoided. It is typically used when the business cycle is on the way up; its use during a depression would be suicidal.

Scheduled Budget Buying   Buying to meet anticipated requirements is planned buying, or **scheduled budget buying**. This policy involves the adjustment of purchase quantities to estimated production or sales needs. Budget buying in suitable quantities will assure the maintenance of planned inventories and the meeting of product schedule requirements without delays in production due to delayed deliveries. It strikes the middle ground between hand-to-mouth buying—with its planned understocking of materials and its occasional delays due to late deliveries—and speculative buying, with its careful overstocking which entails risk as it seeks speculative profits. It represents the best type of buying for the conservative small firm.

Selection of and Relations with Suppliers

Before making a choice of suppliers, the purchaser must know the materials or merchandise to be purchased, including details of construction, quality and grade, intended use, maintenance or care required, and the importance of style features. The purchaser must also know how different grades and qualities of raw materials affect various manufacturing processess.

Factors to Consider in Selecting Suppliers A number of considerations are important in deciding which suppliers to use on a continuing basis. Three of these—price, quality, and general reputation—are explained here.

Price Quotations Quantity price discounts and shipping charges require attention in the comparison of price quotations. Price differences are significant if other factors are equal or do not offset price advantages.

Quality Ratings Some quality differences are difficult to detect, and a number of items varying in quality may be satisfactory. On some types of materials, statistical controls may be utilized by computing and recording the ratio defective of all inbound shipments from a specific vendor. In this way, the purchaser obtains an overall or average quality rating for each supplier. It also enables the purchaser to work with the supplier to upgrade quality or to cease buying from that supplier if quality improvement is not achieved.

General Reputation The supplier's general reputation is gauged by certain abilities and services. For example, can the purchaser depend upon the supplier's ability to meet delivery schedules promptly?

Services provided by the supplier must also be considered. The extension of credit by suppliers provides a major portion of the working-capital requirements of many small firms. Some suppliers provide merchandising aids, plan sales promotions, and furnish management advice. In times of recession, some small retailers have even received direct financial assistance from major suppliers of long standing. Another important service is the provision of repair work by the supplier.

Importance of Good Relations with Suppliers Good relations with suppliers are essential for firms of any size, but they are particularly important to small businesses. Perhaps the cornerstone of good supplier relationships is the buyer's realization that the supplier is usually more important to the buyer than the buyer (as a customer) is to the supplier. The buyer is only one among dozens, hundreds, or perhaps thousands buying from that supplier. Moreover, the buyer's volume of purchases over a year and the size of the individual orders are often so small that the business could be eliminated without great loss to the supplier.

To implement the policy of fair play and to cultivate good relations, the small buying firm should try to observe the following practices:

1. Pay all bills promptly.
2. See all sales representatives promptly, according them a full, courteous hearing.
3. Do not summarily cancel orders merely to gain a temporary advantage.
4. Do not argue over prices, attempting to browbeat the supplier into special concessions and unusual discounts.

5. Cooperate with the supplier by making suggestions for product improvement and/or cost reduction whenever possible.
6. If gifts are returned or reciprocal purchase contracts refused, give a courteous explanation of the reasons underlying the decision.

Small buyers must remember that it takes a long time to build good relationships with a supplier but that good relations can be destroyed by one ill-timed, tactless act.

INVENTORY CONTROL

Inventory control is not glamorous, but it can make the difference between success and failure. The larger the inventory investment, the more vital is its proper use and control. The importance of inventory control, particularly in small retail or wholesale firms, is attested to by the fact that inventory typically represents these firms' major dollar investments.

Objectives of Inventory Control

Both purchasing and inventory control have the same general objective: *to have the right goods in the right quantities at the right time and place.* This general objective requires other, more specific subgoals of inventory control.

Assured Continuous Operations   Efficient manufacturing requires work-in-process to be moved on schedule. A delay caused by lack of materials or parts can cause the shutdown of a production line, a department, or even the whole plant. Such interruption of scheduled operations is both serious and costly. Costs jump when skilled workers and machines stand idle. Given a long delay, the fulfillment of delivery promises to customers may become impossible.

Maximum Sales   Assuming adequate demand, sales are greater if goods are always available for display and/or delivery to the customer. Most customers desire to choose from an assortment of merchandise. Customers who are forced by a narrow range of choice and/or stockouts to look elsewhere may be lost permanently. On the other hand, the small store might unwisely go to the other extreme and carry too large an inventory. Management must walk the chalk line, so to speak, between overstocking and understocking in order to retain customers and maximize sales.

Protection of Assets   One of the essential functions of inventory control is to protect inventories against theft, shrinkage, or deterioration. The efficiency or wastefulness of storekeeping, manufacturing, and handling processes affects the quantity and quality of usable inventory. For example, the more often an article is picked up and physically handled, the more chance there is for physical damage. Inventory items that need special treatment can also spoil or deteriorate if improperly stored.

Minimum Inventory Investment   Effective inventory control permits inventories to be smaller without causing disservice to customers or to processing. This means that the inventory investment is less. It also means lower costs for storage space, taxes, and insurance. And inventory deterioration or obsolescence is less extensive as well.

ACTION REPORT
Inventory—A Hot Potato

To a business, inventory is like a hot potato—no one wants to hold it. In the furniture industry, long setup and production times fuel the problem. Bill Smith, president of Henredon Furniture, has felt the heat at the company's plant in Morgantown, NC. Smith explains:

> The big department stores and the chains don't give you an order at the trade fair. They have to go back home and check inventory first....Only trial and error will tell you whether to multiply the orders you write at the market by three and one-half or four or five to arrive at the proper cutting.
> ...For a store, the ideal is to sell against stock coming....They'd like not to carry inventory. But we have almost compelled them to buy inventory now.

Henredon has one new design which takes from nine to ten months to deliver. Smith concedes, "We haven't shown it because we couldn't make it in time to have the same buyer alive when he received it."

Source: "It Won't Be a Picnic Trying to Copy Us," *Forbes*, Vol. 124, No. 8 (October 15, 1979), pp. 113–115.

Administrative Uses of Inventory Records   The inventory records provide data useful for various administrative uses. For example, the records provide information for determining proper purchase quantities and ordering dates. They also provide information useful for evaluating managerial performance. The *inventory turnover ratio*, which is explained in Chapter 19, is an important tool in such an evaluation. It is a measure of how quickly inventory is sold or placed in production. Too high a turnover as well as too low a turnover can be inefficient.

Controlling Inventory Costs

It is easy to understand how effective control of inventory contributes to the "bottom line," that is, to the profitability of a firm. It is more difficult, however, to understand how to make effective inventory decisions that will minimize costs.

Types of Inventory-Related Costs   Minimizing inventory costs requires attention to many different types of costs. **Order costs** include the preparation of a purchase order, follow-up, and related bookkeeping expenses. **Quantity discounts** must also be included in such calculations. **Inventory-carrying costs** include interest costs on money tied up in inventory, insurance, storage, obsolescence, and pilferage costs. These are costs of carrying items in inventory. There is also a cost of not having items in inventory, or **stockouts**, because of lost sales or disrupted production resulting from the stockouts. Although stockout costs cannot be calculated as easily as other inventory costs, they are nonetheless real.

ABC Inventory Analysis   Some inventory items are more valuable than others and, therefore, more crucial in their effect on costs and profits. For this reason, managers should give most careful attention to those items entailing the largest investment.

One widely used approach, the **ABC method**, classifies inventory items into three categories—A, B, and C. The few high-value items in the A category account for the largest percentage of total dollars and deserve very close control. Category B items are less costly but deserve a moderate amount of attention, because they make up a larger share of the total inventory. Items in Category C contain low-cost items like paper clips in an office or nuts and bolts in a repair shop. Their carrying costs are not large enough to justify close control.

The purpose of the ABC method is to focus managerial attention where it will do the most good. There is nothing sacred, of course, about the three classes. Four classes could be created if that seemed most appropriate.

Reorder Point and Safety Stock   In maintaining inventory levels, a manager must decide the point at which additional quantities will be ordered. Calculating the **reorder point** requires consideration of the time necessary to obtain a new supply, which, in turn, depends on location of suppliers, transportation schedules, and so on.

Because of difficulty in getting new inventory at the exact time it is desired and because of irregularities in withdrawals from inventory, firms also typically maintain a **safety stock**. The safety stock provides a measure of protection against stockouts caused by emergencies of one type or another.

The **two-bin method** is a simple technique for implementing these concepts. Inventories are divided into two portions or two bins. When the first bin is exhausted, an order is placed to replenish the supply. The remaining portion should cover needs until a new supply arrives and also include a safety stock as well.

Kanban Inventory   Reducing inventory levels has been a goal of operations managers around the world. A Japanese concept, known as **kanban system**, or "just-in-time" inventory, enables them to minimize inventory carrying costs by cutting inventory to the bare minimum. New inventory is received, presumably, just as the last item from the existing inventory is placed into service. This, in turn, contributes to their lower costs in production of autos and other products. Many U.S. firms have adopted some form of the kanban system, and small business can likewise benefit from its use.

By keeping inventory at such low levels, a firm minimizes inventory costs. Careful coordination of operations is required, however, to avoid costly stockouts—for example, a mistake leading to the shutdown of a production line. If the inventory is held too low, the firm will suffer in loss of sales or production.

Economic Order Quantity   If a firm could order inventory with no expense other than the cost of the merchandise or material, it would be less concerned about the amount to order at one time. As noted above, however, high carrying costs associated with large orders tend to offset the lower order costs.

The goal is to purchase that quantity which minimizes the total costs of ordering and carrying the inventory. Figure 18–4 portrays the behavior of these costs. The total-costs curve is simply the sum of the carrying and order costs at the various quantity levels.

Figure 18–4   Carrying Costs, Order Costs, and EOQ

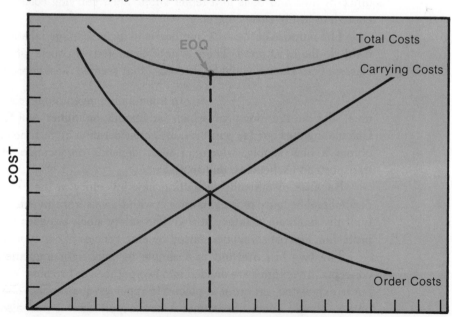

ORDER QUANTITY (UNITS)

The **economic order quantity** is the quantity to be purchased which minimizes total costs, and it is the point labeled "EOQ" in Figure 18–4. Notice that it is the lowest point on the total-costs curve and that it coincides with the intersection of the carrying-costs and order-costs curves. If sufficient information on costs is available, this point can be calculated with some precision.[1]

Inventory Accounting Systems

A small business needs a system for keeping tabs on its inventory. The larger the business, the greater is the need. Also, since manufacturers are concerned with three broad categories of inventory (raw materials and supplies, work-in-process, and finished goods), their accounting for inventory is more complex than that for wholesalers and retailers.

Although some record keeping is unavoidable, small firms should emphasize simplicity of control methods. Too much control is as wasteful as it is unnecessary.

Physical Inventory Method   The traditional method of taking physical inventory is for two people to go from item to item, with one calling off the kind of item and the number of units on hand while the other records this information.[2] Others have improved on this system by using only one clerk, who counts off the items into a dictating machine or a tape recorder. The inventory data sheets can then be typed directly from this recording. Although manual control systems are customarily adequate, the use of computer-aided systems should be adopted by small firms if at all possible.

Perpetual Inventory Method   A **perpetual inventory system** provides a current record of inventory items. It does not require a physical count of inventory. Periodically, a physical count can be made to assure the accuracy of the perpetual system and to make adjustments for such factors as theft. The **stores card** illustrated in Figure 18–5 is the basic control tool in a perpetual inventory system covering raw materials and supplies.

With a separate perpetual inventory card for each raw material or supply item, the firm will always know the number of units on hand. If each receipt and issue is costed, the dollar value of these units is also known.

Use of a perpetual inventory system may be justified in the small factory or the wholesale warehouse. In particular, this is desirable for expensive and critical items—for example, those which could cause significant losses through theft or serious production delays.

Perpetual inventory control for finished goods is similarly available, but the cards used in this case are known as **stock cards** rather than stores cards. Techniques for the use of stock cards are the same as for stores cards.

Figure 18–5   A Stores Card

	Receipts			Issues			Balance on Hand		

STORES CARD

SHAFER SHOE COMPANY

Item: Metal Eyelets

Maximum No. of Pairs   60,000
Reorder Point No. of Pairs   24,000
Minimum No. of Pairs   12,000

Date	Receipts Pairs	Receipts Price per Pair	Receipts Cost	Issues Pairs	Issues Price per Pair	Issues Cost	Balance on Hand Pairs	Balance on Hand Price per Pair	Balance on Hand Cost*
Jan. 1							14,000	$.00400	$ 56.00
2				2,500	$.00400	$10.00	11,500	.00400	46.00
3	48,000	$.00420	$201.60				59,500	.00416	247.60
3				2,000	.00416	8.32	57,500	.00416	239.28
4				2,100	.00416	8.74	55,400	.00416	230.54
7				2,000	.00416	8.32	53,400	.00416	222.22

*Minor discrepancies in this column are due to 5-place rounding in the preceding column. The stores card is used by routing and planning clerks to assure an adequate supply of materials and parts to complete any given factory order.

Retail Inventory Valuation

Retailers can value their inventories at cost or at retail. The retail inventory method requires that starting inventory and purchases be recorded at both cost and retail; sales, net markdowns, and net added markups are to be entered at retail only.[3]

Retail Inventory Valuation Procedure   The procedure may be illustrated with the following data from a small department store recorded for the month of April:

Sales $75,000
Added markups 6,000
Markdowns 2,500
Markdown cancellations 1,800
Purchases .... 45,000 at cost ($81,000 at retail)
Freight in........................... 500
Starting inventory .... 1,000 at cost ($1,800 at retail)

To find the **retail value** of ending inventory for this department store, first tabulate the data so that starting inventory, purchases, freight in, and net added markups can be totaled to provide cost and retail values of goods available for sale during April. Then deduct the total of sales and net markdowns, which are separately recorded at retail, from the total retail value of starting inventory, purchases, and net added markups.

The resulting tabulation is shown below, with $13,100 as the retail value of ending inventory.

	Cost	Retail
Starting inventory................	$ 1,000	$ 1,800
Purchases	45,000	81,000
Freight in.....................	500	
Net added markups		6,000
Goods available for sale	$46,500	$88,800
Sales	$75,000	
Net markdowns.................	700	75,700
Ending inventory (retail value)		$13,100

For balance-sheet purposes, the *cost value* of ending inventory is needed. This unknown amount in dollars, symbolized by X, can be calculated algebraically as follows:

$$\frac{\text{Ending Inventory (Cost)}}{\text{Ending Inventory (Retail)}} = \frac{\text{Goods Available for Sale (Cost)}}{\text{Goods Available for Sale (Retail)}}$$

$$\frac{X}{\$13,100} = \frac{\$46,500}{\$88,800}$$

$$\$88,800X = \$609,150,000$$

$$X = \frac{\$609,150,000}{\$88,800} = \$6,859.80$$

The balance sheet of this department store would show the merchandise inventory at $6,860 (rounded to the closest dollar), which is its value stated in cost dollars.

Primary Use of the Retail Inventory Valuation Method   The retail inventory valuation method was developed primarily for department stores as a basis for *dollar control* of merchandise stocks involving a multiplicity of items in a number of departments. Such inventory conditions, together with a high volume of sales, preclude the use of perpetual inventory cards for each item and also make the use of physical inventory methods arduous and unsatisfactory for control. But the retail inventory valuation method does not contribute to *unit control*.

Advantages of the Retail Inventory Valuation Method   The retail inventory valuation method is approved for income tax reporting. It facilitates the preparation of monthly financial statements, which would be prohibitively expensive if physical inventories were required as their basis. Moreover, this method gives a more conservative balance-sheet evaluation than historical cost data would provide because it relates the inventory values to current sales prices. Hence, the retail inventory valuation method gives valuations equivalent to the lower of cost or market value.

Weaknesses of the Retail Inventory Valuation Method   The retail inventory valuation method has the following weaknesses:

1. Being based on averages and applied on a department-wide or class-of-merchandise basis, this method tends to overvalue certain merchandise items and undervalue others. That is, the inventory value on the balance sheet shows a cost value for total inventory which assumes that all inventory items have the same relation between cost and sales price; this is frequently untrue.

   The retailer ordinarily finds it desirable or necessary to sell merchandise with different gross margins. To the extent that sales are not proportional among the merchandise groups carrying different gross margins, the inventory value computed by the retail inventory valuation method may be distorted. That is, separate inventories, using this method, are required for each "gross margin" class for accuracy.

2. Given very frequent markups and markdowns, the record keeping for the retail inventory valuation method becomes arduous and costly. This is particularly true if separate "gross margin class" inventories are maintained individually under this method.

3. The system also ignores stock shortages and employee discounts, and suffers disadvantages in the proper handling of trade-ins and customer discounts. Of course, physical inventory, used along with this method, helps reveal the "ignored" stock shortages.

The retail inventory valuation method may be an effective system, and it is certainly a unified, integrated system of inventory control in a retail store. Nevertheless, its disadvantages may sometimes outweigh its advantages. Hence, the small retailer should consider carefully both its strengths and its limitations before reaching a decision on its use.

Looking Back

1. The purchasing cycle includes the receipt and evaluation of a purchase request, issuance of the purchase order, maintenance of buying and warehousing records, follow-up of purchases, and receipt and inspection of purchased items.
2. Policies related to purchasing include reciprocal buying, making or buying parts, substituting materials or merchandise, taking all purchase discounts, diversifying sources of supply, hand-to-mouth buying, speculative buying, and scheduled budget buying.
3. Choice of a supplier entails consideration of the supplier's price, quality rating, ability to meet delivery schedules, quality of service, and general reputation. Good relations with suppliers are particularly valuable to small firms.
4. The objectives of inventory control include: assured continuous operations, maximum sales, protection of assets, minimum inventory investment, and administrative uses of inventory records.
5. Maintaining inventory involves a variety of costs, including order costs, carrying costs, and stockout costs. The minimum amount which can be carried depends on the time required to replenish the supply and on the necessary safety stock. Carrying costs are minimized by holding inventory to a minimum, the objective of the kanban system. Total costs are minimized by calculating the economic order quantity, the purchase amount that most economically balances large-order costs and small-order costs.
6. A physical inventory system consists of taking an actual count of items on hand and recording the information. A perpetual inventory system does not require an actual count but provides a current record by recording additions and withdrawals on inventory cards. In retail businesses, the value of inventories may be calculated by using data on beginning inventory, purchases, sales, markups, markdowns, and the ratio of cost to retail prices.

DISCUSSION QUESTIONS

1. What conditions make purchasing a particularly vital function in any given business? If it is important, can the owner–manager of a small firm safely delegate the authority to buy to a subordinate? Explain.
2. Of what value are purchasing records to a small firm?

3. Is reciprocal buying ethical? Wise? Necessary? Explain, with special reference in your answer to a (a) jewelry store, (b) plumbing contractor, and (c) small manufacturer who produces plywood pallets.

4. Under what conditions should the small manufacturer make component parts or buy them from others?

5. Compare the arguments for and against the concentration of purchases with only one or two suppliers.

6. State the factors governing a small manufacturer's selection of a supplier of a vitally important raw material.

7. Does the maximization of inventory turnover also result in the maximization of sales? Explain.

8. Explain and justify the use of the ABC method of inventory analysis. How would it work in an automobile repair shop?

9. What is *kanban*, or *just-in-time* inventory? What are the advantages and dangers of using it in a small firm?

10. Explain the retail inventory valuation method as it would be applied in a small department store.

ENDNOTES

1. See an operations management text for formulas and calculations related to the economic order quantity. One example is James H. Greene, *Operations Management: Productivity and Profit* (Reston: Reston Publishing Company, 1984), Chapter 19.

2. The use of two persons supposedly guarantees the honesty, accuracy, and completeness of the physical inventory, *as recorded.*

3. Initial markup is the excess of initial sales price over the purchase cost of the goods and the pertinent transportation cost. Added markups are increases in selling price above initially marked prices. These may later be cancelled, in part, in which case the difference is the net added markup. Markdowns are reductions below original sales prices. These may be subsequently cancelled, in part, in which case the difference is the net markdown.

REFERENCES TO SMALL BUSINESS IN ACTION

Ford, Joan G. "How to End the Inventory Poker Game." *Inc.*, Vol. 3, No. 5 (May, 1981), pp. 76–79.

A company president realized that customers were maintaining inventories beyond their needs. This article tells how he developed a computer program to reduce these inventories.

"Phoenix." *Forbes*, Vol. 125, No. 8 (April 14, 1980), pp. 122–124.

The inventory experiences of the new Shopsmith Company demonstrate the need for tight inventory control.

Slutsker, Gary. "When Quick Success Is a Mixed Blessing." *Venture*, Vol. 2, No. 10 (October, 1980), pp. 67–69.
> The importance of an inventory control system is demonstrated by the experiences of a small photographic service. The system keeps track of rolls of film while they are being processed by different labs.

Waters, Craig R. "Profit and Loss." *Inc.*, Vol. 7, No. 4 (April, 1985), pp. 103–112.
> A Virginia company, Xaloy, Inc., made substantial savings by shifting to a "just-in-time" inventory system. Problems in operations management were experienced as some personnel found it difficult to adapt to the new system.

_____. "Why Everybody's Talking About 'Just-In-Time'." *Inc.*, Vol. 6, No. 3 (March, 1984), pp. 77–90.
> Many companies, including small ones, are adopting some variation of the "just-in-time" inventory system, thereby reducing inventory levels. Specific cases are reported.

CASE 18

Mather's Heating and Air Conditioning
Selecting and dealing with suppliers

Fred Mather operated a small heating and air-conditioning firm which sold and serviced heating and air-conditioning systems. Over the years the firm had changed from primary reliance on one manufacturer—Western Engineering—as the major supplier to a more balanced arrangement involving three suppliers. In the following discussion with a consultant, Fred described some points of friction in dealing with Western Engineering.

Fred: Western Engineering is so big that it can't be customer-oriented. Why, with my firm they've probably lost $600,000 or $700,000 worth of business just because of their inflexibility!

Consultant: They can't bend to take care of your needs?

Fred: Right. They're not flexible. And part of it, of course, is due to the sales reps they have. They just blew the Mather account. We sold Western equipment mostly until we just got disgusted with them.

Consultant: Did the situation just deteriorate over time?

Fred: True. Finally, after a good period of time, I started getting on them. I'm kind of temperamental. I finally just made up my mind—although I didn't tell them—that in the future our policy will be to sell other equipment also. In essence, what we've done since then is sell more Marshall Corporation and Solex equipment than we have Western.

Consultant: What bothered you about Western Engineering?

Fred: It is really a combination of things. The sales rep, for example. Instead of creating a feeling that he was going to try to take care of you and work with you and be for you, he was always on the opposite side of the fence. It was really strange. Western had certain items that were special quotes to help us be competitive. Well, he was always wanting to take different items off the special quote list every time there was a price change. But we needed every item we could get. This is a very competitive area.

Consultant: What other kinds of problems did he create?

Fred: On paperwork, he would not get it done. Let me give you an example about this sign in front of the business. We bought that sign when we bought the business, and we paid Western for it. About a year later, he came back and said, "Western has a new policy. The sign can no longer belong to the owner, so we will return the money you paid for the sign." I said, "Now that you have operated on my money for a year, the sign doesn't belong to me?" I went along with it, but it was the idea of the thing. They tell you one thing and then do something else.

Consultant: Were there other special incidents that occurred?

Fred: One time we got a job involving $30,000 or $40,000 worth of equipment. I told the rep it *appeared* that we had the job. We had a verbal contract, but that wasn't final. The next thing I knew, the equipment was sitting in Central Truck Lines out here. I hadn't ordered the equipment or anything. Fortunately, we did get the contract. But we weren't ready for the equipment for two more months and had no place to put it. And I ended up paying interest. It irritated me to no end.

Consultant: Was that what made you lean toward the other suppliers?

Fred: The final straw was the Park Lake project—a four-story renovation. I had designed the heating and air-conditioning system myself. I called the rep, intending to use Western equipment, and requested a price. So he called back and gave me a lump sum. There were lots of different items, and they were broken down into groups. I asked him to price the items by groups to provide various options to the purchaser. He replied, "We can't break it out." I said, "What do you mean, you can't break it out?" He said something about company policy. I really came unglued, but he never knew.

Consultant: What did you do about it?

Fred: As soon as I quit talking with him, I picked up the phone and called the Marshall Corporation rep. In just a few hours, we had prices that were broken down as I wanted them. The total price turned out to be $2,500 more, but I bought it! That was the end of Western Engineering as sole supplier.

Questions

1. What services did Fred Mather expect from the supplier? Were these unreasonable expectations?
2. Evaluate Fred's reaction when the Western Engineering rep declined to give him a breakdown on the price. Was Fred's decision to pay $2,500 more for the other equipment a rational decision?
3. Was Western Engineering at fault in shipping the large $30,000 or $40,000 order on the basis of an oral commitment and in the absence of an order? What should Fred have done about it?
4. Are the deficiencies that bother Fred caused by weaknesses of Western Engineering or merely the sales rep who sells for them?
5. Should Fred continue to use three separate suppliers or concentrate more purchases with one of them?

PART V
FINANCIAL AND ADMINISTRATIVE CONTROLS

19 – Accounting Systems, Financial Analysis, and Budgeting
20 – Working-Capital Management and Capital Budgeting
21 – Computerizing the Small Business
22 – Business Risks and Insurance

19

Accounting Systems, Financial Analysis, and Budgeting

Not every small-business manager can expect to be an expert accountant. But every entrepreneur should know enough about the income statement and the balance sheet to recognize optional accounting methods which will work to the advantage of the business's goals. For example, consider the president of a helicopter transportation company who was getting loan rejections due to his negative net worth shown on the balance sheet. The president had left all accounting matters to "a really good tax accountant...It turned out that the company's accountant was 'expensing'—that is, writing off in one year—the entire cost of the major overhauls the company did on its helicopters."

Although the write-off by the accountant was legitimate and helped reduce current taxable income, it was negatively affecting the balance sheet. The company went to another CPA for advice. "The new CPA redid the financial statement for the previous three years, and almost magically the retained earnings account turned positive."

This entrepreneur learned that it is good business to prepare financial statements tailored to the user's needs.

Source: Reprinted by permission of the *Harvard Business Review*. Excerpt from "Managing Financial Statements—Image and Effect" by James McNeill Stancill (March/April 1981). Copyright © 1981 by the President and Fellows of Harvard College; all rights reserved.

Looking Ahead

Watch for the following important topics:

1. Considerations in establishing an accounting system.
2. Selecting alternative accounting methods.
3. Typical accounting statements prepared by a small business.
4. Ratio analysis of accounting statements.
5. Budgeting in small firms.

A strong accounting system provides valuable information for planning, controlling, and evaluating the performance of a small business. Outwardly, a business may appear sound, but actually it may be in poor health. Accounting information is the firm's X ray which allows the entrepreneur to monitor the "medical condition" of the business. Accounting statements, financial ratios, and budgets are important aspects of a complete accounting system. We will examine each of these in this chapter.

MAJOR CONSIDERATIONS UNDERLYING AN ACCOUNTING SYSTEM

An accounting system structures the flow of financial information from the initial transaction to the points necessary to develop a financial picture of business activity. Exactly where these points are depends on the firm and its financial reporting goals. Some very small firms may not even require formal financial statements. Others may need financial statements monthly and want them to be computer-generated.

Regardless of the level of sophistication, any accounting system should accomplish the following objectives for a small business:

1. The system should yield an accurate, thorough picture of operating results.
2. The records should permit a quick comparison of current data with prior years' operating results and with budgetary goals.
3. The records should provide financial statements for use by management, bankers, and prospective creditors.
4. The system should facilitate prompt filing of reports and tax returns to regulatory and tax-collecting agencies of the government.
5. The system should reveal employee fraud, theft, waste, and recordkeeping errors.

Consistency with Accepted Principles of Accounting

An accounting system must be consistent with accepted principles of accounting theory and practice. This means that a business must be consistent in its treatment of given data and given transactions. Since designing an accounting system is seldom done well by the amateur, the services of a certified public accountant ordinarily are required for this purpose.[1]

Larger accounting firms are now paying closer attention to the accounting needs of small businesses. For example, each of the Big Eight accounting firms now has a special division to cater to small firms. The fees charged by these national accounting firms are usually higher than the accountant down the street, but discounts are available.[2] Obviously, fees are an important consideration in selecting an accountant, but there are other major factors in this decision. For example, a recent survey of small businesses by *Inc. Magazine* found personal attention, reputation, and experience to be important criteria for selecting an accountant.[3]

ACTION REPORT
GAAP and Small Business

Generally Accepted Accounting Principles (GAAP) must be observed by large and small business. However, many people believe it is harder for a small business to develop accounting procedures within GAAP standards. For example:

> Privately held Dierckx Equipment Corp...does a lot of leasing as part of its equipment business. GAAP requires that these leases be capitalized, and that has placed Dierckx in the middle of a catch-22 with the banks. If it doesn't capitalize its leases, it's not in compliance with GAAP, and the bank may not like that. If it does capitalize leases, its leverage ratio looks a lot worse, and the banks may not like that. Not only does this GAAP requirement endanger Dierckx' credit rating, but the cost of complying with that *one* requirement is $7,500 annually. Says Financial Vice-President Ray Romano: "It's just a paper entry. It's immaterial. But it adds a lot of bookkeeping time. Our auditors must spend at least three days just going through the lease transactions, and without that requirement that wouldn't be necessary."

There are many proponents for a separate set of standards for small companies. The American Institute of Certified Public Accountants is aware of the problem. Dan Guy, director of auditing research, says, "You can't apply a large-client audit approach in a small-business setting. It doesn't work."

Source: "The World According to GAAP," by Jay Gissen, *Forbes*, Vol. 127, No. 12 (June 8, 1981), pp. 148–149.

Availability and Quality of Accounting Records

An accounting system provides the framework for managerial control of the firm. The effectiveness of the system rests basically on a well-designed and managed recordkeeping system. The major types of accounting records and the financial decisions to which they are related are briefly described below.

1. *Accounts-receivable records.* Records of receivables are vital not only to decisions on credit extension but also to accurate billing and to maintenance of good customer relations. An analysis of these records reveals the degree of effectiveness of the firm's credit and collection policies.

2. *Accounts-payable records.* Records of liabilities show what the firm owes, facilitate the taking of cash discounts, and allow payments to be made when due.

3. *Inventory records.* Adequate records are essential to the control and security of inventory items. In addition, they supply information for use in purchasing, maintenance of adequate stock levels, and computation of turnover ratios.

4. *Payroll records.* The payroll records show the total payments to employees and provide the base for computing and paying the various payroll taxes.

5. *Cash records.* Carefully maintained records showing all receipts and disbursements are necessary to safeguard cash. They yield a knowledge of cash flow and balances on hand. An example of one cash record—summary of daily sales and cash receipts—is shown in Figure 19-1.

6. *Other records.* Among other accounting records which are vital to the efficient operation of the small business are the insurance register, which shows all policies in force; records of leaseholds; and records covering the firm's investments outside of its business.

To safeguard business assets and prevent errors, the accounting records should be accurately maintained, transaction by transaction. No one employee should completely control any given business transaction. For example, cashiering and account collections should be divorced from bookkeeping, and the bookkeeper should never be allowed to authorize purchases.

In addition, data analyses and reports should ordinarily depend upon the efforts of at least two persons. Of course, in a small business using cash registers, the cash register tape provides a double check on cash received by the cashier. Such procedures tend to prevent fraud and errors.

Computer software packages are now available which can be used on the small firm's own personal computer. Most of the simpler software routines fall into one of three categories:

1. Those which are a computerized checkbook, automatically calculating the balance and printing checks.

2. Those that provide a budget and compare actual expenditures with budget expenditures.

3. Those that prepare income statements and balance sheets.[4]

Additionally, there are numerous software packages for specialized accounting needs such as graphs, cash-flow analysis, and tax preparation.[5]

Figure 19–1   Typical Sales and Cash Receipts Summary Form

Date_____

SUMMARY OF SALES AND CASH RECEIPTS

Cash Receipts

1. Sales for cash $_____
2. Collections of cash from previous charge sales $_____
3. Miscellaneous cash receipts $_____
   (Individual receipts attached)
4.   Total cash receipts $_____

Cash on Hand

5. Cash in registers $_____
6. Less beginning petty cash (Minus) $_____
7. Net cash to deposit $_____
8. Cash (short) or over $_____

Total Sales

9. Cash sales $_____
10. Charge sales (Charge slips attached) $_____
11.   Total sales $_____

As an alternative to account keeping by an employee or a member of the owner's family, a firm may have its financial records kept by a certified public accountant or by a bookkeeping or computer service agency that caters to small businesses. Very small businesses often find it convenient to have one and the same firm keep the books, prepare the statements and tax returns, and make the periodic audits. Numerous small accounting firms offer a complete accounting service to small businesses.

Retention of Accounting Records

The life of an accounting record is not necessarily long. Nevertheless, some firms habitually keep all records without considering the future need for them. If a business is quite small and the records can be housed in just a few filing cabinets, the problem is not serious. For most firms, however, there are two weaknesses in such a policy. First, the excess storage equipment and the unnecessary handling of records are wasteful. Second, loading the files with unnecessary material makes it difficult and time-consuming to locate important information when it is needed.

Essential records, including those legally required for possible government audit, must be maintained as long as the actual need exists. The records may have to be kept for three, five, or ten years—or even longer. Nevertheless, every firm should study its needs and retain essential records only for the requisite time periods.

Once retention needs have been determined, the additional problem of reducing the cost of maintaining records should be resolved. The increased usage of personal computers for small-business accounting has helped with the problem of record retention. The floppy disks used by these computers file large amounts of data in a small physical space. These floppy disks are easy to handle and easy to store. Copies of data disks should always be retained, preferably in another location, for backup purposes. Chapter 21 of this textbook discusses these small computer systems.

Physical Protection of Accounting Records

Fires, floods, tornadoes, and other disasters can occur at any time. The loss of all business records in one such disaster could bankrupt a firm. Some precautions are clearly desirable to minimize such dangers. How extensive these should be necessarily depends upon the importance of the records. Financial records may be stored in fireproof safes or cabinets on the premises. Microfilmed copies of the originals, along with other important business documents, might be stored in the firm's safety deposit box. The firm could also build a subsurface storeroom on company premises, separated from the main office and plant, for storing basic or duplicate records. This will involve some expense, but the precautionary measures afford a protection that may be viewed as a type of business insurance.

SELECTING ALTERNATIVE ACCOUNTING OPTIONS

Accounting records can be kept in just about any form as long as they provide users with the data needed and they are legally proper. This implies that the small business has certain options in selecting accounting systems and accounting methods. And this is usually the case. Most entrepreneurs want to minimize the time and effort devoted to developing and managing their firm's accounting systems. However, they should take the necessary time to become aware of current accounting issues and alternative accounting practices.

Three accounting options—cash versus accrual accounting, single-entry versus double-entry systems, and LIFO versus FIFO inventory valuation—are examined in the following sections. These three represent only a few of several alternative accounting methods available to the small business. Other examples are optional accounting periods and depreciation methods.

Cash vs. Accrual Accounting

The major distinction between cash and accrual accounting is the point at which a firm "recognizes" revenue and expenses. The **cash method of accounting** is easier to use and reports revenue and expenses only when cash is received or payment is made. Under the **accrual method of accounting**, revenue and expenses are reported when they are incurred regardless of when the cash is received or payment is made.

The cash method of accounting is generally selected by the very small business, as well as those businesses whose receivables move slowly and who want to help their cash flow by avoiding the payment of taxes on income not yet received. However, the cash method does not provide as accurate a matching of revenue and expenses as most accountants desire.

On the other hand, the accrual method of accounting matches revenues when they are earned against the expenses associated with that revenue. The accrual method involves more recordkeeping but also provides a more realistic measure of profitability within an accounting period.

It should be noted that the small business has the option of using one method for keeping its internal records and another for tax-reporting purposes. The Internal Revenue Service does, however, have some restrictions on changing methods from one year to the next.

Single-Entry vs. Double-Entry Systems

The system of accounts which records financial transactions does not have to be identical in every business. The informational needs of the users will ultimately determine the number of and complexity of the accounts in the system. In the very small business, a single-entry recordkeeping system is still found. It is not, however, a system to be recommended to businesses which are striving to grow and become efficient in financial planning.

A single-entry system neither incorporates a balance sheet nor directly generates an income statement. A **single-entry system** is basically a checkbook system of receipts and disbursements supported by sales tickets and disbursement receipts. The sales and disbursements may be summarized daily and monthly in separate reports, but the checkbook is the focal point of the single-entry of a transaction.

A **double-entry system** of accounting incorporates journals and ledgers and requires that each transaction be recorded twice in the accounts—hence the name double-entry. There are two major advantages of the double-entry system. First, it has a built-in, self-balancing characteristic. If no math errors have been made, the debits recorded will always equal the credits recorded. Second, transactions are recorded in such a way as to provide a natural flow into finished financial statements.

There are basically four components of a double-entry accounting system. These are named below in the order in which they are involved in recording and summarizing financial transactions:

1. *Original source documents.* These would include checks, purchase orders, receipts, etc.
2. *Books of original entry.* These include the general journal and specialized journals such as cash receipts and cash disbursements journals.
3. *Ledger accounts.* These are separate accounts containing the "posting" of the journal entries affecting the ledger balance. These ledger accounts are grouped into asset, liability, capital, income, and expense accounts.
4. *Financial statements.* These are the end products of the financial system and are computed from the ledger accounts.

Introductory accounting textbooks provide considerable information on setting up a double-entry system.[6] Office supply retail stores can provide most of the actual recordkeeping journals and ledgers which are needed. A number of special-purpose forms are available which facilitate manual recordkeeping. For example, there is a One-Write System which uses pre-printed forms so that, when a payroll check is written, the entry is simultaneously entered on the payroll ledger.

FIFO vs. LIFO Inventory Valuation

Small businesses have several accounting options related directly to tax planning. One such option is the selection of LIFO (Last-in-First-Out) over FIFO (First-in-First-Out) inventory valuation. Both FIFO and LIFO are alternatives for reporting the product cost associated with the actual product sold. **FIFO** assumes that the first product in inventory is the first product out of inventory. **LIFO** allows the most recent cost of a product placed in inventory to be charged against revenue regardless of whether that most recent unit was actually sold and delivered to a customer.

During periods of inflation, LIFO appears to be the clear choice. Dan Fensin, a partner in a Chicago accounting firm, argues that LIFO is "the only way to fly...How can anybody ignore a legal way to reduce taxes?"[7] LIFO usually results in reporting higher costs of goods sold and therefore lower operating income. This of course results in lower taxes.[8]

TYPICAL ACCOUNTING STATEMENTS

The preparation of financial statements is made possible by the existence of accurate and thorough accounting records. Four major financial statements of the BLM Manufacturing Company, a hypothetical small corporation, are illustrated in this section. Two of these statements—the income statement and the balance sheet—will be referred to in the discussion of financial ratios later in the chapter.

Income Statement

The **income statement** shows the results of a firm's operations over a period of time, usually one year. Figure 19-2 on page 511 shows the income statement of the BLM Manufacturing Company. A minor variation would be involved in preparing an income statement for a retailing or wholesaling firm rather than a manufacturing firm. Specifically, the "Cost of goods sold" section in Figure 19-2 would make reference to purchases rather than to manufacturing costs.

Balance Sheet

The **balance sheet** is a statement that shows a firm's financial position at a specific date. Figure 19-3 on page 512 shows the balance sheet of the BLM Manufacturing Company as of December 31, 1986. If this firm were a proprietorship or a partnership, the term "Stockholders' Equity" would read "Capital." And the items listed in this section would show individual ownership investments.

Statement of Cost of Goods Manufactured

The **statement of cost of goods manufactured** is a supporting, detailed schedule of the "cost of goods manufactured" entry in the income statement. Figure 19-4 on page 513 shows the BLM Manufacturing Company's statement of cost of goods manufactured. If this company were a retailing or wholesaling firm, no supporting schedule comparable to Figure 19-4 would be required.

Figure 19-2   Income Statement

The BLM Manufacturing Company
Income Statement
For Year Ended Dec. 31, 1986

Sales			$830,200
Cost of goods sold:			
Finished goods inventory, Jan. 1, 1986		$ 77,000	
Cost of goods manufactured		589,350	
Total cost of finished goods available for sale . . .		$666,350	
Less finished goods inventory, Dec. 31, 1986. . . .		102,000	
Cost of goods sold.			564,350
Gross profit on sales.			$265,850
Operating expenses:			
Selling expenses:			
Sales salaries and commissions	$ 57,150		
Advertising expense	38,600		
Miscellaneous selling expense	5,000		
Total selling expenses		$100,750	
General expenses:			
Officers' salaries	$ 46,120		
Office salaries	16,600		
Depreciation—office equipment	3,600		
Bad-debts expense	4,100		
Miscellaneous office expense.	5,580		
Total general expenses		76,000	
Total operating expenses			176,750
Operating income			$ 89,100
Other expense:			
Interest expense			10,000
Net profit before income tax			$ 79,100
Income tax.			17,390
Net profit after income tax			$ 61,710

Figure 19–3   Balance Sheet

The BLM Manufacturing Company
Balance Sheet
Dec. 31, 1986
ASSETS

Current Assets:

Cash		$ 44,480	
Accounts receivable	$ 83,000		
Less allowance for uncollectible accounts	5,000	78,000	

Inventories (at lower of cost or market):

Finished goods	$102,000		
Work in process	52,000		
Raw materials	57,450	211,450	
Factory supplies		8,000	
Prepaid insurance		5,800	
Total current assets			$347,730

Plant Assets:	Cost	Accumulated Depreciation	Book Value	
Office equipment	$ 36,000	$ 16,200	$ 19,800	
Factory equipment	552,000	327,000	225,000	
Buildings	250,000	40,000	210,000	
Land	70,000	—	70,000	
Total plant assets	$908,000	$383,200		524,800

Intangible assets:

Patents	55,000
TOTAL ASSETS	$927,530

LIABILITIES AND STOCKHOLDERS' EQUITY

Current liabilities:

Accounts payable	$ 77,200	
Estimated income tax payable	17,390	
Salaries and wages payable	3,930	
Interest payable	2,500	
Total current liabilities		$101,020

Long-term liabilities:

First mortgage 10% notes payable (due 1991)	200,000	
Total liabilities		$301,020
Common stock, no-par (30,000 shares authorized and issued)	$300,000	
Retained earnings	326,510	
Total stockholders' equity		626,510
TOTAL LIABILITIES AND STOCKHOLDERS' EQUITY		$927,530

Figure 19-4   Statement of Cost of Goods Manufactured

The BLM Manufacturing Company
Statement of Cost of Goods Manufactured
For Year Ended Dec. 31, 1986

Work-in-process inventory, Jan. 1, 1986		$ 40,000
Raw materials:		
Inventory, Jan. 1, 1986	$ 64,000	
Purchases	241,600	
Cost of materials available for use	$305,600	
Less inventory, Dec. 31, 1986	57,450	
Cost of materials placed in production	$248,150	
Direct labor	197,500	
Factory overhead:		
Indirect labor	$38,600	
Factory maintenance	16,000	
Heat, light, and power	23,600	
Property taxes	10,000	
Depreciation of factory equipment	35,200	
Depreciation of buildings	6,000	
Amortization of patents	5,000	
Factory supplies expense	12,000	
Insurance expense	5,200	
Miscellaneous factory expense	4,100	
Total factory overhead	155,700	
Total manufacturing costs		601,350
Total work in process during period		$641,350
Less work-in-process inventory, Dec. 31, 1986		52,000
Cost of goods manufactured		$589,350

Statement of Changes in Financial Position

Formerly known as the "statement of sources and uses of funds," the **statement of changes in financial position** shows how a firm acquired working capital and employed it over the same period covered by the income statement. Figure 19–5 shows the BLM Manufacturing Company's statement of changes in financial position for the year ended December 31, 1986.

Figure 19-5   Statement of Changes in Financial Position

The BLM Manufacturing Company
Statement of Changes in Financial Position
For Year Ended Dec. 31, 1986

Increases in working capital were provided by:
  Operations:

Net profit (per income statement)	$61,710	
Add: Depreciation expense charged to operations	44,800	
Amortization of patents	5,000	$111,510

Working capital was applied to:

Dividends	$18,000	
Purchase of equipment	46,200	
Retirement of long-term notes payable	40,000	104,200

Increase in working capital .... $ 7,310

The net increase in working capital is accounted for as follows:

	Jan. 1 1986	Dec. 31 1986	Working Capital Increase	Working Capital Decrease
Cash	$ 38,000	$ 44,480	$ 6,480	
Accounts receivable (net)	92,000	78,000		$ 14,000
Inventories	181,000	211,450	30,450	
Prepaid expenses and supplies	17,800	13,800		4,000
Accounts payable	56,400	77,200		20,800
Income taxes payable	29,000	17,390	11,610	
Other payables	4,000	6,430		2,430
			$48,540	$ 41,230
Net increase in working capital			—	7,310
			$48,540	$ 48,540

ANALYSIS OF FINANCIAL STATEMENTS

A single item from a financial statement has only limited meaning until it is related to some other item. For example, current assets of $10,000 mean one thing when current liabilities are $5,000 and another when they are $50,000. For this reason, ratios have been developed to relate different income-statement items to each other, different balance-sheet items to each other, and income-statement items to balance-sheet items.

Although numerous financial statement ratios can be computed, only those that are the most practical and widely used for small businesses will be explained here. These ratios will be grouped into four classifications, using the financial statements of the BLM Manufacturing Company for illustrative purposes. It must be emphasized that a careful interpretation of ratios is required to make them useful to a particular firm. A ratio may indicate potential trouble, but it cannot explain either the causes or the seriousness of the situation. Most small firms find it helpful to compare their ratios with their own past experience and with industry standard ratios.

Ratios Related to Working-Capital Position

Adequacy and liquidity of working capital are measured by two ratios: the current ratio and the acid-test (or quick) ratio.

Current Ratio   To compute the **current ratio**, divide current assets by current liabilities. The "banker's rule" for this ratio is "at least two to one" for working capital to be judged adequate. Actually the proper size of this ratio depends upon the type of industry, the season of the year, and other factors. The current ratio of the BLM Manufacturing Company is:

$$\frac{\text{Current assets}}{\text{Current liabilities}} = \frac{\$347,730}{\$101,020} = 3.44 \text{ times}$$

From this it appears that the BLM Manufacturing Company has sufficient cash and other assets which will be quickly converted into cash to pay all maturing obligations.

Acid-Test (or Quick) Ratio   A more severe test of adequacy of working capital is provided by the **acid-test (or quick) ratio**. To compute this ratio, divide current assets less inventories by current liabilities. The exclusion of inventories from current assets is necessary because inventories are in part a fixed-capital investment and are less liquid than other current assets. The BLM Manufacturing Company's acid-test ratio is:

$$\frac{\text{Current assets less inventories}}{\text{Current liabilities}} = \frac{\$347,730 - \$211,450}{\$101,020} = 1.35 \text{ times}$$

The traditional rule of thumb is a minimum of 1 to 1 acid-test ratio. Again it appears the BLM Manufacturing Company's working-capital position is sound.

Ratios Related to the Sales Position

Comparisons between the level of sales and the investment in various asset accounts involve the use of three ratios: inventory turnover, average collection period, and fixed-asset turnover. These ratios indicate the need for a proper balance between sales and various asset accounts.

Inventory Turnover   The **inventory turnover** shows whether or not a company is holding excessive stocks of inventory. When this ratio is computed for a going concern, two questions arise: (1) Since sales are at market prices and inventories are usually carried at cost, which is more appropriate to use as the numerator in the ratio: sales or cost of goods sold? and (2) which inventory figure should be used: an average inventory or an inventory at one point in time?

Logic dictates that the inventory turnover should be computed by comparing cost of goods sold to inventory. As a rule, however, it is better to use the ratio of sales to inventories carried at cost because established compilers of financial ratios, such as Dun & Bradstreet, do this. Thus, the firm can compute a ratio that can be compared to the standard ratio developed by Dun & Bradstreet. It is also better to use an average inventory figure (computed by adding the year's beginning and ending inventories and dividing by 2) if there has been a marked upward or downward trend of sales during the year. The BLM Manufacturing Company's inventory turnover rate is:

$$\frac{\text{Sales}}{\text{Average inventory}} = \frac{\$830,200}{\$89,500} = 9.28 \text{ or } 9.3 \text{ times}$$

If the industry average is 9, for example, it is obvious that the BLM Manufacturing Company is not carrying excessive stocks of inventory. Excessive inventories are unnecessary and reduce business profits.

Average Collection Period   The **average collection period** is a measure of accounts-receivable turnover. A two-step procedure for finding the average collection period for the BLM Manufacturing Company, using 360 as the number of days in a year, is:

$$\text{Step 1: } \frac{\text{Sales}}{360} = \frac{\$830,200}{360} = \$2,306 \text{ average daily sales}$$

$$\text{Step 2: } \frac{\text{Receivables}}{\text{Average daily sales}} = \frac{\$78,000}{\$2,306} = 33.8 \text{ or } 34 \text{ days}$$

If the industry average collection period is 20 days, then it would appear that the BLM Manufacturing Company is experiencing serious collection problems.

Fixed-Asset Turnover   The **fixed-asset turnover** measures the extent to which plant and equipment are being utilized. For the BLM Manufacturing Company, the fixed-asset turnover is:

$$\frac{\text{Sales}}{\text{Fixed assets}} = \frac{\$830,200}{\$524,800} = 1.58 \text{ times}$$

If the industry average is 4 times, this means that BLM's plant and equipment are not being used effectively. This should be borne in mind when considering requests for additional production equipment.

Ratios Related to Profitability

Profitability is the net result of a firm's management policies and decisions. The ratios that may be used to measure how effectively the firm is being managed are: profit margin on sales, return on total assets, and return on net worth (or equity).

Profit Margin on Sales   The **profit margin on sales** gives the profit per dollar of sales. To compute this ratio, divide net profit by sales. For the BLM Manufacturing Company, the profit margin on sales is:

$$\frac{\text{Net profit}}{\text{Sales}} = \frac{\$61,710}{\$830,200} = .0743 \text{ or } 7.43 \text{ percent}$$

If the industry average is 7 percent, BLM's slightly higher profit margin indicates effective management of sales and operations.

Return on Total Assets   The **return on total assets**, or asset earning power, measures the return on total investment in the business. To compute this ratio, divide net profit by total assets. The BLM Manufacturing Company's return on total assets is:

$$\frac{\text{Net profit}}{\text{Total assets}} = \frac{\$61,710}{\$927,530} = .0665 \text{ or } 6.65 \text{ percent}$$

If the industry average is 8 percent, BLM's low rate may indicate an excessive investment in fixed assets even though its profit margin on sales is slightly better than the industry's average.

Return on Net Worth   The **return on net worth**, or return on equity, measures the rate of return on stockholders' investments in the business. To compute this ratio, divide net profit by net worth. For BLM's stockholders the return on net worth is:

$$\frac{\text{Net profit}}{\text{Net worth}} = \frac{\$61,710}{\$626,510} = .0985 \text{ or } 9.85 \text{ percent}$$

If the industry average is 12 percent, it would appear that BLM's return is unsatisfactorily low. It is possible that BLM's return on net worth may be improved by using more leverage, or debt.[9]

Ratios Related to Debt Position

One of the most critical aspects of the financial structure of a firm is the relationship between borrowed funds and invested capital. If debt is unreasonably large when compared with equity funds, the firm may be skating on thin ice. According to the conservative rule of thumb, two-thirds of the total capital in a business should be owner-supplied. In most lines of business, however, the industry standard is somewhat lower.

The ratios that may be used to measure the debt position of a firm are: debt to total assets and times interest earned.

Debt to Total Assets   The **debt to total assets** is a ratio that measures the percentage of total funds that have been provided by a firm's creditors. To compute this ratio, divide the total debts (current liabilities and long-term liabilities) by total assets. The BLM Manufacturing Company's debt ratio is:

$$\frac{\text{Total debts}}{\text{Total assets}} = \frac{\$301,020}{\$927,530} = .3245 \text{ or } 32.45 \text{ percent}$$

It is evident that BLM's debt ratio conforms to the conservative rule of thumb. This means that BLM should be able, if desired, to borrow additional funds without first raising more equity funds.

Times Interest Earned   The **times-interest-earned ratio** measures the extent to which a firm's earnings can decline without impairing its ability to meet annual interest costs. To compute this ratio, divide operating income by interest charges. The BLM's times-interest-earned ratio is:

$$\frac{\text{Operating income}}{\text{Interest charges}} = \frac{\$89,100}{\$10,000} = 8.9 \text{ times}$$

If the industry average is 8 times, it is obvious that BLM's position is strong and that it can cover its interest charges even with a substantial decline in its earnings. This reinforces the previous conclusion that BLM should have little difficulty if it tries to borrow additional funds.

Observance of Accounting Principles and Conventions

In seeking to analyze and interpret financial statements, a manager must remember that certain principles and accounting conventions govern the preparation of accounting statements. For example, *conservatism* is a principle that guides accountants, and the most conservative method available is the one an accountant will typically choose. Another principle governing the preparation of statements is *consistency*. This means that a given item on a statement will be handled in the same way every month and every year so that comparability of the data will be assured. Also, the principle of *full disclosure* compels the accountant to insist that all liabilities be shown and all material facts be presented. This is intended to prevent misleading any investor who might read the firm's statements.

Certain accounting conventions also regulate, in part, the preparation of financial statements. One of these concerns the accrual accounting system mentioned earlier in this chapter. Again, there is a convention governing the balance-sheet valuation of inventory, which may be based on the last-in, first-out (LIFO) method or the first-in, first-out (FIFO) method. Similarly, receivables are valued at their cash value less an allowance for possible bad debts, while fixed assets other than land are valued at their depreciated value based on original cost. Each of these methods results in balance-sheet and income-statement values which may vary from one method to the next and thereby change ratio analysis numbers somewhat.

BUDGETING IN SMALL FIRMS

If your family has ever used a household budget, you are already acquainted with the basic concept of budgeting. Remember how mom and dad agonized over the household budget at the beginning of the month and again sometimes at the end of the month? At the start of the month, they were estimating "income," in the form of salaries and wages, and "outgo" in the form of groceries, utilities, house payments, and braces for Johnny. At the end of the month, they were trying to understand, after looking at the budget and actual income and expenditures, what went wrong!

In a small business the budgeting goals are much the same as in a household—what are the sources of income and how will it be distributed. But the budgeting process in a small business is much more complex. The budget of a small firm is the principal short-range financial plan of the business. It allows the entrepreneur to allocate the firm's scarce funds and to forecast when additional financing may be required.

There are three key budgets used by small businesses—the operating budget, the *pro-forma* (or forecasted) balance sheet budget, and the cash budget. The operating budget and the pro-forma balance sheet budget will be examined in the following sections of this chapter, while the cash budget is presented in Chapter 20 in association with working-capital management.

The Operating Budget

The **operating budget** is a composite plan for each phase of the operation of the business. The operating budget is derived from several other forecasts—the sales forecast, production forecast, purchase forecast, selling and administrative expense forecast, and so forth. These individual "budgets" must be worked-up in order to develop the finished operating budget—usually prepared by months. The operating budget is typically formatted as a budgeted income statement.

Figure 19–6 shows a monthly operating budget for a hypothetical retail firm. This particular pro-forma income statement was prepared with a personal computer using the software contained in *Small Business Management Using Lotus™ 1-2-3*, a workbook supplement to this textbook. Many noncomputer worksheets are also available providing various formats as guides.[10]

Notice in Figure 19–6 how the first line (Sales) reflects a sales forecast of $50,000 for January, fluctuating up and down throughout the year with a $120,000 projection for December. Line number two (Cost of Goods Sold) reflects a 70 percent cost on Selling Price. For example, in May, Sales are forecasted at $60,000; therefore, 70 percent of this amount, or $42,000, is expected to be Cost of Goods Sold. Various other forecasting assumptions are used to generate the budgeted income figures. As you can see from this operating budget, November is expected to be the first "profitable" month of the year ($1,669 in net income).

Pro-Forma Balance Sheet

As stated earlier in the chapter, a balance sheet is a statement of a firm's financial position at a specific date. A pro-forma balance sheet is a forecast of that financial position. It is a budget in the sense that it is a guide to what the firm's future financial position should look like. Figure 19–7 shows monthly pro-forma balance sheets generated by the same software used for Figure 19–6.

Notice that this picture of the firm's overall financial condition shows negative retained earnings at the end of May! It also shows a buildup in the Accounts Receivable (AR) balance from $77,500 in January to $170,000 at the end of December! Both of these projections are a function of the operating budgets and the management policy of collecting receivables.

These two budgets alone do not provide the entrepreneur with sufficient planning tools. Attention must also be given to the cash flow in the business. Unanticipated cash requirements may actually cripple the business prior to reaching the "profitable" month of November! To facilitate the understanding of the interrelationship between the operating budget and the cash budget, the cash budget developed in the next chapter is based on the same hypothetical retail business used to develop the operating budget in Figure 19–6.

We now turn our attention to special considerations in establishing and using all kinds of budgets in a small business. Budgets are not only a valuable planning device, but they are also useful in guiding operations.

Figure 19-6 Operating Budget

	Jan	Feb	Mar	Apr	May	Jun	Jul	Aug	Sep	Oct	Nov	Dec
Sales	50000	70000	100000	75000	60000	50000	50000	50000	70000	90000	100000	120000
Cost of Goods Sold	35000	49000	70000	52500	42000	35000	35000	35000	49000	63000	70000	84000
Gross Margin	15000	21000	30000	22500	18000	15000	15000	15000	21000	27000	30000	36000
Operating Expenses												
Selling and Adm.	15000	20000	35000	21000	18000	15000	15000	15000	25000	35000	25000	30000
Depreciation	500	500	500	500	500	500	500	500	500	500	500	500
Inventory Charge	175	245	350	263	210	175	175	175	245	315	350	420
Operating Income	−675	255	−5850	738	−710	−675	−675	−675	−4745	−8815	4150	5080
Interest Expense	325	346	488	843	756	529	384	343	343	526	811	960
Earnings Before Tx	−1000	−91	−6338	−106	−1466	−1204	−1059	−1018	−5088	−9341	3339	4120
Taxes											1669	2060
Net Income	−1000	−91	−6338	−106	−1466	−1204	−1059	−1018	−5088	−9341	1669	2060

Figure 19-7   Pro-Forma Balance Sheets

BALANCE SHEET	Jan	Feb	Mar	Apr	May	Jun	Jul	Aug	Sep	Oct	Nov	Dec
ASSETS												
Cash	4000	4000	4000	4000	4000	4000	4000	4000	4000	4000	4000	4000
A/R	77500	95000	135000	125000	97500	80000	75000	75000	95000	125000	145000	170000
Inventory	49000	70000	52500	42000	35000	35000	35000	49000	63000	70000	84000	56000
Current	130500	169000	191500	171000	136500	119000	114000	128000	162000	199000	233000	230000
Fixed	20000	20000	20000	20000	20000	20000	20000	20000	20000	20000	20000	20000
(Acc. Depr)	6500	7000	7500	8000	8500	9000	9500	10000	10500	11000	11500	12000
Net Fixed	13500	13000	12500	12000	11500	11000	10500	10000	9500	9000	8500	8000
Total Assets	144000	182000	204000	183000	148000	130000	124500	138000	171500	208000	241500	238000
LIABILITIES & EQUITY												
LIABILITIES:												
Trade Payables	49000	70000	52500	42000	35000	35000	35000	49000	63000	70000	84000	56000
S.T. Bank Notes	41480	58525	101194	90747	63480	46082	41112	41120	63164	97335	115165	137605
Total Current	90480	128525	153694	132747	98480	81082	76112	90120	126164	167335	199165	193605
L.T. Debt	0	0	0	0	0	0	0	0	0	0	0	0
Total Liabilities	90480	128525	153694	132747	98480	81082	76112	90120	126164	167335	199165	193605
EQUITY:												
Common	50000	50000	50000	50000	50000	50000	50000	50000	50000	50000	50000	50000
Retained Earnings	3520	3475	306	253	-480	-1082	-1612	-2120	-4664	-9335	-7665	-5605
Total Equity	53520	53475	50306	50253	49520	48918	48388	47880	45336	40665	42335	44395
Total Liab. & Equity	144000	182000	204000	183000	148000	130000	124500	138000	171500	208000	241500	238000

Budget Revisions

After the budgeted operating statement and balance sheet are prepared, they should be evaluated by the use of key financial ratios such as those that were discussed in the early part of this chapter and others found in financial management textbooks. If the ratio analysis indicates that the budgeted operations will produce unsatisfactory results, the master budget and all supporting schedules must be revised at once. But this revision must still be predicated upon reasonable expectations for next year's operations. On the other hand, if the ratio analysis indicates that the budgeted operations will produce satisfactory results, the master budget may be considered to be completed. Copies can then be prepared and issued to all persons concerned.

Business operation is always full of uncertainties. Thus, actual operations seldom correspond exactly, and sometimes not even closely, to the budgeted operating level. A need for budget revision during the budget year consequently arises. For example, a manufacturer budgets a given product mixture and volume for sales. If actual sales do not conform in total amount and in product mixture, the budgeted sales and the corresponding expense budgets must be revised. Even if forecasted sales volume is achieved, a different sales mixture may require budget revision. Moreover, to obtain sales in a competitive market, anticipated prices may have to be changed. This, too, may occasion a need for budget revision.

In the retail or wholesale establishment, changes in advertising and sales promotion emphasis, changes in style trends, changes in customer clientele, and other changes lead to a similar need for budget revision.

Using the Budget to Control and Reduce Expenses

The budget, when properly used, is perhaps the most effective tool in controlling expenses. By providing a set of standards for expenses of each kind, the budget points up overspending or underspending. To examine the possibilities for controlling expenses, we must first understand the different classifications of expenses discussed below.

Actual vs. Imputed Expense   Those expenses that in fact accrue and require cash outlays are called **actual expenses. Imputed expenses** are those expenses that do not exist in the sense that they can be entered on the books of account and appear on the income statement. Consider, as an example, the interest on the owner's investment in a business. If the owner had invested the money in the stocks or bonds of other corporations or in government bonds, he or she would have received an income in the form of dividends or interest. The theory of imputing the interest expense on the owner's investment lies in the fact that an income which could have been received from another source is lost if the money is tied up in one's own assets. The lost income is the imputed interest expense. The economist refers to imputed expenses as *opportunity costs*. Certainly such imputed expenses cannot properly be included in the income statement. Consideration must be given to them, however, in many business decisions.

Fixed vs. Variable Expenses Those expenses that do not vary in total amount for the accounting period are called **fixed expenses**. For example, a rental charge of $500 per month or a property tax of $1,000 per year are fixed expenses. **Variable expenses** are fixed on a per-unit basis but vary in total amount for month and year with the volume of goods manufactured or sold. As an example of a variable expense, consider machine operators in a factory who work on piece rates and receive a specified amount in dollars and cents per unit of product processed by them. If they process 100,000 units at 5 cents per unit, they receive $5,000. If they process 10,000 units at 5 cents per unit, they receive $500. Thus, the amount of the variable expense—in this case, direct labor—depends upon the number of units made.

This distinction is also important in business decisions. For example, an order might be accepted under some circumstances at a price which would cover variable costs but fail to cover all fixed costs. As a practical matter, many expenses are neither completely fixed nor completely variable in nature.

Functional Expense Those expenses that relate to specific selling and administrative activities of a business are called **functional expenses**. If the amounts recorded by *kinds* of expense in the books of account can be equitably distributed to the functional-expenses categories, then expense control can be achieved. Consider, for example, the expense of "payroll preparation," which is charged to the functional category of "control." This expense does not include the production payroll itself; rather, it involves costs of payroll preparation, distribution of paychecks, and audit. (The payroll cost itself would be distributed to the various pertinent categories.)

A unit of measurement is required for control; this is afforded best, perhaps, by the number of payroll checks written. If the average payroll preparation expense over the past year is taken as standard for budgeting purposes, the actual expense for a given pay period can be compared and discrepancies evaluated. Certainly total payroll expense is not controllable as such, but it can be controlled if allocated equitably to various functional-expense categories.

Controllable vs. Noncontrollable Expenses It is important that managers of small firms stress controllable expenses almost to the exclusion of noncontrollable expenses. Consider a lease with a flat rental. Once a lease has been signed, rental expense is not controllable during the life of the lease. Hence, attention should then be directed to other items of expenses which are controllable.

In the small factory, for example, if a further mechanization of materials handling is possible and the capital expenditure is not prohibitive, the necessary equipment can be installed to reduce expenses. For a given system, however, expense control means that the system must be used more efficiently. For example, employees on hourly rates may be sent home when work is light.

Similarly, delivery expenses are controllable to some extent. The truck driver's salary, truck depreciation, and operating cost can be more effectively used and better controlled if the truck is provided with a two-way radio. In contrast, a retailer subscribing to a delivery service at a fixed amount per month is committed to noncontrollable expense. Accordingly, there is little need for attention to it until time to renegotiate the delivery service contract.

Common Budgetary Control Deficiencies in Small Businesses

Even though budgets are designed to facilitate effective management, they sometimes fail to do so, particularly in the small business. Here are several reasons why small businesses suffer from unsatisfactory budgetary control.

1. *Inaccurate determination of budget standards.* When inaccurate budget standards are set, comparisons of actual results with budgeted amounts are misleading. Management may be lulled into the belief that all is well when, as a matter of fact, costs are uncontrolled and performance is inefficient.
2. *Failure to include all key business activities in the budget.* If desired overall results are to be attained, all business activities of the firm must be incorporated in the budget.
3. *Lack of full support for the budget.* When preparing the budget, managers should consult their subordinates so that the latter will feel that the budget is theirs, too. And when the budget is completed, top management must back it up and convince all employees of the value of the budget as a control system. Subordinates can show their full support by promptly submitting control reports, especially when the budget needs to be revised. Of course, any budget revisions should also be communicated promptly to the subordinates.
4. *Inability to interpret control reports.* Sometimes the manager and the employees find control reports difficult to interpret. Thus, they may fail to detect and to act on controllable expenses that have significant variations between actual and budgeted amounts.

Looking Back

1. A well-conceived accounting system may require the expertise of an accountant. It should be consistent with generally accepted accounting principles and include as a minimum certain accounting records. The retention and physical protection of accounting records are necessary for the proper functioning of the accounting system. The entrepreneur should evaluate the accounting options of cash versus accrual accounting, single-entry versus double-entry systems, and LIFO versus FIFO inventory evaluation.

2. The four accounting statements most typically prepared by a small business are the income statement, the balance sheet, the statement of cost of goods manufactured, and the statement of changes in financial position. The income statement shows the results of a firm's operations over a period of time, usually one year. The balance sheet is a statement that shows a firm's financial position at a specific date. The statement of cost of goods manufactured is a supporting, detailed schedule of the cost of goods produced. The statement of changes in financial position accounts for changes in working capital.

3. Financial statements serve as the basis for computing financial ratios. These ratios can be grouped into those relating to working-capital position, sales position, profitability, and debt position.

4. The three key budgets for a small firm are the operating budget, the pro-forma balance sheet budget, and the cash budget. These budgets are valuable planning and management tools.

5. The budget, when properly used, is an effective tool in controlling expenses. In this regard, first it is important to know which expenses can be controlled and/or reduced. Second, the standards for expenses of each kind must be set so that the manager will know whether overspending or underspending is occurring. Greater attention should be given to major items of expense rather than to minor items.

DISCUSSION QUESTIONS

1. Explain the accounting convention that income is realized when earned whether or not it has been received in cash.

2. Should entrepreneurs have an accounting system set up for their proposed small firms—or do it themselves? Why?

3. What is the relationship between the income statement and the balance sheet?

4. What is the disadvantage of having too low an inventory turnover?

5. Explain the danger in having too high a debt-to-total assets ratio in a small firm.

6. Explain how an operating budget would be useful to the entrepreneur in making business decisions.

7. Explain the tax advantage of using LIFO inventory valuation rather than FIFO. Would this always be an advantage? Explain.

8. What are the major advantages of a double-entry accounting system over a single-entry system?

9. Can "fixed" expenses be controlled? Are they really always "fixed"? Cite some examples for answers to both questions.

10. What is the nature of an expense classification by function? Of what value is it to the manager?

ENDNOTES

1. The entrepreneur who wishes to develop an accounting system should see Bob L. Meisel, *Record Keeping for Small Business* (Houston: Small Business Publications, 1980); and Rick Stephen Hayes and C. Richard Baker, *Simplified Accounting for Non-Accountants* (New York: John Wiley & Sons, 1980). However, a professional review of self-developed systems is recommended.

2. Some practical considerations in selecting an accountant are presented in Raymond J. Lipay, "Selecting an Accountant: Who and How Much?" *In Business*, Vol. 6, No. 5, (September–October, 1984), pp. 38–39.

3. Bradford W. Ketchum, Jr., "You and Your Accountant," *Inc.*, Vol. 4, No. 3 (March, 1982), p. 90.

4. Linda M. Watkins, "Users Find Personal-Accounting Software Doesn't Easily Solve All Financial Woes," *The Wall Street Journal* (March 4, 1986), p. 29.

5. For a discussion of some of the tax software available to the small firm, see Jerry Gibson and Colin Gibson, "Tax Software," *Popular Computing*, Vol. 2, No. 5 (March, 1983), pp. 152–160.

6. An even simpler example of using journals and ledgers can be found in John A. Welsh and Jerry F. White, *The Entrepreneur's Master Planning Guide* (Englewood Cliffs, NJ: Prentice-Hall, Inc., 1983), pp. 265–269.

7. Bradford W. Ketchum, Jr., "Why LIFO's the Only Way to Fly," *Inc.*, Vol. 4, No. 10 (October, 1982), p. 166.

8. There are several possible disadvantages to LIFO and these are discussed in a booklet entitled *LIFO An Implementation Guide* published by Arthur Young, a public accounting firm.

9. For a discussion of how this rate can be broken down into its underlying components, see Kenneth R. Van Voorhis, "The Dupont Model Revisited: A Simplified Application to Small Business," *Journal of Small Business Management*, Vol. 19, No. 2 (April, 1981), p. 45.

10. See for example the Operating Budget in *Financial Records for Small Business*, Bank of America, 1984, p. 14.

REFERENCES TO SMALL BUSINESS IN ACTION

Blotnick, Srully. "Ask the Man Who Hates One." *Forbes*, Vol. 125, No. 2 (January 21, 1980), pp. 94–95.

    The author reports how the financial statements of a small business may distort profitability due to poor recordkeeping practices.

Grabowsky, Alex L. "What to Monitor to Stay in Control." *Inc.*, Vol. 3, No. 3 (March, 1981), pp. 74–76.

    A chief executive officer explains a practical internal monitoring system which has helped him keep track of business operations.

Rashkow, Bertram R. "How to Set the Right Price." *Inc.*, Vol. 3, No. 2 (February, 1981), pp. 54–58.

    This article demonstrates how to re-format the traditional income statement for purposes of comparing alternative price changes.

Sammons, Donna. "Accounting for Growth." *Inc.*, Vol. 6, No. 1 (January, 1984), pp. 75–82.

    This article gives several accounts of experiences which small firms have had with large accounting firms.

CASE 19

Style Shop*

A "tough guy" uses financial and accounting information for decisions

> A friend of mine recently said that 1975 is going to be the year of the tough guys, and that's right. It's for guys and gals who care enough to put everything they've got into what they're doing, and do their best. It's not the year for sitting around and letting everyone else do it for them. It's a good year for challenge and productivity because there is still money there, and there are still people who are ready to spend it. It's up to the tough guys, to the ones who merit being the ones with whom that money is spent![1]

Dorothy Barton, sitting at her desk in the small office just off the Style Shop sales floor, pondered this quotation which happened to catch her eye as she leafed through the latest edition of the *Dallas Fashion Retailer*.

In the women's ready-to-wear business, as in many other businesses, 1974 had been a rough year. It was particularly rough, however, for the attractive, energetic Style Shop owner. Wife, and the mother of four teenage daughters, Mrs. Barton saw her sales fall 12.5 percent from 1973 to 1974; but, more significantly, her net profit plunged 62.5 percent over the same time period. Untold hours she spent on the sales floor catering to her customers' eye for quality and fashion; in the office appealing to manufacturers to ship the next season's orders even though the current ones were yet to be paid; and at the Dallas Apparel Mart buying just the fashions she hoped would fit the needs and desires of her customers. At the same time, she was spending many hours each week in an effort to help her husband get his infant construction business off the ground.

She remembered hearing one "expert" say, "This is not a time for pessimism, nor a time for optimism. This is a time for realism." And an economic prognosticator had indicated that he saw a good future in the industry, despite the economic slowdown. Buyers, he noted, are working a little more cautiously right now. They are still buying, just looking at things a little more carefully.

"But what is 'realism' for me?" she asked herself. "Am I one of the tough guys who can stick it out and 'merit being the one with whom the money is spent!'?"

Style Shop Location and Background

The Style Shop opened its doors on February 12, 1954, in Lufkin, TX, and in 1969 it moved to its present location in the Angelina Mall. The mall

*This case was prepared by Professor Janelle C. Ashley of Stephen F. Austin State University.

contains a major discount chain store, two full-line department stores, and a number of specialty shops. Located nearby are a twin cinema, motel, and junior college. The mall serves as the hub of a trade area extending over a radius of more than 100 miles. The only centers comparable to the Angelina Mall at the time were as distant as Houston, 120 miles to the southwest, and Dallas, 166 miles to the northwest.

Dorothy Barton, the present owner, began with the Style Shop as a part-time accountant in March, 1962. She became a 50-50 partner when the new shop opened in 1969 and purchased the 50 percent belonging to the other partner in January, 1974. She operates the business as a sole proprietorship.

The Style Shop up to 1974

Personnel The style Shop employed four full-time clerks, one alteration lady, and a maid. A former employee and the teenage daughter of Mrs. Barton were frequently called in for part-time work during peak seasons.

Mrs. Flo Gates had been with the shop for 10 years. She worked as a clerk and floor manager and accompanied Mrs. Barton to market. The other three clerks had been with the Style Shop from one to three years each. Personnel turnover and apathy had been problems in the past, but Mrs. Barton was quite pleased with her present work force.

Policies The Style Shop operated with no formal, written policies. Personnel were paid wages and benefits comparable to other workers in similar capacities in the city. They enjoyed a great deal of freedom in their work, flexibility in hours of work, and a 20 percent discount on all merchandise purchased in the shop.

Competition Lufkin had an average number of retail outlets carrying ladies' ready-to-wear for cities of its size. Several department stores and other specialty shops carried some of the same lines as did the Style Shop, but they were all comparable in price. The Style Shop did handle several exclusive lines in Lufkin, however, and enjoyed the reputation of being the most prestigious women's shop in town. Its major competiton was a similar, but larger, specialty shop complete with a fashion shoe department in neighboring Nacogdoches, 19 miles away.

Inventory Control The Style Shop used the services of Santoro Management Consultants, Inc., of Dallas, TX, for inventory control. IBM inventory management reports were received each month broken down into 23 departmental groupings. These reports showed beginning inventory, sales and purchases for the month and year to date, markdowns, ending inventory, and various other information. Cost for the services was $110 per month.

Financial Position It is often quite difficult and sometimes next to impossible to evaluate the "true" financial position of a single proprietorship or a partnership due to the peculiarities that are either allowed or tolerated in accounting practices for these forms of ownership. This is evident in looking at the Style Shop's five-year Comparative Statement of Income (Exhibit 1), the Comparative Statement of Financial Condition (Exhibit 2), plus the 1974 Statement of Income (Exhibit 3) and 1974 Statement of Financial Condition (Exhibit 4). Key business ratios (median) for women's ready-to-wear stores are also given for comparative purposes in Exhibit 5.

Two explanatory footnotes should be added to these statements. The jump in fixed assets between 1970 and 1971 (see Exhibit 2) and the subsequent changes were due in large part to the inclusion of personal real estate on the partnership books. The long-term liability initiated in 1971 was an SBA loan. Caught in a period of declining sales (due in part to the controversy over skirt length and women's pantsuits) and rapidly rising expenses in the new mall location, the Style Shop owners found themselves in that proverbial "financial bind" in late 1969 and 1970. They needed additional funds both for working capital and fixed investments. Since a big jump in sales was anticipated in the new location, additional working capital was necessary to purchase the required inventory. The new tenants also desired fixed-asset money to purchase display fixtures for their new store. They obtained this money through a local bank in the form of an SBA-insured loan.

The Style Shop, 1975

"Certainly there is no longer an arbiter of the length of a skirt or the acceptance of pantsuits," Mrs. Barton mused. "The economic picture is looking brighter. The experts tell us there will be more disposable personal income and a lower rate in inflation. Yet this is a time for 'realism.' Am I a 'tough guy'?"

Questions

1. Evaluate the overall performance of the Style Shop. How good a business was it at the end of 1974?
2. Compute the current ratio for the shop and compare it with the industry ratio. What are the implications?
3. Evaluate the shop's ratios showing the relationships of net profit to net sales, to net worth, and to net working capital.
4. How did the shop's net-sales-to-inventory ratio compare with that of the industry? Explain.
5. Should Mrs. Barton have kept the business or sold it? What are the primary factors to be considered in reaching such a decision?

Exhibit 1   Comparative Statement of Income

Item	1970	1971	1972	1973	1974
Sales	$200,845.43	$213,368.15	$216,927.31	$217,969.59	$190,821.85
Cost of sales	132,838.30	133,527.91	131,900.84	138,427.14	121,689.74
Gross profit	$ 68,007.13	$ 79,840.24	$ 85,026.47	$ 79,542.45	$ 69,132.11
Expenses	60,727.46	70,051.29	67,151.58	69,696.93	65,438.20
Net	$ 7,279.67	$ 9,788.95	$ 17,874.89	$ 9,845.52	$ 3,693.91

Exhibit 2   Comparative Statement of Financial Condition

Item	1970	1971	1972	1973	1974
Current assets*	$38,524.93	$ 70,015.11	$ 66,749.78	$ 58,530.44	$ 68,458.34
Inventory	23,039.00	37,971.00	33,803.00	36,923.00	35,228.00
Fixed assets	7,314.58	86,504.94	83,924.45	80,534.06	63,943.67
Total assets	$45,839.51	$156,520.05	$150,674.23	$139,064.50	$132,402.01
Current liabilities	$35,892.81	$ 19,586.45	$ 20,161.93	$ 31,587.57	$ 55,552.70
Long-term liabilities	none	39,042.90	33,680.07	26,841.76	20,003.45
Total liabilities	$35,892.81	$ 58,629.35	$ 53,842.00	$ 58,429.33	$ 75,556.15
Net worth	9,946.70	97,890.70	96,832.23	80,635.17	56,845.86
Total	$45,839.51	$156,520.05	$150,674.23	$139,064.50	$132,402.01

*Current-asset values include the amounts shown for inventory.

Exhibit 3   Statement of Income

Style Shop
Statement of Income
For Year Ended Dec. 31, 1974

Sales		$190,821.85
Cost of sales:		
Beginning inventory	$ 36,923.00	
Purchases	119,994.74	
	$156,917.74	
Ending inventory	35,228.00	121,689.74
Gross profit		$ 69,132.11
Expenses:		
Advertising	$ 3,034.63	
Auto expense	1,509.63	
Bad debts	(439.83)	
Depreciation	1,580.49	
Freight, express, delivery	2,545.90	
Heat, light, power, and water	1,847.96	
Insurance	1,431.80	
Interest	4,064.25	
Legal and accounting	2,034.74	
Rent	11,220.40	
Repairs	528.98	
Salary	26,227.69	
Supplies	5,138.11	
Tax—Payroll	1,656.18	
Tax—Other	604.62	
Telephone	784.67	
Dues and subscriptions	601.89	
Market and travel	1,066.09	65,438.20
Net profit		$ 3,693.91

Exhibit 4   Statement of Financial Condition

Style Shop
Statement of Financial Condition
Dec. 31, 1974

ASSETS

Current assets:		
Cash on hand and in banks		$ 4,923.92
Accounts receivable		21,306.42
Inventory		35,228.00
Cash value—Life insurance		7,000.00
Total current assets		$ 68,458.34
Fixed assets:		
Furniture and fixtures and		
leasehold improvements	$ 27,749.94	
Less: Allowance for depreciation	9,806.27	$ 17,943.67
Auto and truck		9,500.00
Real estate		20,000.00
Furniture		10,000.00
Boat and motor		2,000.00
Office equipment		2,500.00
Jewelry		2,000.00
Total fixed assets		$ 63,943.67
TOTAL ASSETS		$132,402.01

LIABILITIES AND CAPITAL

Current liabilities:	
Accounts payable	$ 30,413.12
Accrued payroll tax	825.64
Accrued sales tax	1,193.94
Note payable—Due in one year	9,420.00
Note payable—Lot	10,700.00
Note payable—Auto	3,000.00
Total current liabilities	$ 55,552.70
Note payable—Due after one year	20,003.45
Total liabilities	$ 75,556.15
Net worth	56,845.86
TOTAL LIABILITIES AND CAPITAL	$132,402.01

Exhibit 5 Key Business Ratios for Women's Ready-to-Wear Stores

Ratio	1974	1973	1972	1971	1970
Current assets / Current liabilities	2.65	2.81	2.51	2.38	2.50
Net profit / Net sales	2.05	2.30	1.81	1.86	2.18
Net profit / Net worth	8.92	8.53	6.68	7.14	8.73
Net profit / Net working capital	11.43	10.96	8.64	9.98	10.92
Net sales / Net worth	3.82	3.96	3.95	3.76	3.78
Net sales / Net working capital	4.61	4.92	4.73	4.90	4.49
Net sales / Inventory	6.7	6.7	6.6	6.7	6.1
Fixed assets / Net worth	18.3	18.2	18.6	17.5	14.7
Current liabilities / Net worth	49.4	49.2	51.0	54.5	56.5
Total liabilities / Net worth	98.5	100.1	104.0	124.1	125.8
Inventory / Net working capital	73.0	72.3	76.7	71.1	78.3
Current liabilities / Inventory	84.6	87.2	87.0	93.9	86.6
Long-term liabilities / Net working capital	30.1	33.2	29.8	34.0	30.8

Note: *Collection period not computed. Necessary information as to the division between cash sales and credit sales was available in too few cases to obtain an average collection period usable as a broad guide.*

Source: *Dun's Review* (September issues, 1970–1974).

CASE ENDNOTE

1. "Merchandisers Must Provide Leadership," *Dallas Fashion Retailer* (June, 1975), p. 17.

20

Working-Capital
Management and Capital Budgeting

Figure 20-1   George Mason

© 1983 Wiley, Inc., Honolulu

George Mason is president of Crossroads Press, Inc., a Hawaii publishing company, which was incorporated in 1963 with 3 employees. In 8 years, the company grew to employ 33 full-time people.

During these years, Mason encountered numerous money-management problems. He views money management with a common-sense perspective. Concerning his own money management, Mason says, "Last year more than 18% of our pretax profits were from earnings on company cash. Our daily average checking balance so far this year has been $4,300."

Regarding money management by others, he says:

Strangely, many small- and medium-size businesses live with a lot of false impressions about money and banking. I have known some who keep $60,000 to $300,000 in checking accounts; others still haven't heard that a business can put idle money in money-market funds.

Mason was recently honored as Hawaii's Small-Business Person of the Year.

Source: Personal correspondence with George Mason.

Looking Ahead

Watch for the following important topics:

1. Definitions of key financial terms.
2. The cash-flow system in a small business.
3. Managing accounts receivable, inventory, and accounts payable.
4. Capital-budgeting methods in the small business.
5. Considerations in evaluating expansion opportunities.

A small business must carefully plan the use of its financial resources if it is to achieve satisfactory returns and meet its obligations in a timely fashion. By forecasting its working-capital needs, it can determine its short-term financial needs. By capital budgeting, it can evaluate the attractiveness of long-run investment opportunities. In this chapter, we present a practical orientation to the most significant areas of financial decision making in small business.

DEFINITIONS OF KEY FINANCIAL TERMS

The student of financial management must contend with a variety of inconsistently applied financial terms. This problem is noted in a leading financial management textbook with the following comment on the definition of "funds":

> Funds may be defined in several different ways, depending upon the purpose of the analysis. Although they are often defined as cash, many analysts treat funds as working capital—a somewhat broader definition. Other definitions are possible, although the two described are the most common by far. Depending upon the analyst's objective, the definition can be broadened or narrowed.[1]

Another important financial term, "capital," is also used with different meanings. Why so much confusion? The answer probably lies in the differing perspectives of accountants and financial managers. For our purposes in this chapter, the financial terms will be used as defined below.

1. **Capital** denotes all the possessions of a small business which are devoted to the earning of income. It consists of two types: current-asset capital and fixed-asset capital.
2. **Current-asset capital** includes cash and those assets that will be converted to cash within the near future. Accountants generally consider the "near future" to be one year, and we accept this meaning.

3. **Fixed-asset capital** consists of assets intended for long, continued use such as buildings and equipment.
4. **Working capital** is the difference between current assets and current liabilities.
5. **Funds** include money, checks received but not yet deposited, and balances on deposit with financial institutions. A firm's funds do not include such noncash assets as accounts receivable and inventory.
6. **Working-capital management** concentrates on the management of current assets and current liabilities.
7. **Capital budgeting** is the process of planning expenditures whose returns are expected to extend well into the future.

WORKING-CAPITAL MANAGEMENT

The excitement of day-to-day business operations can isolate a small-business manager from potential working-capital problems. Failure to manage working capital usually has devastating consequences. For example, Dun & Bradstreet's study of business failures found that more than one in three had mismanaged operating expenses, receivables, and inventory accounts.[2]

Working capital is a concept representing the *net value* of tangible current assets since, by definition, working capital is current assets minus current liabilities. Therefore, the most logical approach to understanding working-capital mangement is one which analyzes the individual components of working capital: cash, accounts receivable, inventory, and accounts payable.[3]

Managing the Cash Pool

Cash is constantly pumping through the system of a healthy business. It flows out from the checking account of the business to suppliers as payables become due, and back in again as customers buy products and periodically pay off their credit balances. This flow of cash must be managed so that the company can pay its bills on time and buy inventory, supplies, and equipment as needed.

The Nature of Cash Flow Business owners make a serious mistake when they equate cash flow with profit. They must realize that a firm can "go under" with an income statement that shows a profit! Consider this situation: A firm has sales of $100,000 and expenses of $70,000. All sales and expenses are on credit. A simple income statement would show an exciting $30,000 profit. Nevertheless, the firm may be in trouble. If it cannot convert

ACTION REPORT
Profit You Can Spend

Cash problems often seem more troublesome to small firms than to large ones. Two businessmen with big-business backgrounds learned this lesson as they teamed up to run Omega Sports in St. Louis, MO.

Stanley Anonsen, chief executive officer of Omega, previously had 23 years of experience in a $400 million company. Anonsen's partner, John Prentis, had left the presidency of United Missouri Bank to manage Omega.

By 1977, Omega racquetball racquets had sold so well that the company had a cash crisis. Prentis says:

As the presidents of large corporations, we had become used to looking at profit-and-loss statements. Unless there was a problem, we never bothered about cash flow. There was a whole financial staff to monitor specifics. When we tried to run our own business, we had to learn the difference between profit and profit-you-can-spend. We had a terrific P&L, but we had to borrow money to pay our bills.

Omega's major cash-flow problem centered around accounts receivable. Their customers were big enough to demand more time for payment. Omega's short-term solution included additional capital contributions by the partners and an additional bank loan.

Source: Louise Melton, "He Tried to Play the New Game by the Old Rules," *Inc.*, Vol. 2, No. 10 (October, 1980), pp. 68–72.

the $100,000 of accounts receivable into funds at the right time, it will be unable to pay the $70,000 accounts payable when due.

This simple scenario emphasizes the importance of understanding cash flow in a small business and the problems which occur when the flow is not managed properly. Cash must be cycled according to plans in order to make funds available when needed.

In a **cash-flow system,** funds move constantly from one form of capital into another. The challenge for the small-business manager is to have this capital in the optimum form at the appropriate time. This demands effective cash management, a process depicted in Figure 20-2. Notice the varied expenditures of funds. With proper planning, the entrepreneur can regulate the cash inflow to match anticipated cash expenditures. Loans and additional investment may be required at times to keep the flows in balance. The planning process involves the use of cash budgeting which is discussed in the next section.

Figure 20-2   The "Ins" and "Outs" of Cash Management

The Process of Cash Budgeting   Cash budgets differ from income statements in the accounting methods they use. Income statements typically use the accrual method, taking items into consideration before they affect cash—for example, expenses that are owed but not yet paid and income earned but not yet received. **Cash budgets**, in contrast, are concerned more specifically with dollars as they are received and paid out. Depreciation, for example, appears as an expense item on the income statement, but it does not involve a cash payment and therefore does not appear in the cash budget.

By using a cash budget, the entrepreneur can predict and plan the cash flow of a business. An example of a cash budget for a small retail store is shown in Figure 20–3. The business portrayed in this example has projected an uneven monthly sales volume, ranging from $50,000 in January and June to $100,000 in March.

The forecast of monthly sales is the first step in estimating the inflow of cash. These sales figures can be taken from the operating budget which, as discussed in Chapter 19, will typically be developed first. Sales figures and cash receipts are not identical, however, because sales are made on a credit basis. In this cash budget, it is assumed that none of the payments will be received in the month of the sale, that one-half will be received in the month following the sale, and that the remaining one-half will be received in the second month following the sale. Since this business has been in operation for

Figure 20-3 Cash Budget for a Small Business

	January	February	March	April	May	June
Sales	$ 50,000	$ 70,000	$100,000	$75,000	$60,000	$50,000
Cash receipts:						
1 month after sale	$ 27,500	$ 25,000	$ 35,000	$50,000	$37,500	$30,000
2 months after sale	20,000	27,500	25,000	35,000	50,000	37,500
Total cash receipts	$ 47,500	$ 52,500	$ 60,000	$85,000	$87,500	$67,500
Cash disbursements:						
Purchases	$ 35,000	$ 49,000	$ 70,000	$52,500	$42,000	$35,000
Selling and administrative expense	15,000	20,000	35,000	21,000	18,000	15,000
Inventory carrying cost	175	245	350	263	210	175
Interest expense	325	350	492	847	788	567
Taxes	0	0	0	0	0	0
Capital expenditures	0	0	0	0	0	0
Dividends	0	0	0	0	0	0
Total cash disbursements	$ 50,500	$ 69,595	$105,842	$74,610	$60,998	$50,742
Net cash flow	$– 3,000	$–17,095	$– 45,842	$10,390	$26,502	$16,758
Beginning cash balance	4,000	4,000	4,000	4,000	4,000	4,000
Unadjusted ending balance	1,000	–13,095	–41,842	14,390	30,502	20,758
Borrow	3,000	17,095	45,842	0	0	0
Repay	0	0	0	10,390	26,502	16,758
Ending cash balance	4,000	4,000	4,000	4,000	4,000	4,000

some time, the January receipts are based on sales which were made in the previous November and December.

Cash disbursements involve expenditures for a variety of purposes. In this example, we assume that the store has a gross margin of 30 percent. This means that March sales of $100,000 will cost $70,000. The order is placed in February, and the entire amount is paid in the month following the purchase. Therefore, goods sold in March must be paid for in March. Expenditures for selling and administrative activities are self-explanatory. The inventory-carrying cost includes expenditures, such as insurance payments, that vary with the inventory level.

Interest expense represents interest payments on bank loans. As of January 1, this business owed $38,980 to the bank at an interest rate of 10 percent. Additional money is borrowed in months in which there is a negative cash flow, and loans are repaid in months showing a positive cash flow. The company plans to keep a minimum cash balance of $4,000 at all times.

Since the company does not anticipate a net profit during the first six months, there are no projected payments for taxes. Also, there is no plan for purchase of fixed assets or payment of dividends during this time.

As you can see, the company does not achieve a positive cash flow until April. Additional borrowing must be arranged, therefore, in each of the first three months. By preparing a cash budget, the owner of this business can anticipate these needs and avoid the nasty surprises that might otherwise occur.

On those occasions when a small business has idle funds, the cash should be invested. The cash forecast is a basis for anticipating these occasions. If unexpected excess funds are generated, they can be invested also. Many short-term investment opportunities are available. Certificates of deposit and money market certificates are just two of the many vehicles for putting excess cash to work for the firm.

Managing Accounts Receivable

In Chapter 11 some credit activities of small businesses were discussed. At that point, we emphasized the types of credit and the granting of credit with a brief mention of credit-collection techniques. An effective collection system converts accounts receivable to cash at the earliest agreed-upon time. In this chapter we will treat two other aspects of accounts-receivable management: the aging of accounts receivable and the life cycle of accounts receivable.

Aging Accounts Receivable   Many small businesses can benefit from an **aging schedule** which divides accounts receivable into age categories based on the length of time they have been outstanding. Usually, some accounts are current and others are past due. Various collection actions can be used for different-aged accounts. With successive scheduling, troublesome trends can be spotted and appropriate action taken. With experience, the probabilities of collecting accounts of various ages can be estimated and used to forecast cash conversion rates.

Table 20–1 shows a hypothetical aging of accounts receivable. It shows that four customers have overdue payments totaling $200,000. Only Customer 005 is current. Customer 003 has the largest amount ($80,000) of overdue credit. In fact, the schedule shows that Customer 003 is overdue on all charges and has a past record of slow payment (a credit rating of "C"). Immediate attention to collecting from this customer is necessary. Customer 002 should be contacted also. The status of this customer is critical because, among overdue accounts, Customer 002 has the largest amount ($110,000) in the "Not Due" classifications. This customer could quickly have the largest amount overdue.

Customers 004 and 001 need a special kind of analysis. Customer 004 has $10,000 less overdue than Customer 001. However, Customer 004's overdue credit of $40,000, which is 60 days past due, may well have a

Table 20–1   Hypothetical Aging of Accounts Receivable

| Account Status | Customer Account Numbers | | | | | |
	001	002	003	004	005	Total
120 days	—	—	$50,000	—	—	$50,000
90 days	—	$10,000	—	—	—	10,000
60 days	—	—	—	$40,000	—	40,000
30 days	—	20,000	20,000	—	—	40,000
15 days	$50,000	—	10,000	—	—	60,000
Total Overdue	$50,000	$30,000	$80,000	$40,000	0	$200,000
Not Due (beyond-discount period)	$30,000	$10,000	0	$10,000	$130,000	$180,000
Not Due (still in discount period)	$20,000	$100,000	0	$90,000	$220,000	$430,000
Credit Rating	A	B	C	A	A	

serious impact on the $100,000 not yet due ($10,000 in the beyond-discount period plus $90,000 still in the discount period). On the other hand, even though Customer 001 has $50,000 of overdue credit, he or she is overdue only 15 days. Also, Customer 001 has only $50,000 not yet due ($30,000 in the beyond-discount period plus $20,000 still in the discount period) as compared to $100,000 not yet due from Customer 004. Both customers have a credit rating of "A."

In conclusion, Customer 001 is a better potential source of cash; so, collection efforts need to begin with Customer 004 rather than with Customer 001. Customer 001 may simply need a reminder that he or she has an overdue account of $50,000.

The Life Cycle of Receivables Even with timely payment by creditors, the conversion of accounts receivable into cash does not occur instantaneously. The stages of the billing and collection cycle consume a large amount of time. The small-business manager should understand these stages so that tactics can be planned and implemented to minimize the overall cycle time. One clear conceptualization of this life cycle identifies the following five stages:

1. Invoice preparation.
2. Mail transit.
3. Customer processing.
4. Funds remittance.
5. Collection.[4]

Problems may occur in each stage. As an example of stage 1, invoice preparation, the president of a manufacturing company learned of a five-day lag in invoice mailing. The president found that "the shipping office at his plant was batching invoices before forwarding them to the administrative staff for processing and mailing."[5] By processing invoices immediately after they were written, time was reduced and the cash cycle expedited.

Each stage of the life cycle of receivables should be similarly scrutinized. One day saved at each stage means funds will be available five days sooner.[6]

Managing Inventory

Inventory is a "necessary evil" to the financial management system. It is necessary because supply and demand cannot be manipulated to coincide precisely in day-to-day operations. It is an evil because inventory ties up funds which are not actively productive.

Inventory is a bigger problem to some small businesses than to others. For example, by and large, service firms create their "product" as it is sold. Inventories of supplies are, therefore, the only tangible inventory which they have. A manufacturer, on the other hand, has several inventories—raw materials, finished goods, and supplies. Also, retailers and wholesalers, especially those with high inventory turnover rates (such as those in grocery distribution), are continually involved in inventory-management problems.

In Chapter 18 we discussed several ideas related to purchasing and inventory management which were designed to minimize inventory-carrying costs and processing costs. At this point, we wish to emphasize practices which will minimize average inventory levels, thereby releasing funds for other applications. A correct minimum of inventory is the level needed to maintain desired production schedules or a required level of customer service. A concerted effort to manage inventory can trim inventory fat and pay handsome dividends. For example, the Boston-based Superior Pet Products Company tightened its inventory policies and freed up about $400,000 in capital. This released capital also meant a savings of $80,000 in interest expense, which was being paid to finance the inventory.[7]

Staying on Top of Inventory   One of the first tactics of managing inventory to reduce capital investment is to discover what is in inventory and how long it has been there. Too often, items are purchased, warehoused, and essentially lost! A yearly inventory for accounting purposes is inadequate for good inventory control. Items that are slow-movers may sit in a retailer's inventory beyond the time when markdowns should have been applied.

Computers can provide assistance in inventory identification and control. The use of physical inventories may still be required, but only as a supplement to the computer system.

Holding the Reins on Stockpiling   Some small-business managers tend to overbuy inventory. There are several possible reasons for this behavior. First, the entrepreneur's enthusiasm may forecast greater demand than is realistic. Second, the personalization of the business–customer relationship may motivate the manager to stock everything customers want. Third, the price-conscious entrepreneur may overly subscribe to vendor appeal—"buy now, prices are going up."

Stockpiling is not bad per se. Improperly managed and uncontrolled stockpiling may, however, greatly increase inventory-carrying costs and place a heavy drain on the funds of a small business. Restraint must be exercised with stockpiling efforts.

Managing Accounts Payable

Small businesses are legally and ethically bound to pay their debts. This is not debatable. They are also expected to pay their bills when due. However, there may be some flexibility as to the timing of payments. Also, debt obligations can be renegotiated and payment rescheduled. Therefore, financial management of accounts payable hinges on negotiation and timing.

Negotiation   Any business is subject to emergencies, which may lead to a request for the postponement of its payable obligations. If a firm finds itself in this situation, it should so inform its creditors. Usually creditors will cooperate in working out a solution because they are interested in the firm and want it to succeed.

Timing   It would not be surprising to find the motto "Buy Now, Pay Later, Later, Later..." over all entrepreneurs' desks. By buying on credit, a small business is using creditors' funds to supply short-term cash needs. The longer the creditors' funds can be "borrowed," the better. Payment, therefore, should seemingly be made as late as the agreement specifies.

Typically, trade credit will include payment terms which contain a cash discount. For example, terms of 3/10, net 30 would offer a 3 percent potential discount. With trade-discount terms, the entrepreneur's motto

---

ACTION REPORT
Stretching Payables for Cash

Small businesses can experience financial difficulties from rapid growth even with strong profit-and-loss statements. One of these financial difficulties centers on cash flow.

Derma Science Laboratory, Inc., is a manufacturer and retailer of organic cosmetics located near Dallas, TX. Luci Flint and her husband founded the company and "operated on the premise that paying her bills promptly was good business." As the company grew, Mrs. Flint "began to find she was increasingly strapped for cash." Her company was experiencing a classic cash-flow problem.

Her banker advised against a bank loan because it would provide only a temporary solution. Rather, the banker suggested that the Flints control accounts payable to loosen working capital. Mrs. Flint began to calculate how much delay she could build into accounts payable and still retain a good credit rating. A writer states:

> Flint's evaluation of her suppliers and the additional time she devoted to monitoring her payables carefully had impressive results. As the company has grown, accounts payable now average $130,000 and stretch for 45 days. By stretching payables from 22 to 45 days, Flint points out, she has in effect generated $65,000 in interest-free cash from her suppliers, an amount that will grow almost automatically as her purchases increase.

In stretching payments to improve cash flow, a debtor firm must be careful not to delay them beyond the specified due dates. This would violate the contracted agreement and damage the firm's credit standing.

Source: Harrison L. Moore, "Borrow from Stretched Payables," *Inc.*, Vol. 2, No. 7 (July, 1980), pp. 62, 64, 67.

mentioned above may be inappropriate. As an explanation, begin by looking at Table 20–2, which shows the possible settlement cost over the credit period of 30 days. For a $100,000 purchase, a settlement of only $97,000 is required if payment is made within the first 10 days ($100,000 minus the 3 percent discount of $3,000). During the interim between day 11 and day 31, a settlement of $100,000 is required. After 30 days, the settlement cost may even exceed the original amount, as the table indicates.

Table 20–2   An Accounts-Payable Timetable

Timetable (Days after Invoice date)	Account Settlement Costs for a $100,000 Purchase (Terms: 3/10, net 30)
Day 1 through Day 10	$97,000
Day 11 through Day 30	$100,000
Day 31 and thereafter	$100,000 + possible late penalty + deterioration in credit standing

The timing question is: Should the account be paid on day 10 or day 30? There is little support for paying $97,000 on day 1 through day 9 when the same amount will settle the account on day 10. Likewise, if payment is to be made after day 10, why not wait until day 30 to pay $100,000?

It is clear that payment should be made on day 30 if not on day 10. But why would payment be made on day 10 (taking the discount) rather than on day 30 (with no discount)? The answer lies in the concept of **opportunity costs**.[8] Consider carefully the following logic. If the business takes the discount, there is no opportunity cost for the use of the trade credit during the discount period. Likewise, there is no opportunity cost if the credit terms offer no cash discount. Therefore, the justification for taking the discount is in the "opportunity" to earn $3,000 for the 20-day period from day 10 to day 30.

Figures which develop the opportunity costs of a cash discount customarily compute an annualized interest rate which transforms the discount rate into a more meaningful percentage. This computation for the example in Table 20–2 is:

$$\begin{aligned}
\text{Annualized rate} &= \frac{\text{Days in year}}{\text{Net period} - \text{Cash disc. period}} \times \frac{\text{Cash discount \%}}{100\% - \text{Cash disc. \%}} \\
&= \frac{365}{30 - 10} \times \frac{.03}{1.00 - .03} \\
&= 18.25 \times .030928 \\
&= 56.4\%
\end{aligned}$$

By failing to take the discount, the business is losing the "opportunity" to earn the equivalent of 56.4 percent on its money. If funds are short and cannot be obtained easily, however, the small business may find itself paying on the last possible date and incurring the opportunity cost.

CAPITAL BUDGETING IN SMALL BUSINESS

The manager of a going concern must find time to search for alternative prospective investments if the business is to grow. After assessing the availability of expansion capital, the manager must determine the most profitable use of such funds by appraising the alternative investment opportunities open to the small firm.

Capital budgeting assumes that the firm's supply of capital is limited and that it should be rationed in such a way as to provide funds for the best investment proposals. In its broadest sense, capital budgeting includes investments of both a long-range and short-range nature. In this chapter, however, our concern is with long-range financial commitments; and the discussion that follows deals exclusively with long-range movements of funds.

What are some typical investment proposals entailing an outlay of funds that a small manufacturer might be contemplating at one time? Below are some examples.

1. Development and introduction of a new product that shows promise but requires additional study and improvement.
2. Replacement of the company's delivery trucks with newer models.
3. Expansion of sales activity into a new territory.
4. Construction of a new building.
5. Employment of several additional salespersons for more intensive selling in the existing market.

Because capital is insufficient to finance all five investment proposals, the owner–manager must decide which of them must be postponed or rejected and which should be accepted. Both the cost of capital and the absolute limit on the volume of available funds require the rejection not only of proposals that would be unprofitable, but also of those that would be *least* profitable. A ranking of the alternative investment proposals according to their profitability can be made after each proposal has been evaluated.

Traditional Methods of Investment Valuation

Two rule-of-thumb methods of evaluating investment proposals are the payback-period method and the return-on-investment method. In using either of these methods, only net additions to costs or profits are considered. For example, if a partially depreciated machine is to be replaced, the book value of the old machine is ignored except for the purpose of calculating the tax impact of resale at a price differing from book value. Of course, any salvage or trade-in value of the old machine would be considered in computing the investment cost.

The greatest value of these traditional methods lies in their simplicity. They provide a rough check for evaluating an investment. Although they have definite limitations when compared with the more sophisticated valuation tools described later in this chapter, they are widely used and often provide satisfactory answers.[9]

Payback-Period Method   The **payback-period method** shows the number of years it takes to recover the original cost of an investment from annual net cash flows. Suppose that a firm is considering Project A and Project B, each of which requires an investment of $100,000. The estimated annual cash flows (profit plus depreciation) from the two projects are as follows:

Economic Life (Year)	Cash Flow Project A	Cash Flow Project B
1	$50,000	$10,000
2	40,000	20,000
3	10,000	30,000
4	10,000	40,000
5		50,000
6		60,000
	$110,000	$210,000

The payback period for Project A is three years; for Project B, four years. If the firm ordinarily sets three years as its standard payback period, then Project A will be accepted and Project B rejected.

Return-on-Investment Method   The simple **return-on-investment method** evaluates proposals by relating the expected annual profit from an investment to the amount invested. This method is expressed in the following equation:

$$\text{Rate of return} = \frac{\text{Annual profit}}{\text{Investment}}$$

If the expected return on an investment of $100,000 is $20,000, the rate of return will be 20 percent. Such an investment is justified if more lucrative investments are not available and if a return of 20 percent is reasonable in view of the risk involved.

Weaknesses of Traditional Methods   The payback-period method and the return-on-investment method are subject to two major weaknesses. First, they fail to recognize the time value of money.[10] For example, suppose Projects C and D, each of which costs $10,000, had net cash flows listed below. Both projects have a three-year payback, which makes them equally attractive when judged by this criterion. But we know that a dollar today is worth more than a dollar a year from today because the dollar can earn interest during the year. Therefore, Project C with its faster cash flow is more desirable.

Year	Cash Flow Project C	Cash Flow Project D
1	$ 5,000	$ 1,000
2	4,000	4,000
3	1,000	5,000
	$10,000	$10,000

The second weakness of the traditional methods is their neglect of the economic life of a project. Going back to the annual cash flows from Projects A and B listed on page 549, we note that the payback period of Project B is a year longer than that of Project A. But Project B's longer economic life of 6 years provides $100,000 more in total cash flow than Project A. In a similar manner, a simple rate-of-return method gives no indication of the length of time during which that rate of return may be expected to continue.

Theoretically Correct Methods of Investment Valuation

Two valuation methods designed to eliminate the defects of traditional methods are the net-present-value method and the internal-rate-of-return method.

Net-Present-Value Method   **Present value** means the value today of a stream of expected net cash flows, discounted at an appropriate rate of interest. The **net-present-value method** is calculated by means of the following formula:

$$V = \left[\frac{CF_1}{(1+r)} + \frac{CF_2}{(1+r)^2} + \ldots + \frac{CF_n}{(1+r)^n} + \frac{S}{(1+r)^n} \right] - C$$

Where V = excess present value over cost
CF_t = post-tax cash flow in year t (where t is $1, 2, 3, \ldots n$)
S = terminal salvage value
r = selected rate of interest
C = cost of asset/project
n = useful life of asset/project

Note that the present-value symbol, V, represents the net value of the investment over and above the cost of the project and the firm's cost of capital. The selected rate of interest, r, is usually a firm's cost of capital. When the net present value is negative, the project should be rejected. When it is positive, the project should be accepted because the value of the firm increases by the amount of the net present value of the project.

To illustrate, let us calculate the net present value of Projects A and B, previously cited, assuming a 10 percent cost of capital. Also assume that neither project has any salvage value. By using the above formula, the net present value of Project A is calculated as follows:

$$V = \left[\frac{CF_1}{(1+r)} + \frac{CF_2}{(1+r)^2} + \frac{CF_3}{(1+r)^3} + \frac{CF_4}{(1+r)^4} \right] - C$$

Where CF_1 = cash flow in year 1 = \$50,000
CF_2 = cash flow in year 2 = \$40,000
CF_3 = cash flow in year 3 = \$10,000
CF_4 = cash flow in year 4 = \$10,000
$r = 10\%$
$C = \$100,000$
$n = 4$ years

$$V = \left[\frac{50,000}{1.1} + \frac{40,000}{1.21} + \frac{10,000}{1.33} + \frac{10,000}{1.46} \right] - 100,000$$

$$V = [45,455 + 33,058 + 7,519 + 6,849] - 100,000$$

$$V = -7,119$$

With a *negative* present value of \$7,119, Project A should be rejected.[11]

Calculating the net present value of Project B, the formula would be applied as follows:

$$V = \left[\frac{10,000}{1.1} + \frac{20,000}{1.21} + \frac{30,000}{1.33} + \frac{40,000}{1.46} + \frac{50,000}{1.61} + \frac{60,000}{1.77} \right] - 100,000$$

$$V = [9,091 + 16,529 + 22,556 + 27,397 + 31,056 + 33,898] - 100,000$$

$$V = 40,527$$

Since Project B yields a *positive* net present value of \$40,527, this project should be accepted.[12]

Internal-Rate-of-Return Method   In using the **internal-rate-of-return method**, one first finds that rate of return which equates the cost of the investment project with the present value of its expected net cash flows. The formula to be applied is the following, which is basically the same as that of the net-present-value method:

$$C = \frac{CF_1}{(1+r)} + \frac{CF_2}{(1+r)^2} + \ldots + \frac{CF_n + S}{(1+r)^n}$$

Where CF_t = post-tax cash flow in year t (where t is 1, 2, 3, ... n)

$\quad\quad\quad C$ = cost of asset/project

$\quad\quad\quad n$ = useful life of asset/project

$\quad\quad\quad r$ = unknown rate of return

$\quad\quad\quad S$ = terminal salvage value

The internal rate of return on the project may be found by trial and error, starting with any arbitrarily selected rate of interest. Then compute the present value of the cash flows and compare it with the cost of the project. If the present value is higher than the cost of the project, try a higher interest rate and go through the procedure again. Conversely, if the present value obtained is lower than the cost of the project, try a lower rate of interest and repeat the process. Continue this procedure until the present value obtained is approximately equal to the cost of the project. The interest rate that brings about this equality is the internal rate of return of that particular project.

To calculate the internal rate of return for Project A, again assuming that there is no salvage value, we can start with the firm's cost of capital, which has already been given as 10 percent. By substituting 10 percent for r, we find that the present value of the net cash flows of Project A is less than its initial cost of $100,000.

$$V = \frac{50,000}{1.1} + \frac{40,000}{1.21} + \frac{10,000}{1.33} + \frac{10,000}{1.46}$$

$$V = 45,455 + 33,058 + 7,519 + 6,849$$

$$V = 92,881$$

By repeating the procedure with lower interest rates, we find that the interest rate which will equate the present value of the net cash flows with the initial cost of the project is somewhere between 5 percent and 6 percent.

Once the internal rate of return of a particular project is calculated, it can be compared with the firm's current cost of capital (or cost of debt). If the internal rate of return of the particular project is calculated to be the same as the firm's cost of capital, the firm would simply be breaking even if it went ahead with the project. If the calculated internal rate of return exceeds the firm's cost of capital, the project would be profitable. But if the calculated internal rate of return is less than the firm's cost of capital, as is the case for Project A, the result would be a loss.

Criticisms of Theoretically Correct Methods   Even though these methods are theoretically superior to the traditional ones, they are not widely used in small businesses. The typical small-business manager is unaware of the existence of these methods and would not readily understand the underlying reasoning and analysis involved. In addition, the solution of problems through these methods is often time-consuming and may require the use of an electronic computer.

Perhaps the greatest deterrent to the use of theoretically correct valuation methods is the extreme uncertainty that surrounds many investment decisions. If great uncertainty about future demands or costs exists, the use of sophisticated methods may provide little practical guidance. Instead, the small-business entrepreneur may prefer to base decisions on short-run prospects—for example, approving an investment that seems likely to return the invested capital in one or two years.

OTHER CONSIDERATIONS IN EVALUATING EXPANSION OPPORTUNITIES

Having focused on capital-budgeting methods for evaluating investments in expansion opportunities, let us now turn to other considerations that enter into expansion decisions. These considerations involve a firm's growth philosophy, search activity, and approach to financing the expansion.

Growth Philosophy

There are many entrepreneurs who prefer smallness. They are content with their past growth and intentionally ignore further expansion. For example, L. C. Martin, president and chief operating officer of "tiny" Aztec Manufacturing in Crowley, TX, says, "I never really wanted to be rich. What I wanted was to work in a small-company environment, and that's what I've got."[13]

Many other small-business owners, however, carry growth ambitions from the very early days of starting their businesses. Growth is a continuing goal for these entrepreneurs. For example, Carl Karcher, who founded Carl's Jr. Hamburgers in California in 1941, expresses his personal growth philosophy by saying, "If your company decides not to grow, that's the beginning of the end."[14]

But growth is not without its potential problems. Expansion can strain a firm's capital position and damage current operations. It can also spread managerial skills too thinly.

Search Activity

All growth opportunities must be scrutinized carefully. For too long, small business has been saddled with the reputation of making growth decisions without extensive search. Small-business managers have often considered growth opportunities on a one-at-a-time basis. They have been

ACTION REPORT
Growth Pains

Successful growth provides its own unique problems for the small business. Growth strategy must be laid carefully to prevent undue stress on existing operations.

Sandy Ruby's Tech HiFi chain started in 1967 with a few stereo component sales to fellow MIT students. His first stores were all located next to the campuses where his young college customers lived and worked. One writer notes:

> To Ruby's delight, eager young customers snatched components off his store shelves almost faster than Tech HiFi's salespeople could replace them. "We began to think everything we tried would be a winner," he recalls. It was a reasonable assumption: By 1973, six-year-old Tech HiFi had mushroomed into a chain of 16 stores, with sales that topped $12 million.

Ruby's ambition was to grow and the time seemed right. Within a year, 15 new stores were opened near college campuses. However, sales faltered and profits dropped. "Ruby's new stores were scattered all over the map, some in markets too isolated to manage effectively, others in suburbs where Ruby belatedly discovered there was far less enthusiasm for stereo components than in Tech HiFi's usual college locations."

Ruby put a hold on expansion and began to bring overhead under control. The company recovered but not until, according to Ruby, he had lost his own net worth in the business.

Source: Jeffrey Tarter, "Can He Keep His Customers Tuned In?" *Inc.*, Vol. 2, No. 11 (November, 1980), pp. 73–78.

less concerned with ranking a number of growth possibilities than with trying to determine the merit of one particular proposal. Moreover, in the analysis of a single proposal, they have often jumped to a conclusion on the basis of sketchy information. The following case illustrates a behavior pattern of this type:

Mr. E, a dry cleaner, had an opportunity to open a branch dry cleaning store in a new shopping center. After looking at the center, talking to associates, and computing a break-even point, he decided to invest. His demand estimate was based on information given to him by the promoter of the shopping center.

The search for information was both spontaneous and non-programmed. Mr. E had no predetermined approach to the collection of data. He devoted little time to finding sources of information for demand estimates, such as city planning and zoning maps of population. He had no time for such things because of involvement in the day-to-day details of his business. He did not delegate many routine tasks in maintenance, collections, and deliveries.

Similarly, the search for alternatives was neither planned nor programmed. Mr. E did consider the possible purchase of common stock as an alternative to opening the branch store, but the search went no further. Instead of seeking out still other alternatives, he considered only proposals brought to his attention; this was true of the branch-store proposal itself. The issue in this case is whether the delegation of routine tasks would have profited Mr. E. by providing him with time for more concentrated attention to investment alternatives.[15]

The apparent deficiencies in small-business search activity provide an opportunity for improvement in the quality of small-business investment decisions. By breaking out of the pattern of routine activity or by delegating such work to others, the small-business entrepreneur can make more time for the search activity that leads to more profitable expansion.

Friends and acquaintances who are in management positions with other firms are valuable sources of information about expansion opportunities. Many other professionals, such as lawyers and bankers, are also reliable sources of this type of information. Trade journals and publications, such as *The Wall Street Journal*, can also contain notifications of purchase opportunities which represent potential growth developments.

Approach to Financing the Expansion

The financing of expansion is usually a major consideration in growth plans. Financing can be internal or external. Many of the sources of initial financing discussed in Chapter 8 also provide expansion funds. An entrepreneur's past success with a new venture will usually make the financing of expansion easier than start-up financing. However, there can be constraining factors which limit full funding of expansion opportunities. Harold Heinold, now a major marketer of hogs, grew from a small buyer by rapid and aggressive expansion. But still he says, "I never could raise enough money to do the things I wanted to do, never enough to take advantage of all the opportunities that came along."[16]

Realized profits that are plowed back into the business, or **retained earnings**, constitute a major source of funds for financing small-business expansion. Such internally generated funds may be invested in physical facilities or used to expand the firm's working capital. It is likely that the majority of small firms experience an annual growth in net worth as a result of retained earnings.

In using retained earnings, the rate of expansion is limited by the amount of profits generated by the business. In the case of a rapidly expanding small firm, these funds are often insufficient to meet the heavy capital needs.

Financing through retained earnings provides a conservative approach to expansion. The dangers of overexpansion or expansion that is too rapid are largely avoided. Because the additional funds are equity, the firm has no creditors threatening foreclosure and no due dates by which repayment must be made.

The lack of an interest charge on funds secured in this way may create the impression that there is no cost involved in their use. Even though there is no out-of-pocket cost, there is a definite opportunity cost involved. This opportunity cost is the dividend foregone by stockholders. Presumably the stockholders could have reinvested their dividends in other income-generating opportunities.

Looking Back

1. *Capital* refers to the possessions of a business which are devoted to the earning of income. *Current-asset capital* consists of cash and assets that are normally converted to cash within a year's time. *Fixed-asset capital* consists of assets intended for long, continued use such as buildings and equipment. *Working capital* is current assets minus current liabilities. *Funds* refers to cash and includes checks received but not yet deposited and balances on deposit with financial institutions. *Working-capital management* concentrates on the management of current-asset capital and current liabilities. *Capital budgeting* is the process of planning expenditures whose returns are expected to extend well into the future.

2. Working-capital management deals with a firm's current assets and current liabilities. It is particularly concerned with the management of cash flowing into the business (through sales revenue, loans, and so on) and cash flowing out of the business (through material purchases, operating expenses, loan repayments, and so on). These inflows and outflows are reconciled in the cash budget which involves forecasts of receipts and expenditures on a month-to-month basis. If projections indicate a negative cash flow from operations, arrangements must be made to secure additional funds through borrowing or investment.

3. An aging schedule provides a breakdown of receivables by age of the individual accounts. The five stages of the life cycle of receivables are: invoice preparation, mail transit, customer processing, funds remittance, and collection. Periodic inventorying is essential to good inventory control. Stockpiling should be monitored to avoid undue drains on funds. Accounts payable should be paid in accordance with prior agreements but can be negotiated to fit financial situations. Cash discounts can provide a profitable reward for paying accounts earlier than required.

4. The most popular capital-budgeting techniques among small businesses are the payback-period and the return-on-investment methods. The net-present-value method and the internal-rate-of-return method are additional techniques which are considered to be theoretically correct.

5. Small business has various expansion philosophies. Expansion success is facilitated by proper search activity and available financing. Most sources of initial financing can also be approached for expansion support. Retained earnings can be used to finance expansion.

DISCUSSION QUESTIONS

1. Explain the difference between fixed-asset capital and working capital. What is meant by the statement that "working capital is a concept representing the net value of tangible current items"?

2. Explain how a firm may be unable to pay its bills when its income statement shows a profit.

3. What is the principal purpose of aging accounts receivable? Why would an aging schedule show "net-due" credits as well as those which are past due?

4. Can you think of ways to expedite the life cycle of receivables? Give an example of each stage of this cycle.

5. Do you think a business has an obligation to pay its accounts payable before the net due date if it has the funds? Why or why not?

6. Compute the annualized interest rate which represents the opportunity cost on credit terms of "3/10, net 50." Compare this rate with the one in the text on page 546. Explain the difference.

7. What appear to be the principal weaknesses of traditional capital-budgeting methods used by small-business firms?

8. What are the principal advantages of the internal-rate-of-return method and the net-present-value method as compared with the traditional methods of capital budgeting?

9. What is meant by "search activity," and how is it related to investment by small-business firms?

10. Explain the danger in considering investment expansion proposals one at a time (as is done by so many small-business owner–managers) instead of ranking a number of them.

ENDNOTES

1. James C. Van Horne, *Financial Management and Policy* (5th ed.; Englewood Cliffs, NJ: Prentice-Hall, Inc., 1980), pp. 743–744.

2. "Survival Tips for Rough Times," *Nation's Business*, Vol. 68, No. 10 (October, 1980), p. 21.

3. Short-term investments (such as securities) and short-term liabilities (such as notes payable) are additional components of the working-capital equation but are ignored here as they are not a part of the normal operating cycle.

4. William Barent Wemple, "Where Are Your Receivables Right Now?" *Inc.*, Vol. 3, No. 4 (April, 1981), pp. 86–88.

5. *Ibid.*

6. The advantages and disadvantages of several collection techniques are set out in John A. Welsh and Jerry F. White, *Administering the Closely Held Company* (Englewood Cliffs, NJ: Prentice-Hall, Inc., 1980), Chapter 2.

7. "How to Unlock Your Company's Hidden Cash," *Inc.*, Vol. 2, No. 7 (July, 1980), p. 64.

8. An opportunity cost is the value of a lost opportunity. If you see a dollar on the floor and pass it by, your "opportunity," which went unexercised, cost you one dollar!

9. Studies which show the widespread preference for these methods are: Rolf O. Christiansen and Crumpton Ferrell, "Survey of Capital Budgeting Methods Used by Medium-Size Manufacturing Firms," *Baylor Business Studies*, Vol. 11, No. 4 (January, 1981), pp. 35–43; and Donald M. Pattillo, "Capital Investment Practices of Small Manufacturers: America Versus Multinational," *Journal of Small Business Management*, Vol. 19, No. 2 (April, 1981), pp. 29–36.

10. For an unusually clear explanation of the time value of money, see Bertram R. Raskon, "The Longer You Wait for Cash, the Less It's Worth," *Inc.*, Vol. 2, No. 5 (May, 1980), pp. 65–68.

11. The use of interest factors found in present-value tables would facilitate the solution of these problems.

12. Rounding off the denominators in the equation or rounding off interest factors in present-value tables would give slightly different answers.

13. Phyllis Berman, "Close to the Vest," *Forbes*, Vol. 127, No. 9 (April 27, 1981), p. 104.

14. Doris A. Byron, "Carl's Jr.: 306-Unit Restaurant Chain Began as a Hot Dog Cart," *Los Angeles Times*, May 26, 1981, p. 1.

15. Martin B. Solomon, Jr., *Investment Decisions in Small Business*, Small Business Management Research Report. Prepared by the University of Kentucky under a grant by the Small Business Administration, Washington, D.C. (Lexington: University of Kentucky Press, 1963), p. 96.

16. Dick Braun, "One in 17 Grunts Comes from a Heinold Pig." *Farm Journal*, Vol. 105, No. 11 (September, 1981), p. 43.

REFERENCES TO SMALL BUSINESS IN ACTION

Bellegoni, Elvira, and Miriam Weisberg. "Forecast Your Cash Needs." *Inc.*, Vol. 2, No. 9 (September, 1980), pp. 64–67.
> The process and benefits of making cash projection forecasts are demonstrated with data from a small company. The numbers representing cash-flow components are used to develop a 12-month forecast.

Gupta, Udayan. "Locating Those Costly Cash Leaks." *Venture*, Vol. 7, No. 12 (December, 1985), pp. 118–120.
> This article describes the steps taken by several specific small companies to improve their management of cash flow.

Paris, Ellen. "As the Twig Is Bent." *Forbes*, Vol. 127, No. 9 (April 27, 1981), pp. 131, 135.
> This article explains how a conservative expansion philosophy enabled a family business, started in 1906, to become a leading manufacturer of clothing.

Persinos, John F. "The Once and Future King." *Inc.*, Vol. 6, No. 3 (March, 1984), pp. 54–58.
This article explains the major financial problems encountered in an ill-advised major expansion by a well-established small company. The company eventually returned to its original size.

Wemple, William Barent. "Where Are Your Receivables Right Now?" *Inc.*, Vol. 3, No. 4 (April, 1981), pp. 86–88.
The author examines the life cycle of receivables using the real-life experiences of several small businesses. Some suggestions for improving cash flow are provided.

CASE 20

Barton Sales and Service
Managing the firm's working capital

Barton Sales and Service was located in Little Rock, AR. Its owners were John and Joyce Barton. John served as general manager, and Joyce as office manager. The firm sold General Electric, Carrier, and York air-conditioning and heating systems and serviced these and other types of systems as well. It served both commercial and residential customers. Although the business had operated successfully since the Bartons purchased it five years earlier, it continued to experience working-capital problems.

Barton's Financial Structure

The firm had been profitable since the Bartons purchased it. Profits for 1981 were the highest for any year to date. Exhibit 1 shows the income statement for that year.

The balance sheet as of December 31, 1981, for Barton Sales and Service is shown in Exhibit 2. Note that the firm's equity was somewhat less than its total debt. However, $51,231 of the firm's liabilities was a long-term note carrying a modest rate of interest. This note was issued at the time the Bartons purchased the business, and the payments were made to the former owner.

Barton's Cash Balance

A minimum cash balance is necessary in any business because of the uneven nature of cash inflows and outflows. John explained that they needed a substantial amount in order to "feel comfortable." He felt that it might be possible to reduce the present balance by $5,000 to $10,000, but he stated that it gave them some "breathing room."

Barton's Accounts Receivable

The trade accounts receivable at the end of 1981 were $56,753, but at some times during the year the accounts receivable were twice this amount. These accounts were not aged, so the firm had no specific knowledge of the number of overdue accounts. However, the firm had never experienced any significant loss from bad debts. The accounts receivable were thought, therefore, to be good accounts of a relatively recent nature.

Customers were given 30 days from the date of the invoice to pay the net amount. No cash discounts were offered. If payment was not received during the first 30 days, a second statement was mailed to the customer and monthly carrying charges of one tenth of 1 percent were added. The state usury law prohibited higher carrying charges.

On small residential jobs, the firm tried to collect from customers when work was completed. When a service representative finished repairing an air-conditioning system, for example, the rep presented a bill to the owner and attempted to obtain payment at that time. However, this was not always possible. On major items such as unit changeouts—which often ran as high as $2,500—billing was practically always necessary.

On new construction projects, the firm sometimes received partial payments prior to completion of a project. This helped to minimize the amount tied up in receivables.

Barton's Inventory

Inventory accounted for a substantial portion of the firm's working capital. It consisted of the various heating and air-conditioning units, parts, and supplies used in the business.

The Bartons had no guidelines or industry standards to use in evaluating their overall inventory levels. They felt that there *might* be some excessive inventory, but, in the absence of a standard, this was basically an opinion. When pressed to estimate the amount that might be eliminated by careful control, John pegged it at 15 percent.

The firm used an annual physical inventory which coincided with the end of its fiscal year. Since the inventory level was known for only one time in the year, the income statement could be prepared only on an annual basis. There was no way of knowing how much of the inventory was expended at other points and thus no way to calculate profits. As a result, the Bartons lacked quarterly or monthly income statements to assist them in managing the business.

Barton Sales and Service was considering changing from a physical inventory to a perpetual inventory system. This would enable John to know the inventory levels of all items at all times. An inventory total could easily be computed for use in preparing statements. Shifting to a perpetual inventory system would require the purchase of proper file equipment, but that cost was not large enough to constitute a major barrier. A greater expense would be involved in the maintenance of the system—entering all incoming materials and all withdrawals. The Bartons estimated that this task would necessitate the work of one person on a half-time or three-fourths time basis.

Barton's Note Payable to the Bank

Bank borrowing was the most costly form of credit. Barton Sales and Service paid the going rate, slightly above prime, and owed $17,600. The note was a 90-day renewable note. Normally some was paid on the principal when the note was renewed. The total borrowing could probably be increased if necessary. There was no obvious pressure from the bank to reduce borrowing to zero. The amount borrowed during the year typically ranged from $10,000 to $25,000.

The Bartons had never explored the limits the bank might impose on borrowing, and there was no clearly specified line of credit. When additional funds were required, Joyce simply dropped by the bank, spoke with a bank officer, and signed a note for the appropriate amount.

Barton's Trade Accounts Payable

A significant amount of Barton's working capital came from its trade accounts payable. Although accounts payable at the end of 1981 were $38,585, the total payable varied over time and might be double this amount at another point in the year. Barton obtained from various dealers such supplies as expansion valves, copper tubing, sheet metal, electrical wire, electrical conduit, and so on. Some suppliers offered a discount for cash (2/10, n/30), but Joyce felt the credit was more important than the few dollars which could be saved by taking a cash discount. By giving up the cash discount, the firm obtained the use of the money for 30 days. Although the Bartons might wait a few days beyond the 30 days before paying, their suppliers quickly applied pressure. The Bartons could stretch the payment dates to 45 or even 60 days before being "put on C.O.D." However, they found it unpleasant to delay payment more than 45 days because suppliers would begin calling and applying pressure for payment.

The major manufacturers (Carrier, General Electric, and York) used different terms of payment. Some major products could be obtained from Carrier on an arrangement known as "floor planning." This meant that the manufacturer (Carrier) shipped the products without requiring immediate payment. The Bartons made payment only when the product was sold. If still unsold after 90 days, the product had to be returned or paid for. (It was shipped back on a company truck, so there was no expense in returning unsold items.) On items which were not floor-planned but which were purchased from Carrier, Barton paid the net amount by the 10th of the month or was charged 18 percent interest on late payments.

Shipments from General Electric required payment at the bank soon after receipt of the products. If cash was not available at the time, this necessitated further borrowing from the bank.

Purchases from York required net payment without discount within 30 days. However, if payment was not made within 30 days, interest at 18 percent per annum was added.

Can Good Profits Become Better?

Although Barton Sales and Service had earned a *good* profit in 1981, the Bartons wondered whether they were realizing the *most possible* profit. The pressure of inflation and slowness in construction caused by high interest rates were slowing their business somewhat. They wanted to be sure they were meeting the challenging times as prudently as possible.

Questions

1. Evaluate the overall performance and financial structure of Barton Sales and Service.
2. What are the strengths and weaknesses in this firm's management of accounts receivable and inventory?
3. Should the firm reduce or expand its bank borrowing?
4. Evaluate the Bartons' management of trade accounts payable.
5. How can Barton Sales and Service improve its working-capital situation?

Exhibit 1   Barton Sales and Service Income Statement for the Year Ended December 31, 1981

Sales	$727,679
Less: Cost of sales	466,562
Gross profit	$261,117
Less: Selling, general & administrative expense (including officers' salaries)	189,031
Net income before income taxes	$ 72,086
Provision for income taxes	17,546
Net income	$ 54,540

Exhibit 2   Barton Sales and Service Balance Sheet as of December 31, 1981

ASSETS

Current assets:	
Cash	$ 28,789
Trade accounts receivable	56,753
Inventory	89,562
Prepaid expenses	4,415
Total current assets	$179,519
Loans to stockholders	41,832
Autos, trucks, and equipment, at cost, less accumulated depreciation of $36,841	24,985
Other assets—Goodwill	16,500
TOTAL ASSETS	$235,836

Exhibit 2 (Continued)

LIABILITIES AND STOCKHOLDERS' EQUITY

Current liabilities:

Current maturities of long-term debt (see Note 1)	$ 26,403
Trade accounts payable	38,585
Accrued payroll taxes	2,173
Accrued income taxes	13,818
Other accrued expenses	4,001
Total current liabilities	$ 84,980
Long-term debt (see Note 1)	51,231
Stockholders' equity	99,625
TOTAL LIABILITIES AND STOCKHOLDERS' EQUITY	$235,836

Note 1: Short-Term Debt and Long-Term Debt

	Long-Term	Current	Total
(1) 10% note payable, secured by pickup, due in monthly installments of $161 including interest	$ 1,367	$ 1,827	$ 3,194
(2) 10% note payable, secured by equipment, due in monthly installments of $180 including interest	0	584	584
(3) 6% note payable, secured by inventory and equipment, due in monthly installments of $678 including interest	39,127	6,392	45,519
(4) 9% notes payable to stockholders	10,737	0	10,737
(5) 20% note payable to bank in 30 days	0	17,600	17,600
	$51,231	$26,403	$77,634

21

Computerizing the Small Business

Figure 21-1   Anderia Luz

Predefined spreadsheets or templates provide simple worksheets which eliminate the need to start each computer project from scratch. A template can be purchased and used as is, or modified by the user—even by a relatively inexperienced programmer.

Anderia Luz, a secretary at the Master Engineers and Designers consulting firm in Lynchburg, VA, is an inexperienced computer operator who has effectively used templates for spreadsheets. "When I first started doing this, I didn't even know what a spreadsheet was," recalls Luz.

Luz has created a customized spreadsheet to track the firm's 18 employees, capturing information on regular time, overtime, sick time, and "business development" time. This tracking is used to determine "chargeable" time to clients. "About all I have to do is enter the numbers and watch it recalculate," she says.

Source: Reprinted with permission from Personal Computing, September, 1985, pp. 55–59. Copyright 1986, Hayden Publishing Company.

Looking Ahead

Watch for the following important topics:

1. Components of a business computer system.
2. Types of computers based on sophistication and size, and types of computer systems.
3. First-stage and second-stage applications of the computer.
4. Options for the small business that decides to computerize its operations.
5. Ten steps to take when obtaining a computer for the first time.

In years past, computers were used primarily by large governmental agencies and big business. This is no longer the case. Now small firms can also reap the benefits of using a computer. Computers have even become a vital educational tool in our schools and a part of the leisure and recreation activities in our homes.

Probably the four factors contributing most to this remarkable development are lower prices, a greater understanding of what computers can do, advances in computer programs to do the work, and advances in techniques to communicate with the computer. In this chapter, you will see the impact of these four factors as we emphasize the components of a computer system, small-business applications, and special considerations in the decision to computerize.

COMPUTER SYSTEMS

A **computer**, in concept, is a relatively simple device—a machine designed to follow instructions. In reality, it is a complex data processing machine, outperforming humans in the tasks of recording, classifying, calculating, storing, and communicating information. A **computer system** consists of a computer and its related interactive components. The five main components are: hardware (the physical equipment), software (the programs), people (keyboard operator), data (records of transactions or other facts), and support (management commitment).

Figure 21–2 shows a computer user reading the "hard copy" produced by the system printer. This human-readable copy serves as a convenient record of the analysis generated by computer programs. To the right of the printer is a keyboard terminal used for data input and program control

Figure 21–2   A Computer Installation for a Small Business

commands. The screen for viewing input and output operations is stationed atop the floppy disk drive unit. The disk unit is used for input and external storage of data and programs.

Types of Computers and Computer Systems

Different types of nomenclature are given to computers depending on their degree of sophistication and size. A maxicomputer, or **mainframe**, refers to a very large machine capable of processing large amounts of information in a very short time. Mainframes have large internal memories and often cost more than $150,000. The next level of computing power is the **minicomputer** whose cost ranges from $5,000 to $150,000. These computers require special facilities preparation and usually demand ongoing maintenance expense. They do not necessarily require full-time operations personnel or the technical knowledge that a mainframe computer requires. The development of the **microcomputer** (or personal computer), which costs under $5,000, has made computers economically feasible for even the very small business. Microcomputers are "user friendly,"[1] allowing the operator without extensive training and technical expertise to use computers. Microcomputers can be upgraded to provide memory capacity needed to handle day-to-day activities of the small business. Microcomputers now outsell all other types of computers, and the microcomputer of the 1980s has the computing power of the minicomputers of the 1970s.

The so-called **turnkey system** in the computer industry refers to a package consisting of hardware programs and procedures that are produced by the vendor and sold as a unit. A **time-sharing system** refers to the sharing of one computer by several users. Terminals to collect data are located at the office of each user, and the computer runs the programs for all users in sequence. Time-sharing systems allow the small firm the opportunity to use a mainframe or minicomputer since the fee is shared by all users. Disadvantages include delays in getting access to the computer and the problem of finding software suitable for all the diverse users of the system.

The most dramatic changes in computer systems have involved hardware and software. Therefore, we will emphasize these two components in our discussion. However, the remaining three components—data, people, and support—are also important and should be evaluated continually by management.[2]

Hardware

The term **hardware** refers primarily to the computer processor unit and items of peripheral equipment used for data input, data output, and data storage.

The Computer Processor This is the heart of the computer hardware. It consists of a central processing unit (CPU) and memory unit (MU). The electronic circuitry which processes data and the instructions are contained in the CPU. A control unit within the CPU controls the operations, and an arithmetic logic unit performs the calculations. The memory unit of the processor provides temporary storage for data, programs, and intermittent calculations results.

Peripherals Input units supply data to the central processing unit. Input units take various forms. Early input devices were punched cards and punched tapes. Today, the predominant method of data input involves a terminal consisting of a keyboard and video screen. With a keyboard, the data and processing instructions can be entered and displayed on the video screen for editing. The terminal is also used for displaying output from the computer.

Printers are used as a means of obtaining "hard copy" of a computer's output. The less expensive printers are called "dot-matrix" printers. They produce readable copy of lower quality than that produced by the more expensive "letter-quality" printers.

The most popular form of external data storage is the diskette. Commonly called **floppy disks** because of their physical flexibility, these disks are entered into disk drive units to receive data and programs or load existing data programs into the computer. Some small-business computer systems use **hard disks** which are capable of storing larger amounts of information. The reading and writing of data with a hard disk is much faster than is possible with a floppy disk, but the cost is much higher.

Software

The programs for a computer system are called **software**. These are the instructions which operate the hardware. Software is typically divided into two types: system programs and application programs. **System software** includes programs that control the overall operations of the computer including input and output processing. These programs are the link between the hardware devices and the application programs. System software is usually provided by the computer manufacturer. **Application software** consists of programs written for particular business needs. It has been stated that "application software is the most important ingredient of any small computer system." Application programs can be created by the user or purchased as preprogrammed packages. Most small-business users will find the "canned" programs to be the best option.

Before over-the-counter software packages are purchased, it is advisable to evaluate them carefully. A helpful software evaluation checklist is shown in Figure 21–3.

Figure 21–3   Software Evaluation Checklist

1. Do the basic functions of the package meet your requirements for information processing and data management? (What are you seeking to accomplish? Does the package help you reach that goal?)
2. Will this package run on your computer system? What are its requirements for:
   a. main memory
   b. disk drives
   c. printers
   d. input channels
   e. optional hardware
   f. off-line equipment
3. If any extra equipment or features are required, what are the costs and availability of these items?
4. What are the operating-system or language requirements?
5. How well do the detailed capabilities of the package match your requirements?
   a. Does the format and information content of the output meet your needs?
   b. If not, can they be changed with modest cost and limited effort?
   c. Does it contain control procedures and audit trails?
   d. What about file protection and data security?
6. How flexible is the package? Can it be changed, expanded or modified easily?
7. Is the package easy to install and use?
   a. Do you need vendor assistance?
   b. How much user training is needed?

Figure 21–3 (Continued)

    c. Is there extra cost for this training? (Even if there is no direct charge, what is the time cost for the employees involved?)

    d. Is the operating manual well-documented, written in nontechnical, user-friendly language, and complete?

    e. Does the operating manual have sufficient examples of screen formats and printed reports?

8. Is there continuing support the vendor or developer will provide?

    a. What is the cost and availability of additional program assistance if it is needed?

    b. Does your agreement or contract with the vendor consider this issue?

    c. Does the vendor agree to correct any "bugs" found in the program?

9. What is the testimony of other users? (This is the best evidence you can have. Demand user names and talk with them.)

10. What is the total cost of installing and using the program?

    a. Direct cost—selling price of the package

    b. Indirect costs:

        (1) personal training

        (2) modification, adaptation, and change costs

        (3) additional equipment necessary

        (4) installation costs

        (5) annual maintenance and warranty costs

        (6) legal fees for contract and warranty review

        (7) increased audit review and participation

        (8) user personnel removed from normal operations

11. Is the cost worth the expected benefit?

12. What financing options are available?

    a. sale

    b. lease

    c. lease/purchase

    d. Is there a discount for prompt payment?

    e. Is there a discount for multiple installations in the same bank or banking organization?

    f. What is the cost of extra manuals, forms, or other support materials?

    g. If you wish to do so, can you sell the services you produce from use of the package?

13. Summary Report

	Poor	Fair	Good	Excellent
Performance	_____	_____	_____	_____
Documentation	_____	_____	_____	_____
Ease of Use	_____	_____	_____	_____
Error Handling	_____	_____	_____	_____

Source: This appeared in the February, 1984, Newsletter, *Micro Digest*, published by the Center for Banking and Financial Institutions of Baylor University.

COMPUTER APPLICATIONS FOR SMALL BUSINESS

There are three basic reasons for the increasing use of computer systems in small businesses. First, a properly designed computer system can reduce the costs of operating a business. Second, the computer can assist in providing more timely, accurate information for managerial decisions. Third, the computer can improve customer service and thus pave the way for increased revenues.

The benefits of a computer system can be temporarily shrouded by problems which occur when small businesses first change to computer systems. For example, the use of a computer system requires discipline in following procedures, and some employees resist the change from traditional or their own *ad hoc* practices. Also, computer inventory coding often requires lengthy part numbers which may be confusing or time-consuming for salespersons when they record sales. However, the speed and efficiency of computers more than offset these temporary inconveniences. For the first-time users of a business computer system, therefore, it may be wise to acquire some years of experience in first-stage applications only.

First-Stage Applications

In the first stage, computers are used for highly repetitive procedures such as those used for payrolls, billing, accounts receivable, accounts payable, general-ledger systems, word processing, and inventory control. Usually payroll is the first operation to be computerized.

Payroll   The payroll application leads to the preparation of paychecks. The input documents to the computer are attendance and time records. The output documents from the computer, in addition to the paychecks, are statements showing earnings, amount of income taxes withheld, social security taxes, and other payroll deductions. Since computations required for payroll are repetitive, computers have been very satisfactory in performing this function.

Ordering and Billing   Ordering and billing are other business functions that are quickly converted to computerized systems. A vendor may receive orders through a salesperson, by mail, by telephone, or by telegram. The computer can prepare the shipping order with customer codes, names, descriptions of items ordered, and prices in an accurate and very rapid manner. When the billing operation is due, the input document to the computer is a copy of the shipping order. The output document is the invoice prepared for mailing.

Accounts Receivable   To control accounts receivable, management needs information on amounts owed by each customer and the length of time the accounts have been outstanding. The importance of accuracy is obvious. Errors cause loss of revenues and annoyance to customers. The accuracy and speed of computers reduce errors in this function and present a more professional appearance to customers. Accounts receivable computer software provides faster, more accurate customer records. Detailed listings of customers charges and payments plus customer account balances are available in an instant after a request by a user.

Accounts Payable   Computerized accounts payable ledgers supply the user with detailed records concerning vendors and their invoices. Managers are better able to determine where they stand with vendors in terms of payments made and current balances.

General Ledger   Computer software allows the small business to keep up-to-date information on the current month's activity for each general-ledger account. The software enables the user to determine the ending balance for every account and all information necessary for automatic generation of the trial balance, balance sheet, and income statement. Reports can be generated by customer name, customer address, or customer-account balance in a few minutes. The format of financial reports, balance sheets, and income statements depends on the software package purchased by the small business. Figure 21–4 shows the various components of an accounting system for which software has been developed by one successful software business. The original documents—checks, vendor invoices, cash register totals, journal entries, customer invoices, and bank deposits—become the source documents for software processing, culminating in computer-generated financial statements. Two very popular accounting packages selling for under $600 are General Accounting and Peachtree Accounting Software.[3]

Word Processing   The term **word processing** refers to any process that involves textual information and uses such equipment as typesetters, copiers, and automatic typewriters. Once a document has been prepared, the text can be stored on floppy disks. It can then be retrieved, edited, and printed. Word processing is particularly useful where documents go through several drafts before they are finished.

Many word-processing programs can be used with some form of spelling-check program. These programs have a dictionary on their floppy diskettes ranging in size from 20,000 to 80,000 or more words. Two of the more popular word-processing programs are WordStar and PFS: Write which sell for less than $500.[4]

Inventory Control   A computer system can compare stock levels with expected sales for a given period and automatically generate purchase or production orders for needed additional stock. It can keep accurate records of items that are selling rapidly and those that are selling slowly. Thus, it enables

Figure 21-4   Software and the Accounting System

Source: Courtesy of BPI Systems

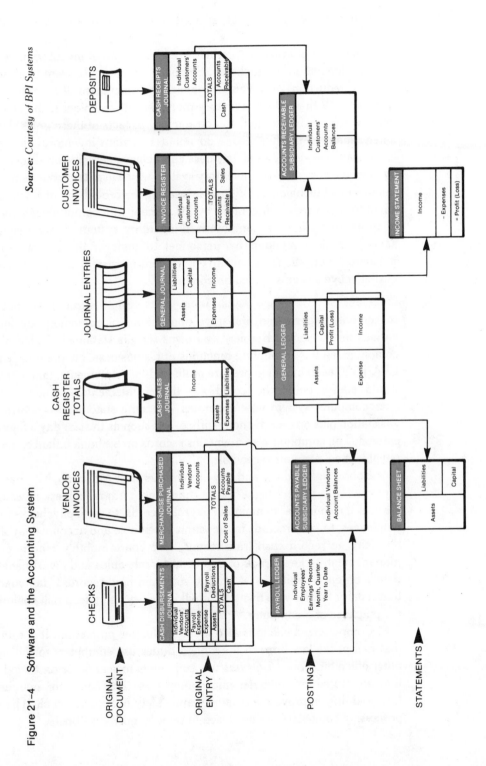

the manager to keep a current, accurate watch on inventory levels and avoid stockouts.

The goals of inventory control are a reduction of inventory investment and an elimination of stockouts. Somehow these goals seem contradictory since a reduction of inventory investment increases the probability of stockouts. With modern inventory-management techniques, the small firm may be able to overcome the contradictory aspects of these goals. Unfortunately, many small businesses do not use modern inventory-management techniques. However, small business can achieve effective inventory control by having a computerized inventory system which uses the modern inventory-management techniques. Without increasing the probability of stockouts, the small firm can reduce inventory by 20 percent with computerized inventory controls. In addition, a computerized inventory system allows a significant savings in time required by personnel to perform the inventory-control function. Unquestionably, an inventory-control system is one of the most cost-effective systems placed on computers.

Examples of First-Stage Application Users Small businesses that have successfully experienced first-stage applications of computers are found in various fields. Marcel Bernier, who owns six gas stations in California, has computerized the accounting functions of his business. He previously paid a CPA $600 each month to prepare profit-and-loss statements, and many days would elapse before he could see these statements. A new $20,000 microcomputer system now generates 7 income statements—one for each gas station plus one for the home office—as soon as the last day's figures are entered. The computer also maintains records on his bank balance, accounts payable, and accounts receivable.[5]

Bobby Hall, a dairy and row-crop farmer near McComb, MS, has found a computer to yield a higher profit than most farm-machinery investments. He uses the computer to maintain payroll records, to write paychecks for nine employees, to keep records for accounts receivable and accounts payable for the dairy, to record cash transactions, to prepare monthly reports on feed management, to keep track of depreciation schedules and investment credit details on each capital asset, and to maintain herd records. Hall concludes that a dairy farmer who owns 125 milking cows and a feed mill could justify the purchase of a computer.[6]

Computerized billing is also found in the law profession. It is estimated that half of the law firms in the United States use computers for billing and other office functions.[7] Lawyers use computers to search for past legal cases that are stored on computer information files. The computer searches are fast, and they improve the reliability and safety of legal research. The word-processing computers are also used to print lengthy case briefs.

Al's Auto Supply in Oklahoma City computerized approximately 30 percent of its 15,000 items in inventory. This store was able to reduce its average inventory investment by 25 percent and to reduce its stockout percentage from 6 percent to 3 percent. The savings quickly paid for the cost of the computer system.[8]

Another example of a business that computerized its inventory-control system is Southwest Tablets Manufacturing Company in Dallas. This business produces writing tablets and notebooks. For this low-profit-margin business, the computer has been helpful in the making of purchasing decisions, in the effective use of production facilities, and in the tabulation of available inventory.[9]

Second-Stage Applications

Second-stage applications involve more advanced uses of computers and usually follow several years of successful first-stage applications. Some second-stage applications involve financial planning, management of information, and market research. These applications would not be recommended for the first-time computer user.

Financial Planning   Financial management involves the management of money. While accounting functions also involve the control of money, a major difference exists between computerized financial-planning systems and computerized accounting systems. The accounting system has many users; therefore, procedures for this system must be clearly defined in order to maintain proper control. On the other hand, financial operations are managed by fewer people—usually high-level personnel. Consequently, the computerized financial-planning system can be flexible and quite varied from one small business to another. Computerized financial-planning systems, though not widely developed, are being used by small businesses.

Like the sophisticated calculator, a computer can be used to calculate cash flow, interest rates, present values, and rates of return for capital budgeting. More important, through financial-planning computer software, the computer can aid in the following financial functions:

1. Forecasting revenues and expenses of the business operation over future years.
2. Analyzing capital expenditures by computing the costs and benefits for different plans of action.
3. Cash planning by keeping current records of cash flows, helping to avoid cash shortages, and properly investing any surplus cash.
4. Credit analysis, which is used primarily by banks and loan agencies to determine the creditworthiness of potential borrowers.

Software packages called electronic **spreadsheets** are the key to this financial-planning activity. Three popular spreadsheet programs that provide rows and columns for entry of numbers are Lotus™ 1-2-3, Multiplan, and VisiCalc.[10] The numbers are entered at certain column and row intersects called *cells*, which are then used in a particular calculation. The spreadsheet allows the manager to play the "what if" game by entering key figures in the appropriate cells, pressing a key, and then seeing the effect of these figures on the total financial structure of the company. Figure 21–5 (beginning on this page and ending on page 578) shows examples of spreadsheets generated by Lotus™ 1-2-3. After supplying certain forecasted figures on the statement of operations and the balance sheet, the program will produce a statement of cash flow.[11] Each time alternative sales figures are entered, for example, the computer will quickly calculate new figures for the financial planner.

Management of Information   Managers need to make decisions based on current, accurate information. They also want information quickly and in a summarized form. Computers can supply information quickly and in any form managers desire. Computers can ease the burden of increased paperwork required by government legislation over recent years.

Figure 21–5   Electronic Spreadsheets

COMMUNITY BALLPOINT PEN CO.
STATEMENT OF OPERATIONS
FIVE YEAR FORECAST

	1	2	3	4	5
SALES	100000	120000	144000	172800	207360
COST	60000	72000	86400	103680	124416
MARGIN	40000	48000	57600	69120	82944
EXPENSES:					
Salaries	17000	21250	26563	33203	41504
Benefits	5100	6375	7969	9961	12451
Trav & ent	840	1025	1251	1528	1867
Dep'n	3000	3000	3600	4320	5184
Interest	3500	3500	3500	3500	3500
Other	2500	2700	2916	3149	3401
Total	31940	37850	45798	55661	67907
PRE-TAX INC	8060	10150	11802	13459	15037
INCOME TAX	3708	4669	5429	6191	6917
NET INCOME	4352	5481	6373	7268	8120

Figure 21-5 (Continued)

COMMUNITY BALLPOINT PEN CO.
BALANCE SHEETS
FIVE YEAR FORECAST

	PRIOR YEAR	1	2	3	4	5
CUR ASSETS:						
Cash	1000	5005	13556	17252	21193	25178
Receivable	10000	16667	20000	24000	28800	34560
Prepaids	750	800	850	900	950	1000
Total	11750	22472	34406	42152	50943	60738
PROPERTY						
Gross	30000	30000	30000	36000	43200	51840
Acc depn	4500	7500	10500	14100	18420	23604
Net	25500	22500	19500	21900	24780	28236
TOTAL						
ASSETS	37250	44972	53906	64052	75723	88974
CUR LIAB:						
Payables	8500	10000	12000	14400	17280	20736
Accruals	2250	2412	2904	3517	4278	5227
Acc tax	2000	3708	4669	5429	6191	6917
Total	12750	16120	19573	23346	27749	32880
L-T DEBT	17500	17500	17500	17500	17500	17500
EQUITY:						
Stock	5000	5000	5000	5000	5000	5000
Ret earn	2000	6352	11833	18206	25474	33594
	7000	11352	16833	23206	30474	38594
TOTAL LIAB						
& EQUITY	37250	44972	53906	64052	75723	88974

The management of information can be used for both long-range planning and operational planning. Long-range planning involves the future financial status of the business. Operational planning usually involves optimization and data analysis to organize daily activities such as the preparation of delivery schedules, truck routes, and purchase orders.

Market Research   Through advanced methods, the computer can evaluate historical data and interpret results of statistical market surveys. These

Figure 21–5 (Continued)

COMMUNITY BALLPOINT PEN CO.
STATEMENT OF CASH FLOW
FIVE YEAR FORECAST

	1	2	3	4	5
CASH SOURCE					
FROM OPER					
Net inc	4352	5481	6373	7268	8120
Add depn	3000	3000	3600	4320	5184
	7352	8481	9973	11588	13304
USE OF CASH					
Purch prop	0	0	-6000	-7200	-8640
CHANGE IN					
WORKING CAPITAL:					
Receivable	6667	3333	4000	4800	5760
Prepaids	50	50	50	50	50
Payables	-1500	-2000	-2400	-2880	-3456
Accruals	-162	-492	-613	-761	-949
Acc tax	-1708	-961	-760	-762	-726
INC(DEC) IN W/C	3347	-70	277	447	679
INC(DEC) IN CASH	4005	8551	3696	3941	3985
CASH-BEG	1000	5005	13556	17252	21193
CASH-END	5005	13556	17252	21193	25178

sophisticated procedures are likely to become invaluable to the progressive small-business manager of the future.

DECIDING TO COMPUTERIZE THE SMALL BUSINESS

If a small business is considering the use of a computer, it should analyze the potential benefits, estimate the costs, and work out an appropriate plan. There are no quick and easy procedures to follow in this decision process. Each business will have a unique set of problems.

The Feasibility Study

As a first step, the small business should make a feasibility study. This study should determine whether the firm has a sufficient work load or need for efficiency to justify the expense of a computer. The cost/benefit analysis is difficult to make, but it is the most important step in the decision-making process. This analysis can be performed by the business owner/manager or by an outside computer consultant.

The feasibility study may indicate that the business should not computerize. If the study shows that the business should computerize, the second step is to decide whether to use a service bureau, to opt for time-sharing, to lease a computer, or to buy a computer. If the firm decides to buy a computer, then it should select the best system for the business.

Service Bureaus

Service bureaus are computer firms which receive data from business customers, perform the data processing, then return the processed information to the customers. The service bureaus charge a fixed fee for the use of their computer. For a small firm desiring a single application and lacking computer experience, the service bureau represents a logical first choice.

Using a service bureau has several advantages. The user avoids an investment in equipment, which will soon become obsolete. The user also avoids the need for specialized computer personnel. Some service bureaus even provide guidance to make it easy for the user to start and expand computer usage. The disadvantages of a service bureau are: slow "turn-around" time in receiving processed information from the service bureau, divulgence of confidential information to outside parties, and difficulty in working with a group unfamiliar with the client company's procedures.

In the past, there have been numerous, small service bureaus. However, today the small service bureaus are having difficulty competing with bigger bureaus that have larger minicomputer systems. The competition between service bureaus will no doubt become even greater in the future.

Time-Sharing

Time-sharing allows a business to have the capabilities of a computer without buying or leasing it. The business pays a variable fee for the privilege of using a computer system. As indicated earlier in this chapter, the user of time-sharing must have at least one terminal in order to input data. The terminal is connected to the time-sharing computer via a telephone line with a device known as a **modem**.

Early time-sharing systems provided computer time for professionals who knew how to operate and to program a computer. With the advancement of software, time-sharing is used more to process data and information for a company by using existing programs. The time-sharing approach is often a good first or second step for small firms that decide to computerize.

ACTION REPORT
Poor Service at Service Bureau

As owner and manager of Jones Fine Furniture, Joe Jones has 15 employees and approximately 2,000 credit customers. Although Jones was at first hesitant to use a computer, he eventually decided to automate some of the day-to-day transactions.

Before automating, Jones was using a ledger card system to keep track of accounts payable and accounts receivable. Copying-machine copies of the bills were made, and the calculation of interest charges was time-consuming. With the encouragement of his son, Jones decided to use a local service bureau that also serviced about five other customers. However, after three years with the service bureau, minor communication problems and occasional delays in mailouts finally convinced him to seek his own computer system.

Jones and his son decided on a microcomputer because it was the least expensive, required little room to house, and seemed capable of meeting the firm's computing needs. Although the accountant learned the system in a week, she disliked the system and left after six months. Jones hired an inexperienced replacement at a much lower salary, and he was delighted when she mastered the computer system in less than a week. The individual operating the computer system was a furniture duster the previous year.

Mr. Jones is much happier with the microcomputer system than he was with the service bureau. "With the service bureau, you were at the mercy of the people who knew how to run their computer system, and delays often occurred. Now I can go in and get a printout anytime I want one," he says. "My system has an audit program that allows me to answer any customer's question about his or her account in a matter of seconds," he boasts.

Source: Personal conversation with the owner's son. Names have been changed.

The advantages of time-sharing include control of company records, more sophisticated applications of programs, and lower cost of installing a working system. The disadvantages include variable costs, waiting time when other customers are using the system, and the need for the user to have some computer ability.

Leasing a Computer

For most businesses, leasing a computer means acquiring possession and use of a computer without buying it. The most common leasing arrangement is the full payback lease. Usually the lease periods are fairly long-term (i.e., for around eight years). A shorter lease period may be more expensive, but it reduces the possibility of having to use outdated equipment. With the current rapid advances in computer technology, some computer users claim that computer equipment becomes outdated every two years!

Two advantages of leasing are the use of a complete computer system without a large initial investment and the availability of consulting help through the leasing company's computer specialists. The disadvantages relate to the length of the lease period and the possibility of having to use outdated equipment. In addition, leasing a computer requires the lessee to have skilled computer personnel.

Buying a Computer

The advantages of buying a computer are obvious. The owner has total control and ownership of the computer. Also, depreciation expense reduces the business owner's taxable income. The disadvantages are the large expense of the computer system, the need for trained computer personnel to operate the programs and maintain the hardware, and the possible obsolescence of the equipment.

For small firms choosing to purchase a computer, the key to creating a successful computer system is a carefully planned approach. It is important for the first-time computer user to look first at the programs, not at the hardware. "The difference between the best and worst hardware is a lot less than it is between the best and worst programs."[12]

Edward Goldfinger lists ten steps for a company to take when considering the purchase of a computer.[13] Frank Greenwood also identifies ten rules of small-business computerization.[14] The ten steps described below involve a blending of these two persons' ideas.

Step 1. Learn about Computers   Visit other firms that are already using computers for similar applications. Ask for a vendor demonstration. Be aware that the changeover will require much time and thought. If possible, hire a "data-processing manager" with experience, or at least place someone in charge of the changeover. In summary, the computer is not an easy way out. If the business is in basic trouble, the computer system will not save it. The computer can help a successful business become more successful.

Step 2. Analyze the Present Manual System   Examine the transactions which involve routine actions. Restudy the routine manual actions to find a more efficient procedure if possible. Having established an efficient procedure, you are then ready to think about introducing a computer.

The detailed study of the business and the areas that might be computerized help to clarify computer needs. This is information that computer vendors need in order to propose ways to computerize a company efficiently.

Step 3. Clearly Define Your Expectations from the Computer System Having reviewed your manual system, decide what you need in a computer system. Be specific in the functions you want the computer to perform. For example, you may decide to computerize mailing lists, accounting payroll, inventory control, or sales analysis. These needs should be outlined for five years in the future. If you are unable to determine your exact needs, you may want to seek help. Possible sources are other small businesses, computer consultants, or an employee with computer experience.

Step 4. Compare Costs and Benefits It is easy to estimate the costs of current manual systems, but it is difficult to estimate the cost of computerization. Estimates should be obtained from several vendors to help determine the cost of changeover. Also, there are hidden costs incurred. For example, the patience and endurance of employees are tested during the conversion.

Step 5. Establish a Timetable for Installing the System A five-year schedule should be made to install the computer system. It is best to automate the simplest manual operations first. Each computerized operation should be working before going to the next. Be aware that transactions are slow. If possible, run the manual system in parallel with the automated system until the rough spots are smoothed out. Be willing to adjust the timetable from time to time as unexpected problems occur.

Step 6. Write a Tight Contract Both the purchaser and the vendor should be willing to sign a formal agreement on the function the computer is expected to perform. The specifications should contain details rather than general summaries of expected performance. Obligations for servicing the equipment should also be clearly specified. The contract should specify what the vendor must do before each step in the payment schedule.

Also, it is usually unwise to agree to field-test *new* equipment. It is best to obtain *established* equipment and programs that have been working in other small businesses.

Step 7. Obtain Programs First, Then Obtain the Computer There are several options for obtaining computer programs:

1. Obtain programs that are already working at other similar small businesses.
2. Hire a programmer to write programs.
3. Hire a consultant who has programs which can serve most business functions.

The manager must make the decision about which alternative is best for the particular business. Once the needed programs are identified, the most economical hardware to run the programs can be obtained.

ACTION REPORT
Software Then Hardware

Claire Lichack, manager of human resource systems at American Express Company's corporate offices in New York, uses the computer to maintain personnel records. She recently converted from an expensive mainframe computer to an IBM personal computer.

Her search for the right personal computer began by studying her personnel management needs and the software which would provide the reports needed. "I wasn't about to buy a machine and then go looking around for software to run on it. I wanted to find the software first, then base the hardware decision on that."

With the personal computer, her department has reduced operating costs by about $120,000 to $150,000 a year. The use of a personal computer rather than a mainframe has also enabled "personnel generalists" to understand the computer so they can have greater access to the personnel data.

Source: Arielle Emmett, "How American Express Saves with PCXT's," *Business Computing,* Vol. II, No. 11 (December, 1984), pp. 22–26. Reproduced with permission.

Step 8. Prepare Your Employees for Conversion   It is commonplace for employees to resist the move to computers. They may feel the computer is a threat to their jobs. Assure employees that the change will be beneficial to the business and consequently beneficial to them. People who are unwilling to become involved should be moved to other departments. A good attitude with interest in the computerization must prevail for a successful transition from manual power to computer power.

Step 9. Make the Conversion   First, assign the responsibilities carefully for the conversion process. The conversion period will require extra work because daily work must continue. Second, remember to convert operations one at a time. Again, if possible, keep the parallel manual system functioning as long as possible. Third, be patient, remembering that pitfalls will occur. Do not plan on using the system until it begins functioning.

Step 10. Reap the Benefits   The goal of the transition is to obtain the following benefits:

1. Earlier, more nearly accurate, and more extensive information.
2. Better organization of information because of the discipline the computer requires.
3. Current information on costs and sales.
4. Current information on inventory levels.
5. Better cash control.

Figure 21–6   The Importance of Computers in the Future

"I don't want to talk to a middleman . . . put
me straight through to the computer!"

Source: From *The Wall Street Journal,* September 9, 1981, p. 25. Permission—Cartoon Features
Syndicate.

THE FUTURE OF COMPUTERS

The use of computers is already evident in stores, airports, banks,
libraries, newspaper plants, law enforcement agencies, hospitals, educational
institutions, business offices, and recreation facilities. Computerized grocery
checkout stands will increase. The stand-alone cash register will continue to
be replaced by computer terminals in retail stores. And there is no reason to
believe that improvements in computer technology will slow in the near
future. Already computer robots are replacing workers in performing repetitive
tasks in manufacturing assembly lines.

The future development of the computer will continue to reduce the time
spent in performing manual tasks and to aid in the decision-making process.
Computers may become as common as the television sets in our homes so
that it will be possible to shop at home via a computer terminal. As
transportation costs continue to rise, computers and video displays will be
used for long-distance sales to customers. It is entirely possible that in the
near future every desk, even in a small business, will have a computer
terminal.

Looking Back

1. The five components of a business computer system are: hardware, software, data, support, and people. The personnel bring the other four components together and are the key to a smoothly operating system.

2. The three basic types of computers based on sophistication and size are: mainframes, minicomputers, and microcomputers (or personal computers). The turnkey computer system consists of hardware, software, and procedures that are produced and sold as a package by the vendor. In the time-sharing computer system, terminals to collect data are located at the business place of each user of the system, and the computer runs the programs for all users in very rapid sequence.

3. First-time users of a business computer system should acquire some years of experience in first-stage applications before proceeding with the second-stage applications. The first-stage applications involve highly repetitive procedures such as those used for payroll, billing, accounts receivable, accounts payable, general-ledger systems, word processing, and inventory control. More advanced uses (or second-stage applications) of the computer involve financial planning, management of information, and market research.

4. The small-business manager who decides that a computer is feasible for business operations has several options: using a service bureau, time-sharing, leasing a computer, or buying a computer.

5. The ten steps to take when obtaining a computer system for the first time are: learn about computers, analyze the present manual system, clearly define expectations from the computer system, compare costs and benefits, establish a timetable for installing the system, write a tight contract with the computer vendor, obtain programs first before obtaining the hardware, prepare employees for conversion, make the conversion, and reap the benefits.

DISCUSSION QUESTIONS

1. Discuss the social problems that arose with the advancement of computer technology.
2. List and define the five components of a business computer system.
3. What types of input units and output units are available in computer systems?
4. What are three types of computers?
5. What is a turnkey computer system?
6. Why have computers become more commonly used in small businesses?

7. Discuss the applications of computers in small businesses.

8. Discuss the advantages and disadvantages of (a) service bureaus, (b) time-sharing systems, (c) leasing computers, and (d) buying computers.

9. List and discuss the ten steps a business should take when obtaining a computer system for the first time.

10. Discuss the future of computers.

ENDNOTES

1. "User friendly" refers to how well an individual can interact with the computer and understand what it is doing. Some of the innovative advances in making computers user friendly are discussed in Sabin Russell, "User Friendlier," *Venture*, Vol. 6, No. 7 (July, 1984), pp. 48–56.

2. An excellent discussion of the human element and data considerations is found in Robert A. Rademacher and Harry L. Gibson, *An Introduction to Computers and Information Systems* (Cincinnati, OH: South-Western Publishing Co., 1983).

3. This ranking appeared in *Business Week*, No. 2830 (February 27, 1984), p. 77.

4. *Ibid.*

5. Edward Goldfinger, "A Manager's Guide to Computer Systems," *Inc.*, Vol. 2, No. 5 (May, 1980), p. 103.

6. "Computer Is as Important as Milk Cows," *Progressive Farmer* (December, 1980), pp. 22–23.

7. "More Law Firms Put Computers to Work to Find Cases, Print Filings, Bill Clients," *The Wall Street Journal*, December 23, 1980, p. 32.

8. K.K. Moore's personal consulting experience. Name and location are fictitious, but the other facts are correct.

9. Goldfinger, *op. cit.*, pp. 105–106.

10. *Business Week* (February 27, 1984), *op. cit.*

11. For more information regarding spreadsheets using Lotus 1-2-3, see Terry Maness, *Small Business Using Lotus 1-2-3* (Cincinnati, OH: South-Western Publishing Co., 1987).

12. "Picking a Small Computer," *Dun's Review*, Vol. 118, No. 2 (August, 1981), p. 72.

13. *Ibid.*

14. Frank Greenwood, "The Ten Commandments of Small Business Computerization," *Journal of Small Business Management*, Vol. 19, No. 2 (April, 1981), pp. 61–67.

REFERENCES TO SMALL BUSINESS IN ACTION

"America's Newest Cottage Industry." *Output* (June, 1981), pp. 19–20.
The growth of computers has seen the flowering of a new breed of entrepreneur—the home-computer owner who turns a hobby to profit by writing software that businesses will buy.

"America's Offices Enter a New Age." *Nation's Business*, Vol. 69, No. 7 (July, 1981), pp. 49–54.

The role of electronic office equipment in increasing the productivity of office functions in small business is discussed in this article.

"A Manager's Guide to Computer Systems." *Inc.*, Vol. 2, No. 5 (May, 1980), pp. 101–106.

This article reports on small businesses that have computerized their business functions.

Kall, Janice. "Small Consulting Firm Solves Its Big Problem." *Business Software*, Vol. 2, No. 1 (April, 1984), pp. 46–51.

This article describes the trial-and-error experiences of a small firm trying to find the best database management system for use in the development and implementation of sales incentive programs for its corporate clients.

"Tapping the Mom and Pop Market." *Information Processing* (October 27, 1980), pp. 165–172.

This article describes the way in which computer makers seek to reach small-business buyers.

CASE 21

The Fair Store*
Contemplating a computerized inventory-control system

The Fair Store of Lott, TX (a small town of less than 1,000 population), has built a reputation as the state's leading retailer of high-quality western wear at moderate prices. Its owner is R. W. Hailey. In the store the atmosphere of the Old West is developed by narrow aisles, crowded racks of merchandise, inexpensive fixtures, and informality in operating procedures. Many customers drive hundreds of miles to this store and, at certain times of the year, stand in line on the sidewalk in order to be admitted.

Fair Store's Sales Personnel

All of the salesclerks at The Fair Store are local people. Many of them are housewives whose husbands are farmers in the surrounding areas. For the most part, the sales personnel are not well-educated and are quite provincial. However, they have always been accustomed to hard work and are pleasant to customers.

Fair Store's Merchandising Practices

In western wear, just as in other types of merchandise, style conscious-ness affects customer demand. Quite a variety of merchandise is sold. Many brands of boots with different price ranges are sold, but The Fair Store's two principal suppliers of handmade boots are Tony Lama and Justin Company.

Breaking the merchandise into groups, Hailey estimates the store's merchandise assortment as follows:

Hats	8%
Jeans, pants, suits, and shirts	20%
Children's boots and cheaper adult boots	15%
Tony Lama and Justin Red Wing Boots	50%
Miscellaneous	7%

The buying of boots has to be done months ahead, usually about six months, because they are handmade. Such a time lag means that purchasing for the Thanksgiving and Christmas markets must come no later than the

*This case was prepared by Professor Kris K. Moore of Baylor University.

previous April or May. Boots, therefore, entail a large inventory investment during the period from June to November. A recent amount purchased from the Justin Company for this market period was $57,507.

Western hats (which are often custom-steamed to the customer's favorite crease) follow the seasonal demand—with straw hats for spring and summer, and felt hats for fall and winter. Hats must be purchased six months in advance. Jeans, pants, suits, and shirts must also be purchased several months in advance.

Fair Store's Inventory Practices

At present the store has no direct methods of inventory control. The sales representatives from Tony Lama and Justin Company bring samples of different styles to Hailey. Hailey then chooses styles that he believes will sell and, with the sales representatives, determines the price and the quantity to be shipped. When the merchandise is received at the store, Hailey helps unpack the goods and mark prices. There is no verification that merchandise received matches the purchase orders. No further record keeping is maintained. Merchandise is shelved, and the amount of a sale is rung up on the cash register when a customer has concluded his or her shopping.

Periodically, Hailey walks through the store and makes a visual check of merchandise, noting low levels of styles and sizes. He then places new orders on the basis of such notes. At year's end, an inventory check is made to determine the information needed for tax returns. The yearly inventory check is time-consuming and costly.

Hailey's Thoughts on Computerizing

After the store grossed over a million dollars in a recent fiscal year, Hailey began wondering how he could use a computer for better control of the business. He was especially interested in 2 areas: (1) controlling the average daily inventory, which had grown from $94,000 to $207,000 in 1 year, and (2) having available in quantity for customers the most demanded sizes of handmade boots. Although sales had increased satisfactorily, the rate of increase was lower than the growth in inventory. Hailey felt that his business would continue to grow at a rapid rate and wondered if a computer would help him with inventory management.

Questions

1. In what areas of inventory management does R. W. Hailey seem to have the greatest problems? What cost savings might be realized by better inventory control?
2. What buying, receiving, pricing, and check-out changes would be necessary to accommodate a computerized inventory-control system? Be specific.

22

Business Risks and Insurance

Figure 22-1   Harry Ball

Going without insurance is a "risky" option for managing a small firm's product liability risks. Nevertheless, escalating policy premiums are encouraging some firms to take the chance. One such business is Sure-Grip International Corporation, a manufacturer of roller skates and skateboards in South Gate, CA. Recently, the firm was confronted with a statement for $40,000 in annual product liability premiums. Its president, Harry Ball, despite fully knowing that one major successful lawsuit could spell doomsday for his firm, takes the position, "I refuse to pay that kind of money for insurance. We'll keep the rest of our insurance, like fire, because it has remained reasonable."

Ball is stepping up quality control as a means to reduce the risk of a product liability claim. He also hopes that plaintiffs will not be as eager to sue if they realize that Sure-Grip has no insurance.

Source: Reprinted with permission, *Inc.* magazine, October, 1985. Copyright © 1985 by Inc. Publishing Company, 38 Commercial Wharf, Boston, MA 02110.

Looking Ahead

Watch for the following important topics:

1. The concepts of risk and risk management.
2. Classifications of business risks.
3. Methods of coping with business risks.
4. Basic principles of insurance.
5. Types of insurance.

It is said that "nothing is certain except death and taxes." Entrepreneurs live with still another certainty—that of taking a risk when operating a small business. Even though most entrepreneurs' personalities are especially suited to cope with business risk, they nevertheless seek to minimize the tension that arises from it. The first step in reducing business-risk tension is to understand the different types of business risks and alternatives for managing them.

Simply stated, **risk** is "a condition in which there is a possibility of an adverse deviation from a desired outcome that is expected or hoped for."[1] Applied to the small-business situation, "risk" translates into losses associated with company assets and earning potential of the business. As used here, the term "asset" includes not only inventory and equipment but also such "assets" as the firm's employees and its reputation. **Risk management** consists of all efforts designed to preserve these assets and the earning power of the business.

Risk management has grown out of insurance management. Therefore, the two terms are often used interchangeably. Actually, risk management has a much broader meaning, covering both those risks that are insurable and also those that are not.

Risk management in the small firm differs from risk management in the large firm. The manager of a small business is usually the risk manager. In contrast, a large firm may assign the responsibilities of risk management to a specialized staff manager. In practicing risk management, the small-business manager should be able to identify the different types of business risks and be able to cope with them. In the next section, we shall discuss the specific nature of the more common types of small business risks.

COMMON SMALL-BUSINESS RISKS

Business risks can be classified in several ways. One simple approach is to list the causes of potential losses. Fire, personal injury, theft, and fraud would be items on such a list. Another system portrays business risks by grouping accidental losses into those which are generally insurable and those which are largely uninsurable. A fire loss would typify the first category; product obsolescence, the second category.

A third system, one which we will use in this text, emphasizes the asset-centered focus of the definition of risk management by grouping business risks into four categories: market-centered risks, property-centered risks, employee-centered risks, and customer-centered risks. Figure 22–2 portrays these four risk categories including examples of each. This classification system encompasses four key "asset" groups for the small business. A substantial loss in any one category could mean devastation for the small business. We will examine the forms of risk associated with each category and identify the possible alternatives for coping with them.

Market-Centered Risks

Some of the most crippling forms of business risks are found in the negative changes occurring within a firm's target market and marketing efforts. Many of these factors directly affect the firm's competitive position and potential for long-term survival. Characteristically, market-related risks develop slowly from day to day until, finally, they become destructive—unlike a fire which ignites and destroys a building overnight. Four examples of market-centered risks are supplier interruptions, deteriorating economic conditions, falling product demand, and product mix neglect. These market-centered risks are generally *uninsurable* through standard insurance policies. Firms can, of course, always practice self-insurance, which we will explain later. Let us examine each of the four examples we have named.

Supplier Interruptions   A small firm is often highly dependent on suppliers to keep its business running smoothly. When major suppliers experience an interruption of their business operations, fall-out from their hard times disrupts the operations of their customers. For example, back in the late seventies there was a coal strike by the United Mine Workers. This strike had a domino effect which quickly resulted in utility companies curtailing the usage of electricity among customers, including numerous small businesses. To many firms, this meant shortening hours of operation; to others, it was a matter of closing down and laying off employees.

Deteriorating Economic Conditions   Periods of high inflation, rising interest rates, declining discretionary income, and recessions are all symptoms of a deteriorating economy and are uncontrollable variables to the small-business manager. Nevertheless, they have a major impact on the small firm's level of risk. Rapidly rising prices for materials and labor, for example, may catch the small firm in a vulnerable position, particularly if it is locked into a fixed price

Figure 22-2   The Wheel of Misfortune

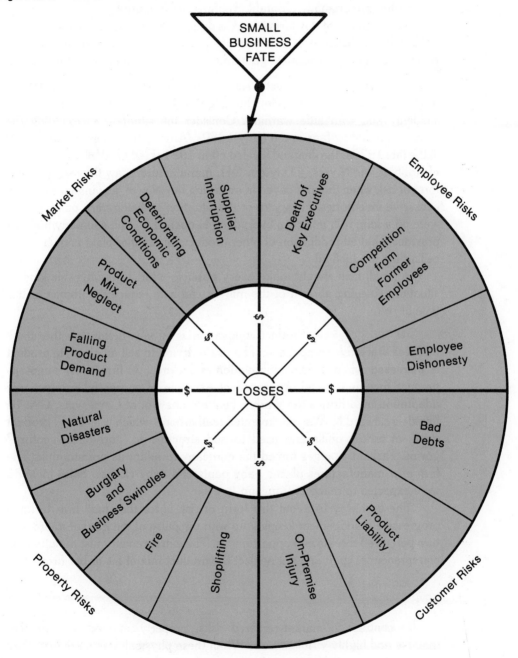

with customers. The increased cost of a bank loan might also be the straw that pushes a marginally profitable venture into bankruptcy.

Management of this form of risk is difficult. Entrepreneurs are extremely vulnerable to this type of risk because much discipline is required to save profits in times of prosperity to guard against a weak working-capital position.

Falling Demand for a Product   As we have discussed in Chapter 10, all products go through a life cycle. Often, however, the downturn in sales occurs suddenly and with little warning. Consider the situation surrounding the demand for ceiling fans in the early 1980s. After experiencing rapid growth in the late 1970s, the demand leveled off in 1981. Fred G. Wall, the president of Robbins and Myers, a Dayton, OH, manufacturer, saw the reality of this form of risk when the roof caved in on ceiling fan growth, leaving his firm with excessive inventories. He spoke of the situation as being very painful. "We were on a long roll, and then everything happened."[2] The company had just previously halted production of other products at another plant converting to ceiling fan production!

A small firm should make every possible effort to escape this kind of situation. Keeping abreast of the market can help reduce the impact of this type of risk.

Product Mix Neglect   Product innovation is a key factor for the small business that stays competitive. The risk of trying to sell an obsolete product is increased when product innovation is lacking. A firm must adapt its product mix to survive! An excellent example of successful product mix adaptation by a firm is the Warren Featherbone Co. of Gainesville, GA. Its founder, Edward K. Warren, invented featherbone, which is a "stay" product made of turkey quills and used to add structure to "turn-of-the-century" gowns. Fashion changes forced the company to adapt its product mix. The firm now manufactures plastic baby pants and baby clothes. Sales in 1986 were expected to reach $25 million.[3]

The best way to avoid this form of risk is for the small firm to have progressive management keeping up with the pulse of the market in order to turn perceived threats into opportunities. The entrepreneur must maintain the entrepreneurial spirit and not neglect the product mix of his or her firm.

Property-Centered Risks

In contrast to market-centered risks, property-centered risks involve tangible and highly visible assets. When these physical assets are lost, they are quickly missed. Most property-centered risks, however, are *insurable*.

Fire Hazards   The possibility of fire is always present. Building, equipment, and inventory items can be totally or partially destroyed by fire. Of course, the degree of risk and the loss potential differ with the type of business. For example, industrial processes that are complex and hazardous or that involve explosives, combustibles, or other flammable materials enlarge this risk.

Fire not only causes a direct property loss, but also may interrupt business operations, resulting in a loss of profit to the firm. During the period when business operations are interrupted, such fixed expenses as rent, supervisory salaries, and insurance charges continue. To avoid losses arising from business interruptions, a business might, for example, have alternative sources of electric power, such as its own generators, for use in times of emergency.

ACTION REPORT
Disaster Fires Up Owner

It was the Fourth of July weekend when Joe Larson and many of his Sparta Brush Company's employees watched the firm's warehouse and plant go up in flames. It was no time for celebration. Neither was it time to lie down and roll over. Larson moved quickly. Fortunately, he had recognized the value of adequate insurance and did not have to worry about financing. Instead, he freed himself from the adjustment process by hiring an independent insurance adjuster and set about the task of putting together a recovery plan.

Customers, suppliers, and employees were given detailed reports about the company's progress. The director of marketing spent his time talking to manufacturers' representatives; some of the staff manned phones from their houses. Machines were repaired by his own machinists on the spot, instead of being shipped off for rebuilding.

In a week's time Larson had the plant "patched-up," and the company was back in limited production. Larson's advice to a manager who has never experienced a fire is "Do a little role-playing. Like a pilot of a small plane, trained to look for emergency landing strips, have a plan."

Source: Reprinted with permission, *Inc.* magazine, December, 1981. Copyright © 1981 by Inc. Publishing Company, 38 Commercial Wharf, Boston, MA 02110.

Under some conditions, a large company can safely *self-insure* against major fire risks. A retail chain store with outlets in many different cities and states, for example, might act as its own fire insurance company. This would require the store management to determine the probability of loss through fire and then set aside a sum, determined by the use of an actuarial method, to meet those losses which are realized. It is clear that the risk would need to be spread so that any one fire would not destroy a substantial portion of the company's property. Total self-insurance, however, is seldom applicable to a small business.

Natural Disasters   Floods, hurricanes, tornadoes, and hail are often described as "acts of God" because of human limitations in foreseeing and controlling them. As in the case of fire, natural disasters may also interrupt business operations. Although a business may take certain preventive measures—for example, locating in areas not subject to flood damage—there is not much one can do to avoid natural disasters. Major reliance is placed upon insurance in coping with natural-disaster losses.

Burglary and Business Swindles   The forcible breaking and entering of premises closed for business with the subsequent removal of cash or merchandise is called burglary. Although insurance should be carried against losses from burglary, it may prove helpful for a business to install burglar alarm systems and arrange for private security services.

Business swindles can amount to hundreds of dollars a year. Small firms in particular are susceptible to swindles. Examples of these are bogus office-machine repairers, phony charity appeals, billing for listing in nonexistent directories, sale of advertising space in publications whose nature is misrepresented, and advanced fee deals. Risks of this kind are avoidable only through the alertness of the business manager.

Shoplifting   The theft of merchandise during store hours costs retail merchants alone upwards of $8 billion a year, and small business is not immune to this danger.[4] It is estimated that one out of three small-business bankruptcies is a direct result of shoplifting by customers or employees.[5] Various precautionary measures may be taken by the small business to minimize shoplifting. These include:

1. Limiting access to certain areas of the business premises.
2. Screening employees carefully.
3. Laying out the facilities to provide good visual coverage.
4. Keeping high-unit-value items in special-security locations.
5. Monitoring shoplifting with special equipment such as closed-circuit television.
6. Educating potential offenders to understand that they will be prosecuted.

Employee-Centered Risks

Employee-centered losses occur indirectly due to employees' personal circumstances or directly through employee actions against the business. A physically sick or injured employee is an example of an indirect loss.

Employee spying, on the other hand, is a direct action against the business and constitutes a major concern for many small businesses. Most employee-centered risks are *insurable*.

Employee Dishonesty   One of the more visual forms of employee dishonesty is employee theft. Estimates of the magnitude of employee theft vary. One Washington attorney has estimated that American workers are stealing more then $800 million a week.[6] There is a strong feeling that small businesses are particularly vulnerable because their anti-theft controls are extremely lax.[7]

Thefts by employees may include not only cash but also inventory items, tools, metal scrap, stamps, and the like. Then there is always the possibility of forgery, raising of checks, or other fraudulent practices. The trusted book-keeper may enter into collusion with an outsider to have bogus invoices or invoices double or triple the correct amount presented for payment. The bookkeeper may approve such invoices for payment, write a check, and secure the manager's signature. In addition to bonding employees, the firm's major protection against employee frauds is a system of internal checks or control.

According to Mick Moritz, who is director of security for United Telephone Systems in Carlisle, PA, there are four contributing factors to employee theft: desire, a rationalization of the action, opportunity, and the perception that apprehension is unlikely.[8] It is mainly the last two factors that small businesses can eliminate.

Death of Key Executives   Every successful small business has one or more key executives. These employees could be lost to the firm by death or through attraction to other employment. If key personnel cannot be successfully replaced, the small firm suffers appreciably and loses profits as the result of the loss of their services.

In addition to valuable experience and skill, there is also the possibility that the executive may have certain specialized knowledge which is vital to the successful operation of the firm. For example, a certain manufacturer was killed in an auto accident at the age of 53. His processing operations involved the use of a secret chemical formula which he had devised originally and divulged to no one because of the fear of losing the formula to competitors. He neither reduced it to writing nor placed it in a safety-deposit box. Not even his family knew the formula. As a result of his sudden death, the firm went out of business within six months. The expensive special-purpose equipment had to be sold as junk. All that his widow salvaged was about $60,000 worth of bonds and the Florida residence which had been the winter home of the couple.

Two answers, at least, are possible to the small firm faced with this contingency. The first of these is life insurance, which is discussed later in the chapter. The second solution involves the development of replacement

---

ACTION REPORT
What Will They Think of Next?

A major employee-centered risk is employee dishonesty. Employee dishonesty usually translates into business losses and can even mean business failure. The nature of employee dishonesty ranges from theft to swindles. In reference to business theft, Sanford Beck, owner of Royal Schutt Inc., a firm specializing in business security, says, "The biggest peril is from trusted people." Consider some of the following incidents:

> ...supervisors had access to time cards and gave out W-2 forms each year. This made it easy for them to keep 18 phantom employees on the payroll, pocket the checks, and endorse them for their own use. One (supervisor) even had a time clock in his garage so he didn't have to rush to work to punch in for his fictitious employees. The five-year scam cost the company nearly $400,000.
>
> ...a manager at a busy branch office of a fast-copying service where $200 and $300 jobs were common...had a receipt book of his own. To steal cash, he simply gave customers a receipt from his book instead of one of the company's numbered forms.
>
> ...a purchasing agent got nickel-and-dime kickbacks on buttons, zippers, and other trim used in such quantity at a successful dress company that over the years he got rich and the company was overcharged $10 million.

Checking out prospective employees and tight control are the two best safeguards against employee dishonesty. Also, according to Saul D. Astor, president of Management Safeguards, Inc., the entrepreneur should "set an example of impeccable honesty."

Source: Reprinted with permission of *The Wall Street Journal,* © Dow Jones & Company, Inc., 1985. All Rights Reserved.

---

personnel. A potential replacement may be groomed for every key position, including the position of the owner–manager.

Former Employees   Good employees are always hard to get; they are even harder to keep. When a business has employee turnover—and it always will—it must be concerned with the risks associated with former employees. This risk is particularly acute with turnover of key executives. They are the more likely candidates to start a competing business or to leave with trade secrets.

Companies are very sensitive to former employee activities. Consider the following risk situation:

> Michael was employed by a company that manufactured equipment and supplies used in hot stamp decorating...Michael met and became friendly with Robert, who owned a company that sold marking tools to Michael's employer.... Michael began ordering patterns and models from a second company, which was

also owned by Robert.... Then Michael and Robert formed a corporation of their own.... Michael quit his job... and began producing and selling material used for hot stamp decorating—in competition with his former employer.... The former employer sued Michael and Robert for misappropriating the manufacturing procedures manual... and other alleged trade secrets.... The judge awarded nearly $200,000 in damages to the former employer.[9]

One common practice to help avoid this kind of employee-centered risk is to require employees to sign employment contracts clearly setting forth the employee's promise not to disclose certain information or use it in competition with the employer.

Customer-Centered Risks

Customers are the source of profit for small business, but they are also the center of an ever-increasing amount of business risk. Much of this risk is attributable to on-premise injury, product liability, and bad debts. Most customer-centered risks are *insurable*.

On-Premise Injury to Customers The small business should be aware of the risks associated with customers' claims against the business originating with an on-premise injury. Because of high store traffic, this risk is particularly acute for the small-business retailer but must be managed by all small businesses. Personal injury liability of this type may occur, for example, when a customer breaks an arm by slipping on icy steps while entering or leaving the business. An employer is, of course, at risk with employees who suffer similar fates; but customers, by their sheer numbers, make this risk larger.

Juries have traditionally favored customers in these types of liability. Consider the following judgments:

> ...An Indiana jury returned a verdict of $2,500,000 for a 6-year-old boy who suffered severe brain injury when a gasoline tank exploded. A construction company had dug up the tank while preparing a site for a new shopping center. The tank, containing gas fumes, was left unattended.
>
> ...In a Kansas supermarket, a 61-year-old woman was reaching for a bottle of Pepsi when a carton of the bottles fell to the floor and shattered. Flying glass struck the shopper's foot. She sued the market and the bottler.... The jury awarded her $86,000.[10]

Good management of this kind of customer-centered risk demands that a regular check of the premises for hazards be conducted. The concept of *preventive maintenance* applies to management of this risk factor.

Product Liability Recent product liability decisions have broadened the scope of this form of risk. No reputable small business would intentionally produce a product which would potentially harm a customer, but good intentions are weak defenses in liability suits.

A product liability suit may be filed when a customer becomes ill or sustains property damage in using a product made or sold by a company. Class-action suits, together with individual suits, are now widely used by consumers in product liability cases. Some types of businesses operate in higher-risk markets. For example, the insulation business has recently been targeted with numerous product claims because of the asbestos scare.

Richard S. Betterley, a consultant, suggests the following steps to help a small company reduce product liability losses:

1. Include thorough and explicit directions for the product's use with each product. Warn customers of potential hazards and keep an eye on promotional material to make sure advertising doesn't undo the company's precautions.
2. Develop procedures for handling consumers' complaints through distributors and at the home office. Prepare a plan to handle the worst possible kind of disaster.
3. Determine whether any of the company's products are too risky to sell, given the consequences of a suit.
4. Test products internally for possible safety problems. Then obtain a "second opinion" from others in the field and consult the company's insurer.
5. Acquaint all employees with the company's concern with product safety.
6. Stay current with legislation and litigation within the appropriate industries.[11]

ACTION REPORT
Lawsuits Bug an Industry

All small businesses should manage product liability risks, but none are any more affected by this kind of risk than exterminators. This is an industry characterized by very small businesses—firms with two or three employees. Rising insurance premiums are placing entrepreneurs of this industry in positions similar to other industries. Richard Lipsey, vice-president of research at Kemco Chemical and Manufacturing Corporation in Jacksonville, FL, says, "I think we are starting into the same position doctors moved into 10 years ago with malpractice problems."

In one year's time, liability insurance costs for the typical "bug doctor" have gone from $1,000 a year to over $4,000. Most suits allege that customers have become ill due to pesticides used by the exterminators.

Source: Reprinted by permission of *The Wall Street Journal,* © Dow Jones & Company, Inc., 1985. All Rights Reserved.

Bad Debts   Bad debts are an unavoidable risk associated with credit selling. Most customers will pay their obligations with no more than a friendly reminder. A few customers will intentionally try to avoid payment. These accounts should be quickly turned over to a lawyer for litigation or be written off.

Customers who fall between the two groups of "quick pay" and "no pay" are the ones who cause the most trouble. These customers may be good customers but, for various reasons, may temporarily experience difficulty and become slow payers. Every effort should be made in an aggressive but courteous manner to offer these customers options which will encourage payment.

COPING WITH SMALL-BUSINESS RISKS

Once a manager is fully aware of the sources of risk in his or her business, programs of risk management can be developed. Three basic alternatives of coping with risks can be pursued individually or in combination. These options are: (1) reduce the risk, (2) save funds to recover from risk losses, or (3) share the risks. Most small businesses rely heavily on sharing business risks via insurance, when they should be using the three options in combination.

Reducing Business Risks

Small-business risks of all kinds can be reduced with sound, common-sense management. Preventive maintenance applied to risk management means eliminating the circumstances and situations which create risk. For example, the small firm needs to take every possible precaution to prevent fires. Possible precautions are the following:

1. *Use of safe construction.* The building should be made of fire-resistant materials, and electrical wiring should be adequate to carry the maximum load of electrical energy which will be imposed. Fire doors and insulation should be used where necessary.
2. *Provision of a completely automatic sprinkler system.* With an automatic sprinkler system available, fire insurance rates will be lower—and the fire hazard itself is definitely reduced.
3. *Provision of an adequate water supply.* Ordinarily this involves location in a city with water sources and water mains, together with a pumping system that will assure the delivery of any amount of water needed to fight fires. Of course, a company may hedge a bit by providing company-owned water storage tanks or private wells.

4. *Institution and operation of a fire-prevention program involving all employees.* Such a program must have top-management support, and the emphasis must always be to keep employees fire-safety conscious. Regular fire drills for all employees, including both building-evacuation and actual fire-fighting efforts, may be undertaken.

Saving to Recover from Risk Losses

Intelligent, personal financial planning usually follows the practice of "saving for a rainy day." This concept should also be incorporated into small-business risk management. It is a difficult practice to follow in a business, but one which will pay dividends. This is a form of risk management frequently called *self-insurance.*

Self-insurance can take a general or specific form. In its general form, a part of the firm's earnings is earmarked as a contingency fund for possible future losses regardless of the source. In its specific form, a self-insurance program designates funds to individual loss categories such as property, medical, or workers' compensation. Some firms, such as the one described at the beginning of this chapter, have moved quite heavily into self-insurance. Consider also Growth Enterprises Inc., a restaurant development company in Basking Ridge, NJ, which saved over $29,000 in its first year of operating a self-insurance program. Suzanne Green, Growth Enterprises's administrative manager, says, "We plan to go back out to the market and compare again. I don't think you can go along blindly with this kind of thing (self-insurance), put it in and say, 'Gee, this is going to work forever.' Self-insurance is not a panacea."[12]

Sharing Risks

Insurance provides one of the most important means of sharing business risks. Too often in the past, the small firm has paid insufficient attention to insurance matters and has failed to acquire skill in analyzing risk problems. Today such a situation is untenable. A sound insurance program is imperative for the proper protection of a business.

Insurance coverage is available for almost anything. Consider these unusual coverages:

1. A graveyard in Pennsylvania insures its tombstones against vandalism.
2. Clergymen carry insurance against suits for giving advice.
3. A nine-foot-long alligator (stuffed) in front of a general store in Ponchatoula, LA, is insured against theft.[13]

Regardless of the nature of the business, risk insurance is serious business. The small-business manager must take an active role in structuring an insurance package.

INSURANCE FOR THE SMALL BUSINESS

It is often apparent that small firms fail to carry sufficient insurance protection. The entrepreneur often comes to such a realization only after a major loss. Careful risk management dictates a study of adequate insurance policies *in advance of a loss* rather than after the occurrence of the event.

Basic Principles of an Insurance Program

What kinds of risks can be covered by insurance? What kinds of coverage should be purchased? How much coverage is adequate? Unfortunately, there are no clear-cut answers to these questions. Probably the best advice to a small-business manager is to seek advice from a professional insurance agent. A reputable, independent insurance agent can provide valuable assistance to small firms in evaluating risks and designing proper protection plans. However, the entrepreneur should enter this consultation as knowledgeable about insurance as possible. Some of the basic principles of insurance are discussed in the next paragraphs.

Identify the Business Risks to Be Covered   Although the common insurable risks were already pointed out earlier, other less obvious risks may be revealed only by a careful investigation. The small firm must first obtain coverages required by law or contract, such as workers' compensation insurance and automobile liability insurance. As part of this risk-identification process, the plant and equipment should be reappraised periodically by competent appraisers in order to maintain an adequate insurance coverage.

Obtain Coverage Only for Major Potential Losses   The small firm must determine the magnitude of loss which it could bear without serious financial difficulty. If the firm is sufficiently strong, it may cover only those losses exceeding a specified minimum amount to avoid unnecessary coverage. It is important, of course, to guard against the tendency to underestimate the severity of potential losses.

Relate Cost of Premiums to Probability of Loss   Because the insurance company must collect enough premiums to pay the actual losses of insured parties, the cost of insurance must be proportional to probability of occurrence of the insured event. As the chance of loss becomes more and more certain, a firm finds that the premium cost becomes so high that insurance is simply not worth the cost. Thus, insurance is most applicable and practical for improbable losses.

Requirements for Obtaining Insurance

Before an insurance company is willing to underwrite possible losses, certain requirements about the risk or the insured must be met. These requirements are explained below.

The Risk Must Be Calculable The total overall loss arising from a large number of insured risks can be calculated by means of actuarial tables. For example, the number of buildings that will burn each year can be predicted with some accuracy. Only if the risks can be calculated will it be possible for the insurance company to determine fair insurance premiums to be charged.

The Risk Must Exist in Large Numbers The particular risk must occur in sufficiently large numbers to permit the law of averages to work and be spread over a wide geographical area. A fire insurance company, for example, cannot afford to insure only one building or even all the buildings in one town. It would have to insure buildings in many other towns and cities to get an adequate, safe distribution of risk.

The Insured Property Must Have Commercial Value An item that possesses only sentimental value cannot be insured. For example, an old family picture that is of no value to the public may not be included among other tangible items whose value can be measured in monetary terms.

The Policyholder Must Have an Insurable Interest in the Property or Person Insured The purpose of insurance is reimbursement of actual loss and not creation of profit for the insured. For example, a firm could not insure a building for $500,000 if its true worth is actually only $70,000. Likewise, it could not obtain life insurance on its customers or suppliers.

Types of Insurance

There are several classifications of insurance and a variety of coverages available from different insurance companies.[14] Each insurance purchase should seek a balance between coverage, deductions, and premiums. Since the trend is toward higher and higher premiums for small businesses, the balancing act becomes even more critical.[15]

Commercial Property Coverage This class of insurance provides protection from losses associated with damage to or loss of property. Examples of property losses which can be covered are fire, explosion, vandalism, broken glass, business interruption, and employee dishonesty.

Most entrepreneurs will see the need for fire coverage and maybe a few other more traditional losses, but not enough small businesses realize the value of **business interruption insurance**. Business interruption insurance protects companies during the period necessary to restore property damaged by an insured peril. Coverage pays for lost income and other expenses of recovery. Proving the extent of lost profits can be difficult. William D. O'Connell of Touche Ross and Company says the process is difficult "because you are trying to reconstruct what never was."[16]

Dishonesty insurance covers such traditional areas as fidelity bonds and crime insurance. Employees occupying positions of trust in handling company funds are customarily bonded as a protection against their dishonesty. The informality and highly personal basis of employment in small firms make it difficult to realize the value of such insurance. On the other hand, the possible loss of money or other property through the dishonesty of persons other than employees is easy to accept. Crime insurance can cover such dangers as theft, robbery, and forgery.

Many commercial property policies contain a **coinsurance clause**. Under this clause, the insured agrees to maintain insurance equal to some specified percentage of the property value.[17] (A percentage of 80 percent is quite typical.) In return for this promise, the insured is given a reduced rate. If the insured fails to maintain the 80 percent coverage, only part of the loss will be reimbursed. To see how a coinsurance clause determines the amount paid by the insurer, assume that the physical property of a business is valued at $50,000. If the business insures it for $40,000 (or 80 percent of the property value) and incurs a fire loss of $20,000, the insurance company will pay the full amount of $20,000. However, if the business insures the property for only $30,000 (which is 75 percent of the specified minimum), the insurance company will pay only 75 percent of the loss, or $15,000.

Surety Bonds   These bonds protect against one kind of market-centered risk. **Surety bonds** insure against the failure of another firm or individual to fulfill a contractual obligation. Surety bonds are frequently used in connection with construction contracts.

Credit Insurance   Some small firms are financially able to insure themselves against certain credit losses. **Credit insurance** protects businesses from abnormal bad-debt losses. Abnormally high losses are those that result from a customer's insolvency due to tornado or flood losses, depressed industry conditions, business recession, or other factors. Credit insurance does not cover normal bad-debt losses that are predictable on the basis of past business experience. Insurance companies compute the normal rate on the basis of industry experience and the loss record of the particular firm being insured.

Credit insurance is available only to manufacturers and wholesalers. It is not available to a retailer. Thus, only trade credit may be insured. There are two reasons for this. The more important reason is found in the relative difficulty of analyzing business risks as compared with analyzing ultimate consumer risks. The other reason is that retailers have a much greater number of accounts receivable, which are smaller and provide greater risk diversification, so that credit insurance is less acutely required.

The collection service of the insurance company makes available legal talent and experience that may otherwise be unavailable to a small firm. Furthermore, collection efforts of insurance companies are generally conceded to be superior to those of regular collection agencies.

In addition, the credit standing of many small firms that might use credit insurance is enhanced. The small firm can show the banker that steps have been taken to avoid unnecessary risks, and thus it might obtain more favorable consideration in securing bank credit.

Credit insurance policies typically provide for a collection service on bad accounts. Although collection provisions vary, a common provision requires the insured to notify the insurance company within 90 days of the past-due status of the account and to turn it in for collection after 90 days.

Although the vast majority of policies provide general coverage, policies may be secured to cover individual accounts. A 10 percent, or higher, coinsurance requirement is included to limit the coverage to approximately the replacement value of the merchandise. Higher percentages of coinsurance are required for inferior accounts in order to discourage reckless credit extension by insured firms. Accounts are classified according to ratings by Dun and Bradstreet or ratings by other recognized agencies. Premiums vary with account ratings.[18]

Commercial Liability Insurance   There are two general classes of this form of insurance—general liability and employers' liability/workers' compensation. **General liability insurance** covers business liability to customers who might be injured on the premises or off-premises or who might be injured from the product sold to them. General liability insurance does not cover injury to a firm's own employees. However, employees using products such as machinery purchased from another manufacturer can bring suit under product liability laws against the equipment manufacturer. For example, a New Jersey court ruled that a machine manufacturer was liable for a worker's injury in a plastics plant when the worker caught his fingers in its machine. A protective guard had been removed, but the court felt that the manufacturer should have foreseen that.[19]

Employer's liability and **workers' compensation insurance** are required by all states to insure employees. As the titles imply, employer's liability coverage provides protection against suits brought by employees who suffer injury. Workers' compensation coverage obligates the insurer to pay eligible employees of the insured as required by workers' compensation law of the state.

Key-Person Insurance   By carrying life insurance, protection for the small business can be provided against the death of key personnel of the firm. This insurance is purchased by the company with the company as sole beneficiary. It may be written on an individual or group basis.

Most small-business advisors suggest term insurance for key-person insurance policies primarily because of lower premiums. How much to buy is more difficult to decide. Stan Meadow, who is a small-business specialist with McDermott, Will & Emery, a Chicago firm, recommends that the best way to determine a key executive's worth is to "calculate what it would cost to bring in someone of equal skill."[20]

ACTION REPORT
Key-Person Insurance

Key-person insurance refers to special life-insurance coverage for top executives. It is most useful, according to Phil Dunne, chief financial officer of Sikes Corporation, for "companies that are highly leveraged or dominated by one person." The Sikes Corporation collected $6.9 million from a key-man policy on Jimmy Sikes, the chief executive officer of the Lakeland, FL, ceramic-tile manufacturer. Sikes had died suddenly at the age of 52 from a heart attack.

The key-man policy had been taken out by the firm in 1976 with yearly premiums of $200,000. Dunne viewed this cost as "...just another cost of doing business." Dunne expects to purchase two more key-man policies for the company. One is on the new chief executive officer and another is for Jimmy Sikes' brother, who is chairman of the board. Dunne feels this type of coverage is still needed. "We don't have somebody who could step right into either one of those jobs, and if—God forbid—something should happen...then we'd need all the help we could get."

Source: "When the Man Is the Company," *Forbes*, Vol. 131, No. 7 (March 28, 1983), pp. 100, 102.

Looking Back

1. Risk management is "an approach to management concerned with the preservation of the assets and earning power of a business against risks of accidental loss." The three ways to manage business risks are: reduce the risk, save to cover possible future losses, and transfer the risk to someone else by carrying insurance. The best solution often is to combine all three approaches.

2. Business risks can be classified by the causes of accidental loss, by insurability, or by type of assets which are preserved with risk management. In using the last system, risks are classified as market-centered, property-centered, employee-centered, and customer-centered.

3. The small firm should carry enough insurance to protect against major losses. Beyond this, the decision on coverage requires judgment that balances such factors as magnitude of possible loss, ability to minimize such losses, cost of the insurance, and financial strength of the firm.

4. To obtain insurance, several requirements must be met. The risk must be calculable in probabilistic terms, the risk must exist in large numbers, the insured property must have commercial value, and the policyholder must have an insurable interest in the property or person insured.

5. The basic types of insurance coverage which the small business might require are: commercial property coverage, surety bonds, commercial liability, credit, and key-person insurance.

DISCUSSION QUESTIONS

1. What are the basic ways to cope with risk in a small business?

2. Can a small firm safely assume that business risks will never turn into losses sufficient to bankrupt it and therefore avoid buying insurance and taking other protective measures? Why?

3. How can a small business deal with the risk entailed in business recessions?

4. Could a small firm safely deal with such hazards as property loss from fire by precautionary measures in lieu of insurance?

5. When is it logical for a small business to utilize self-insurance?

6. Enumerate a number of approaches for combatting the danger of theft or fraud by employees and also by outsiders.

7. Under what conditions would life insurance on a business executive constitute little protection to the business? And when is such life insurance helpful?

8. Are any kinds of business risks basically human risks? Are the people involved always employees?

9. Is the increase in liability claims and court awards of special concern to small manufacturers? Why?

10. What types of insurance are required by law for most business firms?

ENDNOTES

1. Emmett J. Vaughan, *Fundamentals of Risk and Insurance* (4th edition; New York: John Wiley & Sons, 1986), p. 4.

2. Damon Darlin, "Sales Plateau in Ceiling Fans Hurts Concern," *The Wall Street Journal*, Vol. CC, No. 91 (November 8, 1982), p. 2.

3. Eric Mogenthaler, "Featherbone Maker Prospers by Adapting as Product Dies," *The Wall Street Journal*, Vol. CC, No. 101 (November 22, 1982), p. 25.

4. "How Shoplifting Is Draining the Economy," *Business Week*, No. 2607 (October 15, 1979), p. 119.

5. *Ibid.*

6. "How to Foil Employee Crime," *Nation's Business*, Vol. 71, No. 7 (July, 1983), p. 38.

7. See "Crime Prevention for Small Business," *The Small Business Reporter*, Bank of America, 1984, for an extensive discussion of crime in small business.

8. Joanne Kelleher, "A Thief in the Fold," *Inc.*, Vol. 4, No. 6 (June, 1982), p. 96.

9. Fred S. Steingold, "Competing with Your Former Employer," *Inc.*, Vol. 5, No. 1 (January, 1983), p. 91.

10. Fred S. Steingold, "Do Your Business Premises Present a Public Hazard?" *Inc.*, Vol. 5, No. 11 (November, 1983), pp. 189, 191.

11. "Proper Precautions Trim Product Liability Risks," *Inc.*, Vol. 2, No. 5 (May, 1980), p. 131.

12. Donna Sammons, "Risky Business," *Inc.*, Vol. 6, No. 1 (January, 1984), p. 115.

13. "In Insurance, Anything Goes," *Venture*, Vol. 2, No. 10 (October, 1980), p. 20.

14. Much of the terminology used here to describe the different types of insurance is consistent with that used in the new Portfolio Program, suggested by the Insurance Services Office which is a national rating bureau that publishes rates for property and liability insurance. This program introduces simplified policy terminology, effective January 1, 1986.

15. A current assessment of what is happening with insurance can be found in Jill Andresky, "A World Without Insurance?" *Forbes*, Vol. 136, No. 2 (July 15, 1985), pp. 40–43; and David B. Hilder, "Small Firms Face Sharp Cost Hikes for Insurance—If They Can Get It," *The Wall Street Journal*, Vol. LXXVI, No. 25 (August 5, 1985), p. 23.

16. Sanford L. Jacobs, "Business-Disruption Coverage Is Inadequate at Many Firms," *The Wall Street Journal*, Vol. CCII, No. 65 (October 3, 1983), p. 27.

17. It should be remembered that this is value at time of the actual loss.

18. For additional discussion of credit insurance, see Emmett J. Vaughan, *op. cit.*, pp. 602–605.

19. William Steele, "The Product Liability Trap," *Inc.*, Vol. 4, No. 7 (July, 1982), p. 93.

20. Kathleen Mirin, "Key-Man Insurance," *Venture*, Vol. 5, No. 6 (June, 1983), p. 29.

REFERENCES TO SMALL BUSINESS IN ACTION

Cox, Jack. "A Trip Back from the Brink." *Venture*, Vol. 4, No. 8 (August, 1982), pp. 78–80.
The consequences of a lack of adequate fire insurance and no business continuation insurance are described by this account of a partnership manufacturing business which regrouped its operations after a crippling fire.

Crowley, Michael. "Recovering from the Ashes." *Venture*, Vol. 6, No. 3 (March, 1984), pp. 108–110.
This article provides a vivid account of a manager's eyewitnessing of a fire and the recovery strategy after fire completely destroyed a manufacturing plant. Due to careful insurance planning, the company didn't lose a penny.

Green, Richard. "Under the Gun." *Forbes*, Vol. 127, No. 5 (March 2, 1981), pp. 98–99.
This article discusses the history of the Ruger Company, the last of the United States independent gun manufacturers. It includes the comments of its owner on the debt-free philosophy of the company and its insurance problems with product liability claims.

Jacobs, Sanford. "How to Prevent an Employee from Ripping off the Firm." *The Wall Street Journal*, Vol. CXCIX, No. 90 (May 10, 1982), p. 21.
This is a "how to" article based on the experiences of several small businesses related in the article.

Waters, Craig R. "The Private War of James Sullivan." *Inc.*, Vol. 4, No. 7 (July, 1982), pp. 41–46.
The chairman of the board of an insulation business describes his firm's trials and tribulations surrounding more than 1,800 product liability lawsuits directed at his business.

CASE 22

Dale's Lawn Service
Determining insurance needs of a small service business

As Donnie Conner organized his new business, Dale's Lawn Service, he thought about insurance needs and contacted an insurance agent to talk it over. The insurance agent asked Donnie to explain the nature of the business prior to discussing insurance coverage.

Nature of the Business

Donnie explained that he had worked for another lawn-care firm for three years but had decided to begin his own business. In preparation for getting into business, he had acquired 3 riding lawnmowers ($800 each), 5 push lawnmowers ($300 each), 2 hedge clippers ($265 each), 2 edgers ($225 each), a small used pick-up truck ($3,500), a trailer ($1,000), and miscellaneous other equipment.

Donnie planned to provide lawn care for apartments, commercial buildings, and residential properties. In fact, he had been servicing a number of properties on his own time while working for the other employer. The most important part of his business would be performed on the basis of 12-month maintenance contracts. These called for the care of lawns, shrubs, and trees. On some contracts, the rate for three winter months was somewhat lower than the normal monthly rate. However, since some work (such as trimming trees, pruning shrubs, and raking leaves) was necessary in the winter, a few contracts specified a uniform monthly fee throughout the year.

At the beginning, Donnie would be the only person in the business, but he expected to hire other employees when he was able to expand. While he wanted to protect himself against the most important risks which would be involved in the business, he also wished to avoid excessive insurance coverage and to minimize expenses during the early days in the business.

Donnie's Automobile Insurance Coverage

Since Donnie already owned the truck, he had included it with his car on a personal automobile insurance policy. The policy provided for collision coverage ($200 deductible), single-limit liability covering bodily injury and property damage ($50,000), and comprehensive coverage. The agent assured Donnie that his automobile insurance coverage was adequate for business purposes since he used the truck for both personal and business use.

Proposed General Liability Coverage

The agent suggested a $50,000 general liability policy at a premium of $153 per year. Donnie was a little unsure of the wisdom of buying this insurance because he needed to keep all costs to a bare minimum until he became established. On the other hand, he recalled that a mower operated by his former employer once threw a rock that struck a small girl in the face and cut the skin. There was always the outside chance that some such accident could occur because his work was always performed on the property of others.

Proposed Major Medical Insurance

The agent also recommended a major medical policy (with a small deductible) that would cover hospital, surgery, and other medical costs. On major medical expenses, the insurance company would pay 80 percent of the total that exceeded the deductible. Family coverage (for Donnie, his wife Stephany, and his 1-year-old son Caleb) would cost $102 per month, plus a $15 monthly processing fee for the business. (This $15 fee would remain at this level even after Donnie placed other employees under the policy.) When Donnie decided to hire employees, he could add each of them to the policy for approximately $45 per month. The employees would have the option to pay for coverage of their families.

Proposed Six-Month Disability Coverage

If Donnie desired, he could also add a six-month disability clause. The premium on this insurance would run $17 per month. In the event he became disabled through injury or illness, this would pay two-thirds of his weekly salary for 180 days. For example, if Donnie planned to pay himself a $300 weekly salary, he would receive a compensation payment, if disabled, of $200 per week. Donnie was only 30 years old, had good health, and had no prior disabilities. However, most of his financial resources were invested in the business.

Proposed Long-Term Disability Insurance

For disability beyond six months, Donnie could secure a long-term policy which would begin after six months and run as long as he was disabled or until age 65. For the same $200-per-week coverage, the premium would run $42.50 per month. It would take a major accident or very serious illness, of course, to disable him for more than six months. He wondered whether the premium was too much for such an unlikely possibility.

After new employees were hired, they would be covered by the state's workers' compensation plan. Donnie could also elect to be included in that plan. However, the plan protected against only work-related accidents or illnesses, and the total reimbursement for lost wages would be much less than the amount provided by the disability policy. (The law specified a maximum compensation of less than $100 per week and a maximum time period for benefits, the length varying with the type of disability.)

Proposed Theft Insurance

Another hazard faced by the business was the possible theft of equipment. The principal danger, as Donnie saw it, existed while he was using equipment on the job. While he was using one piece of equipment on another part of the property, other items might be stolen from the truck or trailer. A friend of his had lost two lawnmowers in this way. The only available theft insurance had a $200 deductible on each piece of equipment and involved a premium of $40 per month. Donnie wondered whether there was any other way to protect the equipment so that he could avoid this expense.

Donnie's Reactions to the Insurance Proposals

Having reviewed the various policies, the agent asked Donnie which coverages he wanted. Rather than respond immediately, Donnie asked for a few days to think it over.

Questions

1. What general liability insurance, if any, should Donnie Conner buy?
2. Should Donnie take the hospitalization insurance?
3. Should he acquire the short-term disability coverage? The long-term disability coverage?
4. Should he obtain theft insurance for the equipment used in the firm?
5. What other insurance, if any, would be desirable?

PART VI
STATUS AND FUTURE OF SMALL BUSINESS

23 – Governmental Interaction with Small Business
24 – Trends and Prospects for Small Business

23

Governmental Interaction with Small Business

Figure 23-1   Ray Morgan

©*Fred Larson*

Some regulation of business is necessary, but it imposes an especially heavy burden on small firms. Lacking a legal staff, the entrepreneur must try to keep up with requirements of the law. Ray Morgan, owner of Morgan Sanitation, a waste collection company in Algona, IA, has described his predicament:

> Morgan, who only has nine people on his payroll including himself and his wife, says he spends "four or five hours a week doing paper work and trying to keep up on regulations that come out from the Environmental Protection Agency." But it is a losing battle, he says.
>
> He says that, on numerous occasions, he has picked up materials that neither he nor the business he was collecting them from knew had been listed as hazardous. "It's just so time-consuming to try to keep up with all the regs on what materials are dangerous," he notes. "I don't have the time, and the small companies that I deal with don't either. What I hauled a year ago, I may not be able to haul today. But who can afford to subscribe to the *Federal Register* and then spend the time to go through it?"

Source: Mary-Margaret Wantuck, "Moving the Mountain of Paper Work," *Nation's Business*, Vol. 73, No. 11 (November, 1985), pp. 64–65. Reproduced with permission.

Looking Ahead

Watch for the following important topics:

1. Four types of governmental regulation applicable to small business.
2. The burdensome nature of small-business regulation.
3. Attempts to reduce the regulatory burden on small business.
4. Tax responsibilities, tax-saving opportunities, and tax-reform concerns of small business.
5. Types of special assistance provided by government.

As someone put it, "Nothing is sure but death and taxes." Taxes symbolize government, and government is always in the background of business activities. Small business is no exception because small firms interact with government in many ways. In this chapter, we examine both the "plusses" and "minuses" of that relationship.

GOVERNMENTAL REGULATION

Federal laws, as well as state laws, regulate business activity for the benefit and protection of both business firms and the general public. American public policy has long embodied the principle of guaranteed freedom to enter and engage in business. This is part of the economic doctrine which emphasizes the importance of free competition as a method of providing maximum values to consumers.

Maintenance of Free Competition

Of the various laws intended to maintain a competitive economy, perhaps the best known are the federal antitrust laws, especially the Sherman Antitrust Act of 1890 and the Clayton Act of 1914. Both acts were designed to promote competition by eliminating artificial restraints on trade.

Impact of Antitrust Laws   Although the purpose of federal and state antitrust laws is noble, the results leave much to be desired. One would be naive to think that small business need no longer fear the power of oligopolists. These laws prevent some mergers and eliminate some unfair practices, but giant business firms continue to dominate many industries.

To some extent, at least, the antitrust laws offer protection to small firms. For example, a local distributor of petroleum products sued a major oil company and another dealer for $6 million, charging violation of antitrust laws. The suit alleged that the plaintiff was overcharged for gasoline, given unreasonably low allocations of petroleum products, and forced to make one station a nonbrand station. In another case, a small processor of waste material from slaughterhouses, stores, and restaurants sought treble damages of $300,000 and injunctive relief from monopolistic competition. The plaintiff claimed that a larger competitor had begun offering unreasonably high prices for waste products in the plaintiff's territory, far above the prices offered in the defendant's established territory. The suit alleged that the defendant's purpose was to establish a monopoly.

ACTION REPORT
Antitrust Laws Protect Small Firm

Antitrust laws protect small firms from practices of big business which restrain competition. In 1984, the U.S. Supreme Court upheld a $10.5 million judgment against Monsanto Company in favor of a small company, Spray-Rite Service Corporation. Spray-Rite had sued Monsanto when Monsanto, irked by Spray-Rite's cut-rate pricing, refused to renew its contract to distribute Monsanto chemicals. The case struggled through the courts for more than ten years, but the Supreme Court eventually issued a verdict, consistent with the antitrust laws, that protected Spray-Rite's freedom to use discount pricing.

Source: Reprinted with permission, *Inc.* Magazine, August, 1984. Copyright © 1984 by Inc. Publishing Company, 38 Commercial Wharf, Boston, MA 02110.

Impact of Laws on Unfair Competition   In 1914, just prior to the enactment of the Clayton Act, Congress passed the Federal Trade Commission Act. This Act created the Federal Trade Commission (FTC), a body empowered to regulate unfair methods of competition. It seems evident that Congress wished to establish an agency to maintain surveillance over competitive practices and to prevent unfair acts before legal action became necessary. The regulatory authority of the FTC was extended by the Wheeler-Lea Act of 1938 to provide protection to consumers against "unfair or deceptive acts or practices in commerce."

Impact of Price Laws   As an amendment to the Clayton Act, the Robinson-Patman Act of 1936 prohibited price discrimination by manufacturers and wholesalers in dealing with other business firms. In particular, the law is designed to protect independent retailers and wholesalers in their fight against large chains. Quantity discounts may still be offered to large buyers, but the amount of the discounts must be justified economically by the seller on the basis of actual costs. Vendors are also forbidden to grant disproportionate advertising allowances to large retailers. The objective is to prevent unreasonable discounts and other concessions to large purchasers merely because of superior size and bargaining power.

The effectiveness of the Robinson-Patman Act and its benefits to small business have been debated. Some have argued that it discourages both large and small firms from cutting prices and makes it harder to expand into new markets and to pass on to customers the cost savings on large orders.[1]

The majority of states have **unfair-trade practice laws,** known under different titles such as unfair-trade practices acts, unfair-sales acts, and unfair-practices acts. These laws specify that sellers may not sell goods at less than their cost and also specify certain percentage markups. Some of the state unfair-trade laws even cover personal services.

While unfair-trade practice laws ostensibly aim to eliminate unfair price competition, there is a question as to whether they accomplish this objective. The danger in such laws is their tendency to handicap those firms that are able to reduce prices because of their efficiency. Thus, in the guise of preservation of free competition, these laws may actually hold a price umbrella over inefficient, marginal firms, denying freedom of enterprise to efficient firms and penalizing the public accordingly.

Impact of Laws on Rail and Motor Carriers The Interstate Commerce Commission (ICC) was created to regulate the transportation of goods across state lines. However, ICC regulations actually restricted entry into the trucking business and prevented effective competition between truck and rail lines. The following incident provides a humorous but illuminating example of the heavy-handed nature of such regulations:

> In March, 1965, Tom Hilt, of Hilt Truck Line, Inc., of Omaha, got fed up with the knee-jerk reaction of the railroads in automatically protesting every tariff he filed with the Interstate Commerce Commission. With tongue in cheek, Hilt filed a rate for the transport of yak fat between Omaha and Chicago. Sure enough, the Western Trunk Line Committee protested on the grounds that the cost of trucking yak fat far exceeded the proposed rate and was therefore illegal. And, sure enough, the ICC suspended the rate. After 30 days, the Commission found that Hilt had failed to prove the rate legal, and it was disallowed.[2]

In the late 1970s, Congress began the process of deregulation. The Motor Carrier Act of 1980 reduced the degree of regulation of the trucking industry. This step of deregulation opened up some opportunities for small business. For example, a small family business, Love's Trucking, Inc., was founded in Troy, OH, to haul steel between Franklin, OH, and McLean, GA.[3] However, government regulation does not disappear in deregulated industries even though the scope of regulation is curtailed. Love's Trucking, Inc., must still comply with many state regulations, as well as with those ICC regulations which remain. And truckers must still apply to the ICC for permits to operate in particular areas and to haul particular commodities.[4]

Consumer Protection

Insofar as freedom of competition is provided by the laws discussed above, consumers will benefit indirectly. In addition, consumers are given various forms of more direct protection by federal, state, and local legislation.

As mentioned earlier, the Wheeler-Lea Act gave the Federal Trade Commission a broad mandate to attack unfair or deceptive acts or practices in commerce. The FTC's original focus on antitrust practices has been expanded through the years to cover a wide range of business activities: labeling, safety, packaging, and advertising of products; truth-in-lending; fair credit reporting; equal credit opportunity; and many others. States have also enacted laws and created consumer protection agencies to deal with unfair or deceptive practices.

A few examples of the types of trade practices scrutinized by the Federal Trade Commission are: labeling goods as "free" or "handmade"; advertising that offers unreal "bargains" by pretended reduction of unused "regular" prices; and **bait advertising**, in which a low price for an article is advertised merely to lure a prospect into the place of business, whereupon the customer is talked into purchasing a more expensive product.

As still another measure to protect the public against unreasonable risk of injury associated with toys and other consumer products, the federal government enacted the Consumer Product Safety Act of 1972. This act created the Consumer Product Safety Commission to enforce its established goal. The Commission is authorized to set safety standards for consumer products and to ban those goods which are exceptionally hazardous.

Protection of Investors

To protect the investing public against fraudulent devices and swindles in the sale of stocks and bonds, both federal and state laws regulate the issuance and public sale of securities. The federal laws involved are the Securities Act of 1933 and the Securities Exchange Act of 1934. The latter Act established the powerful Securities and Exchange Commission to enforce the regulations provided by both Acts.

Because of the small amounts involved and the private nature of much of their financing, most small businesses are excluded from extensive regulation under federal law. However, they are subject to state **blue-sky laws**. In general, these laws cover registration of new securities; licensing of dealers, brokers, and salespersons; and prosecution of individuals charged with fraud in connection with the sale of stocks and bonds.

ACTION REPORT
Consumer Protection and the Small Firm

Efforts by the Consumer Product Safety Commission (CPSC) to protect the consumer created a major problem for Sprouts, a new small business. Ann Buscho, founder of Sprouts, discovered that her infant daughter's skin rash was caused by an allergy to formaldehyde, a product used in fabrics that are blends and in polyesters. All children's sleepwear contains formaldehyde because pure natural fibers do not lend themselves to flame retardant chemical treatments.

Buscho found that all-cotton clothing solved the rash problem and created a firm to make such clothing for children. Although the clothing was not called "sleepwear," some of it could be used for that purpose. However, the Flammable Fabrics Act requires that all children's sleepwear through size 14 be made from flame-resistant material. Consequently, the CPSC began an investigation of the new firm because of possible violation of the Flammable Fabrics Act. Trying to protect children against a skin rash involved another danger, that of fire. CPSC obviously placed greater emphasis on protection from fire than protection from formaldehyde.

Source: Nora Goldstein, "Do Babies Have Cotton Rights?" *In Business*, Vol. 5, No. 5 (September–October, 1983), pp. 42–44. Reproduced with permission.

Promotion of Public Welfare

Laws that promote the public interest involve environmental protection and licensing procedures for certain professions and types of businesses. A case of sorts can be made for the regulation of almost any business. However, any failure to limit such regulation to the most essential cases erodes the freedom of opportunity to enter business.

Impact of Environmental Protection Laws During the 1970s, numerous environmental protection laws were enacted at the federal, state, and local levels. Specifically, the major laws deal with air pollution, water pollution, solid-waste disposal, and toxic substances. Some of the laws are written in great detail, outlining specific regulatory responsibilities. Other laws confer broad authority on the regulatory agencies. In addition, the federal laws establish minimum standards while state and local governments are free to impose more stringent requirements. As explained in Chapter 14, anti-pollution laws adversely affect some small firms although they may occasionally benefit other firms.

Impact of Laws on Licensing   State governments restrict entry into numerous professions and types of businesses by establishing licensing procedures. For example, physicians, barbers, pharmacists, accountants, lawyers, and real estate salespersons are licensed. Insurance companies, banks, and public utilities must seek entry permits from state officials. Although licensing protects the public interest, it also tends to restrict the number of professionals and firms in such a way as to reduce competition and increase prices paid by consumers.

There is a difference between licensing that involves a routine application and that which prescribes rigid entry standards and screening procedures. The fact that the impetus for much licensing comes from within the industry suggests the need for careful scrutiny of licensing proposals. Otherwise, we may be merely protecting a private interest and minimizing freedom to enter a field of business.

Political Power of Small Business

Although small business is the object of legislation which regulates its activities, it is also a political force which affects the legislative process. Legislators are attuned to the needs of their constituencies, and they recognize small business as a group having votes and political influence. Its political influence is not surprising in view of the large numbers of small businesses and the community leadership roles filled by small-business owners. They are members of the Chamber of Commerce, officers in the Rotary Club, chairpersons of committees to raise funds for hospitals, and leaders in other civic endeavors. Legislators are not inclined to ignore their views.

The sensitivity of political leaders to small-business concerns is indicated by these comments:

> In part, small-business groups are effective because they're seeking special-interest legislation that often doesn't arouse passionate opposition. "Most legislators will follow the line of least resistance," says Iowa State Rep. Darrell Hanson. "The only people paying attention to how the legislator votes are those who asked for the law," he adds. "The only way to lose is to vote against it."
> State Sen. Brian Rude of Coon Valley, WI, adds another reason. "We tend to listen because (small-business people) are our bread and butter," he says. "Joe Smith the car dealer will be talking to 250 of my constituents in the next month, so I want to help him."[5]

These comments suggest that legislators are likely to listen carefully to the opinions of small-business leaders.

Occasionally, the political activities of small firms reflect special interests that conflict with those of the general public:

Local plumbers and electricians have been successful in stirring doubts about polyvinyl chloride (PVC) pipe and conduit. The plastic pipe is easier and cheaper to use than its metal counterparts, thus enabling homeowners to install it themselves. But plumbing and electrical associations, which help write local housing codes, have succeeded in getting PVC pipe banned as dangerous in many locales.[6]

However, we should not assume that all small-business political concern is narrowly self-serving. Many of their interests and causes are entirely consistent with the public interest.

The special needs of small business have been highlighted by White House conferences on small business in 1980 and 1986. These national conferences followed state meetings of small-business owners in which they formulated concerns which were discussed later in the White House conferences. These conferences have placed small business in the spotlight and given it a growing political identity. The awareness of political leaders toward small business was also evidenced in the 1984 election when both the Democratic and Republican parties established small-business councils.

As a result of their political power, small-business owners are in a position to influence the course of legislation and to lobby for passage of favorable laws. The readiness of legislators to act favorably toward small-business needs is evident in the record of Congress following the 1980 White House Conference. They enacted, either partially or completely, some 40 of the 60 conference recommendations.[7] Those in small business exercise their influence not only individually but also collectively through trade associations and more general associations such as the National Federation for Independent Business.

THE BURDENSOME NATURE OF REGULATION ON SMALL BUSINESS

The growth of governmental regulation has reached the point that it imposes a real hardship on the small firm. To some extent, the problems arise from seemingly inevitable "red tape" and bureaucratic procedures of governments.

Even apart from the arbitrariness of regulation, its sheer weight is burdensome to small firms. The contents of the 330-page volume on the Occupational Safety and Health Act (OSHA) alone place unreasonable demands on the funds and productive energies of small companies. The following excerpt from a study by the Small Business Administration provides some understanding of the cumulative burden of regulation:

A Senate Study Group estimated that the annual cost of unnecessary and wasteful regulation ranges between $66 and $475 per U.S. citizen. They also estimated that the number of Federal employees in regulatory agencies has grown from 53,300 in 1973 to 63,700 in 1975—an increase of 14 percent....

Federal regulations have hampered the rate of introduction of new products. The National Commission on Productivity and Work Quality indicated that overregulation has created excessive obstacles to technological process [sic]. Industries that are most heavily regulated are usually dominated by a few large firms. Small businesses cannot survive and, consequently, concentration in the regulated industry may occur. The pharmaceutical industry is an example. Food and Drug Administration procedures delay the introduction of new drugs and discourage small business from competing.[8]

Figure 23-2   The Entrepreneur's View of Regulation

Source: GOOSEMYER by Parker and Wilder, © 1980, Field Enterprises, Inc. Courtesy of Field Newspaper Syndicate.

Attempts to Reduce the Regulatory Burden

The burdensome nature of small-business regulation became increasingly evident during the 1970s. Four recommendations of the 1980 White House Conference on Small Business dealt with improvements in the regulatory process.

The most important law to emerge from the Conference was the Regulatory Flexibility Act of 1980. According to this law, federal agencies must assess the impact of proposed regulations on small business. They are required to reduce paperwork requirements and to exempt small firms or simplify rules when at all possible. The general purpose of the Act is to avoid unnecessary burdensome regulation of small firms. Its usefulness will depend upon the vigor and consistency of its application.

Another law recognizing the regulatory plight of small firms is the Equal Access to Justice Act of 1980. A strengthened version of the 1980 Act was passed in 1985. This law requires the federal government to reimburse court costs for small firms that win cases against regulatory agencies. Incorporated and unincorporated businesses, partnerships, and organizations having a net worth of less than $7 million are eligible for recovery of attorneys' fees.

ACTION REPORT
A Case of Overregulation

The following account by Arthur Levitt, which one may hope is rare, illustrates the tendency toward overregulation:

Billy Halliwell had it made, or at least he thought so. The ingredients were all there for the 11-year-old Roseland, NJ lad to turn a profit from sleepy motorists waiting in predawn gas lines last July. They needed an eye-opener, and Billy provided it from his sister's red wagon laden with coffee and doughnuts. Free enterprise in a most elementary form.

But Billy soon learned the harsh realities that confront millions of small-business owners in this country, namely, that free enterprise is hardly free.

State and local officials soon shut down "Billy's Breakfast" because he lacked a peddler's license, failed to collect state sales taxes and neglected to file a quarterly return with state authorities. Billy was confused by forays from the police department, the local board of health, and the state tax bureau. With the help of his father, William, young Bill spent many hours learning firsthand the ordeals of small-business men and women.

Billy's father estimates that it cost the family close to $1,000 in cash and lost time to guide the youngster through government's bewildering bureaucratic maze. Red-faced officials spent a great deal of taxpayers' money capturing 21 cents—yes, 21 cents—in tax payments from "Billy's Breakfast." Later, the state said its regulations did not apply to Billy's "casual business."

Source: Reprinted by permission of FAMILY WEEKLY, copyright 1979, 641 Lexington Avenue, New York, NY 10022.

The Need for Flexibility in Regulation

Some persons have argued that special consideration in the regulation of small firms is in itself unfair. According to this logic, all competitive firms should "play by the same rules." However, we should note that the marketplace is not perfectly competitive and that the hand of regulation rests more heavily upon small competitors. The Chief Counsel for Advocacy in the Small Business Administration has cited a research study on small business regulatory costs:

The research indicated that average regulatory costs per employee for the median small firm are three times greater than for the median large firm and two times greater than for the median mid-sized firm. When costs of complying with a regulation do not increase proportionately with firm size, small firms bear a disproportionately large share of total regulatory costs and suffer a competitive disadvantage.[9]

Rather than provide a special advantage to small business, therefore, flexibility in regulation serves to minimize a government-imposed handicap.

TAXATION

The primary tax responsibility of a small business is to pay all legally required taxes. In paying taxes, the firm is both an agent and a debtor. As an agent, it withholds and pays taxes owed by others. As a debtor, the firm pays taxes for which it is directly liable.

Tax-Withholding Obligations of the Small Business

The major tax-withholding obligations of a business involve the following taxes:

1. *Income taxes.* Each employee signs a withholding exemption certificate which specifies the number of allowable exemptions. The amounts withheld from salaries and tips are passed on to the government periodically by the employer.
2. *Social Security taxes.* An employer is required to deduct a specified amount of each employee's salary, and this amount is also passed on periodically to the government by the employer.
3. *Sales taxes.* Many state and local governments impose sales taxes. A business firm must collect and pass them on to the appropriate governmental agency.

Major Taxes Paid by the Small Business

The major taxes for which small firms and owners are directly responsible as debtors are the following:

1. *Income taxes.* The federal income tax paid by a business depends on its earnings and on its legal form of organization. According to the Economic Recovery Tax Act of 1981, the corporate income tax rate effective in 1983 and later is: 15 percent on the first $25,000 of net income; 18 percent on the second $25,000 of net income; 30 percent on the third $25,000 of net income; 40 percent on the fourth $25,000 of net income; and 46 percent on net income above $100,000. (The tax bill before Congress in 1986 proposed a rate of 15 percent on the first $50,000 of net income, 25 percent on the next $25,000 of net income, and 34 percent on net income above $75,000.) As explained in Chapter 9, some corporations may qualify as Subchapter S corporations and elect to be taxed as partnerships. In any event, individual owners pay personal income taxes on proprietorship earnings,

partnership earnings, corporate salaries, and corporate dividends. Some states and a few cities also impose income taxes.

2. *Federal excise taxes.* Federal excise taxes are imposed on the sale or use of some items and on some occupations. For example, there is a tax on the sale of certain motor fuels, a highway use tax on trucks which use federal highways, and an occupational tax on retail liquor dealers.

3. *Unemployment taxes.* Firms pay both federal and state unemployment taxes on salaries and wages. The tax rate is usually related to previous unemployment experience.

4. *Local taxes.* Counties, towns, school districts, and other local entities impose various types of taxes. Among these are real estate taxes and personal property taxes. Business licenses are also taxes even though the owner may not recognize them as such.

5. *Estate taxes.* A federal tax is imposed on estates which are passed on to heirs. The amount to be excluded from the inheritance tax increased to $600,000 in 1987. In some cases, families are forced to sell family businesses in order to pay estate taxes.

Tax Savings Through Tax Planning

Tax savings are possible if one knows the law. Legal *tax avoidance*, which is in sharp contrast to illegal *tax evasion*, is both practical and ethical. The small business, while relying primarily on tax experts for assistance, may also supplement this assistance by reference to tax articles in periodicals, pamphlets, books, or loose-leaf tax services. The size of the business, of course, will determine the amount which can be spent in the accumulation of such a tax data library, as well as the time available for its use.

One example of planning to realize tax savings involves using the "investment tax credit." To stimulate investment, the tax law permits a specified percentage of properly qualified investments in new equipment to be deducted from the firm's tax bill in the first year. Buildings and their structural components are excluded from the investment credit. However, careful planning may permit some facilities within the building to qualify for the credit. For example, a small firm may be able to treat alarm systems, special electrical lamps, movable partitions, special plumbing and electrical outlets, and certain types of signs as equipment which will qualify.[10] (The tax bill before Congress in 1986 provided for repeal of the investment tax credit.)

Another way of reducing taxes is to shift from a FIFO (first-in, first-out) to LIFO (last-in, first-out) method of accounting for inventory during a period of inflation. The LIFO method places the recent, higher inventory costs directly into the income statement, thereby reducing the reported income which is subject to tax.

Estate Planning for Business Owners

Special planning is desirable to minimize problems created by estate taxes when a business owner dies. This is particularly true for the family business. It is possible that the need for dollars to pay death taxes can lead to the sale or liquidation of the business. Because of this danger, the entrepreneur needs to plan for the continuation of the business in light of the estate tax law.

As noted earlier, the amount to be excluded from inheritance taxation was raised to $600,000 in 1987. In the case of a very small business, therefore, the tax is not a threat. Numerous small firms, however, have a net worth which exceeds the $600,000 exclusion.

One approach to meeting the estate tax problem involves the purchase of insurance on the owner's life. Proceeds from the policy provide cash for the payment of necessary taxes. However, the size of the premium sometimes makes this a difficult and expensive solution.

Another solution or partial solution to the estate tax problem is found in making an annual gift of a specified portion of the estate to the heirs. The tax law permits such annual gifts without taxation. Over a period of several years, a substantial amount may be thus conveyed without taxation.

ACTION REPORT
Insurance to Pay Estate Taxes

By paying annual life insurance premiums, small-business owners can provide funds to pay estate taxes. The following example shows that the solution may be a costly one:

> In Mars, PA, Harry G. Austin, 65, and his brother John, 55, the only stockholders in $8 million (sales) James Austin Co., a soap manufacturer, pay around $20,000 each in premiums so their 92-year-old company can be passed down to the fourth generation. "Sometimes I think we're really working for the insurance company," says Harry.

Source: "The Death Tax," by Jon Schriber, *Forbes,* Vol. 127, No. 13 (June 22, 1981), pp. 122–126.

Tax Reform for Small Business

The tax system appears to have a number of adverse effects upon small business. The problem areas noted below have been identified in a study on proposed tax reforms for small firms.[11]

Retention of Capital   The present tax system tends to discriminate against small firms by preventing the retention of adequate capital for current operating needs and for survival during recessions. Small firms lack ready access to long-term sources of capital, and this makes the tax erosion of earnings quite serious to them.

Complexity of Tax System   The complexity of the tax system, compounded by the multiplicity of taxes at all levels, the burden of reporting and paying payroll taxes, the difficulty of estimating income and paying taxes in advance, and the expense of professional tax assistance present special problems for small firms.

Incentives for Long-Term Capital   The tax system lacks proper incentives to attract adequate private investment capital to this segment of the economy. Some persons feel that sources of venture and expansion capital have almost disappeared.

Maintenance of Business Independence   The existing tax structure discourages small-business independence by encouraging mergers with larger enterprises on a tax-free basis and forcing the sale of a business to pay estate taxes. An increase in the size of the exemption from estate taxes, legislated in 1981, has eased this problem somewhat.

Financial Security of Business Owners   Even though some provision has been made for retirement plans for business owners, these plans contain complexities that make compliance difficult and expensive. Furthermore, they place unwarranted emphasis on the legal form of organization a business has taken.

SPECIAL GOVERNMENTAL ASSISTANCE

In addition to public policy applying to business generally, some steps have been taken to provide special assistance to small business. Chapter 8, for example, explained the Small Business Administration loan programs and the development and operation of Small Business Investment Companies. Other aspects of special assistance provided by the government are discussed below.

Managerial and Technical Assistance

The provision of management and technical assistance to managers of small firms takes a variety of forms. A series of pamphlets, for example, is published by the Small Business Administration under each of the following titles: (1) *Management Aids*, (2) *Small Business Bibliographies*, and (3) *Starting Out Series*. Appendix B at the end of this book contains a list of publications in each of these areas. In addition, separate publications treat miscellaneous subjects pertinent to small-business management. Research studies of small-business problems have also been subsidized by grants from the Small Business Administration.

Staff personnel both in Washington and in field offices are available for counseling actual or prospective managers of small firms on various management problems. The subjects may range from the evaluation of a going concern to the analysis of plant location or layout requirements. Also, as noted in Chapter 13, the SBA sponsors counseling programs that feature retired business executives and teams of business students.

The Small Business Administration has also created an Office of Advocacy. This office argues the case of the entrepreneur within the federal bureaucracy. Its activities include lobbying, drafting and reviewing legislation, and developing an economic data base for small business.

Assistance in Obtaining Government Contracts

Many small firms serve as subcontractors. Both the Department of Defense and the General Services Administration (the largest contract-awarding agencies) provide active encouragement to prime contractors to engage in subcontracting to small firms. As subcontractors, small firms have the problem of learning who the prime contractors are and what component parts are available for subcontracting.

The Small Business Administration, General Services Administration, and Commerce Department also work with small firms to help them obtain government contracts. SBA field offices advise small firms as to which agencies buy the products they supply, help them get their names on bidders' lists, and assist them in obtaining drawings and specifications for proposed purchases. The SBA also publishes a directory which lists goods and services bought by military and civilian agencies, and it seeks out small companies interested in bidding on purchases on which few small firms have bid in the past.

Set-Aside Programs   Under a **set-aside program**, government contracting officers and SBA representatives review purchase orders to select those which may be set aside for exclusive competitive bidding by small firms. Small firms have participated extensively in set-aside programs. This practice is presumably justified by the increasing technological complexity of material produced by federal agencies and the tendency to favor big business by acquiring systems and goods from a single contractor.

In 1982, Congress passed the Small Business Innovation Development Act. This Act was designed to stimulate technological innovation by requiring certain agencies to set aside a percentage of their research and development dollars for small firms.

Minority Contract Programs One special set-aside program, the **minority contract program**, permits government purchases from minority firms without competitive bidding. The primary objective is business development by awarding contracts and providing managerial, financial, and marketing assistance. Although the program has been criticized because of some reported abuses, supporters still feel it can make a valuable contribution.[12] The program has been modified to encourage the "graduation" of minority firms out of the program into the competitive marketplace. This means that firms entering the program will participate for a specified number of years and then be moved out to make way for new entrants.

ACTION REPORT
A Beneficiary of Government Assistance

After reading about small-business assistance programs, you may wonder what type of business is helped by the government. One firm which did benefit is Welbilt Electronic Die Corporation of New York City. The firm was founded in 1965 by John Mariotta, who was born and raised in New York's Spanish Harlem. Mariotta was joined by Fred Neuberger, a mechanical engineer and refugee from the Nazis in Rumania.

Help from the SBA and other government agencies included the following:

1. An early SBA loan for $25,000 at 7 percent.
2. A later SBA-guaranteed loan (after landing a government contract) for $100,000.
3. A minority-enterprise government contract to make a component of the GE engine which propels the F-104 Phantom jet.
4. A minority-enterprise government contract for cooling kits for the Armored Personnel Carrier.
5. Subsequent loans (which eventually totaled $2.3 million) and loan guarantees (which eventually totaled $3.1 million).

The firm has apparently attained enough experience and momentum to survive. Welbilt has won production contracts in competitive bidding from GE (jet engine parts) and Western Electric (microwave communications equipment). According to founder Mariotta, "This is not a chicken-plucking operation."

Source: "This Is Not a Chicken-Plucking Operation," by Jane Carmichael, *Forbes*, Vol. 128, No. 4 (August 17, 1981), pp. 51–52.

Break-Out Contract Programs   In a related program called the **break-out contract program**, the procuring agency breaks out suitable portions of a larger contract for competitive bidding by small firms. For example, the contract for janitorial services might be broken out of a general contract for housekeeping on a missile installation.

Assistance in Export Sales

To some extent the export-sales problem of small firms is one of information. The Commerce Department has attempted to meet this need by supplying small exporters with an array of technical and general information. The Commerce Department also operates major trade fairs aimed at increasing exports, and it brings foreign customers to visit American plants. The Small Business Administration maintains information on foreign trade and assists small firms who wish to enter foreign markets.

The Need to Improve Governmental Assistance

The governmental programs of small-business assistance have benefited thousands of small firms. At the same time, caution is appropriate in evaluating such programs and in making sure that they provide as much as they promise. Existing governmental programs are obviously no panacea for the various problems of small firms. There is a continuing need for improvement and refinement in these efforts to assist the small-business sector.

The administrator of the SBA, James C. Sanders, has recognized the need for improvement. "The task is to give the SBA new vitality," he says. "If the agency remains static amid changing times and major challenges, it will lose its reason to exist."[13] Its reason to exist was, indeed, challenged in the budget debate during 1984–85, but Congress acted to give it continued life.[14] The consensus holds, therefore, that the SBA is worthwhile in spite of its imperfections.

Looking Back

1. One of the major roles of government is the maintenance of free competition. Legislation varies, however, in terms of its consequences in this area. Although the antitrust laws (including the Sherman Antitrust Act, Clayton Act, Federal Trade Commission Act, Robinson-Patman Act, and state laws) are intended to encourage competition, their general effectiveness has been widely questioned. Governmental regulation also concerns consumer protection, the protection of investors, and the

promotion of public welfare. Small business is also a political force influencing the direction of government policy and regulation.

2. Governmental regulation has become burdensome to small business because of its bureaucratic nature, the excessive paperwork required, and the small firm's lack of time and expertise in responding to regulation.

3. The Regulatory Flexibility Act of 1980 is designed to reduce the burden of governmental regulation of small firms. It requires federal agencies to reduce paperwork requirements and simplify rules applicable to small firms. The Equal Access to Justice Act of 1985 requires the federal government to reimburse court costs for small firms that win cases against regulatory agencies.

4. The tax responsibilities of small firms include withholding income, Social Security, and sales taxes; and paying income, federal excise, unemployment, estate, and local taxes. The present tax system presents possibilities for tax savings that the small business should investigate. The retention of capital, the maintenance of business independence, and the financial security of business owners are problem areas that should be considered in tax-reform programs for small business.

5. Three areas of special governmental assistance to small business are managerial and technical assistance provided through SBA offices, assistance in obtaining government contracts, and assistance in export sales. Programs of governmental assistance have benefited small business in many ways; nevertheless, there is a need for further refinement and improvement in these efforts to aid small firms.

DISCUSSION QUESTIONS

1. Are any of the regulatory roles of government opposed to the interest of small business?

2. The Antitrust Division of the Department of Justice and the Federal Trade Commission have units dealing specifically with small firms and the investigation of their complaints. What is your evaluation of the desirability of such an arrangement?

3. What evidence is there which indicates that small business has political power?

4. Why is governmental regulation burdensome to small firms?

5. How does the Regulatory Flexibility Act of 1980 affect the regulation of small business?

6. Is it inherently unfair to accord special attention to small firms in formulating governmental regulations?

7. In view of the fact that a small business can operate as a proprietorship or a partnership, can it easily avoid any difficulties associated with the corporate income tax?

8. The corporate income tax law permits corporate income up to $100,000 to be taxed at a more favorable rate than corporate income over $100,000. Does this discriminate in favor of small corporations?

9. What are the ethical implications involved when a small business takes advantage of "loopholes" in tax laws? Is there a bona fide distinction between "tax avoidance" and "tax evasion"?

10. What is the "set-aside program" in obtaining federal government contracts? What justification is there for it, if any?

ENDNOTES

1. "The Antitrust Revolution," *Fortune*, Vol. 108, No. 1 (July 11, 1983), pp. 29–32.

2. "The Economic Case for Deregulating Trucking," *Business Week*, No. 2355 (November 2, 1974), p. 86.

3. Ed Barnes, "A Trucking Company Rolls," *Venture*, Vol. 3, No. 1 (January, 1981), pp. 24–26.

4. For a discussion of the status of deregulation, see "Hitting the Brakes: New ICC Chairman Reese Taylor Moves to Halt Trucking-Industry Deregulation," *The Wall Street Journal*, August 5, 1981, p. 46.

5. Damon Darlin, "Small Business, Big Influence," *The Wall Street Journal*, May 20, 1985, p. 71C.

6. *Ibid.*

7. Charles R. McDonald, "It's Time for Conference II," *Inc.*, Vol. 6, No. 7 (July, 1984), p. 14

8. *The Study of Small Business*, a study conducted and prepared pursuant to Public Law 94–305 by the Office of Advocacy, U.S. Small Business Administration, 1977, Part I, p. 39.

9. *Annual Report of the Chief Counsel for Advocacy on Implementation of the Regulatory Flexibility Act* (Washington: U.S. Small Business Administration, 1985), p. 1.

10. Gerald F. Hunter, "Uncovering Tax Credits," *Venture*, Vol. 3, No. 9 (September, 1981), p. 24.

11. The problems identified in this section are those cited in Part III, "The Impact of Taxation on Small Business: A Proposal for Reform," of *The Study of Small Business, op. cit.*

12. For a review of both strengths and weaknesses of this program, see Michael Thoryn, "'Serious Problems' at SBA," *Nation's Business*, Vol. 69, No. 6 (June, 1981), pp. 42–44; and "Can Black Businesses Go It Alone?" *Business Week*, No. 2735 (April 19, 1982), pp. 126–131.

13. Michael Thoryn, "SBA: Confronting Its Own Problems," *Nation's Business*, Vol. 70, No. 8 (August, 1982), p. 32.

14. For a review of the debate, see Jeanne Saddler, "Trimming the SBA," *The Wall Street Journal*, May 20, 1985, p. 78C.

REFERENCES TO SMALL BUSINESS IN ACTION

George, Charles. "Why I Avoid Government Contracts." *Inc.*, Vol. 4, No. 6 (June, 1982), pp. 11–12.

A general contractor explains his avoidance of government contracts because of the Davis-Bacon Act.

Kolbenschlag, Michael. "Fish Story, Chapter 2." *Forbes*, Vol. 126, No. 6 (September 15, 1980), pp. 206–208.

This is the story of a group of independent fishermen who sought governmental protection. The underlying question is the extent to which government should aid small firms facing foreign competition.

Richman, Tom. "Will the Real SBA Please Stand Up?" *Inc.*, Vol. 6, No. 2 (February, 1984), pp. 85–90.

This article describes the experiences of several small businesses which applied for SBA loans.

Wantuck, Mary-Margaret. "Bidding for Fair Play." *Nation's Business*, Vol. 73, No. 9 (September, 1985), pp. 39–40.

A number of small businesses report their problems in selling to the federal government.

CASE 23

The Terrell Company*
Working within legal and governmental controls

The Terrell Company was a small manufacturing company located in Rock Island, IL. It produced chemical coatings which are applied to the unpainted surfaces of farm and construction equipment. The Terrell Company had been in its location only a few years and had been very proud of the fact that it had the latest and most up-to-date equipment for its manufacturing processes and for the safety and well-being of its 80 employees.

When an OSHA inspector appeared to inspect the company's premises, he remarked that its production facility included equipment unlike any he had ever seen. Since fumes emanated from the liquid chemicals flowing through the equipment, the inspector expressed concern for the safety of the employees in this area, particularly as it pertained to flash fires. Although the company's owners attempted to assure the inspector that no hazard existed because the chemicals were neither toxic nor flammable, the inspector cited the company for six violations of OSHA regulations. As part of the citation, the company was fined $300 and was required to correct the violations within 90 days or be subject to further fines and a possible restraining order.

The owners of the Terrell Company immediately contacted their attorney. The attorney advised them that there were two methods of resolving the issue: (1) to work with OSHA officials to reach compliance status, or (2) to contest the alleged violations through a lengthy and costly appeal process.

One of Terrell's owners was particularly livid about the citation and made a series of impassioned speeches about the federal bureaucracy, contacting members of Congress, and "taking the case to the Supreme Court if necessary." Although tending to agree with the owners that the inspector appeared to have been rather arbitrary and capricious in citing the company, the attorney nonetheless encouraged the owners to settle the matter at the inspector level rather than to initiate the appeal process by requesting a hearing. After much discussion, the owners reluctantly agreed to try to work toward a reasonable solution with the inspector.

Terrell, however, experienced considerable difficulty in learning exactly what modifications were needed for compliance. This was because OSHA officials refused to provide Terrell with specifications for equipment that would be acceptable.

After discussions with several manufacturers, it appeared to Terrell's owners that the OSHA regulations would require the purchase of expensive

*This case was prepared by John E. Schoen, Richards Equipment Company, Waco, TX.

additional equipment including enlarged blower fans and fire run-off tanks. The manufacturers of such equipment advised Terrell that it was possible that the blower fans would be challenged by Illinois air-quality officials and that the noise from the motors needed to operate the run-off tanks might exceed OSHA noise pollution standards. The cost of the equipment was estimated between $14,000 and $19,000 and the equipment could not be delivered to the Terrell Company and installed there in less than 150 days.

When Terrell's owners presented this information to the inspector and other members of the OSHA administration, the OSHA officials reiterated that they would not approve or otherwise judge equipment in advance of its installation. The OSHA officials also indicated that they were concerned about violations of OSHA regulations, not state air-quality standards, and that they were fully prepared to cite violations of noise regulations. Finally, these officials commented that the fines for noncompliance might increase to $1,000 per violation per day or $6,000 a day after the 90-day period, so that the owners might prefer to close the plant for 60 to 75 days during the equipment modifications to avoid incurring such penalties.

Thus, it was shortly after the foregoing discussion that the attorney met with a very angry owner of the Terrell Company. Gesturing wildly, the owner said to the attorney:

> Look, we've got to request a hearing on those OSHA violations! I've tried to work with the OSHA officials, but we can't put in $15,000 or $20,000 of modifications and not be sure that will satisfy them. My gosh, that's nearly 30 percent of our net profit; and even if the equipment is all right, the regulations could change in a week, ten days, or a month and we would probably have to buy additional equipment in order to comply! If we have to close for two or three months, I'm not sure we can make a profit this year! I mean, not only the inspector, but the other people in the OSHA administration have admitted that the regulations really do not fit our business format! Surely we can beat this bum rap for less than $15,000.

Questions

1. Should the Terrell Company attempt to contest the alleged violations now if the legal costs of appeal are comparable to the cost associated with compliance?
2. Would the Terrell Company be able to operate in its present condition during the period required for a decision to be rendered on the appeal?
3. What force and effect do OSHA regulations have? Are they merely "one inspector's opinion" of the way Terrell Company should run its business, or are they laws, just as though Congress had passed them?
4. Could the Terrell Company sue OSHA in a court of law for the costs that it will incur or request the court to order OSHA to leave Terrell alone?
5. Could a member of Congress assist Terrell by intervening in this matter? What political pressure, if any, could be brought on the OSHA administration?

24

Trends and Prospects for Small Business

Figure 24–1   Bob Lemons

©Steven Pumphrey

The future for small business is as bright as the capable, confident people who operate small firms. Many of them are building profitable businesses and, in some cases, even bucking unfavorable trends. A few entrepreneurs are presently demonstrating the potential strength of small firms as they cut into the business of national food chains. One of these is Bob Lemons who operates a small food chain in Kansas City. His philosophy is evident in the following account:

> "Give the independent the same size store as the chain, and I firmly believe the independent can whip the chain. I'd rather compete with a chain than an independent any day." Watching Lemons work his way through one of his stores, chatting with longtime female customers and slapping men on the back, one can see why Lemons might be right when he says he suspects his sales per square foot are double that of competitor Safeway.

Source: John Merwin, "A Piece of the Action," *Forbes,* Vol. 134, No. 7 (September 24, 1984), pp. 146–156. Reproduced with permission.

Looking Ahead

Watch for the following important topics:

1. Trends in small-business activity.
2. Competitive strengths of small firms.
3. Problems of small business.
4. Failure and bankruptcy of small firms.
5. Prospects for the future of small business.

After examining the nature of small business and the requirements for good management in the earlier chapters of this book, it is well to inquire about the trends in small-business activity and its prospects for the future. What are its strengths and problems? What is its direction? Although the overall picture contains both bright and dark spots, we hold a relatively optimistic view concerning the future of small business.

TRENDS IN SMALL-BUSINESS ACTIVITY

Reading about government aid and special loans for small companies may lead one to conclude that small business is vanishing. Small firms are sometimes pictured as powerless victims of giant corporations. To understand the truth or error in these views, we must examine the trend of small business in recent decades.

The small-business sector has shown considerable strength over the past two decades. For all industries, small firms (those with fewer than 100 employees) accounted for 39.9 percent of the total employees in 1958 and 40.1 percent in 1977.[1] In some industries, however, small business has declined relative to big business. Figures 24-2, 24-3, and 24-4 show the changes in small-firm employment in wholesaling, retailing, and manufacturing. There is some evident erosion of the small-business position in each of these industries.

Proponents of small business are understandably disturbed by the erosion of the small-business position and are concerned with the need to strengthen the management of small firms. The fact remains, however, that small firms transact a substantial proportion of the total business in the 1980s. As noted in Chapter 3, they still account for 40 to 50 percent of business activity in the United States. In spite of a relative decline in some industries, therefore, small business is far from extinct.

Figure 24-2   Percentage of Employees in Wholesale Firms with Fewer Than 100 Employees

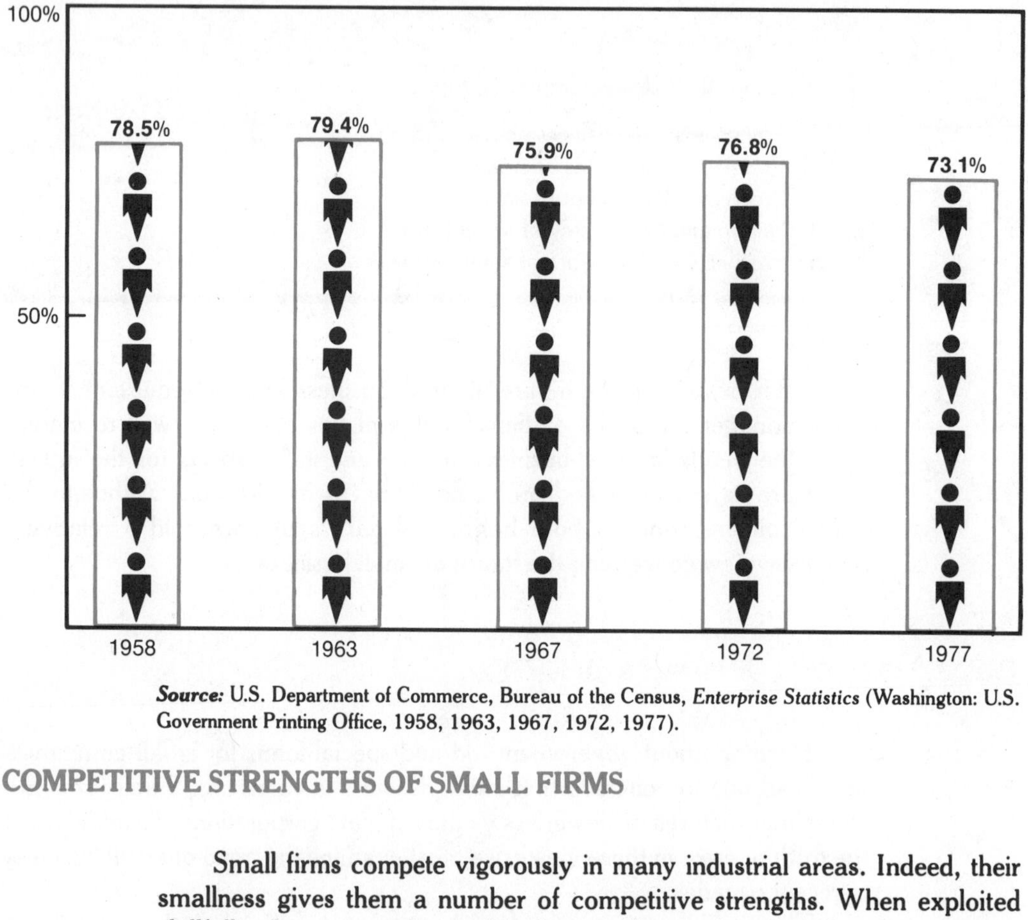

Source: U.S. Department of Commerce, Bureau of the Census, *Enterprise Statistics* (Washington: U.S. Government Printing Office, 1958, 1963, 1967, 1972, 1977).

COMPETITIVE STRENGTHS OF SMALL FIRMS

Small firms compete vigorously in many industrial areas. Indeed, their smallness gives them a number of competitive strengths. When exploited skillfully, these strengths enable them to "carry the attack" to larger firms. Three of these strong points are discussed briefly below.

Knowledge of Customers and Markets

The bureaucratic structure of a large corporation tends to isolate its management from customers and markets. Salespeople have regular contact with the marketplace, but their thinking is several steps removed from the influential decision-making levels of the corporation. Special effort is required to keep decision makers well-informed. Market research, often in sophisticated forms, is a tool designed and used extensively by large firms to probe the market and to reduce corporate ignorance of the market situation.

While it is true that small firms also need good market research, the small-business manager can almost automatically acquire some information that can be gleaned by the manager of a large firm only with great effort. The

Figure 24–3   Percentage of Employees in Retail Firms with Fewer Than 100 Employees

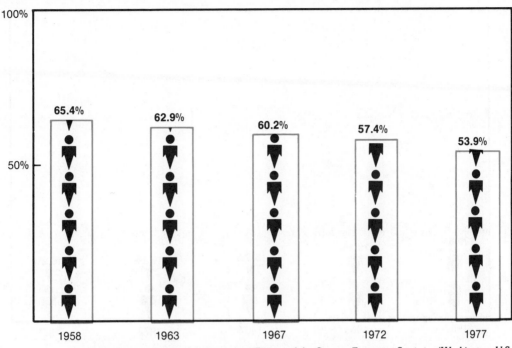

Source: U.S. Department of Commerce, Bureau of the Census, *Enterprise Statistics* (Washington: U.S. Government Printing Office, 1958, 1963, 1967, 1972, and 1977).

small-business manager's closer acquaintance with customers and markets is only a potential strength, however. Both a sensitive awareness of customer needs and a careful observation of market trends are necessary to make this potential strength a reality.

Product and Geographic Specialization

It is impossible to become a specialist in such a broad area as general business management. By narrowing the range of business activity, however, one can develop an expertise in providing needed goals and services. To a greater or lesser degree, the small-business owner specializes. If a sufficiently narrow market segment is selected, the possibility of becoming a true specialist comes closer to reality.

To some extent geographic specialization provides a comparable situation. One can more easily develop a detailed knowledge of a specific locality than of an entire state, region, or country. Chain stores have recognized this handicap in trying to keep up with nimble, independent merchants. This also explains the strength of small business in specialty-shop areas of retailing.

Figure 24–4   Percentage of Employees in Manufacturing Firms with Fewer Than 100 Employees

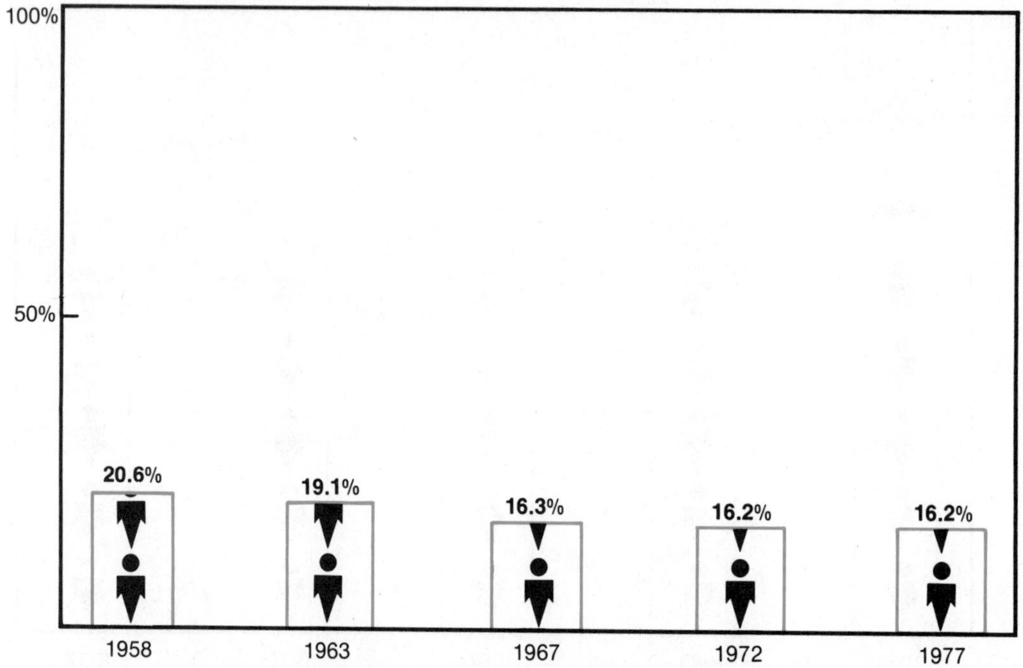

Source: U.S. Department of Commerce, Bureau of the Census, *Enterprise Statistics* (Washington: U.S. Government Printing Office, 1958, 1963, 1967, 1972, and 1977).

ACTION REPORT
Specializing in Small Jobs

Small firms often become strong competitors by specializing. The Seven Sisters Construction Company, an all-female construction firm in California, has chosen to concentrate on relatively small building products. A partner in the company, Tirza Latimer, explains, "We get a lot of jobs that are too small for the big construction firms and too large for the one-person outfits." For example, a current project involves a $92,000 custom-designed house in the San Francisco suburb of Orinda.

Priscilla Danzig, another partner in the company, got into the operation of a construction firm by attending a class in house building and later working as a carpenter. The eight-member firm specializes in home construction, remodeling, and cabinetry. By carefully selecting a market niche, the construction firm has functioned successfully, even managing to earn a profit during its first year.

Source: "Women in Charge; Eight Who Made It," *U.S. News & World Report*, Vol. 88, No. 11 (March 24, 1980), pp. 64–66.

Flexibility in Management

Big business is often pictured as being uniformly more efficient than small business. Such a position, however, is unsupported by the facts. An analysis of the structure of American business reveals many areas in which the optimum-size firm is not large. In his widely read book, *Small Is Beautiful*, E. F. Schumacher argued for small-scale enterprise as a solution for many of today's problems.[2]

Rapid environmental change has become a way of life. Product life cycles become shorter, and innovations appear with greater frequency. Customers grow increasingly fickle and competitors move more quickly. As a result, change is a fact of life for business firms of all sizes. However, a difference exists in the small firm's adaptability. For example, the small firm with a lower investment in fixed assets can resist the snowballing of overhead costs that plague many large firms. And as conditions change, the small firm can make decisions quickly. In contrast, more levels of management must be consulted before making a change in large corporations. The inflexibility of huge organizations is illustrated in a performance review of Sears, Roebuck and Company:

> Sears' biggest problem of all, however, continues to be its ponderous size and the growing unwieldiness that implies—especially in inventories. And there is no easy solution to that, says William S. Hansen, president of the Southern California chain of Buffums'. "It's like the difference between a 747 and a Piper Cub," Hansen notes.[3]

Once again, the small firm's strength is only a potential strength. A prompt decision is not necessarily a good decision. But if the necessary facts are considered, a prompt and correct decision may give the small firm an edge over its large competitor.

SMALL-BUSINESS PROBLEMS AND FAILURE RECORD

A balanced review of future prospects requires us to consider also the darker side of the small-business scene. Small firms face problems, and small firms fail. While we wish to avoid pessimism, we must deal realistically with these matters. Let us now discuss the nature of their problems, their record of failure, and the bankruptcy provisions for those who fail.

Problems of Small Business

In surveys conducted by the National Federation of Independent Business, small-business respondents cite taxes, interest rates, government regulation, and various other issues as their most important problems.[4] There is much variety in their answers. What they consider most critical obviously depends upon the unique features of their businesses. In this section, we review briefly the major problems of small firms; many of these have been touched on in the earlier chapters as having a significant impact on small business generally.

Lack of Managerial Skills and Depth   Perhaps the greatest problem of small-business management is the lack of necessary skills in the management group. In a very small business, the owner is a one-person management team. Top-level decisions, together with lesser tasks of management that assistants cannot accomplish, become the owner–manager's sole responsibility. Unfortunately, this requires a diversity of talents and no individual has superior ability in all areas of management.

The management process is hampered not only by a lack of diversified talents but also by the manager's frequently casual or superficial approach to management problems. The manager often does not understand the intricacies of maintaining adequate business records or of preparing financial statements. Or, if financial data are available, the manager may lack the necessary knowledge or appreciation of their value to interpret and use them effectively.

Personal Lack and Misuse of Time   As mentioned earlier, the owner–manager of a small business frequently bears the management burden alone. In a very small firm, the manager may even help out at the worker level on occasion, packing a rush order or delivering merchandise to a valued customer who insists on immediate service. This means that the manager does not have the opportunity to operate solely at the executive level. This lack of time to manage is accentuated by participation in civic affairs and time devoted to the family, hobbies, and recreational activities. To reduce time pressure, the small-business manager must budget time and exercise reasonable restraint over participation in community affairs.

Difficulties in Financing   A major problem for many small businesses is lack of capital and credit. Long-term capital is a particular need of many small firms. It is obtained by personal investment or by long-term borrowing. Borrowing money to be paid back over a period of ten years or more is difficult for small firms. The banker ordinarily expects funds of this type to come from equity capital. Borrowing from relatives or friends, as an alternative, presents problems because they often expect some voice in the management of the business. And this type of credit can jeopardize the relationship between the parties.

Still another source of long-term capital is the capital markets that are open to large businesses. However, the small firm has only limited access to these markets. Moreover, accepting partners or selling stock may involve the surrender of absolute control over the business, a condition that the original owner may reject. Expansion capital typically must come from personally invested funds or from profits retained in the business.

Overregulation and Taxes Many surveys of small-business problems report governmental regulation and taxation as troublesome areas. In Chapter 23, we discussed the burdensome nature of regulation and the attempt to reduce this burden by increasing flexibility in regulation.

A major problem created by corporate income taxation is the reduction of funds available for reinvestment in the business. This reduction especially hampers small firms because they must rely on earnings as their primary source of expansion capital. Large firms, in contrast, have access to other sources of capital. Even though this principle is recognized in a graduated tax rate system, the impact is still serious for firms which must depend heavily on retained earnings.

Difficulty in Obtaining Qualified Personnel Many small-business managers identify personnel as a major problem area. In most cases, union relationships are not specified as the primary difficulty. Instead, managers often report difficulty in locating properly qualified personnel. Securing well-trained automobile mechanics, television technicians, or pharmacists may pose real problems. For example, the manager of a diesel engine service shop searched for six months to locate a well-qualified parts manager who could also learn to supervise the office and record-keeping activities. Even more difficult for the small business is the recruitment of managerial and professional personnel.

There are numerous other ways in which small-business personnel problems are different. In some industries, for example, the practice of "pattern" bargaining with labor unions tends to impose big-business labor requirements upon small firms. This practice often appears unreasonable to managers of small firms. To illustrate, consider a contract provision limiting employees to a specified type of work. The small firm has greater difficulty in adhering closely to rigid job definitions of this type and needs considerable flexibility in shifting employees from one type of work to another. Some union contracts, it should be noted, have recognized such unique problems of personnel management in small firms.

Weaknesses in Marketing When the small-business owner speaks of the problem of "competition," some aspect of selling is usually stressed. In most small firms, the rigors of competition make the manager painfully conscious of marketing weaknesses. Difficulties in managing the firm's advertising illustrate the nature of the marketing problem. How much should the firm spend on advertising? What media should be used? How can the effectiveness of advertising be measured? For small firms, many of these questions are particularly difficult to answer, and their owners must often guess at the right answer. Channels of distribution, product differentiation, marketing strategy, and other issues likewise constitute significant problems for the small firm.

Failure and the Small Firm

Some unqualified entrepreneurs are doomed from the start. Others who are reasonably well-qualified encounter problems which are too much for them. In either case, the result is failure.

Small-Business Failure Rate Business failure data compiled by Dun and Bradstreet have been used over the years to track the fortunes of business in general and small business in particular.[5] In general, the rate of failure has been low during periods of prosperity and high during economic recessions. For example, the highest rate of failure occurred in 1932, and the rate also increased sharply during the 1981–82 recession.

The frequent citation of failure data has tended to create an erroneous impression about the likelihood of failure.[6] In 1983, for example, 110 firms out of each 10,000 in Dun and Bradstreet's records failed. This means that only 1.1 percent failed. Viewed in this way, one can conclude that chances for success are excellent! The prospective entrepreneur should be encouraged to consider business ownership because of its bright prospects, rather than to shun it because of fear of failure.

Of course, the failure rate would be higher if discontinuances reflecting unsatisfactory operating results were added to those involving loss to creditors. And it is desirable that we should learn from the experiences of those who failed. Caution and apprehension of failure, however, should not be permitted to stifle inclinations toward independent business careers.

The Costs of Business Failure The costs of business failure involve more than financial costs. They include costs of a psychological, social, and economic nature, too.

Loss of Entrepreneur's and Creditors' Capital The owner of a business that fails suffers a loss of invested capital, either in whole or in part. This is always a financial setback to the individual concerned. In some cases, it means the loss of a person's lifetime savings! The entrepreneur's loss of capital is augmented by the losses of business creditors. Hence, the total capital loss is greater than the sum of the entrepreneurial losses in any one year.

Injurious Psychological Effects Individuals who fail in business suffer a real blow to their self-esteem. The businesses they started with enthusiasm and high expectations of success have "gone under." Older entrepreneurs, in many cases, lack the vitality to recover the blow. Many unsuccessful entrepreneurs simply relapse into employee status for the balance of their lives.

However, failure need not be totally devastating to entrepreneurs. They may recover from the failure and try again. Albert Shapero has offered these encouraging comments: "Many heros of business failed at least once. Henry Ford failed twice. Maybe trying and failing is a better business education than going to a business school that has little concern with small business and entrepreneurship."[7] The key, therefore, is the response of the one who fails and that person's ability to learn from failure.

Social and Economic Losses   Assuming that a business opportunity existed, the failure of a firm means the elimination of its goods and services that the public needs and wants. Moreover, the number of jobs available in the community is reduced. The resulting unemployment of the entrepreneur and employees, if any, causes the community to suffer from the loss of a business payroll. Finally, the business that failed was a taxpayer which contributed to the tax support of schools, police and fire protection, and other governmental services.

Causes of Business Failure   Aside from the relatively few cases of fraud, neglect, and disaster, the root cause of business failure is found in managerial incapacity. The weaknesses of management manifest themselves in various ways, however. These manifestations might be thought of as the apparent, or surface, causes of failure.

Root Cause—Inadequate Management   The indictment of the manager is supported by the extensive analysis of business failures conducted by Dun and Bradstreet. Consider, for example, their analysis of reasons for failures that occurred in 1983, as shown in Table 24–1.

In small business especially, management seems to be the number-one problem of the enterprise. The able manager utilizes his or her time wisely and gives proper attention to the various managerial functions. This includes careful attention to customer and public relations, financial planning, employee relations, production control, selling, and other key factors of a business.

Surface Causes   Even though we recognize that management is basically at fault, it is nevertheless profitable to note those areas in which management most frequently finds itself in trouble. For example, a frequently alleged cause of failure is the intensity of competition. Independent grocery stores may be run out of business by efficient chain or supermarket competition. Manufacturers might also encounter new, efficient, well-financed competition for the first time. An efficiently managed existing business,

Table 24–1   Causes of Failures

Neglect		0.6%
Fraud		0.3%
Inexperience, incompetence—evidenced by:		97.8%
Inadequate sales	98.7%	
Heavy operating expenses	26.4%	
Receivables difficulties	5.6%	
Inventory difficulties	1.8%	
Excessive fixed assets	2.8%	
Poor location	0.7%	
Competitive weakness	7.4%	
Disaster		1.3%
		100.0%

Source: The Dun and Bradstreet Business Failure Record (New York: The Dun and Bradstreet Corporation, 1985), p. 15. Since some failures are attributed to a combination of causes, total percentages for the items in the inset column exceed 100.0 percent.

however, is a tough foe for any competitor. Perhaps too much stress has been placed on competition as a cause of failure, although it must be given proper consideration.

Inadequate capital also contributes to business failures. Starting a business on the proverbial shoestring is generally unwise and often leads to failure. Even when initial capital is adequate, the entrepreneur may misuse it. The result is the same—a lack of capital. Sometimes the lack of capital may be only temporary, but the results of overborrowing may still cause failure.

Poor location also causes problems for small firms. The choice of a successful location is partly a science and partly an art. Too many locations are chosen without serious study, careful planning, or adequate investigation. For example, in a particular shopping center three eating establishments were opened in succession. Each one failed, partly because of its choice of location.

Some businesses expand prematurely. Ordinarily, business expansion should be financed from retained earnings or capital contributions of the owners. In periods of prosperity, with reasonable certainty of continued demand, a manufacturer might successfully expand physical facilities through mortgage loans. In any case, expansion calls for careful advance planning. An expanding business should never be top-heavy with debt.

Failure Symptoms   The symptoms of impending business failure are the red flags that alert the entrepreneur. Any one of them may point to trouble. If any of these symptoms are detected, the firm's financial position may be assessed by computing some ratios and comparing them with industry standards. These financial ratios were discussed in Chapter 19.

Deterioration of Working-Capital Position   When a firm's working-capital position is deteriorating, its working capital is becoming inadequate and illiquid. The factors that contribute to declining adequacy and liquidity of working capital include the following:

1. Continuing operating losses.
2. Unusual, nonrecurring losses such as those due to theft, flood, tornado, or adverse court judgments.
3. Payment of excessive managerial bonuses and unearned dividends.
4. Frozen loans to officers, subsidiaries, and affiliates.
5. Overinvestment in fixed assets.
6. Long-term loan payments in excess of proper share of annual profits.

Declining Sales   Sales decline represents a serious situation for any business, large or small. This is true because operating expenses—particularly fixed overhead expenses—do not decline in proportion to sales. Hence, prolonged sales declines result in reduced profits or actual losses.

Controllable factors that may contribute to sales decline include:

1. Inadequate market research to measure sales potential by sales areas or customer groups.
2. Poorly planned advertising and promotional activities.
3. Obsolescent products and product packaging.

Declining Profits   Profits that go downward from month to month or year to year may be attributed to many factors, the most important of which are:

1. Declining sales.
2. Increasing costs of merchandise or raw materials.
3. Higher labor costs.
4. Higher taxes.

Increasing Debts   If current liabilities get out of hand and bills or payrolls due for payment cannot be paid, the firm's situation might deteriorate into involuntary bankruptcy. Nor should a company's fixed, long-term liabilities be allowed to become excessive.

Insolvency and Bankruptcy

A business becomes insolvent when the aggregate value of its assets is not sufficient to pay its debts. There are two major courses of action to take when insolvency exists: to salvage the business through voluntary creditor agreements or creditor arrangements under the Bankruptcy Act of 1978, or to liquidate the business by declaring bankruptcy.

Voluntary Creditor Agreements   If the creditors of an insolvent firm believe that the business can be profitable again, an arrangement permitting continuance of the firm can be made. Such an arrangement may be initiated by either the debtor or a group of its major creditors. The arrangement may take either the form of an extension agreement, a composition settlement, or a combination of both.

Under an **extension agreement**, the creditors of the insolvent business agree to postpone the debtor's payment of obligations for some stipulated period of time. The agreement becomes legally binding upon each of the parties to it. Creditors who do not participate in the extension agreement are not bound by its terms. Therefore, most of the firm's major creditors must become parties to such an agreement if it is to succeed.

In a **composition settlement** the creditors agree to accept reduced amounts due them, on a pro rata basis. The settlement may be either made in cash immediately or postponed to a later date.

Creditor Arrangements under the Bankruptcy Act   The Bankruptcy Act of 1978 (which replaced a bankruptcy law enacted in 1898) provides for the restructuring of the financial affairs of a business.[8] It provides a more flexible approach to reorganizing and continuing the business than was possible under the earlier bankruptcy law. For example, the management of the debtor company is now, in most cases, allowed to retain control, rather than to be automatically replaced. The debtor firm has an exclusive right to propose a reorganization plan within 120 days of filing for bankruptcy. If such a plan is not presented, however, creditors may submit one. All creditors must accept a court-approved plan if it is approved by a majority of each class of creditors—for example, by secured creditors, unsecured creditors, and so on.

The reorganization plan is intended to help those firms which experience temporary financial stress but which are thought to have the underlying strength necessary for long-run success. If a reorganization plan cannot be formulated, the business is liquidated under Chapter 7 of the Act. After the debtor's property has been liquidated and the proceeds distributed, the debtor is legally discharged from further payments on the amounts owed.

PROSPECTS FOR THE FUTURE

In this final section, we turn to the brighter prospects for small business. This involves a review of some of the factors that contribute to the survival of small firms and that also reflect the continuing importance of small business.

ACTION REPORT
Life after Bankruptcy

Debtor companies can sometimes escape liquidation by filing for bankruptcy. Abbott Products of Chicago is one firm which took this route.

Chicago businessman Nelson Carlo spent six months debating whether to close his company, Abbott Products Inc., and seek protection under Chapter 11 of the federal Bankruptcy Code when his business went sour several years ago. The small company, which makes such consumer items as containers and cots, was having cash-flow problems.

Mr. Carlo finally elected to close Abbott in 1982 and seek Chapter 11 court protection from creditors' lawsuits while he worked out a plan to pay his debts and line up new cash sources. Abbott successfully reopened in 1983, but Mr. Carlo says, "Shutting the doors was very hard for me to do. Looking back, I would have saved a lot of money and gotten back on my feet faster if I could have brought myself to make the hard decisions sooner."

Source: Reproduced by permission of *The Wall Street Journal,* © Dow Jones & Company, Inc., 1985. All Rights Reserved.

White House Conferences on Small Business

The 1980 and 1986 White House Conferences on Small Business, as explained in Chapter 23, drew national attention to the role and importance of small business. The first conference was called by President Jimmy Carter and the second by President Ronald Reagan.

The deliberations of the White House Conferences were of general public interest, but they were of particular interest to those who formulate public policy affecting small business. After the Conferences adjourned, their work was followed by informal networks of small-business activists. The net effect, therefore, was to heighten the awareness of small business and to give it a higher priority on the national agenda.

Shift to a Service Economy

One major structural change that favors small business is the shift from a manufacturing to a service economy. The manufacturing segment, in which big business predominates, is currently declining in relative importance. On the other hand, services, retailing, and wholesaling are growing in relative importance. These areas are fields in which small business has traditionally been strong.

Emphasis on Small-Business Courses and Programs

Colleges and universities have greatly expanded their educational emphasis on small business. The teaching of small-business management courses has grown in popularity during the past few years. This emphasis has been encouraged by the SBA-sponsored student consulting programs described in Chapter 13.

The academic field of entrepreneurship and new-venture management has also emerged in recent years. According to Karl Vesper, the number of universities with courses or research centers devoted to entrepreneurship grew from 6 in 1967 to 150 in 1984.[9]

Many leading universities now offer entrepreneurship courses and programs. The surge in such academic offerings is a response to student interest. Dean Elizabeth E. Bailey of the Graduate School of Industrial Administration, Carnegie-Mellon University, is one of many academic administrators who have recognized the increasing demand for training in entrepreneurship.

> She observes an "incredible demand" on the part of students for more education in entrepreneurship. Not all of them want to start their own businesses. Many, she says, "want to know how to be entrepreneurial within the larger corporations."[10]

Strength of Small-Business Associations

Small business has increased its strength by developing associations of small firms. Many of these are trade associations which have worked in the particular interests of various trade groups. The Chamber of Commerce of the United States is another organization which is becoming increasingly effective in its representation of small business as a part of its more general business representation.

One group that represents the interests of small business generally is the National Federation of Independent Business (NFIB), an association with a membership of one-half million members.[11] The NFIB maintains a legislative staff that actively monitors the activities of Congress and supports legislation of interest to small business.

The International Council for Small Business—an association of university business professors, business owners, government officials, consultants, and others directly interested in small business—likewise supports the cause of small business generally and provides testimony regarding proposed legislation.[12] These and other business groups are active in representing the cause of business and in speaking for specific segments of the small-business community.

Growth of Small-Business Periodicals

Many periodicals devote special attention to the needs of small business. *Nation's Business*, for example, is published by the Chamber of Commerce of the United States and places great emphasis on small-business news and programs.

Evidence of a growing interest in small business is found in the launching of new publications. Three new monthly periodicals, *Inc.*, *Venture*, and *In*

Business, started publication in the late 1970s, bringing news and stories of new ventures and entrepreneurship. The fact that three such publications could be launched successfully suggests a widespread interest in entrepreneurship and small business.

A number of business periodicals have added sections or features which highlight small- and medium-sized business. *Forbes,* for example, includes an "Up-and-Comers" section which offers profiles of growing firms. As another example, *The Wall Street Journal* features a "Small Business" column in one issue each week, and, on May 20, 1985, devoted an entire section to "A Special Report on Small Business." Other widely read periodicals, such as *Fortune* and *Business Week,* often spotlight small and growing companies as part of their general coverage of business news.

Continued Support of Governmental Programs

In the preceding chapter, we described many programs of government aid for small business. These aid programs, along with the steps taken by Congress to modify regulatory and tax policies to adapt them to the needs of small firms, represent public policy in support of small business. They reflect an awareness of the vital role played by small firms.

Emergence of Private-Sector Programs and Initiatives

One of the most encouraging factors in thinking of the future prospects of small business is the various initiatives undertaken by private business institutions. Such efforts are diverse, and we can do no more than provide two examples.

The small-business program of the Bank of America illustrates the type of effort that can be undertaken by a single firm. This bank makes a special effort to serve the small-business community of California through its lending programs. It also publishes the *Small Business Reporter*—a series of well-edited monographs on various aspects of small-business management. Some of these are devoted to specific functions or problems of small firms such as cash management, franchising, and management succession. Others present information about particular types of business—apparel stores, restaurants, home furnishings stores, and so on. (The address is: Bank of America, Department 3120, P. O. Box 37000, San Francisco, CA 94137.)

The National Minority Purchasing Council provides an example of cooperative effort among private business concerns. When large corporations become members of this organization, they join a group which attempts to purchase an equitable percentage of services and supplies from minority enterprises. They recognize that minority-owned businesses deserve a chance to compete, and the group strives to make sure they have that opportunity. (The address is: National Minority Purchasing Council, 6 North Michigan Avenue, Room 1104, Chicago, IL 60602.)

ACTION REPORT
NIKE—Triumph of the Entrepreneurial Spirit

Courtesy of Nike, Inc.

The future of small business depends in large measure on the spirit of entrepreneurship. This spirit is alive and often provides a fast track to success.

For example, NIKE shoes did not even exist when its co-founders, Philip H. Knight and William J. Bowerman, became business teammates in 1964. Knight, a former University of Oregon track star, had written a research paper on track shoes while working on his MBA at Stanford in 1960. According to his thesis, the Japanese could do for athletic shoes what they did for cameras. Thus, the game plan was born. On the other hand, Bowerman, his Oregon track coach, had been striving for years to develop a technologically better track shoe. So, in 1964 under the partnership name of Blue Ribbon Sports, Knight and Bowerman began to import the Tiger brand of Japanese-made running shoes and to give the company new designs for shoes.

In 1971, Knight and Bowerman hurdled a dispute with the Japanese manufacturer by contracting out the manufacture of their *own designs* to various Far East factories. They called their new design NIKE and adopted this brand name as their new corporate name. This change obviously worked as NIKE shoes became the largest selling maker of the quality athletic shoe market in the United States. NIKE shoes are still manufactured abroad.

Several winners have worn NIKE shoes—Dan Fouts of the San Diego Chargers, Ingrid Kristiansen, players for the Los Angeles Dodgers, tennis star John McEnroe, NBA basketball stars such as Chicago Bulls' Michael Jordon, baseball's Dwight Gooden, and many others.

But the biggest winner is the entrepreneurial spirit!

The Unflinching Entrepreneurial Spirit

Perhaps the strongest force in achieving a bright future for small business is the unflinching spirit of the entrepreneur. In Chapter 1, we recognized the crucial role played by the entrepreneur—the one who brings new firms into existence and provides leadership for them. Entrepreneurs are creative, talented individuals who provide the backbone for the small-business system. They are also tough individuals who face business problems but who look beyond those problems to find solutions and success in economic endeavor.

Looking Back

1. Small firms now have a somewhat smaller share of the market in some industries than they had earlier. However, they have maintained great overall strength and still constitute an important segment of the economy.
2. The competitive strengths of small firms include knowledge of customers and markets, product and geographic specialization, and flexibility in management.
3. Problems of small business include lack of managerial skills and depth, personal lack and misuse of time, lack of financing, overregulation and taxes, difficulty in obtaining qualified personnel, and weaknesses in marketing.
4. A relatively small percentage of all businesses fail each year. The most important cause of failure is thought to be inadequate management. A business becomes insolvent when the aggregate value of its assets is insufficient to pay its debts. The debtor business firm may make voluntary agreements with creditors, or it may be treated under the Bankruptcy Act of 1978. In the latter case, the firm may be reorganized and continue to function, or it may be liquidated to pay off creditors.
5. Future prospects for small business are bright because of a number of factors. Some of these are the 1980 and 1986 White House Conferences on Small Business, the shift to a service economy, the emphasis on small-business courses and programs, the strength of small-business associations, the continued support of governmental programs, and the unflinching entrepreneurial spirit.

DISCUSSION QUESTIONS

1. What has been the long-run trend of market share accounted for by small business?
2. In what way does knowledge of customers and markets constitute a competitive strength for a small firm?

3. Why can small firms be more flexible in management? How can a large firm achieve similar flexibility?

4. What is the most pressing problem in running a small business? What can be done to alleviate this problem?

5. What would be the diverse managerial skills ideally desirable in the following types of businesses: (a) retail hardware store, (b) photographic studio, (c) wholesale grocery firm, (d) sheet metal shop, (e) retail appliance store, and (f) radio and television repair shop?

6. Why is it unlikely that one individual would have all the necessary specialized managerial skills?

7. Enumerate and describe some of the nonfinancial costs of business failure.

8. Justify the statement that most business failures are caused by management weaknesses.

9. Why is the management of a debtor firm sometimes allowed to retain control during a bankruptcy proceeding?

10. What were the 1980 and 1986 White House Conferences on Small Business, and why were they significant?

ENDNOTES

1. See the Bureau of the Census publication *Enterprise Statistics* for 1958, 1963, 1967, 1972, and 1977 to determine the fluctuation in employment over this period.

2. E. F. Schumacher, *Small Is Beautiful* (New York: Harper & Row, 1973), pp. 64–65.

3. "Why Sears' Profits Tumbled," *Business Week*, No. 2377 (April 21, 1975), pp. 32–33.

4. The National Federation for Independent Business issues a *Quarterly Economic Report for Small Business.*

5. The most comprehensive statistics pertaining to failure and changes in rate of failure are collected by Dun and Bradstreet, a business firm devoted to the analysis and rating of the credit standing of other firms. Failures, as defined by Dun and Bradstreet, include only those discontinuances that involve loss to creditors; voluntarily liquidated firms with all debts paid are excluded. As an example of a Dun and Bradstreet report, see *The Dun and Bradstreet Business Failure Record 1982–1983* (New York: The Dun and Bradstreet Corporation, 1985).

6. Professor M. Z. Massel of De Paul University argues that writers generally have become so preoccupied with the minority of firms which fail that they paint an unnecessarily pessimistic picture of chances for success in business. See Michael Z. Massel, "It's Easier to Slay a Dragon Than Kill a Myth," *Journal of Small Business Management*, Vol. 16, No. 3 (July, 1978), pp. 44–49.

7. Albert Shapero, "Numbers That Lie," *Inc.*, Vol. 3, No. 5 (May, 1981), p. 16.

8. For an explanation of the new Act, see Priscilla Anne Schwab, "Bankruptcy: A New Code May Save Many Firms," *Nation's Business*, Vol. 69, No. 4 (April, 1981), pp. 82–88.

9. "B-Schools Try to Churn out Entrepreneurs," *Business Week*, No. 2831 (March 5, 1984), p. 102.

10. Sharon Nelton, "Molding Managers for the Tests of Tomorrow," *Nation's Business*, Vol. 72, No. 4 (April, 1984), p. 31.

11. NFIB offices are located at 150 West 20th Avenue, San Mateo, CA 94403 and at 490 L' Enfant Plaza East, S. W., Washington, DC 20024.

12. The International Council for Small Business publishes the *Journal of Small Business Management*, with editorial offices at the Bureau of Business Research, West Virginia University, Morgantown, WV 26506.

REFERENCES TO SMALL BUSINESS IN ACTION

Graham, Roberta. "Small Business: Fighting to Stay Alive." *Nation's Business*, Vol. 68, No. 7 (July, 1980), pp. 33–36.

This article describes a number of small firms that are facing severe problems and are fighting to survive.

Mahar, Margaret. "Corporate Cast-offs." *Venture*, Vol. 7, No. 5 (May, 1985), pp. 78–84.

Many corporations are trying to shed excess operations. Quick-footed managers sometimes acquire them before outsiders get the chance. The article describes a number of such cases in which entrepreneurs succeed with operations large corporations found unrewarding.

Ostroff, Jim. "An Update of Venture's Entrepreneurs." *Venture*, Vol. 7, No. 6 (June, 1985), pp. 102–108.

The article gives brief descriptions of several small firms which, for the most part, are thriving. *Venture* has followed these companies over a period of time.

Shell, Roberta W. "Putting A Business Together Again." *Inc.*, Vol. 4, No. 3 (March, 1982), pp. 94–99.

Marine Optical, a Massachusetts manufacturer of metal and plastic eyeglass frames, filed for bankruptcy in 1980. It was able to survive and have a second chance by following this procedure.

CASE 24

Classique Cabinets*
Facing the threat of insolvency and failure

Classique Cabinets was a proprietorship owned and operated by Devlin Toliver and his wife Erika. Located in Zanesville, OH, the business was opened in 1982 to produce handcrafted, custom-designed cabinets for homes and offices.

Devlin was 28 years old and had a high school education. Before starting the cabinet shop, he worked as inventory manager for a lumberyard in Zanesville and as a construction site supervisor. His wife Erika taught second grade and served as part-time bookkeeper for the cabinet operation. The Tolivers had no children.

Location and Facilities

The Tolivers lived in a 2,000-square-foot home, designed and constructed by Devlin, on the outskirts of Zanesville. Zanesville is situated in the eastern part of Ohio, approximately 100 miles from Columbus. If the nearby communities of Crooksville, East Fultonham, and Roseville were included, Zanesville would have a metropolitan population of 50,000.

Classique Cabinets was located adjacent to the Tolivers' home in a five-year-old fabricated metal building. The facility had 3,200 square feet of concrete flooring, 2 overhead bay doors, and a partial skylight. Devlin's woodworking equipment and supplies were valued at $25,000. These were not being depreciated on the income statement prepared by Devlin. However, the income statement shown in Exhibit 1 has been corrected to include depreciation expense. Exhibit 2 shows his balance sheet as of December 31, 1985.

Quality of Devlin's Cabinetwork

Devlin displayed enormous pride in his custom-made cabinets. He commented:

> Craftsmanship has not died out entirely. I make my cabinets the old-fashioned way out of the finest woods and grains. They are built to last a lifetime. Nothing leaves my shop that I'm not proud of. I look upon my cabinets almost as pieces of artwork—not as stamped out assembly-line products.

Classique cabinets were priced at approximately two-and-one-half times the price of mass-milled cabinets sold at home centers and retail building

*This case was prepared by Steve R. Hardy and Professor Philip M. Van Auken of Baylor University.

Exhibit 1   Income Statement of Classique Cabinets

Classique Cabinets Income Statement For Year Ended Dec. 31, 1985		
Income:		
Cabinet operation	$64,638	
Construction	49,760	
Repairs	5,602	
Total revenue		$120,000
Cost of sales:		
Raw materials	$59,438	
Labor	38,970	98,408
Gross margin		$ 21,592
Operating expenses:		
Advertising	$ 562	
Bad-debt allowance	10,260	
Depreciation	15,430	
Fringe benefits—Labor	2,498	
Insurance	1,200	
Office supplies	488	
Salaries	4,678	
Telephone	1,200	
Utilities	2,312	38,628
Net profit (or loss)		($ 17,036)

centers (Payless Cashways, Handy Dan, Sears, and so on). Devlin priced his cabinets at an average of $110 per running foot, which included installation. About 65 percent of Devlin's orders were for homes, with the remaining sales spread fairly evenly among offices for white-collar professionals and financial institutions.

The Market Demand

Devlin made the following comments about the market demand for his products:

> In the three years I have operated Classique Cabinets, I've pretty much creamed the local market. By that I mean that I have landed the easy customers who readily appreciated the quality of my products and didn't worry too much about price. My task now is to search out new customers who either are unaware of the quality of my cabinets or who have not fully considered the long-run value of what I sell.

Exhibit 2   Balance Sheet of Classique Cabinets

Classique Cabinets
Balance Sheet
Dec. 31, 1985

ASSETS

Current assets:		
Cash	$ 2,252	
Accounts receivable*	21,460	
Inventory	9,874	
Total current assets		$ 33,586
Fixed assets:		
Fixtures	$ 1,896	
Machinery and equipment	33,942	
Plant	63,290	
Land	22,700	
Total fixed assets		121,828
TOTAL ASSETS		$155,414

LIABILITIES AND OWNER'S EQUITY

Current liabilities:		
Accounts payable	$15,260	
Note payable (current)	5,000	
Tax provision	2,120	
Total current liabilities		$ 22,380
Long-term liabilities:		
Note payable—Bank	$77,970	
Note payable—Uncle Don	20,000	
Total long-term liabilities		97,970
Owner's equity		35,064
TOTAL LIABILITIES AND OWNER'S EQUITY		$155,414

*Includes approximately $4,000 in bad debts.

Admitting that he had had problems in estimating potential market demand in the Zanesville area and in forecasting future cash flows, he added: "I really don't know to what extent demand for custom-made cabinets in town is currently saturated. I would like to believe that there are plenty of people left who still appreciate quality cabinets that will last a lifetime."

Devlin observed that both the cabinet and construction businesses had been hard hit by high interest rates and a nationwide slump in the construction trade. He said, "Housing starts are way down, and money is extremely hard to come by. The interest rates have also hurt potential customers of mine because handmade cabinets are a luxury which homeowners can postpone."

Operations Management

Devlin had never advertised his services, relying instead on word-of-mouth advertising and the goodwill of past customers. He explained, "Zanesville is a small community. Most people know me personally or at least have heard of my business. After all, I grew up right here in town."

However, Devlin pointed out one disadvantage of being "home grown": *bad debts.* "I have put in cabinets for several friends and social acquaintances who just never got around to paying me," he said. "What am I expected to do, go to their homes with a shotgun to collect?"

When cabinet orders were slow, Devlin spent time with a small home construction business which he operated with two childhood friends. He explained that, although there was very little profit in building homes on a small scale, his occasional construction projects generated the needed cash flow and enabled him to keep his friends employed. He subcontracted out electrical and plumbing work on the homes. He added:

> I really don't have the heart to tell Jessie and Gordon that I'm getting out of the home building business. They have stayed loyal to me and assisted me from time to time with the cabinet shop. Besides, building homes gives me one additional outlet for my cabinets.

Devlin was giving serious consideration to expanding his operations into wood-milling work for local lumberyards and home centers. He explained:

> I've been wanting to become less dependent on products that are so heavily tied to the state of the economy. There are four lumberyards and five retail home centers here in the area which all have a need for milling work—things like fence posts, staircase railings, table legs, and so on. For a total investment of about $8,000, I can be in operation. Milling work is a high-volume proposition and involves at least a 30 percent profit margin because of the high value added. Milling would also complement my cabinet business rather nicely.

However, he had not yet completed any market surveys for a milling operation, though he expressed great confidence that "the demand is there."

Financial Outlook

In evaluating the financial health of Classique Cabinets, Devlin candidly admitted that the business sorely needed a "shot in the arm," having failed to generate a profit in its three years of existence. He felt that cabinet demand was so unpredictable that short-term financial growth would have to come from an alternative business area such as the contemplated milling venture.

In assessing his future outlook, Devlin commented:

> As I see it, I've got just two alternatives: diversify or liquidate. I need to generate and sustain a profitable line of business to overcome bad times in the cabinet and home building markets. Erika has supported me with her teaching income for long enough. Since I'm not drawing a regular salary from Classique Cabinets, our income has been barely enough to scrape by on.
>
> We've both worked too hard to merely subsist on one income. If expansion into wood-milling is not feasible, I would not necessarily be averse to bankruptcy. I have a standing offer to manage Zanesville's largest lumberyard. Although I'd rather be my own boss, I'd be happy enough at the lumberyard, at least temporarily.
>
> In the meantime, I plan to closely study the milling idea and make the go–no-go decision. A lot more thinking is called for.

Questions

1. Assess Classique Cabinet's current financial situation, including short-term solvency, capacity for additional debt financing, and operating expenses.
2. In your estimation, why has Classique Cabinets failed to generate a profit? How optimistic are you about the company's future performance?
3. Should Devlin Toliver invest in the proposed wood-milling venture? Defend your answer persuasively.
4. Do you recommend bankruptcy for Classique Cabinets? If not, present recommendations for helping the company survive financially over the next 6 to 18 months.

COMPREHENSIVE CASE

The Mismatch*
Problems in starting and operating a department store

"Okay, George, here's your opportunity to become an entrepreneur." Bob was speaking to his old fraternity brother George on the telephone concerning George's long-held ambition to own a men's clothing store in Florida. "I am opening a small, specialty department store and I have approximately 1500 square feet available for menswear. I will either sublease you that space, or, if you would rather, I will sell you stock in my corporation and we will use that capital to buy your inventory and fixtures."

George responded enthusiastically, "You could not have called at a better time. The company I am with is having all sorts of problems and I may get laid off. Anyhow, I am sick of New England cold weather. Let me see what I can put together and I will call you back in a few days."

George was a salesman for a company that manufactured golfing and resort sportswear. He had been involved with the wholesale selling of apparel for five years and had always wanted to try the retail end. Being an immaculately groomed dresser himself, he thought he could do well.

Three days later he called Bob. "I can come up with $25,000. If you think that will cover us, I will buy your stock and we will try it. I would rather do that than sublease, as this way I can use your retail experience to help me out."

Although Bob, who had owned successful card and gift shops, had no experience in men's clothing, he calculated that $25,000 might be enough to purchase the initial merchandise and fixtures, so he consented to give it a try. He recommended that George give his resignation notice to his employer in the near future and be prepared to travel to the Atlanta Men's and Boy's Apparel show in four weeks to place orders for their fall opening. The store was scheduled to open in 5 months on October 1.

Bob went to work on the store layout (see Figure 1). He had five departments to lay out in approximately 10,000 square feet of sales floor: cards and gifts, ladies' fashions, menswear, bridal shop, and a restaurant. The store was located in a 55-store enclosed mall and would have both a mall entrance and an outdoor entrance. Since it had previously been occupied by a restaurant, the only preset space was the kitchen area. Therefore, he located the 1000-square-foot restaurant (department 1) adjacent to the kitchen. Knowing that the cards and gifts (department 2) were impulsive merchandise requiring high traffic, that department was placed at the mall entrance. With

*This case was prepared by James W. Halloran and appears in *The Entrepreneur Spirit*, published by Tab Books, Inc.

window exposure from the outside, it was thought ladies' fashions (department 3) would show off well in that area. Bridal and tuxedo (department 4) were placed beside the ladies' fashions. This left the back corner, 1500 square feet, for menswear (department 5). That area also included a brick fireplace and would decorate well for men. Bob, along with the ladies' fashions manager, went to work designing, decorating, and remodeling the restaurant and other departments into an attractive department store. With 80 percent of the store finished, George arrived one week before opening.

Figure 1   The Store Layout

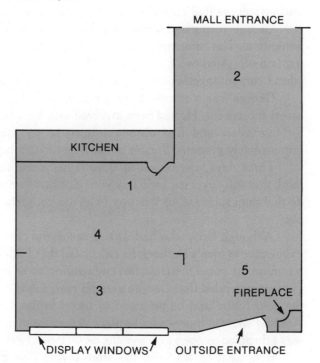

Initial Purchases

The first thing Bob and George did was review the merchandise orders placed in Atlanta for the men's shop. Merchandise for the initial base inventory was ordered at an approximate cost of $20,000. It was broken down as follows:

Original monies		$25,000
Fixtures & equipment	6,300	
Casual slacks, shirts	2,400	
Dress slacks, shirts	1,900	
Sweaters	700	
Belts, accessories	1,225	
Sportcoats	3,900	
Suits	5,600	
Ties, billfolds	2,850	
Total (paid in advance)	$24,875	

In addition, $15,600 of fall and holiday merchandise was ordered for October and November delivery with net 30 day terms.

Bob and George were both somewhat concerned about the suit order. With over 25% of the original order in expensive suits, it cut into the selection presented for more casual wear. In addition, that same percentage was ordered for fall and holiday orders. However, they agreed that, if they were to have a "complete look," the suit selection was necessary. It was also necessary to think about the spring since the orders had to be placed at the mid-October apparel show before any sales history would be realized.

They went to work immediately, unpacking and pricing the merchandise which had been arriving the past two weeks. It was quite noticeable that George's taste in colors and designs was very oriented toward the golf-and-resort look. This concerned Bob because he knew the community, although located in Florida, was composed mainly of engineers from the nearby aerospace industry. However, George was confident it was the right way to go.

The Store Opens

The final week before opening was spent setting up merchandise and adding the finishing touches. Bob became somewhat annoyed at George's meticulous work habits as everything had to be done by plan. With so much to do in such a busy week, it didn't seem appropriate that so much of George's time should be spent in doing a lot of detailed charts and plans until after the opening. The ladies' fashions manager felt the same way. However, Bob thought it should prove advantageous in the long run to have at least one well-organized person in the firm.

Grand opening was set for 7 PM on a Thursday. It was a big affair. Ribbon cutting, champagne, entertainment, and considerable advertising were used to make it a successful evening. George's first customer bought two suits for a total of $450, and everything looked successful.

Unfortunately, the first night was the highlight of the men's department. While the rest of the store performed up to expectations, the menswear floundered. At the end of the fall/Christmas quarter, the total men's department sales were a disappointing $14,560. Since the first year's projections for the department were $150,000, the store had a major problem. The actual figures were as follows:

Sales		$14,560
Less:		
Purchases	−34,375	
Payroll	−11,200 (George plus 1 assistant)	
Share of overhead	−6,450	
Plus: Ending inventory	+27,500	
Net loss	−$9,965	

Of immediate concern was the $18,000 worth of merchandise on order for the spring. They tried to cancel as much as possible, particularly suits; but since most of it had already been cut and was ready to ship, they were obliged to receive over $16,000 (at cost) worth of merchandise.

The January-through-March sales volume quarter was a disappointing $11,700, followed by an equally disappointing April-through-June sales volume period of $13,400. During this period, an additional $4,500 of summer merchandise arrived. Bob looked at the end-of-June figures for the department and knew something had to be done.

October through June

Sales		$39,660
Less:		
Purchases	−54,875	
Payroll	−24,200	
Share of overhead	−17,600	
Plus: Ending inventory	+35,100	
Net loss	−$21,915	

They had already borrowed short-term monies to cover this loss and were now confronted with buying decisions for the upcoming fall. In addition to the financial problems, George continued to show no flexibility in changing plans in mid-stream. He worked everything out based on prescribed formulas he had learned while working for a large corporation. In addition to annoying

Bob and the ladies' fashions manager, two employees had quit over the frustration of working within George's guidelines. Bob called a meeting to confront the problem.

"George, I suggest we liquidate the department. The rest of the store cannot continue to support it and I am not willing to borrow more money to purchase for the fall season. If we liquidate, we can raise enough capital to purchase your stock at the same price you paid for it. We can either expand one of our other departments into that area or carry a limited line of menswear and accessories which will be self-service and will require one-half the investment. I am afraid you will have to go as I cannot afford your salary."

George was confused and disappointed. There seemed to be no other alternatives.

Questions

1. Evaluate George's qualifications for his role as manager of the menswear department.
2. What effect did the location of the menswear department have on its outcome?
3. Should George have subleased the space instead of purchasing stock in the corporation?
4. What problems do you see in the initial purchase plan? What could have been done differently?
5. Do George and Bob have any alternatives to liquidating the menswear department?

APPENDIX A

A FRANCHISE INVESTIGATION CHECKLIST*

The Company

1. Does the company have a solid business reputation and credit rating?
2. How long has the firm been in operation?
3. Has it a reputation for honesty and fair dealing among those who currently hold a franchise?
4. Will the firm assist you with:
   a. a management training program?
   b. an employee training program?
   c. a public relations program?
   d. capital?
   e. credit?
   f. merchandising ideas?
5. Will the firm assist you in finding a good location for your new business?
6. Is the franchising firm adequately financed so that it can carry out its stated plan of financial assistance and expansion?
7. Has the franchisor shown you any certified figures indicating exact net profits of one or more going operations which you have personally checked yourself? (If potential earnings are exaggerated, watch out!)
8. Is the franchisor a one-person company or a corporation with an experienced management trained in depth (so that there would always be an experienced individual at its head)?
9. Exactly what can the franchisor do for you that you cannot do for yourself?

The Product

1. Is it in production and currently available?
2. How long has it been on the market?
3. Where is it sold: what states, cities, stores?
4. Is it priced competitively?
5. Is it packaged attractively?
6. How does it stand up in use?
7. Is it a one-shot or a repeat item?
8. Is it easy and safe to use?
9. Is it a staple, a fad, a luxury item?
10. Is it an all-year seller or a seasonal one?

*From Robert M. Dias and Stanley I. Gurnick, *Franchising: The Investor's Complete Handbook* (New York: Hastings House, 1969), pp. 38–41.

11. Is it patented?
12. Does the franchisor manufacture it or merely distribute it?
13. Do product and package comply with all applicable laws?
14. How well does it sell elsewhere?
15. Would you buy it on the open market on its merits?
16. Is it a product with basic and beneficial qualities, or just a mixture of ordinary raw materials?
17. Will the product or service be in greater demand, about the same, or less in demand five years from now?
18. Is the product manufactured under certain quality standards?
19. How do these standards compare to other similar products on the market?
20. Must the product be purchased exclusively from the franchisor? A designated supplier? If so, are the prices competitive?

The Territory

1. Has the franchise company many available territories?
2. Is the territory completely, accurately, and understandably defined?
3. Is the "exclusive representation" thoroughly spelled out and protected?
4. Does the franchisor guarantee a new holder against any infringement of territorial rights?
5. Is the territory large enough to provide an adequate sales potential?
6. Is the territory subject to any seasonal fluctuations in income?
7. Is the territory above or below statewide average per capita income?
8. Is the territory increasing or decreasing in population?
9. Does the competition appear to be unusually well entrenched in the territory? Nonfranchise firms? Franchise firms?
10. What is the history of any former franchisees or dealers in the territory?
11. How are nearby franchisees doing?
12. Does the franchise company choose the dealer's location or okay the choice?
13. How does the company settle on a location?
14. Does the company lease or sublease premises to its dealers? What are your costs?

The Contract

1. Does the contract cover all aspects of the agreement?
2. Does it really benefit both parties or just the franchisor?
3. What are the conditions for obtaining a franchise?
4. Under what conditions will the franchise be lost?
5. Is a certain size and type of operation specified?
6. Is there an additional fixed payment each year?
7. Is there a percent of gross sales payment?
8. Must a certain amount of merchandise be purchased?
9. Is there an annual sales quota and can you lose the franchise if it is not met?
10. Can the franchisee return merchandise for credit?
11. Can the franchisee engage in other business activities?
12. Does the contract give you an exclusive territory for the length of the franchise or can the franchisor sell a second or third franchise in your territory?
13. Did your lawyer approve the franchise contract after studying it paragraph by paragraph?
14. Under what terms may you sell the business to whomever you please at whatever price you may be able to obtain?
15. How can you terminate your agreement if you are not happy with it?
16. What period does the franchise agreement cover? Is it renewable? And for how long?
17. Can the franchisor sell the franchise out from under you?
18. Is your territory protected?

19. Is the franchise fee worth it? What exactly is the fee for? If the fee includes the cost of equipment or supplies, is it reasonable?
20. Are royalty or other financing charges exorbitantly out of proportion to sales volume?
21. Are your operations subject to interstate commerce regulations?
22. Have you asked your lawyer for advice on how to meet your legal responsibilities? Your accountant?

Continuing Assistance

1. Does the franchisor:
    a. provide continuing assistance?
    b. select store locations?
    c. handle lease arrangements?
    d. design store layouts and displays?
    e. select opening inventory?
    f. provide inventory-control methods?
    g. provide market surveys?
    h. help analyze financial statements?
    i. provide purchasing guides?
    j. help finance equipment?
    k. make direct loans to qualified individuals?
    l. actively promote the product or service?
2. Is there training for franchisees and key employees?
3. How and where is the product being advertised?
4. What advertising aids does the franchisor provide?
5. What is the franchisee's share of advertising costs?
6. Are certain franchisees given preferential treatment with regard to pricing and directed purchases?

APPENDIX B

SBA PUBLICATIONS ON MANAGEMENT ASSISTANCE

The following publications may be obtained at a nominal cost from the Small Business Administration, Washington, DC 20416, or from one of the SBA field offices. (To locate the local address and telephone number of SBA offices, look in the telephone directory under "U.S. Government.")

MANAGEMENT AIDS

Financial Management and Analysis

—MA 1.001	The ABC's of Borrowing
—MA 1.002	What Is the Best Selling Price?
—MA 1.003	Keep Pointed toward Profit
—MA 1.004	Basic Budgets for Profit Planning
—MA 1.005	Pricing for Small Manufacturers
—MA 1.006	Cash Flow in a Small Plant
—MA 1.007	Credit and Collections
—MA 1.008	Attacking Business Decision Problems with Breakeven Analysis
—MA 1.009	A Venture Capital Primer for Small Business
—MA 1.010	Accounting Services for Small Service Firms
—MA 1.011	Analyze Your Records to Reduce Costs
—MA 1.012	Profit by Your Wholesalers' Services
—MA 1.013	Steps in Meeting Your Tax Obligations
—MA 1.014	Getting the Facts for Income Tax Reporting
—MA 1.015	Budgeting in a Small Business Firm
—MA 1.016	Sound Cash Management and Borrowing
—MA 1.017	Keeping Records in Small Business
—MA 1.018	Checklist for Profit Watching
—MA 1.019	Simple Breakeven Analysis for Small Stores
—MA 1.020	Profit Pricing and Costing for Services

Planning

—MA 2.002   Locating or Relocating Your Business
—MA 2.004   Problems in Managing a Family-Owned Business
—MA 2.005   The Equipment Replacement Decision
—MA 2.006   Finding a New Product for Your Company
—MA 2.007   Business Plan for Small Manufacturers
—MA 2.008   Business Plan for Small Construction Firms
—MA 2.009   Business Life Insurance
—MA 2.010   Planning and Goal Setting for Small Business
—MA 2.011   Fixing Production Mistakes
—MA 2.012   Setting up a Quality Control System
—MA 2.013   Can You Make Money with Your Idea or Invention?
—MA 2.014   Should You Lease or Buy Equipment?
—MA 2.015   Can You Use a Minicomputer?
—MA 2.016   Checklist for Going into Business
—MA 2.017   Factors in Considering a Shopping Center Location
—MA 2.018   Insurance Checklist for Small Business
—MA 2.020   Business Plan for Retailers
—MA 2.021   Using a Traffic Study to Select a Retail Site
—MA 2.022   Business Plan for Small Service Firms
—MA 2.024   Store Location "Little Things" Mean a Lot
—MA 2.025   Thinking about Going into Business?
—MA 2.026   Feasibility Checklist for Starting a Small Business of Your Own
—MA 2.027   How to Get Started with a Small Business Computer

General Management and Administration

—MA 3.001   Delegating Work and Responsibility
—MA 3.002   Management Checklist for a Family Business
—MA 3.004   Preventing Retail Theft
—MA 3.005   Stock Control for Small Stores
—MA 3.006   Reducing Shoplifting Losses
—MA 3.007   Preventing Burglary and Robbery Loss
—MA 3.008   Outwitting Bad-Check Passers
—MA 3.009   Preventing Embezzlement
—MA 3.010   Techniques for Problem Solving

Marketing

—MA 4.001   Understanding Your Customer
—MA 4.002   Creative Selling: The Competitive Edge
—MA 4.003   Measuring Sales Force Performance
—MA 4.005   Is the Independent Sales Agent for You?
—MA 4.007   Selling Products on Consignment
—MA 4.008   Tips on Getting More for Your Marketing Dollar
—MA 4.010   Developing New Accounts
—MA 4.012   Marketing Checklist for Small Retailers

—MA 4.013   A Pricing Checklist for Small Retailers
—MA 4.015   Advertising Guidelines for Small Retail Firms
—MA 4.016   Signs in Your Business
—MA 4.018   Plan Your Advertising Budget
—MA 4.019   Learning about Your Market
—MA 4.020   Do You Know the Results of Your Advertising?
—MA 4.021   Specialty Advertising for Small Business
—MA 4.022   Understanding Corporate Purchasing

Organization and Personnel

—MA 5.001   Checklist for Developing a Training Program
—MA 5.004   Pointers on Using Temporary-Help Services
—MA 5.005   Preventing Employee Pilferage
—MA 5.006   Setting up a Pay System
—MA 5.007   Staffing Your Store
—MA 5.008   Managing Employee Benefits
—MA 5.009   Techniques for Productivity Improvement

Legal and Government Affairs

—MA 6.003   Incorporating a Small Business
—MA 6.004   Selecting the Legal Structure for Your Business
—MA 6.005   Introduction to Patents

Miscellaneous

—MA 7.002   Association Services for Small Business
—MA 7.003   Market Overseas with U.S. Government Help
—SBIR-T1   Proposal Preparation for Small Business Innovation Research (SBIR)
—MA5   Women's Handbook

SMALL BUSINESS BIBLIOGRAPHIES

— 1. Handcrafts
— 2. Home Businesses
— 3. Selling by Mail Order
— 9. Marketing Research Procedures
—10. Retailing
—12. Statistics and Maps for National Market Analysis
—13. National Directories for Use in Marketing
—15. Recordkeeping Systems—Small Store and Service Trade
—18. Basic Business Reference Sources
—20. Advertising—Retail Store

—31. Retail Credit and Collection
—37. Buying for Retail Stores
—72. Personnel Management
—75. Inventory Management
—85. Purchasing for Owners of Small Plants
—86. Training for Small Business
—87. Financial Management
—88. Manufacturing Management
—89. Marketing for Small Business
—90. New Product Development
—91. Ideas into Dollars (Inventors' Guide)
—92. Effective Business Communication
—93. Productivity Management in Small Business
—94. Decision Making in Small Business

STARTING OUT SERIES

—0101 Building Service Contracting
—0104 Radio-Television Repair Shop
—0105 Retail Florists
—0106 Franchised Businesses
—0107 Hardware Store or Home Centers
—0111 Sporting Goods Store
—0112 Drycleaning
—0114 Cosmetology
—0115 Pest Control
—0116 Marine Retailers
—0117 Retail Grocery Stores
—0122 Apparel Store
—0123 Pharmacies
—0125 Office Products
—0129 Interior Design Services
—0130 Fish Farming
—0133 Bicycles
—0134 Roofing Contractors
—0135 Printing
—0137 The Bookstore
—0138 Home Furnishings
—0142 Ice Cream
—0145 Sewing Centers
—0148 Personnel Referral Service
—0149 Selling by Mail Order
—0150 Solar Energy
—0201 Breakeven Point for Independent Truckers
—0202 Starting a Retail Travel Agency
—0203 Starting a Retail Decorating Products Business
—0204 Starting an Independent Consulting Practice
—0205 Starting an Electronics Industry Consulting Practice

GLOSSARY

ABC method   a method of classifying inventory items into categories which are of high-value, less costly, and low-cost items

acid-test (or quick) ratio   ratio of current assets less inventories to current liabilities

accrual method of accounting   accounting method by which revenue and expenses are recognized when they are incurred, regardless of when the cash is received or payment is made

advertising   the impersonal presentation of an idea which is identified with a business sponsor and is projected through mass media

affective tie   a tie among entrepreneurs which relates to emotional sentiments in their networking relationships

agency   a relationship whereby one party, the agent, represents another party, the principal, in dealing with a third person

agency power   the power of each partner in a partnership to bind all members of the firm in the exercise of management duties

agents   distribution intermediaries who do not take title to the goods

aging schedule   a grouping of accounts receivable into age categories based on the length of time they have been outstanding

application software   computer programs written for particular business needs and which can be created by the user or purchased as preprogrammed packages

articles of partnership   a written document which states explicitly the rights and duties of partners in a partnership

assorting   the process of bringing together homogeneous lines of goods into a heterogeneous assortment

attitude   a feeling toward an object organized around knowledge which regulates behavioral tendencies

attributes sampling plan   a statistical method of quality control which measures the attributes of a product and checks the acceptability of a small sample of parts to decide about the acceptability of the entire lot

average collection period   a measure of accounts-receivable turnover

average cost   a number obtained by dividing the total cost over a previous period by the quantity sold or produced during that period

average pricing   a pricing approach using average cost as a basis to set price

bad-debt ratio   an expense ratio which is computed by dividing the amount of bad debts by the total credit sales

bait advertising   advertising in which a low price for an article is offered merely to lure a prospect into the place of business, whereupon the prospect is talked into purchasing a more expensive product

balance sheet   a financial statement which shows a firm's financial position (regarding its assets, liabilities, and net worth) at a specific date

benefit variables   segmentation variables that are used to divide and identify segments of a market according to the benefits sought by customers

blue-sky laws   state laws that cover the registration of new securities; licensing of dealers, brokers, and salespersons; and prosecution of individuals charged with fraud in connection with the sale of securities

board of directors   the governing body elected by the stockholders of a corporation

brand   the identification for a product which can be verbalized or expressed in other symbolic forms

breakdown process   a forecasting process which begins with a macro-level variable and systematically works down to the sales forecast (also called a "chain-ratio" method)

break-even analysis   a formal comparison of cost and demand for the purpose of determining the acceptability of alternative prices or for evaluating the prospects for capital investments

break-even point   the point at which total sales revenue equals total costs

breaking bulk   channel activities which take the larger quantities produced and prepare them for individual customers

break-out contract program   a program under which the procuring agency breaks out suitable portions of a large contract for competitive bidding by small firms

brokers   distribution intermediaries who do not take title to the goods

budget   a device for expressing future plans in monetary terms

budget account   a form of consumer credit, sometimes called a Major Purchase Account (MPA), whereby payment is ordinarily spread over a period of three months

buildup process   a forecasting process which calls for identifying all potential buyers in a market's submarkets and then adding up the estimated demand

bulk sales laws   state laws which effectively preclude a debtor from making a secret sale of an entire business before a creditor can take the necessary legal action to collect

business interruption insurance   insurance that protects companies during the period necessary to restore property damaged by an insured peril

business policies   fundamental statements which serve as guides to management practice

capital   all the possessions of a business which are devoted to the earning of income

capital budgeting   the process of planning expenditures whose returns are expected to extend well into the future

capitalization of profit   a process used in the valuation of a business based on its net income whereby the buyer first estimates the dollars of profit that may be expected and then determines the dollar amount of investment which should logically earn the estimated dollars of profit

cash budgets   budgets concerned specifically with dollars as they are received and paid out

cash-flow system   the constant movement of funds from one form of capital into another

cash method of accounting   accounting method by which revenue and expenses are recognized when cash is received or payment is made

chain of command   the superior-subordinate relationship with a downward flow of orders which serves as a channel for two-way communication

channel of distribution   the intermediary system in distribution

chattel mortgage   an interest in personal property given by a buyer to a seller as security for payment of the purchase price

circulating capital   the current-asset items consisting of cash, inventories, and accounts receivable

coercive power   a group's ability to withhold material or psychological rewards

cognitive dissonance   an uncomfortable psychological tension or a feeling of inequity which tends to occur when a consumer has purchased something and then has second thoughts or doubts about the purchasing decision

coinsurance clause   a clause in an insurance policy under which the insured agrees to maintain insurance equal to some specified percentage of the property value or otherwise to assume a portion of any loss

commercial finance companies   institutions that make loans based on securities such as inventories, accounts receivable, equipment, or other items

commission agents (in foreign market distribution)   "finders" for foreign firms wanting to purchase domestic products

committee organization   a variation of the line-and-staff structure which superimposes committees designed to help managers reach necessary decisions by exploring the pros and cons of a given situation

common carriers   transportation intermediaries that are available for hire to the general public

composition settlement   an agreement whereby the creditors of an insolvent business agree to accept reduced amounts due them, on a pro rata basis

computer   a complex data processing machine, outperforming humans in some tasks of recording, classifying, calculating, storing, and communicating information

computer system   a system consisting of a computer and its related interactive components

conditional sales contract   a sales contract whereby legal title to the product does not pass until the customer makes the last payment

consumer credit   the type of credit granted by retailers to final consumers who purchase for personal or family use

continuous operations   production operations that involve long production runs and used by firms that produce a standardized product

contract carriers   transportation intermediaries who transport products on the basis of contracts with individual shippers

contracts   legal agreements in which the parties intend to create mutual legal obligations

controlling   the management function which compares both organizational and individual performance with predetermined standards or expected results

copyright   the registered right of a creator to reproduce, publish, and sell the work which is the product of the intelligence and skill of that person

corporate refugees   individuals who flee the bureaucratic environment of big business (or even medium-size business) by going into business for themselves

corporation   a legal form of business which is an artificial being, invisible, intangible, and existing only in contemplation of the law

corporation charter   the written application for permission to incorporate which is approved by a state official

corrective maintenance   plant maintenance activities which include both the major and minor repairs necessary to restore a facility to good condition

country controlled buying agents   foreign government agencies or quasi-governmental firms empowered to locate and purchase desired goods

credit bureau   an organization of retailers and other firms in a given community which serves its members by summarizing their credit experience with particular individuals

credit insurance   insurance that protects non-retailing businesses from abnormal bad-debt losses

creditor capital   debt capital

culture   mankind's social heritage which includes customary forms of belief and behavior

current-asset capital   cash and other assets that can be converted to cash within one year

current assets   the plus side of the working-capital equation and which includes cash, accounts receivable, and inventories

current liabilities   obligations which must be paid within one year

current ratio   ratio of current assets to current liabilities

daywork   compensation based on increments of time

debt to total assets   ratio of total debts to total assets

delegation of authority   a superior's act of granting to subordinates, on the basis of competence, the right to act or to decide

deliberate search   a purposeful exploration to find a new-venture idea

demographic variables   segmentation variables that refer to certain characteristics which describe customers and their purchasing power

direct forecasting   a form of forecasting which uses sales as the predicting variable

direct loans   SBA loans made for a maximum amount of $150,000

disaster relief loans   SBA loans extended to small businesses after devastating natural disasters

distribution   the physical movement of products and the establishment of intermediary relationships to guide and support the movement of the product

distributor (in foreign market distribution)   a merchant who purchases merchandise from a domestic manufacturer at the greatest possible discount and resells it abroad

double-entry system   accounting system which incorporates journals and ledgers and requires that each transaction be recorded twice in the accounts

dual distribution   distribution that involves more than one channel

earnings approach   a business-valuation approach which centers on estimating the amount of potential income that may be produced by the business in the next year

economic opportunity loans   SBA loans provided to minority and other disadvantaged groups

economic order quantity   the quantity to be purchased which minimizes total costs

elasticity of demand   the degree to which a change in price affects the quantity demanded

elastic demand   the characteristic of demand for a product in which a change in its price produces a significant change in the quantity demanded

entrepreneurial team   a group of two or more individuals brought together to function in the capacity of entrepreneurs

entrepreneurs   people who provide the spark for our economic system by taking risks in starting and/or operating businesses

equipment leasing   leasing of equipment which provides an alternative to equipment purchasing

estate in fee simple   absolute ownership in real property

expert power   a group's ability to be perceived as being in a more knowledgeable position than the individual

export agents   agents who operate in international business in the same manner as a manufacturer's representative, but with the risk of loss remaining with the manufacturer

export management companies (EMCs) companies that act as the export department for several manufacturers of noncompetitive products

export merchants those who purchase products directly from the manufacturer, have the products packed and marked to their specifications, sell the products overseas through their contacts, in their own names, and assume all risks for their accounts

extension agreement an agreement whereby the creditors of an insolvent business agree to postpone the debtor's payment of obligations for some stipulated period of time

external locus of control a psychological characteristic of people who feel that their lives are controlled to a greater extent by luck or chance or fate than by their own efforts

factoring obtaining cash. *before* accounts receivable payments are received from customers by selling the accounts receivable for their full value to a factor

FIFO (First-In-First-Out) inventory valuation system which assumes that the first product in inventory is the first product out of inventory

fixed-asset capital assets intended for long, continued use in the business

fixed assets the relatively permanent assets that are intended for use in a business rather than for sale

fixed-asset turnover the ratio of sales to fixed assets

fixed costs those costs that remain constant in total amount at different levels of quantity sold

floppy disks a form of external data storage which is entered into disk drive units to receive data and programs or load existing data programs into the computer

four Cs of credit character, capital, capacity, and conditions

foreign retailer a retailer located outside the United States to whom selling is accomplished through traveling sales representatives or by direct mailing of catalogs, brochures, or other literature

Foreign Sales Corporation (FSC) a United States corporation selling in international markets that receives tax deferrals (replaced the Domestic International Sales Corporation)

Foreign Trade Zone (FTZ) a site which allows foreign shipments to be received duty-free

founders individuals who are generally considered to be the "pure" entrepreneurs because they initiate businesses on the basis of new or improved products or services

franchise   the privileges contained in a franchise contract

franchise contract   the legal agreement between a franchisor and a franchisee

franchisee   the party in a franchise contract who is granted the privilege to conduct business as an individual owner but is required to operate according to methods and terms specified by the other party

franchising   a marketing system revolving around a two-party legal agreement whereby one party is granted the privilege to conduct business as an individual owner but is required to operate according to methods and terms specified by the other party

franchisor   the party in a franchise contract who specifies the methods and terms to be followed by the other party

free-flow pattern   a type of retail store, curving-aisles layout which makes less efficient use of space than the grid pattern but has greater visual appeal and allows customers to move in any direction at their own speed

functional expenses   expenses that relate to specific selling and administrative activities of a business

funds   money, checks received but not yet deposited, and balances on deposit with financial institutions

general liability insurance   insurance that covers business liability to customers or others who might be injured on the premises or off-premises or who might be injured from the product sold to them

general managers   a class of entrepreneurs who are less innovators and more administrators of their businesses

general partner   any partner in a general partnership or a partner in a limited partnership who remains personally liable for the debts of the business

grid pattern   a type of retail store, block-looking layout which provides more merchandise exposure and simplifies security and cleaning

hard disks   data storage devices which are capable of storing larger amounts of information and which read and write data much faster than floppy disks

hardware   a term which refers primarily to the computer processor unit and items of peripheral equipment used for data input, data output, and data storage

holder in due course   the individual or business who has possession of a negotiable instrument and is not subject to many of the defenses possible in the case of ordinary contracts

imputed expenses   expenses that do not exist in the sense that they can be entered on the books of account and appear on the income statement

income statement   a financial statement which shows the results of a firm's operations over a period of time, usually one year

incubator facilities   facilities that provide shared space, services, and management assistance to reduce initial operational costs of several small businesses

inelastic demand   the characteristic of demand for a product whereby a change in its price does not bring about a significant difference in the quantity demanded

indirect forecasting   a form of forecasting which uses other forecasts to project the sales forecast

inside-out approach   an approach used by potential entrepreneurs in a deliberate search for new-venture ideas by first surveying their own capabilities and then looking at the new products or services they are capable of producing

inspection   scrutinizing a part or a product to determine whether it is good or bad

installment account   a form of consumer credit which normally requires a down payment of the purchase price, with the balance of payments made over a period of months or years

institutional advertising   type of advertising that conveys an idea regarding the business establishment

instrumental tie   a tie among entrepreneurs who find their networking relationship mutually rewarding in a practical way

intermittent operations   production operations that involve short production runs with only one or a few products being produced before shifting to a different production setup (also known as job-order production)

internal locus of control   a psychological characteristic of entrepreneurs who believe that their success depends upon their own efforts

internal-rate-of-return method   investment evaluation where a stream of expected net cash flows is discounted at the rate which results in a zero net present value (NPV)

inventory-carrying costs   costs that include interest costs on money tied up in inventory, insurance, storage, obsolescence, and pilferage costs

inventory turnover   ratio of sales or cost of sales to inventories

kanban system   a system of reducing inventory levels to minimize inventory-carrying costs (also known as "just-in-time" inventory)

LIFO (Last-In-First-Out) inventory valuation which assumes that the most recent cost of a product placed in inventory is charged against revenue regardless of whether that most recent unit was actually sold and delivered to a customer

laws of motion economy principles concerning work arrangement, the use of the human hands and body, and the design and use of tools that are intended to increase efficiency

leading/motivating the management function which involves directing and inspiring those who are part of the organization

lease an agreement whereby a property owner confers upon a tenant the right of possession and use of real property for which the tenant pays rent

legal entity the characteristic of a corporation which permits it to sue and be sued, hold and sell property, and engage in business operations stipulated in the corporate charter

legitimate power recognition of the power of a group (or individual) as right and proper

libel printed defamation of one's reputation

limited partners partners who have limited personal liability as long as they do not take an active role in the management of the limited partnership

limited partnership a partnership which consists of at least one general partner and one or more limited partners

line activities those activities that contribute directly to the primary objectives of a firm

line-and-staff organization an organization structure in which staff specialists exist who perform specialized services or act as management advisers in special areas

linear programming a quantitative tool which involves the use of mathematical algorithms for evaluating the results from several alternative courses of action, each of which contains a number of variables

line organization an organization structure in which each person has one supervisor to whom he or she reports and looks for instructions

liquidation value approach an asset-based approach in the valuation of a business which equates the value of the business with its salvage value if operations ceased

mainframe a maxicomputer, or a large machine which is capable of processing large amounts of information in a very short time and has a large internal memory

management   all the activities undertaken to secure the accomplishment of work through the efforts of other people

management functions   the managerial activities which include planning, organizing, leading/motivating, and controlling

market   a group of customers or potential customers who have purchasing power and unsatisfied needs

marketing   those business activities which relate directly to determining target markets and preparing, communicating, and delivering a bundle of satisfaction to these markets

marketing concept   a consumer-oriented marketing management philosophy

marketing-information systems   an organized way of gathering market-related information on a regular basis

marketing research   the gathering, processing, reporting, and interpreting of marketing information

market segmentation   the process of analyzing one market to find out if it should be viewed as more than one market

market value approach   the approach used in the valuation of a business which relies on previous sales of similar businesses

mechanic's lien   a claim by contractors, laborers, or suppliers against the property if the property owner or tenant defaults in payments for either materials or labor

merchant middlemen   distribution intermediaries who take title to the goods

microcomputer   a personal computer which allows its operator to use it without having extensive training and technical expertise and which can be upgraded to provide the memory capacity needed to handle day-to-day activities of a small business

micromotion study   a refinement of time study which uses a motion-picture camera, rather than a stopwatch, to record the elemental motions, as well as the times

minicomputer   a computer which requires special facilities preparation, usually needs ongoing maintenance and does not necessarily require full-time operations personnel or the technical knowledge that a mainframe requires

minority contract program   a special set-aside program which permits government purchases from minority-owned firms without competitive bidding

modem   a device which connects one computer to another computer via a telephone line

moral tie   a tie among entrepreneurs which involves some type of mutual obligation or commitment in their networking relationships

motion study   a detailed observation of all the actual motions that the observed worker makes to complete a job under a given set of physical conditions

motivations   goal-directed forces within humans which organize and give direction to tension caused by unsatisfied needs

multisegmentation strategy   the marketing strategy used by a business when it recognizes individual market segments that have different preferences and develops a unique marketing mix for each segment

needs   the basic seeds of (and the starting point for) all behavior

negotiable instruments   credit instruments that can be transferred from one party to another in place of money

net-present-value method   investment evaluation to determine the net present value (NPV) of a stream of expected net cash flows at a specified rate of return

networking   the process of developing and engaging in mutually beneficial relationships with peers

new-venture plan   a written plan describing the new-venture idea and projecting the marketing, operational, and financial aspects of the proposed business for the first three to five years

100 percent inspection   inspection of each item in every lot processed

operating budget   a composite plan for each phase of the operation of a business

opinion leader   a group member playing a key communications role

opportunity costs   the value of a lost opportunity

order costs   costs that include the preparation of a purchase order, follow-up, and related bookkeeping expenses

ordinary charge account   a form of consumer credit where the customer obtains possession of goods or services when purchased, with payment due when billed

organizing   the management function which assigns tasks and duties to departmental components and to individual employees and which specifies relationships among departments and individuals

outside-in approach   an approach used by potential entrepreneurs in a deliberate search for new-venture ideas by first looking for needs in the marketplace and then relating those needs to their own existing or potential capabilities

owner capital   ownership equity in a business

participation loans   loans granted by the SBA in cooperation with private banks in which the degree of participation by the SBA ranges up to 90 percent

partnership   a voluntary association of two or more persons to carry on as co-owners a business for profit

patent   the registered right of an inventor to make, use, and sell an invention

payback-period method   method of valuation which shows the number of years it takes to recover the original cost of an investment from annual net cash flows

perception   the individual processes which ultimately give meaning to the stimuli that confront consumers

perceptual categorization   the process whereby consumers attempt to manage huge quantities of incoming stimuli and perceive as belonging together those things which are similar

perpetual inventory system   a system which provides a current record of inventory items and does not require a physical count

personal property   property that is movable in nature

personal selling   promotion delivered in a one-on-one environment

physical distribution, or logistics   the physical movement activities in distribution

planning   the management function which requires decisions about a future course of action and involves goal setting

present value   the value today of a stream of expected net cash flows, discounted at an appropriate rate of interest

preventive maintenance   plant maintenance activities which include inspections and other activities intended to prevent machine breakdowns and damage to people and buildings

price line   a range of several distinct prices at which merchandise is offered for sale

pricing   the systematic determination of the "right" price for a product

primary data new information for which a search is made through various methods

private carriers shippers who own their means of transport

private placement selling of a firm's capital stock to selected individuals

process layout a type of factory layout where similar machines are grouped together

product the total "bundle of satisfaction" which is offered to customers in an exchange transaction

product advertising type of advertising designed to make potential customers aware of a particular product or service and of their need for it

production control procedures that have been developed most extensively in manufacturing which consist of steps designed to achieve the orderly sequential flow of products through the plant at a rate commensurate with scheduled deliveries to customers

product item the lowest common denominator in a product mix—the individual item

product layout a type of factory layout where machines are arranged according to the need for them in the production process

product line the sum of the individual product items that are related

product mix the collection of product lines within a firm's ownership and control

product mix consistency the logical relationship of the product lines to each other

product strategy the manner in which the product component of the marketing mix is used to achieve the objectives of a firm

profit margin on sales ratio of net profit to sales

promotion communication between the business and its target market

proprietorship a business owned and operated by one person

prospecting a systematic process of continually looking for new customers

purchase order an order to buy which, when accepted by a vendor, becomes a binding contract

purchase requisition a formal, documented request from an employee or a manager for something to be bought for the business

purchasing   a process involving receipt of a purchase request, locating a source of supply, issuing a purchase order, maintaining the buying and warehousing records, following up on the purchase order, and receiving the goods

quality circle   a group of employees, usually a dozen or fewer, performing similar or related work, who meet periodically to identify, analyze, and solve production problems, particularly those involving product or service quality

queuing theory   a quantitative tool which consists of the use of calculated probabilities for determining the number of persons who will stand in a line (also known as waiting-line theory)

real property   property which consists of land and buildings and other installations permanently attached to land (also known as real estate)

reciprocal buying   a policy based on the premise that one company can secure additional orders by using its own purchasing requests as a bargaining weapon

reference groups   those groups from which an individual allows influence to be exerted upon his or her behavior

referent power   a group's ability to cause consumers to conform to its behavior and to choose products selected by its members

reorder point   the point at which additional quantities of materials or merchandise should be reordered

replacement cost approach   an asset-based approach used in the valuation of a business which relies on finding the replacement value of the property being purchased

retained earnings   realized profits that are plowed back into a business

return-on-investment method   method of evaluating proposals by relating the expected annual profit from an investment to the amount invested but disregarding the time value of money

return on net worth   ratio of net profit to net worth

return on total assets   ratio of net profit to total assets

revolving credit account   a variation of the installment account whereby the seller grants a line of credit up to a certain amount and the customer may charge purchases at any time if purchases do not exceed this credit limit

reward power   a group's ability to give and to withhold rewards

risk a condition in which there is a possibility of an adverse deviation from a desired outcome that is expected or hoped for

risk management all efforts designed to preserve assets and earning power by managing risk factors

safety stock a level of stock maintained to provide a measure of protection against stockouts

sales forecast the prediction of how much of a product or service will be purchased by a market during a defined time period

sales promotion promotion which provides inducements to potential purchasers of products or services

sales representatives or agents (in foreign market distribution) the foreign counterparts of United States manufacturer's representatives

scheduled budget buying a policy of buying to meet anticipated requirements

secondary data information that has already been compiled

Section 1244 stock a type of stock which can be issued in the initial organization of a corporation which, pursuant to Section 1244 of the Internal Revenue Code, provides certain tax advantages to the stockholder if the stock becomes worthless

segmentation variables labels which identify the particular dimensions that are thought to distinguish one form of market demand from another

self-service layout a type of retail store layout which permits customers direct access to the merchandise

serendipity the faculty for making desirable discoveries by accident

set-aside program a program under which government contracting officers and SBA representatives review purchase orders to select those which may be set aside for exclusive competitive bidding by small firms

simulation a technique which permits the decision maker to gain experience in something resembling the actual situation without taking the risk existing in that situation

single-entry system a checkbook system of receipts and disbursements supported by sales tickets and disbursement receipts

single-segmentation strategy the marketing strategy used by a business when it recognizes that several distinct market segments exist but chooses to concentrate on reaching only one segment

social class a sociological concept in consumer behavior which describes the divisions in a society with different levels of social prestige

software   the programs for a computer system which contain instructions to operate the hardware

span of control   the number of subordinates who are supervised by one manager

speculative buying   the policy of buying substantially in excess of quantities needed to meet actual use requirements in the expectation that prices will go up

spreadsheets   computer programs that provide rows and columns for entry of numbers, which are entered at "cells" and used in a particular calculation to allow the user to analyze actual data and also to play "what if" games

staff activities   those activities which support or help the line activities

state controlled trading companies   businesses in countries that have state trading monopolies

statement of changes in financial position   a financial statement which shows how a firm acquired working capital and employed it over the same period covered by the income statement

statement of cost of goods manufactured   a financial statement consisting of a supporting, detailed schedule of the "cost of goods manufactured" entry in the income statement

statistical inference   the inferring of something about a large group on the basis of facts known about a smaller group

statute of frauds   a law under which sales transactions of $500 or more, sales of real estate, and contracts extending for more than 1 year must be in writing

statutes of limitations   state laws that require creditors to be reasonably prompt in filing their claims

stock cards   the basic control tool in a perpetual inventory system for finished goods

stockouts   not having items in inventory which may result in lost sales or disrupted production

stores card   the basic control tool in a perpetual inventory system covering raw materials and supplies

Subchapter S corporation   a business arrangement which allows stockholders to be taxed as partners and thus avoid the corporate income tax

subcultural analysis   an investigation of culture with a narrower definitional boundary such as age, religious preference, ethnic orientation, or geographical location

surety bonds bonds that insure against the failure of another firm or individual to fulfill a contractual obligation

system software programs that control the overall operations of the computer including input and output processing and are the link between hardware devices and application programs

tenancy at will the condition under which a lease may be terminated at any time upon the request of either party

time-series techniques forecasting techniques which rely on historical data and on quantitative tools

time-sharing system the sharing of one computer by several users where terminals to collect data are located at the office of each user and the computer runs the programs for all users in sequence

times-interest-earned ratio ratio of operating income to interest charges

time study the timing and recording of each elemental motion of a job on an observation sheet

total cost the cost which includes the cost of goods or services offered for sale, the selling cost, and the general overhead cost applicable to the given product or service

trade credit the type of credit extended by nonfinancial firms to customers which are also business firms

trade-credit agencies privately owned and operated organizations which collect credit information on business firms

trademark a legal term describing a word, figure, or other symbol used to distinguish a product sold by one manufacturer or merchant

turnkey system a package consisting of computer hardware and software that are produced by the vendor and sold as a unit

two-bin method a simple technique for maintaining safety stock which divides inventory into two portions; when the first bin is exhausted, an order is placed to replenish the supply while the portion in the second bin should cover needs until a new supply arrives

unfair-trade practice laws laws which specify that sellers may not sell goods at less than their cost and also specify certain percentage markups

unsegmented strategy the marketing strategy used by a business when it defines the total market as its target market

variable expenses expenses that are fixed on a per-unit basis but vary in total amount for month and year with the volume of goods manufactured or sold

variables sampling plan   a statistical method of quality control which measures many characteristics of an item, rather than simply judging the item as acceptable or unacceptable, by taking periodic random samples which are plotted on a chart to discover if the process is out of control and thus requires corrective action

venture capitalist   investment group that invests in new-business ventures

word processing   any process that involves textual information and uses such equipment as typesetters, copiers, and automatic typewriters

work improvement   finding work methods that demand the least physical effort and the shortest execution time at the lowest possible cost

working-capital management   the management of current assets and current liabilities

work sampling   a method of work measurement which provides little operating detail but estimates the ratio of actual working time and downtime

work study   an analysis of equipment and tooling, plant layout, working conditions, and individual jobs

warranty   a promise that a product will do certain things

INDEX

A

ABC inventory analysis, defined, 489
accidental discovery, as basis for new-venture idea, 81–83
accounting: accepted principles of, 503–504; accrual method of, 508; cash method of, 508; double-entry system, 509; single-entry system, 508
accounting options, selecting alternative, 507–510
accounting principles: accepted, 503–504; observance of, 518–519
accounting records, 504–506; physical protection of, 507; retention of, 506–507
accounting statements: balance sheet, 510; changes in financial position, 513; cost of goods manufactured, 510; income, 510; typical, 510–514
accounting system, major considerations underlying, 503–507
accounts: budget, 309; charge, 308–309; installment, 309; past-due, collection of, 313–314; revolving credit, 309
accounts payable: computerized, 572; managing, 545–548; and negotiation, 546; and timing, 546–548
accounts-payable records, 505
accounts receivable: aging, 542–544; computerized, 571–572; and current-asset capital, 203–204; level of, 207; life cycle of, 544; managing, 542–544
accounts-receivable records, 505
accrual method of accounting, 508
achievement, need for, 11–12

acid-test (quick) ratio, 515
actual expenses, defined, 523
advertising, 333–336; bait, 620; defined, 333; ethical, 388–389; frequency of, 335–336; help-wanted, 434; institutional, 334; location of, 336; objectives of, 333; product, 333; types of, 333–335
advisors, board of, 423–424
affective tie, defined, 371
agency, defined, 244
agency power, defined, 237
agency relationships, 244–245
agent, 244, 292
aging schedule, defined, 542
antitrust laws, impact of, 617–618
a percentage of sales (APS), method of funding promotion, 324–325
applicant: evaluation of, 436–438; interviewing, 436–438; testing, 438; unsolicited, 433
application software, defined, 569
applied probability models, as aid in planning, 402–403
articles of partnership, defined, 237
as much as competition spends (ACS), method of funding promotion, 325
asset requirements: calculating, 206–208; cross-checking with break-even analysis, 208–209
assets: current, 203; protection of, and inventory control, 487–488
assorting, defined, 291
assured continuous operations, and inventory control, 487
attitudes, and consumer behavior, 266–267
attorney, choosing, 249–250

attractive small firms, defined, 20
attributes sampling plans, defined, 466
audit, independent, 155
authority: equal, and responsibility, 419; delegation of, 417–419
automated equipment, 193–194
average collection period ratio, defined, 516
average cost, defined, 301
average pricing, defined, 301

B
bad-debt ratio, defined, 314
bad debts, risk of, 601
bait advertising, defined, 620
balance sheet, pro-forma, 520
bankers, as source of information on location, 185
bankruptcy, 649–650
banks: commercial, as sources of funds, 217–220; selection of, 218–220
benefit variables, 110–111; defined, 110
big business, and small businesses, 67–68
billing, computerized, 571
bill of materials, 459
block control technique, 460
board of advisors, alternative to board of directors, 423–424
board of directors: alternatives to, 423–424; compensation of, 423; contribution of, 421; defined, 240; selection of, 422–423; in small corporations, 420–424
branding, 279–280; defined, 279
breakdown process, defined, 123
break-even analysis: and business plan, 94; cross-checking with asset requirements, 208–209; defined, 303; in pricing, 303–305
break-even point, 208
breaking bulk, defined, 291
break-out contract program, defined, 632
brokers, 292
budget: defined, 397; operating, 519–520; revisions, 523; using to control and reduce expenses, 523–525
budget account, defined, 309

budgetary control deficiencies, in small businesses, 525
budgeting: capital, 538; capital, in small business, 548–553; cash, 540–542; in small firms, 519–525
buildings, and evaluating an existing business, 161
buildings and layout, 186–191; and functional requirements, 187–188; and spatial requirements, 187; and structural requirements, 188–189
buildup process, defined, 123
bulk sales laws, defined, 244
burglary, risk of, 596
business: advantages of family involvement in, 32–33; closing deal to purchase, 162; existing, buying, *See* existing business; family. *See* family business; finding to buy, 154; negotiating purchase price and terms of, 162; small. *See* small business; valuation of, 156–160
business decisions, and family decisions, 32
business ethics: and advertising, 388–389; consistency in, 387–388; development of, 387; formal code of, 388; and small business, 386–387
business interruption insurance, defined, 605
business law, and small business, 243–249
business opportunity, finding, 79–80
business owners: estate planning for, 628; financial security of, 629
business plans. *See also* new-venture plan: computer-aided, 94; kinds of, 397–398; long-range, 397; short-range, 397; uses of, 94–95
business policies, 397–398; defined, 397
business suppliers, as sources of funds, 215–217
business swindles, risk of, 596
buyers, benefits of sellers to, 308
buying: making or, 482–483; reciprocal, 481–482; scheduled budget, 485; speculative, 485
buying records, maintenance of, 480–481

C

capital: circulating, 203; creditor, 210; current-asset, 203–204, 537; debt, 210; defined, 537; fixed-asset, 204–205, 537; incentives for long-term, 629; initial, 210–212; loss of, in business failure, 646; owner, 210; promotion-expense, 205; retention of, 629; working, 537

capital budgeting: defined, 538; in small business, 548–553

capitalists, venture, 87–88, 94

capitalization of profit, defined, 158

capital stock, sale of to fund business, 214–215

career risk, 12

carriers, 293

cash, and current-asset capital, 203

cash budgeting, process of, 540–542

cash budgets, defined, 540

cash flow, nature of, 538–539

cash flow forecast, and business plan, 93–94

cash-flow system, defined, 539

cash method of accounting, defined, 508

cash pool, managing, 538–542

cash records, 505

cash requirements, 206–207

certified public accounting (CPA) firms, and management assistance, 367

chain of command, defined, 413

chambers of commerce, as source of information on location, 185

channels of distribution, 289–293; and control, 293; and costs, 292; and coverage, 292; defined, 289; direct, 289; foreign, 294–298; indirect, 289; justifying, 290–292

charge accounts, 308–309; ordinary, 308

chattel mortgage, defined, 309

circulating capital, defined, 203

city: choice of and location, 177–178; growth or decline of, 177

closing, of purchase of business, 162

coercive power, defined, 269

cognitive dissonance, defined, 271

coinsurance clause, defined, 605

collateral arrangements, 217–218

collection: of past-due accounts, 313–314; procedure, 314

commercial banks, as sources of funds, 217–220

commercial finance companies, as sources of funds, 222

commercial liability insurance, 606–607

committee organization, defined, 415

common carriers, defined, 293

communication, effective, 445–446

communication process, 322–323

community developments, and evaluating an existing business, 160

compensation: financial, 332; legislation affecting, 444–445; nonfinancial, 332; of salespeople, 331–332; for small-business employees, 442–445

competition: and evaluating an existing business, 160; extent of local, 178; maintenance of free, regulations for, 617–620; unfair, impact of laws on, 618

competitive strengths, of small business, 640–643

composition settlement, defined, 650

computer: buying, 581-584; defined, 566; future of, 584; leasing, 580–581

computer-aided business planning, 94

computer applications: first stage, 571–575; second-stage, 575–578; for small business, 571–578

computer systems, 566–570; defined, 566; types of, 567–568

conditional sales contract, 217; defined, 309

consultants, management. See management consultants

consumer behavior: and attitudes, 266–267; concepts of, 263–272; and consumer decision making, 271–272; modern roadmap of, 263–272; and psychological concepts, 263–266; and sociological concepts, 267–271

consumer credit, 308–309; defined, 308

consumer decision making, and con-

sumer behavior, 271-272
consumerism, and small business, 386
consumer protection, regulation of, 620
continuous operations, defined, 457
contract, conditional sales, 309
contract carriers, defined, 293
contract construction, and small businesses, 58
contracts, 243-244; conditional sales, 217; government, assistance in obtaining, 630-632
control: and channels of distribution, 293; inventory. See inventory control; quality, 463-467
controllable expenses, 524-525
controlling, 354-355; defined, 354
copyright, defined, 248
copyright protection, 248-249
core marketing activities, 262
corporate charter, 241-242; defined, 242
"corporate refugees," defined, 13
corporations: characteristics of, 239-242; defined, 239; small, and board of directors, 420-424; Subchapter S, 242
corrective maintenance, defined, 462
cost-adjusted break-even stage, 303-305
cost break-even stage, 303
cost control in personal selling, 330-331
costs: average, 301; of business failure, 646-647; of channels of distribution, 292; considerations in pricing, 300-301; of consulting services, 372; inventory, controlling, 488-491; inventory-carrying, 489; location, 179; opportunity, 524; order, 489; reduction of inspection, 465; total, 300; total fixed, 300-301; total variable, 300
coverage, and channels of distribution, 292
craftsman entrepreneur, 20-21; defined, 20
credit: benefits of to sellers and buyers, 308; consumer, 308-309; decision to sell on, 310-313; four C's of, 311-312; investigation of applicants,

312; kinds of, 308-310; limits, 312; in small business, 307-314; sources of information on, 312-313; trade, 216
credit bureau, defined, 313
credit insurance, 605-606; defined, 605
creditor capital, defined, 210
culture, 268-269; defined, 268
current-asset capital, 203-204; and accounts receivable, 203-204; and cash, 203; defined, 537; and inventories, 203
current assets, defined, 203
current product/current market product strategy, 273
current product/new market product strategy, 273
current ratio, defined, 515
customer accessibility, and location, 174, 179
customer-centered risk, 599-601
customer goodwill, building, 332
customers: knowledge of, 640-641; on-premise injury, risk of, 599
customer traffic, amount of, and location, 179-180

D

daywork, defined, 442
debt capacity, unused, 218
debt capital, 210
debt position, ratios related to, 518
debts, increasing, 649
debt to total assets ratio, defined, 518
delegation of authority: defined, 417; and organization of firm, 417-419
deliberate search, as basis for new venture idea, 83-84; defined, 83
delivery terms, and distribution, 293-294
demand: considerations in pricing, 301-302; elastic, 302; elasticity of, 302; factors affecting, 301-302; inelastic, 302
demand for product, falling, risk of, 594
demographic variables, 111-113; defined, 111

departmentation, and organization of firm, 417

development, suburban, and location, 181

development and training. *See* training and development

direct loans, defined, 221

directors, board of, 240

disaster relief loans, defined, 221

discounts, purchase, taking all, 484

discovery, accidental, 81–83

distribution, 289–299; abroad, 294–299. *See also* foreign distribution; channels of, 289–293. *See also* channels of distribution; choosing a system of, 292–293; defined, 289; and delivery terms, 293–294; dual, 290; and materials handling, 293; physical, 289; scope of physical, 293–294; and storage, 293; and transportation, 293

double-entry system of accounting, 508–509; defined, 509

dual distribution, defined, 290

E

earnings, retained, 555

earnings approach, 158–160; defined, 158

economic competition, and small business, 66–67

economic concepts, traditional, 263

economic conditions, deteriorating, risk of, 592–594

economic opportunity loans, defined, 221

economic order quantity, 490–491; defined, 491

education, entrepreneurial, 84–85

efficiency, small business, 68–69

elastic demand, defined, 302

elasticity of demand, defined, 302

employee-centered risks, 596–599

employee participation, in planning, 395–397

employees. *See also* personnel: checking references of, 438; dishonest, risk of, 597; and entrepreneur, personal contact between, 447; former, risk of, 598–599; leasing, 439; physical examination of, 438; referrals

of, 433; small-business, compensation and incentives for, 442–445; sources of, 433–434; training nonmanagerial, 440–441

employment agencies: private, 433; public, 433

entrepreneurial education and experience, 84–85

entrepreneurial roles, defined, 18

entrepreneurial styles, 20–21; defined, 18

entrepreneurial teams, defined, 21

entrepreneurial ventures, 18–20; defined, 18

entrepreneurs: characteristics of, 11–14; craftsman, 20–21; defined, 3; and employees, personal contact between, 447; founding, 18; and need for achievement, 11–12; and need to seek refuge, 13–14; networks of, 368–372; opportunistic, 21; pervading influence of, 447–448; and self-confidence, 12–13; and willingness to take risks, 12

entrepreneurship: readiness for, 14–17; rewards of, 9–11; self-evaluation for, 16–17

environmental conditions, and location, 172–173

environmentalism, and small business, 384–386

environmental protection laws, impact of, 621

equipment: automated, 193–194; factory, 191–192; general-purpose, 191–192; retail store, 192; special-purpose, 191–192; and tooling, 191–194

equipment leasing, defined, 217

equipment loans, 217

equity, ownership, 210

estate in fee simple, defined, 245

estate planning, for business owners, 628

ethics, business. *See* business ethics

executives, death of key, risk of, 597–598

exhibits, and sales promotion, 341

existing business: buying, 152–162; closing deal to purchase, 162; investigating and evaluating, 154–161;

negotiating purchase price and terms, 162; reasons for buying, 152–154

expansion opportunities: approach to financing, 555–556; considerations in evaluating, 553–556; and growth philosophy, 553; and search activities, 553–555

expenditures, promotional, methods of determining, 324–325

expenses: actual, 523–524; controllable, 524–525; fixed, 524; functional, 524; imputed, 523–524; noncontrollable, 524–525; personal, funds for, 205; using the budget to control and reduce, 523–525; variable, 524

experience, entrepreneurial, 84–85

expertise, promotional, sources of, 325–327

expert power, defined, 270

export sales, government assistance in, 632

Export Trading Company Act (ETCA), 298

extension agreement, defined, 650

external locus of control, defined, 13

F

factor, defined, 204

factoring, defined, 203

factory equipment, 191–192

factory layout, 190

failure: causes of, 647–648; costs of, 646–647; and loss of capital, 646; psychological effects of, 646–647; rate, of small business, 646; and small business, 646–649; and social and economic losses, 647; symptoms of, 648–649

family business: and couples, 36–37; culture of, 33–34; defined, 30; and entrepreneur's spouse, 39–41; and family roles and relationships, 35–41; founders of, 35–36; and in-laws, 39; nonfamily members in, 34; and process of succession, 41; and sibling cooperation/rivalry, 38–39; and sons and daughters, 37–38; and transferring ownership, 46–47

family decisions, and business decisions, 32

family involvement in business, advantages of, 32–33

family risk, 12

family roles and relationships, 35–41

feasibility study, in deciding to computerize, 578–579

FIFO inventory valuation, 509–510, 627

financial companies, as small businesses, 59

financial compensation, for salespeople, 332

financial incentives, in small firms, 442–443

financial institutions, as sources of funds, 217–221

financial plan, and business plan, 92–94

financial planning, computerized, 575–576

financial requirements: estimating, 205–210; nature of, 203–205

financial risk, 12

financial security, for business owners, 629

financial statements, analysis of, 514–519

financing, difficulties in, 644–645

financing proposal: defined, 223; points to consider in, 223–226

fire hazards, risk of, 594–596

fixed-asset capital, 204–205; defined, 537

fixed-asset requirements, 208

fixed assets: defined, 204; intangible, 204; minimizing investments in, 209–210; tangible, 204

fixed-asset turnover ratio, 516–517

fixed expenses, defined, 524

fixed security investments, 204

flexible pricing, 305–306

floppy disks, defined, 568

forecasting, as aid in planning, 404

foreign distribution, 294–299; financial incentives for, 298; sales and channels of, 294–298; sources of assistance for, 294

foreign markets, understanding, 294

"foreign refugees," 13

Foreign Sales Corporation (FSC), 298

Foreign Trade Zone (FTZ), 298

founders: defined, 18; as managers, 360–362

four C's of credit, 311–312

franchise: buying, 138–145; cost of, 144; defined, 135; evaluating opportunities of, 145–150; investigating offer, 147; and loss of independence, 144–145; marketing and management benefits of, 143–144; selling, 150–152

franchise contract: defined, 135; examining, 147–150; and restrictions on growth, 144

franchisee: defined, 18, 135; financial assistance for, 142–143; training of, 139–142

franchising: advantages of, 139–144; defined, 135; early, 137–138; in the eighties, 138, frauds, 150; limitations of, 144–145; scope and development of, 135–138; vs. starting an independent business, 138–139; terminology of, 135; types of, 136–137

franchisor, defined, 135

free-flow pattern layout, defined, 190

functional expenses, defined, 524

functional requirements, of buildings, 187–188

funds: defined, 538; from friends, relatives, and local investors, 212–214; locating sources of. *See* sources of funds

G

general ledger, computerized, 572

general liability insurance, defined, 606

general managers, defined, 18

general partner, defined, 238

general-purpose equipment, 191–192; advantages of, 192

geographic specialization, 641

good housekeeping, and plant safety, 462–463

goodwill, building customer, 332

government agencies, as source of information on location, 186

governmental assistance, 629–632; in export sales, 632; managerial and technical, 629–630; need to improve, 632; in obtaining government contracts, 630–632

governmental regulation, 617–626; attempts to reduce burden of, 624; burden on small business of, 623–626; and consumer protection, 620; to maintain free competition, 617–620; need for flexibility in, 625–626; and political power of small business, 622–623; and promotion of public welfare, 621–622; and protection of investors, 620

government contracts, assistance in obtaining, 630–632

government-sponsored agencies, as sources of funds, 221–222

grid pattern layout, defined, 190

growth objective, of small business, 382–383

growth philosophy, and expansion, 553

H

hard disks, defined, 568

hardware, defined, 568

help-wanted advertising, as source of employees, 434

high-potential ventures, defined, 20

hobbies, as basis of new-venture idea, 81

holder in due course, defined, 245

human relationships, effective, in the small firm, 445–449

I

imputed expenses, 523–524; defined, 523

incentives: financial, 442–443; nonfinancial, 443–444; for small-business employees, 442–445

income statement, defined, 510

"incubator organizations," 13

independence: loss of in franchise relationship, 144–145; as reward of entrepreneurship, 10

independent audit, 155

industrial parks, as source of information on location, 186

industrial research: possibilities for, 471; for small plants, 470–471

inelastic demand, 302

information, management of, computerized, 576–577

initial capital, types of, 210–212

initial public offering (IPO), 215
innovation, and small business, 64–65
inside-out approach, defined, 83
insolvency, 649–650
inspection: defined, 465; as method of quality control, 465; 100 percent, 465; points of, 465; reduction of costs of, 465; standards, 465
installment accounts, defined, 309
institutional advertising, defined, 334
instrumental ties, defined, 371
insurance: business interruption, 605; commercial, 606–607; credit, 605–606; general liability, 606; key-person, 607; for small business, 603–607; requirements for obtaining, 604; types of, 604–607
insurance companies, as small businesses, 59–60
insurance programs, basic principles of, 603–604
intermittent operations, defined, 457
internal locus of control, defined, 12
internal-rate-of-return method of investment valuation, 551–552
invention of new product, 81
inventories, and current-asset capital, 203
inventory: managing, 544–545; staying on top of, 545
inventory accounting systems, 491
inventory-carrying costs, defined, 489
inventory control, 487–494; and assured continuous operations, 487; computerized, 572–574; and costs, 488–491; and inventory records, 488; and maximum sales, 487; and minimum inventory investment, 488; objectives of, 487–488; and protection of assets, 487–488
inventory costs: controlling, 488–491; types of, 489
inventory investment, minimum, and inventory control, 488
inventory records, 505; administrative uses of, 488
inventory requirements, 207
inventory turnover ratio, 488; defined, 516
inventory valuation: FIFO, 509–510; LIFO, 509–510; retail, 492–494

investments, fixed security, 204
investment valuation: criticisms of theoretically correct methods, 552–553; internal-rate-of-return method, 551–552; net-present-value method, 550–551; payback-period method, 549; return-on-investment method, 549; theoretically correct methods of, 550–553; traditional methods of, 548–550; weakness of traditional methods, 550
investors: individual, as sources of funds, 212–215; and preparation of business plan, 87–88; protection of, 620

J
Job Instruction Training (JIT), 441
jobs, new, and small business, 62–64
"just-in-time" inventory, 490

K
kanban system, defined, 490
key-person insurance, 607

L
labeling, 280–281
labor supply, adequacy of and location, 176–177
labor unions, and small business, 448–449
law, business. *See* business law
laws of motion economy, defined, 468–469
layouts, 189–191; and building, 186–191; defined, 189; factory, 190; free-flow pattern, 190; grid pattern, 190; process, 190; product, 190; retail store, 190–191; self-service, 191
leading and motivating, 352–354; defined, 352
lease, defined, 245
leasing: of computer, 580–581; of employees, 439; of equipment, 217
legal commitments, and evaluating an existing business, 160
legal organization, options for, 234–236
legitimate power, defined, 270
liability, limited, of stockholders, 241
libel, defined, 249

libelous acts, 249

licensing, impact of laws on, 622

lien, mechanic's, 244

LIFO inventory valuation, 509–510, 627

limitations, statutes of, 244

limited partners, defined, 238

limited partnership, defined, 238

line activities, defined, 414

line-and-staff organization, 414–415; defined, 414

linear programming, as aid to planning, 402

line of credit, and business funding, 218

line organization, 413–414; defined, 413

liquidation value approach, defined, 158

loans: direct, 221; disaster relief, 221; economic opportunity, 221; equipment, 217; long-term, and business funding, 218; participation, 221; Small Business Administration, 221

location: and adequacy of labor supply, 176–177; and amount of customer traffic, 179–180; and availability of raw materials, 176; and choice of actual site, 178–181; and choice of city, 177–178; and choice of region, 175–176; and costs, 179; and customer accessibility, 174, 179; and environmental conditions, 172–173; evaluating geographical, 175–181; importance of, 170–171; and nearness to market, 176; and neighborhood conditions, 180; and resource availability, 173–174; selecting, 171–186; and small manufacturer, 184–185; and small retailer, 182; and small service firm, 182–184; and small wholesaler, 181; sources of information about, 185–186; and suburban development, 181

logistics, defined, 189

long-range business plans, 397

long-term loans, and business funding, 218

losses, social and economic in business failure, 647

M

mainframe computer, defined, 567

maintenance: corrective, 462; plant, 460–463; preventive, 462; role of, in small firms, 460–461; types of, 462

management: defined, 351; flexibility in, 643; outside assistance, 364–374. See also management assistance; small business. See small-business management; time, 363–364; work, methods of, 469

management assistance: and CPA firms, 367; and management consultants, 368; need for outside, 364–365; outside, 364–374; and SBI programs, 365; and SCORE, 366–367; sources of, 365–368

management benefits, of franchise, 143–144

management consultants: common criticisms of, 373–374; cost of services, 372; and management assistance, 368; selection of, 372–373

management functions: defined, 351; in small business, 351–355

management of information, computerized, 576–577

management and operations, and business plan, 91–92

managerial personnel: developing, 441–442; recruiting, 435–436

managers: and decision making, 362–363; founders as, 360–362; professional, 448; time-savers for, 363–364

manufacturers: small, and location, 184–185; as source of information on location, 186

manufacturing, and small businesses, 60–61

marginal firms, defined, 19

market analysis: benefits of, 113; process of, 105–113

market-centered risks, 592–594

marketing, weaknesses in, 645–646

marketing activities: core, 262; defined, 262; for small businesses, 261–262

marketing benefits, of franchise, 143–144

marketing concept, defined, 105

marketing-information systems, 118–120; defined, 118

marketing issues, and business plan, 89–91

marketing management philosophies, 105–106; factors that influence, 106; types of, 105–106; understanding, 105–106

marketing objective, of small business, 382

marketing research, 113–120; computerized, 577–578; defined, 115; nature of for small business, 115; neglect of, 113–114; steps in procedure of, 115–118

markets: defined, 104–105; and evaluating an existing system, 160; foreign, understanding, 294; knowledge of, 640–641; nearness to, and location, 176

market segmentation strategies, 106–113; need for, 107; types of, 107

market segmentation variables, 110–113; benefit, 110–111; defined, 110; demographic, 111–113

market value approach, defined, 156

materials: bill of, 459; substituting, 483–484

materials handling, and distribution, 293

mathematical programming, as aid to planning, 402

maximum sales, and inventory control, 487

mechanic's lien, defined, 244

merchandise, substituting, 483–484

merchant middlemen, defined, 292

microcomputer, defined, 567

micromotion study, defined, 469

middlemen, merchant, 292

minicomputer, defined, 567

mining, and small businesses, 60

minority contract program, defined, 631

mix, promotional, 324

modem, defined, 579

modified product/current market product strategy, 274

modified product/new market product strategy, 274

moral tie, defined, 371

mortgage, chattel, 309

motion economy, laws of, 468–469

motion study, defined, 469

motivations, defined, 266

multisegmentation strategy, defined, 108

N

national emergencies, and evaluating an existing business, 161

natural disasters, risk of, 596

needs, 265–266; defined, 265

negotiable instruments, defined, 245

negotiation, and accounts payable, 546

neighborhood conditions, and location, 180

net-present-value method of investment valuation, 550–551

networking, defined, 368

networks of entrepreneurs, 368–372

new similar product/current market product strategy, 275

new similar product/new market product strategy, 275

new unrelated product/current market product strategy, 275

new unrelated product/new market product strategy, 275

new venture: and accidental discovery, 81–83; creating, 79–85; and deliberate search, 83–84; and education and experience, 84–85; and hobbies, 81; and invention of new product, 81; plan, 85–95. *See also* new-venture plan; refining idea for, 84; sources of ideas for, 80–84; and work experience, 81

new-venture plan: to attract investors, 87–88; benefits of written, 86; and break-even analysis, 94; and cash flow forecast, 93–94; content of, 88–94; defined, 85; and financial plan, 92–94; and operations and management, 91–92; preparing, 85–95; and product and marketing issue, 89–91; and pro-forma balance sheet, 93; and projected income statement, 92; and sales forecast, 92–93

noncontrollable expenses, 524–525

nonfinancial compensation, for sales-people, 332

nonfinancial incentives, in small firms, 443–444

O

objections, overcoming in sales presentation, 329–330

objectives of small business, 381–389; growth, 382–383; marketing, 382; profit, 381–382

100 percent inspection, defined, 465

operating budget, 519–520; defined, 519

operational planning: employee participation in, 395–397; kinds of, 397–398. *See also* business plans; need for formal, 395; neglect of, 394–395; in small firms, 394–400; steps in, 398–400

operations: assured continuous, 487; continuous, 457; intermittent, 457; kinds of, 455–457; production, 455; service, 457

operations and management, and business plan, 91–92

opinion leaders, 270–271; defined, 271

opportunistic entrepreneur, defined, 21

opportunity costs, 524

order costs, defined, 489

ordering, computerized, 571

ordinary charge account, defined, 308

organization structure: committee, 415; formal, 412–415; informal, 415–416; line, 413–414; line-and-staff, 414–415; unplanned, 412–413

organizing, defined, 352

organizing function: and delegation of authority, 417–419; and departmentation, 471; and equal authority and responsibility, 419; fundamentals of, 416–420; how people affect design of, 416–417; and small-business success, 420; and span of control, 419–420

orientation, for new personnel, 440

outside-in approach, defined, 83

overregulation, 645

owner capital, defined, 210

ownership, transferring, and family business, 46–47

ownership equity, 210

P

packaging, 280

participation loans, defined, 221

partners: general, 238; limited, 238; qualifications of, 236–237; rights and duties of, 237

partnership: articles of, 237; characteristics of, 236–239; defined, 236; limited, 238–239; termination of, 238

past-due accounts, collection of, 313–314

patents: application for, 246–248; defined, 246

payback-period method of investment valuation, defined, 549

payroll, computerized, 571

payroll records, 505

perception, 264–265; defined, 264

perceptual categorization, defined, 264

perceptual inventory system, defined, 491

personal expenses, funds for, 205

personal property, defined, 245

personal satisfaction, as reward of entrepreneurship, 10

personal savings, to fund business, 212

personal selling, 327–332; cost control in, 330–331; defined, 327

personnel. *See also* employees: difficulty in obtaining qualified, 645; importance of, 432–433; orientation for new, 440; recruiting managerial and professional, 435–436; recruiting and selecting, 432–439; relationships, informal, 447; selection guidelines, 434–435

personnel manager, use of, 448

physical distribution, defined, 289

physical examination, of employee, 438

physical inventory method, 491

planning, 351–352; defined, 351; estate, 628; operational. *See* operational planning; promotional, 322–327; qualitative tools to aid, 400–404 planning and routing, and production control, 459

plans: business. See business plans; financial, and business plan, 92–94; new-venture. See new-venture plan

plant maintenance, 460–463. See also maintenance

plant safety, and good housekeeping, 462–463

policies: business, 397–398; purchasing, 481–485

political power, of small business, regulation of, 622–623

precipitating events, defined, 16

presentations, sales, 327–330

present value, defined, 550

preventive maintenance, defined, 462

price, selling, calculating, 306–307

price confirmations, 481

price-cutting, 305

price laws, impact of, 618–619

price line, defined, 306

price lining, 306

price quotations, 486

pricing, 299–307; average, 301; break-even analysis in, 303–305; cost considerations in, 300–301; defined, 299; demand considerations in, 301–302; flexible, 305–306; importance of, 300; and price-cutting, 305; special considerations in, 305–306; variable, 305

primary data: defined, 116; search for, 116–118

prime rate, defined, 204

principal, 244

private carriers, defined, 293

private employment agencies, as source of employees, 443

private placement, defined, 214

process layout, defined, 190

process of succession, 41–48; good management in, 47–48; stages in, 42–45

product: building quality into, 463; building the total, 279–282; defined, 272; falling demand for, risk of, 594; invention of new, 81

product advertising, defined, 333

product development curve, 276

production control: balancing sales volume and, 460; defined, 457; and planning and routing, 459; and scheduling and dispatching, 459–460; steps in, 457–460; and supervising and performance follow-up, 460

production operations, 455

production/operations control, 455–460

product issues, and business plan, 89–91

product item, defined, 272

product knowledge, importance of, 327

product layout, defined, 190

product liability, risk of, 599–600

product life cycle, 278

product line, defined, 272

product mix: defined, 272; managing, 275–278

product mix consistency, defined, 272

product mix neglect, risk of, 594

product prices, and evaluating existing business, 161

product specialization, 641

product strategies: current product/current market, 273; current product/new market, 273; defined, 272; modified product/current market, 274; modified product/new market, 274; new similar product/current market, 275; new similar product/new market, 275; new unrelated product/current market, 275; new unrelated product/new market, 275; for small business, 273–282

professional area development groups, as source of information on location, 186

professional personnel: developing, 441–442; recruiting, 435–436

profitability, ratios related to, 517

profit margin on sales ratio, defined, 517

profit objective, of small business, 381–382

profits: declining, 649; as reward of entrepreneurship, 9; and social obligations, 383–384

pro-forma balance sheet, 520; and business plan, 93

programming: linear, 402; mathematical, 402

projected income statement, and business plan, 92

promotion: defined, 322; sales, 336–342. *See also* sales promotion

promotional expenditures, methods of determining, 324–325

promotional expertise, sources of, 325–327

promotional mix, 324

promotional planning, 322–327

promotion-expense capital, 205

promotion of public welfare, regulation of, 621–622

property: personal, 245; real, 245–246

property-centered risks, 594–596

proprietorship: characteristics of, 235–236; defined, 235

prospecting: defined, 327; techniques of, 327–328

protection: consumer, 620; of investors, 620

psychic risk, 12

psychological concepts, and consumer behavior, 263–266

psychological effects, of business failure, 646–647

public employment offices, as source of employees, 433

publicity, and sales promotion, 340–341

public sale, of stock, 214–215

public utilities, and small businesses, 60

public welfare, promotion of, 621–622

purchase of business, negotiating price and terms, 162

purchase discounts, taking all, 484

purchase order: defined, 480; follow-up, 481

purchase requisition, defined, 480

purchasing, 478–487; cycle, 479–481; defined, 479; importance of effective, 478–479; policies, 481–485

Q

quality, building into product, 463

quality circles, 464–465; defined, 464

quality control, 463–467; inspection as method of, 465; in service business, 467; statistical, 466–467

quality ratings, 486

quantitative methods for decision-making: limitations of, 404; value of, 400–401

quantity discounts, 489

queuing theory, defined, 402

R

rail and motor carriers, impact of laws on, 619–620

railroads, as source of information on location, 186

ratios: acid-test (quick), 515; average collection period, 516; bad-debt, 314; current, 515; debt to total assets, 518; fixed-asset turnover, 516–517; inventory turnover, 488, 516; profit margin on sales, 517; related to debt position, 518; related to profitability, 517; related to sales position, 515–517; related to working-capital position, 515; return on net worth, 517; return on total assets, 517; times-interest-earned, 518

raw materials, availability of and location, 176

real estate companies, as small businesses, 59–60

real property, 245–246; defined, 245

receipt of goods, 481

reciprocal buying, 481–482; defined, 481

reference groups, 269–270

references, employee, checking, 438

referent power, defined, 270

refuge, need to seek, 13–14

"refugees": corporate, 13; entrepreneurs as, 13–14; foreign, 13

region, choice of as location, 175–176

reorder point, defined, 489

replacement cost approach, 156–158; defined, 156

research, industrial, for small plants, 470–471

resource availability, and location, 173–174

responsibilities of small business, 381–389; social, 383–389

retailer, small, and location, 182

retail inventory valuation, 492–494; advantages of, 494; primary use of, 493–494; procedure, 492–493; weaknesses of, 494

retail store equipment, 192

retail store layout, 190–191

retail trade, and small businesses, 58

retained earnings, defined, 555

return-on-investment method of investment valuation, defined, 549

return on net worth ratio, defined, 517

return on total assets ratio, defined, 517

revolving credit account, defined, 309

reward power, defined, 269

risk management, defined, 591

risks: career, 12; common small-business, 591–601; coping with small-business, 601–603; customer-centered, 599–601; defined, 591; employee-centered, 596–599; family, 12; financial, 12; losses, saving to recover from, 602; market-centered, 592–594; property-centered, 594–596; psychic, 12; reducing business, 601–602; sharing, 602–603; shifting, 292; willingness to take, 12

roles, entrepreneurial, 18

S

safety, plant, and good housekeeping, 462–463

safety stock, defined, 489

salary levels, in small firms, 442

sales: declining, 649; export, government assistance in, 632; maximum, and inventory control, 487

sales forecast, 120–121; and business plan, 92–93; defined, 120

sales forecasting, 120–125; direct, 124; indirect, 124; limitations to, 121–122; steps in the process of, 122–124; techniques, 124–125

salespeople, compensating, 331–332

sales position, ratios related to, 515–517

sales presentation, 327–330; making, 330; overcoming objections, 329–330; practicing, 328–330

sales promotion, 336–342; defined, 336; and exhibits, 341; and publicity, 340–341; and specialties, 337–340; tools of, 337–342; when to use, 337

sales volume: estimating, 206; and production control, balancing, 460

savings, personal, to fund business, 212

scheduled budget buying, 485

scheduling and dispatching, and production control, 459–460

schools, as source of employees, 433

search, deliberate, 83–84

search activity, and expansion, 553–555

secondary data: defined, 115; external, 116; internal, 116

Section 1244 stock, defined, 240

self-confidence, and entrepreneurs, 12–13

self-service layout, defined, 191

sellers, benefits of credit to, 308

selling, personal, 327–332

selling price, calculating, 306–307

serendipity, defined, 81

service bureaus, 579

service business, quality control in, 467

Service Corps of Retired Executives (SCORE), 366–367; defined, 366

service economy, shift to, 651

service firm, small, and location, 182–184

service industries, and small business, 58–59

service operations, 457

set-aside program, 630–631; defined, 630

shoplifing, risk of, 596

short-range business plans, 397

simulation, as aid in planning, 403

single-entry system of accounts, defined, 508

single-segmentation strategy, defined, 110

site, choice of actual and location, 178–181

small business: activity, trends in, 639; and big business, 67–68; budgeting in, 519–525; budgetary control deficiencies in, 525; burden of regulation on, 623–625; and business law, 243–249; and capital budgeting, 548–553; common risks of, 591–601; compensation and incentives for employees in, 441–445; competitive strengths of, 640–643; computer applications for, 571–578; and consumerism, 386; and contract construction, 58; coping with risks, 601–603; credit in, 307–314; deciding to computerize, 578–584; defined, 55–57; and economic competition, 66–67; effective human relationships in, 445–449; and efficiency, 68–69; and environmentalism, 384–386; and ethical practices, 386–387; failure rate of, 646; and finance, insurance, and real estate firms, 59–60; financial incentives in, 442–443; and innovation, 64–65; insurance for, 603–607; and labor unions, 448–449; and lack and misuse of time, 644; in the major industries, 57–61; major taxes paid by, 626–627; management. See small-business management; management functions in, 351–355; and manufacturing, 60–61; marketing for, 261–262; and mining, 60; and new jobs, 62–64; numerical strength of, 61; objectives and responsibilities of, 381–389. See also objectives of small business, responsibilities of small business; operational planning in, 394–400; political power of, 622–623; problems and failure record of, 643–650; product strategies for, 273–282; prospects for future of, 650–655; and retail trade, 58; role of maintenance in, 460–461; SBA size standards, 56–57; and service industries, 58–59; special contributions of, 61–69; strategy, 389–394. See also strategy; success, and organization principles, 420; tax reform for, 628–629; tax-withholding

obligations of, 626; and transportation and other public utilities, 60; wage or salary levels in, 442; and wholesale trade, 58; White House conference on, 651
Small Business Administration: loans, 221; size standards of, 56–57
Small Business Institute (SBI), 365
Small Business Investment Companies (SBICs), 221–222
small-business management: and changing skill requirements, 358–360; constraints on, 356–357; and decision making, 362–363; distinctive features of, 355–363; founders and, 360–362; inadequate, 647; lack of skills and depth, 644; stages of growth and implications for, 357–358; traditional weaknesses in, 355–356
small corporation, and board of directors, 420–424
small manufacturers: and industrial research, 470–471; problems of, 470–471
social class, defined, 269
social responsibility: and profit making, 383–384; of small business, 383–389
sociological concepts, and consumer behavior, 267–271
software, 569–570; application, 569; defined, 569; system, 569
sources of funds: business suppliers as, 215–217; financial institutions as, 217–222; government-sponsored agencies as, 221–222; individual investors as, 212–215; locating, 210–222
span of control: defined, 419; and organization of firm, 419–420
spatial requirements, of buildings, 187
special purpose equipment, 191–192; advantages of, 192
specialties, and sales promotion, 337–340
speculative buying, defined, 485
spreadsheets, defined, 576
staff activities, defined, 414
standard operating procedure, 398

statement of changes in financial position, defined, 513

statement of cost of goods manufactured, defined, 510

statistical inference, as aid to planning, 401

statistical quality control, 466–467

statutes of limitation, defined, 244

stock: capital, sale of to fund business, 214–215; safety, 489

stock cards, defined, 491

stockholders: death or withdrawal of, 241; limited liability of, 241; rights and status of, 240

stockouts, defined, 489

stockpiling, controlling, 545

storage, and distribution, 293

stores card, defined, 491

strategic niche, finding, 392

strategy: finding niche for, 392; formulating, 389–392; small-business, 389–394; starting point for, 393–394

structural requirements, of buildings, 188–189

structure, organization. See organization structure

Subchapter S corporation, defined, 242

subcultural analysis, defined, 269

suburban development, and location, 181

succession, process of and family business. See process of succession

supervising and performance follow-up, and production control, 460

supplier interruptions, risk of, 592

suppliers: factors to consider in selecting, 486; general reputation of, 486; importance of good relations with, 486–487; selection of and relations with, 485–487

supply: diversifying sources of, 484–485; locating source of, and purchasing, 480

surety bonds, defined, 605

system software, defined, 569

T

taxation, 626–629

taxes, 645; estate, 628; federal excise, 627; income, 626–627; local, 627; paid by small business, 626–627; sales, 626; savings through planning, 627; Social Security, 626; unemployment, 627

tax reform, for small business, 628–629

tax system, complexity of, 629

team, entrepreneurial, 21

tenancy at will, defined, 246

time, lack and misuse of in small business, 644

time management, 363–364

time pressure, problem of, 363

time-savers, for managers, 363–364

time-sharing: of computer, 579–580; defined, 567–568

times-interest-earned ratio, defined, 518

time study, defined, 469

timing, and accounts payable, 546–548

tooling, and equipment, 191–194

total cost, defined, 300

total fixed costs, defined, 300

total variable cost, defined, 300

trade associations, as sources of information on location, 186

trade credit, 216, 308–310; defined, 308; failure to use properly, 216

trade-credit agencies, defined, 313

trademark: defined, 246; registration of, 246

trademark selection, 280

trade suppliers, selection of, 216

traffic, customer. See customer traffic

training and development, 439–442; of managerial and professional employees, 441–442; of nonmanagerial employees, 440–441; purposes of, 439–440

transportation: and distribution, 293; and small businesses, 60

turnkey system, defined, 567

two-bin method, defined, 489

U

unfair-trade practice laws, defined, 619

union, labor. See labor unions

union contracts, and evaluating an existing business, 160

unplanned structure, 412–413

unsegmented strategy, defined, 107